AF559965

A NATION WITHIN A NATION 1877-1937

Pathway to India's Partition

Volume II

A Nation within a Nation 1877-1937

BIMAL PRASAD

Issued under the auspices of the Rajendra Prasad Academy, New Delhi

MANOHAR
2016

First published 2000
Reprinted 2009, 2016

ISBN 81-7304-247-0 (Series)
ISBN 81-7304-249-7 (Vol. II)

Published by
Ajay Kumar Jain *for*
Manohar Publishers & Distributors
4753/23 Ansari Road, Daryaganj
New Delhi 110 002

Typeset at
Kumud Print Service
Boileauganj, Shimla 171 005

Printed at
Salasar Imaging Systems
Delhi 110 035

Contents

Preface

In the previous volume an attempt was made to indicate and analyse the foundations and supports of Muslim nationalism, the major factor behind Partition. The present volume seeks to trace the evolution of that nationalism from its early beginnings in 1870s to the inauguration of Provincial Autonomy in 1937, which marked a major turning point in it. Special attention has been paid to Syed Ahmad Khan's campaign in late nineteenth century to keep the Muslims away from the Congress; the organization of the Simla Deputation and the foundation of the All India Muslim League in 1906; the introduction of separate electorates and weightage for Muslims in 1909; the rise and growth of the pan-Islamic movement and the consequent alliance between Muslim nationalism and Indian nationalism, 1912-22; the resurgence of Muslim (along with Hindu) nationalism after the collapse of the Khilafat movement, 1920-2; the failure of efforts to bring about a rapprochement between the two nationalisms through the Nehru Report 1928-9; the emergence and spread of the Pakistan idea in the 1920s and 1930s and its adoption by M.A. Jinnah, the future founder of Pakistan, as well as Mohammad Iqbal, the greatest poet-philosopher of Muslim nationalism, by June 1937, if not earlier.

Here it may not be inappropriate to mention some of the important points emerging from this study. First, regarding the two nation theory, it has been generally assumed by most historians, that this was first propounded by Iqbal in 1930 and adopted by Jinnah in 1940. This view is no longer tenable. Almost all the leaders of the movement for Muslim awakening and solidarity from the second half of the nineteenth century onwards believed in Muslims being a nation by themselves and actively propagated it through their writings and speeches. Similarly, almost all the leaders of Hindu awakening and solidarity believed in the concept of Hindu nationhood and gave enthusiastic expression to their view. While most of the protagonists of Indian nationalism never accepted the two nation theory, there were not wanting among them leaders who, right up to the mid 1930s, simultaneously espoused the cause of Indian nationalism and that of

Hindu or Muslim nationalism, depending on whether they belonged to the Hindu or the Muslim community. They were apparently oblivious of any serious contradiction between the two and assumed that, with mutual adjustment of the rival claims by the two communities, the latter could amicably co-exist within the same body politic. This was as much true of leaders like Lala Lajpat Rai and Madan Mohan Malaviya on the Hindu side as of Maulana Mohamed Ali and M.A. Jinnah on the Muslim side. By the mid 1930s, however, the issues dividing Indian nationalism on the one hand and Muslim or Hindu nationalism on the other became too sharply defined to allow that position to continue. The adherents of the different nationalisms then turned into bitterly hostile camps.

It was also around that time that the Pakistan idea, implying the separation of the Muslim majority areas from India and the formation of a sovereign State or States on their basis, began to gather momentum. It may, however, be pointed out that this idea did not spring suddenly in 1933, with its forceful advocacy by Rahmat Ali, as is generally believed, but had emerged even earlier and was steadily taking root among the Muslim intelligentsia, particularly the youth, in mid 1920s. While the prominent leaders generally did not talk or write about it at that stage, there were at least two—Lala Lajpat Rai, a Hindu, and Maulana Mohamed Ali, a Muslim—who, without advocating it, anticipated the likelihood of Partition as early as 1924, if the Hindu-Muslim differences in politics were not amicably settled. As for Jinnah, he himself is on record, through his foreword to the booklet containing Iqbal's letters to him in the 1930s (published in 1943) that by June 1937 he, like Iqbal, had, without making it public at that stage, come to adopt a view about the subcontinent's future which, about three years later, found expression in the famous resolution, popularly called the Pakistan Resolution, adopted by the Lahore session of the Muslim League in March 1940.

Jinnah's testimony should enable us to get rid of the notion made popular by so many historians and publicists that the mind of the League's leadership turned towards Partition only after the failure of the Congress to agree to the installation of a coalition ministry in U.P. in 1937, with the cooperation of the League, as agreed upon earlier. For by the time Iqbal wrote to Jinnah (21 June 1937), strongly advocating the application of the principle of self-determination to the Muslim-majority provinces of India—with reference to which Jinnah says that Iqbal's views were 'in consonance' with his own—it was not even clear whether the Congress was going to form ministries in the provinces or not. The Viceroy's statement containing some concession to the Congress viewpoint on the use of special powers by the Governors of the provinces, which opened the way for the formation of Congress ministeries, was still to come. Besides, there had been no understanding—formal or informal—between the Congress and the League leaderships in U.P., stipulating the formation of a coalition ministry, as has been generally assumed so far by most historians.

This underlines the importance of paying much greater attention than has been done so far to the internal sources of inspiration for the Muslim elite and the League leadership instead of concentrating mainly on the attitudes and policies of the Government and the Congress to which the former have been generally supposed to be all along reacting. Throughout history leaders of powerful movements in every country have taken into account the ground realities around them—including the policies of their supporters or opponents—in planning their strategies, but these have never been the most important factors in determining their ultimate objectives or goals. This was also true of the movement inspired by Muslim nationalism and led by the Muslim League. My approach to the various developments covered in the second volume has been conditioned by this consideration. An effort has been made to find out what was going on in the mind of the dominant section of the Muslim elite and why, and to see how that determined the policies of the Muslim League. To the extent British policy or Congress attitude influenced the thinking of the League's leadership on any occasion that has been duly taken into account. However, the primary focus has always been kept on the thinking of the Muslim elite and the League's leadership. How far has this approach succeeded in properly tracing the evolution of Muslim nationalism between 1877 and 1937 and in providing a better perspective on it than has been available so far is for the readers to judge.

Rajendra Prasad Academy, New Delhi
28 February 2000

BIMAL PRASAD

Introduction

IN THE FIRST VOLUME, published a few months back, I have discussed the main foundations and props of Muslim nationalism in India during the period of British rule, with a view to explaining the background of Partition. To recapitulate, these were the legacy of communal consciousness from the past, the economic divide between the Hindus and Muslims in different parts of the country, the ideological and emotional environment of the Muslim elite, Hindu nationalism, the ethos of Indian nationalism and last, but not the least important, British policy of playing off one community against the other. In the present work an attempt has been made to trace the evolution of Muslim nationalism or, as it is customarily called, Muslim politics, from its early beginnings in modern times till it started feeling drawn towards the goal of carving out a separate, sovereign State consisting of the Muslim majority areas of India.

I

In tracing the evolution of Muslim nationalism it seems best to start with 1877. For that year witnessed not merely the setting up of the first significant political organization of Indian Muslims, the National Mohammedan Association of India in Calcutta, under the presidentship of Syed Ameer Ali (1849-1928), one of the prominent leaders of Islamic renaissance in modern times, but also, and more importantly, the foundation of what soon turned out to become the chief instrument as well as symbol of Muslim awakening and solidarity—the Mohammedan Anglo-Oriental College at Aligarh, through the exertions of the greatest leader of that renaissance, Syed Ahmad Khan (1817-98). Both these leaders, without advocating or even envisaging Partition, based their public activities on the assumption that Muslims, although living in the same country as the Hindus and others and interested in its welfare, constituted a nation by themselves and had certain special interests of their own which it was their duty to protect and promote. They in effect stood for Muslims being a nation within a nation, i.e. India. Thus Syed Ameer Ali wrote in course of an article published in a British journal in 1882 that while all the other 'Indian nationalities' in India had prospered under British rule, the Muslims alone—'a nation consisting of upward of fifty millions of souls'—had declined. However, the person who put the greatest emphasis on separate Muslim nationhood and, through his actions as well as speeches and writings, spread it widely among the Muslim elite in the last quarter of the nineteenth century was Syed Ahmad Khan. He can justifiably be described as the prophet of Muslim nationalism in India.

Although deeply moved by the sad plight of the Muslim elite since 1857 Syed Ahmad Khan had in the beginning sought to carry the Hindu elite along with him in his educational work. The emergence of a powerful movement for the replacement of Urdu by Hindi in courts as well as primary schools in U.P., his home-province, in the 1860s, however, changed his perspective. He then came to believe that it would not be possible for Hindus and Muslims to work together in the political field and the promotion of Muslim interests became his exclusive concern. The foundation of the Mohammedan Anglo-Oriental College at Aligarh in 1877 was his greatest achievement in this regard. In his address of welcome presented to the Viceroy, Lord Lytton, on the occasion of the laying of the foundation-stone of the college building by the latter in 1877, he proudly described it as 'the first national institution' for the dissemination of knowledge among Indian Muslims. After the foundation of the Indian National Congress in 1885, he advised the members of the Muslim community to keep strictly aloof from it chiefly on the ground that its major demands such as the introduction of representative parliamentary institutions and the recruitment to the public services through competitive examinations would not suit Muslim interests. For in elected legislatures Muslims would always be outnumbered by three to one and their educational backwardness would stand in the way of their competing successfully against Hindus, particularly hailing from Bengal, Bombay and Madras Presidencies where the latter had the advantage of earlier start in modern education. At the same time he reminded the members of his community that they were the descendents of those who had ruled over India for several centuries. 'Think for a moment', he observed amidst cheers in course of his address to the Muslim elite at Lucknow in December 1887, 'who you are. What is this nation of ours? We are those who have ruled over India for six or seven hundred years.' In his speech at Meerut in March 1888 he spoke even more bluntly and observed that India was 'inhabited by two different nations', who could live in peace only under foreign rule. He also advised the Muslims to ally themselves with their natural friends, the English, a 'people of the book', in order to counter-balance the Hindus who were organizing themselves politically through the Indian National Congress.

In the meanwhile, Syed Ahmad Khan had founded the Mohammedan Educational Congress in 1886, the last part of its name being changed to Conference in 1890. Although its avowed objective was educational advancement of Muslims, it also served the purpose of fostering among the Muslim intelligentsia the feeling of Islamic solidarity. In this respect it is significant that Syed Ahmad Khan delivered his first major address advising the Muslims to keep away from the Indian National Congress at Lucknow in 1887 on the occasion of the second session of the Mohammedan Educational Congress there. Its subsequent annual sessions provided the venue for the launching of two separatist Muslim political organizations—the Mohammedan Anglo-Oriental Defence Association (1893) and the All India Muslim League (1906). While spreading the message of Muslim awakening and solidarity the atmosphere in the M.A.O. College also fostered among its students a feeling of competition with the Hindus. This was a natural role for a college founded with the notion that unless the children of the Muslims elite, descended from the past rulers of India, received higher education on modern lines, Muslims would be left behind by Hindus in the race for status and power under British rule. An idea of the atmosphere pervading the college can be had from the fact that in a debate held in 1889 the overwhelming majority of students voted in favour of the motion holding Akbar rather than Aurangzeb responsible for the downfall of the Mughal empire.

The first political organization founded by Syed Ahmad Khan to oppose the Congress—the United India Patriotic Association (1888)—though predominantly composed of Muslims, had also a few Hindu members, especially those belonging to the big landlord families of U.P. The latter however, soon parted company and the Patriotic Association became practically a Muslim organization, voicing opposition to the Congress demands, particularly the setting up of elected legislatures, and emphasizing the historical as well as political importance of the 'Indian Mohammedan Nation'. After some time Syed Ahmad Khan decided that Muslim interests would be best served by having a purely Muslim organization in name as well as content. The result was the foundation of the Mohammedan Anglo-Oriental Defence Association in December 1893. Theodore Beck, the British Principal of the M.A.O. College, who had been assisting Syed Ahmad

Khan in his political work, became its Honorary Secretary, and it is he who carried on the day to day work of the organization under the guidance of Syed Ahmad Khan. The most significant achievement of the Defence Association was the preparation of a draft scheme of constitutional reforms in Upper India, jointly authored by Beck and Syed Mahmud, son of Syed Ahmad Khan, in 1896 which became famous as the Muslim Manifesto. In view of the fact that the Indian Councils Act of 1892 had already indirectly accepted the elective principle as a basis for the constitution of the legislative councils the Beck-Mahmud paper considered it futile at that stage to oppose the introduction of that principle in India. It, however, emphasized that Muslims in U.P., although constituting only one-sixth of its population, were not socially inferior to Hindus though the latter were in an overwhelming majority. For the Muslims had a long tradition of ascendency and were united by 'a common national sentiment'. On grounds like these it demanded equal representation of Hindus and Muslims in the U.P. Legislative Council as also in local bodies. At the same time it suggested the election of Hindu and Muslim members by electorates consisting exclusively of the members of each community. Thus we see both weightage and separate electorates for Muslims being demanded at least ten years before the famous Simla Deputation presented these very issues to the Viceroy, Lord Minto, in 1906.

Such demands, it may be pointed out, had been prompted not only by a feeling of separateness from the Hindus among the Muslin elite, but also by the poor representation of Muslims in municipal bodies even in towns where they were numerically not negligible in the population and in some cases even where they were preponderant. This was because of the high property qualifications for franchise which favoured the Hindus and the general tendency among both Hindus and Muslims to cast their votes in favour of candidates belonging to their own communities. It must also be noted that the organization led by Syed Ahmad Khan was by no means the only Muslim organization to raise its voice against the introduction of representative institutions on the basis of a uniform franchise. The National Mohammedan Association led by Syed Ameer Ali and the Mohammedan Literary Society led by Nawab Abdul Latif, both based in Calcutta, also made similar submissions to the Government about it in 1890, showing a growing consensus among the Muslim elite on this point. Again, just as in 1906-9, so in 1890-2, British ruling circles were generally sympathetic to the views of the Muslim elite. This was the result not merely of the general British understanding that Hindus and Muslims constituted two distinct communities in India with separate outlooks and interests, but also of the growing realization that Muslims could be of substantial help to the British in meeting the emerging challenge from Indian nationalism, which was considered largely a Hindu show.

The British perception was not entirely baseless. The Indian National Congress, the main organization of Indian nationalists, strove right from its birth in 1885 to draw as many Muslims towards it as possible in order to bolster up its position as the representative organization of the Indian people regardless of the caste, community or region to which they might belong, but largely in vain. There never, of course, was a Congress session which was not attended by some Muslims. A few of them like Badruddin Tyabji (1887) and Rahimtulla Sayani (1896) also presided over those sessions. However, during its early years, as during most of the later, the Congress failed to draw Muslims to it in sufficiently large numbers so as to effectively reply to the charge that it was largely a Hindu organization. Apart from some of the foundations of Muslim nationalism which had already begun conditioning the Indian Muslim mind, the forceful campaign launched against the Congress by the leaders of the movement for Muslim awakening and solidarity, the most prominent as well as active among whom was Syed Ahmad Khan, contributed to this denouement. The growth of communal antagonism in northern India in the wake of the widespread anti-cow-killing riots of 1893 created a favourable atmosphere for the success of such a campaign. All the while, the keen desire on the part of the Congress leaders to draw as many Muslims to their fold as possible led them to deal with the latter as a separate entity deserving special attention and this too contributed to some extent to the strengthening of a separatist consciousness among them.

II

After the passing away of Syed Ahmad Khan (1898) the mantle of Indian Muslim leadership fell on his successors at Aligarh: Mohsin-ul-Mulk (1837-1907), who became the secretary of the M.A.O. College upon Khan's death and Viqar-ul-Mulk (1841-1917) who similarly succeeded Mohsin-ul-Mulk in that position. While, continuing to accord primacy to the work of the College, both these leaders paid greater attention to politically organizing the Muslims than had been possible during the time of their mentor. This was in line with the growing feeling among the Muslim elite that unless Muslims were organized politically, they would not be able to adequately safeguard their interests. The order of the U.P. Government in 1900 permitting the use of Hindi in Devanagari script, along with Urdu, as the language of the courts provided a stimulus to such thinking. The intrusion of Hindi into what was till then the exclusive domain of Urdu was deeply resented by the Muslim elite and they began to think that this would not have been possible if they had a powerful political organization to agitate on their behalf. A greater push towards political organization was provided by the movement against the partition of Bengal in 1905-6. While the Indian nationalists generally looked upon that measure as a device to weaken them by dividing the Bengali speaking people on a communal basis, Muslim leaders generally welcomed it. For the partition had been affected in such a way as to result in the creation of a new Muslim majority province consisting of Eastern Bengal and Assam and many Muslims saw in it prospects of advancement in various fields. As a result of this, while there were always to be found some Muslims in the anti-partition agitation, the bulk of Muslims kept themselves aloof from it. The pronounced Hindu colouring of the anti-partition movement further alienated them from it and they began to look upon it as a primarily Hindu movement aimed at depriving the Muslims of a province where they would be in a clear majority. The pronouncements and activities of the British officials both before and after partition also strengthened that feeling.

Against this background came Secretary of State for India, John Morley's speech in the House of Commons on 20 July 1906, foreshadowing constitutional reforms in India involving expansion of the legislative councils and increased representation therein of Indians based on the elective principle. The Muslim leaders immediately acted in order to ensure the due protection of their interests, as they perceived them, under the coming reforms. Contrary to what was long believed in India and is even now imagined by some, they acted on their own, without any prompting by British officials, though undoubtedly with considerable encouragement and support from them. The result was the waiting upon the Viceroy, Lord Minto, and the presentation of an address to him, at Simla on 1 October 1906 by the famous deputation of Muslim leaders organized by Mohsin-ul-Mulk and led by the Aga Khan. In line with the dominant current of thought among the Muslim elite for quite some time the address pointed out that unless due care was taken the introduction of representative institutions in India might result in placing Muslim 'national interests' at the mercy of 'an unsympathetic majority'. Apart, therefore, from asking for increased Muslim representation in senior government positions, it proceeded to plead that any future scheme of constitutional reforms must be based on separate electorates as well as weightage for Muslims in the legislative councils. These demands were made on the ground that Muslims with their large number (62 millions)—larger than the population of any first class European power except Russia—must be recognized as 'an important factor in the state'. Their representation, it was pointed out, could not be computed on the basis purely of their numerical strength, but must also take into account their 'political importance' and the value of the contribution made by them to the defence of the empire. Note had further to be taken of the position the Muslims had occupied in India only a little more than a hundred years ago and of the fact that the memory of that had not faded from their minds. The address finally pointed out that Muslims constituted a 'distinct community' in India; while they shared many interests with other communities, they had certain special interests of their own which they did not share with any other community.

While the address presented by the Simla Deputation succinctly sums up the assumptions and aspirations of the champions of Muslim nationalism in its early phase, Minto's reply to it is equally significant as showing deep British interest in nourishing that nationalism. Thus he hailed the deputationists as 'the descendants of a conquering and ruling race' and as standard-bearers of 'the inspiration of Sir Syed Ahmad Khan and the teachings of Aligarh'. Although not formally committing the British Government, he expressed his full agreement with their demands for both separate electorates and weightage. The reactions of several other British officials in London as well as Simla showed extreme joy and happiness at the Viceroy's performance.

Encouraged by their success in organizing the Simla Deputation and, still more so, by Minto's response, the Muslim leaders associated with that deputation proceeded to found the All India Muslim League in December 1906. It did not have a very large membership in the beginning, but soon acquired the position of a national organization of Muslims living in different parts of India and made it its chief preoccupation to protect and promote their interests, especially in the context of the ensuing constitutional reforms based on the elective principle, which were likely to put the Hindus in a dominant position.

Contrary to what is generally imagined, right from its birth the League formulated its stand on various issues on the assumption that the Muslims in India were not a minority, but a nation and a nation which was markedly loyal to the British and whose forefathers had ruled over India in the not too distant past. This assumption was brought into the open and forcefully aired in 1908-9 when Morley, after fully applauding Minto for his response to the Simla Deputation, found his liberal conscience revolting against the idea of tailoring an electoral system according to the religious affiliation of the voters. He suggested the election of Muslims in proportion to their share in the total population by mixed electoral colleges. Thus, Syed Ali Imam, in course of his presidential address to the second annual session of the League at Amritsar in December 1908, referred to Muslims and Hindus as 'the conqueror and conquered' and asserted that in spite of living together in the same country for centuries they had continued to maintain their separate identities 'in point of nationality, character and creed'. Several other speakers at that session emphasized this point. Thus, Syed Nawab Ali Choudhry observed that there were definite differences between Hindus and Muslims and their 'interests, aims and objects' could not be the same. Mohammad Ali stressed that religion in India was not merely a matter of personal belief, but had created 'a different outlook on life, different mode of living, different temperament and necessarily different politics'. Syed Ameer Ali, then president of the London Branch of the League, asserted in 1909 that it was not appropriate to describe the Muslims in India as a minority; bound by common ideals and traditions they formed 'a nationality apart from all other people in India'. The Aga Khan spoke in a similar vein and emphasized that no act of Parliament could weld into one 'two nationalities so distinct as the Hindus and the Mohammedans'. At the same time the League leaders adroitly used the loyalty card and repeatedly pointed out that the unwritten Anglo-Muslim alliance, continuing since the time of Syed Ahmad Khan, might receive a severe jolt if their demands for separate electorates and weightage were not conceded.

This argument went well with Minto who was already convinced of the value of Muslim support against the rising tide of Indian nationalism. He patiently worked on Morley and finally succeeded in persuading him to give primacy to British interests over his liberal predilections. Morley included both separate electorates and weightage in the Indian Councils Act of 1909. What is more, while piloting it in the form of a bill he used an argument which fully vindicated the stand of the League leaders and must have appeared as music to their ears. The difference between Hinduism and Islam, he emphasized, was not merely difference in religious faith, but also 'a difference in life, in tradition, in history, in all the social things as well as articles of belief that constitute a community'.

Whatever the arguments used in support of separate electorates and weightage, their introduction did not lead to any immediate spurt of antagonism between the votaries of Indian and Muslim nationalisms as represented by the Congress and the Muslim League. On the contrary, the two organizations moved towards mutual conciliation. On the one hand, the leaders of the Congress, in particular Gopal Krishna Gokhale, the tallest among them, although opposed to weightage, showed understanding of the need for separate electorates, especially in view of the failure of Muslims to secure adequate representation in the legislative councils set up under the Act of 1892, except through nomination. The Congress did adopt resolutions against both separate electorates and weightage more than once, but the speeches delivered on those occasions clearly indicated that its opposition to the former was considerably muted. On the other hand, the leaders of the Muslim League, even while claiming separate nationhood for Muslims and tenaciously clinging to both separate electorates and weightage, repeatedly expressed their desire to work for cooperation between Hindus and Muslims in the political field. They even talked of the growth in the recent past of a common patriotism in India regardless of differences of race and religion as a result of the impact of British rule and the use of the English language all over the country. This seemed to augur well for the growth of cooperation between the two organizations.

III

Ironically, the ground for such cooperation was prepared by the severe Muslim discontent against the British as a result of the annulment of the original scheme for the partition of Bengal in December 1911 and its substitution by another under which the two parts of Bengal proper were again brought together in one province. Aimed at pacifying the Indian nationalists in Bengal who had been carrying on a vigorous agitation against partition and many of whom were turning towards the use of violent means, the Government's decision stunned the Muslim elite who had been feeling elated following the creation of a province with an overwhelming Muslim majority and the introduction of separate electorates and weightage. However, the emergence of disillusionment with the British did not result in any diminution of the feeling of Muslim solidarity and separate nationhood, but just the opposite. The Muslim elite in various parts of the country adopted a common stand against the annulment of partition and made it clear that they were in no way less concerned with it than their brethren in Bengal. The idea of ending the separate political organization of Muslims also did not receive much support.

Several other developments around the time of the annulment of the partition of Bengal further agitated the minds of the Indian Muslim elite and, while strengthening their separate national consciousness, also turned them towards rapprochement with the Congress. The most important among them was the spurt in the Pan-Islamic movement, which had been growing in India, as in several other parts of the world, since the last quarter of the nineteenth century. This centred on concern with the fate of the Ottoman (Turkish) empire, the only surviving centre of Muslim power, whose head, the Sultan, was also recognized as Caliph or head of all Muslims wherever they might be living. This concern particularly came to a head at the time of the Balkan wars (1912), caused by the uprising of the East European Christian subjects of that empire. Along with great sympathy with Turkey, Muslims in India were also swept by a feeling of antipathy towards the European powers in general and Britain in particular for their role in encouraging and aiding the East European rebels against the Ottoman empire. Regardless of their position as subjects of the British empire they generally felt that it was their duty to help the Caliph in his hour of distress in every way they could. The antipathy towards the British was further strengthened by the setback to the movement to raise the M.A.O. College at Aligarh to a Muslim University partly because of failure to raise sufficient funds, but partly also because of the lack of Government's support, on the ground both of the name of the proposed university and its authority to affiliate colleges all over the country. Even stronger anti-British feeling engulfed the Muslims because of what has become famous as the Kanpur mosque incident in 1913: the demolition of a part of a mosque, generally used for washing, in order to facilitate the widening of a road. More and more Muslims now began to feel that the British had scant regard for their religious sensitivities and that, as a consequence, their religion was in danger.

As Muslims became estranged from the Government, the minds of their leaders, particularly of those belonging to the younger generation, turned towards the Congress. There was, of course, no desire to give up separate electorates and weightage or to wind up their separate political organization, the Muslim League, but the leaders of the latter now began to think that instead of banking on the British they would do better by establishing a cooperative relationship with the Congress. In 1913 the League modified its objectives by, among other things, adding to them the attainment of a system of self-government suited to India, thus bringing them broadly at par with the main political objective of the Congress. Its leaders also now began to give greater emphasis in their utterances to the importance of Hindu-Muslim understanding and cooperation. This trend became even more marked after the outbreak of the First World War in 1914 with Britain, France and Russia ranged on one side and Germany and Austria on the other. The internment of a number of prominent Muslim leaders such as Mohamed Ali and Shaukat Ali, generally known as the Ali brothers, and Abul Kalam Azad because of their sympathy with Turkey, which had joined the War on the side of Germany, further alienated the Muslims as a body from the Government and pushed the League near the Congress. The latter, with its keenness to carry Muslims along with it in order to accelerate the march towards self-government, warmly welcomed the prospect of forging an united front with the League. The result was the formulation of the joint Congress-League scheme of constitutional reforms, which became famous as the Lucknow Pact, as it was adopted by the annual sessions of the two organizations, both held at Lucknow in December 1916. Under this pact the Congress agreed to separate electorates as also weightage for Muslims, on a scale higher than that provided under the Act of 1909 in the central legislature as well as in provinces where they were in a minority. In return the League agreed to only 50 per cent representation for Muslims in the Punjab and 40 per cent in Bengal in spite of their being in a majority in the population in both the provinces (Punjab, 54.8 per cent; Bengal 52.6 per cent). The relations between the two organizations now became quite cordial and the atmosphere was full of hope for the future. It was generally expected that the end of the war would be followed by the introduction of a substantial measure of self-government.

The war ended in 1918, but that hope was not fulfilled. On the contrary, repression seemed to have taken precedence over reform in the British scheme of things. This was most poignantly exemplified by indiscriminate firing on unarmed protesters at Jallianwalla Bagh in Amritsar in 1919 resulting in the death of about 400 and injury to about 1200 persons. This left the whole country aghast and all sections of the people regardless of their religion or community seething with discontent. The Muslims had a special cause for grievance because of the treatment being meted out to Turkey after its defeat in the war. Not merely did the Turkish empire come to an end, but plans were afoot to deprive Turkey even of those areas which were inhabited predominantly by the Turkish people. This caused serious disquiet to Indian Muslims as the head of the Turkish Government was their Caliph and they considered it their religious duty to work for the preservation of his dignity and power. They were also alarmed by the prospect of the placing of the holy shrines of Islam in Mecca and Medina under non-Muslim control. Various bodies sprang up in India, headed by the Central Khilafat Committee, to ensure that Turkey was not treated unjustly, as had in fact been promised to them by the British authorities during the war.

Mohandas Karamchand Gandhi (1869-1948) who had returned to India in 1915 after his heroic leadership of the struggle of Indian settlers in South Africa and was hoping to play a similar role in the struggle for freedom in India, saw in this situation a great opportunity for Indian nationalism. He had long been conscious of the fact that there was not much love lost between Hindus and Muslims in India and felt that if that situation continued there was little prospect of the end of British rule over the country in the foreseeable future. If the Hindus were persuaded to take keen interest in the Khilafat question and stand firmly by the Muslims, a change might take place in their mutual relationship, paving the way for early achievement of self-government. He, therefore, became a great champion of the Indian Muslim point of view on that question and got it included as one of the main grounds for the launching of the non-cooperation movement by the Congress in 1920. As a result of it India witnessed—for the first time since the revolt of 1857—a magnificent spectacle of Hindus and Muslims marching together under Gandhi's leadership in 1920-2. However, the movement which produced that spectacle can at best be described as a joint movement led by the forces representing Indian nationalism and Muslim nationalism. For the latter had not merged with the former. Also, while Hindu-Muslim relations in the political field improved for a short while, all was not well with those relations even during the period of the movement. The mass mobilization of Muslims on a purely religious issue, which hardly concerned the country as a whole, upset many Hindus and made them worried about the future, especially in view of the militant tone of some of the prominent Khilafat leaders, particularly the Ali brothers and their professed preparedness to welcome an Afghan invasion of India if its purpose was to free India from British rule. On the other hand, many Muslims felt that Hindus, not excluding Gandhi, had no genuine interest in the Khilafat issue, but were only using it to further the cause of Indian nationalism. Some of them even resented the fact that a purely religious movement of theirs was being led by a Hindu like Gandhi. The already tenuous understanding or friendship between the two communities received a severe jolt as a result of the Moplah uprising of July-August 1921. Although caused primarily by the economic grievances of the Muslim peasantry of the Malabar region of the then Madras Presidency against the Hindu landlords and their protectors, the British, there was also a powerful streak of religious fanaticism behind it and many Hindu temples were desecrated or destroyed and Hindus converted to Islam and killed if they refused. Now all the suspicions which had bedevilled Hindu-Muslim relations in the past reappeared. The situation in this regard was further worsened by Gandhi's indefinite postponement, without consulting the prominent Khilafat leaders, of the projected civil disobedience movement as a result of an unfortunate incident at Chauri Chaura in the Gorakhpur district of U.P. in the beginning of 1922 in which 21 policemen and a relative of one of them were burnt alive by a crowd of Congress supporters. This took the sting out of the non-cooperation movement at a time when the Khilafat issue was far from settled and deeply upset many Muslims who felt let down or betrayed. The British duly utilized the emerging opportunity and the Viceroy now projected himself as a sincere patron of Indian Muslim interests on the Khilafat issue by exerting pressure on their behalf on the authorities in London and duly publicizing it in India, thereby paving the way for the revival of the old Anglo-Muslims understanding. Whatever remained of the Khilafat movement soon petered out as a result of the ending of all temporal authority of the Caliph in 1923, followed by the abolition of the institution of the Caliphate itself in 1924, by the leadership of the new Turkey. Muslim nationalism then reverted to its usual, separatist course with much greater vigour than even before.

IV

The virtual end of the Khilafat movement in 1922 witnessed a powerful communal backlash all over northern India. This backlash had been in the making during the heyday of the Khilafat movement itself. As mentioned earlier, many Hindus were quite worried by the large-scale mobilization of Muslims on a purely religious issue and several other developments in its wake had deepened their fears and anxieties, led them to think more and more in communal terms and increased their distrust and hatred of the Muslims. On the other hand, the Khilafat movement had tremendously strengthened the communal or national consciousness of the Muslims and increased their distrust and hatred of the Hindus. They had now become conscious of the fact that they were Muslims first and then anything else, in a way in which they had never been before in modern times. They also felt that Hindus had not been sincere in their support of the Khilafat movement and that Muslims alone had borne its brunt. The abandonment of the projected civil disobedience movement by the Congress on Gandhi's advice, while the Khilafat issue remained unsolved upset them most seriously. They thought that they had been taken up the garden path and left in the lurch when the going became tough and Gandhi's mood changed. The subsequent abolition of the Caliphate by the new Turkish rulers added to their despair. They naturally wondered what they had received in exchange for all their sufferings during the movement.

Such a situation created considerable communal tension between the two communities Some leaders from both sides initiated movements which further increased such tension. Thus, the Hindus started the *Shuddhi* and *Sangathan* movements, aimed respectively at reconverting those Muslims to the Hindu faith who had been converted from Hinduism to Islam in the recent past and at organizing the Hindus with a view to safeguarding their interests. The Muslims replied by initiating *Tabligh* and *Tanzeem* with the purpose respectively of enlarging the circle of Islam and organizing the Muslims as a community. Outbreak of Hindu-Muslim riots in various parts of north India was the natural result of such activities. Between 1923 and 1927 such riots took a toll of about 450 lives and caused injury to about 5,000 persons.

Themselves the result of heightened communal tension, these riots further aggravated that tension, fouled the political atmosphere and even affected the relations between the top leaders, particularly between Gandhi and his chief Muslim allies, the Ali brothers. It was generally believed in British as well as Hindu circles that the riots had been caused chiefly because of increased Muslim aggressiveness, which was directly traced to the Khilafat movement. Gandhi fully shared this view. He was also conscious of the general feeling among Hindus that he was personally responsible for this because of his championship of that movement. Shortly after his release from prison in 1924 he published a detailed analysis of the Hindu-Muslim problem wherein he emphasized that one of the chief sources of trouble was the fact that the Muslim as a rule was a bully and the Hindu a coward. Muslim leaders naturally resented such a sweeping generalization which implied that Muslims were mainly responsible for starting communal riots. Indeed even before Gandhi's release Mohamed Ali had publicly protested against the tendency to single out Muslims and accuse them of being primarily responsible for starting riots without any impartial enquiry. After the Kohat riots of 1924, when the entire Hindu population of the town had to be evacuated to Rawalpindi, the situation in this regard became worse. Gandhi undertook a fast for 21 days in order to bring about an improvement in the communal atmosphere and achieved some success, at least temporarily. However, as a result of their different assessments of the background and nature of the Kohat riots Gandhi and the Ali brothers now drifted apart. Gandhi was particularly shocked by Shaukat Ali's failure to unequivocally condemn forcible conversions to Islam at Kohat as well as his lack of cooperation in producing a joint report with Gandhi on the Kohat riots, leading to the publication of two separate reports instead of one joint report as planned and expected. This naturally made Gandhi despondent about the prospect of solving the communal problem in the near future.

In the meanwhile, communal tension had been very much aggravated as a result of the working of dyarchy in the provinces under which control over some departments of administration like education, health and local government had been transferred to the control of ministers responsible to the legislatures provided for in the Act of 1919. As these legislatures were constituted on the basis of separate electorates, their members as well as ministers naturally pandered to their constituents, divided on the basis of religion, in order to strengthen their support-base. In such a situation competition and rivalry for the loaves and fishes of office and patronage naturally exacerbated communal tension. This was particularly noticeable in the Punjab and Bengal, the two provinces under dyarchy where Muslims were in a majority in the population. Although they were not in a majority in the legislative councils they were there in substantial numbers and, with the support of official members, commanded a dominating position. Although in a minority, the Hindus had till then been occupying a dominant position in these provinces and they deeply resented the loss of that position now and carried on a tearing campaign against the Muslim ministers. On the other hand, having tasted power, Muslims now wanted their hold on it to be made more secure and demanded that as long as adult franchise was not introduced, the Muslim majority in the population in both the Punjab and Bengal must be reflected in the legislature by providing Muslims with a statutory majority therein. This was totally unacceptable to Hindus. Their argument was that just as Muslims had been given weightage in representation in the provinces where they were in a minority Hindus also must be given weightage in the Punjab and Bengal. The same was to apply to the Sikhs in the former. However, if this was done Muslims would not be able to secure a majority of seats.

On the other hand, after the introduction of dyarchy the centre of Muslim politics had clearly shifted to the Muslim majority provinces, particularly the Punjab, which now came to acquire a dominant voice in decision-making in the Muslim League. M.A. Jinnah, who had joined the Muslim League in 1913, remained its top leader ever since then. However, he could not ignore the Punjabi Muslims, but for whose cooperation the League would have continued to remain a moribund organization as in the recent past when the Khilafat Conference had gained the upper hand. When the revived League met for its annual session at Lahore in 1924, its decisions clearly reflected the shift that had taken place in its power structure. Priority was given to a resolution enumerating the main principles on which India's future constitution was to be based. And those principles clearly stated that while minorities were to be given special consideration in representation, no majority was to be turned into a minority in any legislature—a clear move to ensure Muslim majority in the legislatures of the Punjab and Bengal. In order to safeguard Muslim interests in these provinces against possible encroachment by a Hindu dominated centre, it was further provided that the furture constitution must be based on the federal principle with maximum autonomy to the provinces and strictly limited powers in the hands of the centre. Separate electorates and weightage for Muslims in the provinces where they were in a minority were, of course, to continue. Once these principles were accepted the League session was happy to endorse the demand for a rapid advance towards full self-government in which Jinnah was keenly interested.

Jinnah was also quite keen to revive cooperation between the Congress and the League which had earlier resulted in the signing of the Lucknow Pact (1916) and repeatedly made reference to it in his speeches. Such cooperation, however, could only be on the basis of the acceptance by the Congress of the main demands of the Muslim League as embodied in the principles enunciated at its Lahore session in 1924. Hindu opinion was dead-set against those principles. As communal relations worsened during the post-Khilafat days, Hindu leaders came to the conclusion that the villain of the piece was the system of representation through separate electorates and this must be ended if communal harmony was to be restored. If Muslims were not prepared for this, since separate electorates had been earlier conceded by the Lucknow Pact, the Hindus were prepared to bear with them. There could be no question, however, of their acceptance of a statutory majority for Muslims in the Punjab and Bengal. Lajpat Rai, who was one of the two top spokesmen of Hindu interests—the other being Madan Mohan Malaviya—went to such an extent in opposing that demand that he asserted in 1924 that if the Muslims remained adamant on their demand in that respect, it would be better to divide the Punjab into two provinces—one with a Hindu-Sikh majority and the other with a Muslim majority. He warned at the same time that it would not mean an united India, but an India divided into a Hindu India and a Muslim India. Thus was a partition of India on communal lines envisaged as a solution of the Hindu-Muslim problem as early as 1924 by a prominent Hindu leader belonging to the Congress.

The top leadership of the Congress, as represented by Gandhi, was even keener than Jinnah for a settlement of the Hindu-Muslim problem in order to facilitate India's rapid advance towards self-government. In view of the sharp polarization between the Muslim League and the Hindu Mahasabha, however, the Congress avoided giving a clear lead on a communal settlement, but preferred to work as a mediator between Hindu and Muslim organizations. Its dilemma was real. If it took a stand which did not satisfy Muslims, the latter would be further alienated from it. If, on the other hand, it fully supported the latter's claims, it would lose support among the Hindus who might rally round the Mahasabha, which at that time was making rapid strides and gaining in popular support because of the growing communal discord. The Congress, therefore, contented itself with bringing together all the important leaders of both Hindus and Muslims in unity or all party conferences and encouraging them to come to a settlement. Such conferences, however, failed to produce any result.

By 1925 Gandhi felt so dejected by this situation that he formally withdrew himself from all efforts to find a communal settlement and announced that so far as he was concerned he would work for such a settlement only through prayers to God. The task of bringing about a communal settlement, therefore, fell on the shoulders of other leaders. They could not succeed where Gandhi feared to tread. C.R. Das had taken a bold step by signing the Bengal or Hindu-Muslim Pact with leaders of Muslim opinion in Bengal in December 1923, wherein he had conceded all their demands, but the Pact was not generally liked by the Hindus and was accepted by the Hindu Congressmen primarily out of their regard for Das. At the all-India level the Congress refused even to circulate it amongst its members for eliciting their opinion. At the same time, in spite of its best efforts, it could not succeed in formulating any other suitable scheme acceptable to all concerned. Das too passed away in 1925 taking with him his creation, the Bengal Pact, which was then disowned even by his own followers. Motilal Nehru struggled hard to stem the rising tide of communalism, but without any success, especially in view of the strong opposition mounted by Malaviya and Lajpat Rai, as the leading champions of Hindu interests. The general elections held in 1926 showed both Hindu communalism and Muslim communalism securing significant gains at the cost of the Congress. The assassination of Swami Shraddhanand, the leader of the *Shuddhi* movement, by a Muslim fanatic in December 1926, illustrated the growing impact of communalist propaganda and further vitiated the political atmosphere. By the beginning of 1927 Hindu-Muslim riots, after a temporary abatement due to the shock administered by Shraddhanand's assassination, again made their appearance, adding further to the already heightened communal tension. Hindu nationalism and Muslim nationalism which had so far, by and large, stood side by side now clearly stood face to face, with the Congress more or less in the position of a helpless though concerned onlooker.

V

It is against this background that the leaders of the Congress and the Muslim League initiated a fresh round of negotiations to arrive at a settlement of the communal problem. The key issue in this series of negotiations which went on till 1932 was the League's demand for statutory majority for Muslims in the legislatures of the provinces in which they were in a majority, particularly in the Punjab and Bengal, with strictly limited powers for the central government. As mentioned earlier, this Muslim drive for power in the majority provinces was strongly disliked by the Hindus who had, in spite of their being in a minority, been enjoying a privileged position therein till then. As a minority, they demanded weightage in both Bengal and Punjab at par with the weightage given to Muslims in the provinces where the latter were in a minority. In the Punjab the problem was further complicated by a similar demand on the part of the Sikhs. However, if Hindus and Sikhs had their way, Muslims, with only a slight majority in the population in both the provinces, would not be able to secure a majority of seats in the legislatures. The crux of the matter was that the leaders on neither side were prepared to risk their position among their constituents by making any significant departure from already stated positions. Besides, they thought that since in any case the final decision relating to the nature of the future constitutional arrangements rested with the British it might not be prudent to whittle down their terms. In such a situation the only result of the negotiations among them was a steady widening of the gulf between the two contending communities. In the meanwhile, a section of the Muslim youth and intelligentsia, particularly in the Punjab, moved beyond the demand for a statutory majority and began yearning for a separate sovereign Muslim State consisting of the Muslim majority areas of India, leading some perceptive British observers of the Indian scene to wonder as early as 1931-2 whether a self-governing India would be an united or a divided India.

Ironically, the Congress-League negotiations began in 1927 on a positive note. Following discussions with the then Congress President, Srinivas Iyenger, who had been authorized by the last annual Congress Session (Guwahati, December 1926) to start negotiations with other parties with a view to arriving at a solution of the communal problem, Jinnah, as President of the League, convened a meeting of the prominent Muslim leaders, belonging to various shades of opinion, in Delhi on 20 March 1927 in order to define the Muslim position. This resulted in the formulation of what became famous as the Delhi or Muslim proposals. According to them, Muslims would be prepared to give up separate electorates subject to certain conditions, namely the separation of Sind (with an overwhelming Muslim majority) from

Bombay; the introduction of constitutional reforms in North-West Frontier Province and Baluchistan (both with overwhelming Muslim majorities) at par with those in other provinces; provision for Muslim representation in the legislative councils of the Punjab and Bengal in proportion to Muslim share in the population (small majority) of the two provinces; and Muslim share in the central legislature being fixed at no less than one-third of its total strength.

In the then existing situation, the Delhi Proposals appeared to be a major breakthrough. The Congress Working Committee immediately expressed its appreciation and appointed a high-powered committee to discuss the relevant details with the concerned Hindu and Muslim organizations. The Hindus were expected to welcome the prospect of abolition of separate electorates and the Muslims that of the establishment of their dominance over five provinces where they were in a majority. The atmosphere, therefore, was full of hope. However, snags did not take much time to develop. While Hindus welcomed the substitution of mixed for separate electorates, they were not at all enthusiastic about the provision for Muslim dominance in the provinces where they were in a majority. They were also opposed to the separation of Sind from Bombay on communal grounds, arguing that if a new province had to be created, all relevant factors must be considered and applied not only to Sind, but also to other areas. At the same time they were insistent that Hindu minorities in both Bengal and the Punjab must have weightage in the legislatures at par with that accorded to the Muslims in provinces where they were in a minority and that this privilege should be extended also to the Sikhs in the Punjab. On the other hand, the idea of replacing separate by mixed electorates was not palatable to many of the politically conscious Muslims. The atmosphere of communal tension in the country also remained unabated in spite of the holding of unity conferences at one place or another, making some Congress leaders sceptical about the prospect of arriving at a generally acceptable communal settlement.

In the meanwhile, as a result of widespread dissatisfaction in India with the appointment of an all-British Statutory Commission—popularly known as the Simon Commission because of the name of its chairman, Sir John Simon—and the challenge thrown by the then Secretary of State for India, Lord Birkenhead, to Indian political parties to frame a scheme for a new constitution for India if they could, the consideration of the Delhi Proposals became a part of a much bigger effort. With initiative from the Congress there emerged an All-Parties Conference, which in turn set up a committee consisting of prominent Hindu, Muslim, Sikh and Congress leaders, headed by the veteran Congress leader, Motilal Nehru, to draw up the framework of a new constitutional structure based on consensus among all the parties willing to cooperate. Securing such a consensus, however, became increasingly difficult with the spokesmen of the supposed Hindu, Muslim, Sikh interests continuing to take divergent stands. After a good deal of effort the Nehru Committee did come to a consensus and prepared a report providing for mixed, adult franchise with reservation of seats for minorities on the basis of population and the right to contest additional seats, and for a division of powers between the central and provincial governments in such a way as to tilt the balance in favour of the former. This was also approved by the All Parties Conference. However, consensus in the Nehru Committee and the All Parties Conference was one thing and consensus in the country as a whole quite another. Politically conscious Muslims, with certain exceptions, were by and large hostile to the scheme proposed by the Nehru Report. Jinnah who was even unsure about general Muslim support for the Delhi Proposals, because of the provision for the substitution of separate by mixed electorates, walked warily. He especially felt compelled to do so because of the contemporaneous split in the Muslim League on this issue along with that of the boycott of the Simon Commission. Although he had technically the support of a small majority in the League Council, the other League headed by Mohammad Shafi, had the support of the bulk if the Punjabi Muslim elite, including their most powerful leader, Fazl-i-Husain, on both the contentions issues. Apart from the Punjab, Muslims as a whole were most reluctant to give up separate electorates and were determined to see that they secured statutory majority in both the Punjab and Bengal and at the same time did not have to lose weightage in provinces where they were in a minority. In such a situation Jinnah felt that he could have a chance of winning general Muslim approval for the abolition of separate electorates only if all the other Muslim demands contained in the Delhi Proposals were accepted. Noticing the trend of discussions at the All Parties Conference, which was far from being favourable to those demands, he withdrew from the Conference and left for London. During his absence some of his colleagues cooperated with the Conference and went along with other participants in endorsing the Nehru Report. They justified their action by arguing that from the point of view of Muslim interests the Nehru Report represented an improvement upon the Delhi Proposals. Such an argument, however, did not convince Jinnah, who stuck to the latter and considered the Nehru Report as at best a Hindu response to them, needing to be suitably modified if it had to win general Muslim approval. He most forcefully and cogently presented his views before the National Convention which met in Calcutta in the last week of December 1928 to have a final look at the Nehru Report, as approved by the All-Parties Conference, but to no avail: all his amendments were negatived by a huge majority. Visibly sad and bitter he now adopted a position analogues to that of those Muslim leaders who had been voicing opposition to the Nehru Report from the very beginning.

Most of the historians who have written on the Nehru Report tend to exaggerate its impact on the direction of Muslim politics in India. Actually that politics had had a separatist orientation right from the beginning and that orientation had gone on steadily growing, except for the brief interlude of the Khilafat-non-cooperation movement (1920-2). Even if the Nehru Report had incorporated all the amendments proposed by Jinnah, it is extremely doubtful whether that would have brought about any change in that orientation. All reports confirm that Muslim opinion as a whole was strongly opposed to the substitution of separate by mixed electorates and at the All Parties' meetings no one, not even Jinnah, had suggested any modification of the Nehru Report on that point. The most important impact, therefore, of the failure of the All Parties National Convention to accept Jinnah's amendments was not on the general direction of Muslim politics, but on the role of Jinnah in that politics. This too, however, was not as big or significant as has generally been made out to be by most of the historians in both India and Pakistan. The latter usually contend that Jinnah's disappointment in the National Convention marked the beginning of a major transition in his political career leading him to give up all hope of working out of a ***modus-vivendi*** with the Congress and ending finally in his championship of the demand for Partition and the setting up of a separate sovereign State consisting of the Muslim majority areas of India. Actually, what happened was that in the aftermath of the National Convention Jinnah slightly modified his position—certainly not for the first or the last time—and proposed a charter of Muslim demands which was not significantly different from that formulated by his rivals in Muslim politics. This, among other things emphasized the continued relevance of separate electorates. He, however, continued for quite some time—right upto 1937—to take interest in India's march to freedom and to seek an understanding with the Congress whenever an opportunity presented itself. To see in his disappointment in 1928 the beginning of a major transition in his political career is, therefore, too far-fetched and indeed imaginary.

The same applies to the view, widely popular among historians, that the Congress leadership must be held responsible for driving Jinnah to a new path after 1928. Firstly, as shown earlier, the path was not as new as is generally imagined. Secondly, those who subscribe to such a view fail to realize that if Jinnah had his political compulsions, arising out of his need to regain his credibility as a Muslim leader, so had the Congress leaders. For they had to safeguard their position as leaders of Indian nationalism—something they could not do by just satisfying the Jinnah section of the Muslim League and antagonizing all the rest who were opposed to his amendments but were otherwise supportive of the Nehru Report—and they included most of the Hindus, who were the mainstay of that nationalism. The latter were particularly intrigued by Jinnah's role, or absence of it, in the events taking place during much of 1928. Faced with opposition to his proposals by the Hindu Mahasabha leaders and others, he had absented himself from India during the crucial phase of discussions being conducted under the aegis of the All Parties Conference—apparently in order to gain time for making up his mind and to keep all his options open. During his absence leaders belonging to different shades of opinion cooperating with that Conference, including several belonging to the Jinnah section of the Muslim League, had hammered out a consensus on the basis of the Nehru Report. Indeed some of the prominent colleagues of Jinnah had gone to the extent of describing that Report as an improvement upon the Delhi Proposals. After all this Jinnah returned from London and privately showed extreme annoyance with those of his colleagues who had supported the Nehru Report. Publicly he maintained sphinx-like silence for some time, carefully assessing in the meanwhile the dominant view among the Muslim elite. Sensing the vehemence of their opposition to the Nehru Report he demanded the incorporation in it of the Delhi Proposals in their entirety as a condition for the support of his section of the League (the other section had boycotted the proceedings of the All Parties Conference from the very beginning) and placed amendments to this effect at the All Parties National Convention held in Calcutta in the week of December 1928 for the final ratification of the Nehru Report, but failed to elicit much support. This was because most of its members, numbering over a thousand

and drawn from diverse groups, were extremely reluctant, at that late stage, to reopen matters which had already been settled after protracted discussions. Apart from the Hindu Mahasabha representatives who had adopted a purely negative attitude towards meeting the Muslim League's demands from the very beginning, most of the others too joined in the negative voting on Jinnah's amendments. This was the result of a widespread view, shared also by the Congress leaders, that even the incorporation of Jinnah's amendments in the Nehru Report was not likely to make it acceptable to the generality of Muslim opinion which was irrevocably committed to separate electorates. Besides, with his keenness to re-establish his credibility as a Muslim leader even Jinnah, in spite of his known patriotic zeal and interest in Hindu-Muslim understanding, could not be expected to remain steadfast for long in support of mixed electorates in opposition to the dominant Muslim view. In such a situation the Congress leaders participating in the National Convention, by no means in a majority therein, saw no sense in supporting Jinnah's amendments in the teeth of opposition by an overwhelming majority of delegates. Further, even the securing of majority support for those amendments—an impossible task in any case—could not have led to their incorporation in the Nehru Report. For, according to an earlier decision of the All Parties Conference, any change in the proposals already accepted, could only be incorporated through a unanimous vote. Instead, therefore, of blaming the Congress leaders for not lending support to Jinnah's amendments at the All Parties National Convention and thus contributing significantly to his alienation from Indian nationalism, scholars would do better by examining the realities of the Indian political scene in 1928, dominated by an unending conflict over the irreconcilable claims and counter-claims of not only two communities (some of whose leaders really considered them as two nationalities) as heretofore, but with the recent growth of sectional consciousness among the Sikhs, three. That will help us to understand the constraints of the Congress leadership, which had to steer through such a conflict and retain the support of as large a section of the people as possible for the cause of Indian nationalism.

To say all this is not to imply that the blame for the tragic failure of the All Parties National Convention may more fittingly be foisted on Jinnah or his section of the Muslim League. Just like the Congress leaders he also had to function under certain constraints and could not ignore the dominant Muslim opinion at that time in order to further his pet idea of building a bridge between Indian nationalism and

Muslim nationalism. His credibility as a Muslim leader had been seriously eroded as a result of his initiative in the formulation of the Delhi Proposals, including in particular the provision for the abandonment of separate electorates if some key demands of Muslims were met. Muslims in general were certainly keen on those demands, but they were keen also on retaining separate electorates and not at all prepared to abandon them under any conditions. The Nehru Report, on the other hand, had provided for the abolition of separate electorates and at the same time ignored most of the other Muslim demands. In such a situation Jinnah was not wrong in coming to the conclusion that whatever some of his valued colleagues might feel or say with regard to the Nehru Report, if he had to regain his credibility as a Muslim leader there could be no question of his accepting it without significant modifications therein. The bulk of the delegates assembled in the National convention, on the other hand, for reasons mentioned earlier, refused to be swayed by his most-reasoned eloquence. So the die was cast and Jinnah saw no point in continuing to attend the Convention.

VI

Contemporaneous developments in Muslim politics confirmed Jinnah's assessment of the dominant trend of thought among the Muslim elite. Several months before the holding of the All Parties National Convention preparations had begun for the holding of the All Parties Muslim Conference, which commenced its deliberations in Delhi on 31 December 1928, even while the former was still in session. The old veteran of Muslim politics, the Aga Khan, was at hand to preside over and guide them. Among the participants were the leaders of the Shafi section of the Muslim League, the Khilafat Conference and Jamiat-ul-Ulama-i-Hind together with a large member of Muslim members of the various legislatures, both at the centre and in the provinces. The deliberations resulted not merely in a fresh twelve point charter of Muslim demands but also in the setting up of the All India Muslim Conference, which was led by the powerful Punjab Muslim leader, Mian Fazl-i-Husain, for the next six-seven years, and completely over-shadowed the Muslim League. The demands adopted by the Conference included the setting up of a fully federal system of government with complete autonomy and residuary powers for the constituent states and only those powers for the central government which were specifically allocated to it by the constitution, the continuation of separate electorates, due share for Muslims in the central and provincial cabinets, provision for Muslim majority in the legislatures of the provinces where Muslims were in a majority and the continuation of the then existing weightage for them in the provinces where they were in a minority. Jinnah, not interested in the emergence of another Muslim organization to supplant his own, had declined the invitation to attend the Muslim Conference, but did not differ from its stand on the Hindu-Muslim problem at that stage. He must also have been aware that a different stance would push him further behind in the race for Muslim leadership. Whatever that might be, within three months of the conclusion of the Muslim Conference and its adoption of the twelve point charter of Muslim demands he came forward with what was really a rehash of those demands and became famous as his Fourteen Points. There were only two major points of difference. One was that whereas the Muslim Conference had only asked for due share for Muslims in all cabinets, central as well as provincial, Jinnah mentioned a definite percentage—one-third—for such share. The other was his stipulation that if the Muslims were satisfied that all their demands had been met, they might consider the abandonment of separate electorates. Needless to add, the Muslim Conference leaders fully supported Jinnah's Fourteen Points. It is also significant that though he never joined the Muslim Conference, the two sections of the Muslim League merged together within a year of the formulation of those points. Jinnah's interest in rapid constitutional advance at the centre, however, continued—quite a contrast to the position of most other sectional Muslim leaders, whether belonging to the Conference or the League, who were interested primarily in advance in the provinces. This, for the time being, left him in a rather unenviable position, fully trusted by neither side of the political-communal divide. Yet his general standing as well as personal prestige were so high that his Fourteen Points soon superseded the Muslim Conference's charter as the most authoritative document containing the latest version of Muslim demands and the leaders of the Muslim Conference also showed no hesitation in accepting that.

The hardening of the Muslim side on the communal issue went hand in hand with a similar hardening of the Hindu side. This is borne out by the deliberations of the Hindu Mahasabha's annual session at Surat in March-April 1930, where it went back on its acceptance of the Nehru Report and demanded uniformity of franchise all over the country on the basis of mixed electorates without any reservation of seats. The nature of the then prevailing mood among the Hindus in general at that time can be easily deduced from an exchange of letters between such veteran Muslim champions of Indian nationalism and Hindu-Muslim understanding as M.A. Ansari and Mazharul Haq in September 1929, in which they both felt that Hindus were as much of communalists, if not more, as the Muslims and that there was nothing to choose between the two.

Undeterred by the rising tide of communal consciousness among both Hindus and Muslims, the Congress decided at its Lahore session, held in the last week of December 1929, to jettison the Nehru Report, based on Dominion Status, adopt the goal of complete independence in its place and launch a campaign of civil disobedience in order to achieve it. Such a decision was not totally unexpected and had been indeed foreshadowed a year earlier at the previous annual session of the Congress (Calcutta, 1928) which had provided for all this if Britain failed to concede the demand for Dominion Status before the end of 1929. Even so it served to further alienate Jinnah from the Congress. For although falling in line with such Muslim leaders like the Aga Khan and Shafi so far as the communal problem was concerned, he had continued to work for advance towards Dominion Status through constitutional means and had tried hard to ensure that the Congress desisted from resorting to the campaign of civil disobedience. At the same time the Congress decision also upset most of the Muslim leaders who had thrown in their lot with that organization. The tallest among them, Ansari, refused to accept any executive position in the Congress after the Lahore session and made the strongest possible plea to Gandhi and through him to the other members of the Congress Working Committee to desist from starting the projected campaign in view of the strong current of communal antagonism flowing across the country, but in vain. Gandhi as well as Motilal Nehru and other members of the Working Committee were convinced that they must go ahead with the plan of action decided upon by the Lahore Congress. They agreed with Ansari's analysis of the communal situation, but saw no way of dealing with it through another series of conferences and negotiations with the leaders of Muslim and Hindu communal organizations, which were expected to result not in the settlement of the communal problem, but in worsening it still further, as in the past. On the other hand, they saw hope for the solution of that problem through the participation of Hindus, Muslims and other minorities in the common struggle for freedom. The ensuing civil disobedience campaign, however, failed to achieve that purpose. While the Muslims of the North-West Frontier Province set a most glorious record in the history of the struggle for freedom through their enthusiastic participation in the civil disobedience movement against rather heavy odds, and nationalist Muslim leaders like Ansari and his chief lieutenants also joined the fray at a later stage as a mark of solidarity with other Congressmen in the face of Government's repression, Muslim participation in that movement in India as a whole was not very impressive. Indeed, it would not be wrong to say that most of the politically conscious Muslims kept away from it and even resented the picketing by Congress volunteers of shops owned by Muslims and selling foreign cloth. The Hindus, on the other hand, resented the prevalence of such an attitude among Muslims. The resultant mutual bitterness was poignantly revealed by the severe communal rioting at Kanpur in March 1931, triggered by the refusal of Muslim shopkeepers to down their shutters as part of the widespread protest against the execution of Bhagat Singh, one of the legendary figures in the history of the Indian struggle for freedom. Ansari had precisely anticipated such incidents when pleading against recourse to civil disobedience in 1930 in view of the then highly surcharged communal atmosphere in the country.

While the Congress was preoccupied with the civil disobedience movement, some leaders belonging to the National Liberal Federation had resumed their efforts to arrive at a generally acceptable settlement of the communal problem. In response to their initiative, an informal unity conference met in Delhi in February 1930, followed by a so-called all parties conference in Bombay in May, but with Jinnah insisting on the acceptance of his Fourteen Points as a basis for a settlement and the Hindu Mahasabha leaders strongly opposed to any concessions to Muslims at that stage and declining to even attend the second conference, these efforts failed to produce any positive result. Soon the attention of all concerned was concentrated on the Report of the Simon Commission, published in June 1930, and the first Round Table Conference which met in London a few months later. While the majority of Muslim politicians were happy with some of the recommendations of the Simon Commission, they were quite upset by the failure of that Commission to support all their recent demands. This, according to them, was scant reward for all that they had done to oppose the Congress and support the Government. The latter agreed with them and impressed upon the authorities in London to rectify the shortcomings of the Simon Report from the Muslim point of view. At the same time the Government also saw to it that the Muslim delegates to the Round Table Conference were selected in such a way as to ensure the dominance of persons owing allegiance to Fazl-i-Husain and capable of resisting likely moves from leaders like Jinnah and Shafi for a compromise with the Hindu delegates with a view to facilitating a rapid advance towards self-government at the centre. Even so, Jinnah and Shafi, and even the Aga Khan, showed their readiness to settle with the Hindu leaders on the basis roughly of the Delhi Muslim Proposals, but the opposition of the Mahasabha leaders to those proposals proved an insurmountable hurdle. In the meanwhile, Fazl-i-Husain cracked the whip from Delhi and the Muslim leaders keen on a settlement decided to beat a retreat. So the gulf between the Hindu and Muslim positions remained unbridged, with Muslims insisting on retaining separate electorates as well as weightage in the provinces where they were in a minority and seeking statutory majority for Muslims in Bengal and the Punjab and the Hindus implacably opposed to such demands. With the release of the Congress leaders in early 1931 and the signing of the Gandhi-Irwin Pact in March providing for the suspension of civil disobedience and the participation by the Congress in the Round Table Conference, there began fresh efforts for a communal settlement in which Gandhi took a hand. But, with both the Hindu and the Muslim sides sticking to their old established positions, nothing came out of such efforts either in India or at the second session of the Round Table Conference in London, which Gandhi attended as the sole Congress delegate.

Finally all issues relating to Hindu-Muslim shares in the legislatures were left to arbitration by the then British Prime Minister, Ramsay MacDonald. His award, generally known as the Communal Award, was announced in August 1932 and met most of the Muslim demands. The final outcome was to a great extent conditioned by the pleadings of the then Viceroy, Willingdon, who repeatedly emphasized that if the British wanted to safeguard their position in India they had no option but to keep the Muslims satisfied, for they constituted the one reliable force in India on which the British could depend in stemming the rising tide of Indian nationalism. The Communal Award thus represented a clear victory for the tactics adopted by Fazl-i-Husain and helped to reinforce the traditional view of the dominant Muslim elite that their interests would be served better through friendship with

Britain than aligning with Indian nationalism. It must, however, be added that although the Hindu position was not totally devoid of logic, if considered in the light of the principles of Western democracy, in the then existing historical as well as political contexts in India, the Muslim demands conceded by the British were neither unreasonable nor excessive. The Mahasabha leaders seriously erred by ignoring the realities of the Indian situation and stubbornly refusing to adopt a flexible or pragmatic approach. The Congress leaders, particularly Gandhi, preferred such an approach, but they contented themselves with playing the role of an honest broker or mediator in view of the rigid attitude of the Mahasabha leaders and the apparently wide support for such an attitude among the politically conscious Hindus, who also constituted the mainstay of Indian nationalism.

VII

This was especially unfortunate in the context of the contemporaneous emergence of the Pakistan idea—though the name still remained to be coined—among a section of the Muslim intelligentsia and youth, particularly in the Punjab. That idea owed its birth primarily to the drive of the Muslim elite for power in the provinces where Muslims constituted a majority of the population, including the Punjab and Bengal, where such majority was quite small, untrammelled by any fear of interference by a Hindu-dominated centre—something unavoidable in an undivided India having a system of responsible government. Some Muslim intellectuals in the Punjab thought that one way of dealing with this problem, without necessarily partitioning the country, might be to secure the consolidation of all the Muslim majority areas in the north and north-west into one large state. This was the idea propounded by Mohammad Iqbal, the great poet-philosopher of Muslim nationalism, having his home in Lahore, in his presidential address to the twenty-first session of the Muslim league held in Allahabad in December 1930. Although, contrary to what is generally believed, particularly in Pakistan, he did not advocate Partition, his emphasis on the bond of Islam uniting the Indian Muslims and the need for concentrating the bulk of them in one specified territory contributed significantly to the evolution of the thought-process which finally culminated in overwhelming Muslim support for the idea of Partition.

That idea itself was not entirely new and stray individuals had off and on given expression to it much before Iqbal delivered his Allahabad address. For instance, the two Kheiri brothers, Abdul Jabbar and Abdul Sattar, had propounded it as early as 1917 in course of a paper submitted to the Stockholm Conference of the Second International, and a few others followed suit later. Among the latter was a prominent Congress as well as Hindu leader, Lajpat Rai, who observed in 1924 that if the Muslims continued to insist on asserting their majority rights in certain provinces the way out might be to partition them on communal lines, underlining at the same time that that would mean not an united but a divided India. During the period 1927 to 1932 the Partition idea was no longer confined to stray individuals here and there, but received a much wider airing, particularly in the Punjab. Indeed, in view of this it would be more appropriate to place the emergence of the Partition idea in these years, particularly in 1927-9, rather than in 1933, when it received forceful support and publicity at the hands of an young Punjabi Muslim student at Cambridge, Choudhry Rahmat Ali.

Thus in December 1927, the then Governor of the Punjab, Malcolm Hailey, found that many Muslims of that province had begun thinking that their interests were different from those of their co-religionists living in those provinces where they were in a minority and that it might be desirable to have a separate federation of those areas on northern and north-western India where Muslims were in a majority with the prospect of joining up at a later stage with Afghanistan and perhaps Persia as well. Two years later, while serving as Governor of U.P., Hailey again reverted to this theme and reported that he had been told by Ross Masood, Vice-Chancellor of Aligarh Muslim University, that the differences between Hindus and Muslims in India were really fundamental and they were not likely to live together within the same state once independence was achieved, as Muslims were very much concerned with being swamped by the Hindu majority.

Such impressions are corroborated by the writings and speeches of some Muslims during 1928-9. Thus a book called *The Indian Moslems* by 'an Indian Mohammedan', published in London in 1928, stressed that within the frontiers of India there lived two nations, the Hindu and the Muslim, and that they differed from each other more fundamentally than any two nations in Europe. It was also asserted in that book that Muslims would never get their due unless India was again subdivided as during the pre-Mughal times. In December of the same year a Punjabi Muslim journalist, Maulana Murtaza Ahmad Khan Maikash, wrote a series of four articles in a Urdu daily of

Lahore asserting that the solution of the Indian problem lay in the establishment of a Muslim national homeland consisting of the Muslim majority provinces of north and north-western India. About a year later, a prominent Muslim politician of the Punjab, Nawab Sir Zulfiqar Ali Khan, came out in support of the Partition idea, for the first time including Bengal also in his scheme, in course of his address as chairman of the Reception Committee of the All India Khilafat Conference held in Lahore on 31 December 1929.

Although the demand for Partition had not yet been adopted by any political party, the circulation of the Partition idea was obviously wide enough to lead some British observers of the Indian political scene to conclude that a self-governing India was not likely to remain united and that the ground was being prepared for the emergence of a separate Muslim State out of the body politic of India. Thus a *Manchester Guardian* correspondent reported in that paper dated 19 June 1931 that there were many Muslims who did not believe in the permanence of an united India and looked forward to the setting up of a Muslim State in the north stretching from Karachi to North Bengal. A Cabinet paper dated 1 September 1931 similarly noted that the primary object of the Muslims was the creation of 'a Muslim India'. In April 1932, Lord Irwin, who had relinquished charge as Viceroy of India only about a year ago, opined in a confidential letter that instead of a federal structure, some division of India had better prospect of settling the communal problem. About the same time John Coatman, who had just retired as Director of Public Information in India, wrote in a book surveying Indian politics during 1926-32: 'It may be that the die is already cast and that no united India, as we understand it today, will ever emerge.'

VIII

The trends forming the basis for such a prognosis were considerably strengthened during the next five years (1932-7). The announcement of the Communal Award (1932) by the British Prime Minister significantly contributed to such a denouement. While the Muslim elite were by and large satisfied, without of course publicly acknowledging it, the Hindu elite felt very much aggrieved. This was particularly true of them in Bengal where the Award drastically changed their position—from dominance to dependence. The Indian nationalist press generally looked upon it as another illustration of the old British stratagem to keep the Indian people divided and to prevent as many Muslims as possible from joining or supporting the Congress. The leaders of the Congress by and large shared this approach but, in view of the general Muslim support for the Award, desisted from roundly attacking it as the Hindu Mahasabha leaders were doing and joined hands with the liberal leaders in bringing the opposing sides to the conference table with a view to evolving a generally acceptable alternative to it. When these efforts miserably failed, the Congress, in a bid to safeguard its position among Hindus as well as Muslims, formally adopted a poture of neither accepting nor opposing the Award. However, the intense dislike for the Award on the part of its leaders did not remain a secret as most of them continued to denounce it as highly divisive and anti-national. To some extent this saved the position of the Congress with the Hindu elite, but caused considerable distrust and suspicion among the Muslim elite. In such a situation the return of Jinnah from his self-exile in the United Kingdom to the arena of Indian politics in 1934 filled the Congress leaders with much hope. For although he had returned with the avowed purpose of bringing new life and vigour to the Muslim League, which had been lying in a moribund state for quite some time, it was generally presumed—not without reason—that his old interest in Indian freedom as well as Hindu-Muslim unity was still intact. The result was the holding of detailed talks in 1935, extending over several sessions, between him and Rajendra Prasad, then President of the Congress, with a view to finding out an alternative to the Communal Award. The talks were held in a cordial atmosphere and resulted in a draft agreement between the two leaders, but they got bogged down when it was decided to sound out other concerned parties. Faced with adverse Muslim reaction to the prospect of giving up separate electorates, as provided for in the draft agreement, Jinnah took the position that he could not even place it for consideration before the Muslim organizations until Prasad secured the written concurrence of the most important Hindu Mahasabha leaders, particularly Madan Mohan Malaviya, with all its provisions. Prasad tried hard for this, but failed. As a last resort Prasad suggested to Jinnah that they themselves might sign the draft agreement and secure the approval of their respective organizations, but Jinnah saw no sense in doing so—though he himself had made such a proposal at the start of the talks. So the Prasad-Jinnah talks ended without any constructive result just as several other such talks had done since 1927. As on previous occasions they only added further to bitterness among the parties concerned with each side blaming the other for the failure. A lot of tension was also generated around that time by the powerful advocacy of the Pakistan idea by Choudhry Rahmat Ali in Britain and the subsequent publication of a number of articles on it in the Indian Press, particularly in the Punjab (1933-5).

Such bitterness and tension, far from dying down with the passage of time, received a fresh impetus in 1936 due to the resurgence of the old language controversy—Hindi *versus* Urdu—in a virulent form, occasioned by a chance remark by Gandhi using Hindustani and Hindi as synonymous terms without any reference to Urdu. Protagonists of Urdu questioned the genuineness of Gandhi's championship of Hindustani and accused him of wishing to promote Hindi in the name of Hindustani and actually conspiring with Nehru to crush Urdu. None emerged even from the ranks of the Congress Muslims to publicly defend these leaders. The elections to provincial assemblies in 1937 under the Act of 1935 were fought against this backdrop.

Ignoring all this, a number of scholars have built up a thesis that the political situation in India was quite favourable to the installation of Congress-League coalition ministries in provinces after the elections of 1937. This is assumed to have been particularly true of U.P. where indeed the Congress is supposed to have committed itself to forming such a ministry at a time when the prospects for a Congress victory at the polls did not appear very bright. That such a coalition did not materialize is generally ascribed to Nehru. The failure of the coalition talks in U.P., we are further told, so upset the League leadership that its mind now turned towards Partition as the only honourable goal for the Muslims of India to pursue. These assumptions are based not on fact, but on wishful thinking. As shown above, thanks to the failure of the Prasad-Jinnah talks and the eruption of the language controversy, neither Hindu-Muslim relations nor Congress-League relations had been in any way friendly on the eve of the elections. Those relations had further deteriorated as the election campaign progressed. Jinnah took offence at Nehru's remark that in India the real contest was between two parties—those who wanted to perpetuate British rule and others who were keen on ending it. Asserting that there was a third party in India, namely the Muslims, he declared that the Congress must keep its hands off them and not dare contest from any Muslim seat. Nehru retorted by describing such a stand as not only revealing of a medieval mentality, but also derogatory to the Muslims by implying that they had no interest in securing freedom from British rule. Such exchanges embittered Congress-League relations beyond measure.

This was indeed inescapable. For while the Congress was determined to use the election campaign to heighten the tempo of the Indian nationalist movement and to carry its message to every nook and corner of the country and to every section of its people, regardless of their religious affiliation, the League was equally determined to revive itself and secure recognition from all concerned as the sole representative organization of Indian Muslims. A clash between the two at that point of time, therefore, lay in the logic of history.

Nor is it true that there had been an understanding between the Congress and League in U.P. on the eve of the elections to the effect that they would join together and form a coalition ministry. There had certainly been cooperation between the two organizations in certain constituencies on an informal basis against the candidates of the National Agriculturist Party, their common enemy, just as they had also contested against each other in certain other constituencies. Even Choudhry Khaliquzzaman, the U.P. League leader, who had been very much interested in joining the Congress-led Ministry in U.P. and was sorely disappointed at the failure of the so-called coalition talks, does not claim more than this. In his memoirs, dealing at length with events leading to Partition, all that he claims is that the amicable manner in which the Congress and the League had fought the elections in U.P. 'presaged a future settlement'. It may also be added that when in 1940 the then Viceroy, Linlithgow, first heard of the supposed existence of a Congress-League understanding prior to the elections of 1937 and had the matter thoroughly investigated, the report which he received from impeccable official sources made it clear that there had been no such understanding and that stories regarding it became current quite some time after the event and not 'until the manufacture of Muslim League grievances had been organized'.

Note must also be made of the fact that Congress-League relations had further deteriorated after the elections. The League leadership was most seriously concerned with the inauguration of the Muslim mass contact programme of the Congress, which initially seemed to be making considerable headway and which might have proved the death-knell of the League if it had finally succeeded. Alarm-signals in this regard were coming to the top leadership from various channels. The Congress leadership, on the other hand, was equally seriously perturbed by the most rabid communal propaganda unleashed by the League in course of a bye-election in Bundelkhand (U.P.). Nehru looked upon the use of such tactics as amounting to working for the institution of the dark age in India and felt particularly aggrieved to learn that prominent League leaders of U.P. like Khaliquzzaman were associated with it.

Against such a background, what is surprising is not that the so-called coalition talks in U.P. failed, but that they were held at all. Actually no formal coalition talks were held. What took place were talks not for a coalition between the Congress and the League, but for certain Muslim League leaders joining the Congress Ministry on the condition that the League Party in the U.P. Assembly virtually ceased to function and became an appendage of the Congress. Left to himself Khaliquzzaman might have joined the Ministry even on such terms and had indeed been having talks with the Congress leaders in this regard, without informing Jinnah, but he failed to carry any appreciable number of his colleagues with him and finally backed out and declined the Congress offer.

Thanks to what is generally, but perhaps wrongly, considered as Maulana Abul Kalam Azad's political memoirs, a general impression has been created that what happened in U.P. was the special handiwork of Nehru and that if he had only agreed to having two League leaders, instead of only one, in the Congress Ministry in U.P., the talks with the League leaders would not have broken down. This is totally baseless. As Nehru's detailed letter to Prasad sent just after the breakdown of the talks with the league leaders clearly shows, Nehru, along with several other Congress leaders, including Azad, was willing, however reluctantly, to have two ministers from the League provided the latter ceased to function as a separate party in the Assembly. And the note conveying the Congress terms was handed over to Khaliquzzaman by none other than Azad himself. The Congress strategy in U.P. was not the special handiwork of Nehru alone, though he certainly had a hand in shaping it as the then Congress President, but was broadly in line with the set Congress policy of projecting itself as the chief representative organization of all sections of the Indian people, regardless of the community or the region to which they might belong. It is significant in this respect that the statement that the Congress was not interested in entering into alliance with any other party in the legislatures came as early as 12 February 1937, even before all the results had been announced, and that the author of that statement was not Nehru, but Prasad, who had experience of negotiations with Jinnah in 1935. What happened in Bombay, where the League had done better than in U.P., having won a clear majority of Muslim seats at that time, also points to the same conclusion. Nehru was not present there at all and the negotiations with Jinnah's emissary were carried on by Vallabhbhai Patel and Azad. The latter called off the talks for Congress-League cooperation in forming a Ministry when they realized the Jinnah was not agreeable to letting the League's nominees in it function under the discipline of the Congress Party. That the Congress as a whole, and not just Nehru, was at that time not interested in forming coalitions with the League in the provinces is also made clear by Gandhi's expression of helplessness to do anything in the then prevailing situation, pervaded by darkness all around, in response to Jinnah's suggestion in May 1937 that the former should seriously apply himself to bringing about a settlement of the communal problem, obviously an euphemism for initiating a Congress-League dialogue for cooperation in forming coalition ministries in provinces wherever possible.

As for the result of the failure of the so-called coalition talks in U.P. this has been grossly exaggerated. For it has been argued that it is this failure which turned the mind of the Muslim elite in general and the Muslim League leadership in particular to the Pakistan idea. Actually that idea had begun to draw the attention of both even before the talks on ministry-making in U.P. had reached the final stage. As noticed earlier, the idea of a separate, sovereign State for Indian Muslims after lying in an embryonic stage for several years, had definitely emerged on the Indian political horizon in the late nineteen-twenties and some knowledgeable persons had begun to wonder whether a self-governing India would be able to remain as one united entity. After Choudhry Rahmat Ali's forceful exposition of the Pakistan idea in 1933 in U.K., several articles ardently supporting it had appeared in the Muslim press in India. By 1935 the idea had become so popular that the Aga Khan, writing from Paris to Fazl-i-Husain, used the term 'Pakestan', without fully supporting the idea behind it, to denote the Muslim majority areas of India. It is also significant that in early 1936, G.D. Birla, a leading industrialist as also a close observer of the Indian political scene, informed Linlithgow, then preparing to leave for India to take charge as Viceroy, that the Pakistan idea had begun to catch on and that more and more ambitious Muslim politicians were turning to it.

The leadership of the Muslim league had not remained unaffected by that trend. This is confirmed by Iqbal's letter to Jinnah on 21 June 1937, asserting that the Muslims of north and north-west India, where they were in a majority, must have their own State, on the basis of the principle of self-determination. Although Jinnah's reply to that letter remains untraced, we have Jinnah's own unambiguous testimony, in the shape of his foreword to the book containing Iqbal's letters to him, published in 1943, in which he candidly affirms that Iqbal's views were 'substantially in consonance' with his own and that they finally found expression in what became popularly known as the 'Pakistan Resolution' adopted by the Muslim League at Lahore in March 1940. It is pertinent to remember that when Iqbal wrote the above mentioned letter to Jinnah, the talks on Ministry-making in U.P. had still to reach the final stage. In the face of this evidence it is not possible to argue with any semblance of reason that it is only after the failure of the talks on Ministry-making in U.P. that the League leadership began to think in terms of Partition. Further, the confidential report of Lord Brabourne, then Governor of Bombay, on his talk with Jinnah in early June 1937, indicates that Jinnah had also hit upon the strategy which he was going to follow in order to achieve the new goal. For he clearly told Brabourne that his policy was going to be 'to preach communalism morning, noon, and night'. This was said even earlier than Iqbal's letter to Jinnah. Thus although the year 1937 remains a landmark in the evolution of Muslim politics in India, this has to be ascribed to the transformation in Jinnah's mind—which had by then become an unfailing mirror of the dominant trends in advanced Muslim thinking—rather than to the failure of the Congress-League talks on Ministry-making in U.P.

To say all this is not, of course, to argue that the failure of the so-called coalition talks in U.P. had no significant impact on the course of subsequent developments in India. On the contrary, this provided the League leadership with a powerful weapon with which to preach Muslim nationalism in an extreme form and to deepen the anxiety of the Muslim elite with regard to their future in an undivided India where, it was argued, only those Muslims could look forward to a share in power who would be willing to merge themselves politically with the Hindu majority—a prospect not at all palatable to the Muslim elite who were determined to maintain their separate political identity and at the same time acquire a substantial share in power. Thus though the attraction on the part of the League leadership to the idea of Partition did not originate from the failure of the so-called coalition talks, that failure certainly helped the League leadership in preparing the ground for the enthusiastic adoption of that idea in due course by the generality of the Muslim community as well as the League's membership.

CHAPTER I

Early Assertion of Muslim Nationhood, 1877-1998

In its early phase, Muslim nationalism did not have before it the objective of separation from India or the formation of an independent Muslim State. British rule over India seemed destined to continue for centuries, if not for ever, and such questions naturally did not arise. Attention was, therefore, focused primarily on competition with the Hindus, who constituted the majority community, and appeared to be moving faster than the Muslims in the race for modern education and government employment. The feeling of such competition became particularly acute because of the lingering memory of the so-called Muslim rule over India for several centuries in the past and the extreme reluctance to visualize a situation in which Hindus might acquire a dominant position in the higher echelons of government. Such competition did not necessarily preclude cooperation with Hindus in certain fields. For it was realized that Muslims and Hindus would continue living together in India, as they had been doing for several centuries, and would have to perform many tasks in common. There was no overt antipathy towards Hindus either. On the contrary, while working for the advancement of Muslims, the protagonists of Muslim nationalism also sought the cooperation of Hindus in certain fields and indeed worked for the latter's advancement also. It would not, therefore, be wrong to say that the leaders of early Muslim nationalism looked upon their nation as part of the bigger nation, that was India under British rule. They had not, of course, worked out all the dimensions or implications of such a proposition and sometimes adopted contradictory positions, emphasizing India's composite nationhood at one time and seriously doubting the possibility of the emergence of such nationhood at another. This was inherent in the Indian situation in the last quarter of the nineteenth century when both the unifying and divisive elements of modern nationalism, generated by the establishment of centralized British rule over the whole country and the interplay of modern European ideas and institutions with their traditional Indian counterparts, had begun having an impact on sensitive Indian minds. This need not, however, create any doubt about the emergence of Muslim nationalism, just like that of Hindu nationalism, in the second half of the nineteenth century. It is at the same time important to remember that the natural outcome of such nationalism need not necessarily have been complete separation from India. In any case, this idea emerged much later and was not embedded in Muslim nationalism from the very beginning.

I

The first political organization devoted exclusively to the promotion of what were termed Muslim interests was set up in Calcutta in 1855. Called 'Anjuman-i-Islami' or 'Mohammedan Association', it was led by Mohammed Abdur Rauf, editor of *Durbin*. In his speech of 6 May 1855, at the meeting held to found the organization, he regretted that 'though superior to others in natural energy, boldness of heart, and similar characteristic abilities', and enjoined by the precepts of Islam to remain united, Muslims should be left far behind on the road leading to union. Drawing attention to the decline in the 'strength, wealth and influence' of Muslims he made a plea to the leading men of the community 'to employ their best exertions, without delay or hesitation, for the amelioration of the present and future condition of their brethren, suffering them no longer to sink still further into abjectness and wretchedness'.[1] It is revealing of the general British attitude that while both the leading organs of Hindu opinion in India, *The Hindu Intelligence* and *The Hindu Patriot*, refused to see anything undesirable in this move and indeed welcomed it, rather patronizingly, as signifying the growth of public spirit among Muslims, the British owned *Friend of India* looked upon it as a manifestation of the deep differences between Hindus and Muslims. As the paper put it:

> The Hindoos and the Muhammedans may be said to constitute *two different nations* in India, between whom there is no affinity of interests and not the smallest sympathy of feeling. . . . In all the movements which the Hindoos have made of late years in opposition to their present rulers, and in all those appeals which have been preferred by them against particular measures, though the grievances put forward were common to both classes, the Muhammedans have never united with them on any occasion; . . . .

While deciding to set up an exclusive Muslim political organization, the meeting on 6 May 1855 had also decided that 'no measures should on any occasion be adopted that might, in any manner, appear inimical to the British Government'. Underlining the significance of this decision from the British point of view the *Friend of India* added:

> It seems to wear the appearance of proud submission [on the part of Muslims] to those with whom they once contended on terms of equality, and to whom the dispensation of a higher Power has now given the ascendency. It also precludes all idea of any union with the Hindoo Association [the British Indian Association], which altogether repudiates the principle. To whatever cause we may trace the resolution, it is a token of loyalty which can scarcely fail to prove gratifying to those entrusted with the responsibilities of this empire. Moreover, in an age of Association, the more they are multiplied, the less will be the official embarrassment occasioned by them; and in one aspect, it may be said that *they will serve as a counterpoise to each other*.[2]

In the beginning, the Mohammedan Association did quite well and enrolled more than a hundred members within a few months. It also made representations to the Government on certain Muslim grievances relating the education and government employment. Just like other similar associations, dominated by the Hindus, it condemned the rebellion of 1857, supported the British and congratulated Queen Victoria for taking over the responsibility of Indian governance from the East India Company. However, it did not survive long and soon faded away, largely due to the lack of 'the necessary educational or popular base to sustain its activity'.[3]

The void created by this development in the capital city of the British Indian empire was filled to some extent with the foundation in 1863 of the Mohammedan Literary Society by one of the active members of the erstwhile Mohammedan Association, Abdul Latif Khan (1828-93), generally known as Nawab Abdul Latif. After serving as a Deputy Magistrate in Bengal for several years, he had been nominated during the previous year to the Legislative Council of that province, thus acquiring the distinction of being 'the first Mohammedan ever appointed, and at that time the only one, in any of the Legislatures, Local or Imperial'.[4] Although called a literary society, the Mohammedan Literary Society of Calcutta did not confine itself to purely literary pursuits, but tried to spread among the Muslim elite of Calcutta an awareness of the necessity to make the required adjustments with the new political and social order ushered in by the British and acquire modern or English education with a view to advancing their interests. Far from preaching exclusiveness, it organized an annual get-together, called 'conversazione', of the Muslim elite with European and other non-Muslim citizens in Calcutta. In the absence of any well-organized political organization of Muslims it served as 'a consultative body' for advising Government on all occasions when Muslim interests were involved. It also, on its own initiative, sought to bring to the notice of the Government what it considered to be 'the requirements of the Muhammedan Community' on matters relating to education, legislation, and other similar subjects.[5]

This role was more effectively performed by the National Mohammedan Association (later named the Central National Mohammedan Association), the first significant political organization of Indian Muslims in modern times, founded in 1877 by Syed Ameer Ali (1849-1928), a great scholar and jurist and one of the most prominent leaders of Indian Muslim awakening. As he explained later, in founding this organization he was impelled by a feeling that great changes were in the offing in the system of government and that 'unless the followers of Islam prepared themselves they would soon be outstripped in the political race by their Hindu fellow-countrymen'.[6] The prospectus of the Association issued at the time of its foundation declared that it had been founded with the object of 'promoting, by all legitimate and constitutional means, the well-being of the Mussalmans of India'. While proposing 'to work in harmony with Western culture and the progressive tendencies of the age', it aimed at 'the political regeneration of Indian Muhammedans by a moral revival, and by constant endeavours to obtain from Government a recognition of their just and reasonable claims'.[7]

Although several literary and cultural organizations of Indian Muslims had already emerged, there can be no doubt about the validity of the claim made by the Central National Mohammedan Association in one of its earlier reports that until its formation there did not exist any political organization of Indian Muslims capable of representing to the Government 'the hopes and aspirations, the legitimate wants and requirements of the large body of Muslims in this country, who by their number and homogeneity constitute such an important factor in all questions concerning the welfare of India'.[8]

It is indicative of the nature of early Muslim nationalism in India that the prospectus of the Central National Mohammedan Association took care to mention that the Association did not overlook the fact that the welfare of the Mohammedans was intimately connected with the well-being of 'the other races of India'. It did not, therefore, exclude from its scope 'the advocacy and furtherance of the public interests of the people of this country at large'.[9] According to the Rules of the Association, it was to have two types of members, honorary and ordinary. As regards honorary members, the only qualification provided was that they should be persons 'distinguished for their interests in the Welfare of the Muhammedans of India'. As for ordinary members, it was specifically provided that the Committee of Management had the power 'to elect, in the usual manner, any non-Muhammedan gentleman as an ordinary member of the Association'. It was also laid down that such a member would have the power to vote 'as an ordinary Muhammedan member on any question', except such as might happen to conflict with the interest of any section of the society to which such a non-Muslim member might belong.[10] The bye-laws of the Association provided that its Committee of Management might appoint 'any Muhammedan or non-Muhammedan gentleman' as one of the Honorary Vice-Presidents of the Association, the main criterion being that such a person should be 'taking special and prominent interest in, and affording substantial assistance towards, the promotion of the welfare of the Muhammedans of India'.[11] Two out of the twenty-four members of the Committee of Management were Hindus.[12]

The Association was able to secure considerable support among the Muslim elite. During the first year of its existence it managed to enrol about two hundred members. This number went up to about six hundred by the end of its first five years. Branch organizations sprang up in several parts of the country. Between them they had another eight hundred members.[13] Although it applied itself also to various educational, literary and social activities, its main importance lay in its emphasis on political issues affecting the Muslim elite. Here it concentrated mainly on drawing attention to the poor Muslim share in the higher appointments to government service. For this purpose it submitted a memorandum to Lord Ripon, then Viceroy of India, in 1882. Largely following the line of argument adopted by Hunter in *Indian Muselmans* (1871) the memorial tried to show that the figure of Muslims appointed to high office, as compared to Hindus, continued to fall. Thus it pointed out that while in 1871 the proportion of Muslims to Hindus in the gazetted posts had been less than one-seventh, it had fallen below one-tenth by 1880. It made a strong plea for the redressal of the balance of state patronage as between Muslims and Hindus and suggested that it could be easily done if the Government stopped attaching undue importance to university degrees. If this was not done, 'the Mussalman race' would not be able to come out of its then existing state of 'decadence and depression'.[14]

Ameer Ali, who had evidently drafted this memorial, made more or less the same point in an article entitled 'A Cry from the Indian Muslims', published in *The Nineteenth Century* in its issue of August 1882. Here he stressed that there prevailed at that time 'a very wide and deep feeling of discontent' among Indian Muslims because of the state to which they had fallen as compared to the Hindus. Explaining the reasons for such a feeling he observed:

> Whilst . . . almost all the other *Indian nationalities* have prospered under the British rule, the Muslims alone have declined. . . . In every walk of life, in every matter, whether it concerns the disposal of a post or the dispensing of state hospitality, the Hindu has obtained an influence which he will not willingly share with another. . . . The independent professions make no exception to the rule, and are, for the most part, the monopoly of the Hindus.[15]

Stressing the importance of government employment for Muslims, Ameer Ali added:

> It may seem strange to English readers that I lay so much stress upon State employment as the Keystone of Muslim prosperity. It will be said, not without reason, that this inordinate dependence upon extraneous support betrays a weakness in the national character. It must not be forgotten, however, that *a race of conquerors, who not more than a hundred years ago possessed a monopoly of power and wealth,* has not yet developed commercial and trading instincts. Half a century's degradation has deadened all spirit of enterprise among the Muslims, and the absence of capital is another stumbling-block in their path to commercial success.[16]

Ameer Ali also gave strong expression to the deep resentment of the Muslim elite because of the recent replacement of the Persian script by Devanagari in the courts of Bihar. Although he argued that the change was disliked by both Hindus and Muslims, as the greater part of the former in Bihar (obviously meaning the elite among them) were 'in their manners, their customs, and their modes of amusement, Muslims', he based his plea for a reversal of the Government's decision on the sentiments and interests of the Muslims. The British Government, he further wrote, might probably consider itself strong enough to disregard the sentimental side of the Nagri-Urdu controversy, yet, 'as an act of conciliation and justice, it should abstain from steps which tend still further to ruin the prospects of the Muslims, and place them at a disadvantage with the Hindus'.[17]

Finally, Ameer Ali took up the cause of the spread of modern or English education among the Muslims. The backwardness of Muslims in this respect was, according to him, no longer due to their reluctance to learn the language of an alien race, but to their poverty. Few Muslim parents were in a position to finance the English education of their wards and this was the main cause of so many Muslim students abandoning their studies prematurely. The problem was important enough to warrant the appointment of a commission by the Government to go into the question of Muslim education and devise a practical scheme for it.[18]

The article ended with a fervent plea for the need on the part of the British authorities to correctly understand the state of Muslim feelings and to deal with their 'depressed and despairing condition' in an earnest manner in order to ensure the stability of their rule:

A nation consisting of upward of fifty millions of souls, 'with great traditions but without a career', deprived by slow degrees of wealth and influence . . . must always constitute an important factor in the administration of India. It is this factor which cannot be ignored, and which must be taken into account by the Government in all future projects for the well-being of India.[19]

The Central National Mohammedan Association gradually petered out. While Ameer Ali continued to give expression to the grievances and aspirations of Muslim Indians according to his own light till his passing away in 1928, it was really Syed Ahmad Khan who played the dominant role in shaping Muslim Indians' political attitudes in the second half of the nineteenth century. Indeed, it may not be inappropriate to suggest that the foundation of the Mohammedan Anglo-Oriental College at Aligarh in 1877, under the leadership of Syed Ahmad Khan, was a more important landmark in the evolution of Muslim nationalism in India than that of the Central National Mohammedan Association in the same year under the leadership of Ameer Ali. As has been pointed out in the previous volume, right from the day of its birth, the M.A.O. College became the most potent symbol of nascent Muslim nationalism. The feeling of Muslim pride and solidarity which had inspired its founders comes out clearly in the following lines of the address presented on their behalf to the then Viceroy of India, Lord Lytton, in 1877, at the time he laid the foundation stone of the college building. Describing it as '*the first national institution* for the propagation of learning among the Mussalmans of India', the address asserted:

The College of which your Excellency is about to lay the foundation stone *differs in many important respects from all other educational institutions which this country has seen*. There have before been schools and colleges founded and endowed by private individuals. There have been others built by sovereigns and supported by the revenues of the State. But this is the first time in the history of the Muhammedans of India that a college owes its establishment, not to the charity or love of learning of an individual, not to the splendid patronage of a monarch, but to the combined wishes and the united efforts of a whole community.[20]

Needless to add, Syed Ahmad Khan had freely solicited and received help from Hindus as well as Christians (including the British rulers) in this endeavour. Hindu students also continued to be freely admitted to the M.A.O. College and some Hindus even sat on its managing committee. As his Patna and Jallandhar speeches cited in Volume I testify, Syed Ahmad Khan also wished all his countrymen to regard themselves as members of one nation. There is no doubt, however, about his firm belief that Muslims in India constituted a nation by themselves or about his determination not to countenance any political arrangement or institution which did not recognize this. The fact that Muslims were in a minority in India as compared to Hindus gave an additional edge to such thinking, for the former were likely to be submerged in the vast sea of Indian humanity, if their separate identity was not preserved and certain safeguards not provided for the protection of their special interests. While such a view was repeatedly aired after the foundation of the Indian National Congress in 1885, its expression was certainly not conspicuous by its absence before that event. This comes out clearly in Syed Ahmad Khan's speech in the Indian Legislative Council, on 12 January 1883. Supporting the Government's decision not to go in for 'the system of election pure and simple' while introducing local self-government in India, but to reserve to itself the power of appointing one-third of the members of local bodies, with a view to securing and maintaining 'due and just balance in the representation of the various sections of the Indian population', he observed:

The system of representation by election means the representation of the views and interest of the majority of the population, and, in countries where the population is composed of one race and one creed, it is no doubt the best system that can be adopted. But, my Lord, in a country like India, where caste distinctions still flourish, where there is no fusion of the various races, where religious distinctions are still violent, where education in its modern sense has not made an equal or proportionate progress among all the sections of the population, I am convinced that the introduction of the principle of election, pure and simple, for representation of various interests on the local boards and the distinct councils, would be attended with evils of greater significance than purely economic considerations. . . . The larger community would totally override the interest of the smaller community, and the ignorant public would hold Government responsible for introducing measures which might make the differences of race and creed more violent than ever.[21]

II

Ironically, it was the foundation of the Indian National Congress in 1885, with the objective, among other things, of eradicating all possible racial, credal or provincial prejudices among lovers of the country and promoting 'the fuller development and consolidation of . . . sentiments of national unity' among the Indian people,[22] which set the stage for a much stronger assertion than ever before of the concept of a separate Muslim nationhood.

Although the Congress leaders were quite profuse in their affirmation of loyalty to the British rule, Syed Ahmad Khan did not take much time in realizing that some of the important political demands which they were then making—expansion of legislative bodies on the basis of elections and increased association of Indians with administration on the basis of competitive examinations—would soon land them in conflict with the Government, and push them to the path of political agitation, which he considered harmful to the interests of the country. This, according to him, would be particularly harmful to the interests of the Muslims, for being easily excitable the latter were likely to join such agitation more eagerly than others and in the process hurt themselves much more as they had done at the time of the revolt of 1857. Besides, he considered the political demands of the Congress even otherwise harmful to the Muslims, who were not just numerically a minority and would always be outvoted by the Hindus in open elections, but also educationally backward and hence in no position to compete with the Hindus, particularly the Bengali Hindus, for recruitment to the public services.

Syed Ahmad Khan's opposition to the Congress unfolded itself gradually. In the beginning he kept silent and did not say anything at the time of the first Congress session (Bombay, 1885). He, however, broke his silence before long and published an article in the Aligarh Institute Gazette of 23 November 1886, arguing that the political condition of India was not suitable for the introduction of parliamentary government. Reiterating his argument, first advanced in the Indian Legislative Council in 1883, he asserted that India consisted of a '*mixture of nationalities*' and this would result in the emergence of a permanent division in an Indian parliament between Hindus and Muslims, 'two sections whose interests and prejudices constantly clash, and which differ in a far more radical way than any two parties in England'. If at any time a Parliament actually came into being 'with Hindus and Mohammedans sitting on the two sides of the house, it is probable that the animosity which would ensue would far exceed anything that can be witnessed in England'.[23] At the time of the third session of the Congress (1887) Syed Ahmad Khan launched a much stronger attack on the Congress and positioned himself as an ardent champion of Muslim nationalism in opposition to the concept of an all-embracing Indian nationalism on which the Congress was trying to base itself.

The provocation for this attack was provided by the increased effort on the part of the Congress to draw Muslims towards itself. This had become a problem for it right from its birth. Thus out of seventy-two delegated present at the first session (1885) only two had been Muslims.[24] Sections of the British press, not impressed by the protestations of loyalty by the Congress leaders, immediately pounced upon this limited Muslim participation in the first Congress as an evidence in favour of their assertion that it was largely a Hindu show. Thus the *Times* (London) while recognizing that by the foundation of the Congress India had 'for the first time given proof of the existence of a national life and spirit', also remarked on 1 February 1886: 'One great section of the native population was conspicuously not there. No Muhammedan took any part in the proceedings.' Rebuking the educated Hindus for making 'impractical' demands and indirectly patting the Muslims for keeping out of the Congress, it observed, that if and when the British withdrew from India, 'it would be in favour not of the most fluent tongue or of the most ready pen, but the strongest arm and the sharpest sword'.[25] The leaders of the Congress clearly understood that their claim to speak on behalf of the whole country could not be sustained unless Muslim participation in it increased, and they seriously applied themselves to securing such participation. Their efforts were not wholly without results. The second session (1886) was attended by 33 Muslims out of a total of 431 delegates from British India,[26]— a definite improvement on the situation at the first session, especially when it is remembered that this was in spite of the opposition of Syed

Ahmad Khan as well as of the two leading Muslim associations at Calcutta. The third session (1887), showed a further rise in Muslim participation: 83 out 607 delegates were Muslims.[27] The leaders of the Congress had also succeeded in persuading Badruddin Tyabji, a leading Muslim Barrister of Bombay, to preside over that session. In course of his presidential address he made it clear at the outset that the one factor which had induced him to take up the responsibility of presiding over the Congress session, in spite of his indifferent health, was the earnest desire on his part to prove that not only in his individual capacity, but also as a representative of the Anjuman-i-Islam of Bombay he did not feel that there was 'anything whatever in the position or the relations of the different communities of India—be they Hindus, Musalmans, Parsis or Christians—which should induce the leaders of any one community to stand aloof from the others' in their efforts to secure certain common rights for the good of all. He, of course, admitted it to be undoubtedly true that each one of the various Indian communities had its own peculiar social, moral, educational and even political difficulties to surmount, but so far as general political questions affecting the whole of India were concerned, he was 'utterly at a loss to understand why Musalmans should not work shoulder to shoulder with their fellow countrymen, of other races and creeds, for the common benefit of all'.[28] These words were uttered at Madras on 27 December 1887.

Next day an entirely opposite view was expressed by Syed Ahmad Khan while addressing a large assembly of Muslim landed gentry and government officials at Lucknow on 'the attitude which the Muhammedan community ought to adopt with regard to the political movements of the time'. Eulogising the system of government maintained by the British in India he strongly denounced the Congress for advancing 'monstrous and unreasonable schemes' and urged upon his co-religionists to keep scrupulously away from it. Taking up for detailed analysis the Congress demands for recruitment to the public services through competitive examinations and the formation of legislative bodies through elections, he argued that those demands were not only unsuited to the Indian conditions, but would be particularly harmful to the Muslims. If, for instance, recruitment to the public services were made through competitive examinations, people even from ordinary families might come out successful, but people of good families in India 'would never like to trust their lives and property to people of low rank'. Besides, according to Syed Ahmad Khan, the first condition for the introduction of competitive examination into a country was that all people in that country belonged to one nation, but the case was different in India, which was '*peopled with different nations*'. This was true, he asserted, even if non-Hindus were left alone, for the Hindus of U.P., the Bengalis (by which Syed Ahmad, of course, meant Bengali Hindus), and the Mahrattas in the Deccan did not form one nation. Moreover, the people belonging to these different nationalities did not stand on the same footing so far as the requirements of competitive examination were concerned. Thus, for example, neither the Hindus nor the Muslims of U.P. could successfully compete against the Bengalis. In such a situation, the result of making recruitment to the public services dependent on competitive examination would be to place not only Muslims, but also Hindu nobles, who had not forgotten 'the swords of their ancestors' under the rule of 'a Bengali who at the sight of a table knife would crawl under his chair'. This would affect the peace of the country as the martial races would not tolerate such a situation.

Turning to the Congress demand for making elections the basis for constituting legislative bodies, Syed Ahmad Khan pointed out that this was bound to harm Muslim interests because of the difference in the numerical strength of Hindus and Muslims in India. It could be proved by mathematics that there would be 'four votes for the Hindu to every one vote for the Muhammedan. . . . It would be like a game of dice, in which one man had four dice and the other only one.' If the franchise was limited by making it dependent on the possession of a certain amount of wealth, Muslims again would not be in a position to compete with Hindus, who were certain to have a much larger number of votes. 'In the normal case no single Muhammedan will secure a seat in the Viceroy's Council. The whole Council will consist of Babu so-and-so Chukkerbutty.' This would be resented not only by the Muslims, but also by the Hindus of U.P., in particular the Rajputs, 'the swords of whose ancestors were still wet with blood'. The peace of the country would again be affected, for neither the Muslims nor their 'brave brothers, the Rajputs' could endure such a situation in silence. If a third method of election was introduced and it was stipulated that a certain number of Hindus and a certain number of Muslims were to be elected, the number of such Hindus and Muslims would naturally be proportionate to their share in the total population of the country, again resulting in the situation of one Muslim to four Hindus. Even if a provision was made to have Hindus and Muslims in equal numbers in the legislatures, Muslim interests would still suffer, for, according to Syed Ahmad Khan, among the Muslims there was no person who was equal to the Hindus in fitness for work in the legislatures. He made it clear that he was saying this on the basis of his own experience as a member of the Viceroy's Legislative Council.

Syed Ahmad Khan went on to emphasize that if Muslims did not keep away from the Congress, they would again meet the same fate which their ancestors did at the time of the revolt of 1857. For the demands of the Congress and its agitation in support of such demands were likely to create a condition of widespread discontent in the country. The Government would naturally be watching the situation. So long as the agitation was confined to those sections of the population who would merely be expected to fight with their pens and tongues, it might not take a serious view. But if the Muslims joined such an agitation, it would be duty-bound to suppress them with bayonets, for the Muslims, just like the Rajputs, once they became disaffected, would not confine themselves 'to writing with the pen—*giz, giz, giz, giz, giz*—and to mere talking—*buk, buk, buk, buk*'. Reminding the Muslims of their position as the former rulers of the country and as members of a martial race, Syed Ahmad Khan observed:

> . . . *Think for a moment who you are? What is this nation of ours? We are those who have ruled India for six or seven hundred years* (Cheers).
>
> From our hands the country was taken by Government into its own. . . . Is Government so foolish as to imagine that in seventy years we have forgotten all our grandeur and our empire?. . . We do not live on fish; nor are we afraid of using a knife and fork lest we should cut our fingers (Cheers). Our nation is of the blood of those who made not only Arabia, but Asia and Europe, to tremble. It is our nation which conquered with its sword the whole of India, although its people were all of one religion (Cheers).[29]

When, without reading the text of this speech, Badruddin Tyabji wrote to Syed Ahmad Khan, as also to some others, expressing his inability to understand how the latter justified their stand that the Muslims should keep aloof from the Congress and considering it to be a matter of great pity that 'on matters affecting India as a whole, any section of the Musalman Community should keep aloof from the . . . Hindus and thus retard the progress of India as a whole', Syed Ahmad Khan was not impressed. Tyabji had assumed that aloofness from the Congress was being advocated only on the ground that Hindus being more advanced than the Muslims would profit more from any concessions made by the Government to educated Indians.

He had, therefore, argued that it was the duty of Muslims to raise themselves in the scale of progress rather than to prevent other people from enjoying rights for which they were qualified.[30] To this Syed Ahmad Khan replied that while he did not want either to retard the national progress of India or to prevent other people from enjoying the rights for which they were qualified, he did not consider it obligatory for Muslims 'to run a race with persons with whom we have no chance of success'. Raising a more fundamental point he remarked:

I do not understand what the words 'National Congress' mean. Is it supposed that the different castes and creeds living in India belong to one nation, or can become one nation, and their aims and aspirations be one and the same? I think it is quite impossible and when it is impossible, there can be no such thing as a National Congress, nor can it be of equal benefit to all people.[31]

Deterred neither by this letter nor by Syed Ahmad Khan's speech at Lucknow, Tyabji persisted in his effort to persuade the former that the Congress did not represent the unmitigated evil that he imagined and that Muslim interests would not suffer in any way by joining it. Even he, however, did not contest Syed Ahmad Khan's view that India did not constitute one nation. In course of his next letter Tyabji observed:

Your objection to the Congress is that 'it regards India as one Nation'. Now *I am not aware of any one regarding the whole of India as one Nation* and if you read my inaugural address [at the third Congress Session, Madras, 1887] you will find it distinctly stated that there are numerous communities or nations in India which had peculiar problems of their own to solve, but that there were some questions which touched all those communities and that it was for the discussion of these latter questions only that the Congress was assembled.

Refuting Syed Ahmad Khan's assumption that the Congress represented 'Bengali Babus alone' Tyabji pointed out that it was actually supported by both Hindus and Muslims in Bombay and Madras Presidencies. While Hindus in other parts of the country also supported it, there was 'very considerable opposition' to it on the part of Muslims in Bengal and North-Western Provinces (as U.P. was then called). In such a situation Tyabji tried to persuade Syed Ahmad Khan to the view that the interests of Muslims in India would be better served by working with the Congress. As he put it in the same letter:

We can no more stop the Congress than we can stop the progress of education. But it is in our power by firm and resolute action, to divert the course the Congress shall take and my strong conviction is that the Mussalmans can by united action confine the Congress to such topics only as they may deem desirable or safe for discussion. . . . My policy, therefore, would be to act from *within* rather than from *without*. . . . We should thus advance the general progress of India, and at the same time safeguard our own interests.[32]

This failed to persuade Syed Ahmad Khan to drop his opposition to Muslim participation in the Congress. On the contrary, he now asserted that Hindus and Muslims could never cooperate politically, however cordial their social relations might be. Indeed, he foresaw a violent civil war between them once British rule over India came to an end. This rule, therefore, must remain permanent, in the interest of peace and order in India, and the best way of safeguarding Muslim interests was to work for a close relationship with the British. This line was elaborated in Syed Ahmad Khan's speech at Meerut on 16 March 1888. Here he asserted that while he did not mind the setting up of the Congress by the 'Bengalis', he strongly objected to their 'most unfair and unwarranted interference' with his nation. This interference, according to him, lay in the effort made by the so-called Bengalis to create the impression that the Muslims of U.P. were also with the Congress. According to him, they had put pressure on certain Muslims to join the Congress and even used money to lure them, and then used the presence of such 'hired men' to claim that Muslim noblemen had joined them. Syed Ahmad Khan asserted that this was 'a false accusation' against the Muslim Nation. He also considered it his duty to warn those Hindus of his province who had joined the Congress that they had made a mistake in thinking that by joining the Congress and thereby 'increasing the power of Hindus' they would be able perhaps to suppress those Muslim religious rites which were opposed to their own, and, 'by all uniting, annihilate them'. If the Hindus cherished their religious rites, they could succeed through friendship and agreement and not by pressure. The proposals of the Congress were 'extremely inexpedient', for *India was 'inhabited by two different nations*', even though they drank from the same well, breathed the air of the same city and depended on each other for its life. The truth was that Hindus and Muslims could live in peace with each other only under foreign rule. To quote Syed Ahmad Khan's own words:

Now, suppose that all the English and the whole English Army were to leave India, taking with them all their cannons and their splendid weapons and everything, then who would be rulers of India? Is it possible that under these circumstances two nations—the Mohammedans and the Hindus—

could sit on the same throne and remain equal in power? Most certainly not. It is necessary that one of them should conquer the other and thrust it down. To hope that both could remain equal is to desire the impossible and the inconceivable.

Syed Ahmad Khan added that it was difficult to say whether the Hindus or the Muslims would emerge victorious in the civil war which would ensue once foreign rule came to an end. That rested on the will of God. Lest it be assumed that the balance in such a civil war would be tilted against the Muslims, Syed Ahmad Khan considered it his duty to remind his audience that although the Muslims were less in number than the Hindus and had far fewer people who had received an English education, they must not be considered insignificant or weak. Probably they would be able by themselves to maintain their position. But if they were not able to do so, their 'Muslim brothers, the Pathans, would come out as swarm of locusts from their mountain valleys, and make rivers of blood to flow from their frontier in the north to the extreme end of Bengal'. Whoever came out supreme as a result of such a struggle, this much was certain: 'until one nation had conquered the other and made it obedient, peace cannot reign in the land'. But even this peace would not last long, for some European power or the other would soon attack and conquer India. India had thus 'of necessity' to remain under foreign rule. But the rule of any other European power would be worse than that by the British. It was, therefore, necessary that 'for the peace of India and for the progress of everything in India the English Government should remain for many years—in fact for ever!'

Having established the indispensability of British rule Syed Ahmad proceeded to show how untenable was the Congress demand for representative government. 'The principle of representative government', he affirmed, 'is that it is government by a nation, and that the nation in question rules over its own people and its own land'. There was no instance in the world where a foreign nation after conquering another and establishing its empire over it, had given representative government to the conquered people. Therefore, the demand for representative government on the part of the Congress really meant: 'Abandon the rule of the country and put it in our hands.' It was not at all expedient that the Muslim nation should support such 'monstrous proposals'. Similarly, a conquered people could not lay claim to the highest positions in the regime of the conqueror: if the latter appointed some people to high positions, it would be a favour, but this could not be claimed as a right. The 'Bengalis', not having in any period 'held sway over a particle of land', might not understand such things and go on demanding things beyond their reach, but the Muslims should behave better:

> You can appreciate these matters; but they cannot who have never held a country in their hands nor won a victory. Oh, my brother Musalmans! *I again remind you that you have ruled nations, and have for centuries held different countries in your grasp*. For seven hundred years in India you have had imperial sway. You know what it is to rule.

Once the dynamics of ruler-ruled relationship was understood, Syed Ahmad Khan emphasized, it should be easy for the Muslims to realize that the British rule in India had been quite upright and benevolent; indeed there was no other example of such benevolence in world history. High positions had been given to Indians to the extent they had shown themselves worthy of confidence of the Government. The doors of more such positions were bound to open once Indians convinced the British of their friendship and won the latter's confidence. In any case, this was the most suitable course for the Muslims. The Hindus of the province, because of some wrong notions, had joined in political controversies, but 'Bengali politics' would not be useful for Muslims. On the contrary, they should align with the British. Since the latter were Christians,—'people of the book'—such alliance, Syed Ahmad Khan pointed out, would also be in line with the tenets of their religion. To quote his own words:

> Our Hindu brothers of these provinces are leaving us and are joining the Bengalis. Then we ought to unite with that nation with whom we can unite. No Muhammedan can say that the English are not 'people of the book'. No Muhammedan can deny this: that God has said that no people of other religions can be friends of Muhammedans except the Christians. . . . Now God has made them rulers over us. Therefore, we should cultivate friendship with them, and should adopt that method by which their rule may remain permanent and firm in India, and may not pass into the hands of the Bengalis. This is our true friendship with our Christian rulers, and we should not join those people who wish to see us thrown into a ditch. If we join the political movement of the Bengalis our nation will reap loss, for we do not want to become subjects of the Hindus instead of the subjects of the 'people of the Book'.

Syed Ahmad Khan was confident that if the Muslims followed his advice, remembered their deficiencies in education and wealth as compared to the Hindus, held themselves aloof from the contemporary 'political uproar' and concentrated their energies on advancing themselves in modern education, they would in due course obtain high positions in Government and also acquire wealth. On the other hand, if they followed a contrary course, the Government would keep 'a very sharp eye' on them for they were 'very quarrelsome, very brave, great soldiers and great fighters'.[33]

As Badruddin Tyabji persisted with his plea that participation in the Congress need not harm the Muslims, Syed Ahmad Khan came forward with fresh arguments and greater vehemence to counter that plea. Tyabji pointed out in course of a letter published in the *Pioneer* on 2 April 1888 that as President of the Congress at its third session (Madras, 1887) he had rigidly excluded all questions which were of a purely provincial character or where the Hindus were opposed to the Muslims as a body or *vice-versa*. He further added that the Congress could not be rightly termed a National Congress if any resolution could be carried against the unanimous opposition of either the Hindu or Muslim delegates. In his rejoinder Syed Ahmad Khan opposed the use of the word 'delegate' for Muslims attending the Congress. At least in his own province, he asserted, not even ten Muslims came together to elect anyone of the Muslims who attended the Madras Congress. One Muslim delegate of liberal views had even proudly contended that he had been elected not by Muslims, but by Hindus. Syed Ahmad Khan asked: 'how inappropriate and absurd to apply the word 'delegate' to Muhammedans under such circumstances'. Apparently, according to his way of thinking, only that Muslim could be legitimately considered a delegate who had been elected by Muslims. He also contended that the Congress could not be described as national merely because of the fact that it could adopt unanimous resolutions. It could be called national only if the ultimate aims and objects of the people composing it were identical. As Tyabji had himself admitted that this was not so and that both Hindus and Muslims had their own separate problems and demands, in addition to the common ones which were discussed in the Congress, Syed Ahmad argued that both these communities would also need separate Congresses of their own, which in all likelihood would adopt positions on important issues opposed to one another. Would it serve any purpose, Syed Ahmad asked, if Hindus and Muslims functioned in both types of bodies simultaneously. If they did so, it would only amount to this, that with their conflicting and contradictory aims and objects, the two Congresses would go on fighting each other when they met separately, but when they assembled together in the National Congress, they would say: 'No doubt you are my nation; no doubt you are my brother; no doubt your aims and my aims are one. How do you do, my brother? Now we are united on one point.' Syed Ahmad Khan asked whether 'out of two such nations' whose aims and objects were different, but who happened to agree on some small points, a National Congress could be created. His own answer was: 'No. In the name of God—No.'

Syed Ahmad Khan, of course, admitted that on some minor points in the proposals of the Congress, the Hindus and Muslims might agree, but that, according to him, had hardly any significance. For there were no two things in the world which had nothing in common between them: 'there are many things in common between a man and a pig'. What was important was that there was not one fundamental political principle of the Congress which was not opposed to the interests of Muslims. Recalling his Lucknow speech Syed Ahmad Khan pointed out that if, for instance, the demand of the Congress was fulfilled and the members of the Viceroy's Council were chosen by election, there would be four times as many Hindus as Muslims, all their demands would be gratified, the power of legislation over the whole country would be in the hands of 'Bengalis or of Hindus of the Bengali type', and the Muslims would 'fall into a condition of utmost degradation'. 'I do not like', he added, 'to see my nation fall into this degraded condition. . . .'

Apart from his objection to the nature of the Congress demands, Syed Ahmad also made it clear again that he was fundamentally opposed to Muslims joining any political organization of the type represented by the Congress. The latter had been holding meetings in various parts of the country, attended by growing numbers of ordinary people, to air the grievances of the people and make demands of various sorts on the Government. This was creating a widespread impression among the people that the Government was tyrannical and not responsive to their wishes. If the Muslims joined in such meetings, they would suffer much more than the Hindus. 'What took place in the Mutiny?' asked Syed Ahmad Khan and himself answered: 'The Hindus began it; the Muhammedans with their eager disposition rushed into it. The Hindus having bathed in the Ganges became as they were before. But the Muhammedans and all their noble families were ruined.'[34]

III

Syed Ahmad Khan did not remain content with asserting the separate nationhood of Muslim Indians but also took steps to create organizational structures for fostering the feeling of such nationhood. The role of the Mohammedan Anglo-Oriental College at Aligarh in this respect has already been discussed in Voulme I. Here it will suffice to refer to some of Syed Ahmad's own pronouncements to show that the Aligarh College had been founded not just for educational purposes, but with the broader 'national interests' of the Muslim Indians in mind. Thus in an address presented to Sir John Strachey in December 1880, on behalf of the College Fund Committee and signed, among others, by Syed Ahmad Khan, it was stated:

> We have been guided by a deep-seated conviction that our only chance of success under the British Rule lies in education, that we can never hope to discharge our duties as citizens of a civilised State without acquiring the intellectual training necessary for a proper intelligence of the principles upon which the Government under which we live is conducted. . . . We are proud to see in the objects of our endeavours the elements of loyalty towards the British Rule, as much as a desire to advance our own national interests.[35]

Again, in a similar address presented to Lord Ripon in November 1884, it was stated:

> The aspiration of the founders of this college are purely educational but from education spring those social, political and economic blessings which civilisation brings in its train. The time has happily passed when the Muhammedans of India looked upon their condition as hopeless. . . . Their hopes are now inclined to the prospects of the future, their hearts full of loyalty to the rule of the Queen Empress aspire to finding distinction and prominence among the various races of the vast Empire over which Her Majesty holds sway. It is to help the realisation of these aspirations that the college has been founded. . . .[36]

Syed Ahmad Khan founded several other organizations to enable the Muslims in India to realize their aspirations. Thus, soon after the foundation of the Indian National Congress he founded the Muhammedan Educational Congress (1886); its name was changed to Muhammedan Educational Conference in 1890. Although its purpose was avowedly educational, and it dealt with numerous educational issues every year, it has been rightly pointed out in a recent study that its objective was 'to combine the functions of articulation and aggregation of the Muslims' educational, economic and political interests, while enabling them to define their role in the imperial polity of British India'.[37] It is not without significance that Syed Ahmad Khan delivered his first major speech attacking the Indian National Congress and advising the Muslims to keep away from it on the occasion of the second session of the Mohammedan Educational Congress (1887). Later, an avowedly political organization, the Mohammedan Anglo-Oriental Defence Association, was founded at the annual session of the Educational Conference in 1893. Still later, the All India Muslim League was also born in 1906 at that year's session of the Educational Conference. It was often emphasized in the annual reports of the Conference that its greatest achievement lay in fostering among the Indian Muslims a feeling of solidarity among themselves.[38] This was by no means incidental. Syed Ahmad Khan had this objective in his mind when founding this organization and its mode of functioning—meeting every year at an important city or town containing a sizeable Muslim population, attended by delegates from all parts of the country, with a large contingent of local observers, and ending with a dinner party on the evening of the last day—had been specifically designed to serve this purpose. As Syed Ahmad Khan himself explained in his proposal for the setting up of this body, the main purpose was to provide a forum where Muslims working for the advancement of their 'nation' through education should meet together, know each other and become familiar with the condition of their co-religionists in different parts of the country. He observed:

> It will be admitted on all hands that the condition of our nation, and particularly that of its education deserves much attention and consideration. At present, everywhere something or other is being done for doing good to the nation, but the inhabitants of one province or city are very little acquainted with the modes of thought, intentions and works of those places. People in one district, likewise, know little about the state of education of Muhammedans in other districts. . . . Besides, there is no occasion on which Muhammedans may meet together to converse on the subject of national education, and think over the means with which it may be advanced. In order to better the condition of our nation, it is necessary that we should try to do away with these deficiencies.[39]

Along with the growth of a feeling of solidarity among educated Muslims, there also developed among them a spirit of competition and confrontation with Hindus. Although not directly fostered, such a spirit was the natural end-product of the Aligarh movement, which based itself on the premise that unless Muslims of leading families bestirred themselves and took to modern education, they would be left behind by their Hindu counterparts who were already far advanced in that field. The spirit generated among the educated Muslim youth and intelligentsia by the Aligarh College is illustrated by the debate which was organized by the College Debating Society on the occasion of the fourth annual conference (1889) of the Mohammedan Educational Conference. The subject of the motion was 'That this House is of opinion that the fall of the Mughal empire was due more to Akbar's than to Aurangzeb's policy'. The discussion was quite heated. Some aspersions on the character of Aurangzeb caused offence to his admirers, whose number was obviously much larger than those of Akbar. When the motion was put to vote 119 sided with Aurangzeb and only 36 with Akbar.[40]

However, there was no direct discussion of political issues at the sessions of the Educational Conference. For that purpose Syed Ahmad Khan founded other organizations. His first effort was represented by the United Indian Patriotic Association founded in 1888. Although Syed Ahmad Khan was its moving spirit and the bulk of its supporters were Muslims, it also had some Hindus, particularly those belonging to the families of big landlords, as its members.[41] Its main objectives were (a) to publish pamphlets and other papers in order to remove the impression on the minds of members of the British Parliament and others, sought to be created by the Indian National Congress, that it had the support of 'all the nations of India and the Indian Chiefs and Rulers', (b) to convey to the members of the British Parliament 'the opinions of Muhammedans in general, of the Islamia Anjumans, and of those Hindus and their Societies' which were opposed to the objectives of the Congress; and (c) to work for the maintenance of peace and strengthening of British rule in India.[42] The Patriotic Association issued a number of pamphlets arguing that the objectives of the Congress did not suit the interests of all sections of the Indian people and that its propaganda was likely to create a deep feeling of grievance among the latter. All this would inevitably lead to another mutiny causing great hardship to the people, particularly Muslims, just as had happened in 1857.[43]

The Patriotic Association soon became a purely Muslim organization as its Hindu members slipped away.[44] Not deterred, Syed Ahmad Khan and his Muslim supporters, ably assisted by Theodore Beck, the British Principal of the Aligarh College, continued their fight against the Congress and its programme. When the Congress movement began to have some impact on Government's policy and constitutional reforms, providing for some kind of election to the legislative councils, seemed to be on the anvil, Syed Ahmad Khan and his supporters bestirred themselves. Their labours resulted in the submission to the British House of Commons of a petition in April 1890 on behalf of the Patriotic Association signed by more than twenty-nine thousand Muslims in seventy-one towns opposing the introduction of elections for constituting legislative councils in any form, as demanded by the Congress. It was stated in that petition on behalf of the Indian Muslims that the effect of introducing the elective principle in India would be 'to destroy that even-handed justice' which had been till then the basis of British rule and place them and other minorities under 'an almost intolerable subjection to classes actively hostile to their welfare'.

In support of their plea, the petitioners advanced arguments which remained the bedrock of the dominant Muslim political outlook in India almost till Partition. They, for instance, argued that the Indian Muslims, although only one-fifth of the total number of inhabitants of India, were 'the largest single community' and numbered not less that fifty million souls; the welfare of such a large number of Her Majesty's subjects could not be a matter of indifference to the House of Commons. Further, 'through its history, traditions, bravery and intelligence the Indian Muhammedan nation is a factor of great importance in Indian politics'. The Indian Muslims were not confined, 'like the nationalities of Europe', to any particular area, but were dispersed throughout India among 'the multitude of races and castes inhabiting the continent'. Being in most parts of India in a minority they were likely to be outvoted in any system of elections. This was overwhelmingly proved by what was happening in municipal elections. Besides, in the event of a popular agitation appealing to the religious sentiments of the people, as for example, the agitation against the killing of cows then sweeping the country, 'scarcely a single Muhammedan member representing Muhammedan sentiment could be returned'. A system of proportionate representation would be of no use to Muslims, for 'the Hindus of various races would be in a majority of four to one, and as all matters in the council would be decided by a simple majority, the Muhammedan members would always be inevitably outvoted'.[45]

These arguments as well as the strategy to be followed to convey them to the rulers were further refined by Syed Ahmad Khan in the coming years. In the wake of the persistent Congress propaganda in support of its demand for elected legislative councils and recruitment of Indians to the civil service on the basis of competitive examinations, the aggravation of the Hindi-Urdu controversy and the widespread Hindu-Muslim riots of 1893, he came to the conclusion that the political interests of the Muslims would be served better by a purely Muslim organization, in name as well as content. This was the natural outcome of his conviction that Muslims constituted a separate nation by themselves and, although in a minority, would never consent to be ruled by the majority. In a letter written to the Editor of the *Pioneer* and reproduced in the Aligarh Institute Gazette on 3 October 1893, he summed up the core of his argument:

> Of all countries in the world, India, being the most unhomogeneous, is the least fitted for representative government, and I regard the experiment which the agitation of the Indian National Congress endeavours to make as an experiment full of doubt and disaster to all the nationalities of India, including the Muhammedans, and to them especially, as, although the minority, they are the largest and most united minority, and not unaccustomed, at least by tradition, to resort to arms under oppression by the majority. . . .

In order to show how strongly he adhered to the view that national homogeneity was essential to the success of representative government Syed Ahmad Khan revealed that when the rules concerning the formation of the Governing Body of the Trustees of the Aligarh College were being framed he had taken special care and insisted that its members 'must all be Muhammedans'. He added that he did so in spite of the fact that there were many European and Hindu friends of the college and of himself personally, who 'by their education, sympathy with, and generosity towards, the college, are otherwise eminently fitted to be members of the Governing Body of the College'. They, of course, knew that this rule, stringent as it was, 'as to creed and nationality', was not due to any feelings of bigotry or want of toleration, but due to Syed Ahmad Khan's belief in national homogeneity as an essential condition for representative government.[46]

The foundation of the Mohammedan Anglo-Oriental Defence Association of Upper India followed within three months of the publication of this letter. The decision to found that organization was taken at a small meeting of influential Muslims at the house of Syed Ahmad Khan on 30 December 1893. The main speech was delivered by Theodore Beck, who explained at length the dangers posed to the interests of '*the Indian Muhammedan nation*' by the activities of the Congress, whose objectives were 'to transfer political power from the English Government to certain sections of the Hindu population', and pleaded for an alliance between the Muslims and the British who were 'much better disposed' towards the former than those sections of Hindus who wanted to monopolize power and appointments. According to him, the circumstances of the time demanded that 'the English and the Muhammedans should become united in a firm alliance'. Englishmen and Muhammedans', he added, 'are both in a minority in India, and are therefore both adversely affected by the application of democratic ideas to a country utterly unsuited to them. In their religious beliefs, and in character they have much in common'. He also emphasized that there was only one method to serve genuine Muslim representation in the Legislative Councils: 'the original voters should be Muhammedans, they should elect Muhammedans, and these men again elect a Muhammedan member'. He also drew attention to the problem created by the numerical inferiority of Muslims who were outnumbered one to four by Hindus, and were bound to end up as minorities in the Legislative Councils. However, this need not always be so and indeed the situation might change once the Government recognized the Muslims as 'a separate political factor'. There were already some indications that the process leading towards such recognition had begun. 'The reconciliation committees started by the Local Government after the Azamgarh and Bombay riots, in which the numbers of Hindus and Muhammedans were equal, were a clear recognition of the principle that between rival communities a balance of voting power is necessary.' At the same time Beck warned against adopting the method of political agitation and stressed that the interests of Muslims would best be served by fostering among them the sentiment of loyalty to British rule and presenting their grievances to the authorities in a reasoned manner. The British attitude towards Muslims had considerably changed during the previous ten years due to the anti-Congress stand of their leaders and this would further change for the better if the Muslims eschewed agitational methods and functioned in a loyal manner.[47] The objects of the Association as settled in 1894 were (a) to protect 'the political interests' of Muslims by representing their views to the British people as well as the Government of India; (b) to discourage popular political agitation among Muslims; and (c) to support measures calculated to increase the stability of the Government and the security of the Empire, to strive to maintain peace and to encourage sentiments of loyalty among the people.[48] Theodore Beck was named Honorary Secretary of the Association and did most of its organizational work, of course, under the watchful eyes of Syed Ahmad Khan.

As one of the objectives of the Association was to discourage political agitation among Muslims lest they became discontented with the Government and indulged in actions which invited repression, it was not to affiliate any Anjumans or organize public meetings. It did not even organize meetings of all its members. Only its executive committee met once or twice every year and adopted resolutions on matters likely to affect the political interests of Muslims. Although it never developed into an influential or powerful organization,[49] a perusal of its proceedings will nevertheless be useful in understanding the working of the mind of the dominant section of the Muslim elite working under the leadership of Syed Ahmad Khan. Thus at its meeting at Aligarh in December 1894, it welcomed the despatch of the then Secretary of State for India, Henry H. Fowler, issued in April of the year, rejecting the demand by the Congress for holding simultaneous examinations in India and Britain for selecting recruits to the Indian Civil Service. While doing so, it expressed the view that the holding of such examinations would prove 'most prejudicial to the stability of the British Government, by unduly reducing the number of English administrators, and lowering the character and efficiency of its administration'. Further, in view of the extremely uneven spread of English education among 'the various heterogeneous races and communities' in India, such recruitment to civil service on the basis of competitive examination would be 'a great act of impolicy and injustice' and result in the total exclusion from the civil service of large sections of the Indian population, more particularly the Muslims, Rajputs, Sikhs and other 'martial races' among whom English education had till then made little progress.

Another resolution adopted at the Aligarh meeting opposed the system of competitive examination then in force in the Punjab for recruitment to the posts of Munsiff and Extra Assistant Commissioner in that province, characterizing it as prejudicial to the interests of Muslims and not advantageous to the interests of administration. It was stated in support of this contention that as the proportion of Muslim students studying in the colleges of the Punjab was merely 17.2 per cent in 1886-7 and 18.2 per cent in 1891-2, Muslims were not likely to obtain more than one-fifth of the posts offered for competition. It was further pointed out that since the rate of their progress in higher education was extremely small, notwithstanding the considerable efforts made by them it was 'utterly beyond their power to make such advancement in higher education in the present generation as will enable them to compete on equal terms with the Hindus'. The resolution proceeded to point out that the system of recruitment to public services had grave defects inasmuch as the quickness of mind or memory that enabled a candidate to secure more marks than another one might be less important than any one of the qualities untested by examination such as 'integrity, courage, physique, loyalty of the candidate's family, social position or race'. In the opinion of the Mohammedan Defence Association, therefore, the interests of the public services would be better served by the government prescribing a necessary minimum educational qualification and, subject to that, nominating candidates at its discretion, 'having regard to the character of the candidates so nominated and the fair distribution of the posts among the diverse races of the Province'.

The third important resolution adopted by the Mohammedan Defence Association at Aligarh related to the admission of Muslims into the Engineering College at Roorkie. It was stated in that resolution that the number of Muslims in the engineering profession was extremely small. This was attested to by the fact that between 1858 and 1894, while 580 Hindus had obtained an engineering degree, only 3 Muslims had done so. On the other hand, the engineering profession was 'well adapted to the character of the Muhammedans who have proved themselves capable administrative officers, and are naturally endowed with the physical qualifications which are needed for the work of an engineer'. However, since admission to the Roorkie College depended on success in a competitive examination, Muslims did not have much chance of securing engineering jobs. They constituted only 6 per cent of the student population in colleges throughout India and on that basis could not be expected to get more than one post in sixteen. The Defence Association, therefore, demanded a reservation of certain number of seats for Muslims in the Roorkie College and, in addition, free admission to all those Muslims who had the minimum educational qualifications and were prepared to pay the additional costs involved in educating them.[50]

The most important decision taken at the Aligarh meeting was to request Theodore Beck, in consultation with Syed Mahmud, son of Syed Ahmad Khan, to prepare 'a draft scheme to secure the adequate representation and protection of Mahomedans in Upper India' in Legislative Councils, Municipalities, District Boards, and Local Boards'. This scheme was ready within two years and was published in the *Pioneer* as 'a Mahomedan Manifesto' on 22 December 1896. Although due to certain reasons—the time spent in seeking the views of sympathizers in Britain, the preoccupation of Syed Ahmad Khan and Theodore Beck with a case of embezzlement in the Aligarh College and then their passing away in quick succession (1898, 1899)—it could not be submitted to the Government, as was the original intention,[51] its contents are nevertheless of great significance. For they show that the ideas of separate electorate and weightage were not born suddenly in 1906 at the time of the famous Muslim Deputation to Lord Minto at Shimla, but had already been seriously canvassed at least ten years earlier. Beck had, of course, first propounded them in 1893.

The Mahmud-Beck Paper, as the draft-scheme prepared on behalf of the Mohammedan Defence Association came to be called, recognized that it would be 'useless and foolish' at that stage (i.e. in 1896) to demand the dropping of the elective principle. The Indian Councils Act of 1892 was already on the Statute Book and this was perhaps the major consideration for this recognition, representing a departure from Syed Ahmad Khan's earlier, oft-repeated, stand that the elective system was not suited to Indian conditions. The paper emphasized that in the changed situation, the objective of the Muslims should be 'to secure such a modification of the present rules relating to the Legislative Council as would give them a reasonable and just representation on them'. Taking up first the quantum of representation of Hindus and Muslims on the Legislative Council of North-Western Provinces and Oudh, the Mahmud-Beck Paper opined that although the Muslims constituted only one-sixth of the total population of the province and the Hindus five-sixths, the 'upper and educated classes' of the two communities were divided much more equally. Besides, the 'national sentiments' of the two communities were such that they would both feel humiliated at an overwhelming preponderance being given to the representatives of the other creed. Moreover, the Muslims of Upper India had 'long traditions of ascendency', their social position was not inferior to that of the Hindus, they were more united by 'a common national sentiment' than were the several castes of Hindus, and they would not, rightly or wrongly, in the existing circumstances feel that their position was adequately recognized if they were assigned one out of four seats. The paper, therefore, suggested that it would be best to apportion two seats each to Hindus and Muslims—'a fair way to do *insaf* to the two communities, of which the political status due in the one case to numerical superiority and in the other to historical position, may be regarded as equal'. Roughly the same principle was applied to municipalities and district boards. It was suggested, for instance, that in towns where the Muslims constituted one-fourth or more of the population, 'an even balance should be secured by distributing the seats equally between the Hindus and Muslims'.

Equally significant was the view of the Mahmud-Beck Paper on the nature of the electoral system. It emphatically asserted that unless Hindu and Muslim members of the Legislative Council were elected by separate Hindu and Muslim electorates, Muslims would not be able to have their genuine representatives in the Legislative Council. In the then existing circumstance when the majority of the electors were Hindus, it was natural for them to prefer those Muslim candidates whose views approximated to the former. Thus the Muslims would not only be not represented in the true sense of the term, but would in fact be 'misrepresented'. According to Mahmud and Beck, 'Elementary principles of representative institutions demand that the electors of the Mahomedan members should consist of Mahomedans and the electors of Hindu members of Hindus.' Their scheme, they emphasized, was clearly based on the assumption that the Hindus and Muslims were separate communities and had different interests in the political field. As they put it:

> The above proposals all assume one conditional fact. Namely that *the Muhammedans are for political purposes a community with separate traditions, interests, political convictions and religion*. This is so obvious that it can hardly be denied by any disinterested person who is acquainted with the facts of the case. They are much more a separate community from the Hindus than the Catholics of Ireland are from the Protestants of Ireland. . . . It is not a question here whether the Muhammedans are right or wrong. . . . The point is that they have different views, and any rational system of representation should provide for their expression.[52]

This paragraph succinctly sums up the basic assumption on which the demand for separate electorates for the Muslims was based. This assumption was not put forward for the first time in 1896, but had formed the background of the political attitude and functioning of the dominant Muslim elite ever since 1877, if not earlier. Although Syed Ahmad Khan had at first asked for only nomination and not election, the basis of that demand, was the same. Others had gone beyond nomination and asked for separate electorates also, much before 1896. The necessity for such electorates had dawned upon them so early not merely because of their innate feeling of separateness from Hindus or their belief in the concept of a separate Muslim nationhood, but also because of the generally poor showing of Muslims in elections to local bodies set up as a result of Ripon's decision in 1882. Even in towns in which they constituted a majority, they were not able to elect a substantial number of Muslims. The situation was worse where they were in a minority. And whoever controlled a municipality usually used the powers of appointment to favour the members of his own caste or community. Communal considerations influenced other decisions also.[53] This was largely because of the high property qualifications which deprived many more Muslims than Hindus of franchise. The communal bias of the electors did the rest.

Thus as early as 1884, Syed Ameer Ali, on behalf of the Central National Mohammedan Association, drew the attention of the Governor of Bengal to the plight of Muslims in Calcutta who constituted one-third of the population of that city, but were able to secure only 5 out of 48 elected seats on the Calcutta Municipality. Ameer Ali, therefore, suggested not only the lowering of the property qualifications for franchise, but also a provision 'empowering the local governments to direct the minority to elect their own representatives where the state of feeling or other considerations may render such a step expedient and desirable'.[54] Drawing the attention of the Viceroy during the same year to a letter he had received from a member of the Surat Branch of his Association pointing out the failure of Muslims to secure adequate representation in municipalities in the Bombay Presidency, Ameer Ali observed: 'With two different communities, utterly alien to each other in creed and language, customs and usage, subsisting side by side, you cannot expect one uniform system will work without any friction at all.'[55] In 1888, when constitutional reforms began to be considered, the Central National Mohammedan Association pointed out that while the system of nomination for constituting the legislative councils had not always worked satisfactorily, the introduction of representative institutions also might not work to the advantage of Muslims. This was because of the peculiar position of the Muslims in India and the fact that 'necessarily voting must take place by nationalities and creeds'.[56]

The Patriotic Association, acting under the leadership of Syed Ahmad Khan, was not the only organization which had petitioned the British Government in 1890 against the introduction of elections for constituting legislative councils on the ground that this would hurt Muslim interests. Mention may particularly be made of the representation sent to the Secretary of State for India the same year by the Mohammedan Literary

Society of Calcutta, headed by Nawab Abdul Latif and claiming to be the 'the earliest educational and political organization' of orthodox Muslims. The petition advanced the view that because of 'the peculiar religious and social circumstances of India', the country was not yet fit to have a system of elections. It further stated that if the elective principle was introduced, 'The Mahomedan community, though numbering some fifty millions, will be at the mercy of a strong and compact Hindu majority, whose notions of right and expediency are so different in many vital points from those entertained by the Mahomedans.'[57]

The demand for separate electorates for Muslims naturally emerged from such assumptions and fears once the Indian Councils Act of 1892 made elections, in however indirect a form, a fact of political life in India. The Mahmud-Beck Paper of 1896 thus did not say anything startlingly new, but only expressed a point of view which had been in the making among the dominant sections of the Muslim elite for quite some time. This should enable us to view the similar demands made by the Shimla Deputation ten years later in its proper historical perspective. Again, just as during 1906-9 so also during 1890-2, British ruling circles were generally sympathetic to the separatist Muslim fears and aspirations. Although not yet thinking of separate electorates, they repeatedly emphasized that India was a land of many nationalities and that the Muslims occupied an important place among them and should be provided with adequate representation in the legislative councils. The method agreed upon for this purpose was nomination.

Thus Viceroy Dufferin's Committee on constitutional reforms, while submitting proposals regarding the expansion of the Provincial Councils in October 1888, emphasized that due provision must be made for the presence in them of a fair proportion of members drawn from 'the two great classes, Hindus and Mahomedans, into which the population is divided'. This could be secured through the use of the governor's power of nomination which could be utilized for the purpose of 'adjusting marked inequalities of the election'. The object to be aimed at should be to see that 'the members drawn from the two great classes of the community—Hindus and Mahomedans—should bear to each other a numerical proportion approaching as nearly as may be thought desirable the proportion that Hindus bear to Mahomedans in the Provincial population'.[58] Dufferin himself emphasized in course of a letter dated 12 November 1888 dealing with the problem of expansion of the Provincial Councils that India's population consisted of 'a large number of distinct nationalities, professing various religions, practising diverse rites, speaking different languages'. He particularly mentioned the Muslims and observed that already there were signs that they were 'rising in revolt against the ascendency which they imagine a rival and less virile race is desirous of obtaining over them'.[59] When the reform bill came up for consideration before the Parliament in 1890 several important members referred to Hindu-Muslim differences and the fear of the Muslims of being swamped by Hindu representatives in the legislative councils. Thus Lord Northbrook pleaded for governors being given the discretionary power of nomination in order to enable them to secure adequate representation of people of 'different races and different religions'.[60] Lord Salisbury drew attention to the difficulty of introducing an elective system in a community which was divided into two hostile sections.[61] The Earl of Kimberley cautioned that there was 'a most important body . . . the Mahomedans of India', whose views must be taken into account and warned that there would be great difficulty if the British were guided entirely by 'the Hindoo popular opinion'.[62] Similar opinions were expressed in 1892. Thus J. Maclean observed in course of a debate in the House of Commons on 28 March that it was 'only natural that the Muhammedans should be afraid of what might happen to themselves if they were governed by a legislative body containing a majority of men bitterly opposed to them in race and religion'.[63]

After the reform bill was passed by Parliament and emerged as the Indian Councils Act of 1892, the Secretary of State for India asked the Central and Provincial Governments in India to frame rules and devise means for giving representation to the views of the 'different races, classes and localities'.[64] While Muslims were not clearly mentioned in any category, it was made clear to the Viceroy that it was his duty to see to it that Muslims secured adequate representation in the councils in commensurate with their numbers. The Secretary of State for India Lord Cross told the Viceroy, Lord Lansdowne, in June 1892 that while the Governor-General and the Governors had the power of making nominations, rules and regulations for this purpose should be framed in such a way as to secure 'a fair representation of the Muhammedans'.[65] Queen Victoria also impressed upon Lord Lansdowne the 'importance of securing an adequate representation of the great body of the Muhammedans'.[66] Lansdowne dutyfully informed the Queen that he would bear in mind the latter's wishes and mentioned that direct nominations would afford 'one means of securing proper representation for Mahomedan interests'.[67]

This concern for adequate Muslim representation in legislative councils was not, of course, the result merely of the feeling that Muslims constituted a distinct section of the Indian population and must in fairness have adequate representation, but also of the understanding of their value as opponents of the Congress, whose demands began to appear unreasonable to the British ruling circles right from the start and whose efforts to rally all sections of the India people behind itself seemed to portend a potential threat to the continuance of their rule in India. The British, of course, did not openly take sides in the controversy regarding Muslim participation in the Congress, but did not fail to underline the lack of adequate Muslim presence in the Congress and utilized it to question its representative character. Indeed this often led them to exaggerate Muslim alienation from the Congress. Thus even though two Muslims were present at the inaugural session of the Congress, *The Englishman* (Calcutta), one of the foremost Anglo-Indian newspapers, characterized it as a 'Hindu Congress'.[68] Commenting on the same session *The Times* (London) recognized that 'for the first time, perhaps, since the world began, India as a nation met together'.[69] However, it felt so annoyed at this development that it thought fit to warn the 'Hindu agitators' that it was by force that India had been conquered and it was by force that India must be governed and expressed satisfaction at the supposed Muslim abstention from such 'evil counsels' as those represented by the Congress.[70]

At the highest official level the British were keenly watching the unfolding of the general Muslim attitude to the Congress right from the beginning. Thus, under the instructions of the Viceroy, Lord Dufferin, his Private Secretary promptly informed the Private Secretary to the Secretary of State for India, Lord Cross, in December 1886 of the decisions of both the Central National Mohammedan Association and the Mohammedan Literary Society to decline the invitation of the Congress to participate in its second session being held in Calcutta.[71] In a communication to Cross sent a little later, Dufferin, while mentioning that the Muslims had 'abstained from taking any part in the Indian National Congress', maintained that they had done so entirely on their own volition and not under any pressure from officials. He further added that in his opinion the British could not make a greater mistake than 'to endeavour to sow the seeds of dissention, suspicion, or jealousy between any classes of Her Majesty's subjects'.[72] He himself, however, indirectly admitted later that he had played some role in exciting the jealousy of Muslims against Hindus. For while describing as absurd the allegation in the Indian nationalist press that the anti-Congress posture of 'Mahomedans and many of the higher Hindu Classes' was the result of his 'Machiavellian cunning', he observed: 'The most that I have done has been to express my sympathy with their [Mahomedans'] backward condition, and to exhort them, by the education of the rising generation, to pull themselves up to a level with their Hindu competitors.'[73] That the emerging Hindu-Muslim rift in the political field was found quite pleasing to the British rulers comes out more clearly in the correspondence between the successors of Dufferin and Cross. Thus in the wake of widespread Hindu-Muslim riots on the issue of killing of cows the new Secretary of State for India, Lord Kimberley, wrote to the Viceroy, Lord Lansdowne on 25 August 1893, with evident satisfaction, that in his opinion the cow protection movement made 'all combination of the Hindus and Mahomedans impossible and so cut at the root of the Congress agitation for the formation of a united Indian people', who were to force the British to surrender power into their hands.[74] Many other British officials down the line, of course, believed that even without such riots the emergence of 'a united Indian people' was an impossibility. 'The theory of a "national" movement', wrote Sir Auckland Colvin, Governor of the North-Western Provinces and Oudh, to Duffrin on 24 May 1888, 'is necessarily absurd in India. The Muhammedans, as a body, will not adopt a movement initiated by Hindus, and they detest the claim of the Hindus, whom they dispossessed centuries ago, to return, in whatever guise, to power'.[75]

IV

The Congress, too, while seeking to bring together on one platform the various sections of the Indian people, regardless of their religious, caste or linguistic differences, recognized the fact that the Muslims, because of various reasons, stood in a distinct category and made special efforts to draw them towards itself. It particularly felt compelled to do so as the British used the lack of adequate Muslim participation in the Congress as one of the main grounds for rejecting its claim to speak on behalf of the whole country. Its efforts in this direction did not always end in failure. While tackling this task, however, it was often obliged to take positions which too contributed to the strengthening of the political identity of Muslims as Muslims, a crucial factor in the growth of Muslim separatism or nationalism. Thus there emerged a peculiar paradox: the greater the Congress effort to woo Muslims as Muslims, the stronger their consciousness of the special position held by the members of their community in Indian politics. Sometimes this consciousness was also reflected in certain demands made in the Congress itself by some of its Muslim members.

As mentioned earlier, out of the seventy-two delegates present at the first session of the Congress, only two were Muslims. At the second session held in Calcutta there were thirty-three Muslims out of 431 delegates from British India. In view of the prominence given to this fact by the Anglo-Indian papers in India, the official report of the second Congress, prepared by the reception committee, took special pains to explain it, though it also mentioned that 'the matter was of no importance and need not have been noticed but for the absurd prominence given to it by some of the Anglo-Indian journals'. According to the report, apart from the general backwardness of Muslims in education and their consequent apathy to political issues, a special reason for the lack of sufficient number of Muslim delegates at the Calcutta Congress was the anti-Congress stand adopted by both the important Muslim organizations in Calcutta—the Central National Mohammedan Association and the Mohammedan Literary Society—just on the eve of that Congress.[76]

As a part of their effort to augment Muslim participation in the Congress, its leaders persuaded an eminent Muslim barrister and public worker of Bombay, Badruddin Tyabji, who had not attended the earlier two sessions of the Congress, to preside over the third session held in Madras (1887). The number of Muslim delegates also was slightly better: 83 out of 607. Tyabji took special pains to emphasize that it was 'only partially true' that Muslims had kept aloof from the Congress. As mentioned earlier in this chapter, he also asserted that there was no valid reason for the Muslims to do so.[77] After the session he wrote to important Muslim leaders like Syed Ahmad Khan and Ameer Ali imploring them to end their opposition to the Congress, but to no avail. As noticed earlier, Syed Ahmad Khan, in particular, vigorously continued his anti-Congress campaign. This upset Tyabji to such an extent that he came to the conclusion that if the political atmosphere was not to be vitiated further, it was best to prorogue the Congress for five years after its next session (1888) and to resume it at the end of that period only if the situation appeared congenial. As he explained his thinking in course of a letter to Allan Octavian Hume, generally considered as the founder of the Congress and continuing as its General

Secretary from year to year, the primary object of the Congress was to 'unite the different communities and provinces into one and thus promote harmony', but what had actually happened was just the opposite. Not only had the Mohammedans been divided from the Hindus in a manner they never were before, but the Mohammedans themselves had been split into two factions, the gulf between whom was becoming wider everyday. Tyabji noted that the Nizam and all the leading men of his state had joined the opposition to the Congress, which was led by such well-known persons as Syed Ahmad Khan, Ameer Ali and Abdul Latif. He added further:

> For the purpose of my present argument I assume that all these men are wrong and that we are in the right. Nevertheless the fact exists and, whether we like it or not, we must base our proceedings upon the fact that an overwhelming majority of Mohammedans is against the movement. Against this array it is useless saying that the intelligent and educated Mohammedans are in favour of the Congress. If then the Mussalman community as a whole is against the Congress—rightly or wrongly does not matter—it follows that the movement *ipso facto* ceases to be a general or National Congress. If this is so, it is deprived of a great deal of its power to do good.[78]

Tyabji's proposal to prorogue the Congress was, of course, not accepted by Hume. The latter told the former 'in strict confidence' that he had been enquiring 'town by town and district by district' in northern India wherever there was an appreciable Muslim population and his finding was that out of the Muslims who were intelligent enough to understand political issues, quite a large number were sympathetic to the Congress and only a few opposed to it. He also added that he believed Syed Ahmad Khan to be 'a little mad' and this was, according to him, also the view of 'some of the men in immediate private contact with him'.[79]

The substantial Muslim presence—221 out of 1248 delegates— at the fourth Congress session held at Allahabad (1888)[80] seemed to lend credence to Hume's assessment of the Muslim attitude towards the Congress. That two-thirds of them belonged to the province in which the Congress was held, which was also the home base of Syed Ahmad Khan, who had carried on a virulent propaganda against the Congress during the preceding year, further added to this credence. The speech of Ajudhiya Nath, Chairman of the Reception Committee, as also the response from the audience expressed the general feeling of elation in Congress circles at this development:

. . . I ask you, turn your eyes round this hall and see if it is true that Mohammedans do not sympathize with us. In the last Congress the number of Musalman delegates was eighty-three; now it is more that double this. (Cries of 'Treble! Treble!'). The Mohammedans of Oudh have returned at one meeting fifty-seven delegates, including members of the Royal House of Oudh. Some twenty-seven Mohammedan delegates have been returned by the district of Allahabad, and no less than eleven were returned from a place where you might not have believed that even a single one would be elected. (A voice: 'Aligarh'). Yes, how rightly you have guessed the name? (Laughter and cheers).[81]

The Congress could not, however, ignore the challenge posed by Syed Ahmad Khan's powerful propaganda. The Allahabad Congress adopted a resolution, mooted by Tyabji at the Madras Congress, in order specifically to assure the Muslims that they need have no fear of being outvoted on issues considered vital by them. It provided that no motion would be passed for discussion by the Subjects Committee, or allowed to be discussed at any Congress, to the introduction of which the Hindu or Muslim delegates, as a body, objected, unanimously or near unanimously. Even if a subject was allowed to be discussed, further discussion on it could be disallowed and resolution on it dropped if the Hindu or Muslim delegates, as a body, opposed it unanimously or near unanimously. This was, however, to apply only to subjects on which the Congress had not already formulated its opinion.[82] The fifth Congress session (Bombay, 1889) attended by 1889 delegates of which 254 were Muslims,[83] went a step further to reassure the latter. While proposing a scheme of constitutional reforms, it suggested reservation of seats in legislative councils for minorities according to their proportion in the total population of the province where they resided.[84]

The discussion on this clause was quite interesting and revealing of the diverse strands of thought in the Congress during its early phase on the best means for securing fair representation to religious minorities in the legislative councils. Thus Lala Lajpat Rai supported the minority clause by saying that although it did not matter who represented whom, for all Indians were 'one people and one nation', the clause had been inserted because of the fear lest in some cases, minorities, in whom the feeling of Indian nationhood was not yet as fully developed as it would be after sometime, might have doubts and consider themselves unrepresented if they did not have men of their own communities in the legislatures. 'This will show', he added, 'how sincere we are in guarding not only the real interests but even the possible prejudices of our Mohammedan brethren, and how careful we are to look to the interests of all minorities in every part of the country.' Rev. R.A. Hume suggested that the best way to secure fair representation to minorities was to 'trust the people'. If any deficiencies did crop up, they could be set right by the Government through its power of nomination. Hardeoram Haridas, while agreeing with the view that minorities should be represented in the legislative councils, refused to see any advantage in their being represented only by their own co-religionists, as legislative councils dealt with matters which had hardly anything to do with religion: 'I do not see how the question of a man being a Muhammedan or a Hindu has any relation to the question of the Salt Tax for example.' He further added: 'If we make these divisions in caste or religion I do not know where they will land us. There are so many sections among the Hindus themselves. . . .' Eardley Norton, as the original proposer of the minority clause, stoutly defended it, arguing that it was impossible to ignore the fact that not merely did a 'racial distinction' exist, to a marked degree, but that there were also 'very great differences of opinion on matters theologic'. He asked his colleagues to think what would happen if there were no safeguards for minority representation and the country was swept over by some great wave of a political crisis when Mohammedans would stand on the one side and Hindus on the other. What would then become of the Mohammedans?[85]

Some Muslim members dealt with this problem at greater length. Munshi Hidayet Rasul proposed through 'a very aggressive and defiant speech' an amendment to the effect that in place of proportional representation as provided for in the minority clauses, it should be laid down that in all the councils there should always be as many Mohammedan as Hindu members. This proposal was based on the assumption that Muslims were not merely the equals of Hindus, but greatly their superiors. Syed Wahid Ali Razwi emphasized this point by proposing that instead of providing that there should always be as many Muslim as Hindu members in the councils the Congress should provide that there would always be three times as many Muslims as Hindus. Indeed he argued that if the Congress was to become truly national and representative of the best portion of the nation, 'it ought to be far more Muhammedan than Hindu'. In any case, if the Muslims had, as a body, taken to it in the way Hindus had done, there would have been present at the Congress more Muslims than Hindus, for the Muslims were 'far more independent, energetic, and self-helpful than the Hindus'. He emphatically asserted that the Congress would come to nothing without the hearty support of the 'true Musalmans' who represented 'the generations and dynasties of the old Islamic conquerors'. Once their support became available, however, the Congress would be lifted to that high position which the Muslims occupied among the world's nationalities, a position of dignity and grandeur to which 'the Hindus have never had any pretensions since they were conquered by the Muhammedans, and were thus so reduced and lowered that they are now naturally unfit to execute higher duties and perform the greater works of the present day'. If India was to be represented, it was better for her to be represented by her best and not by her inferior races.

Several Muslim speakers, however, opposed such ideas. Thus Syed Mir-ud-din Ahmad Balki affirmed that people belonging to every creed and caste had the right to be represented just like the Muslims, and there could not be a more just and fair method of election than that based on proportionate representation. Besides, people of different creeds had got together in the Congress for a common objective and that objective was a secular and not a religious one: 'On such an occasion Muhammedans cannot call themselves Muhammedans; nor Hindus, Hindus; but rather forgetting all differences of creed, caste and colour we should call ourselves Indian.' Munshi Naseeruddin Ahmed affirmed that he knew only 'one nation in India, the Indian—all in fact who are born and bred here'. He would feel happy if Hindus, out of generosity, conceded equality of representation to Muslims, but he could never claim it as a right. Indeed, he would be quite happy if the minority clause was removed, for he knew that when the elective system was properly understood, the best men would be elected, no matter whether they were Hindus or Muslims or members of any of the other smaller communities. Two other Muslim speakers, who followed, pleaded to the Hindus to concede equality of representation to Muslims as a graceful concession and observed that this would reassure the latter. On the other hand, another Muslim member strongly opposed this. At first Hidayat Rasul's amendment was put to the vote of the Muslim delegates only. Out of 254 of them only 39 voted either way, 16 for and 23 against. Then the amendment was put to the whole Congress and it was negatived by an overwhelming majority, which the majority of Muslim members also joined.[86]

Seven years later something similar to Hidayat Rasul's proposal was made again by Haji Mohammed Ismail Khan, one of the chief lieutenants of Syed Ahmad Khan.[87] In course of a letter to Rahimtulla Sayani, President-elect of the twelfth session of the Congress (Calcutta,

1896), he suggested that the Congress should adopt a resolution recognizing 'the absolute necessity of equality of number of Hindu and Muhammedan elected members in Legislative Councils, District Boards and Municipalities. . . '. Sayani referred to this in his presidential address and described it as 'a good suggestion'. However, he took the position that so long as the Muslims did not join the Congress movement in the same numbers and with the same enthusiasm as the Hindus, the Congress could not in fairness be asked to carry out such a suggestion.[88] It may be interesting to note that Syed Ahmad Khan approved of Ismail Khan's suggestion. This is not surprising, for it was broadly similar to the proposal made in the Mahmud-Beck Scheme, prepared under his guidance. Syed Ahmad Khan, however, felt that a mere formal adoption of Ismail Khan's proposal by the Congress would 'amount to practically nothing'. According to him, 'the Hindu agitators should also move the Government to sanction the proposal'.[89]

In the meanwhile, after some initial success, the efforts of the Congress to draw to itself Muslims in appreciable numbers had abjectly failed. Thus while at the annual Congress session of 1890 (Calcutta) there were 116 Muslim delegates out of a total of 702 (16.5 per cent), at the Congress session in 1891 (Nagpur) there were only 71 Muslim delegates out of a total of 812 (8.2 per cent). Though at the next Congress session (Allahabad, 1892), there were 91 Muslim delegates out of a total of 625 (14.5 per cent), this was perhaps due to the special exertions of Congressmen in the North-Western Province. For the number of Muslim delegates at subsequent Congress sessions remained constantly small except in 1899 (Lucknow), when the session was again held in that province (311 out of 739, i.e. 42 per cent). Thus in 1893 (Lahore) the Congress session was attended by only 65 Muslim delegates out of total of 867 (7.5 per cent), in 1894 (Madras) by 23 out of 1163 (1.9 per cent), in 1895 (Poona) by 25 out of 1584 (1.5 per cent), in 1896 (Calcutta) by 54 out of 784 (6.9 per cent), in 1897 (Amraoti) by 57 out of 692 (8.2 per cent) and in 1898 (Madras) by 10 out of 614 (1.6 per cent). After a temporary change at the Lucknow Congress (1899), as mentioned earlier, the same trend asserted itself.[90]

The lack of substantial Muslim presence at the Congress sessions has generally been ascribed to the strong stand against that organization by prominent leaders of Muslim opinion like Syed Ahmad Khan, Syed Ameer Ali and Nawab Abdul Latif. While there is no doubt that this must have contributed to keeping the educated Muslims away from the Congress, the fact is that Muslim attendance at Congress sessions was picking up and had considerably improved in 1888 and 1889 in spite of the stand of the Muslim leaders. However, this improvement could not be sustained because of the growing communal antagonism in northern India in the wake of the anti-cow-killing agitation and the widespread Hindu-Muslim riots of 1893. This created a favourable atmosphere for the success of the Muslim leaders' campaign and queered the pitch for the Congress in its early phase.

V

Syed Ahmad Khan passed away in 1898, but his ideological legacy continued to guide the majority of educated Muslims in India. The basic elements of that legacy were that the Muslims constituted a separate nation in India and, although wishing to have friendly relations with other nations in this land, had their own special interests to protect. As they were in a minority of one to four *vis-a-vis* Hindus, and were also educationally backward as compared to the latter, their interests could not be protected by joining the Congress and supporting its demands, particularly those relating to elections to legislative bodies and recruitment to the civil services through competitive examinations, but by an alliance with the British and spread of modern education among Muslims. If elections became unavoidable Muslims must insist on adequate representation for themselves in the legislative councils, based not on their numerical strength, but on their historical importance and military prowess, i.e. their position as the descendants of the rulers of India. Also ways must be found to ensure that Muslim members of the legislative councils were elected only by Muslims. For that alone would ensure the election to the legislative councils of the genuine representatives of Muslims.

Syed Ahmad Khan attached the highest importance to modern education as a means for recovering the lost glory of Muslims and securing for them their due position in the changed situation under British rule. However, he was not opposed to political organization or political action, as is sometimes wrongly believed. Indeed, he had himself been the founder of at least two political organizations—the United India Patriotic Association (1888) and the Anglo-Mohammedan Defence Association of Upper India (1893). What he opposed was political agitation. He feared that such agitation might create discontent among the Muslims against the Government and fill the latter with distrust in Muslims. That, he thought, would be harmful to Muslim interests. However, because of his preoccupation with the building up of the Aligarh College, he had not been able to devote much time to the building up of a political organization and the Defence Association was not in a good shape when he passed away. His successors at Aligarh made it their task to remove that deficiency.

NOTES

1. S.R. Mehrotra, *The Emergence of the Indian National Congress* (Delhi, 1971), p. 212.
2. Ibid., pp. 213-24. Emphasis added.
3. Ibid., pp. 215-16.
4. Abdul Latif, 'A Short Account of My Public Life', in Enamul Haque, ed., *Nawab Bahadur Abdul Latif: His Writings and Related Documents* (Dacca, 1968), p. 160.
5. Ibid., p. 169.
6. Syed Razi Wasti, ed., *Memoirs and other Writings of Syed Ameer Ali* (hereinafter referred to as *Ameer Ali's Writings*) (Lahore, 1968), p. 44.
7. Zafarul Islam, 'A Note on the Central National Muhammedan Association', *The Proceedings of the Pakistan History Conference* (Ninth Session) (Karachi, 1962), p. 85. Islam mentions 1878 as the date of the foundation of the Association, (ibid., p. 84), but we have accepted 1877, the year mentioned by its founder. (See Wasti, n.1, p. 34).
8. Rafiq Zakaria, *Rise of Muslims in Indian Politics* (Bombay, 1970), p. 38.
9. Islam, n. 7, p. 90.
10. 'Rules of the Central National Muhammedan Association', ibid., p. 93.
11. 'Bye-Laws of the Central National Muhammedan Association', ibid., p. 97.
12. Zakaria, n. 8, p. 38.
13. Islam, n. 7, p. 87.
14. Zakaria, n. 8, pp. 17-19. For the text of the Memorial see K.K. Aziz, *Ameer Ali: His Life and Work* (Lahore, 1968), pp. 23-40. A summary is given in Zakaria, n. 8, pp. 17-19.
15. *Ameer Ali's Writings*, n. 6, pp. 165-6. Emphasis added.
16. Ibid., p. 170. Emphasis added.
17. Ibid., pp. 170-1.
18. Ibid., pp. 171-5.
19. Ibid., p. 177. Emphasis added.
20. Shah Muhammed, ed., *The Aligarh Movement: Basic Documents, 1864-1898* (hereinafter referred to as *Aligarh Documents*), III (Meerut, 1978) pp. 699-700. Emphasis added.
21. C.H. Philips and B.N. Pandey, eds., *The Evolution of India and Pakistan 1858 to 1947: Select Documents* (London, 1962), p. 185.
22. See Presidential Address by W.C. Bannerjee at the first session of the Indian National Congress, A. Moin Zaidi and Shaheda Zaidi, eds., *The Encyclopaedia*

of Indian National Congress, (hereinafter referred to as *Congress Encyclopaedia*), I (New Delhi, 1976), p. 46.

23. Bimanbehari Majumdar and Bhakat Prasad Majumdar, *Congress and Congressmen in the Pre-Gandhian Era* (Calcutta, 1967), pp. 81-3. Emphasis added. Syed Ahmad Khan must have drawn comfort from the fact that the leaders of the two leading associations of Muslims in Calcutta—the Central National Mohammedan Association and the Mohammedan Literary Society—also declined the invitation to send delegates to the second Congress session on somewhat similar grounds. Zakaria, n. 8, p. 51.
24. They were R.M. Sayani and A.M. Dharamsi, both occupying important positions in public life in Bombay. See Government of Bombay, *Source Material for a History of the Freedom Movement in India*, II (Bombay, 1958), p. 22.
25. Ibid., pp. 18-21. See also Zakaria, n. 8, p. 49.
26. *Congress Encyclopaedia*, I, n. 22, p. 68.
27. Pansy Chaya Ghosh, *The Development of the Indian National Congress* (Calcutta, 1985; 2nd edn), p. 147
28. *Congress Encyclopaedia*, n. 22, pp. 217-18.
29. For the full text of Syed Ahmad Khan's speech at Lucknow see Bimal Prasad, *Pathways to India's Partition*, I, Appendix I. Emphasis added. It is significant that in its issue of 16 January 1888, *The Times* (London) characterized this as 'one of the most remarkable political discourses ever delivered by a native of India'. See Zakaria, no. 8, p. 53.
30. See Badruddin Tyabji to Syed Ameer Ali, Syed Ahmad Khan and Nawab Abdul Latif, 13 January 1888, *Badruddin Tyabji Papers*, National Archives of India; reproduced in Government of Bombay, *Source Material*, n. 24, pp. 67-8.
31. Syed Ahmad Khan to Badruddin Tyabji, 24 January 1888, ibid., pp. 70-1.
32. Badruddin Tyabji to Syed Ahmad Khan, 18 February 1888, ibid., pp. 71-3. Emphasis added.
33. Full text in Appendix I of the present volume. Emphasis added.
34. A.M. Zaidi, ed., *Evolution of Muslim Political Thought in India*, I (New Delhi, 1975), pp. 65-8.
35. *Aligarh Documents*, III, n. 20, p. 703.
36. Ibid., p. 720.
37. Hafeez Malik, *Sir Sayyid Ahmed Khan and Muslim Modernisation in India and Pakistan* (New York, 1980), p. 218.
38. M.S. Jain, *The Aligarh Movement* (Agra, 1965), pp. 86-91.
39. *Aligarh Documents*, III, n. 20, p. 767.
40. Ibid., p. 803.
41. For the lists of affiliated Muslim Anjumans as also of donors and members see ibid., pp. 924-37.
42. Ibid., p. 909.
43. For the texts of these pamphlets see ibid., pp. 948-1005.
44. Zakaria, n. 8, p. 66.
45. For the full text of the petition as also a statement about the signatures to it see Appendix D in ibid., pp. 378-80.
46. *Aligarh Documents*, III, n. 20, p. 1017.
47. Full text of Theodore Beck's Speech in ibid., pp. 1031-9. Emphasis added.
48. Ibid., p. 1042.

49. Zakaria, n. 8, p. 84.
50. *Aligarh Documents*, n. 20, pp. 1044-7. It may be added here that the general Muslim opposition to recruitment to public services on the basis of competitive examination had already crystallized at the time of hearings by the Public Service Commission, 1886-7. This will be clear from a perusal of the report of the commission. For a summary of the submissions of leading Muslims from different parts of the country see Muhammed Yusuf Abbasi, *Muslim Politics and Leadership in South Asia, 1876-92* (Islamabad, 1981), pp. 86-91.
51. Jain, n. 38, p. 129.
52. *Aligarh Documents*, n. 20, pp. 1063-8. Emphasis added.
53. Zakaria, n. 8, pp. 142-3 and Abbasi, n. 50, pp. 286-9. See also Francis Robinson, 'Municipal Government and Muslim Separatism in the United Provinces 1883 to 1916' in John Gallagher et al., eds., *Locality, Province and Nation: Essays on Indian Politics 1870 to 1940* (Cambridge, 1973), pp. 89-95.
54. Abbasi, n. 50, pp. 284-5.
55. Ibid., pp. 286-7.
56. Ibid., p. 296.
57. Ibid., pp. 298-9.
58. Philips and Pandey, n. 21, pp. 61-2.
59. Abbasi, n. 50, p. 293.
60. Hira Lal Singh, *The British Policy in India* (Meerut, 1982), p. 116.
61. Ibid.
62. Abbasi, n. 50, p. 303.
63. Ibid., pp. 303-4.
64. Singh, n. 60, p. 110.
65. Abbasi, n. 50, pp. 304-5.
66. Ibid.
67. Ibid.
68. Zakaria, n. 8, p. 48.
69. *The Times*, February 1886, cited in ibid., p. 47.
70. Ibid., p. 49.
71. See M.N. Das, *Indian National Congress Versus the British,* I (Delhi, 1978), pp. 266-7.
72. IOR. Mss. Eur, F.130/8 A&B, Duffrin to Cross, 4 January 1887, cited in ibid., p. 268.
73. Dufferin to Cross, 29 October 1888, ibid., p. 271.
74. Ibid., p. 272.
75. Cited in S. Gopal, *British Policy in India 1858-1905* (Cambridge, 1965), p. 193.
76. *Congress Encyclopaedia*, I, n. 22, pp. 68-9.
77. Ibid., pp. 217-18.
78. Tyabji to Hume, 27 October 1888, Government of Bombay, *Source Material,* n. 24, pp. 80-1.
79. Hume to Tyabji, 5 November 1888, ibid., pp. 85-7.
80. *Congress Encyclopaedia*, I, n. 22, p. 239.
81. Ibid., pp. 291-2.
82. Ibid., p. 311.
83. Ibid., p. 324.
84. Ibid., p. 439.

85. Ibid., pp. 348, 358-61.
86. Ibid., pp. 362-72.
87. Zakaria, n. 8, p. 85.
88. *Congress Encyclopaedia*, III, n. 22, p. 90.
89. Zakaria, n. 8, p. 96.
90. Majumdar and Majumdar, n. 23, pp. 98-9. There is a misprint here regarding the session of 1899; the percentage should be 42, but it appears as 4.2; for the correct percentage see ibid., p. 92. It may, however, be pointed out that out of 311 Muslims present at the Lucknow Congress (1899) about 300 belonged to Lucknow itself. So only 11 or so came from the rest of the country, see Annie Besant, *How India Wrought for Freedom: The Story of the Indian National Congress* (New Delhi, 1975; first published 1915), p. 291.

CHAPTER II

Political Organization, Constitutional Recognition and After, 1898-1912

THE MOST prominent among those who inherited the mantle of Syed Ahmad Khan were Syed Mehdi Ali (1837-1907), generally known by his Hyderabadi title 'Mohsin-ul-Mulk', and Mushtaq Husain (1841-1917), generally known by his Hyderabadi title 'Viqar-ul-Mulk'. The former became the Secretary of the Aligarh College shortly after the passing away of Syed Ahmad and was in turn succeeded after his death by the latter. Both of them, following in the footsteps of their master, continued to give primacy to the work of the College, but they paid much greater attention than before to the task of founding a suitable political organization to safeguard Muslim interests as perceived by the leaders of the Aligarh Movement. While doing so, they reflected the growing craving for such an organization on the part of the educated Muslim elite. The latter felt that largely as a result of the growth of the Congress movement their Hindu counterparts had been able to secure significant political concessions from the British, in the form of enlarged legislative councils under the Act of 1892, of which many of the Congress leaders had also become members. They saw no reason why Muslims should not do the same. Indeed, they were convinced that if the Muslims did not take sufficient interest in political organization, they would be left far behind the Hindus in the race for status and power. Some even felt that instead of remaining politically inactive, it might be better for them to join the Congress and make their presence felt there.[1]

Such ideas emerged particularly in the wake of the order of the Lieutenant-Governor of U.P., Anthony MacDonnel, in April 1900, permitting the use of Hindi in Nagari script in the courts of the province. Though the use of Urdu was to continue, Muslims in general felt very agitated over this order and thought that this was a scant reward for all their professed loyalty to the British and aloofness from the Congress. Mohsin-ul-Mulk took the lead in voicing protest against MacDonnel's order, set up an Urdu Defence Association and organized meetings at Aligarh and Lucknow in August 1900. While speaking at the Lucknow meeting he remarked, using words reminiscent of his mentor, Syed Ahmad Khan: 'Though we do not wield the pen and our pen is not powerful which is why we are seldom seen in offices, yet we have the strength to wield the sword, and our hearts are full of love for the Queen. . . .' He could never imagine, he added, that the Government would forsake or ignore the Muslims or allow things on which their life depended to come to grief. Answering the charge of the Government that he and his colleagues were fomenting agitation against it, he observed: 'When an entire nation is aggrieved by some problem there is no need to work up an agitation or to arouse the people. At such a time our duty is to bring public opinion to a moderate level and remove false conceptions about Government's intentions from the hearts of the people.'[2] Such words did not have a soothing impact on MacDonnel's mind. He went down to Aligarh and let it be known to the trustees of the College that Mohsin-ul-Mulk must be made to choose between secretaryship of the college and that of the Urdu Defence Association; if he continued in both the positions the trustees should not bank on financial and other support from the Government. Mohsin-ul-Mulk, wanted to give up the secretaryship of the college, but the trustees persuaded him to give up instead the secretaryship of the Urdu Defence Association. The agitation spearheaded by the latter gradually died down, but this episode hurt the pride of the Muslim leaders and made many of them more than ever convinced of the need for political organization, and some of them even of agitation, to which Syed Ahmad Khan had been so allergic.[3]

This new mood was reflected in the activities of Viqarul Mulk, who emerged from his retirement to work for the Muslim cause in the wake of MacDonnel's order on the use of Hindi and the methods followed by him to suppress the pro-Urdu agitation of the Muslims.[4] He, of course, did not deviate in any respect from the teaching of Syed Ahmad Khan that the future of Muslims lay in loyalty towards the British and not in cooperation with the Congress for the introduction of democratic institutions which could only result in Hindu domination. He observed on one occasion:

> We are numerically one-fifth of the other community. If at any time the British Government ceases to exist in India, we shall have to live as the subjects of the

Hindus, and our property, our self-respect, and our religion will be all in danger. . . . If there is any device by which we can escape this, it is by the continuance of the British Raj, and our interests can be safeguarded only if we ensure the continuance of the British Government.[5]

However, Viqarul Mulk attached great importance to the setting up of a political organization of Muslims and carried out an extensive tour of U.P. in the opening years of the twentieth century with this objective in mind. One of the results of his exertions was the setting up of the Muslim Political Association at Lucknow in November 1901. The aims and objects of this Association were (a) to foster among the Muslims of India the conviction that their well-being and prosperity depended entirely on the stability and permanence of British rule in India; (b) to lay the grievances of the Muslim community before the Government in a moderate and respectful tone and to try to save the Muslims from forming a wrong opinion of any acts of the Government; and keeping in view the aforesaid objectives; (c) to refrain from assuming a hostile attitude towards other communities. It was also made clear that the demands for a representative government and the recruitment to government service through competitive examinations were injurious to Muslims and that it was 'absolutely necessary for the Muhammedans to keep themselves aloof from the Indian National Congress'.[6] The Association hardly made any progress. An effort was made to revive it through a meeting at Saharanpur in 1903, but to no avail.[7]

The partition of Bengal (1905) by Curzon and the powerful agitation against it which followed gave a fresh push to the idea of a Muslim political organization. Although there was ample administrative justification for the partition of Bengal because of its large size and population, there was a major political consideration behind the scheme of partition, as finally adopted, splitting the Bengali-speaking people of the Presidency on strictly communal lines by separating the Muslim majority districts of Bengal from the rest of the Presidency and tagging them on to Assam to form the new province of Eastern Bengal and Assam, where Muslims would be in a majority. That the object was to divide the Bengali-speaking people and thus to weaken one of the major components of the Indian nationalist movement comes out clearly in several official documents long since available to scholars. Thus the Viceroy, Curzon, wrote to the Secretary of State for India, Brodrick, in February 1904:

The Bengalis who like to think themselves a nation, and who dream of a future, when the English will have been turned out and a Bengali Babu will have been installed in Government House, Calcutta, of course bitterly resent any disruption that will be likely to interfere with the realisation of this dream. If we are weak enough to yield to their demand now, we shall not be able to dismember or reduce Bengal again; and you will be cementing and solidifying, on the eastern flank of India, a force already formidable, and certain to be a source of increasing trouble in the future.[8]

Lesser officials were thinking along the same lines. Thus the Lieutenant-Governor of Bengal saw a great political advantage in securing the eastern districts which according to him, constituted 'a hotbed of purely Bengali movement, unfriendly if not seditious in character'. The Home Member of the Government of India felt that it was most desirable to diminish the preponderance of Bengal proper in provincial politics, which he considered an evil. The Home Secretary brought out the political argument in favour of partition most clearly:

Bengal united is a power, Bengal divided will pull several different ways. That is what the Congress leaders feel: their apprehensions are perfectly correct and they form one of the great merits of the scheme. . . . It is not altogether easy to reply in a despatch which is sure to be published without disclosing the fact that in this scheme . . . one of our main objects is to split up and thereby weaken a solid body of opponents to our rule.[9]

As the movement against partition gathered momentum, the British spokesmen openly appealed to Muslim communal sentiments to rally them in favour of the partition scheme. Thus, in course of a speech at Dhaka on 18 February 1904, Curzon remarked:

Partition would make Dacca the Centre and possibly the capital of a new and self-sufficing administration which must give to the people of these districts by reason of their numerical strength and their superior culture the preponderating voice in the province so created, which would invest the Muhammedans in Eastern Bengal with a unity which they have not enjoyed since the days of the old Mussalman Viceroys and Kings.[10]

After the new province came into being (1905) the first Lieutenant-Governor, Bampfyde Fuller, made it his policy to favour Muslims while making appointments to positions in government offices, in order to rectify the situation created by the preponderance of Hindus in them. As his successor, L. Hare, informed the new Viceroy, Minto, 'Fuller had been playing off the two sections of the population against each other'.[11] Hare, of course, continued Fuller's policy of encouraging Muslim recruitment to government offices. This had the full support of Minto. Although he had been primarily instrumental in the acceptance of Fuller's resignation (1906) on account of difference over methods of dealing with the Swadeshi agitation, particularly the singing of *Vande-Mataram* by school students, he clearly saw advantage in building up Muslims to counterbalance the Hindus, who were in the forefront of the Swadeshi movement in Bengal. As he wrote to Morley:

> I have always had great hopes of the Muhammedan population. They have not Bengali [Hindu] gifts of eloquence, and comparatively one hears little of them. But they are made of sterner stuff than the Bengali, and now that they are becoming somewhat alarmed at what they consider Bengali successes, the justice of our safeguarding their interests will become all the more apparent, and ought to be of real assistance to us in dealing with much of the one-sided agitation we have to face.[12]

Although Minto had absolutely no regret regarding the acceptance of Fuller's resignation, he was not at all unhappy at the widespread expression of Muslim feeling against that. 'As long as it does not get out of control', he wrote to Morley, 'it will, I hope, be very useful to us. It shows, at any rate, that there are two sides to the question. . . .'[13] This British policy of openly encouraging Muslim communal aspirations certainly paid rich dividends to the Government.

The creation of a Muslim majority province had, of course, obvious attractions for many Muslims, and it is not at all surprising that both the Mohammedan Literary Society and the Central National Mohammedan Association advised Muslims not to join the anti-partition agitation.[14] However, the pull of Bengali solidarity was also there. A good many Muslims joined the Hindus in opposing partition in the initial phase and there never was a time when there were no Muslims to be found in the ranks of those opposing partition. As has been pointed out in the most authoritative work on the anti-partition movement, 'some amount of Muslim participation can in fact be traced in virtually every aspect of the Swadeshi movement'.[15] However, as the advantages to Muslims in the matter of government appointments and such other matters unfolded themselves, more and more Muslims rallied to the support of the creation of the new province.

Another factor which contributed significantly to this development was the growing Hindu ethos of the Swadeshi movement and the increasing use of Hindu religious symbols, rituals and heroes by its leaders in order to secure mass participation. It has been rightly observed that 'in view of the formidable barriers to unity set up by tradition, British policy and the attitudes of many Hindu nationalists, what is surprising is not the eventual alienation of the bulk of the Muslims, but the extent of their participation in the Swadeshi movement'.[16] Muslim alienation from the anti-partition agitation soon took the form of powerful support for partition. The day on which partition was put into effect (16 October 1905), a Mohammedan Provincial Conference met in Dhaka under the leadership of Nawab Salimullah and hailed the creation of the new province. It also set up a new political organization called the Muhammedan Provincial Union, with Salimullah as patron, with the objective of uniting the Muslims of the new province and furthering their interests. The first anniversary of the partition (16 October 1906) was celebrated by Muslims of the new province as a day of rejoicing. On the other hand, many Muslims expressed resentment at the way boycott of British goods was imposed upon them in various localities by powerful Hindu landlords, sympathetic to the Swadeshi movement. Above all, they deeply resented the acceptance of Fuller's resignation, which was generally thought to be the result of Hindu pressure. The Muslims gathered in a big meeting in Dhaka and strongly protested against it, describing his administration as 'just, sagacious and sympathetic' and the acceptance of his resignation as 'a great injustice' to Muslims.[17] The general Hindu-Muslim divide on the issue of partition led to the growth of considerable tension between the two communities and this resulted in riots at several places. Muslim political consciousness now became much stronger. The acceptance of Fuller's resignation, in particular, had a great impact on the Muslim mind. It led Muslims to ponder, much more seriously than before, on the need for political organization and agitation. They were convinced that it was the Hindus' superiority in this field which enabled the latter to score a success like the acceptance of Fuller's resignation. As Mohsin-ul-Mulk observed in an important letter, there had been a considerable change in Muslim feeling. He was constantly getting letters 'using emphatic language' and pointing out that the Hindus had succeeded due to their agitation and Muslims had suffered because of their silence. They were, therefore, thinking more and more of political organization and agitation. In this connection he referred to a letter he had received from Syed Nawab Ali Choudhry of Dacca, in which the latter had observed:

> . . . uptil now the Muhammedans of Bengal have been careless. They have now begun to feel the consequences of their carelessness. If only the Muhammedans

of Bengal, instead of following the Government, had agitated like the Hindus and had enlisted the sympathies of the Muhammedans of the whole of India, and raised their voice up to the Parliament, they would never have seen these unfortunate consequences.[18]

Lady Minto has recorded a similar impression of the feelings of young Muslims in her *Indian Journal*:

> The younger generation were wavering, inclined to throw in their lot with the advanced agitators of the Congress, then came Fuller's resignation. A howl went up that the loyal Muhammedans were not to be supported, and that the agitators were to obtain their demands through agitation.[19]

II

All this indicates that the leading Muslim disciples of Syed Ahmad Khan were veering increasingly towards political organization. Before setting up a political organization, however, they had a more urgent task to perform, a task, moreover, which they had already taken in hand. This was to present their views to the Government regarding the modality as well as quantum of Muslim representation in the legislative councils and other related matters. The urgency arose from the new Secretary of State Morley's speech on the Indian budget in the House of Commons on 20 July 1906, foreshadowing constitutional reforms, including expansion of the legislative councils and the introduction of the elective principle, the main demands of the Congress. 'I do not say', he declared, 'that I agree with all that the Congress desires, but, speaking broadly of what I conceive to be at the bottom of the Congress, I do not see why anyone who takes a cool and steady view of Indian Government should be frightened'.[20]

Mohsin-ul-Mulk who, as Secretary of the Aligarh College, was considered by many as the natural leader of the Indian Muslims, immediately swung into action. On 4 August 1906, a few days before Fuller's resignation, he sent an urgent letter to W.A.J. Archbold, Principal of the M.A.O. College at Aligarh, then vacationing in Shimla and having easy access to the Viceroy's office, particularly his secretary, Dunlop Smith. Here Mohsin-ul-Mulk drew Archbold's attention to Morley's speech on the Indian budget, and informed him that it was being very much talked of among the Muslims of India who commonly considered it as a great success achieved by the Congress. The Muslims, he added, had already been feeling a little disappointed and many of them, particularly the young and the educated, seemed to be developing sympathy for the Congress. Morley's speech was likely to produce a greater tendency among them to join the Congress. The general complaint of such Muslims was that the Aligarh leaders had hardly done anything to protect Muslim rights. They were particularly worried by the likely consequences of the introduction of elections to legislative councils on a more extensive scale than before and felt that Hindus would 'carry off the palm by dint of their majority' and no Muslim would get into the councils through election. If the Aligarh leaders did not do anything at that juncture, Muslims in general would leave those leaders 'to go their own way and act up to their own personal opinions'. Informing Archbold that a proposal had been made to submit a memorial to the Viceroy in order to draw the attention of the Government to 'the rights of Muhammedans', Mohsin-ul-Mulk asked him for advice on the matter. Imploring him to treat it as 'a very important matter' and to reply as soon as possible Mohsin-ul-Mulk wrote to Archbold: 'You have, there, an opportunity of knowing the opinion of government officials on the matter, and you can thus give me valuable advice in this connection.'[21]

In the absence of knowledge of this letter, historians as well as publicists, particularly in India, had treated Archbold's reply to Mohsin-ul-Mulk dated 10 August 1906, as the starting point of the process which culminated in the famous Muslim deputation to the Viceroy, Lord Minto, on 1 October 1906. On this basis, it had generally been imagined that the whole show had been engineered by the British through the instrumentality of Archbold.[22] However, the text of Mohsin-ul-Mulk's letter became available to scholars in 1960 with the opening of the private paters of John Morley, the Secretary of State for India, deposited at the India Office Library, and of Lord Minto, the Viceroy of India, who had received the Muslim deputation at Shimla, preserved at the National Library of Scotland at Edinburgh. Historians now naturally came to the conclusion that the initiative for the Simla Deputation had been taken not by Archbold, but by Mohsin-ul-Mulk, acting on behalf of the Muslim leaders of the Aligarh School.[23] There could be no dispute over this point.

However, as happened on most of such occasions, while the initiative came from the Muslim leaders it received warm encouragement and support from the British officials, who saw in such an initiative an useful instrument to counterbalance the movement of Indian nationalism, whose success would mean the end of their rule. Thus Mohsin-ul-Mulk's letter dated 4 August, despatched from Bombay, was presented by Archbold to the Viceroy at Shimla through his Private Secretary, Dunlop Smith, on 8 August, and a copy of it was despatched on the same day to the Secretary of State for India in London. While sending it Minto wrote to Morley: 'I have not had time to think over the advisability of receiving the proposed deputation, but am inclined to do so.'[24] Indeed it did not take Minto much time to take the decision to receive the deputation. On 10 August Smith noted on another letter from Archbold, sent on the previous day: 'I have told him H.E. will agree to receive the Deputation.'[25] An early decision was, of course, going to be the major contributory factor to the success of Mohsin-ul-Mulk's efforts for roping in influential Muslims as members of the deputation. That is why he did not want to start the work without receiving Archbold's advice. The latter, fully understanding the implication of Mohsin-ul-Mulk's request, had written to Smith on 9 August: 'If the Muhammedans were informed (*privately*) that a deputation would be received and a statement made what would happen would be that representative Muhammedans from various parts of India would come to Simla and present a carefully drawn up petition.'[26]

After hearing from Smith that the Viceroy would agree to receive the deputation, Archbold wrote to Mohsin-ul-Mulk on 10 August: 'Please remember that if we want to organise a powerful movement in the short time at our disposal, we must expedite matters.'[27] Archbold also helped in drafting and suggested the main points to be included in the memorial to be presented to Minto. All his suggestions, however, were not accepted, showing that although utilizing Archbold's valuable services and soliciting his advice, the Muslim leaders were not by any means acting under his guidance on every point but exercising their own minds regarding safeguarding Muslim interests as they viewed them. Commenting on Archbold's draft, for instance, Mohsin-ul-Mulk wrote to him on 18 August: '. . . I am sure nobody will like the opening phrases which give an assurance of a deliberate aloofness from political agitation in the future.'[28] The Muslim leaders, as we shall soon see, also rejected Archbold's suggestion that adequate Muslim representation in the Legislative Councils might be secured through nomination.

The deputation led by the Aga Khan and consisting of thirty-five leading Muslims—'nobles, jagirdars, taluqdars, lawyers, zemindars, merchants and others', as its members described themselves—presented an address to Minto at Simla on 1 October 1906. After recording their appreciation for 'the incalculable benefits conferred by British rule on the teeming millions belonging to diverse races and professing diverse religions, who form the population of the vast continent of India', the Address emphasized the importance of the Muslim community in India. The Mohammedans, it mentioned, numbered over sixty-two millions, according to the census of 1901. This amounted to between one-fifth and one-fourth of the total population of British India. If a reduction was made for 'the uncivilised portions' of the Hindu community, enumerated under the heads of animists and other minor religions, as well as for those classes who were ordinarily classified as Hindus, but were actually not Hindus, the proportion of Muslims to the Hindu majority would become much larger. On this basis the Address pointed out that under any system of representation, 'a community in itself more numerous than the entire population of any first class European power, except Russia', might justly claim to be recognized as 'an important factor in the State'. It ventured a step further and urged that the position accorded to Muslims in any system of representation 'should be commensurate not merely with their numerical strength, but also with their political importance, and the value of the contribution which they make to the defence of the Empire'. It hoped that the Viceroy would give due consideration to *'the position which they [Muslims] occupied in India a little more than a hundred years ago, and of which the traditions have naturally not faded from their minds'*. Further, it drew the attention of the Viceroy to the fact that although Muslims had till then placed their implicit reliance on the sense of justice and fair-dealing of the British and, had therefore, desisted from doing anything in order to press their demands which might prove embarrassing, a new spirit was gaining ground. Certain recent events had stirred up feelings, particularly among the younger generation, which might, under certain conditions, 'easily pass beyond the control of temperate counsel and sober guidance'.

The Address proceeded to point out that representative institutions of the European type were new to the Indian people and that 'the greatest care, forethought and caution' would be necessary to adapt them to the conditions obtaining in India. In the absence of such care and caution, Muslim 'national interests' were likely to be placed 'at the mercy of an unsympathetic majority'. Since, however, representative institutions had already been assigned an important place in the governance of the country, Muslims, in their 'own national interests', could not afford to keep aloof from them. While expressing the thankfulness of the Muslim community for the representation accorded to it in the legislative councils so far, largely through nomination, the Address mentioned that that representation had been inadequate and had not always carried with it 'the approval of those whom the nominees were selected to represent'. If the method of election was followed, it was unlikely that any Muslim candidate would be elected, unless he was in sympathy with the views of the majority community on all matters of importance. While Muslims could not find fault with the Hindus for favouring persons of their own community or those Muslims who would be expected to vote with them, Muslim interests suffered in the process:

> It is true that we have many and important interests in common with our Hindu fellow-countrymen, and it will always be a matter of the utmost satisfaction to us to see these interests safeguarded by the presence, in our Legislative Chambers, of able supporters of these interests, irrespective of their nationality. Still it cannot be denied that *we Muhammedans are a distinct community with additional interests of our own, which are not shared by other communities*, and these have hitherto suffered from the fact that they have not been adequately represented. Even in the provinces in which the Muhammedans constitute a distinct majority of the population, they have too often been treated as though they were inappreciably small political factors, that might, without unfairness, be neglected. This has been the case, to some extent, in the Punjab; but in a more marked degree in Sind and in Eastern Bengal.

The Address, therefore, suggested that in local bodies as well as in the provincial Legislative Councils and the Imperial Legislative Council, the number of Muslim seats should be fixed, on the basis of considerations mentioned earlier, and special constituencies, consisting only of Muslims, should be created to elect their occupants.

In addition, the Address demanded increased Muslim share in government appointments of all kinds, including judgeships of the High Courts and membership of the Viceroy's Executive Council, and the setting up of a Muslim University 'a subject which most closely affects our national welfare'. The Address concluded by assuring the Viceroy that by assisting the Indian Muslims in the directions suggested he would be 'strengthening the basis of their unswering loyalty to the Throne and laying the foundation of their political advancement and national prosperity'.[29]

The deputationists had no reason to be disappointed with the Viceroy's response. Minto at the outset underlined the representative character of the deputation, 'expressing the views and aspirations of the enlightened Muslim community of India', described them as '*the descendants of a conquering and ruling race*', and hailed them as the standard-bearers of 'the inspiration of Sir Syed Ahmad Khan and the teachings of Aligarh', which according to him, shone forth 'brilliantly in the pride of Muhammedan history, in the loyalty, common sense, and sound reasoning so eloquently expressed in the Address'. Finally, without formally committing the British Government to enlarged Muslim representation and separate electorates, the main demands of the deputationists, Minto expressed his whole-hearted agreement with the views presented in the Address:

> The pith of your Address, as I understand it, is a claim that in any system of representation—whether it affects a Municipality, a District Board, or a Legislative Council . . . —the Muhammedan community should be represented as a community; you point out that in many cases electoral bodies as now constituted cannot be expected to return a Muhammedan candidate, and that if by chance they did so it could only be at the sacrifice of such a candidate's views to those of a majority opposed to his own community whom he would in no way represent; and you justly claim that your position should be estimated not merely on your numerical strength but in respect to the political importance of your community, and the service it has rendered to the Empire. *I am entirely in accord with you* (Applause). Please do not misunderstand me. I make no attempt to indicate by what means the representation of communities can be obtained, but I am as firmly convinced as I believe you to be that *any electoral representation in India would be doomed to mischievous failure which aimed at granting a personal enfranchisement regardless of the beliefs and traditions of the communities composing the population of this continent* (Applause).[30]

This was obviously Minto's way of vindicating the British position of 'entire and resolute impartiality between races and creeds' in India, which he had earlier assured Morley he was going to do in response to the Address of the Muslim Deputation.[31] He was, of course, quite happy with his performance. 'As to the deputation', he wrote to Morley shortly after the event, 'I very much hope you will be satisfied with the reports of my speech. . . . I was very anxious to avoid appearing to take sides, while yet heartily acknowledging the soundness of Muhammedan arguments. . . . As far as I can judge the whole affair was an immense success.'[32] Morley who had earlier told Minto that the Muslim Deputation should provide an 'excellent occasion for indicating our entire and resolute impartiality between races and creeds',[33] whole-heartedly concurred with this view. 'All that you tell me of your Muhammedans', he wrote to Minto in reply, 'is full of interest for me, and I only regret that I could not have moved about unseen at your garden-party. . . . The whole thing has been as good as it could be. . . .' He was particularly pleased to think that after the presentation of its address by the Muslim Deputation, it would not be possible for the 'Cottonians' (sympathisers of the Congress in Britain) to present the Government of India 'as the ordinary case of a bureaucracy *versus* the people. I hope that even my stoutest radical friends will see that the problem is not quite so simple as this.'[34]

Lesser personages commented more candidly on the advantage to be derived by the British from Minto's reply to the Muslim Deputation. Lady Minto recorded in her journal the receipt of a letter from an official on the day the Muslim Deputation had been received: 'I must send your Excellency a line to say that a very, very big thing has happened today. A work of statesmanship that will affect India and Indian history for many a long year. It is nothing less than the pulling back of sixty-two millions of people from joining the ranks of the seditious opposition.'[35] This was not a hyperbole, but a natural reaction of a British official in the context of the contemporary political situation in India as viewed by the Viceroy and the people around him. 'I have been thinking a good deal lately', Minto had written to Morley in May 1906, 'of a possible counterpoise to Congress aims. I think we may find a solution in the Council of Princes, or in an elaboration of that idea, a Privy Council not only of native rulers, but a few other big men to meet, say once a year.'[36] After a few weeks, while expressing his agreement with Morley in the latter's desire to meet reasonable demands for constitutional reform, he again wrote: 'though there are many honest men connected with the Congress movement, I cannot disguise from myself that we are every day being brought more face to face with absolutely disloyal intentions, the ultimate object of which is the overthrow of British administration'.[37] And, as noted by Lady Minto and mentioned earlier in this chapter, in the wake of Fuller's resignation, many Muslims, particularly of the younger generation, were thinking of joining the Congress. Again, as mentioned earlier, Mohsin-ul-Mulk too was worried that the leadership of the Muslims might slip out of the hands of the Aligarh group. The feeling of elation among the British ruling circles at the organization of the Shimla Deputation and Minto's handling of it was thus quite natural.

The same atmosphere prevailed in the camp of the Muslim leaders. They naturally felt encouraged by the British attitude, as reflected in Minto's reply to their Address, towards their demands for separate electorates and weightage, based on the recognition of Muslims as forming a distinct community in India deserving of special position due to historical and other factors. These demands, it is needless to add in view of the facts mentioned in the first chapter, had not been formulated on the spur of the moment, but had been there on the agenda of Muslim politics since 1896, if not earlier. Mohsin-ul-Mulk expressed the feelings of the Muslim leaders in his letter to Dunlop Smith:

> You will allow me on behalf of the Members of the Deputation to assure you that His Excellency's great speech in reply to the Address, embodying as it does a clear and sympathetic recognition of the rights of the Muhammedans of India, as a distinct community, based on a generous appreciation of their political importance as being inferior to that of no others, has put a new heart in us, and will always, with gratitude, be treasured by us and our posterity as a historic declaration of the policy of the Indian Government.[38]

The assumption underlying the Muslim demands has been summed up best by the Aga Khan, who had formally led the deputation and read the Address. 'Now in 1906', he writes, 'we boldly asked the Viceroy to look facts in the face: we asked that *the Muslims of India should not be regarded as a mere minority, but as a nation within a nation* whose rights and obligations should be guaranteed by statute'.[39] This finally came about in 1909, but the ground for it was prepared by the Simla Deputation in 1906.

III

In the meanwhile, the success of the Simla Deputation hastened the process, already underway, of the emergence of an all-India Muslim political organization. In a way the one led directly to the other. For it became obvious to the leaders of the deputation that since they had secured separate electoral recognition they 'must have the political organization to make that separate representation effective'.[40] Indeed, the need for such an organization had been felt by the Muslim leaders even while organizing the Simla Deputation. Mohsin-ul-Mulk had at one stage informed Archbold that Muslim leaders might not like him 'to represent their cause to the Government without the means of a political association'.[41] Although the Address was presented without forming any political association, the need for such an association continued to be felt. As Mohamed Ali wrote in his introduction to the summary of the proceedings of the Foundation Conference of the All India Muslim League: 'Before a communal representation, side by side with territorial representation, could be fairly demanded, the community must point out to the Government a representative body of men whom, as such, it could unhesitatingly accept'.[42]

Both at Lucknow, where the contents of the Address were finalized, and at Simla, where the Address was presented to Minto, the Muslim leaders who had assembled for the occasions seriously discussed the ways and means for setting up an all-India organization. It was decided at Simla that it was best to deal with this matter at Dhaka at the time of the forthcoming annual session of the Mohammedan Educational Conference in December 1906. Accordingly, the All-India Muslim League was founded at Dhaka on 30 December 1906, with the following objects:

(a) To promote among the Musalmans of India feelings of loyalty to the British Government, and to remove any misconception that may arise as to the intention of Government with regard to any of its measures.

(b) To protect and advance the political rights and interests of the Musalmans of India, and respectfully to represent their needs and aspirations to Government.

(c) To prevent the rise among the Musalmans of India of any feelings of hostility towards other communities without prejudice to the other objects of the League.[43]

Needless to add, the last object was merely for cosmetic purposes, as made clear by the conditional phraseology used. The first two were the real objects. In Nawab Salimullah's scheme for the Muslim All-India Confederacy, which was circulated among the Muslim leaders in November 1906 and served as the basis for the scheme adopted for the All-India Muslim League, only two objects had been mentioned. They were considered two sides of the same coin: 'the sole object and purpose of the Association shall be, whenever possible, to support all measures emanating from the Government and to protect the cause and advancement of the interest of our co-religionists throughout the country'. An anti-Congress stance was implicit in such write-up. This came out clearly in Salimullah's explanation of the *raison d'être* of an all-India Muslim political organization:

(a) To controvert the growing influence of the so-called Indian National Congress, which has a tendency to misinterpret and subvert the British rule in India, or which may lead to that deplorable situation, and (b) to enable our young men of education, who, for want of such an association, have joined the Congress camp, to find scope to exercise their fitness and ability for public life.[44]

The main argument behind such objects and stance was explained at length by Viqar-ul-Mulk in course of his presidential address to the foundation meeting of the League. Muslims, he emphasized, had not yet forgotten the tradition of their recent rule in India and elsewhere and were more intimately acquainted than others in India with the relationship that should subsist between the rulers and their subjects. They should, therefore, accept it as a rule of their conduct that 'the plant of the political rights of a subject race thrives best in the soil of loyalty, and consequently the Musalmans should prove themselves loyal to their Government before they can ask for recognition of any of their rights'. There were other cogent reasons, Viqar-ul-Mulk added, for supporting the British. The lives and property, honour and religion of Muslims were all bound up with the stability of British rule. For if that rule ended, there could be no escape from the domination of Hindus, who, for historical reasons, could not be depended upon to show any interest in the protection of Muslim interests or honour. As Viqar-ul-Mulk put it:

> The Musalmans are only a fifth in number as compared with the total population of the country, and it is manifest that if at any remote period the British Government ceases to exist in India, then the rule of India would pass into the hands of that community which is nearly four times as large as ourselves. Now, gentlemen, let each of you consider what will be your condition if such a situation is created in India. Then our life, our property and our faith will all be in great danger, and when even now that a powerful British administration is protecting its subjects, we the Musalmans have to face most serious difficulties in safeguarding our interests from the grasping hands of our neighbours, instances of which are not rare in any province or District, then *woe betide the time when we become the subjects of our neighbours, and answer to them for the sins, real or imaginary, of Aurangzeb who lived and died two centuries ago, and other Musalman conquerors and rulers who went before him.*

This, it was clarified, did not necessarily mean any hostility towards Hindus. Viqar-ul-Mulk emphasized that as their neighbours, it would always be one of the first duties of the Muslims to reat the Hindus with fairness and courtesy and without prejudice to their legitimate rights and interests, carry on an intimate social intercourse with Hindus and avoid all forms of hostility towards them. He went a step further and declared that there was no quarrel between the Muslims and the Congress; nor did the Muslims oppose everyone of the latter's acts or views. He indeed expressed thanks to the Congress for its efforts to secure certain advantages that all Indians shared. It was possible, he added, that in future Muslims might even consider some of the programmes of the Congress as justified. All this, however, did not in any way dilute his firm conviction that Muslim interests and honour were bound up with the fortunes of the British. If the Congress leaders failed to restrain their followers and the latter's growing hostility to the British resulted in spreading sedition in the country, 'the Musalmans of India would be called upon to perform the necessary duty of combating this rebellious spirit, side by side with the British Government, ***more effectively than by the mere use of words***'.[45]

We need not read too much into these protestations of loyalty to the British on the part of the founders and early leaders of the Muslim League. They were not fundamentally different from similar protestations on the part of the founders and early leaders of the Congress: partly an expression of genuine feelings and partly a matter of necessity in the context of the contemporary situation. In any case, the Muslim League leaders, just as their counterparts in the Congress, pursued their own interests and objectwes even while making these protestations. It is, of course, a fact that these interests and objectives very often converged with British interests and objectives. This was the basis of the unwritten alliance between their promoters. But the Muslim leaders were no stooges of the British and did not function at the latter's orders. Indeed, there were occasions when they acted against the known wishes of the British rulers.

While it is a fact that some of the key-figures among the founders of the League had maintained contact with the leading British officials in India and kept them informed of what was going on, there is absolutely no evidence to suggest that the British in any way either inspired the foundation or influenced the shape of the organization which eventually emerged.[46] Thus, for instance, wrote the Aga Khan to Dunlop Smith shortly after the reception of the Muslim Deputation:

> In order to reach the definite objects mentioned by the Deputation. . . . I have asked all members . . . to form a permanent committee, and I have given to my old friend Nawab Mosin-ul-Mulk, who as you know is a most loyal and zealous Muhammedan, certain instructions regarding the methods by which he is to proceed. . . .
>
> I have also asked him not to move in any matter before first finding out if the step to be taken has the full approval of Government privately, as otherwise, unintentionally, he might be led to do something or other that would leave the Government in an inconvenient situation.[47]

However, as has already been noticed, the organization which was finally founded was based not on any scheme prepared by the Aga Khan, but on that prepared by Salimullah. Mohsin-ul-Mulk was, of course, a confident of both, but he, as well as his close colleague, Viqar-ul-Mulk, who together played a key role in the foundation of the Muslim League, were guided by the general sentiment among the Muslim leaders of their school of thinking. The urge for an all-India political organization of Muslims was not suddenly born in the wake of the Simla Deputation, but had been there since the turn of the century, though there is no doubt that the success of the Simla Deputation facilitated its fulfilment. It would not, therefore, be wrong to say that the foundation of the Muslim League was not the result of any British machination, but represented the natural culmination of the dominant pattern of Indian Muslim thought and action since the foundation of the Central National Mohammedan Association of India at Calcutta and the Anglo-Oriental Mohammedan College at Aligarh in 1877.

IV

The greatest achievement of the Muslim League in its early years was the torpedoing of Morley's scheme to secure Muslim representation in the legislative councils, proportionate to their numbers, through mixed electoral colleges, constituted on the basis of a territorial franchise. This was the result of his search for a formula which would 'at once satisfy Muslim expectations, roused by Minto's promises, without violating his own Liberal revulsion against making religious affiliations the primary criteria for election'.[48] The Muslim League leaders mounted a vigorous campaign both in India and Britain against Morley's scheme. They were clear and emphatic that they would not be satisfied without separate electorates and larger representation than their numerical strength warranted. One of the highlights of this agitation was the large number of meetings, some of them attended by thousands of Muslims, held in different towns of northern India. Muslim shops remained closed in Lucknow and Dhaka on the days of the meetings. This type of agitation was a new phenomenon in the evolution of Muslim politics in India in modern times. The leaders of the Muslim League, of course, rightly took the stand that their basic demands had already been conceded by Minto and Morely's scheme represented a departure from that position. They must have also felt encouraged by the knowledge that Minto, conscious of his commitment to them, was strongly opposed to Morley's scheme. Even so, both the spread and the intensity of the agitation were 'really indicative of the depth of Muslim feeling in favour of separate electorates'.[49] The agitation also confirmed that the leaders of Muslim nationalism were acting on their own volition and not on the prompting of the British rulers, as has very often been imagined by Indian historians. The success of this agitation, epitomised by the abandonment of Morley's scheme and the acceptance of both separate electorates and weightage for Muslims in the Legislative Councils under the Act on 1909, was a great victory for early Muslim nationalism. It set the seal of constitutional recognition on the position of Muslims in India as 'a nation within a nation', and immensely facilitated their march towards independent nationhood.

The main arguments advanced by the leaders of the Muslim League in favour of their demands for separate electorates and weightage in 1908-9 also strengthened the ideological foundations of Muslim nationalism. Thus Syed Ali Imam, in his presidential address to the second annual session of the Muslim League, held at Amritsar in December 1908, remarked that in spite of Muslim rule over India for centuries, Hindus and Muslims had maintained their different identities intact: 'Centuries rolled by but the conqueror and the conquered in point of nationality, character and creed suffered not from their political association. Characteristics of race and religion and political and social ideals of the two presented irreconcilabilities.' The result was that the two communities, 'from the truly social point of view', were as far apart in the twentieth century as they were a thousand years ago. Time had not worn out any of the angularities that characterized their social systems when they first came face to face. Indeed, according to Imam, apart from 'ethnic diversity of character', the two communities had 'nothing in common in their traditional, religious, social and political conceptions'.[50] Reacting strongly against the widespread use of Hindu rituals and symbols in the anti-partition agitation in Bengal, he observed:

> I cannot say what you think, but when I find the most advanced province of India put forward the sectarian cry of 'Bande Mataram' as the national cry, and the sectarian Rakhibandhan as a national observance, my heart is filled with despair and disappointment; and the suspicion that, under the cloak of nationalism, Hindu nationalism is preached in India becomes a conviction.[51]

While moving from the chair the resolution opposing Morley's scheme of election of a certain number of Muslims through mixed electoral colleges on the ground that it would preclude the election of the 'real representatives of minorities' and ensure the return of such members as were 'only mandatories of majorities',[52] he also objected to the proposed quantum of representation given to the Muslims. The latter had been provided representation in the ratio of 1 to 3 Hindus. Ali Imam observed that this might be in accordance with the numerical strength of the two communities, but was 'certainly not justified by the social, traditional, and religious considerations attaching to the Indian Muhammedans'. According to him, the test of mere numbers was 'dangerous and misleading'. For the first time introducing the Pan-Islamic connections of Indian Muslims as one of the factors behind their political status, he remarked: 'As a community, the Muhammedans contribute largely to the defence of the Empire and have also the weight of their Pan-Islamic relations to enhance the value of their position in India.'[53]

Speaking in support of this resolution, other important leaders made similar speeches. Thus Syed Nawab Ali Choudhry, one of the most prominent leaders of the pro-partition movement in Bengal, observed: 'It sounds very well to hear that the Hindus and Muhammedans should work together in harmony, but past events are a criterion to assure us that a difference exists between the Hindus and the Muhammedans, and that their interests, aims and objects cannot be one.'[54] Mohamed Ali, later to become famous as Maulana Mohamed Ali, remarked that Morely had failed to recognize one of the most important differences between Britain and India. This difference was that in India the line of cleavage between various political interests was 'not territorial but denominational'. Besides, in India, the religious faith of a man did not only stand for his relationship with his Maker, and was not merely a matter of spiritual difference. In the course of many centuries it had become a matter also of strong temporal difference and stood for 'a different outlook on life, different mode of living, different temperament and necessarily different politics'.[55]

Ameer Ali, as President of the London Branch of the Muslim League, went even further in emphasizing the difference between the two communities and referred to them as different nationalities or nations. Thus in his letter to *The Times*, dated 14 January 1909, he emphasized that the rank and file of the two communities in India were 'widely divided in habits, customs, and traditions of race and religion'. Besides, their political objectives were different: the Hindus were most anxious to preserve and extend the ascendency they had gained while the Muslims aspired to obtain a share of the benefits promised to India by British rule. 'Under existing conditions and in the present state of feeling among the general body of the two nationalities', he added, the system of election through joint electoral colleges proposed by Morley would lead to 'constant friction, heart-burning, and complaints. In certain localities . . . worse results may be apprehended.'[56] In his presentation before Morley on 27 January 1909, as the leader of a deputation on behalf of the London Branch of the League, he further elaborated this argument and emphasized that it was wrong to treat the Muslims in India as a minority. Their population was quite substantial and, bound by certain common ties, they constituted a distinct nationality and should be treated at par with the other major nationality (i.e. Hindus) in India. To quote his own words:

> It has been said that the Muhammedans form a minority among the population of India. There, they do not equal in numbers the other great community which inhabits India, but they are seventy million souls, fifty-three of whom are under British rule. They have common ideals, and by traditions of race and religion form a nationality apart from all other people in India. To call them a minority is a misapplication of the term, and to regard them in that light would be an injustice to the Mussalman people. We form a nationality as important as any other, and our wishes, sentiments and interests should, we conceive, form as important factors in the consideration of policy and measures as those of any other.[57]

In support of the contention that the Muslims deserved to be treated at par with the Hindus, Ameer Ali pointed out that 'the vast masses of low-caste people' were only nominally Hindus. If they were excluded from the Hindu figures in the census, the disparity in size between the Hindu and Muslim populations 'would not strike as so great or so disproportionate'. In any case, the principle of proportional representation, Ameer Ali emphasized, would be fatal to Muslim interests. Whatever might be the value of proportional representation in countries where the people were homogeneous, it was wholly unsuited to India; for under such a system the representation of Muslims would be 'completely swamped'. Note must also be taken of the fact, Ameer Ali added, that the Muslims shared the burden of defending the empire to the same extent as other Indians and perhaps sent a larger number of soldiers to the Indian Army than that sent by all the rest of the Indian population. He did not ask for parity for Muslims with Hindus in representation to the legislative councils, but emphasized that the representation of Muslims should be 'not only adequate, but substantial' in order to give them 'an effective voice' in the deliberations of the councils. With this in view he suggested that the number of Muslim members in the various councils should be so fixed that if they joined the 'non-partisan members' (an euphemism for the official and nominated members) they should be able to carry their motion on any particular question.[58] At a luncheon meeting of the London League on 23 February 1909, Ameer Ali, in his presidential address, went a step further and declared that the impending reforms could be successfully implemented 'only by recognising the differences between the two nations and their equal importance as factors in the administration of the country'.[59]

The Aga Khan, the permanent president of the All-India Muslim League, fully endorsed such views. In an interview published in *The Times* on 15 February 1909, he observed: 'An Act of Parliament cannot weld into one, by general machinery, two nationalities so distinct as the Hindus and the Muhammedans'. The relations between the two communities, according to him, were such that if one secured predominant political power or was in a position to impose its will on the other, it would 'always not only be liable but compelled by religious and social circumstances to exert that authority'.[60]

Ironically, Morley, with all his liberal convictions, openly expressed his agreement with such propositions. This is amply borne out by his speech in the House of Lords on the occasion of the second reading of the Indian Councils Bill on 23 February 1909, while announcing the abandonment of his scheme of mixed electoral colleges and the acceptance of separate electorates, as suggested by Minto, together with much larger weightage than that suggested by the latter. Morley defended his *volte-face*, prompted by the strong support for the Muslim demands by the conservative sections of the British press and Parliament, by underlining the difference between Islam and Hinduism. That difference, he emphasized was not a mere difference of religious faith, but 'a difference in life, in tradition, in history, in all the social things as well as articles of belief that constitute a community. . . '[61]

V

Needless to add, while fighting for separate electorates and weightage, the leaders of the Muslim League also played the loyalty card. Thus, the resolution against Morley's scheme of election through mixed electoral colleges adopted by the Aligarh Session (December 1908) of the Muslim League declared that unless that scheme was modified to provide for representation on a purely denominational basis, it would 'mark the first breakdown of that implicit faith which Musalmans have so long placed in the care and solicitude of Government whose just pride and profession have been to hold the scales even'.[62] Mian Mohammad Shafi, one of the prominent League leaders in the Punjab, in his first of four letters sent to Dunlop Smith in January 1909 on the ensuing constitutional reforms, affirmed that in dealing with important problems of that type he looked at them from what might be called 'the Anglo-Muhammedan point of view'. This was because he was sincerely convinced that the interests of the Muslim community in India were 'absolutely identical with those of the British Government, and the Anglo-Indian community'.[63] In another letter he remarked that the Muslims constituted 'the really and truly loyal section' of the Indian population.[64] When Shafi learnt that Morley had an interview with the King-Emperor in which the question of protection of Muslim interests was discussed, he wrote to Dunlop Smith that that news would have sent 'a thrill of gratitude to His Majesty' in the hearts of millions of Indian Muslims. 'I assure you', he further wrote, 'that all this will bind the Muhammedan community still closer to the British rule with the silken chains of sincere gratitude and loyalty, and will strengthen the Anglo-Muhammedan bond of union a hundred-fold.'[65] In the same letter Shafi conveyed special thanks to Minto for 'the generous and noble support His Lordship is extending to our backward—but sincerely loyal—community in their struggle for self-preservation and self-defence against an aggressive majority'. He assured Minto that the latter had won, 'not only the sincere gratitude, but deep affection of the entire Muslim community in India'.[66] Ameer Ali used the supposed Muslim loyalty to the British as an additional ground for buttressing the League's demand that the size of Muslim representation on the legislative councils must not be limited to the proportion of Muslims in the Indian population. As he put it in his letter to *The Times,* dated 14 January 1909:

> The importance of a nation cannot always be judged on numerical considerations. Whatever may be the view regarding the historical and political position of the Muhammedans, to which the Government in India attaches some value, Muhammedan loyalty is an asset to the Empire which I venture to submit ought not to be lightly put aside.[67]

The British did not lightly put it aside. Minto at any rate was fully alive to the value of Muslim loyalty. Without this assumption it would be very difficult for anyone to explain his whole-hearted support to the Muslim demand for separate electorates as well as weightage in representation on the ground of the political importance of the Muslim community in his response to the Simla Deputation in October 1906.

His letters to Morley on that deputation, to which reference has been made earlier, clearly indicate his happiness at the availability of the Muslim card in dealing with the Indian nationalist agitation, particularly in Bengal. In the controversy over Morley's scheme of mixed electoral colleges, Minto consistently took the stand that it would be impolitic to deviate from the promises he had made at Simla. That turned him into a strong opponent of Morley's scheme. That the loyalty factor was one of the major considerations behind Minto's stand is borne out by the following extract from one of his letters to Morley, explaining the attitude of Muslims towards the latter's scheme:

To put it briefly, they say that large Hindu majorities will enable Hindus not only to elect their own man but a Muhammedan as well, and that being so a Muhammedan may be elected representative of advanced Hindu political inclinations, and not at all of bonafide Muhammedan interests. Moreover, *the old fashioned Muhammedans who are such a loyal mainstay to us,* are not likely to push themselves forward and will be left in the lurch, if opportunity is given for the election by manipulated Hindu votes to secure seats for a younger Muhammedan generation that is being drawn into the vortex of political agaitation.[68]

Both Minto's strong opposition to Morley's scheme and the significance attached by him to the Simla Deputation come out clearly in his letter to a former Viceroy of India, Lord Lansdowne:

The 'electoral colleges' are absolutely impossible—mad and distinctly contrary to pledges I had given to the Muhammedans, and of which the Government of India approved. We simply cannot have them. I am so glad you saw the meaning of the deputation to me—it was by far the most important event that has happened during my time.[69]

Even after Morley agreed to abandon his scheme and provide for separate electorates Minto kept up the pressure on him. Thus in April 1909, he wrote to Morley: 'Muhammedan electorates are absolutely necessary—if we retreat at all from that view, we shall have an infinitely worse trouble than anything that can arise from Hindu opposition.'[70] As has been observed by an admirer of both Minto and Dunlop Smith, Minto was here reflecting the latter's view that 'in the last resort the Government had more to fear from Muslim than from Hindu hostility on account of the *greater basic loyalty of the Muslims to the British Raj*'.[71]

That Muslim loyalty was an invaluable asset and further that there was a tremendous advantage in keeping the Muslims and Hindus divided was also realized by British non-officials in India, and they saw the use of separate electorates in securing that objective. This was duly communicated to the decision-makers. Thus wrote Lovat Fraser, editor of *The Times of India*, to Dunlop Smith after a conversation with the Aga Khan:

I am sure you realise, as keenly as he appears to do, that probably our greatest danger in India is the likelihood of an *entente*, so much desired by many of the younger and abler Muhammedans, between Hindus and Musalmans. Men like the Aga firmly feel that, in pressing for large separate treatment for Muhammedans, they are fighting our battle much more than their own. We have far more to lose than the Moslems by an *entente* between Islam and Hinduism.[72]

There is thus considerable justification for the general Indian view that the provision for separate electorates and weightage under the Act of 1909 represents an excellent illustration of the British policy of divide and rule, adopted with a view to keeping Muslims away from the Indian nationalist movement. Minto's ardent as well as persistent championship of separate electorates owed much to that consideration. The same applies also to certain sections of the British press and Parliament, who lent their strong support to the Muslim demands. However, the British had not invented those demands. Besides, they were also genuinely convinced that the arguments of the Muslim leaders were sound.

Whatever that might have been, there is no doubt that separate electorates turned out to be an invaluable source of support to Muslim nationalism and played a crucial role in shaping its evolution in the coming years. They symbolized, as nothing else did, the position of Muslims in the then Indian society—'a nation within a nation' as the Aga Khan put it. That position, of course, was already a fact of life and did not suddenly emerge in 1909. But the constitutional recognition of that position under the Act of 1909 solidified it and made it difficult for the Muslims to be absorbed by the growing current of Indian nationalism. On the other hand, it provided the starting point of that politico-constitutional process which, step by step, within less than forty years, culminated in the birth of Pakistan. This is not to suggest either that the course of that process was already set in 1909 or that anyone knew or even thought about its culminating point. All that lay in the future. Besides, both the course of the process and its final outcome were brought about not by separate electorates alone, but by their conjunction with several other variables.

VI

Surprising though it may seem, the years immediately following the introduction of separate electorates and weightage for Muslims in the various legislatures did not witness any exacerbation of conflict between the forces of Indian nationalism and Muslim nationalism, represented respectively by the Indian National Congress and the All India Muslim League, but just the opposite. The leaders of the Congress realized that whether they liked separate electorates and weightage or not, these had become a reality with which they had to live. They also knew how keen the British were to keep the Muslims on their side and realized that the Congress must do whatever was possible to draw the latter to the side of Indian nationalism in order to ensure its success. The leaders of the Muslim League, on their part, thought that once separate electorates and weightage had been secured, there was no point in continuing an antagonistic relationship with the Congress. They also realized that even with separate electorates and weightage Muslims and Hindus had to live together in the same country and face many common problems.

That the Congress and the Muslim League, in spite of their different stands on the issue of separate electorates and weightage, were able to move towards each other in quest of understanding and cooperation so soon after their introduction, was also partly due to the fact that, contrary to what has been generally imagined, the Congress at that time was not too strongly opposed to separate electorates, though the same cannot be said about its attitude towards the large weightage provided by the regulations made under the Act of 1909. This is clearly borne out by the stand of Gopal Krishna Gokhale, then its most prominent leader, in course of his speech on the budget in the Imperial Legislative Council on 29 March 1909, well after Morley's announcement of the abandonment of his scheme of proportional representation of Muslims through mixed electoral colleges and its substitution by separate electorates and weightage. He then revealed that he had communicated his opinion in favour of limited separate electorates to the Secretary of State for India as early as September 1908. According to him, the 'most reasonable plan' was first to throw open a substantial minimum of seats to election on the basis of territorial constituencies, in which all qualified to vote could do so without any distinction of race or creed. Subsequently the Government could hold supplementary elections for a few additional seats in order to rectify the imbalance, if any, in the representation of minorities, and these should be confined to the latter. Since this was also the proposal of the Government of India and Morley seemed to have fallen back on it after the abandonment of his own scheme, Gokhale saw no ground for complaint. On the contrary, he saw an advantage in providing for composite election by all communities up to a certain point and then prevention of injustice to minorities by giving them special supplementary electorates of their own. He was, of course, opposed to placing Hindus and Muslims in watertight compartments and did not consider it at all feasible. However, he not only saw no objection to the introduction of separate electorates in the absence of unity between Hindus and Muslims, which could not be denied, but even felt that this would promote their coming together. As he put it:

> My Lord, it has been urged by some of my countrymen that any special separate treatment of minorities militates the idea of union of all communities in public matters. Such union is no doubt the goal towards which we have to strive, but it cannot be denied that it does not exist in the country today, and it is no use proceeding as though it existed when in reality it does not. Not only this, but unless the feeling of soreness in the minds of minorities is removed by special separate supplementary treatment such as is proposed by the Government in India, the advance towards a real union will be retarded rather than promoted.[73]

Gokhale also answered those who criticized the plan of separate electorates as recommended by the Government of India on the ground that under it Muslims would have the opportunity to vote twice, once in general territorial electorates and then in separate, communal electorates. The matter, he pleaded should be looked at 'in a large way and in a practical spirit'. For the objective was 'not to secure a scientific accuracy of method, but to obtain substantially just and satisfactory results'. Then there was the question of quantum of representation. Under the plan of the Government of India, Muslims were to be given slightly larger representation than their proportion in the population warranted. This did not bother Gokhale. According to him 'a member more or less for either the Hindus or the Muhammedans' was not a matter of much consequence in the given situation. For neither the existence of Government was going to depend on the votes of the non-official members of the legislative council nor were the members of the Government to be drawn from the latter. The most important advance envisaged under the reforms was the power conferred upon members of the legislative council to raise discussion on administrative matters, and for that purpose the exact proportion of members returned by any community was 'a matter of small importance'.[74]

Gokhale was, however, opposed to the excessive demand for weightage being then made by the leaders of the Muslim League. This is borne out by his speech at Poona on 11 July 1909 on the Hindu-Muslim question. Therein he showed his deep understanding of the importance of this question by stressing at the very outset that it was one of two or three most important questions that lay at the very root of India's national regeneration, and as regards the difficulties it represented, it exceeded all. 'The worst of the situation', he added, 'was that over the greater part of India the two communities had inherited a tradition of antagonism, which though it might ordinarily be dormant, broke forth into activity at the smallest provocation. It was that tradition that had to be overcome.' On the other hand, 'there could be no future for India as a nation, unless a spirit of cooperation of a sufficiently durable character was developed and established between the two great communities, in all public matters'. The question of Hindu-Muslim relations, therefore, had to be handled with great care, forbearance and self-restraint. In the then existing situation, Gokhale again saw no escape from the introduction of separate electorates on a limited basis, as suggested both by himself and the Government of India. That, according to him, was the only course which reasonably safeguarded the interests of all communities and prevented injustice to any one of them in practice. However, when matters went beyond it and some of the leading spokesmen of the Muslim community demanded a larger representation than they were justly entitled to on grounds such as special importance and higher loyalty, Gokhale felt that it became the duty of the other communities to protest strongly against such claims.[75]

The regulations made under the Act of 1909 also appeared quite unjust to Gokhale. According to him, the weightage for Muslim representation in the Imperial Legislative Council was 'so excessive as to be not only unjust but monstrously unjust'. Although Muslims formed only one-fifth of the population of the Bombay Presidency, three out of four members of that Council from there for the next three years were going to be Muslims. The situation was more or less similar with regard to other parts of the country. There was provision for three members in the Imperial Council from the Punjab. It was expected that in the beginning all three would be Muslims, with Hindus, constituting nearly half of the population, sometimes having no representative and sometimes only one. What hurt even more was the great difference in qualifications for franchise between Muslims and others. Thus, for example, in the city of Bombay, while every Muslim who had an annual income of Rs. 135 had a vote in the election of a member to the legislature council, no Hindu or Parsee, however wealthy or whatever his position in other respects, could vote unless he was a member of the three of four public bodies which had been called upon to return a member. 'And it is the same everywhere. The distinction is too glaring and hurts very much in practice.'[76]

It is this feeling which was reflected in the resolution on the council reform adopted by the twenty-fourth session of the Congress held in December 1909. While appreciating the efforts of both Morley and Minto, which, according to it, had resulted in 'a fairly liberal measure of constitutional reforms', it placed on record its 'strong sense of disapproval of the creation of separate electorates on the basis of religion'. Expressing its dissatisfaction with the regulations framed under the Act it particularly referred to 'the excessive and unfairly preponderant share of representation' given to Muslims and 'the unjust, invidious, and humiliating distinctions' made between Muslims and non-Muslims in matters relating to electorates, franchise and qualifications of candidates.[77] While a large number of speakers dilated upon these defects, the butt of their criticisms was directed not towards separate electorates as such but towards these two points underlined in the reasolution.[78] Madan Mohan Malaviya, who presided over that session, summed up in his address the general Congress attitude on the matter of separate electorates for Muslims. Taking his cue from Gokhale, he observed:

> We were prepared to agree that a certain amount of representation should be granted to them; that they should try to secure it through the general electorates, and that if they failed to obtain the number of representatives fixed for them, they should be allowed to make up the number by election by special Muhammedan electorates formed for the purpose.
>
> The Regulations which have been published, however, not only provide that they shall elect the number of representatives which has been fixed for them on a consideration not only of their proportion to the total population but also of their alleged political importance, by special electorates created for the purpose, but they also permit them to take part in elections by mixed electorates, and thereby enable them to secure an excessive and undue representation of their particular community to the exclusion to a corresponding extent of the representatives of other communities.[79]

A still more moderate line was adopted by the next annual session of the Congress (1910). There was a serious difference of opinion among the members of the Subjects Committee whether the resolution of the last annual session on the subject of council reform should be reaffirmed or not, and the Committee debated this matter at three sittings. The resolution as finally adopted was a compromise between the opposing views.[80] It recognized the necessity of providing for a fair and adequate representation in the legislative councils for Muslims and other communities where they were in a minority, but disapproved the regulations promulgated in 1909 to carry out that object by means of separate electorates. In particular it urged upon the Government to remove the 'anomalous distinctions' between the different sections of the Indian people in matters relating to franchise and qualifications of candidates.[81] As a part of the same compromise the Congress also adopted a resolution deprecating 'the extension or application' of the principle of separate electorates to municipalities, district boards or other local bodies.[82] It is interesting that the mover, the seconder and the supporter of that resolution were all Muslims. M.A. Jinnah who moved the resolution, though it necessary to make it clear that he had not wished to speak, but he agreed to do so 'in response to the wishes of a great many leaders of the Congress'. He also thought it fit to add that he was not representing the Muslim community, nor did he have any mandate from that community, but only expressing his 'personal views . . . and nothing more'. Mazharul Haq, who was a member of both the Congress and the League, emphasized that he was in both the organizations because he believed in the unity of India. In order to provide a bridge between the Congress and the League, on the one hand he asked the former to accept separate electorates for the Imperial and Provincial Councils, as they were already there and, on the other hand, asked Muslims to stop there and not demand their extension to local bodies.[83]

Next year (1911) Gokhale again made it clear that in his opinion, separate electorates for Muslims were necessary in view of the failure of sufficient number of Muslims to get into the legislative councils under the Act of 1892, except through nominations. Speaking in the Imperial Legislative Council on Malaviya's resolution asking for the appointment of a committee to suggest changes in the regulations made under the Act of 1909, he affirmed: 'I think, at our present stage, special electorates cannot be avoided. . . .' He, of course, also reiterated his objection to over-representation of Muslims in the legislative councils, but stressed the impraticability of any step to reduce it at that stage. 'You cannot', he observed, 'take away from the Muhammedan community today what you gave them only yesterday, and I would say to my Hindu brethren, make the best of the situation in the larger interests of the country.' In any case, he emphasized, in the councils, as they were constituted then, weight of numbers did not decide anything. That might become important in future, but at that stage it did not really matter which community had how many members in the councils. It was, therefore, best to leave such questions alone for sometime.[84] Gokhale's views could not be ignored by other Congress leaders. While the annual Congress session of 1911 reiterated the moderate resolution on council reforms adopted in 1910,[85] the next Congress session (1912) did not do so, but merely contented itself with reiterating the resolution deprecating the extension or application of separate electorates to local bodies.[86] The next Congress (1913) did not reiterate even that resolution.[87]

VII

In the meanwhile, the Muslim League, too, was moving towards conciliation and accommodation with the Congress. It has been generally assumed that this process began with the annulment of the partition of Bengal in December 1911 and the growing Indian Muslim interest in the developments in Turkey and Persia. Actually, it began right on the morrow of the foundation of the League. This was facilitated by a change in its top leadership. Mohsin-ul-Mulk passed away in October 1907 and his successor at Aligarh, Viqar-ul-Mulk, had to remain preoccupied with affairs of the College. In their place emerged leaders like Ali Imam and Shah Din, who were anxious to build bridges with the moderate leadership of the Congress.[88] The new trend was reflected in the address of Sir Adamji Peerbhoy, the president of the first annual session of the League held at Karachi in December 1907. He failed to understand, he declared, 'why the Muhammedans should in the advancement of their own interests injure those of any other people. It is no part of the purpose of this League to oppose the progress of other communities or to be aggressive towards them in any direction whatever. We respect all who work for the common good of the country'.[89] This trend of thought was reflected in the modification by the Karachi session of the third objective of the League. At Dhaka this had been spelled out as preventing 'the rise among the Mussalmans of India of any feeling of hostility towards other communities'. Now this was changed to promoting 'friendly feelings between the Mussalmans and other communities'.[90]

Even while opposing proportional representation through mixed electoral colleges and insisting on separate electorates and weightage, and using the separate nationhood of the Indian Muslims as the main ground for this demand, the Muslim League leaders were also, in their own way, preparing the ground for cooperation with the Hindus. Thus, for instance, Ali Imam, while emphasizing the socio-cultural differences between Hindus and Muslims in course of his presidential address to the second annual session of the League, held at Amritsar in December 1908, to which reference has been made earlier, also dilated upon the growth of a common patriotism among the educated Indians, regardless of religious or racial differences, as a result of the British rule and the common use of the English language. This is what he said:

> Hindu or Muhammedan, Parsee or Christian, intellectually the educated Indians have drawn nourishment from one and the same feeding-bottle, the great liberalising influence of the great British race. With all the theological, social and ethnic differences between communities in India, it is futile to question the fact that the educated Indians, of whatever race they may be, have acquired a common attitude of thought relating to the land of their birth. There seems to be unanimity in the sentiments of love for the mother country. . . . We, the educated Mussalmans of India, have no less love for the land of our birth than the members of the other communities inhabiting the country. India is not only the land of our birth, we are tied to her by the sacred association of age. We yield to none in veneration of and affection for our motherland.[91]

After the League's success in securing separate electorates and weightage, its sessions continued to be marked by these dual trends. On the one hand, it demanded safeguards for what it considered special Muslim interests. On the other hand, its leaders also emphasized the need for conciliation and accommodation with Hindus. Thus the third annual session of the League, held in Delhi in January 1910, placed on record 'its deep sense of appreciation' of the Indian Councils Act (1909) and the regulations made under it (which provided for separate electorates and weightage) and offered its 'grateful thanks' to the Government for them.[92] By another resolution it demanded the extension of separate electorates to 'all self-governing bodies'.[93] It also expressed the view that the number of Muslims employed in the various branches of public service was 'absolutely inadequate' and strongly urged the Government to give the Muslim community that share in the public service to which it was entitled by reason of both its importance and numerical strength.[94] Further, it deplored 'the attempts made in certain quarters to damage the importance of Urdu as the principal vernacular of India' and recorded its view that the preservation and advancement of Urdu language and literature were essential for the general progress of the country.[95] By another resolution it reiterated the necessity of 'a separate Muhammedan university of their own for the Indian Mussalmans' and emphasized the desirability of raising the Aligarh College to the status of such a university.[96]

At the same session which adopted these resolutions, howeve, the Aga Khan, as the permanent President of the League, delivered an address which was remarkable, among other things, for its stress on the necessity of Hindu-Muslim cooperation, while working at the same time to protect special Muslim interests. Said the Aga Khan:

> I have no hesitation in asserting that unless Hindus and Muhammedans cooperate with each other in the general development of the country as a whole and in all matters affecting their mutual interests, neither will develop to the full its legitimate aspirations or give full scope to its possibilities. In order to develop their common economic and other interests, both should remember that one is the elder sister of the other, and that India is their common parent; religious differences should be naturally reduced to the minor position, as such differences have been in America and Western Europe.[97]

Ameer Ali, who had played a leading role in the agitation for separate electorates, expressed similar sentiments in his presidential address, which was read in his absence:

> . . . I sincerely trust that the two great communities whom the Reforms mainly affect will decide to work together in harmony and concord for the good of their common country. They have to live together, to progress together, and in evil days to suffer together. The Mussalmans have established their right to be in the land by a longer domicile than the Normans in England; many of them have the same blood in their veins as their Hindu fellow-countrymen. There is no reason whatever why, in spite of difference of religion, customs, habits of life and ideals, they should not cooperate in the great task which lies before them both, of promoting the welfare of India under the aegis of the British Crown. National development, even the fulfilment of the dream of self-government, depends on the cooperation of both races in a spirit of amity and concord.[98]

Thus we see the idea of 'a nation within a nation' being operationalized by some of its most prominent leaders immediately after the promulgation of separate electorates and weightage. Just like Syed Ahmad Khan, both the Aga Khan and Ameer Ali frequently asserted that Indian Muslims constituted a nation and must be treated as such.

At the same time they looked upon India as a whole also as a nation and wished both Muslims and Hindus to cooperate to advance its welfare. However, separatist politics was taking its toll. The agitation for separate electorates, just as the agitation against the partition of Bengal, had resulted in the general worsening of Hindu-Muslim relations. As a result of discussions among Sir William Weddenburn, who presided over the twenty-fifth session of the Congress held at Allahabad in December 1910, Sir Pherozeshah Mehta, a veteran Congress leader, the Aga Khan and Syed Ameer Ali, it was decided to hold a conference of selected leaders of the Congress and the Muslim League at Allahabad just after the close of the twenty-fifth session of the Congress in order to arrive at 'a friendly settlement of differences' between Hindus and Muslims.[99] The conference, formally convened by Wedderburn,[100] met on the appointed day (31 December 1910), chaired initially by him and then by the Aga Khan. The points for discussion were provided by a memorandum prepared by Ameer Ali in London with some additions made by certain Muslim leaders in India. These included the extension of separate electorates and weightage to local bodies, and an understanding regarding cow-killing and the playing of music before mosques. It was also demanded that since the Muslims would be in a minority in the legislative councils, 'no question should be urged which the Muslims, as represented by the Muslim League, may look upon as detrimental to their communal interests'. The conference, however, failed to produce any agreement. The only result of its deliberations was the appointment of a committee consisting of eight Hindus and seven Muslims, with one Hindu and one Muslim as joint convenors to further consider the matters raised at the conference and make recommendations on them. The committee proved to be a non-starter, and there is no evidence of its having ever met to consider the subject entrusted to its care. One of the most serious hurdles in its way was, of course, the difference between the two sides on the weightage provided to Muslims by the regulations framed under the Act 1909. This became clear when Madan Mohan Malaviya, himself a member of the committee, moved a resolution in the Imperial Legislative Council proposing the appointment of a committee to report on the changes to be introduced in the regulations made under the Act of 1909 so as to remove some of the anomalies created by it, as also to ensure real non-official majority in the provincial councils. Although he withdrew the resolution, this proved to be the death-knell of the move for Hindu-Muslim conciliation initiated by the Allahabad Conference. For the leaders of the Muslim League were now convinced that a powerful section of the Congress leadership was bent upon ending separate electorates.[101]

VIII

What could not be accomplished either by the Allahabad Conference or by the committee formed by it was brought about as a result of certain events which temporarily alienated the Muslims in general and the votaries of the Muslim League in particular from the Government and prepared the ground for their cooperation with the Congress. At the same time, however, they also very much strengthened the feeling of Muslim solidarity and nationhood. This predicated that any understanding between the Congress and the Muslim League, whenever it materialized, would have to be on terms which did not run counter to the sentiment of Muslim nationalism or require its merger with Indian nationalism.

Mention may here be made of annulment of the partition of Bengal through a royal pronouncement on the occasion of the Coronation Darbar held in Delhi on 11 December 1911, in spite of repeated affirmations by the leading spokesmen of the British Government that partition was a settled fact which could not be unsettled. Inspired primarily by the desire to end the continuing political unrest in Bengal,[102] it had a traumatic impact on the Indian Muslim mind. This impact was felt not only by the Muslims of Eastern Bengal, who had gained considerable advantages, particularly in the field of education and employment, during the short span of six years that the partition had been in force,[103] but by Muslims all over the country.[104] They thought that the partition had been annulled, without any regard for Muslim feelings, because of the increasingly violent struggle of the Hindus in Bengal. Their feeling was succinctly expressed by Viqar-ul-Mulk when he remarked: 'The policy of the Government is like artillery passing over the dead bodies of the Muslims, without realizing whether any life remained in the bodies and whether they would be hurt.'[105] He now openly declared that the old Muslim policy of relying on Government's support must come to an end. 'What we should rely on, after the grace of God', he observed in course of an article in the Aligarh Institute Gazette on 20 December 1911, 'is the strength of our right arm, for which we have, before us, the example of our worthy countrymen.'[106] However, when some educated Muslims began to question the validity of the old Muslim policy of keeping aloof from the Congress and to suggest that Muslim interests might be better served by joining the bigger body, Viqar-ul-Mulk, representing the majority view among the Muslim elite, rejected that suggestion. This, in his view, meant that the Muslims should disband their 'own national organization' and join the larger group, 'just as a river loses its identity in a vast ocean'. He further added: 'It is true that many a time disappointments point the way to suicide, and the suggestion that we should join the Congress is a result of similar disappointments—for which the present Government is responsible—but suicide is never advisable.'[107]

Viqar-ul-Mulk's stand was based on unassailable logic in the context of the ideology of Muslim nationalism. The Muslims had supported the partition of Bengal not out of loyalty to the British, but in order to safeguard their own interests as a separate nationality in India. Now that the British, for their own reasons, had annulled that partition, it did not follow that the Muslims, howsoever dissatisfied with that action, should suddenly forget their separate nationhood, disband their national organization and merge with the Congress. Nawab Salimullah explained the rationale behind the East Bengali Muslim support for partition in course of his presidential address to the fifth session of the Muslim League, held at Calcutta in March 1912:

> The partition gave us a great opportunity to bestir ourselves, and it awakened in our hearts the throbbings of a new national life. I hope, gentlemen, you will believe me when I assure you that the Mussalmans of East Bengal supported the partition, not out of enmity to our Hindu brethren or at the bidding of the Government, but because we felt sure that the new administrative arrangements in East Bengal would afford us ample opportunities for self-improvement. . . . We came to realise for the first time in our history that we too had rights and privileges as British subjects, and that it was only necessary for us to put our own shoulders to the wheel to free ourselves from the state of servile dependence on a dominant community in which we had been living before the partition.[108]

That feelings of Muslim solidarity and separate nationhood were not confined to the leaders of the older generation but equally engulfed the young radicals is borne out by Mohamed Ali's speech at the same session. Moving a resolution to record the League's 'deep sense of regret and disappointment at the annulment of the partition of Bengal in utter disregard of Muslim feeling', he observed that it might seem strange that though not born a Bengali he was moving that resolution. However, as he considered the Muslim community in India as one, he thought that 'when the interest of a portion of the community suffered, the remaining portions shared the same feeling of trouble. This lesson of unity, they had learned from the Hindus, who made the question of Bengal an All-India question.'[109]

The general Muslim reaction to a remark made by the Under-Secretary of State for India, Edwin Montagu, on 26 April 1912, while piloting the Government of India Bill in the British Parliament (with a view to giving effect to the Delhi announcement regarding Bengal) shows how strong the feeling of Muslim nationality was in India at that time. Montagu had observed that the Muslims of East Bengal were the descendants of Hindu converts or were Hindu converts themselves, and had 'little or no relation except that of religion with those three-fifths of the Muhammedan population of India outside the limits of Bengal, who constitute so largely the fighting races of the north'.[110] This almost raised a hornet's nest. Protests poured in from various parts of India. And they were couched in terms which constituted a strong reassertion of Muslim nationhood. Thus the Madras Presidency Muslim League affirmed that irrespective of their origin, Indian Muslims had, 'by reason of their common religion, traditions, usage and Government', become welded into 'a solid and homogeneous mass of people with distinctive features of their own'. The Bengal and Bombay Leagues declared that Indian Muslims constituted 'a homogeneous nationality'. Wazir Hasan, a rising Muslim leader of U.P., chastized Montagu for his aspersions on the 'homogeneous nationality' of the Indian Muslims, who had already got united in order to safeguard their 'national interests against the rapidly growing Hindu domination'. The Council of the All India Muslim League expressed its strong resentment at Mantagu's attack on the solidarity of Muslim 'nationality'.[111] Matiur Rahman, author of the most authoritative history of the Muslim League in its early phase, has aptly observed: 'The cry of Muslim nationality had never been so loudly and emphatically proclaimed by such a large section of the educated Muslims.'[112]

NOTES

1. See Shan Muhammed, ed., *The Indian Muslims: A Documentary Record* (hereinafter referred to as *Muslim Documents*), I (Meerut, n.d.), pp. 3-23; Syed Sharifuddin Pirzada, ed., *Foundations of Pakistan: All India Muslim League Documents* (hereinafter referred to as *League Documents*), I (Karachi, 1969), Introduction, pp. xxix-xxxi.

2. Cited in Jamilud-din-Ahmad, *Muslim Political Movements: Early Phase* (Karachi, 1963), p. 26.
3. S.M. Ikram, *Modern Muslim India and the Birth of Pakistan* (Lahore, 1965), pp. 86-8.
4. Ibid., p. 88.
5. Ibid., p. 117.
6. *Muslim Documents*, n. 1, pp. 40-1.
7. Ibid., pp. 38-9.
8. Curzon to Brodrick, 17 February 1904, IOR, Curzon Papers, cited in S. Gopal, *British Policy in India, 1858-1905* (Cambridge, 1965), pp. 270-1.
9. Ibid., pp. 269-70.
10. Cited in Shila Sen, *Muslim Politics in Bengal, 1937-1947* (New Delhi, 1976), p. 33.
11. Minto to Morley, 15 August 1906, IOR, Mss. Eur. D 573/9, Morley Collection.
12. Ibid.
13. Minto to Morley, 22 August 1906, ibid.
14. Rafiq Zakaria, *Rise of Muslims in Indian Politics* (Bombay, 1970), pp. 100-1.
15. Sumit Sarkar, *The Swadeshi Movement in Bengal, 1903-1908* (New Delhi, 1973), p. 426.
16. Ibid., p. 424. See also Amales Tripathi, *The Extremist Challenge* (Bombay, 1967), pp. 64-76.
17. Sen, n. 10, pp. 35-6.
18. Mohsin-ul-Mulk to W.A.J. Archbold, 18 August 1906, reproduced from Minto Papers in Syed Razi Wasti, *Lord Minto and the Indian National Movement* (Oxford, 1964), pp. 231-2.
19. Mary, Countess of Minto, *India, Minto and Morley 1905-1910* (London, 1934), p. 45.
20. Ibid., pp. xxiii-xxxiv.
21. Mohsin-ul-Mulk to Archbold, 4 August 1906, Enclosure to Minto to Morely, 8 August 1906, n. 11, Morley Collection.
22. See, for instance, Asoka Mehta and Achyut Patwardhan, *The Communal Triangle in India* (Allahabad, 1942), p. 62; Rajendra Prasad, *India Divided* (Bombay, 1946), p. 112; B.M. Choudhry, *Muslim Politics* (Calcutta, 1946), p. 15; Ram Gopal, *Indian Muslims* (Bombay, 1959), p. 97; and G.N. Singh, *Landmarks in Indian Constitutional and National Development,* I (Delhi, 1973), pp. 179-80 (sixth reprint).
23. See Zafrul Islam, 'Two Historic Letters', *Journal of the Punjab University Historical Society* (Lahore), June 1960; Wasti, n. 18, pp. 63-4; and M.N. Das, *India under Morley and Minto* (London, 1964), pp. 164-5.
24. Minto to Morley, 8 August 1906, n. 11, Morley Collection.
25. Das, n. 23, p. 166.
26. Ibid.
27. Mehta and Patwardhan, n. 22, p. 62.
28. Wasti, n. 18, p. 231.
29. Text of the Address in Morley Collection, n. 11; reproduced in Appendix II to this volume. Emphasis added.
30. Ibid. Emphasis added.
31. Minto to Morley, 29 August 1906, Morley Collection, n. 11.
32. Minto to Morley, 4 October 1906, ibid.

33. Secretary of State to Viceroy, Telegram, 27 August 1906, IOR, D 573/28, ibid.
34. Morley to Minto, 26 October 1906, Morley Collection, n. 11.
35. Mary, Countess of Minto, n. 19, pp. 47-8.
36. Minto to Morley, 28 May 1906, Morely Collection, n. 11.
37. Minto to Morley, 2 August 1906, ibid.
38. Mohsin-ul-Mulk to Dunlop Smith, 7 October 1906, ibid., reproduced in Martin Gilbert, *Servant of India* (London, 1966), p. 57.
39. Aga Khan, *The Memories of Aga Khan* (London, 1954), p. 93.
40. Ibid., p. 95.
41. Mohsin-ul-Mulk to Archbold, 18 August 1906, Wasti, n. 18, p. 231.
42. Mohamed Ali, *Green Book, No. 1* (hereinafter referred to as *Green Book*) (Lucknow, 1907; *Freedom Movement Archives*, Karachi University), pp. 5-6.
43. Ibid., p. 11.
44. *League Documents*, n. 1, Introduction, pp. xlviii-xlix. It is not surprising that after the circulation of Salimullah's plan the *Friend of India* (Calcutta), a British owned paper, commented: 'In short what the Nawab of Dacca wants to see is an avowedly anti-Hindu organization which shall make no pretence of friendship or alliance with representative Hindu bodies', Editorial, 13 December 1906, cited in Mafizullah Kabir, 'Nawab Salimullah and Muslim Politics, 1871-1915', *Bangladesh Historical Studies*, Vol. II, 1977, p. 192.
45. Mohamed Ali, n. 42, pp. 9-10. Emphasis added.
46. See Matiur Rahman, *From Consultation to Confrontation: A Study of the Muslim League in British Indian Politics, 1906-1912* (London, 1970), pp. 40-4.
47. The Aga Khan to Dunlop Smith, 29 October 1906, Gilbert, n. 38, p. 57.
48. Stanley A. Wolpert, *Morley and India* (Berkeley, 1967), pp. 192-3.
49. Rahman, n. 46, pp. 121-2.
50. League Documents, n. 1, pp. 43-4.
51. Ibid., p. 51.
52. Ibid., p. 59.
53. Ibid., p. 61.
54. Ibid., p. 67.
55. Ibid., p. 70.
56. K.K. Aziz, *Ameer Ali, His Life and Work* (Lahore, 1968), p. 311.
57. Ibid., p. 316.
58. Ibid., pp. 316-20.
59. Rahman, n. 46, p. 113.
60. Ibid.
61. C.H. Philips and B.N. Pandey, eds., *The Evolution of India and Pakistan, 1858 to 1947: Select Documents* (London, 1962), p. 87.
62. League Documents, n. 1, p. 59.
63. Mohammed Shafi to Dunlop Smith, 8 January 1909, Gilbert, n. 38, p. 177.
64. Do, 13 January 1909, ibid., p. 181.
65. Do, 18 January 1909, ibid., p. 183.
66. Ibid., p. 185.
67. Aziz, n. 56, p. 314.
68. Minto to Morley, 31 December 1908, D 573/18, Morley Collection, n. 11. Emphasis added.
69. Minto to Lansdowne, 21 January 1909, cited in Das, n. 23, p. 237.

70. Minto to Morley, 7 April 1909, D 573/19, Morley Collection.
71. Gilbert, n. 38, p. 173. Emphasis added.
72. Lovat Fraser to Dunlop Smith, 20 July 1909, ibid., p. 202.
73. R.P. Patwardhan and D.V. Ambekar, eds., *Speeches and Writings of Gopal Krishna Gokhale*, I (Poona, 1962), p. 149.
74. Ibid., pp. 149-50.
75. Ibid., II (Bombay, 1966), pp. 307-12.
76. Gokhale to Wedderburn, December 1909, Cited in B.R. Nanda, *Gokhale: The Indian Moderates and the British Raj* (Delhi, 1977), pp. 349-50.
77. A.M. Zaidi and Shaheda Zaidi, eds., *The Encyclopaedia of Indian National Congress* (hereinafter referred to as *Congress Encyclopaedia*), V (New Delhi, 1978), pp. 545-6.
78. For the speeches on the resolution on council reform see ibid., pp. 327-71.
79. Ibid., pp. 307-8.
80. Ibid., p. 567.
81. Ibid., p. 703.
82. Ibid., pp. 568, 704.
83. Ibid., pp. 647-8.
84. Patwardhan and Ambekar, n. 73, II, pp. 76-9.
85. *Congress Encyclopaedia*, n. 77, VI (New Delhi, 1979), p. 237.
86. Ibid., p. 361.
87. For the texts of resolutions adopted at the annual Congress session of 1913 see ibid., pp. 441-9.
88. Rahman, n. 46, p. 50.
89. *League Documents*, n. 1, p. 21.
90. Rahman, n. 46, p. 51.
91. *League Documents*, n. 1, p. 47.
92. Ibid., p. 120.
93. Ibid., pp. 129-30.
94. Ibid., p. 126.
95. Ibid., p. 132.
96. Ibid., p. 135.
97. Ibid., p. 97.
98. Ibid., p. 110.
99. See Sir William Wedderburn's presidential address at the twenty-fifth session of the Congress, *Congress Encyclopaedia*, V, n. 77, p. 691.
100. Ibid. There is no confirmation here of Rahman's assertion (n. 46, p. 211) that Wedderburn only invited Hindu leaders after the Aga Khan had invited the Muslim leaders and no one on the Hindu side came forward to issue corresponding invitations to Hindu leaders. On the contrary, Wedderburn clearly stated in his presidential address that at the request of the Aga Khan, Pherozeshah Mehta and Ameer Ali, he addressed a letter to 'some of the leading representatives of the various communities in different parts of India explaining the proposal and inviting their cooperation'.
101. Rahman, n. 46, pp. 210-13.
102. Lord Hardinge, *My Indian Years, 1910-1916* (London, 1948), pp. 36-7.
103. Sufia Ahmed, *Muslim Community in Bengal, 1884-1912* (Dacca, 1974), pp. 288-9.

104. See Rahman, n. 46, pp. 236-51.
105. Ikram, n. 3, p. 118.
106. Ibid.
107. Ibid., p. 119.
108. *League Documents*, n. 1, p. 235.
109. Ibid., p. 250.
110. Cited in Rahman, n. 46, p. 257.
111. Ibid., pp. 257-8.
112. Ibid., p. 258.

CHAPTER III

Pan-Islamism to Indian Nationalism, 1912-1922

THE ANNOUNCEMENT of the annulment of Bengal's partition, which, as noticed in the previous chapter, gave a severe jolt to the Muslim elite, came at a time when they were being engulfed by the rising tide of Pan-Islamism. The historical roots as well as the main elements of the ideology of Pan-Islamism have already been discussed in Volume I and need not detain us long here. It should suffice to mention that the Islamic elite had been increasingly exercised over the developments in the Islamic world outside India since the last quarter of the nineteenth century. They were particularly concerned with the fate of the Turkish Empire, the last great bastion of Islamic power in the world, whose ruler was also the Caliph or head of all Muslims. The Young Turk Revolution in Turkey (1908) and the Persian revolution of the same year had also excited their younger sections and filled them with ideas of democracy and self-government. This was followed in quick succession by Italy's attack on Tripoli, then a part of the Turkish Empire (1911), Russian pressure on Iran (1911) and the uprising of the East European peoples within the Turkish regime (1912), resulting in what became famous as the Balkan wars.

All this very much upset the Muslim elite in India and made them worried about the future of the Turkish Empire. As a gesture of goodwill towards the Turks, they sent a medical mission to Turkey in 1912 under the leadership of M.A. Ansari. Some well-known Muslim Leaders like Mohamed Ali, Shaukat Ali, Mushir Hussain Kidwai and Abdul Bari set up an organization called *Anjuman-i-khuddam-kaaba* (Society of the Servants of the Kaaba) in 1913, with the objective of protecting the Muslim holy places from encroachment or invasion by non-Muslim powers. This concern with the future of the Turkish Empire and the preservation of Muslim control over the holy places of Islam went hand in hand with the growth of anti-European feeling in general and anti-British feeling in particular. For it was generally assumed that the

European powers had entered into a conspiracy to destroy the Turkish Empire and that the British Government too was aiding and abetting it.[1] This alienated a growing number of politically conscious Muslims from the British and paved the way for an understanding between the Muslim League and the Congress. Pan-Islamism thus became a bridge between Muslim nationalism and Indian nationalism.

I

The Muslim League as well as the new organs of radical Muslim opinion like *Al-Hilal* (edited by Maulana Abul Kalam Azad), *The Comrade* (edited by Maulana Mohamed Ali) and *Zamindar* (edited by Maulana Zafar Ali Khan) gave forceful expression to Pan-Islamic sentiments. Thus the fifth session of the Muslim League held in March 1912, while placing on record its deep sympathy with the people of Iran, declared that the latter were connected with the Indian Muslims by 'the closest ties of blood, religion and a common culture'.[2] It also expressed its deep abhorrence of Italy's invasion of Tripoli.[3] The next annual session of the League, held in March 1913, drew the attention of the British Government to the 'massacres and outrages . . . perpetrated by the Balkan invaders amongst the Mussalman population of Macedonia' and deeply regretted the attitude of 'Christian Europe', which might result in the destruction of 'the Mussalman power in Europe' and the integrity and honour of the Ottoman Empire.[4] Analysing the situation in the Turkish Empire in the wake of the Balkan wars and the Indian Muslim attitude towards it, the *Comrade*, observed in 12 October 1912:

> The combined aggression of the Balkan states against Turkey is bound to create a profound impression throughout the Islamic world. If the Montenegrin attack brings about a general war, every Muslim will feel an irresistible call of duty to help those who will have to carry on a life and death struggle in defence of their honour and their rights. The feeling would be as strong and natural as the spiritual and moral ties that unite the followers of Islam. . . . No Mussalman, in whose breast there exists the least fraternal feeling that has been the glory of his creed, can see unmoved the struggle of his fellow Muslims in a just and noble cause.[5]

This was by no means an isolated observation. As the *London Times* correspondent in India reported in his paper, it was difficult to take up any Indian Muslim paper without noticing that the sufferings of Muslims in other countries, the conspiracy of the Christian powers against Muslim States, the necessity of subscribing generously to the Turkish war fund, and the obligation of all Muslims to be ready to act together in defence of the faith formed 'practically the sole topics for discussion'. The correspondent added that the strong feeling of solidarity with fellow-Muslims in Turkey was also putting a severe strain on the loyalty of 'what we have always regarded as perhaps the most loyal community'.[6] The Viceroy, Lord Hardinge, agreed with this view. In a letter to an English friend, he observed:

> The Muhammedans of this country are already in a very agitated frame of mind owing to events in Tripoli and Asia, and I am already receiving telegrams protesting against the aggressive action of the Balkan States. . . . The Pan-Islamic idea in this country is spreading very fast, and, although the Muhammedans have hitherto been very loyal to Government, the action of England in the concert of Europe is being very closely watched and any action on our part hostile to Turkey is certain to create trouble in the future.[7]

The movement for the setting up of a Muslim university, with the power to affiliate colleges all over India, which gathered momentum at this time, also contributed substantially to the growth of Muslim national consciousness and the alienation of the Muslim educated elite from the Government. This movement had been born in 1898, when after the death of Syed Ahmad Khan, his important colleagues and disciples founded Sir Syed Memorial Fund to raise the Aligarh College to a University. For a variety of reasons, including the failure to raise sufficient funds, factional fights at Aligarh and the unsympathetic attitude of the Government, the movement could not make much headway.[8] After sometime, however, it was reborn in 1910. Although, the third annual session of the Muslim League, held in Delhi in January 1910, had adopted a resolution urging the setting up of 'a separate Muhammedan University', the movement really began afresh in right earnest with an appeal by the Aga Khan at the annual session of the Muhammedan Educational Conference held in December 1910 at Nagpur. The Sir Syed Memorial Fund Committee was now replaced by the Muslim University Foundation Committee, with the Aga Khan as president and Viqar-ul-Mulk as Secretary. The Aga Khan as well as other important Muslim leaders undertook an extensive tour of the country and succeeded in collecting handsome donations. The fourth annual session of the League held at Nagpur in December 1911 did not adopt any resolution on the Muslim University issue. This was obviously a strategic move, designed to impart to the movement a non-political character. This, however, could not disguise the fact that the Muslim University movement was 'initiated, controlled and conducted by the League leaders both at the All-India and provincial levels'.[9] Besides the President and the Secretary, sixteen of the twenty-one Vice-Presidents and three of the four Joint Secretaries of the Muslim University Foundation Committee were members of either the executive committee or the council of the Muslim League.[10]

In the speeches and writings in support of the movement there was an inevitable emphasis on the glories of the Muslim past and the separate cultural identity of the Muslims,[11] essential ingredients of the Muslim national consciousness. It is, however, worth noting that there was no anti-Hindu element in the Muslim University movement. There was, of course, a friendly rivalry in fund collection with the contemporaneous Hindu University movement. The spirit in which that competition was carried out can be imagined from the fact that the Aga Khan made a handsome donation to the Hindu University fund and this gesture was reciprocated by the Maharaja of Darbhanga, President of the Hindu University Society.[12]

The Muslim University Foundation Committee was fairly successful in its drive for funds. By August 1911 it had secured pledges for rupees twenty-five lakhs and actually collected nearly four lakhs.[13] The Government of India was quite sympathetic to the setting up of this University, but the Secretary of State objected both to the name of the University and the plan to give it power to affiliate colleges all over India. So the scheme fell through for the time being. After 1912, the leaders of the Muslim University Movement, most of whom were also leaders of the Muslim League, were bitterly disappointed and turned into 'the most bitter critics of the Raj'.[14]

A similar result was produced by the demolition of a portion of a mosque in a congested part of Kanpur, known as Machhli Bazar, in July 1913, in order to improve the alignment of a road named after the then Lieutenant-Governor of U.P., James Scorgie Meston. This caused considerable resentment among the Muslims not only in Kanpur, but all over India. The resentment was perhaps all the greater because an earlier plan for improving the alignment of the same road had been modified in order to save a temple from demolition. The U.P. Government's argument that what was demolished was only the 'Washing House', which was not really a part of the mosque and did not have any sanctity attached to it, did not assuage Muslim feeling in any way. The same applied to the Government's offer of land on the other side of the mosque. Muslim Leaders and papers took the position that only Muslims knew what was a part of a mosque and what was not, and such matters could not be decided by the Government. The dominant feeling among the former was that the Government in its arrogance was not caring for the religious sensibilities of the Muslims. The Muslims were not prepared to tolerate this. *The Comrade* and *Al-Hilal* played a very prominent role in spreading this view. Matters came to a head on 3 August 1913, when after a public meeting a large number of Muslims marched to the site of the mosque with a view to rebuilding the demolished portion. When the crowd failed to disperse and instead indulged in throwing stones on the policemen, the District Magistrate ordered firing. This resulted in rather heavy casualties: 18 persons killed and 27 wounded. Criminal cases were started against the rioters and 105 persons were put up for trial before the Sessions Court. This further aggravated the situation and Muslim feeling all over the country became deeply estranged from the Government. The matter became serious enough for the Viceroy, Lord Hardinge, to intervene. He went to Kanpur in October 1913, and, after receiving a Muslim deputation and talking to the leading members of the Muslim community, ordered the restoration of the disputed land to the mosque and the withdrawal of all cases against the rioters.[15] Although this assuaged Muslim feeling to some extent, the scars created by the demolition and the police firing were bound to remain for quite sometime. How serious had the situation become is borne out by a note dated 2 September 1913, by Syed Ali Imam, a former President of one of the annual sessions of the Muslim League, and at that time Law Member of the Government of India, wherein he remarked that the Kanpur mosque incident had 'greater potentiality for trouble than any since 1857'.[16]

The change in Muslim feeling in India towards the Government as a result of the various developments mentioned here—the annulment of the partition of Bengal, the difficulties of Turkey, the failure of the Muslim University movement and the Kanpur mosque incident—was very well summed up by the *Manchester Guardian* in a leader on 'The Indian Government and the Moslems' after the Viceroy's intervention in the Kanpur mosque issue:

> For seven or eight years before the Balkan War the Government of India pursued towards the Muslim Community a policy of unmistakable, often avowed, preference. The higher officials, everywhere, it appeared, were acting upon the assumption that Muhammedans' loyalty, encouraged by special concessions, could be relied upon as an offset to the aggressive nationalism of Hindu politicians, and that in consequence the burden upon the Executive would be materially lightened.

During the past twelve months events have occurred to overturn this assumption, and it would be true to say that Lord Hardinge's Government is confronted with a situation hardly less grave than that of the Hindu unrest between 1905 and 1909.[17]

II

As Muslims became estranged from the Government, their minds turned more and more towards the Congress. They realized that there was no point in pursuing the old policy of looking up to the British. Instead, Muslim interests, they thought, would be better served through self-help and cooperation with the Congress. This was particularly true of the younger leaders of the League representing the new members from the middle class who flocked to it in the wake of the ferment created by some of the developments during 1911-13. Developments in the Islamic world outside India had a particularly exhilarating impact on the minds of these younger leaders. Their political horizons were widened and they began to yearn for self-government. They had, of course, no desire to dissolve the Muslim League. The Muslim identity in politics, of which the League was the most important symbol, had to be maintained. But it was growingly felt that the League should work more earnestly than before for building bridges with the Congress, for neither Muslims nor Hindus could make satisfactory progress without mutual cooperation. Nor could they march towards self-government, fast emerging as their common goal. Mohamed Ali gave expression to this new feeling in the very first issue of *The Comrade* (14 January 1911):

It is our firm belief that if the Mussalmans or the Hindus attempted to achieve success in opposition to, or even without the cooperation of, each other, they will not only fail, but fail ignominously. . . . We may not create today the patriotic fervour and the fine national frenzy of Japan with its forty millions of homogeneous people. But a concordaat like that of Canada is not beyond the bounds of practicability. It may not be a love marriage, born of romance and poetry. But *marriage de convenance*, honourably contracted and honourably maintained, is not to be despised.[18]

This trend of thought received considerable fillip from the fact that non-Muslim public men and press generally shared the Muslim concern with the events in Tripoli and the Balkans. Unlike the Muslims, they had, of course, no religious ground to feel attached to the Sultan-Caliph, but they looked upon the Turkish Empire as a great Asian power and felt deeply sympathetic towards it in view of the European onslaught on its integrity. There was also the feeling that it was the duty of non-Muslims in India to sympathize with their Muslim countrymen who were deeply grieved because of the plight of Turkey. Thus a meeting of Hindus was organized in Calcutta in November 1912 under the presidentship of Bipin Chandra Pal, one of the most prominent leaders of the radical section of the Congress, to express sympathy with Turkey.[19] In his presidential address to the twenty-seventh session of the Congress held in December 1912, R.N. Mudholkar gave expression to the 'profound sorrow and sympathy' which the Hindu and all non-Muslim Indians felt for their Muslim brethren in the great misfortune which had overtaken the Caliphate and the struggle for existence which the Turkish Empire had to carry on against a powerful combination. He further added that it should be possible to satisfy the just and legitimate aspirations of the Christian provinces of the Turkish Empire without destroying the existence or the importance of Turkey or subjecting her to the humiliating condition of powerlessness.[20] The Indian nationalist press also adopted a similar stance towards Turkey. According to the *Mahratta* (17 November 1912), for instance, the main cause of the troubles of the Turkish Empire was the fact that the Europeans wanted to preserve Europe for themselves. It asked whether they were prepared also to leave 'Asia for the Asiatics' and 'Africa for the Africans'. The *Tribune* (6 November 1912) looked upon the defeat of Turkey as a great blow to Asia.[21]

The changed mood among the Muslim elite was reflected in the resolution adopted by the national council of the Muslim League in December 1912, recommending the adoption of the following as the objects of the League:

1. To promote and maintain among Indians feelings of loyalty towards the British Crown;
2. To protect and advance the political and other rights and interests of the Indian Mussalmans;
3. To promote friendship and union between the Mussalmans and other communities in India; and
4. Without detriment to the foregoing objects, the attainment of *a system of self-Government suitable to India* by bringing about, through constitutional means, a steady reform of the existing system of administration, by promoting national unity and fostering public spirit among the people of India and by co-operating with other communities for the said purposes.[22]

These objects were significantly different from those in vogue since 1906-7. Thus, as per the first object now adopted, the League was no longer concerned with removing any misconception that might arise among Muslims as to the intentions of the Government. Besides, instead of promoting the loyalty of Indian Muslims towards the British Government, the League now was to work for the promotion of *Indian* loyalty towards the British Crown. The second object dropped the League's earlier concern with presenting Muslim aspirations before the Government in temperate language. According to the third objective, the League was not to be content with merely promoting 'concord and harmony' between the Muslims and other communities in India, but was to work for the promotion of 'friendship and union' between them. Besides, this was no longer to be subject to the fulfilment of the first two objects. The fourth object, the attainment of self-government, through, among other things, the promotion of 'national unity among the people of India', was entirely new and showed the significant shift that had taken place in the thinking of the League's leadership.

Yet, if there was change, there was also continuity. This came out clearly in the discussion over the proposed changes. The changes in the second and third objects were adopted without any opposition. However, Mazharul Haq, an ardent Indian nationalist and one of the most important Congress leaders at that time in Bihar even though a member of the Muslim League, opposed the first object as being not radical enough. Why should the Muslims, of all the people in India, he asked, make it their speciality to proclaim their loyalty to the British. He was supported by M.A. Jinnah, again an important Congress leader, who had not yet joined the League, but had begun taking interest in it and attended some of its sessions. According to him, the protestation of Muslim loyalty reflected upon the loyalty of other people in India. Their objection, however, was over-ruled by a large majority and the change, as proposed, was adopted.

The discussion on the fourth object was even more significant. One of the old leaders of the League, Muhammed Abdullah, opposed the mention of self-government. He obviously thought it was too radical an object to be made a part of the creed of the League. On the other hand, Mazharul Haq wanted the phrase 'suitable for India' after self-government to be substituted by 'on colonial lines'. This would have made the League's object exactly similar to that of the Congress. Jinnah, however, opposed this amendment. He pointed out that although a Congressman, he was convinced that the Congress was wrong in seeking self-government on colonial lines and a day would come when it would change its creed and adopt the phraseology suggested for the League. Conditions in India were different from those in the British colonies and, therefore, what was suitable for them might not be found suitable for India. Besides, as self-government was only an ideal for the future and not immediately in the offing, there was no sense in the League committing itself to any particular form of it so much in advance. The future leader of the League and founder of Pakistan was perhaps keeping his options open. The object as proposed was, of course, adopted.[23]

Along with changes in the objects of the League, notice must also be taken of significant changes made in its rules and regulations, adopted with a view to broadening its base. Thus the annual membership fee was reduced from Rs. 20 to Rs. 5. The educational qualification required for membership was changed from the ability for 'reading and writing with felicity' to just literacy, which could be claimed by any one just on the basis of his ability to sign his name in any language. The maximum number of members of the council was raised from 40 to 150. It was also provided that any Muslim association within British India or outside could be affiliated to the League. Last, but not the least important, it was decided to eliminate the clause fixing the maximum number of members of the All-India League at 800. At the same time an effort was initiated to tighten the organization of the League by providing that it would be the duty of the League to ensure that activities of its various branches should be in line with those of the parent body.[24]

The sixth annual session of the League held at Lucknow in March 1913 endorsed all these changes. At the same time it adopted a resolution putting on record its firm belief that 'the future development and progress of the people of India depend exclusively on the harmonious working and cooperation of the various communities'. Further, the resolution deprecated 'all mischievous attempts to widen the unfortunate breach between the Hindus and Mussalmans' and expressed the hope that the leaders of both sides would periodically meet together 'to restore the amicable relations prevailing between them in the past and find a *modus operandi* for joint and concerted action' on matters of public interest.[25]

Mohammad Shafi, who had presided over this session, took great pains in his address to emphasize the importance of Hindu-Muslim unity. While dilating on this theme, he declared that 'the warm blood of Indian patriotism courses through the veins of Indian Mussalmans with the same vitality as is the case with those articulate classes whose patriotic spirit finds loud expression from the public platform and in the press'. The 'evolution of a common Indian nationality', he added, was something 'which all genuine well-wishers of the country must sincerely long for'. Till that became an accomplished fact, it was quite natural on the part of the Indian Muslims to seek to protect their communal interests by securing their due share in the administrative and legislative machinery of the country. This need not, however, prevent Hindus and Muslims from cooperating to safeguard 'the vital interests of the motherland', on which there were no differences between them and dealing with those common problems whose solution depended mainly on united action by them. Mutual confidence and goodwill resulting from such action would bring about 'complete harmony of feeling and unanimity of views' even regarding matters on which there were differences between the two communities at that time. Everyday which passed without such action was a day lost to the 'sacred cause of Indian nationality'.[26]

After the close of the League's session Shafi continued his efforts in this direction. In April 1913 he issued a circular to all papers reiterating his plea that the time had come for Hindus and Muslims to end their internecine conflicts and work for the dawn of a new era of peace and goodwill in the country. Here he repudiated the view held by some Hindus that the policy of inter-communal cooperation proclaimed by the Muslim League did not reflect a genuine desire for Hindu-Muslim *entente* for the good of the country, but was the result of Muslim resentment at the disastrous consequences of the Balkan Wars on their co-religionists in Turkey, and reiterated the need for united action on issues on which such action was possible.[27] This was followed by a similar letter from Sir Wazir Hasan, Honorary Secretary of the Muslim League. 'It is obvious', he observed in that letter, 'that we are bound to each other by ties of common nativity and progress of India must necessarily mean the progress of all.' He suggested a meeting of four representatives from each of the two communities in every province to prepare a plan for joint action by them.[28] Hailing this suggestion, *The Comrade* remarked: 'The most reassuring, as indeed the most impressive, feature of the Indian situation today is a general desire for some organised movement towards the growth of better relations between Hindus and Mussalmans.'[29]

At the next session of the Muslim League, held at Agra in December 1913, its President, Sir Ibrahim Rahimtulla, again emphasized the urgent need for Hindu-Muslim unity. Referring to the goal of self-government recently adopted by the Muslim League, he observed:

> Everyone must recognise that no form of self-government is possible in India unless the two principal communities, the Hindus and the Muslim, are closely and consciously united. What can be a nobler aim, a loftier goal than to endeavour to secure India united! Once we become sincerely and genuinely united, there is no force in the world which can keep us from our heritage; without such union, the Indians will have to wait indefinitely for the realisation of their fondest hopes.[30]

The religious scholars or the *Ulama,* who had become politically active as a result of the ongoing Pan-Islamic movement in the country, shared such sentiments. How strong was the desire among the Muslim elite for cooperation with the Congress can be imagined from the report of an intelligence officer of the Government in the middle of 1912 that he had been informed by a reliable correspondent that the latter had not met a single educated Muslim who did not favour 'combination between Muslim politicians in India and the Hindu Congress Party'.[31] Viceroy Hardinge also conceded in a communication to the Secretary of State, Crewe, that the Government was not in a position to count on the loyalty of the Muslims who were prepared to join 'any other faction in opposition to the Raj'.[32]

In view of the emergence of such views among the Muslim elite and their growing impact on the new generation of League's Leadership, some of the older leaders found it embarrassing to continue in their positions. This was symbolized by the resignation of the Aga Khan in 1913 from the permanent presidency of the League.[33] And in came Jinnah, who had been active so far only in the Congress, that same year.[34] The majority of the active members of the League, however, were not prepared to dilute in any way their firm adherence to separate electorates in order to forge a joint front with the Congress. The issue came to the fore at the Agra session itself (December 1913). As had been done at the earlier sessions, a resolution was moved recording the opinion of the League that it was absolutely necessary to extend the principle of communal representation to local bodies in order to secure 'the adequate and effective representation' of Muslims on them. Mohamed Ali moved an amendment suggesting that the consideration of that question be postponed for a year. His main ground for making this suggestion was the need to meet the Congress half-way which had that year desisted from adopting any resolution opposing the extension of separate electorates to local bodies. Jinnah strongly supported this suggestion. Even the Aga Khan lent his support. The supporters of the resolution, however, remained firm. Finally, voting had to be resorted to. While the main resolution secured 89 votes, Mohamed Ali's amendment could muster only 40.[35] The new rising leadership as well as the old established one must have taken note of these figures.

This difference on extension of separate electorates did not in any way affect the strong desire of almost all sections of the League's Leadership to forge a cooperative relationship with the Congress. The latter strongly welcomed this trend. The President of the twenty-eighth annual session of the Congress (1913), Nawab Syed Mahmud, made a pointed reference to the proceedings of the sixth annual session of the League held in March 1913 and strongly welcomed some of its notable decisions like the adoption of self-government as one of its goals and the adoption of a resolution expressing the urgent need for Hindu-Muslim unity.[36] Following the lead of its president, the Congress desisted from adopting a resolution opposing the extension of separate electorates to local bodies. It further adopted a resolution putting on record its 'warm appreciation of the League's adoption of self-government for India as one of its goals as also the expression of its belief that the political future of the country depended upon the harmonious working and cooperation of the various communities in India'.[37]

III

The trend towards Congress-League rapprochement became stronger after the outbreak of the First World War in 1914, with Britain, France and Russia on one side and Austria and Germany on the other. Turkey proclaimed neutrality in the beginning, but a little latter joined Germany. Just like Hindu and Sikh revolutionaries, a number of Muslim revolutionaries saw in the war an opportunity to secure India's freedom with the help of Turkey and Germany, and risked their lives for the fulfilment of this objective.[38] Muslims working through the constitutional method adopted a dual policy. On the one hand, they did not hide their sympathy for Turkey. On the other hand, as subjects of Britain, they also considered it their duty to proclaim their loyalty to the latter and to wish it victory in the war. At the same time they expressed the hope that Britain would ensure that no damage was done to the Muslim holy places located within the Turkish Empire and that they were not placed under any non-Muslim control. This was the line adopted by the leading Muslim princes, political parties and newspapers.[39] The general Muslim attitude towards the war was very well explained by Mohamed Ali in an article in *The Comrade* dated 7 November 1914. 'It would be hypocrisy', he observed, 'to disguise the fact that love of Turkey and her people is to the Indian Mussalmans a deep and abiding sentiment and that millions of them revere the Sultan as their Caliph.' However, he explained, the Muslims also realized that they formed 'a large and responsible section of the people of India', and were subjects of the British Crown. They were, therefore, ready to perform their duty in the war in a 'manly and ungrudging spirit'. They recognized that the conflict between Turkey and Britain, however unfortunate, had nothing to do with religion, but was a purely secular conflict. They might sympathize with the Turks in their difficulties, but were not bound by any temporal or spiritual obligation to back them in every mundane quarrel of theirs.[40]

The British, of course, did not take such protestations at their face value. Sir Reginald Craddock, Home Member of the Government of India, conveyed to Hardinge the remark made by the Maharaja of Darbhanga, that the Muslims were 'praying for the British in the day and for the Germans at night'. Craddock did not take this remark literally, for he knew that the Maharaja liked to be amusing. He did, however, took care to convey to the Viceroy that the Maharaja's impression about there being a strong pro-German feeling among Muslims was confirmed by many 'well-disposed' Muslims.[41] In a memorandum prepared for the Secretary of State for India, Theodore Morrison, a former Principal of the Aligarh College and at that time a member of the Secretary of State's Council, thus analysed the Indian Muslim sentiment for Turkey:

> This sentiment was not due solely to religion or what is called religious fanaticism. It is rather a kind of patriotism for which we have no exact analogy. Islam is more than a religious belief. It is a *Kultur*, a civilisation, a society conscious of its separate existence. . . . To this civilisation or society Muhammedans feel an attachment which is very like patriotism and similar to what Western Europe in earlier days felt for Christendom. . . . They have seen one Muhammedan Kingdom after another go down before the onset of Christian powers and they live in dread of seeing the final collapse of the temporal power of Islam.[42]

Morrison went on to cite the words of Syed Ahmad Khan spoken to him some twenty years earlier, the purport of which was that the Muslims were haunted by the fear that they might become, like the Jews, a people without a country of their own, and their heart went out 'in passionate sympathy' to those who were taking 'the last stand against overwhelming odds'.[43] The British, therefore, saw danger in the spread of the Pan-Islamic ideology and interned almost all its leading champions like Abul Kalam Azad, Mohamed Ali, his brother Shaukat Ali, and Zafar Ali Khan and suppressed the leading organs of radical Muslim opinion like the *Al-Hilal*, *The Comrade* and *Zamindar* in spite of their protestations of loyalty to the British cause in the war.

All this further alienated the bulk of politically conscious Muslims from the British, strengthened in them the urge for self-government, and turned them towards the Congress, which was working for the realization of the same objective side by side with extending support to Britain in the war. This facilitated the rise to the top position in the Muslim League of such leaders like Mazharul Haq and Jinnah who were also among the important leaders of the Congress. At Jinnah's suggestion the League decided, in spite of strong opposition by conservative elements, to hold its next annual session in December 1915 in Bombay where the Congress too was holding its session. Mazharul Haq, who presided over the League's session, made a most fervent plea for Hindu-Muslim unity. Taking a position both as an Indian and as a Muslim, he declared that on a question relating to the welfare of India and of justice to India, he was 'not only an Indian first, but an Indian next and an Indian to the last, an Indian and an Indian alone'. On the other hand, if any matter arose on which there was a divine injunction, he 'could not even consider, let alone accept as correct, anything conflicting with that injuction, no matter on what mundane authority it was based'. On such an occasion, he would be 'not only a Muslim first, but a Muslim next, a Muslim to the last and a Muslim and nothing but a Muslim'. Implicit in this description of his dual position was the proposition that on political issues there was hardly any scope for difference between a Muslim and a non-Muslim. Underlining this point further Haq asserted that if people looked sufficiently deeply into the different questions affecting India, they would find hardly any which did not affect all equally. 'The truth is', he emphasized, 'that in all essential matters such as legislation, taxation, administration of justice, education, we are all in the same boat, and we must sink or swim together.' Differences could arise from time to time, but these would not in any way affect 'the essentials of our corporate life as citizens of a common land' and could be easily solved by a little sobriety of judgement, based upon the principle of give and take. Making a plea for a radical change of outlook on the part of the Muslim League, he further added:

For too long we have relied upon others. It is quite time that we got rid of unreliable and temporary props, stood upon our own legs and became a self-reliant people. For too long has our policy been regulated by distrust and dominated by fear. We have unnecessarily feared and distrusted the Hindus. We have had an unholy awe of authority; and we have never placed any faith in ourselves, but have made ourselves dependent on others. All this must be changed. This policy has kept us from enjoying our rightful share in the public life of our country, to the great detriment of our best interests. We must have independence, and open our eyes in the fresh air.[44]

This session of the League appointed a 71-member committee, with members from every province, to formulate a scheme of constitutional reforms. While performing this task, the committee was authorized to confer with other political organizations or committees subject, of course, to due regard being paid to the needs and interests of Muslims. Jinnah, who moved the resolution embodying this decision, made it clear in his speech that the committee was expected to work in collaboration with a similar committee appointed by the annual Congress Session of 1915, which had just concluded in Bombay. This was natural, he asserted, as the Congress and the League were 'the two chief representative political organizations of India'. After they had jointly formulated a scheme of reforms they could go to the authorities and assert that these were the reforms which they demanded 'in the name of United India'.[45]

As in the past, this desire for cooperation with the Congress did not mean that the League was in any way prepared to whittle down its commitment to separate electorates. This became clear when the same session again adopted a resolution reiterating the League's stand that such electorates must be extended to local bodies. Neither Haq nor Jinnah opposed it.[46] This was a clear signal to the Congress that if it was keen on an agreement with the League, it would have to give up its opposition to separate electorates. The Congress, in its keenness to forge a united front with the League, was not averse to such a compromise. The test came soon enough in March 1916 when in U.P. a provision was made for separate representation of Muslims in municipalities. An important Congress leader, Madan Mohan Malaviya, voiced his strong opposition to this measure, but other Congress leaders, notably Motilal Nehru and Tej Bahadur Sapru, realizing the danger such an attitude posed to the ongoing negotiations for building up a joint Congress-League front, extended support to it. 'In order to make it possible for the Muslim community to cooperate with us . . .', declared Tej Bahadur Sapru, who had himself condemned separate electorates in 1909, 'and in order to remove at least one of the several causes of friction, I should not grudge separate representation to the Muslim Community'.[47]

This presaged the shape of things to come. The Congress-League Scheme or, as it was popularly known, the Lucknow Pact—since the Scheme was adopted by the annual sessions of the two organizations, both held in December 1916 at Lucknow—provided for not only separate electorates, but also weightage. In the negotiations the Congress side accepted them in principle for Muslims in provinces where they were in a minority without much difficulty. Whatever negotiations took place related to the quantum of weightage in the various provinces.[48] The figures finally agreed upon represented an advance over the position under the Act of 1909. So far as the minority provinces were concerned the Muslims were to have 25 per cent in Bihar and Orissa (population 10.5 per cent), 33.3 per cent in Bombay (population 20.4 per cent), 15 per cent in Central Provinces (population 4.3 per cent), 15 per cent in Madras (population 6.5 per cent) and 30 per cent in U.P. (population 14 per cent). In exchange for this, Muslims had to remain content with only 50 per cent of seats in the Punjab where their population was 54.8 per cent and 40 per cent in Bengal where there population was 52.6 per cent. For the Central Legislative Council the percentage of Muslim representation was fixed at 33.3. It was also provided that Muslims would vote only through separate electorates. As a further concession to the Muslims it was provided that no bill or resolution introduced by a non-official member of any council affecting any community would be proceeded with if three-fourths of the members of that community declared their opposition to it.[49]

As for other provisions of the Lucknow Pact, mention may be made of the fact that it demanded that four-fifths of the members of central as well as provincial legislative councils should consist of elected members. It also demanded that not less than one-half of the members of the Executive Council at the centre as well as in the provinces should be elected by the elected members of the legislative councils. The presidents of the legislative councils were to be elected by their members. The central legislative council was to have purview over the entire field of administration, except foreign affairs and defence.

Similarly, a provincial legislative council was to have within its purview all matters relating to the internal administration of the province. India was to be treated at par with the Dominions.[50]

Needless to mention, the significance of the Lucknow Pact lies not so much in the general political demands made by it as in the understanding reached between the Congress and the League regarding those demands. The Congress, no doubt, had to make major concessions to the League by not only recognizing both separate electorates and weightage for Muslims, which it had so far declined to do, but also by agreeing to quite a generous quantum of weightage. Besides, it also agreed to the Muslims having the right to block the passage of any bill or resolution in any council if the bulk of the members of their community wanted to do so. Above all, by negotiating and signing the Lucknow Pact, the Congress recognized the Muslim League as the representative organization of Indian Muslims and, by implication, compromised its own position as the representative organization of all Indians, irrespective of the religion or region to which they might belong. All this lent great strength to the separate political identity of the Indian Muslims. However, the League too made vital concessions. It did not for instance hark back to the days of Syed Ahmad Khan when the demand was that the Muslim share in every council should not be less than 50 per cent. Besides, if it insisted on securing more seats for Muslims at the Centre and in the provinces where they were in a minority, it agreed to forego the majority in the councils in the Punjab and Bengal, to which the Muslims were entitled on the basis of their population. Regarding Bengal in particular, its concession was exceptionally generous. For the Muslims were turned from a majority into a minority. Above all, the League pledged to work in cooperation with the Congress in the name of united India. This was a tremendous gain for the Congress and represented the fulfilment of one of its most deeply cherished dreams.

All this was fully realized by the Congress leadership and this was at the back of their mind when they agreed to the terms of the Lucknow Pact. Bal Gangadhar Tilak, while soliciting support for the Pact at the Congress Session, summed up the feelings of the entire Congress leadership when he observed:

> It has been said by some that we have yielded too much to the Muslims. I am sure I represent the sense of the Hindu community all over India and I say that we could not have yielded too much. I would not care if the rights of self-government are granted to the Muslim community only. . . . I would not

care if those rights are granted to any section of the Indian community. . . . We have to fight against a third party and therefore it is very important that we should stand united on this platform, united in race, united in religion and united as regards all shades of different political opinions. We have forged this weapon of unity and that is the most important event of the day.[51]

The League leaders fully reciprocated such sentiments at the annual session of their organization. In his presidential address Jinnah, while analysing the Indian problem, referred to the 'unifying process' going on in the country as a result of British rule, particularly the spread of Western education. This, according to him, was creating, out of the vast diversities of race and religion, 'a new India, fast growing into unity of thought, purpose and outlook, responsive to new appeals of territorial patriotism and nationality, stirring with new energy and aspiration and becoming daily more purposeful and eager to recover its birth-right to direct its own affairs and govern itself'.[52] Pointing to the future he remarked: 'Be the time near or distant, the Indian people are bound to attain to their full stature as a self-governing nation. No force in the world can rob them of their destiny and thwart the purpose of providence.'[53] Wazir Hasan, Secretary of the League, in his report to the annual session of his organization on the making of the Lucknow Pact correctly described the spirit which animated the members of the committees, appointed respectively by the Congress and the League, at their joint session held at Lucknow on 25-7 December 1916. 'The exact numbers of population and of representations', he noted, 'were considered, but this was a small matter compared with the vitally important matter of the national life which both the committees inhered, and the supreme interests of India as a nation were recognized as that before which all else must yield.'[54]

All, of course, did not view the problem of distribution of seats between Hindus and Muslims in the councils in this light. After the terms of the Lucknow Pact were made public, there came forward many critics, both among Hindus and Muslims, who thought that the other side had got away with unjust gains. They were full of forebodings for the future. If the size of weightage for Muslims in provinces where they were in a minority worried many Hindus, their counterparts among the Muslims were worried by the denial of Muslim majority in both Punjab and Bengal. The extent of this denial appeared particularly galling in the latter. In the then prevailing atmosphere, however, such critics did not get any wide support among either Hindus or Muslims, except in Bengal, where almost all Muslim organizations were united in their opposition to the Lucknow Pact.[55]

IV

The years immediately following the adoption of the Congress-League Scheme of reforms witnessed further cooperation between the Congress and the League. The severe Hindu-Muslim riots over cow-killing in Bihar and eastern U.P. in 1917 failed to produce any adverse impact on such cooperation. The continued internment of the Ali brothers and other Muslim leaders added considerably to widespread Muslim discontent with British rule. The Congress shared the League's interest in the release of the Ali brothers and adopted a resolution demanding it at its annual session in December 1917.[56] Mohandas Karamchand Gandhi, then working his way to national leadership after acquiring fame for his glorious leadership of the Indians in South Africa, won many Muslim hearts by his championship of the cause of the Ali brothers. Indeed in January 1918, he seemed to be planning a big fight for their release as a means of spreading political awakening in India and cementing Hindu-Muslim unity. How serious he was is clear from the fact that he took steps to get his name removed from the bank accounts of his *ashram* at Sabarmati (near Ahmedabad) to save them from being forfeited by the Government in case of struggle. Asking a trusted inmate of the *ashram* to take steps in this regard he wrote: 'I am likely to have a battle royal over Mohamed Ali. If India carries out my plan, the Government of India will be properly humbled. Hindus and Muslims, never united, will become so, mother cow will be safe and we shall hear the triumph of non-violence proclaimed all over the world.'[57] Although for some reason the fight was not started, Gandhi carried on a vigorous campaign on behalf of the Ali brothers through letters to high government functionaries as well as public speeches.[58] By the end of 1918 he was beginning to be recognized in certain influential sections of Muslim leadership as a spokesman of Muslims. M.A. Ansari, who had led the medical mission to Turkey in 1912 and had been chairman of the reception committee for the annual session of the Muslim League held in Delhi in December 1918, hailed him as a 'dauntless champion of Muslims' rights' and the 'acknowledged intrepid leader of India . . . who is never afraid to speak out the truth and who has, by his noble actions, endeared himself, as much to Mussalmans as to Hindus'.[59] When Gandhi gave a call for *Satyagrah* against the Rowlatt Act (1919) Muslims participated in large numbers at various places. The feelings between the two communities were so cordial that the famous Arya Samaj leader, Swami Shraddhanand, was invited to address Muslims from the pulpit of the Jama Masjid in Delhi. In Calcutta Hindus joined Muslims in a meeting in the famous Nakhoda mosque. The same thing happened in the chief mosque at Allahabad.[60] 'Though the Rowlatt Act sits like a dreadful nightmare on our breasts', aptly observed the editor of the *Amrit Bazar Patrika,* 'it has united both Hindus and Muslims in a way which has never been witnessed. Is it not a miracle that Hindus should preach in the Masjid and Muslims should enter Hindu temples?'[61]

Such miracles were partly the result of the widespread feeling of resentment, shared by both Hindus and Muslims, at the state of affairs in the country after the end of the First World War, when repression took prercedence over reform in the British scheme of things. This feeling became still sharper after the massacre at Jallianwala Bagh (Amritsar; April 1919) which, according to Government's own estimate, left nearly four hundred dead and twelve hundred wounded. Mohamed Ali gave expression to the prevailing mood when, soon after his release from prison, he addressed the vast concourse gathered for the annual session of the Congress at Amritsar in the last week of December 1919. Making a reference to the role of Brigadier General R.E.H. Dyer, whose order to fire at the unarmed people assembled at Jallianwala Bagh had resulted in the massacre, Mohamed Ali declared: 'He has fired not only on those people put fired into our hearts. He has created a new fire and out of that new fire a nation of Hindus and Muslims is being created before you today.'[62]

The 'nation of Hindus and Muslims' was being created not only by the Rowlatt Act and the Jallianwala Bagh massacre, but also, indeed much more so, by the deep Muslim concern for the future of Khilafat and the holy places of Islam. Turkey was among the defeated powers and there were reports that it was not only to be deprived of all its possessions populated by non-Turkish peoples, but even of some populated by Turks. This was most disturbing to Indian Muslims who had long looked upon the Sultan of Turkey as their Khalifa or Caliph, supposed to be not merely the spiritual, but also the temporal head of all Muslims wherever they might be residing. The Indian Muslim leadership took the position that their Caliph must have adequate power in order to be able to perform his responsibilities as the head of all Muslims. They also contended that the stewardship of the holy places of Islam must not pass into non-Muslim hands. Britain, ruling over such vast numbers of Muslims, was expected to work for the fulfilment of these wishes. This much had been promised by British statesmen during the war. Any departure from this, therefore, would not merely be an unjust act, but also involve a serious breach of promise. The dominant Indian Muslim leadership turned it into a major religious issue, indeed a matter of life or death for Muslims.

While there is no doubt about the serious Muslim concern with the future of the Caliphate and the holy places of Islam, scholars are not agreed as to the real motivation of the Indian Muslim leadership in giving so much importance to this issue. Some feel that behind this move was the desire of a section of the new leadership of the Muslim League 'to ensure that the Muslim identity remained the powerful guise to adopt in Indian politics that it had been'.[63] As for the *Ulama*, who provided the driving force behind the Muslim agitation on the Khilafat issue, it is held that they 'just wanted to control Indian Muslims'.[64] Similarly, there is a view that the main purpose of the Khilafat movement was to unite the Muslim community politically through the use of religious and cultural symbols and use the 'united, Pan-Indian Muslim constituency' thus created to ensure 'genuine Muslim participation in the Indian nationalist movement'. Muslim unity, according to this reasoning, would offset their minority status and enable them to bargain from a position of strength and secure the necessary political concessions from the Congress.[65] The common point in both these views is the assumption that the Khilafat movement was not a spontaneous movement created by religious and Pan-Islamic feelings, but artificially engineered for certain political purposes by scheming leaders who used religious symbols to rouse the passion of their followers. Such an interpretation, it has been rightly contended by Mushirul Hasan, 'ignores the importance of religious symbols in Indian Islam; underestimates the sense of religious unity among Muslims . . .; and takes no account of the religious ties between the Indian Muslims and their co-religionists in other parts of the world'. The last mentioned factor, according to this view, 'provided the driving force behind Pan-Islamic ideology generally and the Khilafat movement in particular'.[66]

While emphasizing the religious factor, however, it will not be appropriate to completely ignore the quest for power which had always been a major factor, along with the feeling of a religious bond with the Muslims outside India, behind the Pan-Islamic movement in India. Because of the close association of Islam with political power in the Muslim historical tradition and the total lack of such power in British India, Indian Muslims drew considerable psychological comfort from the existence of powerful Muslim states outside India and became seriously alarmed whenever there was a threat to their continued existence. The Turkish empire was the greatest source of such comfort because of its extent and power, apart from the fact that its Sultan also bore the title of Caliph and was considered the head of all Muslims. There also developed the view that the existence of the Muslim states outside India added to the political importance of the Indian Muslims and entitled them to greater weight in political matters than that warranted by their proportion in the population. This was mentioned often by Indian Muslim leaders and sometimes also by senior British officials. While religious sentiment was the most important factor, the political or power factor was never absent from the minds of Indian Muslim leaders on any occasion in the history of the Pan-Islamic movement in India. This was also true of the Khilafat movement. This should be clear from the speeches and writings of Mohamed Ali and other stalwarts of the Khilafat movement in India who repeatedly emphasized that the Khalifa must have adequate temporal power in order to be able to discharge his responsibilities as head of all Muslims and protector of their holy places. Thus, referring to the position of the Khalifa in course of a letter to a Hindu journalist, Mohamed Ali observed:

> . . . The Sultan of Turkey is something more than the ruler of the Ottomans. He is . . . an Emperor and Pope in one, and combining in himself as the successor or Caliph of our Prophet . . . the two-fold function which is the logical sequence of the most rational abhorrence that Islam has for any lacerating separation between things temporal and things spiritual. . . . You must remember Islam is not only a religion in the ordinary sense, but also a theocracy, a Government, though it be the Government of God Himself.[67]

A somewhat similar view was expressed by Hakim Ajmal Khan in course of his presidential address to the twelfth annual session of the Muslim League held in December 1919. The Muslim representations on the Khilafat issue, he emphasized, were based on the ground that temporal power was 'the chief factor of the Khilafat. . . . The Khilafat must not be reduced to the position of His Holiness the Pope at Rome, with his influence extending to spiritual confines only.'[68] How the continuation of the temporal power of the Caliph was seen to be related to the political importance of the Muslims in India is best illustrated by the resolution on Turkey adopted by the eleventh annual session of the Muslim League held in December 1919. It outlined the reasons for conveying to the British Government the 'true sentiments of the Muslim Community' regarding the policy to be adopted towards Turkey as follows:

. . . the fact that the Indian Muslims take a deep interest in the fate of their co-religionists outside India, and that *the collapse of the Muslim Powers of the world is bound to have an adverse influence on the political importance of the Mussalmans in the country*, and the annihilation of the military powers of Islam in the world cannot but have a far-reaching effect on the minds of even the loyal Mussalmans of India. . . .[69]

V

Gandhi had realized quite early in his political career (while still in South Africa) that 'there was no genuine friendship between the Hindus and the Mussalmans' and that this constituted the most serious obstacle in the path of India's advance towards self-government.[70] He now saw in the deep Muslim concern for the future of the Caliphate a golden opportunity, an opportunity of a lifetime, to end Hindu-Muslim antagonism and forge unity between the two communities. He did not visualize any difficulty in this as, according to him, the Muslim demands were quite just and the British were honour-bound to fulfil them. As he explained at a meeting in Bombay in April 1920, Muslim hearts were sore as they had never been before. If the Hindus failed to sympathize with them on that occasion, the great opportunity for cementing Hindu-Muslim unity would vanish, never perhaps to come again.[71] Ignoring the power factor in the background of the movement he concentrated purely on its religious motivation in his public utterances and emphasized that if Hindus and Muslims had to live together as members of one nation, they must share each other's agony. He gave expression to these views again and again in his speeches and writings in 1919-20. The following extract from an article published in September 1919, succinctly sums up his point of view:

The Turkish question concerns eight crores of Indian Muslims; and a question that concerns nearly one-fourth of the nation must concern the whole of India. It is impossible that one of the four limbs of the nation be wounded and the rest of the nation remain unconcerned. We cannot be called one nation, we cannot be a single body, if such a wound has no effect on us.[72]

The cause of Hindu-Muslim unity was definitely advanced, at any rate for the time being, by Gandhi's exertions. The leaders of the Khilafat movement, working in the name of the Central Khilafat Committee, openly recognized him as their leading spokesman and he was invited to address several conferences held under that body. After the announcement of the terms of the Treaty of Severs (1920), which confirmed the worst fears of the Indian Muslims and not only deprived Turkey of her non-Turkish possessions but also of certain areas inhabited preponderately by Turks and placed the Muslim holy places under British and French mandates, Gandhi placed before the Central Khilafat Committee a programme of non-cooperation with the Government. This programme was launched under his leadership on 1 August 1920, several weeks before the Congress met in a special session in Calcutta to consider it. At that session, the Khilafat wrongs were bracketed with the Punjab wrongs (arising out of the British failure to atone for the Jallianwala Bagh massacre) as grounds for the non-cooperation movement, whose objective was declared to be achievement of Swaraj. During the year and a half which followed (September 1920-February 1922) India witnessed joint action by Hindus and Muslims in different parts of the country from one end to the other. This was indeed an unique experience for the country, never to be repeated again, at any rate to the same extent.

Yet, with all this, it is well to remember that the Khilafat-non-cooperation movement could at best be described as a joint struggle and not a common struggle. The forces of Indian nationalism and Muslim nationalism had only formed an united front; they had not merged into one nationalism. To put it in another way, the leaders of Muslim nationalism had joined the stream of Indian nationalism, but they had not abandoned Muslim nationalism. On the other hand, the leaders of the Congress looked upon their championship of the cause of Khilafat primarily as a gesture from the Hindus to the Muslims. Neither side donned a purely Indian identity. This appeared quite natural in the context of the contemporary Indian reality and no eyebrows were raised or protests registered at this role of the leaders. Obviously, it was considered quite natural at that time for a particular leader to function simultaneously as an Indian leader and a Hindu or a Muslim leader. Indian nationhood itself was looked upon as a federation of various faiths.

Thus throughout 1919-20 Gandhi as well as Mohamed Ali and other Muslim leaders were appealing to and speaking on behalf primarily of their own co-religionists. While pleading for 'joint and firm action' before the terms of the Turkish Peace Treaty were published, Gandhi, for instance, observed in August 1919: 'I know what the Muhammedans feel, but I have no status to voice specially their feelings.'[73] While addressing a predominantly Muslim meeting in Bombay in September

1919, he remarked: 'I can enter into your feelings for I know what Hindus would feel if their religious honour was at stake. I know that with you Khilafat is all in all today. I am sure, therefore, that you have the whole of the Hindus with you in this your just struggle.'[74] While extending support to the appeal of the Lucknow Muslim Conference for the observance of 17 October 1919 as Khilafat day, Gandhi made a special appeal to Hindus:

It goes without saying that it is the bounden duty of the Hindus and other religious denominations to associate themselves with their Muhammedan brethren. It is the surest and simplest method of bringing about the Hindu-Muhammedan unity. It is the privilege of friendship to extend the hand of fellowship, and adversity is the crucible in which friendship is tested. Let millions of Hindus show to the Muhammedans that they are one with them in sorrow.[75]

Again, in course of a letter to the press Gandhi expressed the hope that 'every Hindu, man and woman, will observe the 17th instant and thus put a sacred seal on the Hindu-Muhammedan bond'.[76] In order to mobilize Hindu support to the Muslims on the Khilafat issue Gandhi also began to emphasize that such support would turn out to be an effective means of cow-protection. He, of course, did not want Muslim abstention from cow-killing to be made a condition for Hindu support to the cause of the Khilafat, but had no doubt that such support would so overwhelm the Muslims that they would give up cow-killing on their own volition. The decision of certain Muslims not to kill cows apparently added strength to this line of argument.[77]

The Muslim leaders, on their part, made no secret of the fact that their main concern was the fate of Turkey and that for them it was a religious issue for which they would not mind any sacrifice. A pamphlet written by Mushir Hussain Kidwai and entitled *The Future of the Muslim Empire* (1919) made a succinct exposition of the Muslim point of view. The following extract can serve as an illustration:

The disintegration of Turkey—the last Muslim Empire—will be a direct challenge to Islam. It will mean that the Muslims are to be made homeless, like the Jews. But the Muslim nation is so constituted that it cannot exist like the Jews. It is bound to enter into a deadly struggle with all those forces which would tend to bring it to that position. . . Muhammed (peace be upon him) did not allow himself to be crucified. He took the sword against the world of enemies who sought to exterminate his religion and his people. No League of Nations can be superior to the command of God, and it is the command of God to Muslims to safeguard Islam even with the last drop of their blood.[78]

Such an approach was particularly strengthened by the active participation of a large number of Muslim theologians, generally called the *Ulama*, in the Khilafat struggle. Their religious and educational role in the Muslim society, through innumerable mosques and *Madrasas*, endowed them with considerable influence among its various sections, particularly the masses in villages and small towns, and put tremendous value on their support for any cause they chose to spouse. The Western educated Muslims who had recently assumed a position of leadership in their community's politics were conscious of this and enthusiastically welcomed their support to the Pan-Islamic cause, which was equally dear to both. Thus the *Ulama's* role in Muslim politics increased, particularly during the days of the Khilafat movement. According to Mushirul Hasan, most of the *Ulama* favoured cooperation with the Congress and the Hindus only 'because of the vital necessity of enlisting their support for the Khilafat campaign'.[79] Further, the large-scale participation of the *Ulama* 'heightened the religious aspects and weakened the anti-colonial dimension of the Khilafat movement'.[80] Several scholars have gone beyond it and underlined the contribution made by the Khilafat movement to the growth of Muslim separatism.[81] Recently, however, there has been an effort to draw attention to the positive contributions made by the Khilafat movement to the growth of the anti-imperialist struggle in India; Hasan himself has modified his earlier assessment and drawn attention to 'the process which enabled the Khilafat movement, in spite of its Pan-Islamic concerns, to merge itself into a general political struggle that far outstripped its original limitations'.[82]

As there is still a widespread tendency among the Indian elite to decry the Khilafat movement because of its use of religion in politics, it seems pertinent to point out that during those days it were not the leaders of the Khilafat movement alone who were inspired primarily by religion. Gandhi, the greatest leader of the Indian freedom struggle, was in a somewhat similar position. Answering a question from a correspondent whether he was not mixing religion and politics, Gandhi through an article in *Navajivan,* dated 30 January 1921, pleaded guilty to the charge and affirmed that in his view not a single activity in the world should be independent of religion. He further added that it was because religion had not been introduced into our politics that there had been so much delay in winning freedom.[83] Although here he apparently meant religion in a broad sense and not Hindu religion in particular, he did not fight shy of speaking in the name of Hindu religion. Indeed, he often justified his support for the Khilafat movement by mentioning his religious obligation as a Hindu. Thus in the same issue of his paper, to which reference has been made above, he wrote about Khilafat:

> I feel very much about this issue because I am a staunch Hindu. If I wish to see my religion protected against seven crores of Muslims, I must be ready even to die for their religion. Similarly, for the Hindus as well freedom will remain a meaningless ideal until Hindus and Muslims develop unity of heart; till such time cow-protection will remain an impossibility.[84]

The point is that religious motivation or appeal to religion need not necessarily lead to discord in a multi-religious society. During 1920-2 most of the Congress as well as Khilafat leaders made an appeal to the religious sentiments of the Hindus and Muslims. But that by itself did not lead to any discord between them and create any fissures in the non-cooperation movement. Gandhi, in spite of his repeated description of himself as a staunch Hindu whose main source of inspiration was religion, and his constant use of Hindu religious symbols, was willingly accepted as their leader by Muslims. Similarly, Muslim leaders like the Ali brothers and Maulana Azad continued to speak as staunch Muslims and to emphasize the religious duty of Muslims to fight for restoring the honour of the Caliph, but that did not come in the way of their commanding respect and regard from Hindus. The use of religious symbols did not create any barrier so long as these leaders were working together and fighting for the interests and aspirations of both Hindus and Muslims. Indeed theirs was the most magnificent essay in Hindu-Muslim cooperation in the entire history of the Indian subcontinent.

VI

To say this is not to imply that so far as Hindu-Muslim relations were concerned everything was perfect during the period of the Khilafat movement. Thanks to the historical and socio-political background of those relations, this was just not possible. Even during the heyday of that movement many Hindus were worried because of the large-scale mobilization of Muslims for a cause which did not seem to concern India in any way and the apparently aggressive and violent tone of the speeches of some of the Muslim leaders in support of that cause. Such people were particularly upset by Maulana Mohamed Ali's speech at

Madras on 2 April 1921 in which he was reported to have observed that if the Afghan Amir invaded India it would be the duty of Indian Muslims to support him. While this was widely publicised, what he had actually said was that if the Afghan Amir were to invade India with a view to subjugating its people, it would be the duty of the Muslims to resist him. If, however, the Amir invaded India in order to fight with those who had subjugated the Indian people and who wanted to crush Islam, it would be the duty of Indian Muslims not merely to refuse to assist the Government, but also to 'gird up their loins and fight the good fight for Islam'.[85] Many Hindus noticed or remembered only the end-portion of Mohamed Ali's statement and treated it as part of a design to re-establish Muslim hegemony over India. 'I am convinced' wrote Brij Narain 'Chakbast', a famous Urdu Poet, to Tej Bahadur Sapru on 28 April 1921, 'that at this stage the Hindus must raise their hands and thwart all such attempts'.[86] The Viceroy noted with glee: 'All the discussion which has taken place on the Afghan question . . . has tended in my opinion to weaken the non-cooperation movement, and particularly the Hindu-Muslim agreement. The Hindu naturally loathes the idea of an Afghan invasion: the Muslim—that is Muhammed Ali—loves it'.[87] Gandhi did his best to allay Hindu apprehensions and affirmed that his own attitude towards an Afghan invasion was not much different from that of Mohamed Ali. For he would consider it his duty to assist the Amir of Afghanistan if he waged a war against the British Government. This he would do by telling the Indian people that 'it would be a crime to help a Government which had lost the confidence of the nation to remain in power'.[88] It is, however, a moot point whether these words had the desired impact on the majority of politically conscious Hindus.

On the other hand, although the majority among the leading Muslim *Ulama* who were active in the Khilafat movement supported Gandhi's leadership and expressed their agreement with him in his insistence on non-violence, a section of the Khilafat leadership headed by Maulana Hasrat Mohani differed from them and held the view that their religion permitted the use of violence against the enemy where necessary. Some even felt unhappy at the dominant role of Gandhi, a Hindu, in the Khilafat movement, which they regarded as a purely religious movement of Muslims. At the back of their mind there was also a feeling that the Khilafat movement had failed to acquire the required force and vehemence primarily because of the mild, cautions leadership of Gandhi. Thus at the All-India Khilafat Conference held at Meerut on 7 to 10 April 1921, some *Ulama* objected to the involvement of Hindus in the Khilafat movement and demanded that the scope of the movement be defined according to the injunctions of the *Sharia*. Although this objection was not supported by the majority,[89] it showed the unease in some Muslim circles at the leading position in the *Khilafat* movement being occupied by a Hindu.

Gandhi aptly described the state of Hindu-Muslim unity around May 1921 as 'a daily growing plant, as yet in delicate infancy, requiring special care and attention'.[90] For Hindus and Muslims were both continuing to show signs of mutual distrust. As Gandhi noted:

> I know that there is much, too much distrust of one another as yet. Many Hindus distrust Mussalman honesty. They believe that Swaraj means Mussalman raj, for they argue that without the British, Mussalmans of India will aid Mussalman empire in India. Mussalmans on the other hand fear that the Hindus, being in an overwhelming majority, will smother them.[91]

'There is no doubt', Gandhi again wrote two months later, 'that the cement binding the two is yet loose and wet.' He went on to add that the Muslim masses did not still recognize the same necessity for Swaraj as Hindus did; the former also did not flock to the public meetings in the same numbers as did the Hindus. This process, he stressed, could not be forced. Sufficient time had not passed for 'the national interest to be awakened among the Mussalmans'.[92] A little latter, he spoke even more frankly:

> Let us not ignore the fact that it is not yet possible to induce Mussalmans to take interest in Swaraj except in terms of the Khalifat. It is sad but it is true. The two communities have remained so long estranged; the Mussalmans had unconsciously almost come to think that India was not their home. The peril to the Khilafat has opened their eyes. The Hindus can take note of the fact, help their Mussalman countrymen and help themselves, and thus for all time cement Hindu-Muslim union.[93]

On the other hand, many Muslims complained that Hindu Congressmen did not show much interest in the Khilafat movement. The President of the Khilafat Committee of Unnao (U.P.), Syed Mahmud, for instance, wrote to Gandhi:

> It is a matter for regret that the Hindu leaders in district generally feel a sort of estrangement from their Mussalman neighbours and both the Hindu and Mussalman workers in several districts are fired with the ambition of personal advancement and claim a superiority which is the most dangerous poison to

real unity. The result is that the Hindu workers hardly take any active part in the *Khilafat* movement, and the gulf thus gets wider. The Congress Committees are doing nothing so far as propaganda work is concerned, and they think that their work is quite different from that of the *Khilafat* Committees.[94]

It soon became clear that apart from differences among the rank and file Hindu-Muslim components of the non-cooperation-Khilafat movement, even the top leaders were finding it difficult to move on the same wavelength. The apparently violent tone of some of the speeches of Mohamed Ali and his brother Shaukat Ali,[95] were found embarrassing by Gandhi. When the former issued a statement clarifying what they had said and affirming their peaceful intent, it was generally believed, not without reason, that they had done so at Gandhi's behest.[96] This began to be described as an apology and seriously affected their prestige. Many Muslims felt quite sore with Gandhi far having led them to that position.[97] When Gandhi did not attend the All-India Khilafat Conference held at Karachi in July 1921, under the presidentship of Mohamed Ali—that being the first such conference missed by him—it was generally believed that this was due to his want of sympathy with the line adopted there. The most notable resolution adopted by the Karachi conference declared that in the then existing circumstances the Holy *Shariat* forbade Muslims to serve or enlist themselves in the British Army or to raise recruits for it. The resolution further added that it was incumbent on all Muslims in general and all *Ulama* in particular to carry this 'religious commandment' to every Muslim soldier in the British Indian Army.[98] When the Government arrested and prosecuted the Ali brothers, along with Dr. Saifuddin Kitchlu and four others in September 1921, and they were all sentenced to rigorous imprisonment for two years, on various charges, including tampering with the loyalty of the Indian soldiers, Gandhi strongly protested and reiterated the stand of the Ali brothers. Thus, for example, in a speech at a public meeting on 19 September 1921, he declared that according to him it was a sin for any Indian to serve either in the British Army or in any of the civil departments of the government, adding that if it was an offence to make such a declaration in public, then he had indeed committed such an offence many a time without number.[99] Part of the reason for such a forthright declaration was Gandhi's desire to refute the notion, widely prevalent in India at that time, that the Muslims were to be left alone to bear the brunt of Government's repression.[100]

As far as Hindu-Muslim relations were concerned, the situation became much worse after the Moplah rebellion in the Malabar district of the then Madras Presidency in August 1921. Although primarily an uprising of oppressed Muslim peasantry against Hindu landlords and their protectors, the British Government, it was also propelled by religious fanaticism. The goal was not merely the ending of the landlords' oppression, but also the setting up of an Islamic State or Khilafat.[101] While a few poor Hindus had joined the rebellion at the initial stage and there was an effort on the part of its leadership to prevent any general attack on the Hindus, it was marked, at the later stages, with a considerable amount of communal frenzy: every Hindu was treated as a potential, if not an actual, enemy and presented with the option of death or conversion to Islam. Although exact figures are not available, it has been estimated, on the basis of reliable contemporary authority, that a minimum of 1,000-1,500 were converted; it is, of course, not known how many preferred death to conversion.[102] It was officially stated by Government spokesmen that the number of persons killed by the rebels was between 500 to 600.[103] Although it was not specifically mentioned, it must have been generally assumed that an overwhelming majority of them were Hindus. According to official estimates, Moplah casualties in the rebellion were 2,337 killed and 1,652 wounded; those who surrendered or were captured numbered 45,404. Non-official sources, however, put the number of the Moplahs killed as more than 1,000.[104]

The spokesmen of the Government generally underplayed the economic grievances of the Moplahs and highlighted the acts of communal frenzy perpetrated by some of the rebels, describing these as the inevitable result of the Khilafat propaganda. This is, for instance, how the official report for the year 1921-2, prepared by the Central Buraeu of Information of the Government of India, describes the Moplahs:

> The Malabar territory of Madras Presidency, in addition to some two million Hindus, contains about a million persons, of mixed Arab and Indian decent, who under the name of Moplahs, have acquired an unenviable reputation for crime perpetrated under the impulse of religious frenzy. Fanatical Muhammedans, poor and ignorant, under the thumb of a bigoted priesthood, they are prone to sudden waves of religious mania, which inspires them with the simple desire to win the martyr's crown after killing as many non-Hindus as possible. Systematic attempts have been made to improve their educational and economic status: but progress is slow, and meanwhile, the soil is only too responsive to the seed sown by the religious agitator.[105]

After emphasizing that in 1921 the Khilafat propaganda filled the minds of the Moplahs with the dream of setting a Khilafat kingdom, the report goes on to emphasize that although the Government had to suffer heavy losses because of Moplah attacks on public property, including telegraph and railway lines, it were the Hindus who suffered most:

> The main brunt of Moplah ferocity was borne not by Government, but the luckless Hindus who constituted the majority of the population. Somewhat naturally they did not join a purely Muslim revolutionary movement, and accordingly paid a bitter price for this loyalty when the temporary collapse of Government authority placed them at the mercy of their savage neighbours. Massacres, forcible conversions, desecration of temples, foul outrages upon women, pillage, arson and destruction—in short, all the accompaniments of brutal and unrestrained barbarism, were perpetrated freely until such time as troops could be hurried to the task of restoring order throughout a difficult and extensive tract of country.[106]

Writings in the contemporary press, particularly the sections dominated by British interests, followed the same line. This is well illustrated by the following lines appearing in a report in *The Times of India*, which was also carried by the *Leader*, in September 1921:

> A special feature of the present outbreak was that the rebels had separated themselves into three groups: Looters, Murderers, Proselytisers. The Looters looted all Hindu houses, the Murderers committed the horrible crime of murder whenever occasion arose and the Proselytisers carried on with all their energy their propaganda, most reprehensible indeed, of forcible conversion of Hindus. Every Moplah in Ernad seemed to be entirely in sympathy with the movement. . . . Not a single Moplah has been looted by these bands and it is very doubtful whether any Hindu house has been left unmolested in the whole of Ernad and Walluwanad. The plight of the Hindus at Nilambur and other places is simply tragic. Women fearing for their lives, and more for their modesty, have taken shelter in forests, and it is reported that some have had ultimately deliveries in the forests on account of fear. . . . Almost all the Hindu homes have been vacated and many have fled miles to Calicut and other places.[107]

Such publicity could not but have an impact on people's attitudes. The traditional Hindu stereotype of a Muslim as particularly prone to be fanatical, aggressive and violent now acquired a new shine. 'The Muslim lion and the Hindu lamb', commented the *Indian Mirror* (Calcutta), 'will lie down together, but the lamb will be inside the lion.'[108] Enthusiasm for Hindu-Muslim unity now visibly waned among Hindus. Many of them felt that it had been a blunder on the part of

Gandhi to have supported the Khilafat movement, which had strengthened the religious fanaticism of the Muslims and made them more aggressive than ever before. 'The doings of the Moplah bands', observed C. Rajagopalachari, a close associate of Gandhi, 'have made man, woman and child among the Hindus here lose faith in Hindu-Muslim unity . . . nothing can make up for the universal feeling of distrust and hatred that has taken the place of Hindu-Muslim amity that had been built up with so much trouble.'[109]

The general Hindu misgivings were further strengthened by the attitude of some Muslim leaders. Although several prominent Muslim leaders like Maulanas Abdul Bari and Azad condemned forcible conversions and declared them to be opposed to the principles of Islam, there was a tendency among certain other leaders to rationalize the actions of Moplah rebels and avoid criticizing them in any way. This is best illustrated by the observations of Maulana Hasrat Mohani, one of the prominent leaders of the radical wing of the Khilafat movement. Delivering his presidential address to the fourteenth annual session of the Muslim League held at Ahmedabad in December 1921, he remarked:

> You are probably aware that Hindu India has an open and direct complaint against the Moplahs, and an indirect complaint against all of us, that the Moplahs are plundering and spoiling their innocent Hindu neighbours; but possibly you are not aware that the Moplahs justify their action on the ground that, at such a critical juncture, when they are engaged in a war against the English, their neighbours not only do not help them or observe neutrality, but aid and assist the English in every possible way. They can, no doubt, contend that, while they were fighting a defensive war for the sake of their religion and have left their homes, property and belongings and taken refuge in hills and jungles, it is unfair to characterise as plunder their commandeering of money, provisions, and other necessities for their troops from the English or their supporters.[110]

Hasrat Mohani did not utter a word regarding forcible conversion. This was, however, the one issue which was creating the greatest anguish in the Hindu mind. Even those Hindus who were deeply interested in Hindu-Muslim unity were seriously exercised over it. One of them wrote to Gandhi shortly after the outbreak of the Moplah uprising:

> I am a staunch believer in Hindu-Muslim unity. But this Moplah outbreak has raised doubts in me. Success in the Khilafat means strength to Islam. Strength to Islam means attempts at conversion. Have we not often been given the

choice between Islam and the sword? Can people such as the Moplahs learn the beauty of non-violence? And even if they appreciate non-violence for the sake of their faith, will they not use violence for the sake of spreading their faith? My belief in the necessity of Hindu-Muslim unity is there. But do you not think that the questions I have raised are relevant?[111]

Gandhi, while publishing this communication in *Young India* dated 29 September 1921, felt constrained to admit that the questions raised here were 'indeed relevant', particularly because they had occurred to 'so sane' a person as his correspondent. He, however, went on to argue that the Congress championship of Khilafat would have been wrong if Islam was based on force, but this was not a fact; there was no sanction in the Koran for forcible conversion.[112] A few weeks later he returned to the subject of the Moplah rebellion with a long essay in *Young India* (20 October 1921). Describing the rebellion as a test for both Hindus and Muslims, he asserted that the Hindus must have the courage and the faith to feel that they could protect their religion in spite of such 'fanatical eruptions'. On the other hand, the Muslims should not confine themselves to a verbal disapproval of the 'Moplah madness' and 'must naturally feel the shame and humiliation of the Moplah conduct about forcible conversions and looting', and work hard to ensure that such things might become impossible 'even on the part of the most fanatical among them'.[113] No Muslim leader spoke in this vein.

It is remarkable that both Hasrat Mohani and Gandhi, though speaking from opposite sides at the annual Congress session at Ahmedabad in December 1921, admitted that Hindu-Muslim unity was not yet a fact of life in India. The former wanted a resolution to be adopted by the Congress as well as the League session calling for independence being made the objective of those organizations. This was to replace Swaraj or self-government, which could mean Dominion Status or independence depending on circumstances. Mohani's argument was that independence alone would rid the Muslim mind of the fear of Hindu domination. Although such a resolution was rejected by both the Congress and the League, what he said in course of his presidential address to the League session about the Muslim fear of Hindu majority and the way it might be removed with the coming of independence shows the limits of Hindu-Muslim understanding after more than a year of joint effort in the non-cooperation movement:

The generality of Mussalmans, with few exceptions, are afraid of the numerical superiority of the Hindu. . . . Fortunately this fear is such that it will be automatically removed with establishment of the Indian Republic; for while the Mussalmans, as a whole, are in a minority in India, yet nature has provided a compensation in the fact that the Mussalmans are not in a minority in all provinces. In some provinces, such as Kashmir, the Punjab, Sind, Bengal and Assam, the Mussalmans are more numerous than the Hindus. This Muslim majority will be an assurance that in the United States of India, the Hindu majority in Madras, Bombay and the United Provinces will not be allowed to overstep the limits of moderation against the Mussalmans.[114]

This was nothing but pinning hope on the theory of hostages to assure Hindus and Muslims of protection against each other. The other point made by Mohani in this connection is equally interesting and shows the depth of distrust between the two communities. So long as India did not become fully independent, he argued, the Hindus would continue to be suspicious that 'in case of a foreign invasion, the Mussalmans would aid their co-religionist invaders'. Once, however, the Indian Republic, 'shared in common by Mussalmans and Hindus', came into being, the ground for Hindu suspicion would be removed; 'for no Mussalman would desire that the power of even a Muslim foreigner should be established over his country'.[115] The following from the concluding paragraph of Hasrat Mohani's address is further indicative of the fact that all was not well even in the relationship between the Congress and the League and that there was an undercurrent of distrust in spite of fervent declarations on the need for Hindu-Muslim unity:

In my opinion, gentlemen, the most pressing necessity of Hindustan is the conclusion of a definite compact between the Congress and the League. The Congress should not enter into any negotiations with the Government concerning *Swaraj* (i) until the minimum Muslim demands with regard to the *Khilafat* are satisfied; (ii) on the other hand, the Muslims should definitely bind themselves to the assurance that, even though their demands with regard to the *Khilafat* are satisfied, the Mussalmans of India will stand to the last by the side of their Hindu brethren for the attainment and preservation of Indian independence. Such a compact is all the more necessary because there are signs that the enemies of Indian independence . . . are concentrating all their efforts on wrecking Hindu-Muslim unity and creating distrust and misunderstanding between the two communities.[116]

Gandhi, while opposing Mohani's motion on independence at the Congress session, mentioned the lack of Hindu-Muslim unity as one of his principal grounds for doing so. 'We cannot do a tiny thing', he observed, 'but want to think of a very big thing—this is the meaning of Hasrat Mohani's resolution. . . . We have not even fully achieved Hindu-Muslim unity. And we want to talk of big things in advance of it.' Proceeding further, he asked: 'Who is here who can say today with confidence, 'Yes, Hindu-Muslim unity has become an indissoluble factor in Indian nationalism'?[117] Commenting on the proceedings of the Congress a little latter Gandhi reiterated this point more than once. Thus in the *Young India* dated 5 January 1922, he wrote: 'There is still much left to be desired as to Hindu-Muslim Unity.'[118] In an article on independence in the same issue, he again observed: 'We have not come to our own. There is still mutual distrust between Mussalmans and Hindus.'[119]

Gandhi, of course, underlined the many positive developments in Hindu-Muslim relations in the wake of the Khilafat-non-cooperation movement. The fact that since 1919 the Muslim League and the Khilafat Conference held their sessions at the same place and about the same time as the Congress was itself of great importance. This enabled Hindus and Muslims 'to learn a great deal from each other and to strengthen their friendship'. At Ahmedabad (1921) this process had gone still further because Hakim Ajmal Khan presided over the Congress session as well as that of the Khilafat Conference. 'The Khilafat camp and the Congress camp', wrote Gandhi, 'thus came so close to each other that nobody would think of them as separate camps'.[120] He took special pleasure in mentioning 'the daily increasing amity' between Hindus and Muslims which he noticed during the Khilafat Conference and Muslim League sessions. The presence of a large number of Muslims on the dais at the Congress session and of Hindus at the dais of the Khilafat Conference and Muslim League sessions was an 'impressive spectacle' and its memory 'worth treasuring by all'. Yet Gandhi, with his usual mastery of the nuances of a situation, also took care to remark: 'Though Hindu-Muslim relations are thus improving, we are not free from dangers. There still remain in our paths many deserts to be crossed, many forests, valleys and hills. The road has yet to be cleared, metalled and rolled.'[121]

VII

The road was indeed 'cleared, metalled and rolled', but after its direction had been fully reversed. Indeed, as noticed earlier, the process of reversal had already begun under the shadow of the Moplah rebellion. Ironically, a step taken by Gandhi himself further contributed to that process. That was his decision to indefinitely postpone the civil disobedience movement which had been scheduled to be launched in the Bardoli district of Gujarat. First planned for the last week of November 1921, the launching had been postponed till the middle of February 1922 as a result of incidents of violence in Bombay on the occasion of the visit of the Prince of Wales to that city in the same month that the movement had to be launched. While the eyes of the whole country were fixed on Bardoli in anticipation of the planned movement, a serious incident involving violence on the part of supporters of non-cooperation took place on 5 February 1922 at a place called Chauri-Chaura in the Gorakhpur district of U.P. A sizeable crowd of Congress workers and sympathizers having been provoked by police firing had, after the policemen had exhausted their limited ammunition, set fire to the police station and, along with it, burnt to death twenty-two persons, including twenty-one policemen and an younger son of one of them. Gandhi, already full of misgivings regarding the Indian people's ability at that stage to organize an active movement strictly on the basis of non-violence and worrying because of sporadic incidents of violence connected with the non-cooperation-Khilafat movement, now decided that the time was not yet ripe to start the projected civil disobedience movement. So instead of the movement being launched on 12 February 1922, there appeared on that day a resolution adopted by the Congress Working Committee, under Gandhi's guidance, suspending it. This suspension was to continue till the atmosphere in the country became 'so non-violent as to ensure the non-repetition of popular atrocities' as witnessed at Chauri-Chaura and other places. While normal Congress activities on the basis of non-cooperation with the Government were to continue, Congress workers were advised to stop all activities specially designed to court arrest and imprisonment and to concentrate on constructive activities.[122] This decision was confirmed by the All India Congress Committee on 25 February 1922.[123]

While suspension of the programme of civil disobedience at a time when the political barometer in the country was touching the boiling point baffled and upset most of the Congress leaders, including some of Gandhi's closest associates, its impact was particularly severe on those Muslims who had cast their lot with him primarily because of his espousal of the Khilafat cause. They felt let down and betrayed.[124] Some Muslim leaders now began to openly attack Gandhi and his methods, including his insistence on non-violence and constructive activities. At an important conference of the *Ulama*, held at Ajmer, in the first week of March 1922, Maulana Abdul Bari made a violent speech, and Gandhi had to rush to that place to explain matters to him. This did the trick at least for the time being and the Maulana issued a statement adhering to non-violence. The *Civil and Military Gazette* (Lahore) published a report in the middle of March 1922 from Calcutta purporting to sum up Hasrat Mohani's grievances against Gandhi. According to it, Hasrat Mohani was reported to have wondered why Gandhi himself had not been arrested. He was also reported to have asserted that 'although the proportion of Hindus to Muhammedans in India was four to one, yet, 95 per cent of those who had gone to jail in connection with the agitation were Muhammedans'. Mohani later denied having made such observations, but some others were hold enough to openly attack Gandhi. Thus Mushir Hussain Kidwai, in course of a letter to the *Leader* in the middle of March 1922, observed:

> I cannot help reminding Mr. Gandhi that his programme of removing untouchability or picketing liquor shops or boycotting councils and Universities or even of wearing nothing but Khaddar cannot have the slightest effect on the *Khilafat* question. The idea of converting all Indian Muslims to Jainist beliefs may be a very good method of solving the *Khilafat* question for India, but, fortunately, for Islam it is not practicable.[125]

While such statements caused a good deal of confusion among the votaries of the Khilafat movement, the strong religious motivation of the movement kept it going for sometime more. Indeed, the vitality of the Khilafat movement still 'continued to lend non-cooperation a formidable appearance'.[126] In the meanwhile, however, the Government of India headed by the Viceroy, Lord Reading, had begun considering ways and means of detaching Muslims from the non-cooperation movement. In this effort, Reading's path was lighted by the Muslim member of his Executive Council, Mohammad Shafi. In a memorandum dated 2 November 1921, handed over to the Viceroy, he pointed out that the failure of the Indian agitation against the partition of Bengal during 1905-8 had been due 'mainly to the fact that the Muslim community in India as a whole supported Government throughout that troublesome period'. Conversely, it was the participation of a large section of the Muslim community in the non-cooperation movement 'due exclusively to the wounding of their religious feeling' that had made the situation so dangerous. The situation could be immensely improved by modifying the terms of the Turkish Peace Treaty in favour of the Turks, and thereby removing the sole reason for Muslim participation in the non-cooperation movement. Debunking the impression in certain circles in Britain that the *Khilafat* movement was not religious but part of the political movement for Indian Swaraj he observed:

The Russian Bolshevik menace and Mr. Gandhi's non-cooperation movement being the two dangers which the British Empire has at present to face, and a revision of the Turkish Peace Terms on reasonable lines being the one remedy calculated effectively to meet both these dangers, it is of the highest moment to the British interests that such revision should be brought about at an early date. Indeed, I am confident that such a step will help to restore the pre-war Anglo-Muhammedan Union. . . .[127]

Reading saw the point and immediately forwarded Shafis' memorandum to the Secretary of State for India, Montagu, with a suggestion that it might be circulated among the members of the British Cabinet.[128] Finally, on 28 February 1922, the Viceroy sent an official telegram to the Secretary of State for India imploring the British Government to get the Treaty of Severes modified in such a way as to meet the most important demands of the Indian Muslims, namely, the evacuation of Constantinople, the maintenance of the Turkish Sultan's suzerainty over the holy places and the restoration of Ottoman Thrace, including the sacred Muslim city of Adrianople, and the unreserved restoration of Smyrna. The fulfilment of those demands, the telegram emphasized, was of 'the greatest importance to India'. The Viceroy also pressed for permission to publish this telegram immediately as it was so important for the Government of India 'to range itself openly on the side of Muslim India'.[129]

Reading was particularly keen to have this telegram published before Gandhi's arrest, which had already been decided upon. After Montagu's permission was obtained, the telegram was published on 8 March 1922. Gandhi was arrested two days later. As Montagu had authorized publication without consulting either the Prime Minister or Cabinet, he had to resign. Because of his resignation, many more people came to learn and talk about the Viceroy's telegram than it might have otherwise happened. Although for quite sometime the Viceroy had been assuring successive deputations of Muslim leaders who called on him that he wanted the terms of the Turkish Peace Treaty to be modified in line with Muslim aspirations, the telegram provided solid proof of the fact that he had actually conveyed his views to the British Government. This was the Viceroy's main purpose in sending the telegram and getting it published.[130]

That purpose was fully served, particularly because of the wide publicity given to Montagu's resignation and its background. As a result, the Viceroy appeared to many Muslims in India as a knight in shining armour, valiantly fighting for the fulfilment of their demands. There were, of course, some Muslims who felt that the Viceroy's telegram did not go far enough, as it did not mention Arabia, Mesopotamia and Palestine, which were also the objects of Indian Muslims' concern at that time. However, by and large there was a feeling among Indian Muslims that the Viceroy was doing his best to get their demands fulfilled. Most of them were already extremely unhappy at the indefinite postponement of civil disobedience at Gandhi's instance. Now they began to think that Muslim interests would be better served by working with the Government. Within a fortnight of the publication of Reading's telegram to Montagu the Director of Information of the Government of India informed the British Government in London that it had produced a marked effect on Muslim opinion, which might shortly separate itself from the non-cooperation movement.[131] About a month later Shafi confirmed the accuracy of this prognosis. As he reported to Reading on 20 April 1922:

> The effect produced in All-India Muslim circles by this telegram, and the news of Mr. Montagu's resignation, has indeed been widespread and profound. The conviction has now been brought home to all Muhammedans that they had been misled into believing that the Government of India were not earnest in their advocacy of the Indian Muslim views. The moderate section of the community are delighted, for their faith in the Government of India has been completely vindicated. The members of the left wing of the *Khilafat* Party, who had joined Gandhi's movement, have now cried halt to their activities. Indeed, the process of separation between their party and the non-cooperation movement has, as I expected, already commenced.[132]

Shafi substantiated this by pointing out that all Khilafat activities of an anti-British character had come to an end. The tone of the Indian Muslim press had changed 'for the better'. A large number of meetings had been held in different parts of the country where resolutions had been adopted recording the gratitude of the Indian Muslim community to the Viceroy. In a few *hartals* that had taken place in some of the towns of northern India in the wake of Gandhi's conviction, during the celebration of the National Week (6-13 April), the majority of Muslim shopkeepers had refrained from joining and kept their shops open. A famous Muslim fair near Lahore (known as the *Chiraghan* fair) which could not be held during the earlier two years because of the Khilafat movement, was held that year 'on a bigger scale than ever'. A meeting held at Lucknow at the house of a loyal Muslim supporter of the British cause had the distinction of being attended by such luminaries of the Khilafat movement as Maulana Abdul Bari and M.H. Kidwai. After the meeting, the former wrote to Shafi expressing his and his party's gratitude to the Viceroy and to Montagu and promising to stop all anti-British activities. Shafi was also informed that Bari had despatched telegrams to the Central Khilafat Committee at Bombay and the Bengal Khilafat Committee asking them to stop anti-British activities. Further, he despatched Kidwai to Bombay in order to convey his message personally to the President of the Central Khilafat Committee, Chhotani. On his return from Bombay Kidwai had written to Shafi enclosing cuttings from the *Bombay Chronicle* containing texts of his letter and interview in which he had referred to the excellent impact of the Government's action on the Indian Muslim mind. Shafi was naturally pleased by all this and concluded his letter by expressing his conviction that the desired modification of the terms of the Turkish Peace Treaty was bound to restore the old, pre-Khilafat bond between the Government and the Muslims:

> These healthy signs, even among the ranks of the left wing of the *Khilafat* Party, are indicative of material improvement in the situation and are, to my mind, conclusive evidence of the fact that modification of the Turkish Peace Terms on the lines suggested by the Government of India will restore the previously existing Anglo-Muhammedan unity in this country, will break the back of the non-cooperation movement, and the entire Indian Muslim Community once again will be at the back of the British Government in this country and the prospect of restoration of normal conditions will thus become definite and certain.[133]

Information from some other sources available to Reading confirmed the impression created by Shafi's note. The Viceroy conveyed to the new Secretary of State for India, Viscount Peel, a few weeks later that such information indicated in a stronger measure than he had ever expected the tendency of Muslims in India to abstain from active co-operation with Hindus as a result of the impression created on their minds by the Government of India's telegram dated 28 February 1922. This, according to him, was primarily responsible for comparative peace in India since the arrest and imprisonment of Gandhi. As he put it:

Private letters have been shown to me which have really surprised me, for I had scarcely anticipated that some of the men against whom we were then proposing to institute criminal proceedings would now be working privately to bring about Muslim cooperation with the Government of India. I have never myself exaggerated the importance of the telegram. . . . Some of my more enthusiastic adherents tell me that it will cause definite and open secession of the Muhammedans from the non-cooperation movement. I dare not expect quite so much, but I have already evidence of its great effect, and we must never lose sight of it when trying to understand why there has been so much peace and tranquility in India since Gandhi's arrest. . . . Wherever we had trouble with the non-cooperationists it was caused by the Muhammedans and, indeed, at least 75 to 80 per cent of the political prisoners were Muhammedans. . . . When word was passed to this turbulent Muhammedan Community to cease from demonstrations and disturbances, the more peaceful era began and I hope will continue.[134]

The Viceroy was not wrong in marking the virtual end of the Khilafat movement by mid-1922. He also spared no effort to ensure that it did not get any chance to revive itself during the coming months. As discussion began in Europe regarding revision of the terms of the Treaty of Severes because of the victories of the Turkish nationalist forces over those of Greece, the Viceroy continued to press for consideration being given to the Indian Muslim point of view and the adoption of a sympathetic attitude towards Turkey. Thus, in a telegram to Peel in July 1922, he again recalled that 'the violent disturbances of the past were mainly by truculent and fanatical Muhammedans and not by Hindus'. Emphasizing that it was difficult, if not impossible, for non-cooperation to be effective without cohesion between Hindus and Muslims, he observed:

At the present moment certain of the most important Khilafat leaders are working to bring about cooperation with Government of India and with His Majesty's Government, and if they succeed, it will have great importance in Indian politics. A little encouragement from His Majesty's Government and more particularly any sympathetic words you may utter would be most valuable. It is certain that non-cooperation is on the decline and its leaders are making and will make great efforts to regalvanise it into life. If at this juncture we are able definitely to break the Muslims away from it, we shall have struck what I believe will be a fatal blow to the most powerful hostile movement we have had to encounter since the Mutiny.[135]

Again, within less than a fortnight the Viceroy telegraphed to the Secretary of State for India: 'Believe me we cannot exaggerate the importance of getting the Indian Muslims on our side. Every day and every hour impress this upon me.'[136] The Secretary of State was, of course, quite sympathetic to this view, as is evident from his reply to the Viceroy's telegram of 13 July: 'I read with the greatest possible satisfaction your impressions of the weakening of the bond between the Muhammedan and the Hindu. . . .'[137] Contrary to the opinion of some scholars,[138] however, it was not so much pleadings by the Viceroy and the Secretary of State for India, as the military victories of the new Turkey and the course of European politics which determined the contents of the Treaty of Lausanne, providing several vital concessions to Turkey, which was finally signed on 24 July 1923 and replaced the Treaty of Severes.[139] Whatever that may be, there is no doubt that the Treaty of Lausanne had a generally soothing impact on the majority of politically conscious Muslims so far as their attitude towards the British Government was concerned. This was quite natural. For although the future of the holy places of Islam was not yet solved to their satisfaction, most of Turkey's demands had been conceded. As Reading noted, the British attitude during the negotiations leading to the signing of the Lausanne Treaty had 'certainly had a beneficial influence on the situation in India' and had caused the moderate Mohammedans to move away from the extremists and range themselves with the Government.[140]

Even before the signing of the Lausanne Treaty the Khilafat movement in India had received a severe blow from the new Turkey. The Grand National Assembly at Ankara had, in November 1922, abolished the Sultanate with retrospective effect from 16 March 1920. Although the institution of the Caliphate was not abolished, the Caliph ceased to have any temporal power, which was now vested in the Grand National Assembly. In a further assertion of its authority after about three weeks, the latter deposed the reigning Caliph and selected his cousin as the new Caliph. As the Khilafat movement had been based on the view that the Caliph must have adequate temporal authority in order to properly discharge his duty as head of all Muslims, the abolition of the Sultanate left that movement gasping for breath. Whatever life was left in it was finally extinguished in March 1924 when the Turkish National Assembly abolished the institution of the Caliphate and banished from Turkey the then Caliph and all members of his family. The leaders of the Khilafat movement, whose credibility had already come into question because of the serious financial scandals surrounding them as well as the widespread feeling that the Government of India had done more for Turkey by securing a revision of the terms of the Turkish Peace Treaty than the Khilafat movement, now found the ground completely cut from under their feet. If there was no Caliphate, what could be the justification for a pro-Caliphate movement? With the end of the Khilafat movement there came also the end of the brief cohabitation of Muslim nationalism with Indian nationalism. Muslim nationalism now reverted to its original, separatist course, in a more intensified form than ever before.

NOTES

1. See Yuvaraj Deva Prasad, *The Indian Muslims and World War I* (New Delhi, 1985), pp. 8-25.
2. Syed Sharifuddin Pirzada, ed., *Foundation of Pakistan: All India Muslim League Documents* (hereinafter referred to as *League Documents*), I (Karachi, 1969), p. 255.
3. Ibid.
4. Ibid., pp. 279-80.
5. Shan Muhammed, ed., *The Indian Muslims: A Documentary Record* (hereinafter referred to as *Muslim Documents*), III (Meerut, 1980), p. 131.
6. Ibid., p. 135.
7. Lord Hardinge to Lord Sanderson, 5 October 1912, ibid., p. 126.
8. For details see Gail Minault and David Lelyveld, 'The Campaign for a Muslim University, 1896-1920', *Modern Asian Studies*, 8, 2 (1974), pp. 145-89.
9. Matiur Rahman, *From Consultation to Confrontation: A Study of the Muslim League in British Indian Politics, 1906-1912* (London, 1970), p. 214.
10. Ibid.
11. Ibid., p. 221
12. Minault and Lelyveld, n. 8, p. 161.
13. Ibid., p. 162.
14. Mushirul Hasan, *Nationalism and Communal Politics in India, 1916-1928* (New Delhi, 1979), p. 59.
15. See Prasad, n. 1, pp. 34-41.
16. *Muslim Documents*, n. 46, V (Meerut, 1981), p. 53.
17. Ibid., p. 97.
18. Cited in Syed Razi Wasti, *The Political Triangle in India, 1858-1924* (Lahore, 1976), p. 175.
19. Ibid., pp. 174-5.
20. A.N. Zaidi and Shaheda Zaidi, eds., *The Encyclopaedia of Indian National Congress* (hereinafter referred to as *Congress Encyclopaedia*), VI (New Delhi, 1979), p. 313.
21. See Sheila Rani, 'Indian Public Opinion and the Crisis in the British Empire', unpublished Ph.D. Thesis, University of Delhi, 1985, pp. 343, 346.
22. *League Documents*, n. 2, p. 258. Emphasis added.
23. See Rahman, n. 9, pp. 272-4.
24. Ibid., pp. 267-70.
25. *League Documents*, n. 2, p. 281.

26. Ibid., pp. 267-270.
27. *Muslim Documents*, IV, n. 5, pp. 203-4.
28. Ibid., p. 205.
29. Ibid., p. 206.
30. *League Documents*, I, n. 2, p. 305.
31. Cited in Hasan, n. 14, p. 63.
32. Ibid.
33. Ibid., pp. 61-2. For the text of the Aga Khan's letter of resignation, dated 3 November 1913, see *Muslim Documents*, IV, n. 5, pp. 67-70.
34. The facsimile of Jinnah's application for League's Membership dated London, 10 October 1913, can be seen in 'Sharif-al-Mujahid, *Quaid-Azam Jinnah* (Karachi, 1981), p. 461.
35. *League Documents*, I, n. 2, pp. 315-17.
36. *Congress Encyclopaedia*, n. 20, VI, pp. 407-8.
37. Ibid., p. 442.
38. For details see Prasad, n. 1, pp. 126-49.
39. Ibid., pp. 43-87.
40. *Muslim Documents*, n. 5, pp. 11-12.
41. Ibid., p. 9.
42. Cited in Prasad, n. 1, p. 45.
43. Ibid.
44. *League Documents*, n. 2, pp. 334-5.
45. Ibid., pp. 353-4.
46. Ibid., pp. 357-9.
47. Hasan n. 14, pp. 74-5.
48. Hugh F. Owen, 'Negotiating the Lucknow Pact', *Journal of Asian Studies*, Vol. XXXI, No. 3, May 1972, pp. 576-8.
49. Ibid., p. 584.
50. For the text of the Congress-League Scheme, see *League Documents*, n. 2, pp. 392-7.
51. Cited in T.V. Parvate, *Bal Gangadhar Tilak* (Ahmedabad, 1958), p. 353.
52. *League Documents*, n. 2, p. 374.
53. Ibid., p. 376.
54. Ibid., p. 379.
55. For details see Hassan, n. 14, pp. 88-94; and Owen, n. 48, pp. 578-84.
56. *Congress Encyclopaedia*, n. 20, VII, p. 249.
57. *Collected Works of Mahatma Gandhi* (hereinafter referred to as *CWMG*), XIV (Delhi, 1965), p. 160.
58. See ibid., pp. 51, 120, 141, 161, 193, 280-1, 321, 335, 373-4, 383; also XV, pp. 94-5, 133-4, 220, 231, 296, 342, 404.
59. Speech by M.A. Ansari at Muslim League Meeting, Delhi, 30 December 1918, cited in Judith M. Brown, *Gandhi's Rise to Power* (Cambridge, 1972), pp. 156-7.
60. For details see Hasan, n. 14, pp. 115-17; R. Kumar, ed., *Essays on Gandhian Politics: The Rowlatt Satyagraha, of 1919*, pp. 281-2; and Gail Minault, *The Khilafat Movement* (Delhi, 1982), pp. 70-1.
61. Motilal Ghose to Mohamed Ali, 14 April 1919, Mushirul Hasan, ed., *Mohamed Ali in Indian Politics: Select Writings*, II (New Delhi, 1983), p. 220.
62. Ibid., p. 299.

63. See Francis Robinson, *Separatism Among Indian Muslims* (Delhi, 1975), p. 292.
64. Ibid.
65. Minault, n. 60, p. 2.
66. Hasan, n. 14, p. 133.
67. Brown, n. 59, p. 193.
68. *League Documents*, n. 2, p. 528.
69. Ibid., p. 500.
70. M.K. Gandhi, *Autobiography* (Ahmedabad, 1969), p. 334.
71. *CWMG*, n. 57, XVI, p. 310.
72. Ibid., XVI, p. 104.
73. Gandhi to Abdul Bari, 27 August 1919, ibid., p. 70.
74. Ibid., p. 151.
75. Ibid., p. 207.
76. Ibid., p. 227.
77. Ibid., pp. 305, 308, 323.
78. Cited in P.C. Bamford, *Histories of the Non-Cooperation and Khilafat Movement* (Delhi, 1974), p. 142.
79. See Mushirul Hasan, 'Religion and Politics in India: The *Ulama* and the Khilafat Movement', in Mushirul Hasan, ed., *Communal and Pan-Islamic Trends in Colonial India* (New Delhi, 1985; 2nd edn), p. 27.
80. Ibid., p. 31.
81. See, for instance, Prabha Dixit, 'Political Objectives of the Khilafat Movement in India' and Ali Ashraf, 'Khilafat Movement: A Factor in Muslim Separatism', ibid., pp. 51-81, 82-100.
82. See Mushirul Hasan, 'The Khilafat Movement: A Reappraisal' in Ashgar Ali Engineer, ed., *Islamic Perspective,* Vol. II, Issue II, July 1986, pp. 16-35. See also Ashgar Ali Engineer, 'The "Ulma" and the Freedom Struggle' in the same Journal, pp. 1-15. For a thorough as well as sympathetic account of the Khilafat movement see B.R. Nanda, *Gandhi: Pan-Islamism, Imperialism and Nationalism in India* (Bombay, 1989).
83. *CWMG*, n. 57, XIX, (New Delhi, 1966), p. 300.
84. Ibid., p. 304.
85. Bamford, n. 78, pp. 28-9.
86. Cited in Hasan, n. 14, p. 191.
87. Reading to Montagu, 19 May 1921, IOR, Mss. Eu. 238/3, Reading Collection.
88. *CWMG*, n. 57, XX (New Delhi, 1966), p. 59.
89. Bamford, n. 78, p. 166.
90. *CWMG*, XX, p. 89.
91. Ibid., p. 90.
92. Ibid., p. 436.
93. Ibid., XXI (New Delhi, 1966), p. 10.
94. Ibid.
95. Bamford, n. 78, pp. 53-4.
96. *CWMG*, XX, pp. 536-8.
97. Reading to Montagu, 7 July 1921, Reading Collection, n. 87.
98. Bamford, n. 78, p. 171.
99. *CWMG*, XXI, pp. 147-8.

100. Reading to Montagu, 6 October 1921, Reading Collection, n. 87.
101. See K.N. Panikkar, *Against Lord and State: Religion and Peasant Uprising in Malabar, 1836-1921* (Delhi, 1989), pp. 191-200. Also Stephen Frederic Dale, *Islamic Society on the South Asian Frontier: The Mappiles of Malabar, 1498-1922* (Oxford, 1980), pp. 209-18; Conrad Wood, *The Moplah Rebellion and its Genesis* (New Delhi, 1987), pp. 237-40; M. Gangadhar Menon, *Malabar Rebellion, 1921-1922* (Allahabad, 1989), pp. 423-84; and Robert L. Hardgrave, JR, 'The Mapilla Rebellion, 1921: Peasant Revolt in Malabar', *Modern Asian Studies*, Vol. XI, n. 1 (1977).
102. Wood, n. 101, p. 215.
103. Ibid., p. 214.
104. K.N. Panikkar, ed., *Peasant Protests and Revolts in Malabar* (New Delhi, 1990), p. xxvii.
105. L.F. Rushbrook Williams, *Indian in 1921-1922* (Calcutta, 1922), p. 73.
106. Ibid., p. 74.
107. Panikkar, n. 104, pp. 423-4.
108. Minault, n. 60, p. 148.
109. C. Rajagopalachari to Gandhi, 8 September 1921, Nanda, n. 82, p. 319.
110. *League Documents*, n. 2, pp. 559-60.
111. *CWMG*, n. 57, XXI, p. 216.
112. Ibid., p. 217.
113. Ibid., pp. 320-1.
114. *League Documents*, n. 2, p. 359.
115. Ibid.
116. Ibid., p. 563.
117. *CWMG*, n. 57, XXII (New Delhi, 1966), pp. 107-8.
118. Ibid., p. 137.
119. Ibid., p. 144.
120. Ibid., p. 147.
121. Ibid., pp. 147-8.
122. Ibid., pp. 377-8.
123. Ibid., pp. 468-9.
124. Nanda, n. 82, pp. 345-6; 357-8.
125. Bamford, n. 78, p. 192-4.
126. Rushbrook Williams, n. 105, p. 103.
127. Enclosure to Reading to Montagu, 3 November 1921, Reading Collection, n. 87.
128. Ibid.
129. H. Montgomery Hyde, *Lord Reading* (London, 1967), pp. 371-2.
130. Ibid., p. 372.
131. Rushbrook Williams to Lloyd Evans, 22 March 1922, Reading Collection, n. 87.
132. Enclosure to Reading to Viscount Peel, 26 April 1922, ibid.
133. Ibid.
134. Reading to Peel, 13 July 1922, ibid.
135. Reading to Peel, 16 July 1922, ibid.
136. Reading to Peel, 27 July 1922, ibid.
137. Peel to Reading, 2 August 1922, Reading Collection, 238/5.

138. See, for instance K.K. Aziz, *The Making of Pakistan: A Study in Nationalism* (London, 1967), p. 36, who holds the view that the pressure of Indian Muslims exerted through the Khilafat Movement forced the British Government to modify its attitude towards Turkey.
139. See A.C. Niemeijer, *The Khilafat Movement in India, 1919-1924* (The Haque, 1972), pp. 153-4.
140. Reading to Peel, 14 December 1923, Reading Collections, n. 87.

CHAPTER IV

The Communal Backlash and Resurgence of Muslim Nationalism, 1922-1927

THE END of the Khilafat movement witnessed a powerful communal backlash over most of northern India. Writing in the first half of September 1924, Lala Lajpat Rai, one of the prominent leaders of the Congress, thus summed up the situation since 1922:

> ... for the last three years Hindus and Mussalmans have been at daggers drawn with each other to an extent never before known under British rule. All attempts to stem the tide have so far proved ineffectual. All efforts for finding a solution have been fruitless. It cannot be denied that at the moment of writing, the relations between the two communities are strained almost to the breaking point. Communal riots and scuffles are of more frequent occurrence than ever before. Mutual distrust and suspicion has reached the Nth point. Even in Congress circles, in spite of much hugging and cooing, the relations between the leaders of the two communities are not free from distrust and suspicion.[1]

Ironically, the Khilafat movement, which brought Hindus and Muslims together in the fight against the British, had itself contributed to this denouement. By calling upon Muslims to offer supreme sacrifice for a cause which was purely religious, of significance to Muslims alone, it had heightened their community consciousness in a way in which nothing had done before. The issue of Indian freedom was, of course, there, but this did not provide the chief motivation for their participation in the movement. The situation was somewhat similar on the Hindu side; it was no secret that most of the Hindu participants in the non-cooperation movement did not have any interest in the Khilafat issue. K.K. Aziz is not wrong in remarking that although Indian Muslims had long since been conscious of being a separate religious group, it was only in the aftermath of the Khilafat movement that they 'felt, with unprecedented intensity, that they were Muslims first and Indians afterwards'.[2]

The heightened Muslim consciousness received a rude shock when Gandhi decided not to start the civil disobedience movement, as planned, in February 1922, without any consultation with the Khilafat leaders, thereby taking the sting out of the non-cooperation movement at a time when the Khilafat issue appeared nowhere near solution. The widely publicized Viceroy's telegram to the Secretary of State in March 1922, supporting the Indian Muslim stand on that issue, on the other hand, made many Muslims, including some leaders of the Khilafat movement, feel that the British were sympathetic to their cause and that it might be more productive, from the Muslim point of view, to revert to the erstwhile unwritten but firm alliance with the British rather than continuing with the new *entente* with the Congress and the Hindus. The Treaty of Lausanne, signed in 1923, helped to further strengthen this type of thinking. Whatever ground there might still have seemed to remain for a policy of alliance with the Congress and Hindus finally vanished when the new rulers of Turkey, under the leadership of Mustafa Kamal Pasha, abolished the Caliphate and banished the Caliph from their land. The end result of such developments was the creation of a feeling of 'bitter disillusion' and 'a sullen sense of betrayal' among the Muslim community as a whole.[3]

The heightening of a separate Hindu consciousness went hand in hand with that of a separate Muslim consciousness. While the former was as old as the latter and had continued, in some form or the other, even after the foundation of the Congress, it acquired much deeper roots as well as wider appeal in the wake of the Khilafat movement. The scale of mass mobilization among Muslims on a purely religious issue and of concern to them alone, the apparently violent tone of the speeches of several Muslim leaders, notably the Ali brothers, and their declaration of welcome to a possible Afghan invasion of India, even though in opposition to the British, caused serious misgivings in many Hindu minds and made them apprehensive of possible efforts for the revival of so-called Muslim rule over India or, at any rate, of Muslim fanaticism which might make life difficult for Hindus in several parts of India. Some of the incidents taking place in course of the Moplah uprising of 1921, particularly the attacks on Hindu temples, killing and conversion to Islam of Hindus, and the disinclination of some Muslim leaders to condemn the Moplahs for such incidents, further strengthened Hindu suspicions. The *Shuddhi* movement, aiming at the reconversion to Hinduism of such Muslims as had been earlier converted from that faith, going on in a subdued form in some parts of northern India ever since the foundation of the Arya Samaj, now acquired a new vigour. Along with it was added the movement for *Sangathan*, calling upon Hindus to organize themselves to face Muslim aggression, which was generally supposed in Hindu circles to be the main cause of the communal riots that were then occurring with increasing frequency, particularly in northern India. The All India Hindu Mahasabha, lying generally dormant since its foundation in 1915, now acquired a new life and began to hold its annual sessions on a regular basis.

Shuddhi and *Sangathan* on the Hindu side were matched by *Tabligh* (expansion of Islam) and *Tanzeem* (organization) on the Muslim side. While several Khilafat leaders remained steadfast in their attachment to Indian nationalism and Hindu-Muslim unity, some others like Maulana Abdul Bari and Saifuddin Kitchlu became growingly involved with *Tabligh* and *Tanzeem*. The *Shuddhi* and *Sangathan* movements were similarly led or patronized by such starlwarts of Indian nationalism as Swami Shraddhanand, Madan Mohan Malaviya and Lala Lajpat Rai. These movements increasingly drew a large number of adherents and soon acquired a dominant position in the political life of the country, leaving non-cooperation as well as Khilafat far behind. A confidential report of the Government of India thus described the situation:

> The Hindu *Shuddhi* movement, though it illustrates the appearance . . . of a militant Hinduism, proposed merely to purify and restore to the fold Hindus converted to Islam or other creeds. Muhammedan bigotry replied, and, as is characteristic of the Muhammedan in action, by a method at any rate more openly aggressive, with the *Tabligh* movement, which aims at the 'enlargement' of Islam. The divines and clerics being thus engaged with Shastric and Quranic war cries on either side, the Hindu and Muhammedan politicians intervened with the rival schemes of mobilisation known as *Sangathan* and *Tanjeem*.[4]

II

This communal backlash in the aftermath of the non-cooperation-Khilafat movement aggravated tension between Hindus and Muslims in northern India. They came to blows on such issues as cow-killing, which the Hindus resented, and music before mosque at the time of prayer, to which the Muslims objected. While the former was an old issue the latter cropped up in the aftermath of the Khilafat movement.[5]

This was indicative of the new mood prevailing among the Muslims at that time. The year 1923 witnessed communal riots in such far-flung places as Amritsar, Multan, Panipat and some other areas in the Punjab; parts of Sind; Jabbalpur in C.P.; and Gonda, Agra, Rai Bareili and Saharanpur in U.P. The riot at Saharanpur, marked by loot, arson and murder, was particularly severe.[6] An even more severe riot took place at Kohat in North-West Frontier Province during the following year. While the Muslims had been provoked by a poem penned by a Hindu and a Hindu too had fired the first shots, the reprisal from the Muslim side was so severe that the entire Hindu population, constituting a tiny minority in the town, felt compelled to migrate to Rawalpindi.[7] Calcutta witnessed rioting on a much bigger scale in 1926, resulting in 151 dead and 1,400 injured.[8] During the five-year period between 1923 and 1927, in all about 450 persons lost their lives and 5,000 persons were injured as a result of communal riots.[9]

Although these riots arose out of local causes, and were not master-minded by any political party,[10] there can be no doubt that they were primarily caused by the acute tension between Hindus and Muslims prevailing in India during the post-Khilafat days. 'It takes very little' observed Reading in a telegram to Peel in August 1923, 'to produce a flame of rage between Hindu and Muhammedan now and, in spite of the efforts of some of the leaders, the chasm between the two seems to widen'.[11] In the wake of the Kohat riots (1924) the Viceroy again gave his assessment that in spite of the genuine efforts of Gandhi and other leaders, there seemed at that moment 'no possibility of these two communities living in amity together throughout India'.[12] A year later he informed the new Secretary of State for India, Birkenhead: 'I see no sign of a decrease in the intensity of feeling between the two communities.'[13]

Themselves caused by the then prevailing tension between Hindus and Muslims, the communal riots further aggravated that tension. They also affected the attitudes of and relations between prominent leaders, notably between Gandhi and the Ali brothers. The attribution of responsibility for the communal riots made its own contribution to the worsening of the political atmosphere. It was generally assumed by top government officials as well as Hindu leaders that the apparently aggressive attitude of the Muslims, much strengthened in the wake of the Khilafat movement, was the prime factor behind the riots. The argument was that, on the one hand, the Khilafat movement had made the Muslims conscious of their strength in a way in which nothing else had done in modern times and, on the other, the failure of that movement had left them frustrated and angry and turned them inevitably on the usually mild and weak Hindus, whom they traditionally looked upon as their enemies. 'The external cause for Muslim discomfort', wrote the then Governor of the Punjab, Malcolm Hailey, in 1924, 'has been removed, and Muhammedan eyes are now turned back on their home conditions, but with new ideas of their own position and power for agitation. The Indian is still in the tribal and communal stage; and the Muslim's activity turns first against the Hindu.'[14] Madan Mohan Malaviya, an important Congress leader who growingly identified himself with the Hindu Mahasabha, observed in course of his presidential address to the all-India annual conference of that organization held at Gaya (Bihar) in December 1922: 'The breaches in the past were due mainly to the weakness of the Hindus. Bad elements among the Muhammedans, feeling sure that the Hindus were cowards, attacked them.'[15]

Surprisingly enough, Gandhi, who did not maintain any relationship with the Hindu Mahasabha and attached the highest importance to Hindu-Muslim unity, describing it often as a necessary condition for India attaining freedom, also thought along similar lines. Released from prison in February 1924, he realized that the Hindu-Muslim tension had reached new heights. After deep study and reflection, he dealt with 'its cause and cure' in course of a long article published in his weekly, *Young India*, covering almost the whole issue dated 29 May 1924 and emphasizing the urgency of Hindus and Muslims both adopting the path of non-violence in settling their disputes. While observing that both Hindus and Muslims had suffered from communal riots, he went on to add:

> There is no doubt in my mind that in the majority of quarrels the Hindus come out second best. My own experience but confirms the opinion that the Mussalman as a rule is a bully, and the Hindu as a rule is a coward. I have noticed this in railway trains, on public roads, and in the quarrels which I had the privilege of settling. Need the Hindu blame the Mussalman for his cowardice? Where there are cowards, there will always be bullies.[16]

Both Malaviya and Gandhi broadly suggested the same remedy for the prevailing malady. Posing the question as to what constituted *Hindu Dharma* (religion) in course of his presidential address to the Hindu Mahasabha session at Gaya (December 1924) Malaviya answered: 'It told them to respect other religions, to be tolerant and never to be aggressive. But it also enjoined upon them not to hesitate for a moment to lay down even their lives, if their *Dharma* was attacked.'[17] In course of his article in *Young India* in May 1924, Gandhi, after describing the Muslim as a bully and the Hindu as a coward, referred to the recent rioting at Saharanpur (U.P.) and remarked:

> They say that in Saharanpur the Mussalmans looted houses, broke open safes and, in one case, a Hindu woman's modesty was outraged. Whose fault was this? Mussalmans can offer no defence for the execrable conduct, it is true. But I as a Hindu am more ashamed of Hindu cowardice than I am angry at the Mussalman bullying. Why did not the owners of the houses looted die in the attempt to defend their possessions? Where were the relatives of the outraged sister at the time of the outrage? Have they no account to render of themselves? My non-violence does not admit of running away from danger and leaving dear ones unprotected. Between violence and cowardly flight, I can only prefer violence to cowardice.[18]

When a learned Hindu philosopher, Bhagwan Das, after reading Gandhi's article, asked him to explain the cause of such a difference in the nature of Hindus and Muslims, especially in view of the fact that most of the Muslims, being converts from Hinduism, belonged to the same racial stock as the Hindus, Gandhi explained that it was religion which had brought about the difference. As he put it:

> Though the majority of the Mussalmans of India and the Hindus belong to the same 'stock', the religious environment has made them different. I believe and I have noticed too that thought transforms man's features as well as character. The Sikhs are the most recent illustration of the fact. The Mussalman, being generally in a minority, has as a class developed into a bully. Moreover, being heir to fresh traditions, he exhibits the virility of a comparatively new system of life. Though, in my opinion, non-violence has a predominant place in the Koran, the thirteen hundred years of imperialistic expansion has made the Mussalmans fighter as a body. They are therefore aggressive. Bullying is the natural excrescence of an aggressive spirit. The Hindu has an age-old civilisation. He is essentially non-violent.[19]

Not to talk of Muslims in general, even Gandhi's followers or admirers among Muslims would not have felt happy at the public airing of such views on his part. This must have been anticipated by Gandhi. That in spite of such anticipation he felt compelled to write in the way he did shows that he must have been deeply touched by the accounts of riots which he had received since his release from prison and in most of which Hindus were generally supposed to have been at the receiving end. Besides, while he continued to assert that his championship of the Khilafat cause had not been a mistake, he had perhaps a nagging feeling that there might be some validity in the general Hindu thinking that that movement had been responsible for strengthening the aggressive trait among Muslims and that he must share responsibility for this. As he mentioned in his article on Hindu-Muslim tension referred to earlier, he had received many letters and messages from Hindus conveying this. Their gist, as he himself, summed it up, was as follows:

> You asked the Hindus to make common cause with the Mussalmans on the Khilafat question. Your being identified with it gave it an importance it would never have otherwise received. It unified and awakened the Mussalmans. It gave prestige to the Maulvis which they never had before. And now that the Khilafat question is over, the awakened Mussalmans have proclaimed a kind of *Jehad* against us Hindus.[20]

Whatever doubt Gandhi might have had about the validity of this charge disappeared after the Kohat riots in early September 1924. The fast for twenty-one days which Gandhi undertook in Delhi on 18 September for restoring Hindu-Muslim unity also represented a penance on his part for his responsibility for causing pain to Hindus. On the day the fast began, when Mahadev Desai, his close confidant and secretary, asked him where his error lay for which he was doing that penance, Gandhi replied:

> My error! Why, I may be charged with having committed a breach of faith with the Hindus. I asked them to befriend Muslims. I asked them to lay their lives and their property at the disposal of the Mussalmans for the protection of their holy places. Even today I am asking them to practise *ahimsa*, to settle quarrels by dying but not by killing. And what do I find to be the result? How many temples have been desecrated? How many sisters come to me with complaints?... Hindu women are in mortal terror of the Mussalman *goondas*. In many places they fear to go out alone. I had a letter from.... How can I bear the way in which his little children were molested?[21]

III

The Kohat riots not merely strengthened Gandhi's guilt-consciousness *vis-a-vis* Hindus, but also created a gulf between him and the Ali brothers, whose friendship and trust, in spite of occasional differences, had been such a great factor behind his influence over Muslims during the days of the Khilafat movement. When Mohamed Ali was released from prison in 1923, he was still full of Gandhi and saw in him the only hope for India's salvation. Asking Saifuddin Kitchlu to try to rouse the people with the slogan 'Back to Gandhi', he remarked: 'It is Gandhi, Gandhi, Gandhi that has got to be dinned into the people's ears. . . .'[22] In course of his presidential address to the Cocanada session of the Congress held in December 1923, he described Gandhi as 'the most Christ-like man of our times' and reaffirmed his faith in the latter's leadership in the most glowing terms.[23] While fasting for twenty-one days in Delhi in September 1924 after the Kohat riots, Gandhi stayed in the house of Mohamad Ali, who took a leading role in assembling prominent leaders of Hindus and Muslims with a view to committing them to work for the restoration of communal harmony between the two communities. However, below the surface, the two leaders had started drifting apart. As noticed earlier, Gandhi made no secret of the fact that he shared the widespread view prevailing in official as well as Hindu circles that Muslim intolerance and aggression had been the main factor behind the riots at that time. On the other hand, even before Gandhi was released, Mohamed Ali had publicly expressed his unhappiness with such a view remarking, in course of his presidential address to the Cocanada session of the Congress (December 1923), that 'it would neither be fair nor productive of any satisfactory result if either community is saddled with all the guilt and denounced without an adequate enquiry'.[24] At his instance the Bombay session of the Muslim League (December 1924) adopted a resolution on the Kohat riots which caused great displeasure to Gandhi. While deploring very deeply the Kohat tragedy and the great loss of life and property there, the Muslim League, through that resolution, felt it to be its duty to place on record that the sufferings of the Hindus of Kohat were 'not unprovoked', and that, on the contrary, they had offered 'gross provocation' to the religious sentiments of the Muslims and had been the first to resort to violence. It went on to point out that although the sufferings of the Hindus were very great, 'it was not they alone that suffered'. Further, it advised the Muslims of Kohat to invite the Hindu residents of that place to return and 'to settle their differences with the Mussalmans of the place honourably and amicably'. It also expressed its trust that while the Hindus would in future avoid provoking the Muslims the latter would refrain from resorting to violence. At the end it condemned the failure of the authorities to take proper steps to prevent the tragedy at Kohat and protect the lives and property of Hindus and Muslims there.[25] Seeing this resolution on 31 December 1924, Gandhi remarked to Mahadev Desai: 'Nothing could be a greater eye-opener than this.'[26] Gandhi apparently found it inappropriate or embarrassing to discuss this matter face to face with Mohamed Ali, for when the latter called on him the next day it was not touched upon.[27] However, he felt too strongly about it to keep silent and wrote to Ali the same day, forcefully expressing his unhappiness at the Muslim League's resolution on the Kohat tragedy, drafted by the latter:

You have meant well but you have done badly. Your resolution reads as if Hindus richly deserved what they got. You state as fact that provocation was from Hindus, that violence too was commenced by them. You state that the Hindus' suffering was great, (but) the Hindus were not the only ones to suffer, meaning thereby that others suffered almost equally. . . . You make the League ask the Mussalmans to invite the Hindus to go to Kohat and to settle their differences with the Mussalmans honourably and amicably. This means that the Hindus are the offenders in the main. . . . You then proceed to invite the Hindus not to provoke and ask the Mussalmans not to resort to violence. This means that there was extraordinary provocation by the Hindus. . . . Your condemnation of the Government coming at the end in the language it is couched has no force whatsoever and you have made no case for condemnation either.

Gandhi also pointed out that Mohamed Ali had 'erred grievously' by his failure to refer to the destruction of temples in the resolution. 'I have read the resolution again and again', said Gandhi, 'and the more I read it the more I dislike it.'[28]

Mohamed Ali's reply to Gandhi's letter is not available, but the former published a lengthy explanation of the background and nature of the Muslim League's resolution in his paper, *The Comrade*, in January 1925. Therein he pointed out that the League was not an organization consisting almost entirely of Muslims of his own way of thinking and that he had to prepare his draft keeping this in view and also in a great hurry in the midst of an ongoing session of the subjects committee of the League a couple of hours past midnight. He, however, firmly stood by the main thrust of that resolution and saw no need to offer any apology for his role in drafting it:

Now, while I was, and am personally content with saying nothing about the provocation offered by a Hindu and another Hindu's resort to firearms, and to let the whole thing be investigated by the National Panchayat or by some equally impartial board of arbitrators, I cannot say that the Mussalmans, who have been assailed so persistently on all sides as a community responsible for outbreaks of violence against unoffending Hindus, are unreasonable if they repudiate such accusations and declare that their actions, however guilty, are not unprovoked, that it is not they in every case who first resort to violence, and that if the Hindus suffer grievously, they do not suffer alone. This is what was sought to be conveyed by the resolution that I had drafted, not as my own, but as the one which I could hope with a great effort to make acceptable to the Muslim League. . . .[29]

Gandhi must have seen this rejoinder and may not have been amused. He had a much worse experience with Shaukat Ali. When after the despatch of Gandhi's letter to Mohamed Ali on 1 January 1925, referred to above, Mahadev Desai talked of Shaukat Ali's 'shamelessness', Gandhi observed: 'The cat will be out of the bag by the end of the year.' 'Rather by the end of two or three months, Bapu!', said Desai. 'Still better then', commented Gandhi.[30] This conversation was obviously related to Shaukat Ali's behaviour during the enquiry into the Kohat riots. Gandhi and Shaukat Ali wanted to visit Kohat for an enquiry (on behalf of the Congress) into the background and nature of the riots, but were not allowed by the Government of India to do so. They, therefore, had to content themselves with visiting Rawalpindi, where the Hindus of Kohat had taken shelter. They did so twice, once in December 1924 and again in February 1925, but came to different conclusions and all efforts to hammer out a joint statement failed. Summing up the differences between them Gandhi observed in course of his letter to Shaukat Ali on 23 February 1925:

I have twice read your comments and I see the wide gulf that separates us in the affair. I am prepared to strongly condemn the publication of the poem [derogatory to Islam] but I am unable to condone the looting and arson. I do not endorse your opinion that the pamphlet was the cause of the conflagration. The ground was already prepared. I cannot treat conversions as lightly as you seem to do. In my opinion the Khilafatists have greatly neglected their duty. . . .[31]

Finally, when all efforts to remove the differences failed, Gandhi and Shaukat Ali published their separate statements on 19 March 1925.[32] Presenting a comparative study of the two statements in *The Comrade* in April 1925, Mohamed Ali rightly regretted their publication, showing the differences between the two leaders 'in a manner which everyone knowing the state of the country could predict without much perspicacity would be exploited by large sections of the two contending communities in the Punjab'.[33]

This was an understatement. For the differences between Gandhi on the one hand and the Ali brothers on the other in relation to the

Hindu-Muslim problems were bound to be exploited by interested parties with a view to accentuating the differences between the two communities not merely in the Punjab but in the whole country. Even more significant was the impact of these differences on Gandhi himself. He had been working in collaboration with the Ali brothers ever since the beginning of the Khilafat-non-cooperation movement in 1919-20; his espousal of the Khilafat cause and his friendship with the Ali Brothers, who had come to symbolize that cause in Indian eyes, had endowed him with a unique position in the country; and he was the one leader who was extremely popular among Muslims as well as Hindus. All this, however, soon changed. The Kohat riots and their aftermath, including the Muslim leaders' perception of their background considerably upset and demoralized Gandhi. He felt particularly sad at his failure to secure a modification of Shaukat Ali's views, thereby necessitating the publication of two separate reports. Gandhi was perhaps even more shocked as well as saddened by Shaukat Ali's lack of interest and prevarication on the issue of forcible conversion of Hindus, particularly married women, during the Kohat riots and his efforts to tutor witnesses at Rawalpindi so that the full picture was not revealed to Gandhi.[34]

As Mahadev Desai informs us, Gandhi's whole effort during the enquiry (February 1925) into the background and nature of Kohat riots was to find out if the pamphlet attacking Islam was the sole cause of the bloodshed or there was some other cause too and whether the widespread arson and plunder at Kohat represented a spontaneous outburst on the part of Muslims because of an acute provocation or was the result of previous planning for revenge. How much importance Gandhi attached to these issues is borne out by his remark to his close confidants at the end of the enquiry: 'I have done the most valuable work in the year.' He further added: 'I made such a closely searching cross-examination after many long years.' In answer to a query by Mahadev Desai, Gandhi mentioned that he had not exerted himself so much while enquiring into some earlier important occurrences like those in Champaran (1917) and the Punjab (1919). 'But this time', he observed, 'I feel as if I used all my art of cross-examination, so that the witnesses might not even feel that they were being under it.'[35]

Before this cross-examination Shaukat Ali had warned the Muslim witnesses: 'Whatever be your internal differences, you must not betray them in your evidences this time.' However, this advice was not heeded by all. One of the important witnesses, Peer Kamal, informed

Gandhi that conversion of Hindus to Islam was a regular feature of life at Kohat. A few of them were converted every Friday. The converted included married women also. 'But the difficult question then arises as to whose wife a converted woman should be. According to the *Shariat* she cannot be allowed to go back to her husband.' Referring to this statement Gandhi remarked to Desai and Jairamdas Daulatram, a Congress leader of Sind, who had also accompanied him to Rawalpindi: 'Didn't you mark it? In what a casual and nonchalant manner he was talking! As if there was nothing wrong in it.' Turning to Shaukat Ali for the latter's views on conversion and perhaps seeing Shaukat Ali trying to avoid answering this question directly, Gandhi remarked that it was 'really a shocking affair' and indeed 'preposterous' for a man like Shaukat Ali to go to an *Ulama* for answers to such questions. Shaukat Ali explained that he had no command over *Hadis*. As he did not know Arabic he had to find its meaning from someone else. Gandhi asked how it was possible to support an action 'against which both our reason and our heart revolt'. He made several other remarks to prod Shaukat Ali. The latter, however, gave only 'evasive and halting replies'.[36]

The trauma on Gandhi's mind caused by reports of conversion at Kohat and Shaukat Ali's refusal to condemn it in spite of repeated prodding on his part came out in this remark of Gandhi while talking to Vallabhbhai Patel after his return from Rawalpindi: 'I wish I could wind up all other work and tie myself down to the Ashram. How long can a man live in this filthy political atmosphere? It seems politics is not for a man like myself.' He was even more forthcoming in his address to the ashramites on 10 February 1925. 'I am now', he observed, 'in the position of a man who is shocked to find a snake under his quilt and gives it a thorough shaking and sweeps his whole room clean.' Explaining that he had come to learn amazing things about Kohat which he did not know before and that he was disclosing that to the ashramites as it was question of one's religion, he came to the issue of conversion. According to him, this was the root cause of the Kohat riots. For when the Hindus awoke to the alarming pace of conversion this was disliked by the Muslims who were looking for an opportunity for revenge. The offending pamphlet came handy to them and they fully utilized the opportunity. He went on to observe:

If all the thirty crores of Hindus turned Muslims after a full knowledge of Muslim scriptures or their own intellectual convictions, I would not feel the loss so much. I would then be content to be the only Hindu on earth. But it passes my endurance, when people are made Muslims by bribery or coercion, as was the case there. I am talking all this to you in order to make you firmer in your loyalty to your religion. . . . My only object is to wake you up, to alert you today in the holy early hours of the morning. And that I do, because it is possible that you may have to face a similar situation some day. If a child, a boy or a girl, is kidnapped from the Ashram, you should not interpret my principle (of non-violence) crudely and sit silent as spectators.[37]

Such talks, implying that Hindus in almost all parts of India lived under a threat of kidnapping and conversion by Muslims, could not have been music to Muslim ears. That Gandhi nevertheless indulged in such talk shows the depth of his repugnance to forcible conversions to Islam for which he got incontrovertible evidence at Kohat as also apprehensions regarding the future. The failure of the Ali brothers to unequivocally condemn such conversions must have made him despair about the possibility of re-establishing Hindu-Muslim friendship in the near future or even entering into a meaningful dialogue with Muslim leaders regarding a solution of the Hindu-Muslim problem.

III

Apart from communal riots the other major factor which contributed significantly to the worsening of Hindu-Muslim relations and the consequent resurgence of Hindu as well as Muslim nationalism was the working of the reformed constitution, embodied in the Government of India Act of 1919 and providing for the partial introduction of democratic government in the provinces. The provincial legislatures had been considerably enlarged, with a wider franchise than before and having a majority of elected members. Under a scheme known as Dyarchy, the subjects of provincial administration were divided into two parts—reserved and transferred. The former, covering such subjects as law and order, revenue and finance remained directly under the control of the Governor who administered them with the help of members of his Executive Council. The transferred departments, covering such subjects as education, health and local government, were placed in charge of ministers responsible to the legislature. Though these ministers also functioned under the overall supervision and control of the Governor, they enjoyed considerable autonomy in promoting schemes of their choice and in dispensing favours and patronage. This naturally led to an intense struggle among politicians for the loaves and fishes of office and competition among their hangers-on for patronage. It also led to complaints and counter-complaints regarding a particular minister unduly favouring the members of his own community and ignoring or harming those of the others.

One result of the introduction of Dyarchy was the shift in the centre of Muslim politics from the Muslim minority provinces like U.P., Bihar and Bombay to the Muslim majority provinces, the Punjab and Bengal. For here Muslims had the largest number of seats in the legislative councils and were in a position to utilize the reformed constitution to the advantage of their community. Hindus, who had earlier occupied a position of predominance because of their educational and economic superiority, had to contend now with the new reality of Muslim power. Their interactions were quite bitter and made a major contribution to the aggravation of communal tension not merely in the Punjab and Bengal, but in the whole country. At the same time Muslims, having tasted power under the new dispensation, began to think of ways to further consolidate it and safeguard it against possible encroachment by a future, democratic central government dominated by the Hindus. The working of Dyarchy thus marked a watershed in the evolution of Muslim politics in India.[38]

We may turn first to the Punjab, where Muslims were in a particularly strong position, owning large tracts of land, especially in the western part of the province where they constituted the overwhelming majority of the population, and having a fairly large representation in the police and other civil services as well as the army. They had been helpful to the British in the latter's conquest of the Punjab and the troops supplied by them had, along with those supplied by the Sikhs, played a major role in enabling the British to re-establish their rule after the rebellion of 1857, particularly in Delhi. During the First World War more than 50 per cent of the recruits for the British Indian Army came from the Punjab. Although the Sikhs of the Central Punjab and the Hindu jats of Ambala Division also contributed significantly, the largest number of recruits, out of Punjabi soldiers, came from the Muslims of Western Punjab. Almost all the recruits, whatever their community, belonged to agricultural families. The British, always conscious of what they owed to those families, favoured them in various ways. The first significant measure in this regard was the Punjab Land Alienation Act (1900), which barred the transfer of agricultural land to non-agricultural families and thereby saved it from being occupied by moneylenders, even though the peasants might default in paying back their loans. The government's bias towards the agricultural classes came out most vividly in the distribution of seats for the Punjab Legislative Council under the Act of 1919, the overwhelming majority of seats being allocated to rural areas. The interests of the rural areas were further safeguarded by providing for residential qualification for candidates, who had to reside in a particular area for four years before becoming eligible to be a candidate for election from that area. The grant of franchise to all ex-servicemen also strengthened the rural classes, for most of the soldiers came from them.[39]

In view of all this it is not surprising that the Punjab Legislative Council was dominated by landlords, majority of whom were Muslims. The council consisted of 94 members, 71 elected and 23 nominated. Out of the elected members, 32 (5 urban, 27 rural) were Muslims, 20 non-Muslims (7 urban, 13 rural) and 12 Sikhs (1 urban and 11 rural). Besides, there were seven constituencies representing special interests like the Punjab University, industry, commerce and landholders.[40] In the first council, constituted in 1920, Muslims, with 35 members (including three representing special constituencies) formed the largest group.[41] As the bulk of them had come from rural areas, they were known as belonging to the rural bloc. While the Muslims dominated this group some Hindu jat members from the Ambala Division also worked with them, besides a few Sikh members from Central Punjab.

The person who provided leadership and a degree of cohesion to the members of the rural block was Mian Fazl-i-Husain (1877-1936), elected to the Punjab Legislative Council from one of the landholders' constituencies and appointed Minister for Education and Local Government in 1921. He held that position till 1926, when he was appointed as a Revenue Member of the Governor's Executive Council. Although he owned a small estate in Gurdaspur district, he belonged essentially to a service family: his grandfather had served in the Sikh Army and his father had risen to the post of District Judge under the British. Educated at Lahore and Cambridge and a well-established lawyer, he was selected as Minister not because he was one of the biggest landlords, but because he was the ablest and most prominent Muslim politician elected to the Punjab Legislative Council, his senior Mohammad Shafi having moved to the centre in 1919 as a member of the Viceroy's Executive Council. The fact that he had built up a reputation as a liberal and a moderate Indian nationalist, being the leader of both the Muslim League and the Congress before the latter launched the Khilafat-non-cooperation movement, was an added qualification. That movement had also given a call for non-cooperation with the legislative councils and it was to the advantage of the British Government to have a liberal and nationalist Muslim as a minister.

The same consideration governed the appointment of Lala Harkishen Lal as a minister from the Hindu side, who too had been active in Congress politics in pre-non-cooperation days.[42]

As Minister for Education and Local Government, Fazl-i-Husain made a tremendous contribution to the socio-economic development of the Punjab. Having long been associated with the management of the Islamia College in Lahore before he became a Minister, he had developed a keen interest in education and regarded it as the key to progress. Under his stewardship there was an all-round progress of education in the Punjab from the primary to the college stage. He took special pains to see that as many districts as possible implemented the provisions of the Compulsory Education Act of 1919. The result was that the number of primary schools multiplied manifold. At the same time a number of Government secondary schools were established in many districts. In order to make college education available to the children of not so well-off families, Fazl-i-Husain provided for the opening of an intermediate college in each district. Apart from starting Government schools and colleges wherever possible, provision was also made for grants-in-aid to needy schools on a most generous basis, in some cases going up to 90 per cent. Liberal provision was made for grant of free studentships and scholarships at all levels. As a result of all these measures education spread even to the most backward districts of the province. While in 1920 only 2.42 per cent of the population in the Punjab received instruction in any educational institution, by 1926 the percentage had risen to 6.71. Fazl-i-Husain saw to it that institutions of local self-government were established in areas (both rural and urban) where they were not functioning before and were further strengthened where they already existed by increasing in them the ratio of elected members and providing for non-official heads in district boards. He also did a lot for the extension of medical relief to rural areas, providing for at least one dispensary for every 100 square miles or every 30,000 of the population.[43]

Fazl-i-Husain contributed to the political development of the Punjab by founding the party system within the Legislative Council. As mentioned earlier, the Muslim members, together with some Hindus and Sikhs, generally worked under his leadership and were known as the Rural Party without, of course, having anything like a written constitution or rules and regulations. In 1923 he went a step further and founded the Punjab National Unionist Party with a similar support-base as the Rural Party. Apart from such items as the attainment of

Dominion Status, the working of the reformed constitution, removal of illiteracy, encouragement of local self-governing institutions and promotion of indigenous industries, its aims and objects included, among others, the following items which would largely benefit the Muslims, without specifically naming them:

(4) To provide equal opportunities of advance to all, and to direct, in an increasing measure, the beneficent activities of Government to backward classes and areas with a view to enabling them to make good the leeway produced by an ill-conceived or inadvertent policy of neglect in the past;
(5) To secure a fair distribution of the burden of provincial taxes between agricultural and other classes;
(6) To secure a just and fair representation of all classes and communities in the public services of the provinces;
(7) To check the exploitation of economically backward classes by economically dominant classes.[44]

As the Muslims, particularly in the Western Punjab, where they constituted the overwhelming majority of the population, were economically as well as educationally backward as compared to Hindus, particularly in the urban areas, Government measures aimed at helping the backward sections of society would inevitably benefit the generality of Muslims. This enabled Fazl-i-Husain to claim that his policies were meant to help uplift the backward sections of society without any distinction of religion. In an address to his supporters in 1930 he remarked:

> I formulated no new political creed; I simply tried in my own humble way to carry out what I understood at the time when I was in the Congress was the Congress programme (hear! hear!). We in the Congress before the Reforms stood out for what? To help the backward. . . . What did I do as a Minister? Nothing more than carry out the Congress programme that had been formulated before the Reforms.[45]

There is no doubt, however, that, as underlined by David Page, many of Fazl-i-Husain's measures were 'more exclusively to the advantage of Muslims'. In 1921 he introduced a system of reservation in admission to Medical College and Government College at Lahore, distributing seats among Muslims, Hindus and Sikhs in the ratio of 40:20:20. This would naturally benefit the Muslims who had formed only a little over 15 per cent of admissions to the Government College, Lahore. Their share in admissions to Medical College was much less: out of 65 students who passed the first examination in Medicine in

1917, only six were Muslims; and out of 45 who passed the second, only four were Muslims. A similar quota was also fixed for recruitment to medical and educational services. However, no attempt was made to introduce such a quota to recruitment to the police force which was dominated by Muslims. The same objective of helping Muslims to improve their position lay behind the Municipal Amendment Act of 1923, which 'redistributed seats where communal electorates already existed and redrew electoral boundaries where joint electorates were still in operation'. As a result of this measure while Hindus also gained in some municipalities Muslims for the first time secured a majority in some of the larger municipalities like Lahore and Ambala. By 1930 the Muslim share in the total number of municipal seats went up from 44 to 49 per cent.[46]

As the bulk of Fazl-i-Husain's supporters in the Punjab Legislative Council belonged to the Muslim community there was nothing surprising in the fact that he undertook special measures to promote their interests. For only a few Hindus and Sikh members had joined his party and when the chips were down the majority of even these could not be counted upon to support him. This became clear in March 1923 when Raja Narendra Nath, the leader of the urban Hindu bloc in the council, moved for a cut in Fazl-i-Husain's salary, charging him with neglecting the interests of non-Muslims in local bodies and bringing down the efficiency of Government by favouring members of his own community in recruitment and promotion. Although Fazl-i-Husain put up a strong defence of his policies, he hardly got any support from any Hindu or Sikh member even of his own party, with the exception of Lala Harkishen Lal and Sunder Singh Majithia, both of whom were in the Government. Apart from them the only non-Muslim to support the Government was L.K. Rallia Ram, a nominated Christian. Thus Raja Narendra Nath's motion was supported by 23 Hindu and Sikh members and opposed by 47 Muslims and British officials. After describing this episode with a view to pinpointing the 'reality of political power' in the Punjab Council on which Fazl-i-Husain based himself, Page aptly observes: 'It was the Muslim bloc on which he ultimately relied and, because this bloc was the most substantial bloc working the Reforms, it was the Muslims who obtained the maximum amount of official support.'[47]

Considering the dynamics of parliamentary government in a society torn by communal cleavages this was quite natural, almost inevitable. The then Governor of the Punjab, Malcolm Hailey, wrote in a confidential letter:

I . . . admit that much has been done that seems to offend against the canons of clean administration; there has been a good deal of pandering to sectional and communal spirit in the administration of transferred departments. But no conceivable system of advance in representative institutions would prevent this; we cannot expect of India, any more than we could expect of the majority of other countries, that it would spring into the position of England in the twentieth century. Wherever representative institutions are in process of development, the majority will claim its rights and exercise its advantages.[48]

However natural the exercise of power in the interest of the Muslim majority on the part of ministers drawing their support from it, the Hindus could not but feel deeply resentful, especially as they had, in spite of their smaller number, enjoyed a privileged position in the pre-reform era because of their educational and economic superiority. The result was acute communal tension. 'It is true', Hailey reported to the Viceroy in January 1925, 'that this tension permeates every walk of life; one never escapes it in any sphere of work, and it is the ordinary subject of conversation in the provinces.'[49] The growing resentment among Hindus at the working of Dyarchy in the Punjab is best illustrated by a memorandum submitted to H.D. Craik, Chief Secretary to the Punjab Government, on 16 April 1925, by Raja Narendra Nath, President of the Punjab Hindu Sabha, wherein he observed, with reference to the prospects for further constitutional reforms:

The next ten years should be utilised not in making great and rapid advance towards responsible self-government but in preparing the way for better and more harmonious relations between the communities and in mitigating the evils which the working of the Reforms Scheme has brought to light and for the creation of some of which it is mainly responsible. The proper time for provincial autonomy will be when no community is influenced by the desire of separation. To introduce provincial autonomy hedged round by communalism of all sorts is to sow the seed of the plant of self-government with the seed of a pernicious creeper which will eventually destroy the plant.[50]

The memorandum had been approved by a largely attended meeting of the Punjab Hindu Sabha. Lala Sewak Ram, a member of the Punjab Legislative Council, had also attended that meeting and gone there with the text of a speech which he could not deliver for lack of time. That text, which Narendra Nath had appended to his memorandum, went even further in opposing constitutional reforms unless they were accompanied by the abolition of communal electorates and vividly illustrates the difficulty of many Hindus in reconciling with the emerging reality of a Muslim dominated government in the Punjab:

The way the Hindus have been treated during the last four years' regime of the Reformed council, I would be voicing the views of many Hindus when I say that Government of India Act should be absolutely repealed. I rather go back to good old days when Hindus and Muhammadans lived in peace, rather than have these reforms. It is said that provincial autonomy be granted. Sir, the minority has come to the conclusion that abolition of communal electorate is at present out of question. If the abolition of communal electorates is out of question, then from the Hindu point of view the provincial autonomy in the Punjab is out of question. Under these circumstances, we want a strong Central Government.[51]

IV

Just as in the Punjab, in Bengal too the working of Dyarchy contributed significantly to the polarization of politics on communal lines and the emergence of a separate Muslim bloc in the Legislative Council. The British played a major role in bringing this about. We, of course, may not wholly agree with Page that there is no better example of the power of patronage available to the Government under the Act of 1919 than that provided by the 'creation in Bengal between 1924 and 1927 of a homogeneous community working closely with the Government out of the disparate material of pre-1920 Muslim politics'.[52] For the 'disparate material' remained so for some more time and complete Muslim homogeneity in politics in Bengal materialized only about two decades later under the impulse provided by the demand for India's Partition and the leadership of Jinnah. It must also be noted that apart from the atmosphere of communal tension prevailing in the country, the growth of Muslim awareness of their position as the majority community in Bengal and their determination to acquire a corresponding position in government and politics and the general Hindu reluctance to accept this were also important factors in facilitating communal polarization under Dyarchy. There can be no doubt, however, that faced with the Swarajist challenge in the Bengal Legislative Council in 1924-5, the British actively promoted the secession of Muslims from Indian nationalist ranks and succeeded in depriving the Swarajist bloc of its entire Muslim component, except just one member, by the time new elections were held in 1926.

As the Congress had boycotted the elections to the first Council under the Reforms Act, held in 1920, managing it did not pose any serious problem to the Government of Bengal. The situation, however, drastically changed after the elections to the second Council, held towards the end of 1923. The Swaraj Party, which had been formed by a section of Congressmen in 1922 after the failure of the non-cooperation movement, had a strong base in Bengal, built up under the dynamic leadership of C.R. Das. The objective of the Swaraj Party was to enter the councils with a view to obstructing the working of the reformed constitution. Das realized that his party could achieve its objective only if it entered the Council in strength. Although, in spite of their being in a minority the Hindus or non-Muslims, as they were described in the Government regulations, had secured 46 out of 85 elected seats, the Muslims had been awarded 39 seats.[53] The Swarajist objective, therefore, could not be achieved without winning a sufficient member of Muslim seats. As in other parts of the country, Muslim enthusiasm for the Congress, because of the latter's support of the Khilafat cause, had withered away. The attention of politically conscious Muslims was now, by and large, centred on their sectional problems and demands. The fact that in spite of their being in a minority of the population of Bengal, the Hindus, because of their educational and economic strength, dominated all spheres of politics and administration was a particularly sore point with most of the Muslims. Even the Muslim leaders who had negotiated the Lucknow Pact with the Congress in 1916 had been content with only 40 per cent of seats in the Bengal legislature for the members of their community. The Act of 1919 also did not go beyond 45 per cent in fixing Muslim share of the elected, territorial seats. Being a wise and imaginative leader Das recognized the genuineness of Muslim grievances in Bengal and, in 1923, entered into a pact with some of their prominent leaders with a view to solving them. This became famous as the Hindu-Muslim Pact or the Bengal Pact. Under it the Swaraj Party agreed that representation to the Legislative Council would be through separate electorates and based on population (thereby ensuring a Muslim majority). In local bodies whichever community was in a majority in a particular district would have 60 per cent of seats and the minority community 40 per cent. The question whether elections to local bodies would be by separate or mixed electorates was to be decided in future, after ascertaining the views of both the communities. Muslims were to have 55 per cent of government posts. Until that position was achieved, their recruitment would have to be larger than the figure stipulated and might go up to 80 per cent. The Legislative Council would not adopt any resolution affecting the religion of any community unless such a resolution had the support of three-fourth of the elected members of that community.

Processions were to be forbidden from performing music before mosques. Muslims were to remain free to kill cows.[54]

Muslims in Bengal could not have asked for better terms. However, the Pact was not popular in Hindu circles and even some of the closest colleagues of Das were not free from misgivings about it. He secured their consent and cooperation primarily because of his outstanding position in Bengal and the force of his personality. He also used incontrovertible arguments. Thus during the debate on the Pact at the Provincial Political Conference at Serajgunj in northern Bengal in June 1924 he observed: 'If the Hindus do not behave magnanimously, they can never earn the confidence of the Muslims. In that case, there shall be no unity between Hindus and Muslims. Without Hindu-Muslim unity, our demand of Swaraj shall ever remain a slogan, and never be transformed into a reality.'[55]

Although the Bengal Pact was formally approved by the Swaraj Party in December 1923, its terms had already been settled and were widely known throughout Bengal. They had the desired impact on the electorate, the Swaraj Party winning 47 elective seats out of which 26 were non-Muslim and 21 Muslim seats. That meant more than 50 per cent seats in both these categories. Even the great moderate leader, Surendranath Banerjee, who had been a Minister during the previous Council, was defeated by an young, not so well-known Swarajist—B.C. Roy.[56] 'Bengal', ruefully observed the *Statesman*, the mouthpiece of British capital in Calcutta, on 1 December 1923, 'has declared itself Swarajist. In every kind of Bengal constituency, the Swarajists have triumphed. Even the Muhammedan electorate, which was considered to be a safe asset for Government, has been rent asunder.'[57] Eulogizing the statesmanship of C.R. Das which had enabled the Swaraj Party to win so many Muslim seats in Bengal Abul Kalam Azad, remarks in his memoirs: 'The way he solved the communal problem of Bengal is memorable and should serve as an example even today.'[58]

The Swaraj Party followed up its success in the Council elections by capturing a majority of seats in the reformed and expanded Calcutta Corporation in April 1924. Particularly noteworthy was its success in Muslim constituencies where it won 10 out of 15 seats. Das was himself elected Mayor and Hussain Shaheed Suhrawardy, a highly educated young man belonging to the leading Muslim family of Calcutta, became Deputy Mayor. Even an younger person, Subhas Chandra Bose, who had made a name for himself by resigning from the Indian Civil Service three years before, became the Chief Executive Officer.

He too, like Das, had a Muslim as his Deputy—Haji Abdur Rashid Khan, a prominent non-cooperator. Out of the first appointments to various positions in the office of the Corporation 25 went to Muslims and only 8 to Hindus.[59]

Control of the Calcutta Corporation not merely added to the prestige of the Swaraj Party but also provided it with considerable power of patronage and financial resources. Above all, it provided ample opportunities for constructive work which the new authorities of the corporation fully utilized. The use of Khadi was encouraged. Apart from the Swarajist Councillors and Aldermen who went to the Corporation clad in Khadi, Khadi was made the official uniform for all the employees. Primary schools and dispensaries were started in all wards of the city. Children belonging to poor families were supplied with free milk. Within ten years the number of primary schools started by the corporation went up to 232.[60] The Government of Bengal in its report for 1921-7 recognized the good work done by the Calcutta Corporation under Swarajist leadership. 'There is great keenness', it noted, 'on medical and public health work, and the zeal for free primary education is shown by the large number of new schools which have been started during the last few years.'[61]

Such activities, however, were confined to the Calcutta Corporation. So far as the Legislative Council, the main arena of provincial politics, was concerned the Swaraj Party followed a policy of obstruction, aimed at proving the failure of the reformed constitution. When, as the leader of the largest party in the Council, Das was invited by the Governor to head a ministry for the administration of the transferred departments, he conveyed to the latter that his party had decided against accepting office and added: 'The members of this party are pledged to do everything in their power by using the legal right granted under the Reforms Act to put an end to the system of Dyarchy.'[62] The Swaraj Party failed to bring an end to the system of Dyarchy, but it did succeed remarkably in obstructing its smooth functioning and in showing that it did not enjoy the support of the majority of members of the Bengal Legislative Council. This it did by securing enough support from the elected members of the Council, both Hindu and Muslim, including those who did not belong to the Swaraj Party, in support of motions to refuse Ministers' salaries on three successive occasions: March 1924, August 1924 and March 1925. The Governor had no option left except suspending the working of Dyarchy and himself taking over the administration of the transferred departments.

Indian nationalism, however, had to pay a heavy price for this success of the Swaraj Party in Bengal. On the first two occasions that ministers' salaries were outvoted, both the ministers happened to be Muslims. Some sections of the Muslim press used this to show that the move of the Swaraj Party was motivated by a communal bias. Thus attacking Das, *Islam-darsan* wrote in 1924:

He has opposed Muslim interests in the Council with all his might—the two Muslim Ministers (Mr. A.K. Fazlul Huq and Mr. A.K. Guznavi) have been forced to resign through the administrative reforms for Bengal being withdrawn due entirely to Mr. C.R. Das's envy, animosity and impetuousness.[63]

Such an approach received almost open support from the Government, which made strenuous efforts to detach Muslims from the Swaraj Party so as to make it impossible for the latter to obstruct the working of Dyarchy. As Lytton, then Governor of Bengal, has himself recorded, the two Muslim ministers 'worked their power of patronage for what it was worth, and brought what pressure they could upon the members of their own community'. Their main argument was that the Hindu-dominated Swaraj Party was trying to bring down a Muslim ministry and it was the duty of all the Muslim members of the Council to unite against the Hindus.[64] Lytton, of course, does not mention that his officials gave the ministers every possible assistance, and interceded with the members of the Council on their behalf. As J.H. Broomfield points out, the official members of the Bengal Government had already concluded that 'their best hope of breaking the Swaraj Party lay in encouraging communal divisions'.[65] With that end in view, a Muslim supporter of the Government, Khan Bahadur Musharruf Husain, was persuaded to move a motion early in the first session of the Council calling for the implementation of the Bengal Pact's provisions relating to employment by recruiting Muslims up to 80 per cent of the vacancies in Government till their share in government service reached 55 per cent. It was calculated that this would place Das in a tight corner, and so it really did. For if he supported the motion, it would be difficult for him to carry with him all his Hindu supporters many of whom had no liking for the Pact. On the other hand, if he opposed the motion, it would provide ammunition to those Muslims who had been arguing that Das had not been sincere in promising more government jobs to Muslims. Das was able to get out of this predicament by securing an adjournment of the discussion of Musharruf Husain's motion on the ground that he had yet to place the Pact before the country. It is remarkable that he was able to secure this adjournment with the backing of a majority of Muslim as well as Hindu members of the Council. The success of the Swaraj Party in Muslim constituencies in the elections to the Calcutta Corporation held after this episode showed that the majority of Muslims in Bengal continued to have faith in Das's leadership in spite of what had happened on Musharruf Husain's motion. Some damage, however, had certainly been done. The Swaraj Party's opponents among Muslims utilized the opportunity to argue that Muslim interests would not be served by following Das. 'Had Mr. C.R. Das', observed the *Muslim Hitaishi* on 4 April 1924, 'really desired that the Pact would be put into practice, he and his party would certainly not have proposed to postpone indefinitely the resolution of Khan Bahadur Musharruf Husain.'[66]

While Das was shown as either insincere in promising more government jobs to Muslims or incapable of implementing his promise, the Government came forward to show that it was keen to enlarge Muslim representation in government service. Here its path was lighted by Sir Abdur Rahim, a former judge of the Madras High Court, who had been appointed a member of the Governor's Executive council in Bengal. In a minute dated 27 July 1925, he recalled the background of the motion moved by Musharruf Husain and pointed out that 'the best prospect for Government seemed still to lie in the Muhammedan quarters'. He also argued that keeping in view that background the Government was committed to taking steps to advance the position of Muslims in government service—an issue which, because of the circumstances then prevailing in Bengal, had acquired 'considerable dynamic political force'. The Government accepted Rahim's advice. In October all government departments were instructed to increase Muslim recruitment and in December 1925 that order was made public. 'Its effect was to intensify communal ill-feeling.'[67]

The Government of Bengal also did its best to encourage Muslims to organize themselves separately from the Hindus as a political force, particularly in the districts. The Political Department instructed the district officers to back those local Muslim associations which supported the Government. Smaller Muslim organizations were to be encouraged to merge themselves with the leading such association in each district. Where such an association did not exist, the district officers were to encourage their formation. In October 1925 the Divisional Commissioner of Dacca reported that a new Islamia Anjuman was seeking recognition in place of the already existing District Muslim Association. He was of the opinion that such a recognition need not be given, but he was overruled by the political department; the latter was impressed by the fact that the new organization aimed at organizing Muslims for election to all public bodies and ensuring that Muslim candidates for election to the Legislative Council did not seek the support of the Swaraj Party. With the same purpose of developing Muslims as a separate political force in Bengal, the Government encouraged the formation of peasant organizations and cooperative societies in the rural areas as these were expected to be dominated by Muslims and likely to foster their separatist political aspirations.[68] The rising class of prosperous Muslim peasantry, known as *Jotedars*, enthusiastically responded to this move as they were keenly interested in securing a dominant voice in the local bodies, which had till then been dominated by the Hindu zamindars. Apart from the general political atmosphere surcharged with communal tension in the country and the encouragement received from the Government, promoters of separate Muslim organizations for political purposes in the rural areas received considerable support from the fact that the Swaraj Party, dominated by Hindu landlords, failed to support measures for improving the lot of the peasantry. This became clear from the general Swarajist opposition to the Bengal Tenancy Amendment Bill which was brought forward by the Government in December 1925.[69]

If Das had been alive such a denouement might have perhaps been prevented, but he had passed away on 16 June 1925. Those who inherited his mantle did not have the necessary stature or authority to override the dominant urges of a majority of their followers in the Swaraj Party. These urges did not result merely in the Swarajist opposition to the Bengal Tenancy Amendment Bill but also in the repudiation of the Bengal Pact itself, fathered and nurtured by Das with much care and attention and constituting his most important contribution to the political development of Bengal. It was no secret that the Bengal Pact was not popular among the Hindu *bhadralok* who dominated the Swaraj Party. The Government officials had not been wrong in reporting that the Pact was so favourable to the Muslims that it had raised 'intense resentment among a very large section of the Hindu community'.[70] Although Das had been able to carry the day because of the force of his personality, opposition to the Pact had not died down but had only gone underground. Once he passed away it came out in the open. The Calcutta riots of April 1926 further strengthened the general feeling of hostility towards the Pact among the Hindu middle class. At the Bengal Provincial Conference held at Krishnagar on 22-3 May

1926, a resolution for abrogating the Pact could not be passed by the Subjects Committee only because of the casting vote of the president of the Conference, B.N. Sasmal. After his resignation (due to strong opposition by some delegates) and subsequent dissolution of the conference by the President of the Bengal Provincial Conference (J.M. Sen Gupta), a section of delegates assembled together (under the presidentship of J. Chaudhary) and adopted a resolution rescinding the Pact on the ground that it was 'based on communalism'.[71] Although this resolution became infructuous as a meeting of the Bengal Provincial Congress Committee held in Calcutta on 13 June 1926, declared that the meeting at Krishnagar on 23 May last under the presidentship of Chaudhary was not a meeting of the Bengal Provincial Conference, the former neither reaffirmed the Bengal Pact nor refused to do so, as has been surmised by some.[72] What the meeting did was to adopt a resolution, moved by S.N. Biswas, saying that the B.P.C.C. 'should not now consider the question of rescission, revision or modification of the Hindu-Muslim Pact of Bengal having regard to the present state of feeling in the country'.[73] The mover of the resolution explained that if the members of the B.P.C.C. decided to rescind the Pact they would be wounding the feeling of Muslims and if they decided to reaffirm it they would be incurring the approbrium of the Hindus. It was, therefore, better for them, as members of the Congress, to adopt an attitude of neutrality.[74] Whatever that might have been, there is a no doubt that by the middle of 1926, if not earlier, the Bengal Pact was virtually dead and no longer a factor in the politics of Bengal. Co-operation between Hindus and Muslims was, by and large, a thing of the past. The bulk of the Hindu middle class stayed with the Swaraj Party, but the Muslim middle class, in rural as well as urban areas, though not yet united among themselves, definitely moved away from it. There could be no question for them to belong to a Hindu-dominated party. *The Servant of India* aptly summed up the position in its issue of 24 June 1926:

> And the Pact? It is dead as mutton. No one wants it and no one can appeal to it without imperilling his chances at the election. The Hindus as a body are sick of it and in their existing temper will make short work of the public career of any among them who proposes a large[er] share of the public employment and of representation on public bodies for the Muslim brethren than at present. The Muslims, on the other hand, are confident, thanks to the unwearied efforts of Sir Abdur Rahim, of securing, with their unaided exertion and without entering into a bargain with the Hindus, all that any pact might give them in the best of circumstances.[75]

Hindus generally believed that both Abdur Rahim and his son-in-law, Hussain Shaheed Suhrawardy, had been busy, behind the scenes, inciting Muslim mobs to attack Hindu processionists and shops in Calcutta during the communal riot of April 1926, with a view to ensuring their victory in the elections expected to be held towards the end of the year. 'How long' and 'what next' would they need, asked the *Forward* in its issue of 29 April 1926, 'to ensure the safe return to Abdur Rahim's thirty followers in the ensuing elections'.[76] The confidential records of the Government of India for that year show that the belief in Hindu circles regarding the role of Rahim and Suhrawardy in the riots was not baseless.[77] Even those who did not share this belief felt, like the editorial writer of Annie Besant's paper *The New Age*, that the 'inflammatory communal propaganda' carried out by Rahim and his followers 'must have contributed to the production of an atmosphere favourable for such outbursts'.[78] In May 1926 Rahim formed the Bengal Muslim Party, with a view to organizing Muslims for the coming elections. The objective was to secure a dominant place for Muslims in the Legislative Council. The role played by such Hindu organizations as the Arya Samaj and the Hindu Sabha in the riots helped. Above all, however, was the appeal of Islamic solidarity. Rahim went to the elections in November 1926 with a simple question: 'Mussalmans! who are you going to vote for? For the servants of Rahim (Worshippers of God) or for the slaves of Rama (Hindus)?' The answer was most favourable. Out of 39 Muslim seats, only one went to the Swaraj Party, the rest were captured by those who were pledged to give priority to Muslim interests.[79]

The growing Muslim antipathy towards Hindus ran parallel with a similar growth of Hindu antipathy toward Muslims. A Hindu landlord of Bankura, S.K. Sahana, recorded his happiness at seeing Hindus no longer at the receiving end in communal riots and opined that there was no hope of abiding friendship between Hindus and Muslims until the former convinced the latter that they would get 'force for force, roughness for roughness and hooliganism for hooliganism from the Hindus'.[80] The most telling illustration of the growing antipathy of Bengali Bhadralok towards Muslims is provided by the transformation which took place in the outlook of Sarat Chandra Chattopadhyay (1876-1938), the leading Bengali novelist of the twentieth century, whose works are generally noted for their liberal outlook; and who was also president of the Howrah District Congress Committee since 1921.[81] The political atmosphere of the post-Khilafat period and, more particularly, the Calcutta, Pabna and Dacca riots of 1926,[82] ignited by Muslim objection to Hindu religious processions with music before mosques, had apparently brought about a radical change in his outlook. In a speech on the 'Current Hindu-Muslim Problem', delivered at the Bengal Provincial Conference of 1926, he sharply attacked the search for Hindu-Muslim unity, describing it as a mirage, and called upon the Hindus to realize their responsibility for the liberation of their motherland and to concentrate on bringing all sections of Hindus together for this purpose:

> The truth is that if Muslims ever say that they want to unite with Hindus, there is no greater hoax. The Muslims came to India to plunder it, not to establish a kingdom. They were not satisfied merely with looting, they destroyed temples, they demolished idols, they raped women. The insult to other religions and the injury to humanity were unimaginable. Even when they became Kings they could not liberate themselves from these loathsome desires. Even Akbar, who was famous for his tolerance, was no better than notorious emperors like Aurangzeb. But today it seems that these practices have become an addiction. . . .[83]

According to Chattopadhyay, Hindu-Muslim unity was 'a bombastic phrase' and did not serve any purpose. Hindus need not waste their energy on bringing about an 'unnatural union between Hindus and Muslims', but concentrate on achieving unity 'within their own community', particularly by ending the distinction between high and low castes. Hindus must also understand that India was 'the homeland of the Hindus' and it was the duty of Hindus alone to free the country from the yoke of foreign rule. Muslims, on the other hand, looked towards Turkey and Arabia. Their hearts were not in India. To appeal to them in the name of the motherland was 'as pointless as talking to a brick wall'. Chattopadhyay clarified that saying all this did not mean that he would not be pleased if Hindus and Muslims came together and began to respect each other. All that he was saying was that if it did not come about and if there were no signs that it would ever come about, there was no use weeping about it; it did not mean the end of the world. If Hindus applied themselves whole-heartedly to the task of achieving freedom, it would matter little if 'a few dozen Muslims' lent their support or not. 'The Muslims will never truly believe that India's freedom will bring them freedom too. They will only accept this truth when their obsession with their religion weakens.'[84] Rajat Kanta Ray is not wrong in underlining that such a speech shows that 'psychologically speaking, the Hindus and Muslims were becoming two truly different peoples, parted by a deep chasm of mutual hatred'.[85]

V

Muslim politics at the central or all-India level was naturally conditioned by the trends in the provinces as well as the inclinations of the top leadership. As mentioned earlier, the All-India Khilafat Conference which had become the most powerful organization of Muslims during 1920-2 suffered a decline in the following years, its top leaders moving in different directions and the issue of Khilafat itself losing its significance after the abolition of that institution by the Turkish National Assembly. This created a favourable situation for the revival of the All-India Muslim League which had gone into the background during the heyday of the Khilafat movement. Here the key role was played by M.A. Jinnah.

Jinnah had begun his political career as a Congressman. When the Muslim League was being born at Dacca (December 1906) he was busy working as secretary to Dadabhai Naoroji, President of the annual Congress session being held about the same time in Calcutta. While several Muslim leaders of the Congress, without leaving it, joined the new organization, Jinnah held strictly aloof, changing his mind only in 1913. By that time, as seen in an earlier chapter, the orientation of the League had been modified due to the new winds blowing in Muslim politics since 1911-12. Elected the Permanent President of the League[86] because of his stature and position in the public life of the country, he utilized that position to bring the League closer to the Congress, without of course, ignoring Muslim interests. In spite of various twists and turns, this remained his policy for quite a long time. As the Aga Khan, the leader of the famous Muslim deputation to Minto in 1906 and one of the founders as well as the first permanent president of the League, recalled later:

> Who then was our doughtiest opponent in 1906? A distinguished Muslim barrister in Bombay, with a large and prosperous practice, Mr. Mohammed Ali Jinnah. . . . We had always been on friendly terms, but at this juncture he came out in bitter hostility towards all that I and my friends had done or were trying to do. He was the only well-known Muslim to take up this attitude, but his opposition had nothing mealy-mouthed about it; he said that our principle of separate electorate was dividing the nation against itself, and for nearly a quarter of a century he remained our most inflexible critic and opponent.[87]

This need not be taken literally. Although Jinnah was never enamoured of separate electorates, he never attacked it either. On the contrary, as early as 1909, he gave it his qualified support[88] and in

1916 secured its acceptance by the Congress through the Lucknow Pact. Jinnah was, however, definitely opposed to the policy of those leaders of the League who endeavoured to keep Muslims estranged from Indian nationalism and close to the British imperial power. Being a firm adherent of the path of constitutional agitation, he differed sharply from Gandhi in 1920 on the issue of non-cooperation and overwhelmingly outvoted and jeered by the delegates, Muslim as well as Hindu, at the annual Congress session at Nagpur in December 1920, he left that organization never to return. This did not, however, cool his patriotic ardour or turn him into a votary of exclusive Muslim nationalism. The Muslim League too joined the Congress and the Khilafat Conference in supporting non-cooperation with Government and Jinnah was a lonely figure in 1920-2. However, he did not contest the election to the central legislature of which he had been a member from Bombay Muslim constituency since 1910. Further, he did whatever he could to secure the objectives of the non-cooperation movement even though keeping out of it, for he shared as much as any one else the national indignation at the Khilafat and Punjab wrongs. He also joined hands with some other leaders in trying to bring about a reconciliation between the Congress and the Government. However, he was temporarily not at the centre-stage of politics and concentrated mostly on his legal practice. When the non-cooperation movement lost steam in 1922-3, he again became active. Along with a section of the Congress who contested elections to the legislatures in the name of the Swaraj Party, he also stood for election to the central legislature from his old seat in Bombay as an independent in 1923 and won unopposed. As the elected leader of a group of unattached members (seventeen in number) he worked in close collaboration with Motilal Nehru who headed a group of 41 Swarajist members. Together the two groups were known as the Nationalist Party. With the Government bloc of 36 members in a house with a total membership of 101, the Nationalist Party was able to win on several occasions in its bid to push forward the general Indian demand for further advance towards self-government. Jealous of his independence as ever, Jinnah never merged the identity of his group with that of the Swaraj Party and rather used his group's strength in the Central Assembly to sometimes play a balancing role between the Government and the Swaraj Party, but he desisted from toeing the Government line or adopting a communal stance. The latter was in any case not practical politics as his Independent Party consisted largely of Hindus; indeed the Swaraj Party had more Muslim members (eight out of forty-one) than the Independent Party (three out of seventeen).[89]

At the same time Jinnah also sought to revive the Muslim League, which had gone into hibernation, with he himself functioning as its Permanent President but out of accord with most of its members who were active in the non-cooperation movement. Although its annual session had been held in 1921, no such session could materialize in 1922. At Jinnah's initiative the League assembled on 31 March for its fifteenth session, under the presidentship of Ghulam Mohammad Bhurgri, but had to be adjourned on the next day for lack of quorum (requiring the presence of only 75 members).[90] The adjourned session met more than a year later at Lahore in May 1924. Thanks to the efforts of Fazl-i-Husain there was no problem of quorum there. However, most of the members present were from Lahore and the neighbouring districts, there being barely two dozen members from outside the Punjab.[91]

Jinnah's motivation in persuading the League's Council to hold the session at Lahore was partly to solve the problem of quorum and partly to secure support for his policy of pushing forward the demand for further constitutional advance. As Muslims were enjoying power in the Punjab, they were expected to throng the session in large numbers and also to support Jinnah in his quest for further constitutional advance. This he was able to secure, but in the process he had to fully accommodate the Punjabi Muslim viewpoint which attached the highest importance to full provincial autonomy with a federal government at the centre with strictly limited powers, and the safeguarding of the Muslim majority position therein on the basis of population and separate electorates. It is significant that the resolution (no. II) reflecting these Punjabi Muslim preoccupations—as indeed those of the Muslims in other Muslim majority provinces—was given precedence over that (no. III) demanding further constitutional advance. This was a clear indication of the fact that, thanks to Dyarchy, the centre of gravity in Muslim politics had passed from the Muslim minority provinces like U.P. and Bombay to Muslim majority provinces, chiefly the Punjab and, to some extent, also Bengal.

Resolution III declared that the reforms introduced by the Act of 1919 were 'wholly unsatisfactory and altogether inadequate', particularly in the absence of any provision ensuring the responsibility of the executive to the elected representatives of the people in the legislatures and urged the adoption of immediate steps for the establishment of full responsible government, 'having regard to the provisions of Resolution II'. That resolution specified the following six 'basic and fundamental principles' of any future constitution of India that might be agreed upon:

(a) The existing provinces of India shall be united under a common government on federal basis so that each province shall have full and complete provincial autonomy, the functions of the central government being confined to such matters only as are of general and common concern.
(b) Any territorial redistribution that might at any time become necessary shall not in any way affect the Muslim majority of population in the Punjab, Bengal and North-West Frontier Province.
(c) The mode of representation in the legislature and in all other elected bodies shall guarantee adequate and effective representation to minorities in every province, subject, however, to the essential proviso that no majority shall be reduced to a minority or even to an equality.
(d) Full religious liberty, i.e. liberty of belief, worship, observances, propaganda, association, and education shall be guaranteed to all communities.
(e) The idea of joint electorates, with a specified number of seats, being unacceptable to Indian Muslims, on the ground of its being a fruitful source of discord and disunion and also of being wholly inadequate to achieve the object of effective representation of various communal groups, the representation of the latter shall continue to be by means of separate electorates as at present, provided that it shall be open to any community at any time to abandon its separate electorates in favour of joint electorates.
(f) No bill or resolution or any part thereof affecting any community, which question is to be determined by the members of that community in the elected body concerned, shall be passed in any legislature or in any other elected body, if three-fourths of the members of that community in that particular body oppose such bill or resolution or part thereof.[92]

This resolution became something like a charter of Muslim demands and the principles mentioned therein were reiterated on many an occasion whenever any proposal relating to advance towards self-government came up. It may be mentioned here that although the adoption of the six principles at the Lahore session of the League in 1924 reflected the emerging importance of the Muslim majority provinces, the interests of the Muslims in the minority provinces were not ignored. This is borne out by the willing acceptance by the Punjab leaders of the viewpoint of the Muslims of the minority provinces while deliberating upon resolution II. Clause (c) of that resolution, as it emerged from the subjects committee, ran as follows:

> The basis of representation in the Legislature and in all other elected bodies shall be population, except that very small minorities may be given representation in excess of their numerical proportion in those cases in which they would remain entirely unrepresented in the absence of such exceptional treatment, subject however to the essential proviso that no majority shall be reduced to a minority or even to an equality.

This was manifestly to safeguard the interests of Punjabi Muslims who were keen to prevent their majority position in the legislature from being diluted in any way by any provision in favour of Hindus and Sikhs of their province as minorities requiring special treatment just like the Muslims in the minority provinces. However, when the resolution was placed before the special session it was realized that clause (c) as it then stood would hurt the interests of the Muslims of the minority provinces. This led Ziauddin Ahmad of U.P. to move for its replacement by the clause which finally found place in the resolution, safeguarding the interests of Muslims in minority as well as majority provinces. The amendment was supported by several important Punjabi leaders, including Fazl-i-Husain, and adopted by a comfortable majority (126 to 83).[93]

While taking steps to revive the Muslim League, Jinnah also ensured the continuance of its earlier policy of cooperation with the Congress and Hindus, symbolized by the Lucknow Pact (1916), in spite of the general atmosphere of communal antagonism then prevailing in the country. Thus in his presidential address to the resumed fifteenth session of the League at Lahore he adopted an extremely conciliatory tone towards the supporters of the non-cooperation movement and made an impassioned plea for Hindu-Muslim unity:

> Many mistakes have been made, blunders have been committed, a great deal of harm has been done; but there has come out of it a great deal of good also. The result of the struggle of the last three years has this to our credit that there is an open movement for the achievement of *Swaraj* for India . . . the ordinary man in the street has found his political consciousness, and realised that self-

respect and the honour of the country demand that the government of the country should not be in the hands of any one except the people of the country. But while that demand is a just one, and the sentiment only natural and requiring every encouragement, we must not forget that one essential requisite condition to achieve *Swaraj* is political unity between the Hindus and the Mohammedans. . . . *Swaraj* is an almost interchangeable term with Hindu-Muslim unity. If we wish to be free people, let us unite, but if we wish to continue slaves of bureaucracy, let us fight among ourselves and gratify petty vanity over petty matters, Englishmen being our arbiters.[94]

In line with this approach, the Lahore session of the League appointed a committee, consisting of its most prominent leaders, to frame a scheme for a new constitution of India in consultation with a similar committee or committees appointed by other political organizations of the country.[95] Nothing came out of it, but this did not dampen the keenness of the League's leaders for a cooperative approach to the solution of India's problems. When the League met for its sixteenth session in Bombay in December 1924, its president, Sayed Riza Ali, referred to Gandhi, who had been released early in the year, as the 'one great unifying influence of which the country ought to take the fullest advantage'. While affirming his differences with Gandhi, he further remarked that every patriotic Indian would readily acknowledge that Gandhi had done more than any other Indian to instill among India's teeming millions a feeling of nationalism. Concluding his address he remarked: 'Whatever the obstacle in our way, a common bond unites all of us who have started on the march towards the goal. And that bond is service of the motherland.'[96]

It was, however, not to be expected that the general atmosphere of communal antagonism then prevailing in the country would not find any reflection in the proceedings of a political organization like the Mulsim League. Sir Abdur Rahim, president of its seventeenth session held at Aligarh in December 1925, became a medium for such reflection. As mentioned earlier, Rahim, in cooperation with the British officials, had been active for quite sometime in organizing the Muslims of Bengal as a separate political force. The speech which he delivered at Aligarh was in marked contrast to those of his predecessors and indeed also of his successors in that office until the late thirties. Referring to the failure of some Englishmen to realize the necessity of separate political organizations of Hindus and Muslims, he remarked:

The fact . . . is that the Hindus and Mussalmans are not two religious sects like the Protestants and Roman Catholics of England, but form two distinct communities or peoples, and so they regard themselves. Their respective attitudes towards life, their distinctive culture, civilisation and social habits, their traditions and history, no less than their religion, divide them so completely that the fact that they have lived in the same country for nearly a thousand years has contributed hardly anything to their fusion into a nation.[97]

This, however, did not yet become a constant refrain in the proceedings of the League. Shaikh Abdul Qadir, president of the eighteenth session held in Delhi in December 1926, spoke in most rational terms and reminded 'the dreamers' among both Hindus and Muslims that Hinduism and Islam had to live side by side and could not destroy one another. The only rational course open to the two parties, according to him, was 'mutual toleration and respect for the feelings of one another'. The gist of his address, in his own words, was that the Congress and the Muslim League should both 'come together and devise ways and means of acting in harmony wherever possible, and of agreeing to differ in a friendly way when such difference becomes inevitable'.[98]

The professed keenness of the Muslim League leadership for a settlement of the communal problem did not, however, imply any preparedness to whittle down its terms for such a settlement as embodied in the second resolution adopted by its Lahore session in 1924 and reiterated thereafter. The essence of these terms was that while the gains made by the Muslims through the Lucknow Pact (1916) in the shape of recognition of separate electorates and weightage for them in representation to legislatures in Muslim minority provinces were to continue, the scheme of representation in the Muslim majority provinces should be such as to ensure the reflection of their majority in the legislatures. Besides, the future constitution of India must be based on full provincial autonomy with a federal government at the centre with strictly limited powers.

VI

The leaders of Hindu public opinion, on the other hand, had come to the conclusion that separate electorates represented the villain of the piece so far as the communal problem was concerned. As communal tension mounted they began to urge the abolition of separate electorates with a view to ensuring peace and harmony in the country. If the Muslims were not prepared to give up separate electorates these might continue but should in no case, as demanded by the leaders of Muslim opinion, be extended to local bodies and other institutions or agencies. Besides, while the Hindu leaders would not mind Muslim majority emerging in any legislature in India through general territorial constituencies based on population, they were not prepared to countenance the ensuring of Muslim majority in any province through specially contrived electorates on a communal basis. If separate electorates continued, the Hindu leaders demanded weightage for the representation of Hindus (and in the Punjab also of Sikhs) on the same pattern on which Muslims enjoyed weightage in provinces in which they were in a minority. But if this was conceded, Muslims with a slender majority in the Punjab (56 per cent) and Bengal (52 per cent) might not be able to secure a majority of seats in the respective legislatures and this they were not prepared to accept. Besides, while Hindus were not opposed to provincial autonomy, they did not at all favour a weak central government with limited functions.

Behind these differences with the Muslims on constitutional issues there lurked deeper fears and suspicions in the Hindu mind *vis-a-vis* Muslims. As mentioned earlier, these were caused by the latter's passionate interest in the Khilafat issue, seemingly of no concern to India as a whole, the declaration of some Muslim leaders that they would welcome an Afghan invasion of India if its purpose was to free India from British rule, incidents involving religious fanaticism perpetrated by Muslims at several places in Malabar during the Moplah uprising, and the general reluctance of many of the Muslim leaders in the rest of the country to condemn them. Such developments created in the minds of many Hindu leaders serious doubts regarding the prospects for Hindu-Muslim unity in India. At the same time a feeling grew that the primary loyalty of Muslims was to their community and not to India, and that such loyalty was so strong that in the event of a clash between India and a Muslim power, Muslims in India would side with the latter. Indeed some even felt that the Muslims in India might combine with their co-religionists abroad in a bid to reestablish Muslim rule over the country. Such feelings were most forcefully expressed by the great Irish Theosophist and a former President of the Congress (1917), Annie Besant, in 1922. While arguing that India would have a better future as a part of 'a world-wide Commonwealth of free nations' rather than as an 'isolated and independent country,'[99] she observed:

> Another serious question arises with regard to the Muhammadans of India. If the relation between Muslims and Hindus were as it was in the Lucknow

[Pact] days, this question would not be so urgent though it would even then have almost certainly arisen, sooner or later, in an independent India. But since the Khilafat agitation, things have changed and it has been one of the many injuries inflicted on India by the encouragement of the Khilafat crusade that the inner Muslim feeling of hatred against 'unbelievers' has sprung up, naked and unashamed, as in years gone by. . . . If India were independent, the Muslim part of the population—for the ignorant masses would follow those who appealed to them in the name of their Prophet—would become an immediate peril to India's freedom. Allying themselves with Afghanistan, Baluchistan, Persia, Iraq, Arabia, Turkey and Egypt and with such of the tribes of Central Asia who are Musalmans, they would rise and place India under the rule of Islam. . . .[100]

The great poet, Rabindra Nath Tagore, too was full of misgivings on the question of Muslims' loyalty to India in case of attack by a Muslim power. This is borne out by the following extract from an interview with him published by a Bengali paper in 1924:

. . . another very important factor which, according to the poet, was making it almost impossible for the Hindu-Mohamedan unity to become an accomplished fact was that the Mohamedans could not confine their patriotism to any one country. . . . The poet said that he had very frankly asked many Mohamedans whether, in the event of any Mohamedan power invading India, they would stand side by side with their Hindu neighbours to defend this common land. He could not be satisfied with the reply he got from them. He said that he could definitely state that even such men as Mr. Mohamed Ali had declared that under no circumstances was it permissible for any Mohamedan, whatever his country might be, to stand against any other Mohamedan.[101]

Such thoughts were apparently so widespread among Hindus that some Muslim leaders occasionally used them to threaten the former. This is illustrated by the following observation at a public meeting in Lahore in 1925 made by Saifuddin Kitchlu, one of the most prominent leaders of the non-cooperation-Khilafat mevement, who had later become actively associated with the *Tanzeem* movement:

If we remove British rule from this country and establish Swaraj, and if the Afghans or other Muslims invade India, then we Muslims will oppose them and sacrifice all our sons in order to save the country from the invasion. But one thing I shall declare plainly. Listen, my dear Hindu brothers, listen very attentively! If you put obstacles in the path of our *Tanzeem* movement, and do not give us our rights, we shall make common cause with Afghanistan or some other Musalman power and establish our rule in the country.[102]

It is not known who among the Hindu leaders of the Congress shared the fears and suspicions prevalent among the politically conscious members of their community regarding likely Muslim political behaviour in the future. There is no doubt, however, about the feelings of Lala Lajpat Rai who, while maintaining his position as one of the most prominent leaders of the Congress, was along with Malaviya and some other Hindu leaders of that organization, also actively associated with the Hindu Mahasabha, and had emerged as one of the most powerful exponents of the Hindu point of view in politics during the years following the Khilafat movement.

Obviously upset by certain happenings during the Khilafat movement, mentioned earlier, he, while incarcerated in the Lahore Central Prison during 1921-2, devoted himself most seriously to a study of Islamic history and theology. This filled his mind with misgivings about the future of Hindu-Muslim relations. Particularly distressing to him was his discussion with a fellow Muslim prisoner and a prominent religious divine and Khilafatist leader of the Punjab, Maulvi Habib-ur-Rahman. Asked to define 'the limits within which, in strict conformity with religious injunctions, Muslims could cooperate with Hindus', the Maulvi replied, in effect, that 'the believers could certainly remain in partnership with infidels in turning out the alien Christian rulers, but not beyond the achievement of the objective'.[103] The impact this had on Lajpat Rai's mind is revealed by a letter sent by him from prison in 1922 to another prominent Congress leader, belonging to the Hindu community, C.R. Das, who was to preside later over the annual Congress session that year in December. Stating that Hindu-Muslim unity was one of the matters which had been troubling him 'very much' of late and on which he wanted Das to think carefully, he observed:

> I have devoted most of my time during the last six months to the study of Muslim history and Muslim law, and I am inclined to think, it [Hindu-Muslim unity] is neither possible nor practicable. Assuming and admitting the sincerity of the Muhammedan leaders in the non-cooperation movement, I think their religion provides an effective bar to anything of the kind. . . . There is no finer Muhammedan in India than Hakim [Ajmal Khan] Saheb, but can he or any other Muslim leader override the Quran? I can only hope that my reading of Islamic Law is incorrect, and nothing would relieve me more than to be convinced that it is so. But if it is right, then it comes to this, that although we can unite against the British, we cannot do so to rule Hindustan on democratic lines. What is then the remedy?[104]

The apparently bleak prospect for Hindu-Muslim unity was particularly worrisome to Lajpat Rai in view of the widespread apprehension among a section of the Hindus that Muslims in India might at some future date align with the large number of Muslims living in other countries in the neighbourhood of India and pose a threat to Hindus. Thus, he further remarked in his letter to Das:

> I am not afraid of seven crores [of Muslims] in Hindustan, but I think the seven crores of Hindustan plus the armed hosts of Afghanistan, Central Asia, Arabia, Mesopotamia and Turkey will be irresistible. I do honestly and sincerely believe in the necessity or desirability of Hindu-Muslim unity. I am also fully prepared to trust the Muslim leaders, but what about the injunctions of the *Quran* and *Hadis*? The leaders cannot override them. Are we then doomed? I hope not. I hope your learned mind and wise head will find some way out of this difficulty.[105]

Lajpat Rai's worries continued after his release from prison in 1923. He was deeply upset when Mohamed Ali, in course of his presidential address to the annual Congress session at Cacanada (1923), 'tentatively' placed before it a suggestion made by 'an influential and wealthy gentleman' (later assumed by many to be the Aga Khan,[106] for years president of the All-India Muslim League). The suggestion was to arrive at a settlement between leading Hindus and Muslims and 'divide the country into separate areas where Hindu and Muslim missionaries could respectively work' among the untouchables. This virtually amounted to a proposal to divide the untouchables into Muslims and Hindus and was offered as a solution to a problem which could easily furnish a ground for complaint of unfriendly action if 'communal activities' were not amicably adjusted.[107] Sensing danger to the Hindu community in this proposal Lajpat Rai immediately set up an *Achchut Uddhar* committee, with himself as president, which became active in the Punjab, Delhi and U.P., with financial support from Jugal Kishore Birla.[108] The Congress had, of course, taken up the work of ameliorating the condition of the depressed classes as a part of its constructive programme at its Nagpur Session (1920), but it had not yet gathered momentum.

Lajpat Rai's thinking was also conditioned by the widespread communal riots during 1923-4 and the demand of Muslim leaders of the Punjab that the shortcomings, from their point of view, in the Lucknow Pact (1916), which had dealt mainly with the demands of the Muslims in the provinces in which they were in a minority, should be removed and in provinces in which Muslims were in a majority that majority must be reflected in the legislatures. He was also irked by their demand for the extension of separate electorates to local bodies and proportionate representation for Muslims in the educational institutions and the services. Such demands created considerable tension and resentment among the politically conscious Hindus and they became convinced that unless separate electorates were abolished Muslim demands would go on proliferating and Hindu-Muslim unity would become totally unattainable. Lajpat Rai, increasingly full of misgivings because of the developing political situation in the Punjab and the growing estrangement between Hindus and Muslims there, fully shared this view, though he continued to believe that the cause of Hindu-Muslim discord was not merely political, but also religious (a throwback to his view communicated to C.R. Das in 1922). That the main cause of Lajpat Rai's misgivings in 1924 regarding the prospects for Hindu-Muslim unity was the then prevailing political situation in the Punjab comes out clearly in his observations in course of a series of thirteen articles by him on the Hindu-Muslim problem published in *The Tribune* (Lahore) and some other newspapers in November-December 1924:

> People outside the Punjab have no idea to what extent the principle of communal representation has been or is being pushed in Punjab. Practically all social relations between Hindus and Muhammedans, and Sikhs and non-Sikhs have ceased. All three communities have their separate clubs, separate organisations and separate colleges. Even in sporting clubs or social functions all three communities insist on communal representation.[109]

Lajpat Rai's portrayal of the political situation in the Punjab found corroboration in a speech before the Punjab Legislative Council delivered about the same time by Malcolm Hailey, then Governor of that province. In course of that speech Hailey mentioned the fact that 'in every sphere of life and activity, in social matters, in almost every question of administration, in the management of local affairs, in the conduct of education, even in the current discussion of questions of law and justice, the communal question intervenes'.[110]

Lajpat Rai was particularly worried by the demand of Muslim leaders that their community's majority in the Punjab be reflected in the provincial legislature. He did not see how this demand could be fulfilled in view of the fact that the Muslims did not command an overwhelming but merely a bare majority in the Punjab and just as they had been given increased representation in provinces where they were in a minority, Hindus and Sikhs would also, as minorities in the Punjab, demand increased representation there. Even if the Hindus were excluded from this consideration on the ground that they would be effectively represented in the legislature because of their large size, the same could not be said about the Sikhs. And justice demanded that the increased representation for Sikhs should not be at the cost of Hindus, who were themselves in a minority, but at the cost of Muslims who constituted the majority. If that was done, how would Muslims secure a majority? The Muslims could not 'have everything in their own way'. Even if somehow they had their way, would the Sikhs, who were 'the rulers of the province' when the British conquered it and were 'virile, strong and united', agree to occupy 'the entirely subservient position' to which they would be reduced if the Muslim demand for domination was met? If nothing else helped, they might oppose Swaraj itself. In view of this if the Muslims still insisted on having a majority in the provincial legislature, the only way to satisfy them was to partition the Punjab into two provinces—Western Punjab with a Muslim majority and Eastern Punjab with a non-Muslim majority. Lajpat Rai went further and suggested that if the Muslims persisted in their demand to have their own government where they were in a majority, they might be given four such states—North-West Frontier Province, Western Punjab, Sindh and Eastern Bengal. '*But it should be distinctly understood*', significantly added Lajpat Rai, '*that this is not a united India. It means a clear partition of India into a Muslim India and a non-Muslim India.*'[111]

This, of course, does not mean that he was in favour of such a division, but only that he feared that if the Muslims persisted with their demand for Muslim dominance in the Punjab and Bengal, it might become impossible to maintain the unity of India. Concluding this series of articles, he remarked: 'Let us live and struggle for freedom as brothers whose interests are one and indivisible. . . .'[112] In another series of articles on the political situation in India published in the *Hindustan Times* in March 1925, he observed:

> Any solution effective for national purposes and safeguarding against the danger of dividing the provinces on the basis of Hindu and Muhammedan majorities will appeal to me. But from a close study of the mentality of Muslim leaders, I am afraid, they are determined to have their own way. In that case, I will rather let them negotiate with the Government than agree to propositions which to me mean fatal to the very purpose for which an understanding is desired.[113]

It remains to add that Lajpat Rai strongly opposed not only the creation of provinces on the basis of Hindu or Muslim majorities, but also the continuation of separate electorates, which he considered the root of all communal troubles in India and the chief impediment in the way of the emergence of a united Indian nation. He also thought that in view of lack of will for communal political organization among other communities, particularly the Hindus, the Muslims' insistence on separate representation, not merely in the legislatures, but all along the line, including the services and educational institutions, was motivated by their desire to become 'the dominating communal entity in India'.[114]

VII

The Congress, with its claim to represent the entire Indian people, regardless of the community or the region to which particular persons or groups might belong, found itself on the horns of a dilemma. If it took a stand in favour of Muslim demands, it faced the danger of losing support of the majority of politically conscious Hindus. In this connection it could not but take into account the growing popularity of the Hindu Mahasabha, some of whose meetings around that time drew more people than those held under its own auspices.[115] On the other hand, if it refused to concede those demands, it faced the danger of further alienating the Muslims from Indian nationalism. In such a situation it often avoided taking a clear stand and (with the sole exception of C.R. Das in Bengal) confined itself largely to bringing together the respresentatives of Hindu and Muslim opinion in unity or all-party conferences and trying to persuade them to come to a settlement.

The imperative need for Hindu-Muslim unity was, of course, always recognized by almost all Congress leaders, most of all by Gandhi. As has been noticed earlier, the Congress had joined hands with the Muslim League in 1916 in formulating the Lucknow Pact and in 1920 adopted the Khilafat issue as one of its major planks while charting the path of non-cooperation primarily with that perspective in mind. Writing to Hakim Ajmal Khan, then president of the Congress, on 12 March 1922—his first letter from prison—Gandhi again stressed the supreme importance of Hindu-Muslim unity. 'We all now realise', he observed, 'as we have never realised before that without that unity, we cannot attain our freedom. . . . Divided, we must ever remain slaves.'[116] As Hindu-Muslim relations rapidly deteriorated throughout the country, C.R. Das in course of his presidential address to the annual Congress session held at Gaya in December 1922 stressed that the Congress should commence its work for the next year by 'a clearer declaration of the rights of the different communities in India under the Swaraj Government'. Referring specifically to Hindus and Muslims, he called for 'a clear and emphatic confirmation' of the Lucknow Pact and, along with it, 'an emphatic recognition of each other's rights'. There was also need, according to him, for each side to remain prepared to make some sacrifice in favour of the other.[117] Das as well as the delegates who heard his address were, however, preoccupied with the issue of entry into the legislative councils, which Das himself advocated, in contravention of the earlier Congress decision while launching the non-cooperation movement. In the context of the charged atmosphere, generated by the debate on that issue, with stalwarts ranged on both sides, it is not surprising that no one paid attention to Das's proposal to take steps to delineate the rights of different communities under the Swaraj constitution. As Das, along with Motilal Nehru and other leaders, went ahead with their plan of council-entry in spite of the rejection of his proposal by the Gaya Congress, and formed the Swaraj Party for this purpose, and a split in the Congress seemed imminent, a special Congress session had to be held in Delhi in September 1923 to deal with the problem. A solution was found through a formula, devised by Maulana Mohammad Ali and accepted by that session, continuing the official Congress policy of boycott of legislative councils but permitting individual Congressmen who wished to do so to contest elections to them. At the same time the Congress also turned seriously to the Hindu-Muslim problem. M.A. Ansari, Chairman of its Reception Committee, drew the attention of the assembled gathering towards this problem in very forceful words and underlined the damage caused to Indian nationalism by the leadership's neglect of it in the recent past:

The Recent unfortunate happenings in various places have strengthened my conviction that in the first instance we did not devote sufficient attention to a matter whose importance demanded our best efforts. Misled by superficial appearances, we became content with what really was but a courteous *entente*. As if the neglect itself was not most deplorable, there arose differences in the Congress and drove this vital necessity of national life out of our minds. So, far from consolidating Hindu-Mulsim unity, we seem open to the charge of having helped to consign it to oblivion.[118]

Maulana Abul Kalam Azad, in his presidential address, spoke in a somewhat similar vein and remarked that while the rest of the world was turning its ears to tales of freedom, in India the cries heard were 'save Hindus from Mussalmans' and 'save Mussalmans from Hindus'. In order to put an end to such a state of affairs he suggested the setting up of a committee of selected members from the two communities to prepare a draft pact to be submitted to the next session of the Congress.[119] The special Congress session accepted this suggestion and appointed a committee of three eminent leaders, belonging respectively to Hindu, Muslim and Sikh communities, to prepare a draft National Pact, circulate it among leading members of different communities and, after considering their views, submit their report for consideration at the next session of the Congress. The committee was to consist of Lajpat Rai, Sardar Mehtab Singh and M.A. Ansari, who was also designated convenor of the group.[120]

Mehtab Singh could not attend due to ill health, but Lajpat Rai and Ansari immediately set themselves up on the task assigned to them and were able to prepare a draft National Pact for submission to the next Congress session (Cacinada, December 1923). The draft showed agreement between the two leaders on 'complete Swaraj for India' as the objective and the form of government under Swaraj to be 'democratic and of the federal type'. They also agreed that Hindustani would be the national language of India with permission to write it in Urdu or Devnagari script. The State would ensure full religious liberty to all the citizens and would not show preference to any religious denomination. All citizens, irrespective of their race or religion, would bear responsibility for India's defence. Considering it necessary to afford adequate protection to the interests of the minorities, the two authors of the draft National Pact also agreed that the various communities would have separate representation in the legislatures, both state and federal. Here, however, the agreement ended. Ansari wanted the principle of separate electorates to be extended to municipalities and local boards also, but Rai did not agree to this. The latter also suggested that there should be a time-limit after which separate electorates should be abolished. Moreover, he was of the view that representation throughout the country should be based on the numerical strength of each community in a constituency. He also wanted a special provision for the representation of Sikhs and some other communities such as Christians and Parsis, who were in a very small minority. Ansari suggested that while large minorities such as Sikhs and Christians might be given special representation only in the federal legislature, very small minorities such as Parsis might be given such representation in both federal and state legislatures.

Both Ansari and Rai agreed that in order to achieve national unity and out of regard for the religious feelings of their Hindu compatriots Muslims should bind themselves to give up cow-slaughter except on the occasion of Id-ul-Zoha, when it should be done in such a manner as not to injure the feelings of Hindus. No music would be allowed in front of places of public worship at such time as might be fixed by local, mixed conciliation boards. Ansari also suggested the incorporation of a clause stipulating that no bill or any clause thereof or any resolution affecting any community—which question was to be determined by the members of that community in the legislature concerned—would be proceeded with if three-fourth of the members of that community in the particular legislature, federal or state, opposed it.[121]

While the National Pact was still in the making, C.R. Das, as mentioned earlier, had taken the bold step of formulating the Bengal Pact. Its terms have already been discussed and need not detain us here. It will suffice for our purpose to note the treatment it received, along with the draft National Pact, at the hands of the majority of delegates attending the annual Congress session at Cacanada in December 1923. The resolution dealing with the two pacts, as it emerged from the subjects committee, asked the committee appointed by the Delhi session to call for further opinions on the draft of the National Pact as also on the Bengal Pact and submit its report to the All India Congress Committee for its consideration within the next three months. Motilal Nehru, who moved that resolution in the open session, took pains to clarify that no pact had actually been concluded and the pacts mentioned in the resolution were merely drafts which were being submitted to the country in order to elicit public opinion. He had to make this clarification as he had noticed a 'great outburst of alarm in many provinces' and the leaders had received 'wire after wire in protest'. His own position was that his head was for some kind of pact although his heart felt differently, for a real solution lay not in a pact but in mutual goodwill. The latter was also the position of some others. The main opposition was, however, directed to the inclusion of the Bengal Pact in the resolution and an amendment was moved for its deletion. Hardayal Nag, who moved it, declared that it was 'a hurriedly formed and ill-considered document'. A heated debate ensued. Apart from the mover of the main resolution, Motilal Nehru, the amendment was opposed by such important leaders as Sarojini

Naidu and M.A. Ansari, among others. C.R. Das, the author of the Bengal Pact, made a most forceful intervention against the amendment. Explaining that the resolution did not commit the Congress to accepting it, but only to circulating it to elicit the reaction of the general public, he burst out:

What is this misapprehension about? Is Bengal debarred from making that suggestion? Is any human being in India to be deprived of his undoubted right to press before the Congress his suggestion? Is the Bengal Provincial Congress Committee to be deprived of its right to place its suggestion before the Congress? You may delete 'the Bengal National Pact' from the resolution but I assure you, you cannot delete Bengal from the history of India, from the history of the Indian National Congress (Cheers). Bengal demands the right of having her suggestion considered. You may throw it out after considering it.

All this eloquence, however, failed to sway the majority of delegates. The same fate befell the sober reasoning of T.K. Sherwani who pointed out that he himself had never supported the idea of a National Pact in the past but he opposed the deletion of the Bengal Pact from the resolution on the ground that it would create an impression among Muslims in general that the Congress was opposed to even considering a document which gave just rights to them. After four hours of discussion the President put the amendment to vote and declared it lost. As the voting figures were fairly balanced a division was challenged. The pandal was cleared of all visitors and voting took place again. The amendment was carried by 678 votes to 458 against. The main resolution was then put to vote and declared carried by 775 votes to 205 against.[122] The Congress leadership must have taken note of these figures. The list of persons who voted on either side is not available and some of those who voted for the amendment could be Muslims like, for instance, Yakub Hussain, who had spoken in support of it. It can, however, be safely presumed that most of the supporters were Hindus and reflected the general Hindu dislike for the Bengal Pact. The message was loud and clear: the Congress leadership, while dealing with the Hindu-Muslim problem, could not take Hindu support, even within their organization, for granted.

Released shortly after this, on health grounds, in February 1924, Gandhi took sometime to recuperate his health and study the fast deteriorating political-communal situation. As mentioned earlier, he came out with his detailed analysis of that situation in *Young India* in its issue dated 29 May 1924. The main purpose of that article was to prepare the ground for a fruitful dialogue between the leaders of the two communities with a view to bringing about a reconciliation between them. With this end in view he tried to remove the prevailing misunderstanding about the most prominent leaders from both sides. Thus he most warmly praised Madan Mohan Malaviya, Lajpat Rai and Swami Shraddhanand on the one hand and Maulana Abdul Bari and the Ali brothers on the other. Similarly, while referring to the *Shuddhi* and *Tabligh* movements he remarked that while genuine movements of conversion, motivated by religious conviction, might be permissible, no one could be allowed to revile other religions in that process. On the then burning issues of cow-slaughter and music before mosques he advised both Hindus and Muslims to practise tolerance and restraint. Referring to cow-slaughter he remarked that although he regarded cow-protection as 'a central fact of Hinduism', he failed to understand the general Hindu antipathy towards Muslims on that score while nothing was said about the daily slaughter of cows for Englishmen. In any case, communal riots in the name of cow-protection had not saved a single cow, but had only resulted in more slaughter. Apart from treating cattle properly and not selling them to butchers, Hindus must befriend the Muslims and leave it to their honour to save the cow. Just as the Hindus could not compel Muslims to stop killing cows, Muslims could not stop Hindus from playing music before mosques at the point of the sword. The only proper thing for them to do was to trust to the good sense of the Hindus. As a Hindu Gandhi advised Hindus to show due regard to the sentiments of Muslims on this point and condemned the action of those Hindus who deliberately played music or performed *arati* at the time of prayer in the mosques in order to irritate them. At the same time he cautioned Muslims that they should never expect to stop Hindu music by force.

On purely political issues, Gandhi recognized the need for a pact, but considered the restoration of friendly feeling between the members of the two communities as conditions precedent to it. For this, the first thing necessary was for all to agree that no disputes, religious or otherwise, between the communities should be sought to be settled through a recourse to violence. Appealing to the leaders of the two communities in this connection, he remarked that the masses would not want to fight if the leaders did not. As for the nature of the pact regarding such matters as representation in legislatures Gandhi's prescription was that Hindus, as the majority party, should not bargain, but leave the pen in the hands of a person like Hakim Ajmal Khan and abide by his decision. The same approach should be adopted with regard to other minorities like the Sikhs, Christians and Parsis. Hindus must be satisfied with the residue after all the minorities had had their share. This was, in Gandhi's opinion, 'the only just, equitable, honourable and dignified solution. Hindus, if they want unity among different races, must have the courage to trust the minorities'. Gandhi, however, opposed communal representation in employment to various government services. That would be 'fatal to good government'. On this basis Gandhi looked forward to an immediate solution of the Hindu-Muslim problem, which he considered the most urgent problem before the country:

> For me the only question for immediate solution before the country is the Hindu-Mussalman question. I agree with Mr. Jinnah that Hindu-Muslim unity means Swaraj. I see no way of achieving anything in this afflicted country without a lasting heart unity between Hindus and Mussalmans of India. I believe in the immediate possibility of achieving it, because it is so natural, so necessary for both, and because I believe in human nature. . . . The key to the situation lies with the Hindus. We must shed timidity or cowardice. We must be brave enough to trust.[123]

All this was written on the basis of the adage: trust begets trust. Trust between Hindus and Muslims, however, was the most difficult thing in the India of 1924 to secure. From Bihar Rajendra Prasad ruefully reported more than two months after the publication of Gandhi's article on the Hindu-Muslim problem that in the eyes of some Muslims of the province there was not one truthful and honest Hindu there. The number of such Muslims was, hopefully, not large, but they kept on writing in the newspapers, which were read by all, big and small, and no one opposed them.[124] Then came the news of severe rioting at Kohat. In a statement issued on 18 September 1924, the day he began his fast, Gandhi explained that the recent events had proved unbearable to him and his helplessness was even more unbearable. Nothing evidently that he said or wrote could bring the two communities together. He hoped that his fast would work as an effective prayer to both Hindus and Muslims not to commit suicide. He also appealed to all the communities, including Englishmen, to meet and end that quarrel which was a disgrace to religion and to humanity. 'It seems as if God has been dethroned. Let us reinstate Him in our hearts'.[125]

Under the shadow of Gandhi's fast a unity conference, convened by Maulana Mohamed Ali, then president of the Congress, and attended by about three hundred delegates representing the different communities in India, met in Delhi under the chairmanship of Motilal Nehru from 26 September to 2 October. According to one of the participants, the general impression was 'far from satisfactory'. There were terms and counter-terms proposed by opposing groups 'who seemed to have met together to strike a bargain rather than achieve unity'.[126] Before the conference ended, however, it was able to adopt a number of resolutions asking for sanity in communal relations, more or less on the lines indicated by Gandhi in his article on the Hindu-Muslim problem published on 29 May 1924. Indeed, the resolution moved by Shaukat Ali on 27 September incorporating these ideas and adopted by the subjects committee of the conference was assumed by some to have been drafted by Gandhi himself, though he was not present at the conference.[127]

Thus the conference emphatically declared that the utmost freedom of conscience and religion was essential and condemned the desecration of places of worship, regardless of the faith to which they might belong, and all kinds of religious persecution or compulsion. Similarly it deplored all religious quarrels then going on between Hindus and Muslims. Hindus, it declared, must not expect to stop cow-slaughter through the use of force. Nor could Muslims expect music before mosques to be stopped by force. As regards conversion from one religion to another, the conference declared that while every individual or group was at liberty to convert or reconvert another by argument or persuasion, it had no right to do so or prevent its being done by force, fraud or other unfair means such as the offering of material inducement.[128] The members of the conference were fully aware that political differences constituted a major factor behind the religious quarrels, but no effort was made to tackle them. The resolutions, indicating as they did a consensus in favour of certain general principles of a salutary nature among the leading figures in the public life of the country, had some use in the then charged atmosphere, but the proceedings of the conference were, on the whole, more indicative of differences between the leaders representing the different communities than of agreement or even keenness to reach such agreement. Apart from general declarations, the only concrete measure the conference adopted was to appoint a Central National Panchayat with Gandhi as chairman and convenor to enquire into and settle all disputes and differences between the different communities. This Panchayat hardly ever functioned. One of the participants in the Conference, Rajendra Prasad, has thus summed up its outcome:

The conference seemed to promise some improvement in the country's atmosphere. It appeared as if members of all communities had resolved to be good and cordial towards one another. It would have been a great thing if that effect could prove lasting, but, alas, it was not to be and the hopes which this improvement raised in people's minds were belied by future events.[129]

Gandhi was keen to utilize the apparent improvement in the general atmosphere to hammer some agreement on the political issues dividing the different communities. An opportunity for this came at the meeting of an all parties conference at Bombay on 21and 22 November, convened by Maulana Mohamed Ali as president of the Congress, mainly with a view to voicing the nation's protest against the repressive policy of the Government symbolized by the arrest of Subhas Chandra Bose and some other prominent Swarajist leaders in Bengal. On the second day the conference adopted a resolution moved by Gandhi appointing a large representative committee to prepare a scheme of Swaraj, including the solution of the Hindu-Muslim question and other similar questions in their political aspects and to report not later than 31 March 1925.[130] This committee, known as the All Parties Conference Committee, met in Delhi on 23 and 24 January 1925, under the presidentship of Gandhi, who had assumed the presidentship of the Congress in December 1924. He had apparently high hopes from this committee. Its deliberations, however, only helped to highlight the serious differences between the Hindu and Muslim leaders at that time.

The occasion was provided by the discussion on Gandhi's motion (which was eventually carried) to appoint a subcommittee to suggest the lines of agreement between Hindus and Muslims and also prepare a scheme for Swaraj. While Malaviya welcomed the appointment of a subcommittee to bring about political unity he did not think the time was yet opportune for the appointment of a sub-committee to deal with the Hindu-Muslim question and prepare a Swaraj scheme. Apart from the fact that Hindu and Sikh organizations had not yet formulated their demands, Muslims too, according to him, had not formulated what their demands really were. Hindu opinion, from the very beginning, was opposed to communal representation and recent experiences had further deepened their conviction on that point. As Hindus had agreed to the Lucknow Pact (1916) they would continue to honour it, but there could be no extension of the principle of communal electorates. In any case there was no need for appointing a committee unless Muslims fully explained in what ways they wanted a modification of the Lucknow Pact. This drew a pointed reply from

Jinnah. He remarked that he had not gone to that meeting to say what the Muslims wanted, but to sit with others as co-workers. The need of the hour was to put their heads together not as Hindus or Muslims, but as Indians. The leaders were free to decide whether they wanted to discuss or wanted to wait. The choice was theirs. On the second day of the meeting (24 January), however, Jinnah explained at length what the Muslim view was. The Lucknow Pact, he said, had been a necessary step in the march towards self-government, but that did not mean that the Pact could not be revised. Facts had to be faced. The large bulk of both Hindus and Muslims had no real confidence in each other. The Muslims wanted to ensure that their majority was not diluted in the Punjab and Bengal, as had been done by the Lucknow Pact. In other provinces the interests of minorities should continue to be safeguarded acording to the principles enshrined in the Lucknow Pact. Lajpat Rai, explaining the Hindu point of view, remarked that if the Lucknow Pact had to be revised in the interest of the country, such revision should not be confined merely to the figures of representation but extend also to the fundamental character of representation. Communal representation, according to him, was a negation of nationalism and was practically dividing the country into watertight compartments. If the principle of communal representation was extended, it was difficult to say how many further divisions and subdivisions might be created. The Congress predicament in the face of such divergent views was best expressed by Motilal Nehru who declared that he was constitutionally incapable of thinking communally, but thoroughly agreed with both Jinnah and Rai.[131]

As the meeting was coming to a close Jinnah again stressed the urgency of speedily settling the Hindu-Muslim problem in view of the ensuing debate on the report of the Reforms Enquiry Committee in the Central Assembly. As much was made of Hindu-Muslim differences he was keen to be able to tell the Government on that occasion that those differences had been settled and they stood united in their demands. Gandhi commented that Jinnah's purpose would be served by the publication of the subcommittee's report.[132] This hope, however, could not be fulfilled. The subcommittee divided itself into two groups—one for preparing a Swaraj scheme and the other for settling the Hindu-Muslim problem. The former was able to prepare a report, but the latter failed to do so. According to Gandhi, the best solution might be to accept the Muslim demand for majority of seats in the legislatures in the Punjab and Bengal, but to do away with separate electorates.[133] This was apparently not acceptable to the representatives of either Hindu or Muslim opinion. After several informal meetings at which no settlement could be reached a formal meeting was fixed for 1 March 1925. However, out of fifty-three members only fourteen found it possible to attend. Lajpat Rai was absent and Jinnah came for a few minutes from another meeting he was attending at that time. As Gandhi and Motilal Nehru explained through a press statement issued next day, the attendance was 'too meagre for coming to any decision'. The meeting, therefore, decided to adjourn its proceedings *sine die* with the provision that another meeting could be called on a requisition by a majority of the members of the subcommittee.

'That the subcommittee', said Gandhi and Nehru in their joint statement, 'has not been able to reach any decision is no reason for individuals or groups to relax their efforts towards a solution.'[134] A day or two later, writing for the issue of *Young India* dated 5 March 1925, Gandhi further explained that the subcommittee failed in its endeavours because the atmosphere for a reasonable solution was lacking and each side distrusted the other. He added, however, that there was no cause for despair: 'The present failure may be a stepping stone to success, if those who can trust and who have no fear of one another will be true to their faith and try to work at a solution.'[135] Gandhi was obviously not merely consoling and exhorting others, but also himself. He had pinned great hope on the labours of the subcommittee of the All Parties Conference Committee, but its proceedings had only helped to exhibit the wide chasm separating the Hindu and Muslim positions instead of bridging them. About the same time, as seen earlier, he was facing failure on another front: carrying Shaukat Ali, a close comrade of yester years, with him on the report of enquiry into the Kohat riots. Gandhi's exercise in self-consolation and exhortation, however, failed to produce the desired result. On the same day that it appeared in print (5 March 1925) he observed in course of an interview to the press in Bombay that he saw no Hindu-Muslim settlement materializing in the near future as no lasting settlement could be had by higgling. The Hindu-Muslim problem had become 'an insoluble puzzle'. 'I propose', he added, 'to keep out of it, holding myself available whenever wanted.' In the meanwhile, the spinning-wheel and the fight against untouchability were more than enough for him to occupy his time and that of those who thought like him.[136]

In answer to a question relating to the Hindu-Muslim problem Gandhi remarked about a month later (*Young India*, 2 April 1925) that he did not despair of the future and that order was bound to come out of the then prevailing chaos. This could be expedited by 'watching, waiting and praying'. If this was done the evil that had come to the surface would disappear much quicker than if, 'in our haste and impatience, we would disturb the surface and thus send the dirt to the bottom again instead of allowing it to throw itself out'.[137] In an interview published in *The Bombay Chronicle* on 13 April 1925, he reiterated this view more clearly, observing that he did not see any immediate prospect of achieving much so far as inter-communal unity was concerned and that he was inclined 'to leave the question to work itself out'. According to medical opinion, he pointed out, some diseases were best left alone; the more they were treated, the worse they would become. The communal trouble at that time, appeared to have developed that character.[138] Speaking at a public meeting in Calcutta on 1 May 1925 he went further and admitted his 'incompetence' to deal with that trouble, implying that even if it was amenable to treatment he did not consider himself capable of providing it. He was so upset by the rampant communal tension that he remarked: 'If it is to be our lot that before we can come together, we must shed one another's blood then I say the sooner we do so the better it is for us'.[139]

That Gandhi, with all his devotion and commitment to non-violence, could utter such words shows not merely his deep feeling of disgust and despair at the then prevailing communal situation, but also his feeling of utter helplessness in dealing in any meaningful way with that situation. For he had come to realize that, barring a few exceptions, neither Hindus nor Muslims were then in a mood to listen to him or to follow his advice. As he explained to a Khilafat Conference at Patna on 22 September 1925, in such a situation the only recourse left to him was 'pray and pray to God'. This was also the reason, according to him, why, unlike in 1921, when he was so fond of speaking on Hindu-Muslim unity, four years later he was confining himself largely to Khadi and Charkha. Why should he speak to someone who was not prepared to listen to him?[140] Gandhi pursued the new line so seriously that he refused to say anything publicly even on the occasion of extensive Hindu-Muslim rioting in Calcutta in April 1926. When G. D. Birla raised some queries in this connection Gandhi replied to him on 16 April:

> I shall answer your questions regarding the Hindu-Muslim riots, but the replies are not for the Press. I have told you that I have no influence at all now over the Hindus, at any rate over that class among them which interests itself

in these disturbances. My views, therefore, are misunderstood. Hence I believe that it is best for me to say nothing.[141]

Perhaps in order to rationalize his silence Gandhi went on believing that the Hindu-Muslim question had to 'solve itself'.[142] He even thought that the situation was getting worse only in order to get better in due course. 'Hindus and Muslims', he wrote to Jawaharlal Nehru, 'are going more and more away from each other. But this thing does not disturb me. Somehow or other, I feel that the separation is growing in order only to bring them all closer later on.'[143] This was nothing but wishful thinking or perhaps an unconscious rationalization of his own position of inactivity on the Hindu-Muslim problem.

VIII

Whatever that might have been, there can be no doubt that no other Congress leader could succeed where Gandhi feared to tread. Except C.R. Das none had a comparable understanding of the nature of the communal problem in India and none including Das (whose influence was largely confined to Bengal) had that hold over the imagination of Hindu masses and elite all over the country which alone could enable a leader to work out a communal settlement, acceptable to Hindus as well as Muslims at that time. Das passed away on 16 June 1925. The burden, on the Congress side, of dealing with the communal problem fell on Motilal Nehru, leader of the Swaraj Party in the Central Assembly and, in view of Gandhi's voluntary silence, the sole spokesmen of the Congress on political issues. Himself absolutely free from any communal bias or prejudice, he battled heroically to somehow calm the rising communal tension in the country, but he battled in vain. The backdrop was provided by the increased tempo of Hindu-Muslim rioting during 1925-6 at several places from Rawalpindi to Calcutta. Sometimes rural areas were also affected.[144] In such a situation even the Hindu and Muslim leaders associated with the Congress fell apart.

Nehru's difficulty in carrying them together was best illustrated by the decision of some Muslim members of the Swaraj Party in the Central Assembly, in March 1926, to move a motion, without any discussion with the party leadership, favouring the extension of constitutional reforms to the North-West Frontier Province. This had been done at the instance of Muslim members from that province, but this was not to the liking of the Hindu members of the Swaraj Party, notably Lajpat Rai who had joined it in January 1926. Nehru tried to keep the differences on this question under wrap by mentioning the lack of adequate notice to the Party regarding the motion in question and raising the more substantial point that the Swaraj Party could not ask for the extension of Dyarchy to a new area while denouncing it in the rest of the country. When this failed to dissuade the Muslim members of his party from moving that motion, he came out with a formula calling for the introduction of constitutional reforms, as desired by the Swaraj Party and debated earlier in the Assembly, to the whole country, including North-West Frontier Province. The Muslim members, however, remained far from mollified and felt that Nehru had taken such a stand in order to placate Lajpat Rai whose cooperation he required in order to deal with the opposition to his leadership mounted by Malaviya. They held this view particularly because of a rider to the suggested resolution, namely, 'subject to any redistribution of the provinces', which had been added at the instance of the Hindu members of the Party.[145] Even Gandhi's support to Nehru's position proved of no avail. On the other hand, the Hindu members of the Swaraj Party too were unhappy with the position adopted by the leadership in order to accommodate the wishes of the Muslim members. 'The situation thus developed was this', said Nehru in course of a statement to the press, explaining his position, 'that neither the Mussalmans nor the Hindus were in favour of the alternative adopted by the Party with a view to satisfy both'.[146]

It must here be added that as far as the Muslim members of the Swaraj Party were concerned they did not suspect Nehru to be himself swayed by communal considerations. What they objected to was his perceived inability to put up an effective fight against those Hindu leaders who were so swayed.[147] Nehru soon discovered that this was the general feeling among most of the Muslim leaders associated with the Congress, who also thought that most of the Hindu leaders of the Congress were hostile to Muslims and communalists at heart. Writing to Gandhi in April 1926 after attending a conference of leading Congress and Khilafatist leaders in Delhi Nehru reported:

> All Hindu Congressmen with the exception of yourself, Jawahar and me were condemned as open enemies of Muslims, being members of or sympathisers with Hindu Sabha and the Sangathan and Shuddhi movements. The three of us were excepted from this sweeping condemnation but were not absolutely absolved from blame. The gravamen of our offence was that we kept silent when it was our duty to speak out.[148]

It was claimed in contrast, Nehru continued, that none of the Khilafatist leaders had deviated from nationalism or taken any part in the communal strife. This led to 'a few acrimonious passages at arms' between Mohamed Ali and Motilal Nehru. For the latter was not prepared to agree with the sweeping condemnation of almost all Hindu Congressmen nor with the general commendation of all Khilafatists. As a result of this some heat was generated in the discussion and that militated against a calm and dispassionate consideration of the situation in the country at that time. No definite proposal emerged for restoring friendly relations between Hindus and Muslims as each side waited for the other to evolve a formula for this purpose. Nehru also reported in the same letter that Hakim Ajmal had told him in an intimate conversation that there had been a change in his (Ajmal Khan's) attitude towards the Hindu-Muslim problem and that he had come to believe that 'the entire blame rested with the Hindus'. Nehru also learnt from Ajmal Khan that though he himself was opposed to such a move, the Khilafatist leaders had almost made up their minds to set up a 'a Mussalman Party for the protection of Mussalman interests as against not only the outside Hindu movement but also against the anti-Muslim activities of Congressmen'.[149]

The forebodings contained in Nehru's letter to Gandhi were confirmed by the proceedings of the special session of the All India Khilafat Conference held at Delhi on 8 and 9 May 1926. Ajmal Khan, as chairman of the Reception Committee, delivered a speech which showed that he was a changed man. The Hindus, he declared, had been excited by the happenings in Malabar and Kohat and thereafter started the *Shuddhi* and *Sangathan* movements. However, Muslims too had suffered in the past from communal riots at certain places, but they had not started any activity as a consequence of it. Deploring that while the Muslims had no communal organizations, Hindu organizations were jeopardizing the very existence of Islam, he appealed to Hindus to reconsider their programme and not to push the Muslims into the ditch of communalism. In his presidential address Syed Suleman Nadvi remarked that while the Khilafat Conference had in the past worked for Islam abroad, the time had come for it to work also for the protection of Islam against the high-handedness of the other communities in India. Abdur Rahman Dojanwe, in his address to the conference on the first day, declared that they had gathered together there to deliver funeral orations on Hindu-Muslim unity. According to him, slavery was ingrained in Hindu blood and the Hindus could not bear to see the Muslims free. Whatever religion was against freedom should be crushed and annihilated. Every Muslim should be told that to extend the hand of friendship to a Hindu would be construed as a sign of weakness. No separate Muslim party was formed for the protection of Muslim interests, but this session of the Khilafat Conference changed the creed of that organization and added to its earlier objects the object of striving 'to safeguard the religious, educational, social, economical and political interests of Indian Mussalmans and to reform and organise them'. In addition, a resolution was adopted calling upon the Central Khilafat Committee to take all necessary steps to protect the rights and properties of Muslims whenever these came under attack in any part of the country. When the mover of this resolution, Maulana Zafarul Mullick, in course of his speech, used the word 'brethren' for Hindus, uproarious scenes followed. Several persons stood up and demanded the withdrawal of the 'objectionable' word. Calm was restored only after the intervention of the President and Maulana Shaukat Ali.[150]

It must be pointed out here that the proceedings of the special session of the Khilafat Conference in May 1926 should not be taken to imply that all the leaders associated with that conference and the movement it represented believed in the line adopted there. The Ali Brothers, of course, fully supported it and, on the basis of the position they occupied in that organization, it may even be assumed that they had actually inspired it. This is also substantiated by the proceedings of the conference. Mohamed Ali himself had moved the resolution specifying the new creed of the Khilafat Committee and Shaukat Ali had strongly supported a resolution moved by Mohammad Shafi condemning the leaders of the Hindu Mahasabha for their *Sangathan* activities. While doing so the latter had eulogized his fellow Khilafatists for furthering the national cause 'in spite of the Hindus'. The Hindus, he added, had been misled by England and turned from national activities to communal strife and aggression. He advised both Muslims and Hindus to live in a state of friendship with each other, but if Muslims were attacked by the Hindus or members of any other community, their right response should be 'to pay back in the like manner'. There was, however, at least one delegate at the conference, one Sirajuddin, who opposed this resolution as also the one calling upon the Khilafat Committees to exert themselves to protect the rights of the Indian Muslims.[151] Maulana Abul Kalam Azad was present at the Conference, but chose not to speak. One great veteran of the

Khilafat movement who was not present at the conference, but who strongly protested against the new line was M.A. Ansari, who felt provoked by it to resign forthwith from the Central Khilafat Committee, as indeed from all sectional or communal organizations. In his letter of resignation from the Khilafat Committee he observed:

> After the retrograde turn given to the Khilafat Committee at the special session, held at Delhi last May, I had felt I could no longer remain a member of that body. But on my return from England in June, I found that communal passions had run amuck and threatened to utterly destroy all that was noble and fine in this unfortunate motherland of ours. . . . As an Indian owing allegiance first to the motherland, I feel I must sever my connections with all communal or sectional political organisations.[152]

Motilal Nehru faced even greater difficulties in dealing with the tide of Hindu nationalism or communalism, especially in view of the leadership provided to the latter by such towering leaders as Malaviya and Lajpat Rai, who like the Ali brothers, also occupied an exalted position inside the Congress. Besides, he could not ignore the fact that although the Congress claimed to represent and actually had in its ranks members belonging to all religions communities in India, Hindus constituted the overwhelming majority of its membership and they could not always be counted upon to remain immune to the general atmosphere prevailing in the country.

The situation for the Congress became particularly critical because of elections to the councils due to be held towards the end of 1926. As a result of Gandhi's efforts the differences between the two wings of the Congress (pro-changers and non-changers) had been settled; the Swarajist programme had been accepted by the Congress and it had been decided that the next elections would be fought in the name of the Congress. At the same time, however, some leaders of the Hindu Mahasabha too began to think of that organization putting up candidates for elections. In the context of the general communal atmosphere then prevailing in the country the Hindu Mahasabha had been gaining in popularity and if it joined the electoral battle it could pose a serious threat to the Congress. Keeping this in mind, Nehru adopted a conciliatory line towards the Mahasabha. Along with the then Congress President, Sarojini Naidu, he attended its ninth annual session held at Delhi in March 1926, with a view mainly to dissuading it from deciding to put up candidates for election to the councils. Thinking that the session would last only for two days (13 and 14 March) he had planned some other programme for the 15th. It so happened, however, that the session continued for three days and the issue of elections came up only on the third day. Nehru was absent, but a note left by him was read out at the session by Lala Dunichand. In this note Nehru pointed out that while the objective of the Sabha was to work for Hindu solidarity regardless of the political opinions held by the members of the community, by contesting elections it would be creating further divisions in its ranks. He also pointed out that after all the overwhelming majority of the Congress consisted of Hindus and even mentioned the fact that Muslim participation in it had recently further declined. In any case, because of the system of separate electorates then in vogue in the country, only those Hindu candidates could be elected by Hindus who could be counted upon by the voters to safeguard the interest of the Hindu community. Instead of putting up candidates for elections and thereby creating a division among Hindus on political lines it would be better for the Sabha as a whole to join the Congress which was a great national organization. As Nehru put it:

> It is no use concealing the fact that the Indian National Congress is predominantly a Hindu organisation. It started and developed as such, and whatever accession of strength it received from the Mussalmans from time to time is fast decreasing by the revival of independent Muslim organisations. In spite of all vicissitudes of fortunes that it has passed, the Indian National Congress remains, and will always continue to be, the premier national institution of the country. Why is it at all necessary to usurp its functions and confer them on newly started Hindu organisations? What is there to prevent the Hindu Mahasabha as a whole to enlist itself in the ranks of the national institution? I have heard complaints that the Congress does not look after the interests of Hindus. Does the true remedy lie in opposing your great national institution for communal advantages, or is it to be found by supporting it for the good of all communities?[153]

Nehru's reasoning and eloquence had no impact on most of the delegates attending the session. They confirmed and adopted a resolution already passed by the Working Committee of the Mahasabha in August 1925. That was to the effect that normally the Hindu Mahasabha should not put up candidates for election, but in case of apprehension that the election of any particular candidate might be injurious to Hindu interests, it should be the duty of Hindu voters to oppose such a candidate. Further, a provincial Hindu Mahasabha could put up its own candidates where this step was considered necessary for the protection of Hindu interests.[154] Failing to convert the leadership of the Hindu Mahasabha to his point of view and alarmed by its growingly strident communal propaganda along with that on the Muslim side, Nehru hit on another plan. Taking Abul Kalam Azad as a joint signatory he issued a statement on 1 August 1926, calling for an end to the 'indiscriminate mixing up of the political and religious issues' and the deliberate inculcation of 'a national consciousness and a national atmosphere', with a view to relegating religious and communal conflicts to a subordinate plane. Referring to the new trend in the Hindu Mahasabha movement on the one side and of the Muslim communal organizations on the other the statement emphasized the need for urgent action on the part of those who still retained their balance. Keeping this in view, the statement announced the decision of the signatories to found a new organization to be called the Indian National Union. Its membership would be open to all persons who did not belong to any communal organization and who believed that communalism was a negation of nationalism and that continued communal conflicts would inevitably lead to political, economic and social ruin.[155] The plan was supported by several well-known persons, notably Tej Bahadur Sapru, V.S. Srinivasa Sastri, Hakim Ajmal Khan, Sarojini Naidu and M.A. Ansari,[156] but hardly took off the ground and was overtaken by other developments, in particular the ensuing elections to the councils which naturally took most of the time of the persons who were expected to organize the new body. Those persons also knew that whatever its long-term utility, this was not going to help in any way in the coming elections. 'It has had a very good reception in the Press both Indian and English', wrote Nehru to his son, Jawaharlal, then abroad, referring to the statement, 'but from its very nature is bound to do us more harm than good at the elections which it is now certain will be fought on communal lines'.[157]

IX

The activities of Malaviya, particularly in U.P., constituted the main cause for Motilal's worry. The latter informed Jawaharlal that almost all the important Congress workers had joined Malaviya, and except for two, there was not a man on whom he (Motilal) could thoroughly rely. This made the political prospect very gloomy for the Congress in U.P.[158] An old rival of Motilal, Malaviya had been one of the veteran leaders of the Congress, well-known for his championship of supposedly Hindu interests and actively engaged in revitalizing the Hindu

Mahasabha. He believed neither in the Gandhian programme based on non-cooperation nor in the Swarajist programme, based on obstructionism inside the councils and keeping away from office. In February 1926 he resigned from the Independent Party in the Central Assembly in order to work for the formation of one strong Nationalist Party, which was to follow the policy of responsive cooperation with Government, implying acceptance of office under Dyarchy. Under the banner of the new party Malaviya launched a vigorous attack on the Swarajist programme, which the Congress as a whole had recently adopted.[159] Gandhi had announced retirement from political work for the whole of 1926 and Motilal had to bear the brunt of Malaviya's attack. Most of the Congress workers with a marked concern for Hindu interests naturally tended to flock to Malaviya. That all did not do so was because Lajpat Rai still clung on to the Swaraj Party which he had only recently joined. He shared with Malaviya the mantle of Hindu leadership, but had a stronger position than Malaviya inside the Congress. Unlike Malaviya, who was a moderate in politics and had kept aloof from non-cooperation, Lajpat Rai had joined the non-cooperation movement and also suffered imprisonment. His remaining with the Swaraj Party was a great source of strength to it. With his reputation as a veteran fighter for freedom since the pre-Gandhian era and his power of eloquence in both speech and writing quite at par with Malaviya's, he was more than a match for the latter. Thus a few weeks after Malaviya had visited Lahore and given an address attacking the Swaraj Party Lajpat Rai addressed a large gathering at the same place and forcefully rebutted all of Malaviya's charges.[160] The advantage of Lajpat Rai's association with the official Congress leadership was, however, soon lost. Not less concerned than Malaviya with Hindu interests and the widely perceived failure of the Congress to appreciate or protect them, he also did not fully agree with the functioning of the Swaraj Party, particularly its recent decision to withdraw from the Central Assembly. In view of all this, he could not sustain for long his separation from Malaviya and resigned from the Swaraj Party on 14 August 1926. Next month the two leaders joined hands together to form the Independent Congress Party with a view to contesting the ensuing elections under its banner. Although not wholly unexpected in the context of his known views and predilections, this shift in Lajpat Rai's position was highly significant, indicating as it did the growing disenchantment in certain Hindu circles with the official leadership of the Congress because of its alleged failure to safeguard Hindu interests.

Lajpat Rai did not make any effort to hide the fact that he fully shared this disenchantment. In his letter of resignation from the Swaraj Party addressed to Motilal Nehru, he observed:

> There are certain matters on which my differences with you are almost fundamental. The angle of vision with which we two look at the questions relating to matters on which Hindus and the Muslims differ is entirely different and often brings us into a conflict. Slowly and gradually I have come to share the belief of many other Hindus that the Swaraj Party as at present constituted is distinctly harmful to the Hindus. . . .[161]

With Lajpat Rai and Malaviya working together in the elections held in November 1926, with a view to safeguarding Hindu interests, the going became really tough for the official Congress candidates in Hindu constituencies. Communal propaganda was the order of the day. According to Motilal Nehru, he was publicly denounced by persons working under the auspices of 'the Malaviya-Lala gang' as anti-Hindu and pro-Muslim. Privately voters were told that he was a beef-eater and cooperating with Muslims 'to legalise cow-slaughter in public places at all times'.[162] This was said about the tactics of the people belonging to the Independent Congress Party in U.P. and has often been cited in works dealing with politics in the twenties. The communal atmosphere, however, was so pervasive in northern India at that time that at one stage Motilal Nehru himself sought to use the communal card in an indirect way. He made a vain effort to capture the Agra Hindu Sabha and during the elections encouraged the use of anti-Malaviya material issued by some extreme champions of Hindu orthodoxy. Besides, he also took the precaution of putting up candidates at several places in U.P. who might be found acceptable by the communally-minded voters among the Hindus. At least there was one such candidate whom Malaviya himself extolled.[163] In Bengal some Congress candidates went much further and showed no scruples in openly pandering to Hindu communal sentiments.[164] B.N. Sasmal, a former president of the Bengal Provincial Congress Committee, who was denied the Congress ticket because of his opposition to the then dominant group in the Bengal Congress and stood as an independent candidate for election to the provincial council from the Midnapur district, publicly and in writing alleged the use of such tactics against himself by the Swarajist workers of his constituency. According to him, an anonymous leaflet entitled 'Hindus, Be Careful', circulated in his constituency alleged that he was a supporter of prohibition of music before mosques and had voted in favour of giving 80 per cent of government jobs to Muslims. Another leaflet, bearing the names of some prominent Hindu citizens of Midnapur, alleged that he had refused to pay subscription for *Saraswati Puja*, that he had no objection to becoming a Muslim, and that he had shown respect for those Muslims who had broken many temples and ruined the chastity of many Hindu women.[165]

The election results showed that these tactics had helped the Congress in Bengal, but not in U.P., where it faced a debacle. Its strength in the U.P. Council was reduced from thirty-one to sixteen. In several other provinces the results were similar. In the Punjab the Congress had to be content with two seats in contrast to Lajpat Rai's nine. In C.P., its strength was reduced from thirty-five to seventeen (bringing to an end its dominant position there) and in Bombay from twenty-five to twelve. The Congress did well in Bihar and Madras, having raised its strength in the former from eight to thirty-five and in the latter from ten to forty-seven. In the Bengal Council the Congress retained its earlier position in purely numerical terms, but, unlike in 1923, when it had fifteen Muslim members, it had to be content with a single Muslim member in its ranks.[166] The Congress did badly in Muslim seats in other provinces also. In the Punjab no Muslim had stood on a Congress ticket, but this was a continuation of the precedent set in 1923. In C.P. the Congress had captured one Muslim seat in the provincial council and also one in the Central Assembly in 1923. In 1926, however, it had no such luck. In U.P. while eleven Muslims had contested on Congress ticket and four of them returned in 1923, in 1926 six contested out of which only one got elected. In northern India only Bihar presented a different picture. Fourteen Muslims had contested on Congress ticket and six out of them were returned. In addition the Congress was able to get elected four Muslims in the Madras Council and two Muslims in Bombay. In the Central Assembly, the Congress, with thirty-eight members, retained its position as the largest party, but with fewer Muslim members. In contrast to eight Swarajist Muslim members in 1923, it had only three Muslim members returned on Congress ticket in 1926.[167] On the other hand, several Hindu colleagues of yester years were now sitting separately as members of the Nationalist Party led by Malaviya. At the same time, most of the Muslim as well as Hindu members now separated from Jinnah and his Independent Party virtually ceased to function.[168]

This was indeed a severe blow for the Congress, the flag-bearer of the ship of Indian nationalism, which was being stormed by the forces of Hindu as well as Muslim nationalism. Indeed, the situation looked so grim and foreboding, particularly with Gandhi in voluntary retirement from politics, that Motilal seriously considered calling it a day and joining Gandhi in retirement, fearing the worst, namely the capture of the Congress at its coming annual session at Gauhati in the last week of December 1926 by forces loyal to Malaviya and Lajpat Rai. 'I am thoroughly disgusted', he wrote to Jawaharlal, 'and am now seriously thinking of retiring from public life. What is worrying me is how to occupy my time.'[169] At the same time Gandhi was 'so sickened with the election propaganda' that he did not like to attend the Gauhati Congress session. Motilal, however, kept on pressing him to attend, thinking that his presence at the Congress was essential, 'if only to give it a decent burial'.[170] Motilal did not tell Jawaharlal, but must have calculated that Gandhi's presence at Gauhati would be of great help in stemming the expected onslaught on his leadership. Gandhi listened to Motilal's entreaties and did attend. Aware of his full backing for the elder Nehru or perhaps realizing that the capture of the Congress was at that time beyond their capacity, his opponents stayed their hands. Some of their leading figures such Lajpat Rai, M.R. Jayakar and N.C. Kelkar did not go to Gauhati at all. M.S. Aney and B.S. Moonje did attend, but sat like silent spectators. Only Malaviya spoke against the Swarajist programme and made a plea for moderation and acceptance of office under Dyarchy, but that line did not draw much support.[171]

One other possible reason for the smooth proceedings of the Gauhati Congress session could have been the assassination of Swami Shraddhananda, one of the most prominent leaders of the *Shuddhi* and *Sangathan* movements, by a Muslim fanatic on 23 December 1926, just three days before the commencement of that session. All sections of public opinion among both Hindus and Muslims, with only a few exceptions, condemned that dastardly act. For a moment there was a realization, as if in a flash, what communal propaganda could lead to. Hindus, of course, were very angry and bitter, but their leaders spoke in a sober tone and decried communal propaganda. Gandhi, who moved the resolution of condolence (the first resolution to be taken up by the Congress), declared that the sinner was not Abdul Rashid, who had committed the assassination, but the leaders of Hindu and Muslim opinion. The resolution expressed horror and indignation at the assassination of Swami Shraddhananda and paid tribute to him as 'a brave and noble patriot who dedicated his life and his great gifts to the service of his country and of his faith and espoused with fearless devotion the cause of the lowly, the fallen and the weak'. It was seconded by Mohamed Ali and supported by the elder Nehru and Malaviya. While all the three joined in paying tribute to Swami Shraddhananda, the differences in their political outlook came through in their speeches. Thus Mohamed Ali made it clear that while he associated himself whole-heartedly with the condemnation of the atrocious deed, he would not be true to his faith and therefore to the nation if he did not say that 'the same value would not be put by the Mussalmans as by the Hindus upon every part of Swami Shraddhananda's life-work'. The elder Nehru stressed that dissension between Hindus and Muslims had gone too far and should not be allowed to go further if people wanted to avoid the utter ruin of both the communities. 'It is up to us now to cry halt to the communal movements and communal writings. Let us stop this disgraceful state of things.' Malaviya referred to the Swami's pioneering role in the *Shuddhi* and *Sangathan* movements and emphasized that those people who wrote in the press that Swami Shraddhananda was a great enemy of Islam must bear their share of responsibility for the crime; such acts could not be stopped until the writings which poisoned the people's minds were stopped. In this connection he mentioned that a press cutting had been placed in his hand showing that a meeting of Muslims had approved of the crime.[172] Speaking before the Hindu Mahasabha session, also held at Gauhati a couple of days later, Malaviya spoke more forcefully, emphasizing that the Swami did not in any way act wrongly by starting the *Shuddhi* and *Sangathan* movements and called upon Hindus to continue to work for them. The resolution of condolence adopted by the Mahasabha recalled 'with pride' that Swami Shraddhananda had become a victim of the assassin's bullet 'for no other reason than his honourable devotion to and dauntless courage in carrying on the sacred work of Shuddhi and Sangathan'.[173]

Reference to the Swami's assassination was also made at the annual session of the Muslim League, which commenced in Delhi on 29 December 1926. Shaikh Abdul Qadir in his presidential address to the session deplored the assassination and declared that the person responsible for it 'could not have rendered a greater disservice to Islam or lent a stronger impetus to the Shuddhi propaganda', than he had done by that 'foul deed'. The session adopted a resolution of condolence expressing its 'profound regret at the horrible outrage'. At the same time, however, it also deplored and condemned the assault by a section of Hindus on Muslims in Delhi, one of whom had subsequently succumbed to the injuries inflicted upon him.[174]

Apart from the Hindu demonstrations in Delhi to which reference had been made in the League's resolution, there were no major outbreaks of violence or rioting in any other part of the country. This showed that at least in the immediate aftermath of the murder, Hindus in general had listened to the pleadings of Hindu as well as Muslim leaders to remain calm and avoid any action which might further exacerbate communal tension. Yet, nuances in the reactions of those very leaders and their political parties, mentioned above, show that even in that hour of shock and horror they could not really get over their differences over the communal issue. This was not a good augury for the maintenance of an atmosphere of communal peace and harmony in the country for any length of time. Besides, as the Viceroy (Lord Irwin) reported to the Secretary of State in the second half of February 1927, though the outward manifestations had been comparatively restrained, a 'strong under-current of hostility' continued to exist between the two communities as a result of the Swami's assassination.[175] Besides, the popular press, particularly in the Indian languages, continued to fan communal feelings. The result was that Hindu-Muslim relations became 'more difficult and dangerous than ever, as the direct result of Swami Shraddhananda's murder'.[176] During February-March 1927 the old spectacle of recurring communal riots, big as well as small, appeared again. The most serious of these was the riot at Kulakathi in the Barisal district of Bengal on 2 March on the issue of music before mosque. Police had to open fire as a result of which fourteen rioters lost their lives and seven were injured.[177] Not surprisingly did the Secretary of State for India exultingly write to the Viceroy in the last week of February 1927: 'I have a feeling that if you handle the situation with subtlety, a very promising political prospect may now develop. The Swarajists are down. The Hindu-Muslim dissensions have destroyed Gandhi's dream.'[178] This was certainly not an overdrawn picture.

NOTES

1. Lala Lajpat Rai, *Writings and Speeches*, ed. Vijaya Chandra Joshi, II (New Delhi, 1966), pp. 170-1
2. K.K. Aziz, *The Making of Pakistan: A Study in Nationalism* (London, 1967), p. 115.
3. Home Pol. En. 82/1925, Part I, National Archives of India.

4. Ibid.
5. Jawaharlal Nehru, *An Autobiography* (New Delhi, 1984; first published 1936), p. 135.
6. L.F. Rushbrook Williams, *India in 1923-24* (Calcutta, 1924), p. 258.
7. *Indian Annual Register*, 1924, II, pp. 26-32.
8. Kenneth McPherson, *The Muslim Microcosm. Calcutta, 1918-1935* (Wiesbaden, 1974), pp. 89-95; and Suranjan Das, *Communal Riots in Bengal, 1905-1947* (New Delhi, 1991), pp. 75-91.
9. For details of casualties in Hindu-Muslim riots between 1923 and 1927 see *Indian Statutory Commission*, Vol. IV (London, 1930), pp. 108-20. A province-wise abstract is available in David Page, *Prelude to Partition* (Delhi, 1982), p. 74.
10. 'It is not at the present juncture', said a confidential report of the Government of India in 1925, 'in the interest of any political party, however, disaffected, to promote Hindu-Muslim riots'. Home Pol. File 140-1925, National Archives of India.
11. Viceroy to Secretary of State, 30 August 1923, IOR, Mss. Eur. E. 238/6, Reading Collection.
12. Viceroy to Secretary of State, 18 September 1924, IOR, Mss. Eur. E. 238/7, ibid.
13. Viceroy to Secretary of State of India, 3 September 1925, IOR, Mss. Eur. E. 238/8, ibid.
14. Malcolm Hailey to Perceival Landon, 29 September 1924, IOR, Mss. Eur. E. 220/6B. Hailey Collection.
15. *The Indian Annual Register*, 1922, p. 343.
16. *The Collected Works of Mahatma Gandhi* (hereinafter referred to as *CWMG*), XXIV (New Delhi, 1967), p. 142.
17. *The Indian Annual Register*, 1922, n. 15.
18. *CWMG*, n. 16, pp. 589-90.
19. Ibid., pp. 270-1.
20. Ibid., p. 136.
21. Mahadev H. Desai, *Day to Day with Gandhi: Secretary's Diary,* Vol. IV (Varanasi, 1969), p. 195.
22. Mohamed Ali to Saifuddin Kitchlu, 30 September, 1923, IOR, Mss. Eur. E. 220/7A, Hailey Collection.
23. *Congress Presidential Addresses*, ed. A.M. Zaidi, IV (New Delhi, 1988), p. 132. It is a revealing commentary on the social background of Muslim politics in India in the twenties that in order to satisfy his orthodox followers Mohamed Ali felt obliged to clarify soon after that however pure Gandhi's character might be, 'from the point of view of religion' he must be considered inferior to a Muslim regardless of the level of the latter's character. See B.R. Ambedkar, *Pakistan or the Partition of India* (Bombay, 1946; 3rd edn.), p. 296.
24. Zaidi, n. 23, pp. 210-11.
25. Syed Sharifuddin Pirzada, ed., *Foundation of Pakistan: All India Muslim League Documents* (hereinafter referred to as *League Documents*), II, pp. 28-9.
26. Desai, n. 21, V (Varanasi, 1970), p. 111.
27. Ibid.
28. Ibid., pp. 111-12.
29. Shan Muhammad, ed., *The Indian Muslims: A Documentary Record* (hereinafter

referred to as *Muslim Documents*), VIII (Meerut, 1985), pp. 88-9; for the full text see pp. 78-92.

30. Desai, n. 26, p. 112.
31. *CWMG*, XXVI (Delhi, 1967), pp. 190-1.
32. For the texts of the respective statements by Gandhi and Shaukat Ali see Desai, n. 26, pp. 343-52 and 353-60. Gandhi's statement can also be seen in *CWMG*, XXVI, n. 31, pp. 341-4.
33. *Muslim Documents*, n. 29, p. 20.
34. J.B. Kriplani, *Gandhi: His Life and Thought* (New Delhi, 1970), pp. 102.
35. Desai, n. 26.
36. Ibid., p. 262.
37. Ibid., pp. 263-5.
38. See Page, n. 9, pp. 36-41.
39. Ibid., pp. 46-59.
40. Home Public, No. 145, 10.06.1920, National Archives of India.
41. *Report of the Administration of the Punjab, 1922,* p. 7.
42. See Azim Husain, *Fazl-i-Husain: A Political Biography* (Bombay, 1946), pp. 1-128.
43. Ibid., pp. 130-44.
44. Ibid., pp. 154-5.
45. Ibid., p. 175.
46. Page, n. 9, pp. 70-1.
47. Ibid., pp. 71-2.
48. Hailey to Lytton (Acting Governor General), 22 June 1925, IOR, Mss. Eur. E. 220/7B, Hailey Collection.
49. Hailey to Reading, 22 January 1925, ibid., 7A.
50. Punjab Civil Secretariat, Annual Confidential File No.14 (Political/General) of 1925, ibid., 7B, p. 6.
51. Ibid.
52. Page, n. 9, p. 44.
53. The rest of the 139 member strong Legislative Council consisted of representatives of special constituencies like Europeans, Anglo-Indians, Calcutta University, landholders and trade and commerce, besides a number of nominated members. See J.H. Broomfield, *Elite Conflict in a Plural Society: Twentieth Century Bengal* (Bombay, 1968), p. 128.
54. AICC Papers. File 1/1924. Nehru Memorial Museum and Library. Also in A. Karim, *Letters on Hindu-Muslim Pact*, Appendix A. (Calcutta, 1924).
55. Gautam Chattopadhyaya, *Bengal Electoral Politics and Freedom Struggle 1862-1947* (New Delhi, 1984), pp. 75-6.
56. Rajat Kanta Ray, *Social Conflict and Political Unrest in Bengal, 1875-1927* (Delhi, 1984), p. 317.
57. Cited in Chattopadhyaya, n. 55, p. 76.
58. Maulana Abul Kalam Azad, *India Wins Freedom: The Complete Version* (Hyderabad, 1988), p. 23.
59. McPherson, n. 8, pp. 79-81.
60. Subhash Chandra Bose, *The Indian Struggle* (Calcutta, 1944), pp. 95-6.
61. Cited in Leonard A. Gordon, *Bengal: The Nationalist Movement, 1876-1940*, pp. 215-16.
62. Prithwis Chandra Ray, *Life and Times of C.R. Das* (Landon, 1927), p. 199.

63. Mustafa Nurul Islam, *Bengali Muslim Public Opinion as Reflected in the Bengali Press, 1901-1930* (Dacca, 1973), p. 83.
64. Earl of Lytton, *Pundits and Elephants* (London, 1942), p. 252.
65. Broomfield, n. 53, p. 253.
66. Cited in ibid., p. 255.
67. Ibid., pp. 270-1.
68. Ibid., pp. 271-3.
69. Ray, n. 56, pp. 336-8. See also Chattopadhyaya, n. 55, pp. 93-4.
70. Government of India, Home Pol. 25 of 1923, National Archives of India.
71. *The Indian Quarterly Register*, 1926, I, pp. 417-21.
72. See, for instance, Ray, n. 56, p. 352, where the author says that the meeting of the Bengal Provincial Congress Committee reaffirmed the Bengal Pact; and Chattopadhyaya, n. 55, p. 96, who says that the majority at the meeting voted against the resolution seeking endorsement of the Pact.
73. *The Indian Quarterly Register*, n. 71, p. 88.
74. Ibid.
75. Ibid., p. 99.
76. Cited in Sheela Sen, *Muslim Politics in Bengal, 1937-1947* (New Delhi, 1976), p. 59.
77. See Ray, n. 56, pp. 357-8.
78. Sen, n. 76, p. 59.
79. Broomfield, n. 53, pp. 279-80.
80. Ibid., p. 278.
81. Manik Mukhopadhyaya, ed., *The Golden Book of Saratchandra: A Centenary Commemorative Volume* (Calcutta, 1977), pp. 414, 425.
82. For an account of the riots see Das, n. 8, pp. 76-102.
83. Joya Chatterji, *Bengal Divided: Hindu Communalism and Partition, 1932-1947* (New Delhi, 1995), p. 271, see also pp. 173-80.
84. Ibid., pp. 272-3.
85. Ray, n. 56, p. 361.
86. The Permanent President of the Muslim League was elected for three years at a time and was distinct from the President of an annual session whose authority was limited to that session only. See 'Rules and Regulations of the All India Muslim League', in Shamsul Hasan, *Plain Mr. Jinnah* (Karachi, 1976), Appendix, p. 309.
87. The Aga Khan, *The Memoirs of Aga Khan: World Enough and Time* (London, 1954), p. 94.
88. See Jinnah's letter to the *Times of India*, Mail Edition, 10 February 1909, reproduced in Shamsul Hasan, n. 86, Appendix III, pp. 337-40. Here Jinnah welcomed Morley's scheme of electing members of legislatures in India through mixed electoral colleges consisting of both Hindu and Muslim representatives, describing it as 'the most excellent scheme', but suggested that Muslim proportion in such colleges should be raised from one-fourth to one-third, with a view to ensuring the election of the 'real representatives of Muslims'. 'If this is not feasible', said Jinnah, 'then I am afraid we must resort to communal representation.' He, however, added that the electorate should be left free to choose its representative, regardless whether he was a Muslim or a non-Muslim. In most cases a Muslim would be elected, but there could be occasions when a non-Muslim might be considered better to represent Muslims.

89. Page, n. 9, pp. 109-10
90. *League Documents*, n. 25, pp. 572-3.
91. See Mohamed Ali's article on the Muslim League and the Congress published in *The Comrade* in December 1925 and reproduced in *Muslim Documents*, VIII, n. 29, p. 50.
92. *League Documents*, n. 25, pp. 578-9.
93. Ibid.
94. Ibid., p. 577.
95. Ibid., p. 580.
96. Ibid, II, pp. 19, 24-5.
97. Ibid., 41, 44.
98. Ibid., pp. 87, 95.
99. Annie Besant, *The Future of Indian Politics: A Contribution to the Understanding of Present-Day Problems* (Adyar, 1922), pp. 294-5.
100. Ibid., pp. 301-6.
101. *The Times of India*, 18 April 1924; cited in Ambedkar, n. 23, pp. 268-9.
102. *The Times of India*, 14 March 1925; cited in Ibid., p. 264.
103. Feroz Chand, *Lajpat Rai: Life and Work* (New Delhi, 1978), pp. 478-9; also p. 425.
104. Cited in Ambedkar, n. 23, p. 268.
105. Ibid.
106. Feroz Chand, n. 99, p. 435.
107. *Congress Presidential Addresses*, IV, n. 23, p. 180.
108. Feroz Chand, n. 99, pp. 435-6. See also pp. 487-8.
109. Lala Lajpat Rai, n. 1, p. 206.
110. Cited in ibid., pp. 206-7.
111. Ibid., pp. 212-13.
112. Ibid., p. 221.
113. Ibid., p. 237.
114. Ibid., p. 246.
115. According to a confidential memorandum of the Home Department, Government of India, the meetings on the occasion of the annual session of the Hindu Mahasabha held at Belgaon in the last week of December 1924 were reported to have been more largely attended than those of the Congress, which too held its session at the same place under the presidentship of Gandhi. See Home Pol., En. 82/1925, n. 3. National Archives of India.
116. *CWMG*, XXIII (New Delhi, 1967), pp. 88-91.
117. *Congress Presidential Addresses*, n. 23, pp. 64-5.
118. *Indian Annual Register*, 1923, Vol. II (8th issue), p. 192.
119. Ibid., p. 195.
120. Ibid., p. 206.
121. Ibid., Vol. II Supplement (7th issue), pp. 105-8.
122. Ibid., pp. 121-8.
123. *CWMG*, XXIV, n. 16, pp. 136-54.
124. Rajendra Prasad to M.K. Gandhi (in Hindi), 2 August 1924, AICC Papers, No. 150/1924, Nehru Memorial Museum and Library.
125. *CWMG*, XXV (Delhi, 1966), pp. 171-2.
126. M.R. Jayakar, *The Story of My Life*, II, 1922-5 (Bombay, 1959), p. 445.
127. See *CWMG*, XXV, n. 120, pp. 214-15.

128. *The Indian Quarterly Register*, 1924, II, pp. 25-32.
129. Rajendra Prasad, *Autobiography* (New Delhi, 1994; first published 1957), pp. 225-6.
130. *CWMG*, XXV, n. 120, pp. 341-2.
131. *The Indian Quarterly Register*, 1925, I, pp. 65-70.
132. Ibid.
133. *CWMG*, XXVI, n. 31, pp. 162, 215.
134. Ibid., pp. 217-18.
135. Ibid., p. 219.
136. Ibid., pp. 233-4.
137. Ibid., p. 443.
138. Ibid., p. 503.
139. *CWMG*, XXVII (Delhi, 1968), p. 6.
140. Ibid., p. 214.
141. Ibid., XXX (New Delhi, 1968), p. 298.
142. Gandhi to Satis Chandra Mukherji, 17 April 1926, ibid., p. 304.
143. Gandhi to Jawaharlal Nehru, 23 April 1926, ibid., p. 345.
144. For details see *Indian Quarterly Register*, 1926, II, pp. 75-84.
145. See Page, n. 9, pp. 132-5.
146. *Selected Works of Motilal Nehru* (hereinafter referred to as *SWMN*) V, Ravinder Kumar and Hari Dev Sharma, eds., (New Delhi, 1993), p. 470. For full texts of Nehru's two statements issued in March 1926, clarifying his position on the issue of constitutional reforms in the NWFP. See ibid., pp. 466-76. Nehru's statements along with those by others may also be seen in *The Frontier Question in the Assembly, being the Statements of Pandit Motilal Nehru, M.L.A., Maulvi Shafi Daudi, M.L.A. and Syed Murtenza, M.L.A.* (Delhi, 1926).
147. See Page, n. 9, p. 134.
148. Motilal Nehru to Gandhi, 28 April 1926, *SWMN*, n. 146, p. 40.
149. Ibid., pp. 40-2.
150. *Indian Quarterly Register*, 1926, I, pp. 409-12.
151. Ibid. Even before the Khilafat Conference, Mohamed Ali had, in course of his speech at a meeting of Muslims at Jama Masjid (Delhi) on 23 April 1926, declared that no Khilafatist would go to the legislative councils on the Congress ticket and, if otherwise elected, would not submit to the Congress discipline. Some other speakers at the same meeting had explained that Muslims could not fight both the Government and the Hindus, and that it was better for them to devote their attention only to the Hindus. Irwin to Birkenhead, 5 May 1926, IOR, Mss. Eur. C152/2, Halifax Collection.
152. Mukhtar Ahmad Ansari to Maulana Shaukat Ali, 16 July 1926, Mushirul Hasan, ed., *Muslims and the Congress: Select Correspondence of Dr. M.A. Ansari, 1912-1935* (New Delhi, 1979), p. 19.
153. *SWMN*, n. 146, 408; full text, pp. 407-9.
154. *Indian Quarterly Register*, 1926, I, p. 406.
155. *SWMN*, n. 146, pp. 635-8.
156. Ibid., p. 635.
157. Motilal Nehru to Jawaharlal Nehru, 5 August 1926, ibid., p. 110. The Viceroy had foreseen several months earlier that the elections were going to be dominated by the communal issue. See Irwin to Birkenhead, 28 April 1926, Halifax Collection, n. 151.

158. Motilal Nehru to Jawaharlal Nehru, *SWMN*, n. 146, p. 110.
159. *Indian Quarterly Register*, 1926, I, pp. 51-3.
160. Ibid., pp. 57-64.
161. *Indian Quarterly Register*, 1926, II, p. 51. See also 'Differences with the Swaraj Party', Lala Lajpat Rai, n.1, pp. 316-22.
162. Motilal Nehru to Jawaharlal Nehru, 2 December, 1926, *SWMN*, n. 146, p. 182.
163. Page, n. 9, pp. 135-6. See also Richard Gordon. 'Hindu Mahasabha and the Indian National Congress, 1915 to 1926', *Modern Asian Studies*, IX, 2 (1975), p. 189. It may be worth noting that in some of his election speeches Motilal Nehru reiterated the line adopted by him in his appeal to the Hindu Mahasabha in March (1926), namely, that the Congress had a large number of Hindus as its members and could be relied upon not to do anything to jeopardize Hindu interests, see *SWMN*, n. 146, pp. 488-9. The Viceroy was not wrong in interpreting it as saying that the Congress was as good a Hindu body as one could want, see Irwin to Birkenhead, 23 September 1926, Halifax Collection, n. 151.
164. Ray, n. 56, p. 363.
165. Ibid., p. 364.
166. Broomfield, n. 53, p. 280.
167. Page, n. 9, pp. 136-9.
168. J. Coatman, *India in 1926-27* (Calcutta, 1928), pp. 46-7.
169. Motilal Nehru to Jawaharlal Nehru, *SWMN*, n. 146, p. 164.
170. Motilal Nehru to Jawaharlal Nehru, 9 December 1926, ibid., p. 187.
171. Motilal Nehru to Jawaharlal Nehru, 6 January 1927, ibid., p. 194.
172. *Indian Quarterly Register*, 1926, II, pp. 312-14.
173. Ibid., pp. 355-7.
174. *League Documents*, n. 25, pp. 95-6.
175. IOR, Viceroy to Secretary of State, Telegram P. No. 91-S, 19 February 1927, Mss. Eur. C152/8, Halifax Collection, n. 151.
176. Coatman, n. 168, p. 13.
177. Ibid., pp. 14-15. See also *Indian Quarterly Register*, 1927, I, pp. 81-4.
178. Birkenhead to Irwin, 24 February 1927, C152/3, Halifax Collection, n. 151.

CHAPTER V

The Widening Gulf and Emergence of the Pakistan Idea, 1927-1932

AT THE END of 1926, in the wake of the assassination of Swami Shraddhanand, all the major political parties had emphasized the need for a settlement of the Hindu-Muslim problem. It was natural, therefore, that 1927 saw the beginning of an apparently serious search for such a settlement, which continued in some form or the other till 1932. The result, however, was just the opposite. The more the effort for a settlement, the farther the two communities moved from each other. Finally, when all efforts to arrive at an agreed solution failed, the main issues of contention between them had to be settled through an award by the British Prime Minister. In the meanwhile, the steadily widening gulf between the political elites of the two communities, the growing preoccupation of most of the Muslim politicians in the Punjab with securing a dominant position in the governance of their province as a natural corollary to the Muslim majority in its population and with ensuring that Punjab remained free from interference by a Hindu dominated centre, and the increasing emphasis on the centrality of Islam in determining a Muslim's political outlook as well as identity led to the emergence of the Pakistan idea, though the name still remained to be coined.

In trying to understand how and why this happened it is pertinent to remember that the tide of Hindu as well as Muslim nationalism propelled by the communal backlash in the aftermath of the Khilafat movement had not abated by 1927, but was continuing in full force. The separate political organizations of the two communities had acquired an upper hand and an organization like the Congress, claiming to represent both the communities, was not in a position to ignore them or their views while dealing with the Hindu-Muslim problem. The people leading the communal organizations were full of suspicion and distrust of each other's intentions and not really keen to follow the path of accommodation and compromise. Apart from their long-standing sectional prejudices, fears and aspirations, their behaviour was powerfully conditioned by the presence of a third party—which was also the dominant party—namely, the British. By the very nature of things, most of the discussions for the settlement of the Hindu-Muslim problem related to the distribution of power between the two communities under the new constitutional set-up that was to take the place of the Montagu-Chelmsford reforms and the British were the final arbiters of that set-up. So each party tried to pitch its demand higher than what might have been reasonable under the given circumstances in order to influence the British and gain more for the community. Because of their strategic position the British could easily play one community against the other and this they always did. This further contributed to the heightening of communal tension among the elites of the two communities. What Jawaharlal Nehru writes about the political situation in India in this respect on the eve of the elections to the Councils in November 1926 applies equally to the situation after those elections:

> On the one side, there were the Muslim fears of a Hindu majority; on the other side Hindu resentment at being bullied, as they conceived it, by the Muslims. Many a Hindu felt that there was too much of the stand-up-and-deliver about the Muslim attitude, too much of an attempt to extort special privileges with the threat of going over to the other side. Because of this, the Hindu Mahasabha rose to some importance, representing as it did Hindu nationalism, Hindu communalism opposing Muslim communalism. The aggressive activities of the Mahasabha acted on and stimulated still further this Muslim communalism, and so action and reaction went on, and in the process the communal temperature of the country went up.[1]

The heightened communal tension among the two elites further aggravated and was in turn aggravated by growing communal antagonism among the lower middle classes and the masses, frequently resulting in communal riots. The period between 1927 and 1932, which witnessed efforts for a communal settlement was very much marked by such antagonism and rioting. In his opening address to the Shimla session of the Indian Legislature on 29 August 1927, the Viceroy, Lord Irwin, was not exaggerating when he remarked that during the seventeen months that he had been in India, the whole landscape had been overshadowed by the hovering clouds of communal tension leading to large-scale rioting in which between 250 and 300 persons had lost their lives and over 2,500 were injured.[2] The first six months of 1927-8 (April to September 1927) witnessed 25 riots—ten in the United Provinces, six in the Bombay Presidency, two each in the Punjab, the Central Provinces, Bengal, Bihar and Orissa, and one in Delhi. The total casualties were over 100 persons killed and over 1,000 persons injured.[3] The issues around which most of these riots took place were the same which had bedevilled Hindu-Muslim relations during the previous five years, namely cow-slaughter and music before mosque.

Along with communal rioting, Hindu-Muslim antagonism at the mass level also took the form of murderous attacks by individuals belonging to one community against those of the other. Some of the most serious incidents of this nature took place in the Punjab in the summer of 1927 on the occasion of the *Rangila Rasul* agitation. In May 1924, a Punjabi Hindu had published a pamphlet in Urdu under the title *Rangila Rasul* (The Gay Prophet), containing a scurrilous attack on the personal character of Prophet Mohammed. In July the Punjab Government ordered prosecution and a case was filed against Rajpal, the author of the pamphlet. The case dragged on for more than two years. In January 1927, Rajpal was sentenced to a rigorours imprisonment for eighteen months and a fine of Rs. 1,000. The Sessions Court upheld the conviction, but reduced the sentence to six months. The High Court, on appeal, remitted even this reduced sentence and acquitted Rajpal on 4 May 1927, on the plea that the section (153-A) of the Indian Penal Code under which the prosecution had taken place was not intended to bar all discussion of the character of a deceased religious leader. The case had by then received wide publicity and the acquittal of Rajpal aroused a storm of protest against the judgement among Muslims not only in the Punjab but in the whole country. The judge who had delivered the judgement, Dalip Singh, a Christian having some relations among Sikhs, was widely attacked and demands were made for his dismissal. The Hindu press, on the other hand, eulogized his independence and judicial competence. The editor and proprietor of the *Muslim Outlook* were prosecuted for a particularly intemperate attack on Dalip Singh. This was followed by another attack in the character of the Prophet in an Arya Samaj paper called *Risala Vartman*.[4] Feelings among Muslims ran so high that at one stage Hindus in Lahore were reported, on the highest authority, to be in a state of alarm.[5] Communal tension spread to some other towns in northern India also. A mammoth meeting of Muslims was organized in Delhi opposite Jama Masjid at which very strong speeches were made by some of their prominent leaders, including Maulana Mohamed Ali. He declared that a Muslim lost his senses if the Prophet was insulted or his life reviled. The meeting adopted a resolution, moved by Mohamed Ali, asking the Government to move the Privy Council against the judgement delivered by Dalip Singh or indicate its willingness to amend the Indian Penal Code so that it might not be possible to deliver such judgements in future. In the meanwhile an ordinance should be issued to deal with the situation.[6] At Allahabad the Muslims made an unprecedented demand that no marriage procession of Hindus be taken out on any public street during Muharram, regardless whether there was any mosque on it or not. In exasperation Motilal Nehru remarked: 'The Mussalmans of India have gone mad.' He soon found that the Hindus too were not in any better frame of mind and got tired of intervening in local disputes between the two communities, remarking ruefully: 'They have all lost their heads.'[7]

The situation was, for the time being, saved from deteriorating further by the then Governor of the Punjab Hailey's assurance to the Muslims that if the matter was not settled satisfactorily by the courts, the Indian Penal Code would be suitably amended.[8] This was followed by the judgement by a Division Bench of the Punjab High Court in the *Risala Vartman* case pointing out that attacks on the character of the Prophets and founders of religions were punishable under the concerned article of the Indian Penal Code. Even so the Government felt compelled to amend that code (by adding a new section—295-A) in order to remove all ambiguity in this matter. This had 'a certain tranquillising effect' and put an end to what remained of the agitation on the *Rangila Rasul* issue. Besides, communal writings now became more restrained.[9]

The situation improved slightly during the twelve months ending with 31 March 1929 mainly because public attention was generally focused on the general boycott of the Indian Statutory Commission headed by Sir John Simon and popularly known as the Simon Commission. Even so there were no less than 22 riots during those months in which over 200 persons died and about a thousand got injured. The number of casualties swelled largely because of serious rioting in Bombay in February 1929 in course of which 149 persons lost their lives and 739 got injured. The army had to be called and firing resorted to on no fewer than 11 occasions.[10] Riots continued during 1929-30, though their number came down, only 12 of them being large enough to be reported to the Government of India. Among them the most serious was the riot in Bombay which continued sporadically for three weeks during April-May 1929 and caused thirty-five deaths and about two hundred other casualties. The murder of Rajpal, the author of *Rangila Rasul,* by a Muslim at Lahore in April caused a good deal of communal tension, which came to the fore again when the man convicted for that crime was executed.[11]

For much of the time during 1930-1 the civil disobedience movement under Gandhi's leadership provided the main focus of excitement and interest and the country was generally free from the ravages of communal riots. In the last week of March 1931, however, Kanpur became the scene of severe rioting, indeed the worst which India had experienced for many years.[12] Ironically, the circumstances associated with the civil disobedience movement itself provided the immediate background for these riots. Although the Pathans of the North-West Frontier Province under the leadership of Khan Abdul Gaffar Khan, popularly known as Frontier Gandhi, played a memorable role in that movement and a number of Muslims in the rest of India also joined it, on the whole Muslim participation in it was quite minimal. Indeed, the generality of Muslims, apart from those in the North-West Frontier Province, regarded it as a purely Hindu movement, with which they had no concern, and resented the picketing of their shops selling foreign cloth. On the other hand, Hindus resented this attitude of the Muslims. This naturally aggravated communal tension and bitterness. This is forcefully brought out by the report (23 May 1931) of the Commission of Enquiry into the Kanpur riots appointed by the U.P. Government:

> Whether the Muslims [of Kanpur] were organised or not, it is obvious that during the civil disobedience movement in 1930 the two communities came more definitely face to face with each other than they had been before. The Congress Hindus generally were irritated with the Muslims for standing aloof from what they believed to be a national movement and Hindu traders in Cawnpore were jealous of Muslims carrying on business as usual. The Muslims, on the other hand, were getting exasperated with what the Secretary of Upper India Chamber of Commerce in his evidence calls the tyranny of the Congress. . . .
>
> . . . . It is in the increasing embitterment of feeling between the two communities that the cause of the outbreak has to be sought, and the cause of that embitterment is to be found in the course taken by the civil disobedience movement. . . . It had become in Cawnpore a Hindu movement with Muslims actively or passively in opposition.[13]

This is fully corroborated by the Committee of Enquiry appointed by the Congress at its Karachi session (March 1931) which submitted its report to the Congress President in October 1931. After describing the growth of communal movements among both Hindus and Muslims in Kanpur since 1922, the Committee observed:

> Thus, since the stopping of the Non-cooperation Movement in 1922, mutual distrust had been growing between the two communities. The year 1930 instead of improving the communal situation made matters worse. The Hindus, especially at Cawnpore, felt a grievance against their Muslim brethren for not only keeping aloof from the National Movement but also, in collusion with the enemies of the country, trying to stand in its way. The Muslims, on their side, felt little enthusiasm for Swaraj in the hands of people whom they associated with the communal movements of the previous seven years and even thought that Congress interference with their business, when they had kept away from the movement, was unjustifiable. Distrust went on developing, and, with it, bitterness of feeling. Thus a magazine had been created which waited only for a spark to burst any time into conflagration.[14]

The Kanpur riot was by no means an isolated incident. Before it, between January and March 1931, riots had taken place at Basti, Varanasi, Mirzapur and Agra (all in U.P.).[15] The riot at Kanpur, however, was one of unprecedented fury which rapidly engulfed the whole city and even areas beyond it. For three days the situation was totally out of control and there were widespread murders, arson and looting. The number of verified deaths was 300, but it was estimated that actually between four and five hundred persons had died.[16] The total number of buildings destroyed or seriously damaged was more than 500. This included 23 mosques and 37 temples.[17] Hailey, then Governor of U.P., considered the Kanpur riot as 'certainly the worst' in his experience in India.[18] The ineptitude or indifference of the District Magistrate at the initial stage contributed significantly to the ferocity of rioting and its heavy toll—a fact recognized by the U.P. Government in its resolution on the report of its Enquiry Commission. Ganesh Shankar Vidhyarthi, the most prominent Congress leader of Kanpur and then President of the U.P. Provincial Congress Committee, who had rescued many Muslims along with Hindus from the rioters, was killed by a Muslim mob while trying to pacify it.[19]

I

It was against this background of growing communal tension and recurring Hindu-Muslim riots that the leaders of the various political parties, notably the Congress, Hindu Mahasabha and Muslim League, carried on their intermittent negotiations for a settlement of the communal problem. If this is kept in view, nobody need be surprised at the failure of these negotiations or at the fact that instead of leading to a solution of the communal problem, these negotiations further aggravated it. Even if all the leaders concerned were keen on a settlement—something not beyond doubt—they could not but take into account the sentiments and views of their constituents and would not dare go too far in a contrary direction. This was not a background favourable to a real give and take without which no settlement was possible.

On the other hand, the steady growth of communal tension itself provided the spur to efforts for a settlement. There was a feeling in certain circles that things had gone too far and that efforts must be made to reverse the path. A royal commission on further constitutional reforms was in the offing and it was realized by important leaders particularly those belonging to the Congress and the Muslim League that a major advance towards responsible government was not possible unless they presented an united front. Keeping this in view, the annual sessions of almost all the major political parties, held in the last week of December 1926, had called for such efforts. Proceeding in the light of the resolution adopted by the Congress session at Gauhati, the Working Committee of that organization at its informal meeting in Calcutta on the first of January 1927 authorized its president, Srinivas Iyengar, to convene a conference of the Hindu and Muslim members of the Central Assembly and the Council of State in Delhi 'at the earliest opportunity' to consider ways and means of promoting Hindu-Muslim unity. After consultations with several leaders in Delhi, Iyenger found it more expedient to start separate discussions with the prominent Hindu and Muslim members of the Central legislature. Jinnah was among the leaders present at the discussion with Muslim leaders, marked by 'a full and frank presentation' of their point of view.[20] The discussions with both the Hindu and Muslim leaders centred round the issue of separate versus mixed electorates.[21] The discussions took place on 17 March 1927.[22] Three days later, on 20 March 1927, there assembled 30 prominent Muslim leaders at Western Court, New Delhi, at the call of Jinnah and under his chairmanship. They included leaders representing varying shades of opinion in the Congress and the Khilafat Conference as well as the Muslim League. After protracted discussions they agreed, as announced by Jinnah, to accept elections by mixed electorates provided the following four conditions were met:

1. Sind (having a Muslim majority) to be separated from the Bombay Presidency and constituted into a separate province;
2. Reforms to be introduced in the North-West Frontier Province and in Baluchistan (both having overwhelming Muslim majorities) on the same footing as in any other province in India;
3. In the Punjab and Bengal (with small Muslim majorities) the proportion of representation of a community in the legislature to be in accordance with the population of that community;
4. and in the Central Legislature Muslim representatives not to be less than a third of the total.

It was also provided that Muslims in Sind, North-West Frontier Province and Baluchistan would be willing to grant the same concessions to the Hindu minorities there which the Hindus agreed to grant to Muslims in provinces where they were in a minority. These proposals, which became famous as the Delhi Proposals, were subject to ratification by the Muslim organizations concerned. The question of Muslim share in the services and other questions with regard to safeguards concerning any bill or resolution which might affect the religion, customs or usages of either community or affect inter-communal interests, were also discussed by the meeting, but postponed for further consideration and were to be taken up after there emerged unanimity of opinion on the main propositions.[23]

The Delhi Proposals represented a major breakthrough. If all parties concerned adopted a cooperative approach, there was a reasonable chance of their success in bidding good bye to separate electorates, which had bedevilled Indian politics and stood like a high and thick wall between Hindus and Muslims, especially since 1919, but which politically conscious Muslims had come to regard as their most valuable asset. At the same time the proposals safeguarded the vital Muslim interests and aspirations by providing for the emergence of five Muslim dominated provinces, including those of the Punjab and Bengal, the most cherished goal of Muslim India since the introduction of the Montagu-Chelmsford reforms. 'Jinnah's bold and patriotic initiative', aptly observes Tara Chand, 'had at last interjected a ray of light into the encircling gloom. The way seemed to be opened to communal understanding and Swaraj.'[24] Such a hope was further strengthened by the warm welcome accorded to the Delhi Proposals by the Congress Working Committee. At its meeting in Delhi on 21 March, it 'cordially' appreciated those proposals and appointed a high-powered sub-committee consisting of Srinivas Iyengar, Motilal Nehru, Maulana

Mohamed Ali and Sarojini Naidu to discuss the details with the representatives of Hindu and Muslim organizations.[25]

The attitude of leaders of Hindu opinion, however, was not encouraging. The Hindu members of the Central Legislature met on 23 March under Malaviya's chairmanship and settled the principles which were to form the basis for future discussion on the constitutional problem. These were mixed electorates for elections to all legislatures; reservation of seats on population basis in all legislatures; and safeguards for the protection of religious and quasi-religious rights in the constitution. The question of redistribution of provinces 'on linguistic and other essential bases' was to be left open for consideration. This was obviously intended to be a reply to the Muslim demands for the separation of Sind from Bombay and bringing the constitutional setup in North-West Frontier Province and Baluchistan at par with that in other provinces. The thinking of the Hindu leaders was more bluntly expressed by *The Hindustan Times* (Delhi) which was at that time controlled by persons like Malaviya and Lajpat Rai. It condemned what it called 'the spirit of petty bargaining' which, in its opinion, had inspired the Delhi Proposals and wondered how persons like M.A. Ansari, Mohamed Ali and Jinnah had given their assent to them. The paper asked in what way was the establishment of mixed electorates connected with the separation of Sind from Bombay or the introduction of reforms in North-West Frontier Province and Baluchistan. It went on to assert that Muslims felt that by accepting mixed electorates, as demanded by Hindus, they were entitled to expect a price for this in the shape of more power in Sind, Baluchistan and North-West Frontier Province. The Hindu leaders, it clarified, were asking for mixed electorates not because it would mean more power to the Hindus but because such electorates, while fully protecting the legitimate interests of the minorities, would help in the growth of the spirit of nationalism and in eliminating rather than emphasizing the differences prevailing between the different sections of the Indian people. The paper further observed that if Muslims wanted the separation of Sind to ensure more power for themselves, there were Hindus who would like to readjust the boundaries of the Punjab and Bengal in order to eliminate Muslim majorities from them.[26]

Jinnah, through a statement to the press on 29 March, clarified that the Delhi Proposals were interdependent and could only be accepted or rejected in their entirety. It would not do, as the Hindu leaders had attempted, to accept one part and reject another. Referring to the decision taken at the meeting of the Hindu members of the Central Legislature on 23 March to appoint a committee to frame definite proposals after consulting leaders of Hindu opinion, he hoped that the country would give the fullest consideration to the offer made by the Muslim leaders in a calm atmosphere without any heat or passion. He also emphasized that the most notable feature of the Muslim offer was its recognition that separate electorates could only be got rid of by 'a thorough adoption of the system of give and take'. Apparently addressing Muslims as well as Hindus, he further remarked:

> The question of separate or mixed electorates is after all a method and a means to an end. The end in view is that Mussalmans should be made to feel that they are secure and safeguarded against any act of oppression on the part of the majority, and that they need not fear that during the transitional stage towards the fullest development of national government the majority would be in a position to oppress or tyrannise the minority, as majorities are prone to do in other countries.[27]

These words failed to remove suspicion and distrust from the minds of the bulk of those Hindu and Muslim politicians who were primarily guided by communal or sectional considerations. This is best illustrated by the treatment meted out to the Delhi Proposals by the Hindu Mahasabha at its tenth session held at Patna from 16 to 18 April 1927. It resolved that in view of the fact that the Muslim community as such had not yet endorsed the Delhi Proposals, which were in any case subject to ratification by Muslim organizations, and of Jinnah's statement that they had to be either accepted or rejected as a whole, without any modification, no useful purpose would be served by expressing any opinion on them at that stage. It added that it would be premature and harmful for the All India Congress Committee also to consider those proposals At the same time, it accepted mixed electorates and reservation of seats, as basis for discussion, but with the proviso that the latter would have to be for a fixed period only and based not merely on population, but also on such variables as voting strength or taxation. Further, it deprecated any attempt to constitute new provinces or legislatures for the purpose of giving a majority therein to any particular community. According to it, the question of the creation of new provinces should be considered, if necessary, 'independently of any proposals and exclusively on their merits'.[28]

On the other hand, there were rather strong expressions of protest by various Muslim organizations, individual leaders and organs of the press against the offer made in the Delhi Proposals to give up separate electorates. Among these were also some who belonged to the group of 30 Muslim leaders whose deliberations had given birth to those proposals. Indeed, immediately after their publication, one or two of the participants wrote to the press denying that they had agreed to the abandonment of separate electorates and saying that they could not accept the system of mixed electorates on any terms.[29] Three weeks later, notable participant, Sir Abdul Qaiyum, the most prominent Muslim League leader in the North-West Frontier Province and a prominent member of the Central Assembly, said in course of a statement to the press that if the Muslims desired to maintain their identity they should not allow themselves to be merged in the Hindu majority. 'A joint electorate under the existing circumstances', he added, 'will be an unequal combination, disadvantageous to the weaker side'.[30] The Muslim press generally commented in this strain. Not surprisingly, the Viceroy reported to the Secretary of State that 'whatever Hindus might think about the proposed conditions for joint electorates, there was little chance of their finding favour with the Mohammedans'.[31]

Among others to protest against the offer to give up separate electorates under certain conditions were the Muslim members of the Madras Legislative Council. Meeting on 28 to 30 March 1927, they came to the conclusion that under the then existing conditions, mixed electorates, particularly in their province, would not only prove detrimental to the political advancement of the Muslims, but also jeopardise their interests and hamper the friendly relationship that existed between Hindus and Muslims.[32] In course of his presidential address to a special meeting of the Punjab Provincial Muslim League held at Lahore on 1 May, Mian Mohammad Shafi, one of the prominent members of the group of 30 Muslims who had met at Delhi on 20 March before the enunciation of the Delhi Proposals, gave a lengthy oration on the impracticability of giving up separate electorates under the then existing conditions. According to him, such a step was certain to prove not only a cause of friction between Hindus and Muslims, but also fatal to the cause of Indian nationalism and productive of difficult and complicated administrative problems for the Government. The meeting adopted not one but three resolutions supporting separate electorates.[33] One week later, on 8 May, Sir Abdur Rahim, declared, in course of his presidential address to the Bengal Muslim Conference, that any change from separate to mixed electorates under the then existing conditions would seriously endanger Muslim interests.[34] Prominent Muslim leaders of Bihar and Orissa, meeting at Patna on the same day, came to a similar conclusion.[35]

Undeterred by such adverse reactions, the All India Congress Committee, at its meeting at Bombay on 15 and 16 May, came up with a positive response to the Delhi Proposals by adopting certain principles as the basis for the future constitution of India which broadly tallied with those proposals, with some modifications and additions here and there. These principles, contained in a resolution moved by Motilal Nehru and adopted by the A.I.C.C., included representation in all legislatures through mixed electorates, with reservation of seats on the basis of population. Reciprocal concessions in favour of minorities, including Sikhs in the Punjab, might be made by mutual agreement so as to give them more representation in the legislatures concerned than they would be entitled to exactly on the basis of their population in any province. The mention of Sikhs in the Punjab represented a significant modification of the Delhi Proposals which stipulated for representation in the Punjab (as also in Bengal) strictly in accordance with population and talked of reciprocal concessions or weightage only in connection with Sind, Baluchistan and North-West Frontier Province on the one hand and the Muslim minority provinces on the other. With regard to the separation of Sind from Bombay and the introduction of constitutional reforms in Baluchistan and North-West Frontier Province, the resolution adopted by the A.I.C.C. (incorporating an amendment moved by M.R. Jayakar) endorsed in substance the demands put forth in the Delhi Proposals, but couched them in a slightly different language. Thus the A.I.C.C. declared that the time had come for the redistribution of provinces on a linguistic basis and demanded the separation of Sind from Bombay in that context, along with the creation of Andhra and Karnataka also as separate provinces. With regard to introduction of constitutional reforms in Baluchistan and North-West Frontier Province, it was stipulated that along with various measures of administrative reform, care should also be taken to introduce therein an adequate system of judicial administration. With a view to reassuring the Muslims, as also other minorities, that they needed to have no worry regarding any interference with their religion or culture in a free India, the A.I.C.C. stipulated in its resolution that liberty of conscience would be guaranteed in the future constitution and that no legislature, central or provincial, would have the power to make any laws interfering with such liberty. Liberty of conscience, the resolution went on to clarify, meant liberty of belief and worship, freedom to carry on religious education and propaganda, with due regard to the feelings of others and without interfering with similar rights of others. It further provided that no bill, resolution, motion or amendment regarding inter-communal matters would be moved, discussed or passed in any legislature, central or provincial, if a three-fourth majority of the members of either community (Hindus or Muslims) affected by it in that legislature was opposed to it. After the resolution was declared carried unanimously, Sarojini Naidu, a famous poetess and a former President of the Congress, rising to congratulate the house, observed that by accepting Jinnah's proposals Congressmen had truly proved themselves to be the natural spokesmen of India.[36]

III

In spite of such declarations it must have been obvious to all concerned that the communal problem was still far from being solved. In fact, as the agitation against the Punjab High Court's judgement on the *Rangila Rasul's* case showed, communal tension had gone on increasing even while the Delhi Proposals were under discussion. Indeed, the conflicting reactions of the leaders and organs of the two communities towards those proposals, particularly those relating to the abolition of separate electorates and the creation of Muslim dominated provinces, had perhaps contributed further to the growth of such tension. The Viceroy at any rate thought it to have been the case. Shortly after the announcement of the Delhi Proposals he wrote to the Secretary of State that these were likely to widen rather than diminish the breach between the two communities.[37] A few days later, he again conveyed to the Secretary of State that his impression was that the Delhi Proposals represented largely a 'manoeuvring for position' and that there was 'not much prospect of a real agreement emerging'. According to him, it would be premature to assume, just on the basis of the Delhi Proposals, that the Muslims had accepted the principle of mixed electorates. Analysing the motivations of leaders behind the Delhi Proposals he observed:

> From what I have heard I should judge there were two very different forces which contributed to this *ballon d'essai.* Jinnah finds his position as nominal leader of what is practically a Mohammedan Party most precarious. Some form of compromise with the Hindus is not only demanded by his political beliefs, but is probably an essential condition of his retaining position as a political leader. Some Mohammedans, on the other hand, may possibly have thought this move a useful means of sowing dissensions among the Hindus, reckoning that the Congress Party must welcome it, while the Nationalists led by Lajpat Rai and Malaviya were not likely to accept the essential

conditions about Sind, Baluchistan and North-West Frontier Province. It would, in any case, exhibit the Muslims in a reasonable light, and the subsequent failure to reach agreement would be attributed to intransigence of Hindus.[38]

The Viceroy's calculation that Hindus and Muslims would not be able to come to an agreement seemed vindicated by April-May 1927, when the Hindu Mahasabha and certain Muslim leaders and organizations attacked the Delhi Proposals from opposite sides. And all the while, communal tension in the country as a whole, fuelled partly by these differences and partly by the agitation on the *Rangila Rasul* case, seemed to be increasing. At one stage the Viceroy toyed with the idea of calling the leaders of both sides to a conference, but desisted from such a move thinking that it might do more harm than good: 'it sometimes looks as if', he told the Secretary of State, 'every attempt to narrow the issue only results in widening the gulf'. This had already happened as a result of the Delhi Proposals.[39] He wrote again more than a month later regarding 'the eternal question of communal strife':

> I don't think the position gets any better as between the two communities. We have, it is true, got through the Bakr-Id festival, but only at the cost of plastering the danger-spots with an overwhelming show of force, and everything that I hear leads me to think that the strain is undiminished. None of these agreements, so called, have cut much ice and at any moment therefore we must continue to expect trouble.[40]

Surprising though it may appear, Motilal Nehru, thought more or less on the same lines as the Viceroy. In a letter to Jawaharlal 11 days after the announcement of the Delhi Proposals, which he described as a 'very reasonable move' on the part of the Muslim leaders, he observed: 'The communal feeling in country is daily in the increase and things have come to such a pass that any honest attempt to allay that feeling has the inevitable result of flaring it up'.[41] A little over a month after successfully piloting the resolution in the all India Congress Committee broadly accepting the Delhi Proposals, Motilal privately confessed his own lack of enthusiasm for those proposals because their limited objectives, as he perceived them, related primarily to the presentation before the ensuing royal commission of India's case for responsible government:

> The Hindu-Muslim question is no doubt most important; but I am not sure that the solution we are working for will take us to any appreciable distance on the road to Swaraj. The sole objective of Jinnah and the Maharaja

of Mahmudabad [a close associate of Jinnah] is to get as much as possible out of the coming Statutory Commission. It is obvious that with all the communal bitterness and strife prevailing on all sides the Statutory Commission is not expected to fulfil the expectations of even those who have faith in it. I have unfortunately no faith in it and am convinced that it will give nothing even if the Hindus and Mussalmans all over the country begin to fall on each other's neck. I am, therefore, not very keen on a Hindu-Muslim unity which has so limited a scope and objective. That the Delhi-Bombay proposals [so called after the A.I.C.C. meeting at Bombay in May 1927] mark a step in the right direction admits of no doubt but it leaves those people cold who are not concerned with Council elections and do not see their salvation coming that way.[42]

It is possible that Motilal Nehru had persons like Gandhi in view when he wrote this letter. For Gandhi continued to hold firmly to his opinion that unless there was a change in the attitude of the people at large resolutions and agreements would not be of much use in changing the situation. When the then Congress President, Srinivas Iyenger, telegraphically informed him of the unanimous adoption by the All India Congress Committee at Bombay on 16 May 1927, of the resolution broadly accepting the Delhi Proposals, Gandhi sent his wishes for success in Iyenger's efforts to improve the communal situation, but observed, with reference to the resolution, that he was 'not enthused over it because of the wretched atmosphere about us'. He then added: 'Our best resolutions come to naught because we seem to have lost the power of taking the people with us. Of what use will be our resolutions if the people continue savagely to break one another's heads'?[43] A couple of days later Gandhi wrote to another important Congress leader, M.A. Ansari, in the same vein:

I see nothing but devilry going on under the garb of religion. Not until we learn to become men and therefore instead of breaking heads for the vindication of supposed rights, we learn to refer to arbitration matters even of attacks upon our right, supposed or real, and until we cease to think of Government interference, shall we have real peace or real Swaraj. Anything short of that gives me no satisfaction.[44]

In an article on Hindu-Muslim Unity published in *Young India* on 16 June 1927 Gandhi openly expressed the view that the A.I.C.C. resolution on the Delhi Proposals had left him unmoved. This was because in his view Hindus and Muslims had neither changed their hearts nor had they shed fear of each other. Any compromise in such a situation must be 'a mere make-shift'.[45] 'No special legislation', he wrote again in *Young India,* dated 14 July 1927, 'without a change of heart can possibly bring about organic unity. And when there is a change of heart no such legislation can possibly be necessary'.[46] Such ideas found an echo in the hearts and minds of some other leaders also, who realized that apart from negotiations regarding distribution of seats in the legislatures something must also be done to change the outlook of people in both the communities who continued to go on rampage in one part of the country or another on such issues as cow-slaughter and music before mosque.

The initiative in this regard was taken by the leaders of the Khilafat Conference at a time when the communal temperature of the country, particularly in the north, had risen very high in the wake of the agitation against the Punjab High Court's decision on the *Rangila Rasul* case. The Hindu Mahasabha as well as the Congress responded favourably and the result was the convening of a Conference of prominent Hindu and Muslim leaders, generally called the Unity Conference, to discuss the then prevailing communal situation and find out a remedy for it. It met at Simla on 30 August 1927 and appointed a committee, which became known as Simla Unity Committee, consisting of prominent Hindu and Muslim leaders, in order to devise measures to bring about an improvement in the communal situation. They also issued an impassioned appeal to people to desist from doing anything which might cause a further deterioration in the communal situation. To what extent that situation had deteriorated by 1927 was very well brought out in the opening lines of that appeal:

> We the undersigned deplore the communal differences that have most unfortunately grown up among our people and have created so much mistrust of each other that on the slightest provocation or misunderstanding, some of our countrymen, Hindus and Mussalmans, come to blows and trivial incidents develop into heart-rending tragedies, involving loss of innocent life and property and embittering still further the relations between the two communities. It will be the greatest folly, indeed a sin, to fail to realise the extreme gravity of the situation. Apart from the impossibility of making any political advance in such circumstances, peaceful social existence itself is threatened.[47]

The atmosphere at the Conference itself had been far from congenial. According to information reaching the Viceroy, the tone of some of the speeches delivered there was 'so intemperate that it nearly led to a communal riot in the committee room'.[48] What followed, therefore, was not surprising. The Unity Committee, appointed by the Conference, met at Shimla for full one week (16 to 22 September) under the chairmanship of Jinnah and having among participants such stalwarts as Malaviya, B.S. Moonje, Mohamed Ali, Ansari, Azad and others. Rival Hindu and Muslim drafts both on cow-slaughter and music before mosque were brought up and discussed, but no agreement could be arrived at.[49] Shortly after this Srinivas Iyenger, as Congress President, took the initiative and convened another Unity Conference at Calcutta in the last week of October 1927. Where the Shimla Conference had failed, the Calcutta Conference succeeded. Thanks to Iyenger's efforts Hindu and Muslim leaders, after long discussions spread over two days, were able to agree on a common stand not only with regard to cow-slaughter and music before mosque, but also the issue of conversion and re-conversion from one religion to another. Thus the conference resolved that every individual or group was at liberty to convert or re-convert another by argument or persuasion but must not attempt to do so or prevent its being done by force, fraud or other unfair means. Persons under 18 were not to be converted, unless it was along with their parents or guardians. On the issue of music before mosque it was agreed that Hindus were at liberty to take processions and play music before mosques at any time for religious or social purposes. At the same time it was stipulated that there should be no procession nor special demonstration in front of mosques nor should the music played in front of such mosques be of such a nature as calculated to cause annoyance, social disturbance or offence to the worshippers in the mosques. Similarly Muslims were to be at liberty to slaughter cows in exercise of their rights in any town or village in any place not being a thoroughfare nor one in the vicinity of a temple nor one exposed to the gaze of Hindus. However, having regard to the deep-rooted sentiment of the Hindu community in the matter, an earnest appeal was made to Muslims to so conduct the cow sacrifice as not to cause annoyance to Hindus in the towns or villages concerned.[50]

The All India Congress Committee, met in Calcutta from 28 to 30 October, immediately after the Unity Conference and adopted the latter's resolutions on conversions, music before mosque and cow-slaughter.[51] They were reiterated at the annual session of the Congress held in Madras in the last week of December 1927. At the same time the Madras Congress Session also reiterated the resolution regarding mixed electorates and reservation of seats adopted by the A.I.C.C. at Bombay in the middle of May. All of them were made part of the same resolution on Hindu-Muslim unity and designated respectively as

'Political Rights' and 'Religions and other Rights' respectively. Sarojini Naidu who moved that resolution described it as 'the most vital, the most epoch-making of all the resolutions that have been passed or will be passed in this historic and epoch-making Congress'. Most of the speakers spoke in this vein. Some opposition was, of course, voiced by a few members seeking to represent the Hindu point of view, but when Malaviya himself stood up to warmly support the resolution, all opposition died down and it was carried unanimously amidst shouts of *Alla-O-Akbar, Vandemataram* and *Mahatma Gandhi Ki Jai*. Ansari, the new President of the Congress, remarked jubilantly to a cheering audience: 'Today you have not only laid the foundation of a free India, but you may consider that you are well on the way to win it'.[52]

The Madras Congress took two other important decisions. Firstly, it resolved to boycott the Indian Statutory Commission (popularly called the Simon Commission after the name of its Chairman, Sir John Simon) whose appointment had been announced on 8 November 1927, with a view to submitting proposals for the next instalment of constitutional reforms and which was looked upon as a great national affront because of its all-British membership. At the same time, it asked its Working Committee to draft a Swaraj Constitution for India in consultation with similar committees to be appointed by other organizations in the country.[53] This was its response to a challenge thrown by the then Secretary of State for India, Lord Birkenhead, who had observed that if Indians could frame a constitution acceptable to all parties, the British would be willing to consider it.

The Muslim League Session in Calcutta from 30 December 1927 to 1 January 1928 adopted broadly similar resolutions.[54] The spirit animating the session can be guessed from the fact that those present there included Malaviya, the great Hindu leader, and at the invitation of the President he also addressed it, calling upon those present to be united and have confidence in each other, always remembering that they were Indians first and Hindus and Muslims afterwards. In his concluding remarks Jinnah, as President, made a particularly warm reference to Malaviya. 'I welcome Pandit Malaviya', he said, 'and I welcome the hand of fellowship extended to us by Hindu leaders from the platform of the Congress and the Hindu Mahasabha.' That, he added, was more valuable for him than any concession which the British could make.[55]

Yet, with all this bonhomie, the League session was careful enough to emphasize in the resolution approving the Delhi Proposals that under the then existing circumstances, representation of Muslims through separate electorates was inevitable, and the Muslims would not accept any scheme involving the surrender of that 'valuable right' unless and until Sind was 'actually' constituted into a separate Province and reforms were 'actually' introduced in the North-West Frontier Province and Baluchistan.[56] Besides, the leaders present at the League session took special pains to emphasize the gains which Muslim would make if the Delhi Proposals gained universal acceptance. In this connection it is remarkable that Azad who, while speaking at the Madras Congress in support of those proposals had emphasized the gains for national unity to be secured through the abolition of separate electorates,[57] in his speech at the League session emphasized the power which would come to Muslims through their control of the Muslim majority provinces provided for in those proposals. Dilating on that point, he observed that the Muslims had sold away their interests through the Lucknow Pact (1916) and that the Delhi Proposals for the first time opened the door for the recognition of their real rights in India. He further added:

> The separate electorates granted by the Pact of 1916 only ensured Muslim representation, but what was vital for the existence of the community was the recognition of its numerical strength. . . . Their existing small majority in Bengal and the Punjab was only a census figure; but the Delhi Proposals, for the first time, gave them five provinces of which no less than three . . . contained a real overwhelming Muslim majority. . . . There would be now nine Hindu provinces against five Muslim provinces; and whatever treatment Hindus accorded Muslims in the nine provinces, Muslims would accord the same treatment to Hindus in the five provinces. Was not this a great gain? Was not a new weapon gained for the assertion of Muslim rights?[58]

In fairness to Azad, it must be recorded that, as recapitulated by Sarojini Naidu who addressed the League Session after him, he had also emphasized that Muslims should not look at the Delhi Proposals in the petty spirit of traders.[59] In spite of such exhortations Jinnah, the great realist, was not sure that a majority of Muslims in the country were really behind the Delhi Proposals which, among other things, included preparedness on their part to give up separate electorates, looked upon by them as their most valuable asset. Speaking after Azad he observed: 'We have got a majority in this House, but shall we be able to carry the majority in the country? Nothing will please me more, but at the same time, it will be fair to say that I am not so sure that I am satisfied that the majority of Musalmans throughout the country are in favour of it. That remains to be decided. . . .'[60]

Jinnah's as well as Azad's hesitation in assuming majority Muslim support for the Delhi Proposals was not groundless. As mentioned earlier, Muslim organizations in several provinces had raised their voices against them. The situation became more difficult for Jinnah after the issue of boycott of Simon Commission got joined with that of abolition of separate electorates. Jinnah, along with a host of other prominent political leaders in the country belonging to different parties, expressed his unhappiness at the all-British membership of the Simon Commission and considered it an affront to Indian's dignity. However, unlike the Congress leaders, he did not immediately announce a boycott of that Commission. Even after his pleadings with the Viceroy to get the membership of that commission broadbased by the addition of at least two Indian members to it failed to produce any result,[61] he was at pains to assure Irwin as late as middle of December 1927 that he had till then made no public utterance which bound him to boycott the commission on the ground of its personnel.[62] He further told the Viceroy that 'he had been very careful to close no doors and that unless he went on agitating, other people who were against him would gain ground'. The Viceroy naturally concluded that all this represented 'a bit of manoeuvring'.[63] However, if no satisfactory step was taken by the Government to assuage Indian opinion there was no doubt as to what Jinnah's decision would be, namely boycott of the Simon Commission. On the other hand, there were several other leaders of the Muslim League, notably in the Punjab, who were opposed to any talk of boycott, as they considered that inimical to Muslim interests. These were the leaders who were also opposed to the Delhi Proposals chiefly on the ground of its offer to give up separate electorates. Thus opposition to the boycott of Simon Commission went hand in hand with opposition to the Delhi Proposals. 'The advocates of a Separate Electorate', wrote Hailey, then Governor of the Punjab, to a friend, 'realise that they can only secure its maintenance through the Commission; they deprecate boycott not so much as a question of principle as because it might close to them a unique opportunity for gaining this particular end'.[64]

Hailey, of course, was playing an active role, behind the scenes, in encouraging the Muslim leaders of the Punjab to pursue this course. 'I have for some time', he informed the Viceroy, 'been urging the Punjab Muslims to take this opportunity to assume the leadership in Muslim politics. . . .'[65] The Punjab Muslim leaders, barring a few notable exceptions, did all they could to fulfil Hailey's expectations. As noted earlier, they had taken the lead in opposing the Delhi Proposals.[65a] Soon after the public announcement of the appointment of the Simon Commission and the talk of its boycott by prominent Indian leaders, the Punjab Muslim League adopted a resolution by 22 votes to 4 declaring that it was not in the interest of the country in general and the Muslims in particular to boycott the Commission. Reporting this to Hailey, Firoz Khan Noon, Minister of Local Self-Government in the Punjab, remarked: 'I think on the whole it is quite satisfactory'.[66] The next step of the Punjab League leaders was to carry the struggle to the all-India body. Jinnah and his supporters wanted the annual session of the League to be held at Madras, which was also the venue selected for the annual Congress session, but the Punjab League leaders, supported by their U.P. comrades in the League Council, succeeded in ensuring that the session would be held at Lahore under the presidentship of their own leader, Sir Mohammad Shafi, so the decision to be arrived at would be according to their wishes. 'The one thing that is counting with them', gleefully recorded the Viceroy, 'is communal electorates, and they are not going to run any risk of having their counsels deflected on this point by men of the Jinnah type'.[67] Not to be so easily out manoeuvred Jinnah got convened another meeting of the League's Council on 11 December 1927. The Jinnah camp now proposed Calcutta as the venue for the annual session, but the Shafi camp insisted on Lahore, as Abdur Rahim, the Bengal League leader, had also opted for boycott of the Simon Commission. Out of 300 members only 23 were present. Out of them 13 voted for Lahore and 10 for Calcutta. However, a large number of members had sent their votes by proxy: 74 in favour of Calcutta and 41 in favour of Lahore. So the decision went in favour of Calcutta by 84 votes to 54.[68] The Muslim League split into two parts, those opposed to Calcutta as venue of the League session forming their own separate Muslim League and deciding to go ahead with the session at Lahore as planned earlier.

That session met at Lahore from 31 December 1927 to 1 January 1928. As expected Shafi, in his presidential address, strongly opposed the proposed abolition of separate electorates and declared that under the then existing conditions the introduction of mixed electorates, with or without reservation, 'would be certain to furnish a periodical cause for friction between the two communities, and would, in consequence, be in the highest degree injurious to the cause of Indian nationalism'. As regards the Simon Commission he called upon all concerned to settle their differences and present a united demand before it. 'A unanimous demand thus made would be irresistible, no matter what the constitution of the Royal Commission might be.' The session adopted resolutions along these lines. The first resolution invited the leaders of all non-Muslim communities in India to come to a satisfactory settlement with the Muslim community so that a united demand might be placed before the Statutory Commission or the British Parliament or both. The second resolution declared that neither the proposals formulated by some Muslim leaders in their individual capacities at Delhi on 20 March 1927, in their original form, nor in their amended form as passed by the Congress session at Madras, were acceptable to the Muslims of India.[69]

Voices of dissent from the Delhi Proposals regarding separate electorates were heard even at the Calcutta session of the League. Thus the Chairman of the Reception Committee, Mujibur Rahman, while supporting the boycott of the Simon Commission, made a strong plea for the retention of separate electorates. Describing them as 'the corner-stone of Muslim politics' under the then existing conditions in India, he observed:

> When each community is assured that its interests and privileges are safe in the hands of the common state that we have succeeded in evolving, there will be, I believe, no necessity and no cry for separate electorates. The day we long for is yet to come. Between the two great communities of India, there is still 'doubt, hesitation and pain'. Let us recognise, honestly and frankly, the existence of mutual jealousy and suspicion; let us agree to be represented through the medium of separate electorates.[70]

Perhaps such observations were at the back of his mind when the Viceroy concluded that the Lahore session of the League represented 'real Muslim opinion'.[71] Whether it was so at that point of time or not, subsequent developments certainly enabled it to acquire that position.

IV

As per the decision of the Madras session of the Congress (1927), M.A. Ansari, as its president, invited a number of political organizations, including the Muslim League (Jinnah Group), the Hindu Mahasabha and the National Liberal Federation, to send representatives to an All Parties Conference in order to initiate discussions for framing a new constitution for India. The first session of this Conference began in Delhi on 12 February 1928 and continued for ten days, but with the (Jinnah) League and Mahasabha representatives taking opposite stands on the main issues, failed to produce any concrete result. The hardening of the Mahasabha's stand was particularly noticeable: its spokesmen observed that they would rather stick to separate electorates than agree to a redistribution of provinces.[72] Perhaps reacting to it, Jinnah said on 21 February that he had no authority from the League to agree to anything and that what he had said at the conference merely represented his personal views. This shattered Motilal who thought that a number of decisions had already been arrived at on issues which were not so controversial.[73] 'Thus it was', he informed Gandhi, 'that the long sittings and elaborate discussions occupying ten days came practically to nothing.'[74] The Conference adjourned after appointing a committee to meet again on 8 March. Motilal was left wondering whether it might not be better to agree to some kind of separate representation in order to hold together all the conflicting elements of the Conference 'even for a time'.[75]

The same story repeated itself when the adjourned session of the All Parties Conference met in Delhi on 8 March 1928. According to Jawaharlal Nehru, who was present, the Conference witnessed 'a battle of a few extremists on either side—Jinnah and his group on one side and the Hindu Mahasabha on the other—the others had little say except when they got angry'.[76] The Mahasabha leaders again adopted an adamant attitude, reiterating that they considered separate electorates as lesser evil than the creation of new Muslim majority provinces. The Conference, coming to a deadlock, adopted the usual device in such situations and adjourned after appointing two committees, one to examine the financial aspects of the separation of Sind from Bombay and the other to look into the question of the nature of electorates.[77] Jinnah found himself in a rather difficult situation. On the one hand, his hopes of reaching an agreement with the Hindus had failed. On the other, he found himself isolated from the great majority of Muslims both on the subject of boycott of Simon Commission and that of accepting joint electorates.[78] He found a way out by withdrawing the League's representatives from the All Parties Conference and sailing for Britain before its next meeting in Bombay on 19 May.

As the date set for the start of the Bombay session of the Conference came near, Motilal was not amused by the prospect of Jinnah's absence. 'The Muslim League without Jinnah', he observed, 'is impossible to get at and will probably take no part in the Conference.' He was, however, determined to make 'a violent effort' to make the Bombay session a success and not be deterred by the obstructionist attitude of the Hindu Mahasabha:

If we can get the Muslim and Liberal League to be present in respectable numbers we shall achieve the maximum success that can reasonably be achieved. The Hindu Sabha should really have been kicked out in Delhi but if that was not done there is no reason why we should not adopt a stronger attitude in Bombay. To repeat an old story, it is no use allowing a diseased limb to dangle by your side and obstruct your movements. There is I think still a chance of all others coming to some sort of an agreement and we must concentrate upon this.[79]

This was easier said than done. There was no favourable response from the (Jinnah) Muslim League to repeated requests to it to attend the Bombay session. When it became clear the Jinnah would not postpone his departure for Britain in order to participate in the Bombay Conference, Motilal wired him to nominate a person or persons who could deputise for him in his absence, but received no reply.[80] Efforts to persuade other important Muslim League leaders to attend the Conference in their individual capacities also failed in several cases.[81]

The main result of the Bombay session of the All Parties Conference was the appointment of a committee with Motilal Nehru as chairman and nine other members to consider and determine the principles of a constitution for India. In handling its assigned task the committee was expected to give 'fullest consideration' to the resolutions of the Madras Congress (1927) together with those of the Hindu Mahasabha, the Muslim League and other organizations and suggestions that might be made thereafter.[82] Out of the ten members appointed to the Committee the report was signed by only eight—Motilal Nehru, S. Ali Imam, Tej Bahadur Sapru, M.S. Aney, Sardar Mangal Singh, Shuaib Qureshi, Subhas Chandra Bose and G.R. Pradhan.[83] Of the remaining two, M.R. Jayakar resigned at the very start, pleading ill-health, and N.M. Joshi, a trade union leader, neither attended any meeting nor signed the report. Ali Imam, Subhas Chandra Bose and G.R. Pradhan also did not attend most of the meetings. The remaining five—Motilal Nehru, M.S. Aney, Tej Bahadur Sapru, Shuaib Qureshi and Sardar Mangal Singh—attended the meetings of the Committee more or less regularly.[84] Jawaharlal Nehru, though not a member of the Committee, worked closely with his father most of the time, not merely preparing notes for him, but also joining him in drafting the report;[85] he also compiled statistics relating to population figures, community-wise, in different districts of the Punjab and Bengal (given in Appendix A and B of the Report) on the basis of the census of 1921.[86] Although the report of the Committee has been generally known as the Nehru Report after the name of its chairman, who drafted most of it, Tej

Bahadur Sapru also had had a hand in drafting it, particularly those portions of it which dealt with Indian States, Dominion Status versus Responsible Government, and the Depressed Classes.[87]

The Nehru Report, submitted to the president of the All Parties Conference, Ansari, on 10 August 1928, accepted Dominion Status for India and provided for a system of government based on the principles of the rule of law, fundamental rights and parliamentary democracy, with universal adult franchise, both at the centre and in the provinces. The word federation or federal was nowhere used, implying an unitary bias. However, the Report contained detailed lists of subjects specifying the respective jurisdictions of the central and provincial legislatures, with no provision for concurrent powers. It was not indicated where the residuary powers were to lie, again giving rise to the presumption that they were intended to lie with the central government.[88] With regard to the communal and other controversial matters, the Report laid down that there would be joint or mixed electorates throughout India. There would be no reservation of seats for the House of Representatives (lower house at the Centre) except for Muslims in provinces where they were in a minority and for non-Muslims in North-West Frontier Provinces. Such reservation, however, would be in strict proportion to the Muslim population in every province where they were in a minority and in proportion to the non-Muslim population in the North-West Frontier Province. The Muslims or non-Muslims, where seats were reserved for them, would have the right to contest additional seats. As for the provinces, it was laid down that there would be no reservation of seats for any community in the Punjab and Bengal. In provinces other than the Punjab and Bengal there would be reservation of seats for Muslim minorities on population basis, with the right to contest additional seats. In the North-West Frontier Province there would be similar reservation of seats for non-Muslims with the right to contest additional seats. Reservation of seats where provided would be for a fixed period of ten years. Sind would be separated from Bombay and constituted into a separate province after such enquiry into the financial position as might be considered necessary. Parts of Karnataka, except the small islands on the other side of the Mysore territory, would similarly be separated from the provinces in which they were then included and formed into a single, separate province. The North-West Frontier Province, and all newly-formed provinces, would have the same form of government as the other provinces in India.[89]

There was no mention of Baluchistan in the last mentioned recommendation, perhaps by oversight. The omission was rectified by the All Parties Conference at its session at Lucknow (28-31 August 1928), convened to consider the Nehru Report, where it was unanimously resolved to add Baluchistan after North-West Frontier Province.[90] Among the other decisions of the Lucknow All Parties Conference mention may be made of a clearer and stronger support for the separation of Sind from Bombay.[91] Another notable feature of the Lucknow Conference was the support extended to the provisions of the Nehru Report relating to the Punjab by the delegates from that province, including leaders belonging to the Khilafat Conference and the Muslim League (Jinnah Group). A similar support was extended to the provisions relating to Bengal by Akram Khan, the Muslim League leader, and J.M. Sen Gupta of the Congress, respectively on behalf of Muslims and Hindus of Bengal. This was to some extent offset by the observation of Shaukat Ali that the Central Khilafat Committee continued to stand by its earlier stand in favour of reservation of seats for Muslims in the Punjab Legislature and the statement of the Akali leaders, Master Tara Singh and Giani Sher Singh, on behalf of the Sikhs, demanding the introduction of proportional representation in the Punjab.[92]

In spite of such dissenting notes, the proceedings of the Lucknow Conference were, on the whole, marked by an atmosphere of cordiality and bonhomie. The chairman of the Reception Committee, Maharaja of Mahmudabad, who was also an important leader of the (Jinnah) Muslim League, expressed the hope that the members of the Conference, would show the same spirit which had been exhibited by the people who signed the Lucknow Pact in 1916 and that all parties would extend unqualified support to the Nehru Report. Ansari, who as Congress President presided over the Conference, underlined its historical significance as well as that of the publication of the Nehru Report. One of the resolutions adopted by the Conference placed on record the 'grateful appreciation' of the Conference for the work done by the members of the committee who had drafted the Nehru Report. That was moved by Lajpat Rai and supported by a host of speakers including Malaviya, Shaukat Ali, Annie Besant, Mohammad Yakub, Giani Sher Singh and M.C. Chagla. There was only one dissenter, Maulana Hasrat Mohani, who found little in the Report to fall in love with, but had difficulty in completing his speech due to protesting voices raised by other members of the Conference.[93] In an interview to the press on 1 September 1998, Ansari expressed great satisfaction at the success achieved by the Lucknow Conference.[94]

Even outside the Conference, the immediate reactions to the Nehru Report were generally favourable. The Viceroy reported to the Secretary of State shortly after its publication that it had 'a pretty good press in India, even from the English newspapers'. The Viceroy, however, went on to add that most people thought that 90 per cent of Muslim opinion which, according to him, was not represented at the Lucknow Conference, would have nothing to do with joint electorates; even among the remaining 10 per cent, represented by the Khilafatists and Jinnah's followers, there would be some dissensions. As for Jinnah himself (who was still abroad), the Viceroy did not see how he could refuse to accept joint electorates in view of the acceptance in the Nehru Report of the two pre-conditions contained in the Delhi Proposals in March 1927, namely the separation of Sind from Bombay and the extension of constitutional reforms to North-West Frontier Province. There could be some opposition on the ground of incompleteness of reservation (this obviously referred to Punjab and Bengal) but the opponents might compromise by staying away from the All Parties Conference. 'Unless enough of his followers object', the Viceroy surmised, 'Jinnah will, I should guess, swallow the proposals whole.'[95] In another communication to the Secretary of State (meant for Sir John Simon) in the first week of September the Viceroy remarked: 'At the moment the atmosphere, as a result of the Nehru Report and the Lucknow Conference, is one that is temporarily depressing to those who have stood by us.'[96]

This depression was not entirely groundless. Those who had formed a rival Muslim League under Shafi's leadership had, of course, kept away from the Lucknow Conference and made it clear that, apart from other demands, they were not prepared to give up separate electorates under the then existing conditions and further that they wanted statutory majority for Muslims in the legislatures of both the Punjab and Bengal. There was, however, considerable support for the Nehru Report among those Muslim leaders who had participated in the Lucknow Conference. As pointed out by M.C. Chagla, (then Secretary of the Bombay Provincial Muslim League), who was present at the Conference, most of the Muslim League leaders attending it had supported the Nehru Report. Among them were three members of the subcommittee appointed by the League to confer with representatives of other political parties for drafting a constitution for India. Chagla further pointed out that on all the points on which the Nehru Report differed from the League's resolution of December 1927, the former represented an improvement upon the latter from the Muslim point of view. Illustrating this with reference to reservation of seats for the Muslim majority in the Punjab and Bengal, he argued that while with reservation Muslims would secure only 55 per cent of seats, without reservation their share could go up to 65 to 75 per cent. As for the League's demand that Muslims should get one-third of the seats in the Central Legislature, Chagla said that he did not see what difference it made whether Muslims there were one-third or one-fourth. A minority would be a minority even if it were a minority of one. All that the Muslims had to safeguard was their fundamental rights and these were guaranteed to them by the proposed constitution.[97] Similar views were expressed by some of the Khilafatist leaders from the Punjab such as Mohammad Alam and Saifuddin Kitchlu (also one of the secretaries of the All India Muslim League). While the former described the Lucknow Conference as a complete success, the latter described its resolutions regarding the solution of the communal problem as most reasonable and added: 'Joint electorates, no reservation of seats for the majority, reservation of seats for small Hindu and Muslim minorities only for ten years in the provinces, distribution of provinces on linguistic basis and similar other recommendations are bound to create a sense of true nationalism in the country.'[98]

The most prominent Khilafatist leaders, however, were the Ali brothers. Mohamed Ali was in Europe when the Lucknow Conference was held, but Shaukat Ali was present and he turned out to be the most bitter critic of its decisions. 'The ideal of independence and unity', he wrote in course of a lengthy note in *Hamdard* dated 3 September 1928, 'that inspired our hearts and gave us strength has almost vanished after the [Lucknow] session of the All Parties Conference.' Making a personal attack on Ansari, Shaukat Ali asserted that as chairman the former exhibited 'extraordinary magnanimity coupled with weakness' to opponents of Muslim interests, but exactly the opposite to their champions. He further asserted that the treatment meted out to proposals on behalf of representative Muslim organizations by Ansari could not be expected 'even under the chairmanship of an extremely undesirable non-Muslim chairman'. He particularly took objection to the failure of the Conference to provide for statutory Muslim majority in the Punjab Legislative Council. Ansari's rejoinder failed to mollify Shaukat Ali, who again came to the charge and asserted that Motilal Nehru and his Committee had, 'intentionally or unintentionally, treated Muslim point of view with undeserved contempt'.[99] The President of the Central Khilafat Committee, Maulvi Muhammad Shafee Daoodi, also adopted a similar line and accused Ansari of not giving him a chance at the Conference to press for the Muslims in minority provinces to be given reservation for an unlimited period and not only for ten years as decided upon. In another statement he asserted that although Muslims were keen to cooperate with other communities in India in the struggle for freedom, one thing was certain: 'they cannot surrender themselves to the mercy of the party bent upon assuming the role of a dictator and cannot think for a moment that they have to live in India on their sufferance'.[100]

From reports reaching the Viceroy it was clear that an overwhelming majority of politically conscious Muslims thought along similar lines. Before the Lucknow Conference began its deliberations, he informed the Secretary of State that practically all Muslim members of the Assembly were opposed to the Nehru Report.[101] The situation, according to him, remained the same after the Lucknow Conference.[102] Although Motilal Nehru continued to claim, in private as well as publicly, that the report carrying his name was acceptable to the bulk of Muslims of the Punjab and Bengal and that Muslims in the minority provinces could be mollified by some minor concessions',[103] he knew that securing general Muslim approval for the Report was not easy. In such a situation his mind turned to Jinnah who was still in Europe, but expected to return soon. Writing to a common industrialist friend and sympathizer a day before making the above-mentioned claim, Nehru asked him to 'rope in' Jinnah the moment he landed in Bombay. 'So much depends upon Jinnah', he wrote further, 'that I have a mind to go to Bombay to receive him.' If he succeeded in securing the necessary funds within the next few days, he also hoped 'to create a strong opinion among the Mussalmans [in favour of the Nehru Report] to greet Jinnah on his arrival'.[104] However, so strong was the general Muslim dislike of the Nehru Report that it was beyond Nehru's capacity or any one else's to create such an opinion. And Jinnah must have been fully aware of this.

V

It had been an act of great courage on Jinnah's part to have taken the lead in formulating the Delhi Muslim Proposals, involving as they did the offer to give up separate electorates, which Muslims in general had come to regard as their most valuable asset. The offer, however, had been made strictly subject to certain conditions. Although Jinnah continued to stick to that offer in spite of the general Muslim reservation about it, it was too much to expect that, because of his known patriotic fervour and keenness for Hindu-Muslim concord, he could be persuaded to agree to the abolition of separate electorates without the fulfilment of those conditions. Indeed, there is evidence to suggest that much before the publication of the Nehru Report, Jinnah's position as a Muslim leader was becoming shaky, with Muslims increasingly expressing their unhappiness at the offer of giving up separate electorates and the Hindu Mahasabha taking up a rigid stand against the conditions set forth in the Delhi Muslim Proposals for such an offer. 'Everybody who comes to see me', the Viceroy informed the Secretary of State in early March 1928, 'seems to agree on one thing, which is the extreme discomfort in which Jinnah is finding himself, as he contemplates the possibility of being politically swallowed by the Congress Party and forfeiting completely any hold he might have had on Muslims.'[105] After the publication of the Nehru Report and the deliberations of the Lucknow Conference the Viceroy again wrote about Jinnah: 'From several quarters I hear that he is very uncomfortable and it is not quite off the map that he might later find it his duty to return to the Muslim camp and platform.' The Viceroy of course added that he found this difficult to believe for, in his opinion, Jinnah was 'more heavily committed [to joint electorates] than most'.[106] If, however, he was willing to lead a united Muslim party, the large majority of the Muslim members of the Central Assembly would consent to follow him. 'But it would have to be on Muslim majority opinion terms.'[107]

Since withdrawing from the All Parties Conference parleys in March 1928, Jinnah had kept strictly aloof from its proceedings and spent several months abroad since May. When he returned to India in October he left no one close to him in doubt that he was not at all pleased with the Nehru Report. When Chagla went to receive him in his cabin on landing at Bombay he found the latter in a furious mood. 'What right', asked Jinnah, 'did you have to accept the Nehru Report on behalf of the Muslim League? Who authorized you?' After some discussion he agreed to reserve judgement and place the matter for consideration before the Legaue.[108] In the meanwhile, he avoided committing himself either way. A meeting of the League's Council at Lucknow on 11 November 1928 proved inconclusive and contented itself with merely thanking the Nehru Committee and did not record its acceptance of the Nehru Report.[109] The League's annual session held in the last week of December at Calcutta was finally expected to decide this matter, but failed to do so: 'It was composed of warring elements and Jinnah's position was not very strong.'[110] Jinnah was opposed to the Nehru Report but the president of that session, Maharaja of Mahmudabad, was in favour of accepting it;[111] indeed he had already done so at the Lucknow All Parties Conference. The League session resolved the problem by appointing a delegation consisting of 23 of its prominent members to participate in the All Parties National Convention meeting in Calcutta at the same time to give the final approval to the Nehru Report. According to the guideline given to the delegation, it was to 'take into consideration and attach due weight' to the earlier resolutions of the League on the communal question and to endeavour to 'bring about an adjustment of the questions between Hindus and Mussalmans arising out of the Nehru Report'.[112] Both the Maharaja of Mahmudabad and Chagla (who moved the resolution appointing the delegation) underplayed the differences between the Nehru Report and the League's resolution of December 1927 and pointed out that they could be settled through negotiation. Asking those present to approach the subject in a spirit of broad-mindedness, the former observed that the differences between the Hindu majority and the Muslim minority had narrowed themselves down to issues that were 'few and not essentials of any first principles'. According to him, those issues were only three: reservation of seats for Muslims where they were in a majority; whether the constitution should be federal or unitary; and the proportion of reservation for Muslims in the Central Legislature. These were all issues, he emphasized, which could be settled through friendly negotiation.[113] Chagla spoke in a similar vein and emphasized that it was only in two or three respects that the Nehru Report differed from the League's proposals; it would be for the members of the League's delegation to consider whether the modifications introduced by the Nehru Report were more beneficial to Muslims than the League's proposals and how far the Report safeguarded their rights and interests.[114] Jinnah himself did not deliver any speech, but it was clear that Chagla's resolution was his handiwork. When Haji Abdullah Haroon moved an amendment asking for the appointment of a committee to examine the Nehru Report from the point of view of Muslim interests, Jinnah persuaded him to withdraw his amendment.[115] It is remarkable that in spite of differences among the League's leaders present at the Calcutta session, no one harked back to separate electorates.[116]

The League's delegation decided to move a number of amendments to the Nehru Report of which the really important were three: Muslims to be given one-third representation in the Central Legislature; Muslims to have reservation of seats on the basis of their population in the Punjab and Bengal, subject to review after ten years; and residuary powers to be vested in the provincial legislatures. The subcommittee of the National Convention appointed to meet the delegates of the Muslim League and Central Khilafat Committee rejected all these amendments. On centre-province relationship, however, the committee was willing to accommodate Jinnah halfway. While recording its opinion in favour of the residuary powers vesting in the Central Legislature, it had no objection to the revision of the details regarding the distribution of powers between the central and provincial legislatures.[117] Undeterred by that experience, Jinnah moved the same amendments at the open session of the Convention on 28 December 1928. Characterizing the Nehru Report as 'neither helpful nor fruitful in any way whatsoever' and reminding his listeners that the moment was 'very critical and vital to the interest not only of the Mussalmans, but to the whole of India' and that a Hindu-Muslim settlement was 'absolutely essential' to India's progress, he made a most reasoned and forceful presentation.

Speaking first on the demand for the reservation of one-third representation for Muslims in the Central Legislature Jinnah referred to the contention of the authors of the Nehru Report that even without any reservation Muslims were likely to secure one-third of the seats in the Central Legislature. He asserted that the method proposed by the Report was neither fair to the Muslims of the minority provinces nor did it guarantee that Muslims would indeed secure one-third of the seats. For it envisaged the Muslims of the Punjab and Bengal securing more seats in an open contest than their numbers warranted and the Muslims of the minority provinces securing seats reserved strictly according to their proportion of the population. This amounted to giving more to the rich, i.e. the Muslims of the Punjab and Bengal who would in any case secure the largest share of Muslim representation, and restricting the Muslims of the minority provinces to their proportion of the population. Instead of this, Jinnah suggested that Muslims in the Punjab and Bengal be restricted to representation strictly according to their proportion of the population and the surplus distributed among those belonging to the Muslim minority provinces like Bombay, Madras and U.P., 'the centre of Muslim culture and heart'.

Taking up the next Muslim demand that in the event of adult franchise not materializing Muslims in the Punjab and Bengal should have seats reserved for them in the provincial councils on the basis of population, subject to a review after ten years and without the right to contest any more seats, Jinnah drew attention to the patent fact that the Muslim share of representation in the legislatures of those provinces had been much less than their share of the population. He also stressed that the establishment of adult franchise was not within the range of practical politics in the near future. His third important amendment was that the form of the Indian constitution should be federal, with residual powers vesting in the provinces. In this connection he specifically referred to clause 13-A of the Supplementary Report issued by the enlarged Nehru Committee describing it as 'most pernicious' and calling for its deletion and also revision of the schedules included in the Nehru Report specifying the central and provincial subjects. The new clause had made explicit what was implicit in the Nehru Report and provided for sweeping emergency powers for the central government, including the power to suspend or annul an act, legislative as well as executive, of a provincial government. It was also provided that the Supreme Court would have no power to interfere with the actions of the central government under this clause.[118] 'This question', said Jinnah while speaking on relations between the centre and the provinces, 'is by far the most important from the constitutional point of view and the future development of India and has very little do do with the communal aspect.'[119] Although containing an obvious understatement regarding the bearing of the centre-province relationship on the communal problem at that time, these were indeed prophetic words so far as India's constitutional development in general was concerned.

All of Jinnah's reasoned eloquence, however, failed to persuade the overwhelming majority of his listeners totalling about 1,200 and representing diverse parties all over the country. Only Tej Bahadur Sapru, though a member of the Nehru Committee, supported him, but mainly on one point—the demand for one-third Muslim representation in the Central Legislature. Even so, the support was based not on the merit of the demand but on the consideration of satisfying Jinnah in the interest of a settlement. This is what Sapru said:

The simple position is that for the sake of settlement you are invited by Mr. Jinnah, however illogically and unreasonably, to agree to this proposition, which I consider is not inconsistent with the Nehru Report (Voice: 'No' and some interruptions) Speaking for myself I would like you to picture Mr. Jinnah, whom I have known intimately for fifteen years. If he is a spoilt child, a naughty child I am prepared to say, give him what he wants and be finished with it.[120]

As for the reservation of seats for Muslims on the basis of population in the Punjab and Bengal, Sapru asked Jinnah to reconsider his position on that issue. On the issue of centre-province relationship he agreed that there was room for improvement in clause 13-A providing for suspension of the provincial constitution and that the two schedules containing the lists of central and provincial subjects could also be modified. He, however, categorically stated that, having regard to the conditions in India, it would not be wise to vest the residuary powers in the provinces.[121] Speaking immediately after Sapru, C.Y. Chintamani, rose up to announce the decision of the Council of the Liberal Federation making it mandatory for every member of that body present at the Convention to vote for residuary powers being vested in the Centre.[122] Rallia Ram, a leader of the Christian community, who spoke after Sapru, also opposed Jinnah's demand for reservation of seats for Muslims. If that demand was accepted, he said, other communities like the Sikhs, the depressed classes and the Indian Christians would come forward with the same and no 'national unification' could take place.[123] Rev. J.R. Banerjee spoke in the same vein.[124]

The star speaker after Sapru, however, was M.R. Jayakar who, matching Jinnah's reasoned eloquence and speaking from the Hindu point of view, strongly opposed acceptance of his amendments. He argued that a number of prominent Muslim leaders, including those belonging to the Jinnah section of the Muslim League, had already accepted the Nehru Report. On the other hand, 'a large bulk' of Muslims, who were with the rival League led by Shafi were totally opposed to joint electorates. The same applied to some other Muslim leaders, who were going to meet under the presidentship of no less a person than the Aga Khan. There was, therefore, no prospect of winning over the support of the entire Muslim community for the Nehru Report by accepting Jinnah's amendments. On the other hand, many parties and groups had accepted that Report, which was in the nature of a compromise, by surrendering their 'valuable rights and privileges'. In contrast, Jinnah had withdrawn the League's cooperation from the Nehru Committee at an early stage, had gone abroad and, on return, kept completely silent on the merits of the Report. Besides, the Report had behind it 'the greatest common measure of agreement in the country'. If Jinnah's amendments were accepted at that late stage, several other parties might be upset and feel compelled to revive their claims and counter-claims. Jayakar went on to add:

The Report, in other words, is like an edifice which has been completed by careful skill and consideration by the leading men in the country. If you take away any brick—it may [be] three or four—out of the foundations on which it is firmly resting, it is sure to disturb the edifice, and you must not complain if later on you find that the whole structure topples down. . . . It is not so much a question of the Muhammadans getting a few more seats in the Legislature. It is the question of opening the Report once more so as to revive claims which have received a quietus in a spirit of give and take.[125]

Replying to the debate, Jinnah again asked for acceptance of his amendments on the ground that this would help secure wider Muslim support for the Nehru Report and significantly contribute to Hindu-Muslim unity. Making an impassioned plea he observed:

What we want is that Hindus and Mussalmans should march together until our object is attained. Therefore it is essential that you must get not only the Muslim League but the Musalmans of India and here I am not speaking as a Musalman but as an Indian. And it is my desire to see that we get 7 crores of Musalmans to march along with us in the struggle for freedom. Would you be content with a few? Would you be content if I were to say, I am with you? Do you want or do you not want the Muslim India to go along with you?. . . . We are dealing in politics. We are not in a court of law and therefore it is no use resorting to hair-splitting and petty squabbles. These are big questions and they can be settled only by the exercise of the highest order of statesmanship and political wisdom.[126]

Not surprisingly, in view of what had happened the previous evening when the League leaders had met the members of the Convention's subcommittee, consisting of the top leaders of various parties, Jinnah's arguments failed to move the majority of the members of the Convention. All the three amendments moved by him were put to vote and rejected.[127] This was the end of Jinnah's participation in the Convention though it continued till 1 January 1929. Looking sad and disappointed he retired to his hotel after the voting on his amendments on the 28 December 1928 and left Calcutta the next day, remarking to a friend at the railway station: 'This is the parting of the ways.' These words, supposed to have been uttered to a friend (and not recorded anywhere) in a moment of disappointment and conveyed by the latter to a Western author of a hagiographical study of Jinnah more than a quarter of a century later,[128] need not be taken seriously. The same applies to a remark, supposed to have been made by Jinnah in 1938 and recorded by a Pakistani journalist about thirty years later, to the effect that the former had been working for the setting up of a sovereign Muslim State since 1928.[129] As the following pages will show, the erstwhile 'ambassador of Hindu-Muslim Unity',[130] even though leading an avowedly sectional or communal organization, continued to take keen interest in matters of national importance and seek a *modus-vivendi* with the Congress whenever an opportunity presented itself for several years after 1928. It is, therefore, purely imaginary to see the beginning of a major transition in Jinnah's political life in 1928.

Some have argued that the Congress leadership acted foolishly by not supporting Jinnah's three amendments to the Nehru Report at the National Convention. For the acceptance of those amendments would have resulted in the abolition of separate electorates, thereby ruling out the possibility of Partition. Ironically, one of the most prominent protagonists of this view has been Khaliquzzaman who, from his base in U.P., actively worked for several years in the movement for Pakistan, migrated to it shortly after its creation and held several high positions there:

> The heavens would not have fallen if a few amendments that were proposed had been generously accepted and the sad chapter of communal bickering and disharmony closed. The shortsightedness of Hindu politicians on this occasion could not be surpassed. The Muslims had offered to deprive themselves of the most valuable right of separate electorates in favour of joint electorates, which farsighted statesmanship would have tried to secure at any cost, but events were leading up to something else which fate had ordained.[131]

This has been written on the basis of hindsight. But even in December 1928 it was not difficult to imagine that his failure to secure the desired terms for Muslims at the National Convention would leave no option for Jinnah—unless he was prepared to commit political suicide or give up his long-cherished aspiration of leading the Muslims—but to join hands with Shafi and others like him who were strongly attached to separate electorates as well as anti-Congressism. The point to consider then is why no serious attempt was made by Motilal Nehru and others working with him in the All Parties Conference and Convention to persuade the majority to accept Jinnah's amendments, thereby securing his support for the replacement of separate by mixed electorates—the prize which all Congress and Hindu leaders so keenly desired and which was so vital for India's future. The reasons for their negative approach were spelled out in Jayakar's speech opposing Jinnah's amendments. That must have been the reason why Motilal did not feel the need for speaking up himself in the debate. Those reasons briefly were that it was too late in the day to introduce any significant change in the proposed constitutional structure built up after lengthy consultations with so many leaders and groups. Then there was the question of how much support could Jinnah muster among Muslims for the Nehru Report even after his amendments had been accepted, for as was generally estimated, an overwhelming majority of politically conscious Muslims remained firmly wedded to separate electorates. The greatest difficulty was the stiff Hindu and Sikh opposition to the price for hypothetical giving up of separate electorates. As the 1926 elections had shown, communal sentiments had established a firm foothold among the Hindus and the Hindu Mahasabha had emerged as a powerful force in Indian politics. On the other hand, general Muslim support for mixed electorates, even with Jinnah's help, was extremely doubtful. In such a situation, the leaders of the All Parties Conference decided that they should retain Hindu and Sikh support and not do anything to lose it. Indeed, the decision had been taken much before the meeting of the National Convention. Jinnah's style of dealing with the All Parties Conference was also not such as to create confidence among Congress leaders regarding his likely moves. A certain feeling of distrust in his intentions was shared by a number of top Congress leaders. This was caused primarily by the fact that while deeply attached to the cause of Hindu-Muslim unity as well as to India's freedom, he was equally, or perhaps even more, attached to his position of supreme leadership of the Muslim community and not prepared to do anything to compromise it in any way. Thus, while anxiously waiting for Jinnah to land in Bombay in October 1928 and hoping against hope that somehow he might be persuaded to extend his support to the Nehru Report, Motilal wrote to Gandhi:

> But for one weakness he is thoroughly sound. He is always afraid of losing his leadership and avoids taking any risks in the matter. This weakness often drives him to support the most reactionary proposals. In reality he has no following at all and his so-called followers are men who fully understand his weakness and bend him to their own will. After he has played into their hands, it pays them to groom him as a great leader of the Mussalmans. He

cannot of course always defend his attitude when talking freely with me and other friends. His one explanation is: 'My dear fellow I have to take these fools with me.'[132]

Minus Motilal's lampooning of the relationship between Jinnah and his followers, Ansari's attitude towards Jinnah was not very different. Referring to Jinnah's possible intentions in the summer of 1927, for instance, he wrote thus to Sarojini Naidu, one of Jinnah's greatest admirers in the Congress: 'I believe he is a nationalist at heart, turned into a communalist by the exigencies of the time (like Jayakar), but I have little faith in any one who can change his conviction so readily to suit the circumstances.'[133] Jinnah's haughty and disdainful manners created a further barrier between him and the top Congress leaders.

Jinnah's haughtiness was, of course, more than evenly matched by Motilal Nehru's arrogance. Thus, elated by the prospect of support by the Khilafatist leaders in the Punjab and Bengal for the Nehru Report, he remarked in a private letter that after that whatever remained of the Hindu-Muslim question would be easily settled 'by throwing a few crumbs here and there to the small minorities'.[134] Little did he realize that Muslims of the minority provinces had more than the required strength to create a hostile atmosphere for the Nehru Report in the whole country so far as the Muslims were concerned.[135] It is significant that of the two chief campaigners against the Nehru Report—Shaukat Ali and Shafee Daoodi—one came from U.P. and the other from Bihar. When Ansari remarked that Motilal's 'cold reception' to Jinnah whom Ansari had persuaded to call on the former at the time of the sessions of the National Convention, had been 'a great disappointment', Motilal replied: 'What Mr. Jinnah said on the occasion left me cold and I could not work up an artificial warmth to please him.'[136]

The heart of the matter was that if Jinnah had his compulsions, so had Motilal Nehru and his close colleagues. Indeed what Motilal wrote about the former applied, again minus the lampooning, equally to him. In the post-Khilafat, and more particularly post-1926 India, Motilal could not ignore strong Hindu and Sikh opposition to reservation for majorities (which the League demanded for Muslims in the Punjab and Bengal), especially when it was not certain that even with that concession most Muslims would agree to give up separate electorates. The Punjab issue was the most crucial. If there was provision of reservation for Muslim majority, the Sikhs were not prepared to give up their claim to reservation and, as a minority, reservation with weightage. But if this was conceded, it might not be possible to ensure Muslim majority. For Hindus, too, were, a minority in the Punjab and they would not agree to part with seats from their quota to meet the Sikh claims. Weightage for Muslims in the minority provinces also became difficult to retain for the same reason. For if this was done, how could the Sikhs be denied weightage in the Punjab. In this connection it must be remembered that the Madras Congress Session (1927), while accepting the Delhi Muslim Proposals, had specifically mentioned that in case of weightage, the guiding principle would be reciprocity, and further that in the event of reservation being provided for Muslims in the Punjab, due consideration would be given to the representation of the Sikhs 'as an important minority'. Besides, while the Muslims preferred a weak centre or a centre with limited powers, all others preferred just the opposite. Only on one point, i.e. one-third representation for Muslims in the Central Legislature—supported also by Sapru—it might have been possible for Motilal to accommodate Jinnah. He had had a secret understanding with Lala Lajpat Rai, who had played a crucial role in securing the support of the Hindu Mahasabha for the Nehru Report, that while during the run up to the National Convention the latter would go on taking a hard line on all the Muslim demands so that these could be reduced to the minimum at the Convention, he would try to persuade the Hindu Mahasabha delegates to agree to that one demand. As fate would have had it, however, Lajpat Rai passed away before the meeting of the National Convention and the Hindu delegates, going by his public stance during the last days of his life, stood firmly against all of Jinnah's major amendments, including the one dealing with one-third Muslim representation at the centre. Motilal talked to some important Hindu Mahasabha leaders. Jayakar was agreeable, provided the other Muslim demands were given up. This was also more or less the position of Moonje. But Malaviya took the line that such a concession would not go well with the majority of Hindus. So Motilal decided to remain silent at the Convention even though remaining convinced that one-third Muslim representation in the Central Legislature would not make any practical difference to the Hindu majority therein.[137] Even if he had broken his silence and spoken, like Sapru, in favour of this demand, that would not have made any significant difference to the outcome. For it is doubtful whether the majority at the Convention would have agreed with him, particularly in the absence of support from any powerful Hindu leader. And, according to a resolution of the All Parties Conference at Lucknow (August 1928) which had approved the Nehru Report, any change in that Report could be brought about only by 'the consent and agreement of all the parties'.[138]

Almost all important leaders of the Congress understood the hard reality, namely the indispensability of general Hindu support for any successful effort at constitution-making, and fully supported the Nehru Report regardless of their misgivings on one point or another. More than a year after the conclusion of the National Convention, Ansari who, as President of the Congress in 1928, had presided over both the All Parties Conference at Lucknow and the National Convention at Calcutta and was in a key position to influence their decisions as well as the contents of the Nehru Report, surmised that the failure to secure Muslim approval for the Nehru report had been caused primarily by the inability of the Congress leadership to firmly stick to the resolution of the Madras Congress Session (1927) on the communal problem:

> I have not the slightest doubt that if we had stuck to it we could have gradually overcome the opposition of the Hindu Mahasabha and Hindu-Muslim unity would have been an accomplished fact by now. But, we wanted to be just and fair and in our effort to do justice and bring greater harmony and unity in the shape of the Nehru Constitution, I am afraid we lost at Lucknow and Calcutta what we had gained at Madras.[139]

This was, however, wisdom after the event. While the Nehru Report was under preparation Ansari had fully backed the elder Nehru. The most important departure in the Nehru Report from the Delhi Muslim Proposals related to reservation of seats for the Muslim majority in the Punjab and Bengal. Shaukat Ali was not wrong when he accused Ansari of pressurizing Shuaib Qureshi, a member of the Nehru Committee, not to insist on such reservation.[140] As Motilal informed Gandhi, facing an impasse on this issue, particularly because Sapru also supported Qureshi, he (Motilal) called in Ansari, who was 'very favourably impressed' with the provisions in the draft Nehru Report prepared by Motilal regarding the Punjab and Bengal and 'spent two days in trying to convince Shuaib'.[141] The latter was, of course, not convinced. Qureshi's viewpoint was shared by several Muslim leaders, notably Shaukat Ali and Shafee Daoodi.[142] Regardless of such opinions Ansari was full of undiluted praise for the Nehru Report. This is, for instance, how he referred to it in his presidential remarks at the All Parties Conference at Lucknow (August 1928) especially convened to consider it:

India has gone through many and varied phases of the struggle for liberty, but never in the chequered history of this country's fight for freedom had representatives of all schools of political thought assembled together to draw up a definite scheme of our constitution. That has now been done by the [Nehru] Committee. It is in itself a historic event, and when we see the background of the dark events of the last few years, resulting in the spasmodic and ineffective attempts to introduce some light into the darkness of wilderness, of confused aims and objects in which we had lost ourselves, and of complacent challenges that were being thrown at us both from within the country and beyond the seven seas, I need hardly tell you that that Report becomes a doubly historic event.[143]

After the conclusion of the Lucknow Conference, Ansari spoke on 1 September 1928, with a tremendous sense of fulfilment: 'It has been the proudest day of my life to feel that Providence bestowed on me this good fortune. It was far more than I deserved. I feel that my life work, i.e. the bringing of the unity of all people has been achieved.'[144] When Shaukat Ali criticized the Nehru Report for not honouring the earlier decision of the Congress so far as Muslim demands were concerned, Ansari asked 'if a better alternative be handy, why should it not be adopted'?[145] Again, in his presidential address to the All Parties National Convention delivered on 22 December 1928, he described the criticism of the recommendations of the Nehru Report in certain Muslim circles as 'based on ignorance of the real import of the recommendations and on a confusion of the rights of the minorities with the principles of representation'. He, of course, admitted that minorities had their concerns and they had been protected in other countries of the world, but asserted that the constitution outlined in the Nehru Report gave to Indian minorities 'more real and solid safeguards' than had been granted by the League of Nations to the newly constituted states of Europe.[146]

The other leader who could have influenced the Nehru Committee, particularly its chairman, was Gandhi. Although in semi-retirement from politics and seldom opening his mouth on Hindu-Muslim questions in public, he continued to be looked upon by Motilal Nehru as a great source of support and kept informed by him of the major developments in politics behind the scenes. In one of his letters to Motilal as early as the first week of March 1928, Gandhi clearly stated that although he himself was opposed to both separate electorates and reservation, he did not see how the Congress could back out of the commitment made in its resolutions on the latter:

I am of the same opinion that I expressed years ago at Delhi that we should not be party to separate electorates or to reservation of seats, the latter should be by mutual voluntary arrangement if such is necessary. But unless the Mussalmans agree, there is no going back by us on reservation of seats. The Congress is committed to it. I think, therefore, that we must simply adhere to the Congress resolution and expect Hindus and Mussalmans to carry out that resolution. If the All Parties Conference cannot discover another method acceptable to all, we must simply work out the Congress formula.[147]

After the publication of the Nehru Report, however, Gandhi hastened to extend his public congratulations to Motilal and his colleagues for bringing out 'the very able and practically unanimous report' on a very vexed question. Although the Report had departed from the earlier Congress stand on reservation of seats for Muslims and it was by no means clear that the formula devised by it—adult franchise—was acceptable to all as a substitute for it, that did not in any way affect the warmth of Gandhi's congratulations. 'In the matter of the constitution', he observed, 'the main thing was not to present perfect recommendations but to secure unanimity for the recommendations that might in the circumstances be considered the best possible.'[148] At the National Convention he was a great source of support to Motilal, whose pressing request had been primarily responsible for his presence in Calcutta at that time.[149]

That leaders like Ansari and Gandhi considered it their duty to back Motilal Nehru so unreservedly shows that they realized that he had done the best under the then prevailing circumstances and that the Nehru Report could not be significantly improved upon from the point of view of safeguarding the interests of the minorities in the face of opposition on the part of the majority. The authors of the Nehru Report, however, sought to sugar-coat this hard reality by referring to lofty principles or ideals, going to the extent of underestimating the seriousness of the communal problem itself. 'If the fullest religious liberty is given', it was observed in Chapter II of the Report 'and cultural autonomy provided for, the communal problem is in effect solved, though people may not realise it.'[150] In the next chapter, the Report emphasized that once India became free the communal problem would cease to occupy the centre of the stage and parties would be formed in the country chiefly on the basis of economic programmes. 'We shall then find Hindus and Muslims and Sikhs in one party acting together and opposing another party which also consists of Hindus and Muslims and Sikhs. This is bound to happen if we once get going.'[151] Observations like these have led several scholars in recent years to conclude that the authors of the Nehru Report had no understanding of communal problem in India and that they were generally guided by abstract considerations in complete disregard of the then existing situation in India. Others have imagined the preponderant influence of the younger Nehru on his father as the likely cause of such fascination for abstract principles. Actually the authors of the Nehru Report were firmly grounded in reality and knew what they were doing. They realized that they could not ignore the sentiments of Hindus, the mainstay of Indian nationalism and constituting the overwhelming majority in the Congress, especially when their demands were strictly in conformity with the principles and practices of democratic government to which the Congress had been traditionally committed. They particularly saw no reason to do so in order to satisfy a section of Muslim opinion, which in any case did not reflect the sentiments of politically conscious Muslims in general, wedded as the latter were irrevocably to separate electorates and dependence on the British authorities for safeguarding their interests. There is no doubt that the Nehru Report signally failed to solve the communal problem and bring the Hindus and Muslims together and indeed left behind a trail of unprecedented acrimony and bitterness among them. The main cause of this failure, however, has to be seen not in the failure of the Congress leadership to stand up to the Hindu Mahasabha, or lack of understanding of the nature of the communal problem in India on the part of its authors, or the undue influence of the younger on the elder Nehru, as has been done in some recent studies,[152] but in the irreconcilable claims and counter-claims made on behalf of not two, as heretofore, but three major communities of India (Hindus, Muslims and Sikhs) and the obvious compulsions of the Congress leadership.

VI

While the All Parties National Convention was coming to a close, arrangements were proceeding to hold the first session of the All Parties Muslim Conference, which began in Delhi on 31 December 1928, under the presidentship of the Aga Khan, who had returned to lead the Indian Muslims after a lapse of 15 years. The initiative for holding this conference had been taken, in the context of the widespread Muslim discontent with the Nehru Report, by the Shafi section of the Muslim League together with some prominent Khilafatist leaders and Muslim members of the central and provincial legislatures, who felt the need for an united Muslim organization to articulate the sentiments and demands of the Indian Muslims more effectively than was possible through the then existing Muslim organizations, including the two sections of the Muslim League. With the exception of leaders from the Jinnah section the Muslim League and the Congress, almost all other important Muslim leaders, including those belonging to the Jamiat-ul-Ulama-i-Hind, participated in its deliberations. The presence of a large number of Muslim legislators, both from the centre and the provinces, added significantly to the representative character of the conference.[153] Its most important result was the formulation of certain principles which, the Conference declared, must be incorporated in a constitution if it was to be accepted by the Muslims:

1. A federal system of government with complete autonomy and residuary powers for the constituent states, the central government having control only of such matters of common interest as might be specifically entrusted to it by the constitution.
2. No bill or resolution regarding inter-communal matters to be moved, discussed or passed by any legislature, central or provincial, if this was opposed by three-fourth majority of the members of either Hindu or Muslim community affected by it.
3. Muslims not to be deprived of their right, without their consent, to elect their representatives, which under the then existing conditions were essential for a really representative government.
4. Muslims to have their due share in central and provincial cabinets.
5. In Muslim majority provinces, Muslims to have majority in the legislature and other statutory self-governing bodies.
6. In provinces where Muslims were in a minority, they were to continue to have the same representation which they enjoyed at that time.
7. Muslims to have the right of one-third representation in the central legislature.
8. Sind to be constituted into a separate province with the Hindu minority therein being given special representation in the legislature similar to that enjoyed by the Muslims where they were in a minority.
9. Constitutional reforms to be introduced in North-West Frontier Province and Baluchistan with Hindu minorities therein being given adequate and effective representation in the legislatures.

10. Muslims to be given adequate share in all services of the state and on all statutory self-governing bodies, having due regard to the requirements of efficiency.
11. Adequate safeguards to be provided for protection and promotion of Muslim education, language, religion, personal law and charitable institutions, with due share in grants-in-aid.
12. No change in the constitution to be possible without the concurrence of all the units constituting the Indian Federation.[154]

These principles became the guiding lights of the bulk of the politically minded Muslims in their negotiations with the Government as well as the Congress during the next six-seven years (1929-35). These were also the years when the All India Muslim Conference, meeting from year to year, continued its existence and functioned as the dominant or most representative organization of Indian Muslims, superceding, though not supplanting, the Muslim League and other organizations engaged in protecting or promoting Muslim interests. The fact that it had, among its constituents, most of the Muslim members of the central and provincial legislatures added to its strength and helped to underline its representative character. The patronage of the Aga Khan, who was a venerable figure among the Muslim elite since the days of the Simla Deputation (1906) and had a good rapport with some of the leading political figures in Britain, ensured British recognition and support for the Muslim Conference. This went far in strengthening its position among the Muslim elite, who, except during the heyday of the Khilafat movement, always had an eye for such support. The Muslim Conference generally worked under the guidance of Fazl-i-Husain, a towering personality with exceptional political abilities, who had shown his mettle in the Punjab and, after a distinguished career there both as a Minister and a Member of the Governor's Executive Council, been appointed a Member of the Viceroy's Executive Council in 1930. This not only ensured the Government's continuing recognition and support, but also enabled the various sections represented in it to work together as a cohesive force. The devoted labours of Maulvi Muhammad Shafee Daoodi, an old veteran of the Khilafat Movement and a former Congressman and Swarajist, who became the organizing secretary of the Conference, contributed a good deal to its continued functioning from day to day.[155]

Jinnah was the one important Muslims leader conspicuous by his absence from the Muslim Conference and his section of the Muslim League the one important Muslim organization not represented there.

He obviously looked upon his section of the Muslim League as the most representative organization of the Indian Muslims, with himself as its most authentic spokesman, and saw no reason to contribute to the emergence of another organization with similar claims. Thus replying to the letter of invitation sent by the Secretary of the Muslim Conference Jinnah, while keeping his final decision pending until the forthcoming session of the Muslim League and in the meanwhile seeking certain clarifications, made it clear that he did not think there was 'any reason or occasion' for the convening of such a conference and that in his opinion 'everybody should rally round the All India Muslim League'.[156] At its annual session held in Calcutta in the last week of December 1928, the League echoed these sentiments and recorded that 'it would be disastrous to Muslim interests if rival and ad-hoc organizations of the nature of the Conference were set up at every crisis in the history of the community'.[157] So far, however, as the approach to the Hindu-Muslim question was concerned there was no major difference now between the National Conference and the Jinnah section of the Muslim League or between their top leaders, the Aga Khan on the one hand and Jinnah on the other: both were bound together by a deep distrust of the Congress. Commenting on the success of the first session of the Muslim Conference (1928) the Aga Khan observes:

> The unanimity of this Conference was especially significant, for it marked the return—long delayed and for the moment private and with no public avowal of this change of mind—of Mr. M.A. Jinnah to agreement with his fellow-Muslims. Mr. Jinnah had attended the Congress Party's [actually the National Convention's] meeting in Calcutta shortly before, and had come to the conclusion that for him there was no future in Congress or in any camp—allegedly on an all-India basis—which was in fact Hindu dominated. We had at last won him over to our view.[158]

Jinnah's change of mind did not remain secret for long. The widespread Muslim hostility towards the Nehru Report, particularly after the outright rejection of his proposed amendments to it by the National Convention and the success of the All India Muslim Conference did not leave him much choice in the matter, especially in view of the growing question mark on his credibility as a Muslim leader. As has been pointed out by Sharif al Mujahid in his admiring critique of Jinnah's political role, 'these two developments not only seriously undermined but even controverted most demonstrably Jinnah's claim to League, not to speak of Muslim, leadership'.[159] Jinnah, of course, still remained the unchallenged leader of his section of the Muslim League, though not of the undivided League or the Muslims of India as a whole. The problem, however, was that the section of the League led by him had been deserted by many of its earstwhile leaders and those who remained were sharply divided among the ones who were for supporting the Nehru Report, subject to the incorporation in it of Jinnah's amendments, and others who were totally opposed to it.[160] The thinning of its ranks as well as the divisions therein were vividly exposed to public gaze when efforts to hold the adjourned session (December 1928, Calcutta) of the League in Delhi in March 1929 dismally failed and the session had to be adjourned again because of irreconcilable differences among those present.[161] It had to remain in that condition till the next session in December 1930. The only concrete result of the Delhi Session was the formulation and enunciation, by Jinnah, though not their acceptance by that session (because of its adjournment), of his famous Fourteen Points in the shape of a draft resolution. Actually the points numbered fifteen, but '*Fourteen Points*' became famous perhaps because that looked more impressive, conforming as they did in form to President Wilson's celebrated Fourteen Points.[162] The last point mentioned that in the then existing circumstances separate electorates for Muslims were inevitable and could not be abolished without their consent. Such consent, it was further stipulated, would not be available until the Muslims were satisfied that their rights and interests were satisfied in the manner indicated in the other points. The latter were substantially the same as the principles enunciated by the All Parties Muslim Conference held earlier under the chairmanship of the Aga Khan. There was only one difference. While the All Parties Muslim Conference had demanded due representation of Muslims in all cabinets, central and provincial, Jinnah demanded that no cabinet, whether central or provincial, was to be formed without at least one-third of its members being Muslims.[163] Unlike the Delhi Muslim Proposals, therefore, the so-called Fourteen Points represented Jinnah's efforts, not to bridge the gulf between the Hindus and Muslims, but to reunite the Muslims under his own leadership. That was the reason why those points incorporated with slight cosmetic changes here and there, all the principles enunciated by the All Parties Muslim Conference in Delhi held earlier. Jinnah himself thus explained the background of those Points while moving his draft resolution before the adjourned session of the League on 30 March 1929:

I want to make one thing quite clear. There is an impression that the draft resolution which I put before the Council of the League contains my personal ideas. That is not correct. I have only carried out the task entrusted to me by the Council on the 3rd of March to consult the various groups and schools of thought as far as possible and place before them a draft which would command the support of a large body of people. I have, therefore, taken the ideas from various persons in accordance with these instructions and, to the best of my ability and judgement, I have tried to place a draft which in my opinion carries with it the majority's opinions.[164]

The formal merger of the Shafi section of the League with the League led by Jinnah did not take place before February 1930,[165] but there is no doubt that so far as their attitude towards the Hindu-Muslim question was concerned, the two Leagues were practically united by March 1929 when Jinnah's Fifteen or Fourteen Points were enunciated.[166] Even the reunited League, however, was no match for the All India Muslim Conference where Fazl-i-Husain called the tune. Jinnah's credentials as a Muslim leader continued to carry a question mark for several years more. This was due as much to his recent efforts for Hindu-Muslim understanding, even at the cost of separate electorates, as to his continued interest in speeding up India's advance towards Dominion Status, an objective for which the Congress leaders too were working. Most of the Muslim politicians, particularly in Muslim majority provinces, were keen on constitutional advance in the provinces and not at all interested in the early establishment of Dominion Status, which would inevitably result in the emergence of a Hindu-dominated centre. This was clearly the position of the Punjabi Muslim leadership, headed by Fazl-i-Husain, and most of the Muslim politicians, active in the provincial arena, subscribed to it. Besides, for achieving their objective, they banked more on British support than on joining hands with the Congress for mounting combined pressure on the British. Jinnah, on the other hand, even while underlining his rejection of the Nehru Report and on the way to formulating his Fourteen Points, joined hands with the Congress and Hindu leaders in defeating the Government in Central Assembly in early March 1929 on the issue of the '*National Demand*' for early Dominion Status spearheaded by Motilal Nehru. This indeed led the Viceroy to guess that in the renewed efforts which the Congress leaders were expected to make soon to arrive at some accommodation with dominant Muslim opinion, alienated by the Nehru Report, on the constitutional issue, they would have 'the earnest support of Jinnah'.[167]

Motilal Nehru, however, had no use for Jinnah, especially after he had raised his terms for a settlement, through his Fourteen Points. Instead, Nehru looked for support to the newly formed All India Muslim Nationalist Party, consisting largely of Muslims belonging to the Congress, and formed by the All India Nationalist Muslim Conference held at Allahabad in July 1929, under the presidentship of Abul Kalam Azad. Its objects, amongst others, were 'to promote among Muslims a spirit of nationalism, to develop a mentality above communalism, and to inspire in them greater confidence in Indian national ideas'.[168] When Gandhi could not get anything positive from meeting Jinnah on 12 August 1929, as also the Ali brothers (at the prompting of Sarojini Naidu), and remarked that his mind was 'in a whirl' and the atmosphere 'too foggy' for him to see clearly,[169] Motilal commented:

> He [Jinnah] is simply trying to reinstate himself with his followers by making preposterous demands. I can understand the atmosphere being too foggy for you but I am quite clear in my own mind that the only way to reach a compromise with the truly nationalist Mussalmans is to ignore Mr. Jinnah and the Ali brothers completely. All three of them are totally discredited and have no following worth the name.[170]

Parallel to the adoption by leaders like Jinnah and the Ali brothers of the line chalked out by the Aga Khan and Shafi was the stiffening of the negative attitude of the Hindu Mahasabha leaders towards a settlement of the communal problem. This was illustrated by the proceedings of the Surat session of that organization (30 March to 1 April 1929), when it went back on its acceptance of the Nehru Report and insisted on uniformity of franchise for all communities in every province and representation through mixed electorates everywhere without any kind of reservation.[171] It is not, therefore, surprising that even some prominent Congress Muslim leaders came to believe that the communal feeling had become as strong among the Hindus as among the Muslims. Thus wrote Mazharul Haq to Ansari:

> I entirely agree with you that the Hindus are as much communalists as the Muslims. In my long life I have come to the conclusion that there is nothing to choose between the two. The only difference that I find between the two is that the Hindus are more united and more organised and that they have developed a political sense for their community. I wish to God that we had also the same sight to see things clearly.[172]

With this understanding of the Hindu mind Haq, whose devotion to the cause of Hindu-Muslim unity had become legendary, at any rate in Bihar, his home-province, was now giving priority to the cause of unity among Muslims. 'The first thing that I would urge', he wrote further to Ansari, 'is to bring about reconciliation between the opposing forces among the Muslims.' It may, however, be mentioned here that although Haq did not qualify the word 'Muslims', his main pre-occupation seems to have been unity among those Muslim leaders who had earlier worked together with the Congress. His feeling was that if four or five Muslim leaders became friends again such unity could be achieved. In this connection he thought first of ending the alienation of the Ali brothers from the nationalist camp and offered his own services in the matter.[173] Ansari's response to this suggestion underlines the wide gulf which had by then emerged between the two sections of Muslim leaders earlier wedded to the Congress ideology and programme and led respectively by the Ali brothers on the one hand and Ansari and Azad on the other. According to Ansari a compromise between the two sections was 'very difficult, if not impossible'. In this connection he recalled that he and his friends had made several attempts during the past year—at Lucknow, Patna and Calcutta—to come to an understanding with the Ali brothers, but failed. They had drifted apart 'gradually but surely', and finally the Ali brothers found themselves in the company of leaders like the Aga Khan and Shafi. Ansari ruefully added:

> The willingness with which they [the Ali brothers] associated themselves with people whose only distinction is that they have always been reactionary in regard both to Indian and Muslim affairs was surprising. Mohammad Ali actually seconded the resolution proposed by Sir Mohammad Shafi at the All Parties Muslim Conference at Delhi. The Ali brothers still stand by the resolution which no sensible Indian can entertain seriously but which they regard as the minimum of Muslim demands. This is not all. They have developed a point of view from which everything that is said or done by a Hindu or Nationalist Muslim appears to them to be the direct result of Hindu Mahasabha influence. Their new mentality admits of only two divisions in India, Hindu and Muslim, and not Nationalist and reactionary or non-cooperating and cooperating.[174]

VII

While communalism was thus gaining ground among both Hindus and Muslims the Congress turned its attention to launching another mass struggle for accelerating the march to freedom. This had been predicated as early as December 1928 by the Calcutta session of the

Congress which had considered the Nehru Report. That report, as indicated earlier, had prepared the framework of a constitution for India on the basis of Dominion Status, but several younger leaders of the Congress, notably Jawaharlal Nehru, Subhas Chandra Bose and Srinivas Iyengar, considered that derogatory to India and wanted the Congress to demand 'Complete Independence'. With Gandhi's active intervention, a compromise was worked out at the Calcutta Congress under which Dominion Status might be acceptable to the Congress if offered before the end of 1929. However, if such an offer did not materialize, the Nehru Report would lapse and the Congress would adopt complete independence as its goal and start a campaign of civil disobedience in order to achieve it. As the end of 1929 drew close, therefore, these decisions appeared imminent. Although moving close to the Aga Khan and Shafi on the line to be adopted on the communal problem, Jinnah, unlike those leaders, was as keenly interested in the early inauguration of self-government on the basis of Dominion Status as were the top Congress leaders like Gandhi, Motilal and Ansari. On the other hand, he did not relish the start of a civil disobedience movement, but wanted that objective to be secured through discussion and negotiation between the British and Indian leaders. Thus on 19 June 1929, he wrote to the new British Prime Minister, Ramsay MacDonald drawing attention to the developing political situation in India, particularly the growing momentum of the independence movement, and underlining the urgency of taking effective steps to restore India's faith in Britain. In particular Jinnah suggested two measures: a declaration of British policy of granting self-government to India on the basis of Dominion Status and the convening of a conference in London consisting of prominent Indian leaders and British officials for devising a suitable constitutional scheme for that purpose.[175] Later on, when the Viceroy's announcement on 1 November 1929 about the convening of a Round Table Conference in London as also the declaration that in Britain's view the attainment by India of Dominion Status was the natural issue of India's constitutional advance failed to satisfy the Congress, Jinnah did whatever he could to break the impasse between the Congress and the Government. On the one hand, he met the Patel brothers, Vithalbhai and Vallabhbhai, in Bombay in the second week of November and urged them to use their influence with Gandhi to moderate his stand, or, at any rate, persuade him to talk to Jinnah and the elder Patel—Vithalbhai—before taking the final plunge towards civil disobedience.[176] On the other hand, he joined hands with Sapru and Vithalbhai Patel in urging the Viceroy to hold a conference with Gandhi and Motilal along with themselves with a view to breaking that impasse.[177] Such a conference, held in Delhi on 23 December 1929, failed to produce the desired result. Gandhi and Nehru insisted on a firm commitment by the Viceroy that the purpose of the proposed Round Table Conference would be to frame a constitution on the basis of Dominion Status. When the Viceroy found himself unable to do so, Jinnah joined Sapru in urging Gandhi and Nehru to agree to Congress participation in the Round Table Conference regardless of this difficulty, but to no avail.[178] Jinnah naturally felt quite unhappy and bitter at the failure of all his efforts to avert civil disobedience and prepare the ground for substantial constitutional advance towards self-government, at the centre as well as in the provinces, through discussion and negotiation between Indian leaders and British representatives. This further deepened his alienation from the Congress leadership.[179]

Among other prominent leaders made unhappy by the failure of the talks with the Viceroy, the most important, from the Congress point of view, was Ansari, the leader of the Congress Muslims and founder of the Muslim Nationalist Party.[180] He was not happy when the Lahore Congress session (December 1929-January 1930) decided to jettison the Nehru Report, adopt complete independence as its goal and launch a campaign of civil disobedience with that aim in view. Although, out of loyalty to old colleagues, particularly Gandhi and the elder Nehru, he did not publicly oppose those decisions, he disassociated himself from all executive positions in the Congress, declining to be General Secretary and member of the Working Committee and resigning from the presidentship as also the membership of the executive of the Delhi Provincial Congress Committee. With his deep attachment to Congress as well as Indian nationalism, he could not countenance any step beyond this. As he explained to one of the prominent nationalist Muslim leaders of U.P., he and persons of his way of thinking could not think of leaving the Congress or weakening it in any way. Stressing that in any democratic institution the will of the majority must prevail, he added: 'To leave the Congress would be to commit political suicide, to oppose the Congress would be a crime'. According to him, the nationalist Muslims had no other option left to them except to continue in the Congress, without holding any executive position in it, and do their best to strengthen the recently formed Muslim Nationalist Party, the only channel left for their political activities. For they could join neither the liberals, who did not believe in any action apart from passing resolutions and signing protests nor the Muslim communalists from whom they had extricated themselves 'with the greatest difficulty and a good deal of struggle'.[181]

At the same time Ansari considered it his duty to make a last ditch effort to persuade Gandhi and other leaders at the helm of the Congress to desist from launching the projected civil disobedience movement in the then prevailing situation, particularly on the communal front. 'Hindu-Muslim unity', he reminded Gandhi, on the eve of the meeting of the Congress Working Committee called for drawing up the programme for the ensuing movement, 'is not only one of the basic items in our programme, but according to my firm belief and conviction, *the one and only* basic thing'. Recapitulating the efforts made for a settlement of the communal problem since 1927 and their failure and also taking into account such other factors as the enrolment of members and volunteers for the Congress and collection of funds he emphasized that the country was 'not the least ready for starting a campaign of civil disobedience in any shape or form'. This view was supported on the basis of a detailed comparative analysis of the political situation in 1930 and 1920 when the non-cooperation movement had been launched, leading to the conclusion that the situation in 1930 was 'quite the reverse of what it was in 1920'. One of the five points included in this analysis—the second—related to Hindu-Muslim unity: while 1920 saw the 'highest water-mark reached in Hindu-Muslim unity', 1930 represented the 'lowest water-mark reached in Hindu-Muslim disunity'.[182]

Ansari's plea fell on deaf years. His letter was seen by both the Nehrus, and then read out to the other members of the Working Committee. As Gandhi reported to Ansari, no one thought that there was anything to justify a departure from the decision taken by the Lahore Congress. Gandhi as well as the Nehrus had come to believe that while Hindu-Muslim unity continued to be important, it could not be achieved by arranging more meetings and conferences between Hindu and Muslim leaders in the then prevailing atmosphere. Active participation in the struggle for freedom was more likely to be fruitful in this respect. As Gandhi put it:

> I agree that the Hindu-Muslim problem is the problem of problems. But I feel that it has to be approached in a different manner from the one we have hitherto adopted—not [as] at present by adjustment of the political power but by one or the other acting on the square under all circumstances. Give

and take is possible only when there is some trust between the respective communities and their representatives. If the Congress can command such trust the matter can proceed further, not before. But meanwhile the third party—the evil British power—has got to be sterilized. There will be no charter of independence before the Hindus and the Muslims have met but there can be virtual independence before the charter is received.[183]

Motilal wrote to Ansari in a somewhat similar vein, but in a sharper language, after having 'very carefully read and re-read' the latter's letter to Gandhi. While he fully agreed with Ansari in giving due importance to Hindu-Muslim unity, he made clear his disagreement with the latter both as to the reasons for the failure of their efforts till then in that regard and the direction in which further efforts had to be made. Asserting that the line which the Congress leaders had followed in the past was fundamentally wrong he observed:

It is my firm conviction that Hindu-Muslim unity cannot be achieved by preaching it. We have to bring it about in a manner which will accomplish it without either Hindus or Muslims realising that they are working for unity. This can only be done on an economic basis and in the course of the fight for freedom from the usurper. . . .

You say the country is not ready for civil disobedience. If so, when and how are you going to make it ready? Do you believe that in the present temper of the so-called leaders of the two communities it is possible to arrive at any formula? Even if it were possible which I seriously doubt how far will the existence of that formula on paper seriously carry us in our conflict with the foreign Government?. . . I have definitely come to hold the opinion that no amount of formula based upon mutual concessions which those making them have no right to make will bring us any nearer Hindu-Muslim unity than we are at present.[184]

Such a stand, born partly from tiredness with a long series of conferences and negotiations on the communal problem in the preceding years with no positive result and partly from the pressure of the younger elements in the Congress who were impatient for a struggle, dismayed and upset the nationalist Muslims beyond measure. For it meant the determination of the dominant Congress leadership to go ahead with civil disobedience regardless not only of the absence of Hindu-Muslim unity but also of the anticipated apathy if not hostility of the generality of Muslims towards such a movement and the advice of the senior-most nationalist Muslim leader against it. Khaliquzzaman, for instance, found himself quite disappointed and worried after reading Gandhi's reply to Ansari and remarked:

> Uptil now we thought Hindu-Muslim unity was the pillar over which the superstructure of the constitution of free India was to be laid, but from Mahatmaji's letter one can infer that while recognising the utility of such a unity he does not consider it *sine qua non* for a fight for independence. If we accept the formula laid down therein we indirectly proclaim to the Muslim community to find its champions in people who believe that communalism in India is a fact.[185]

What Khaliquzzaman wrote immediately after also deserves to be quoted, for it shows how difficult the Hindu-Muslim problem appeared as early as 1930 to a prominent Muslim leader still wedded to Indian nationalism and actively associated with the struggle for freedom: 'No one can deny that in time to come nationalism would grow and envelope every one of its sons—Hindus and Muslims—but that would certainly require ages. Those who believe in the ultimate unity of communities may as well believe in the ultimate unity of nations, and start with internationalism rather than with nationalism.'[186]

Another Muslim leader with a similar background, Tasadduq Ahmad Khan Sherwani, agreed with every word used by Ansari in his letter to Gandhi on 13 February 1930, and also found Gandhi's reply to it 'most disappointing'.[187] Syed Mahmud, known for his closeness to Jawaharlal Nehru, narrated most poignantly his experience at the meeting of the Congress Working Committee at Ahmedabad on 14 February which decided to go ahead with the programme of civil disobedience. He wrote that he placed all the difficulties in the way of the adoption of such a programme, particularly mentioning in this connection that the Government would organize Muslim riff-raff to create troubles and after a dozen of such riots Hindu workers of the Congress would join in communal conflicts and desert the civil disobedience movement. To this Gandhi replied that he realized this but it could not be helped; they had to march ahead, there was no other alternative. 'I read contempt', added Mahmud, 'in the faces of great leaders for the Muslims. They thoroughly deserve contempt, I know but even then it pained me.'[188]

It cannot be said with any certainty whether this is a true picture of the top Congress leaders at that time or merely a reflection of the goings on in the mind of a sensitive Congress Muslim leader torn between his deep loyalty to the Congress and the feeling that Ansari's arguments were really sound and the Congress would have served the cause of the country better by postponing the projected movement. Whatever that might be, if leaders like Gandhi and the Nehrus showed impatience with those arguments—which might have appeared to

Mahmud as contempt for Muslims—this could be because they must have wondered what more they were expected to do to satisfy their Muslim friends and create an enthusiasm in them for the movement except to plan another series of conferences and negotiations on the communal problem which, given the then existing atmosphere, were sure to again result in failure and lead to even greater acrimony than had been produced by such conferences in the recent past.

In this connection it may be mentioned that at Lahore, while adopting complete independence as its goal and declaring the Nehru Report to have lapsed, the Congress had adopted a resolution on the communal problem with a view to reassuring the minorities, particularly the Sikhs and Muslims. Through it the Congress affirmed its belief that in independent India communal questions could only be solved on 'strictly national lines'. At the same time, taking into account the dissatisfaction among Sikhs, Muslims and other minorities with the solution of the communal problem proposed in the Nehru Report, the Congress deemed it necessary to assure them that it would accept no solution of that problem in any future constitution unless it gave 'full satisfaction to the parties concerned'.[189] The resolution was thus cleverly drafted. While the first part was expected to appeal to the Hindu majority, the second part was intended to satisfy the minorities. It is not clear, however, as to how the two parts could be reconciled. For while the Hindu majority desired a solution on strictly national lines, without making any distinction among the country's citizens, the Muslim and Sikh minorities wanted special safeguards in their favour, whose nature might vary from province to province. Besides, as noticed earlier, it was not easy to reconcile the claims and counter claims of Muslims and Sikhs in the Punjab, not to mention other minorities in the country. Regardless of these difficulties, the Congress apparently thought that it had devised a formula on the basis of which it could appeal to all sections of the Indian people to play their due role in the ensuing struggle. So it went on reiterating it whenever questions were raised by minority groups, particularly Muslims, regarding its attitude towards the communal problem. Thus, responding to a press report from Delhi in April 1930 indicating that there was still doubt in the minds of some Muslims about the attitude of the Congress towards the Nehru Report and the communal problem, Motilal Nehru, as Acting President of the Congress (since the arrest of Jawaharlal, who was the President) wrote to the Chairman of the Reception Committee of the 9th session of the Jamiat-ul-Ulama to be held at Amroha (U.P.) in early May, reiterating the Congress position. He recalled the resolution of the Lahore Congress declaring the Nehru Report to have lapsed and affirming that, in the future, the Congress would not accept any solution of the communal problem which was not acceptable to the Muslims and other minorities.[190] In June 1930 the Congress Working Committee reiterated this position and expressed the hope that Hindus and Muslims jointly participating in the struggle against foreign rule would establish a spirit of camaraderie which would work as 'an effective safeguard against all communal differences'.[191]

Gandhi went beyond even Motilal Nehru and the Congress Working Committee in reassuring the Muslims and other minorities regarding their position. In course of an article entitled 'Hindu-Muslim Unity' published in *Young India* on 24 April 1930, written with a view to clarifying his attitude towards the communal question, he affirmed that there had been no change in his previously held views on that question and that he continued to believe that there could be no freedom without, among other things, communal unity. The only non-violent way to achieve it was 'for the Hindus to let the minority communities take what they like'. Going further he declared that he would not hesitate even to 'let the minorities govern the country'. He saw no risk in such a solution. For under a free government the real power would be held by the people. If people worked in a disciplined manner and for the common good, the mightiest government could be rendered impotent.[192]

The main purpose behind airing such views must have been to create enthusiasm among Muslims for the ensuing civil disobedience movement, but that was not achieved. Thanks to the charismatic leadership of Khan Abdul Gaffar Khan, who became famous as the Frontier Gandhi, the most spectacular demonstration of Muslim participation in that movement took place in the North-West Frontier Province. Troops had to be called in to restore order in Peshawar in April 1930, followed by other towns like Kohat, Bannu and Dera Ismail Khan. In August the whole province had to be put under martial law.[193] This had immediate repercussion in the Punjab. The firing by British troops at Peshawar, as also the fact that the city had temporarily passed into the hands of Congress volunteers, had resulted in 'a good deal more Muslim sympathy for the Congress cause'. Although a number of leaders, Muslim as well as Hindu, had been arrested by way of precaution, the Governor could not be sure about the situation in towns like Lahore and Amritsar: 'they are like pots on the boil: and there is no knowing when they will boil over'.[194] The Governor of U.P. also was 'very much concerned about the possibility of a landslide on the part of Muslims'. Soliciting the assistance of the Nawab of Chhatari, then Home Member in the province, in preventing such a landslide he observed: 'I think at the moment the Muslim position is so important that it is necessary for you to do anything you can in that direction.'[195] Writing to the Home Member, Government of India, a few days later Hailey reported that in U.P. the news of happenings in Peshawar had aroused the sympathies of Muslims.[196] The Home Member too was worried on the same account. 'I think our main anxiety at the moment', he wrote to the U.P. Governor, 'is the possibility of defection of Muslims under the influence of Congress misrepresentations'.[197] Mohamed Ali, who claimed that he was doing his best to keep the Muslims out of the civil disobedience movement, told the Viceroy during a meeting on 12 May that the happenings at Peshawar had 'inevitably disturbed Muslim feeling'.[198]

Another notable victory for the Congress was the open support extended to the civil disobedience movement by the annual session of the Jamiat-ul-Ulama-i-Hind at Amroha (U.P.) in spite of the pleadings of the Nawab of Chhatari, who had made a special trip to Deoband for this purpose, staying in the famous Muslim theological seminary itself despite considerable personal inconvenience.[199] After discussions lasting three days, it declared on 7 May 1930, that here was no reason why the Muslims should keep aloof from the Congress and appealed to the Muslims to cooperate with the Congress in carrying out the non-violent struggle for freedom with 'courage, zeal and determination'.[200] As Government mounted severe repression against the Congress, Ansari and his group of Muslim leaders in the Congress also put on shelf their reservations about the wisdom of starting the civil disobedience movement and began to play their due role in it. At the request of the then acting President of the Congress, Vallabhbhai Patel, Ansari rejoined the Working Committee in August and was arrested during the same month. Syed Mahmud had already been arrested at the end of June. Sherwani, Azad, Khaliquzzaman, Hasrat Mohani, Saifuddin Kitchlu, Rafi Ahmad Kidwai, S.A. Brelvi and a host of smaller leaders went through imprisonment for varying periods for their participation in the movement.[201] Apart from North-West Frontier Province, Muslims in the Punjab and Delhi also joined the movement in appreciable numbers. Thus out of 882 persons convicted in Delhi between April and November 1930, 88 were Muslims. In the

Punjab the number of Muslims convicted was between 600 and 700.[202] These figures should help us modify the widely held view that the Muslims had kept completely aloof from the civil disobedience movement.

Yet the fact cannot be denied that, taking the country as a whole, Muslim participation in the civil disobedience movement was not numerically significant or impressive. This became particularly conspicuous in U.P.[203] until then regarded, justifiably, as the leading centre of Indian nationalism as well as Muslim separatism. Successive confidential reports by the Viceroy underline the absence of Muslims in any appreciable number among the ranks of the civil resisters in India as a whole. Thus on 24 April 1930 he informed the Secretary of State for India that one of the most important features of the political situation at that time was that 'the Muhammedans as a community have kept aloof from the [civil disobedience] movement'.[204] The situation in Peshawar in the last week of April caused the Viceroy 'very serious anxiety',[205] but he was soon relieved by general Muslim restraint in the rest of the country and wrote after a few days: 'The Muslims are so far standing pretty well aloof.'[206] A week later he reported that although Muslims in general had been shaken by the events in Peshawar, they were till then 'all right'. A report prepared by an intelligence officer and enclosed with the Viceroy's letter noted: 'All sections of Muslims are enthusiastic in their support of the [Round Table] Conference and strongly opposed to civil disobedience.'[207] Writing about four weeks later the Viceroy again remarked: 'Muslims generally are holding quite steady. . . .'[208]

There may be some element of exaggeration in these reports, born of a feeling of relief, indeed elation, at the thin Muslim participation, except in the North-West Frontier Province, in the civil disobedience movement, but in substance they are accurate and represent a hard reality of the political situation in India in 1930.[209] There was nothing surprising in this. Muslim presence in the Indian nationalist movement, as noticed in the earlier chapters of this book, had always been thin right from the birth of the Congress in 1885. This trend had been reversed for a short while during the temporary convergence of the aims of the rising tide of Pan-Islamism and Indian nationalism between 1912 and 1922, more particularly during the heyday of the Khilafat-non-cooperation movement in 1920-2, but, for a variety of reasons mentioned in the previous chapter, had reasserted itself after the end of that movement. Since then, Muslims had been steadily moving away from the Indian nationalist movement and all efforts to bring them closer had miserably failed with the gulf between the Hindus and Muslims growing wider day by day. Against this background what is surprising is not that Muslims, with the exception of those in the North-West Frontier Province, did not participate in the civil disobedience movement of 1930 in appreciable numbers, but that they participated in it at all and did so, in whatever numbers, in all parts of the country. And among them were front rank leaders like Ansari, Azad, Khan Abdul Gaffar Khan and a host of others, who would make any nation proud.

VIII

While the Congress was busy planning and launching the civil disobedience movement, the leaders of the National Liberal Federation, notably Tej Bahadur Sapru, tried to hammer out a settlement of the communal problem by bringing together the leaders of the leading political parties in a small, informal Unity Conference at Birla House, New Delhi, towards the end of February 1930. The Congress kept out of it, but leaders of other parties, including the Muslim League and the Hindu Mahasabha, attended. The speeches delivered showed a keen desire to bury all misunderstanding and distrust and prepare a fresh basis for settlement.[210] Nothing concrete, however, came out of this effort. Jinnah was quite enthusiastic about the idea of such a conference, but thought that his Fourteen Points provided a sound basis for a settlement.[211] Even Sapru, however, had strong reservations about several of those points and was particularly opposed to residuary powers for the provinces and statutory reservation for Muslims in cabinets and public services as well as separate electorates.[212] The Hindu Mahasabha leaders, on the other hand, thought that there was no need at all to organize such a conference at that time.[213] While they participated in the Delhi Conference because of the pressure of the liberal leaders, they adopted quite a rigid attitude and refused to consider any significant concession to the Muslim side. When in March some leaders met in a consultative meeting to thrash out the terms of an agreement, the Mahasabha leaders refused to join in that effort. When another All Parties Conference, so-called, met in May in Bombay they again refused to attend it. In their absence, the liberal Hindu leaders—themselves opposed to some important Muslim demands as embodied in Jinnah's Fourteen Points—could not claim to speak on behalf of the Hindus. So the Conference broke up with Jinnah's remark that there was nobody with whom he could enter into a pact: 'I am prepared to take responsibility for the Muslims but where are the representative Hindus who would take such responsibility for their communtiy.'[214] However, it would not be correct to put all the responsibility for the failure of the unity conferences in Delhi and Bombay in 1930 on the rigid attitude adopted by the Hindu Mahasabha leaders. Their rigidity was evenly matched by that of Jinnah and the majority of Muslim leaders who, however sweetly and reasonably they might talk about the need for a communal settlement, remained firmly glued to Jinnah's Fourteen Points which even the Hindu leaders belonging to the Liberal Federation were not prepared to accept. The Viceroy's comment on the proceedings of the Delhi Unity Conference provide a glimpse of the mood of the Muslim leadership at that point of time:

> . . . I am told that those Muhammadans, like Sir Ali Iman, who have never taken the communal point of view hitherto, are now apparently coming into line with Jinnah, who himself is more of a communalist now than he has been since he revived the All India Muslim League in the summer of 1924. Even the Nationalist Muhammadans, therefore, seem to be tending more and more to be Muhammadans first and Nationalists afterwards, and this development is pretty sure to be reflected in future Indian constitutional conferences.[215]

Jinnah, it must be put on record, was still trying to function, as in the past, both as an Indian nationalist and a Muslim nationalist. A few weeks before the Unity Conference there was a move to unite all Muslim members of the Central Assembly under one party with Jinnah as leader, but the latter refused to join such a party as he did not want to part with Sir Purshotamdas Thakurdas, a Hindu industrialist, who belonged to his (Jinnah's) Independent Party.[216] He told a deputation which called on him with that proposal on behalf of the Central Muslim Party in the Central Assembly on 25 January 1930, that he did not favour it at that juncture.[217] Even after the failure of the Delhi Unity Conference to produce any positive result Jinnah did not neglect his role as an Indian nationalist leader although at the same time carefully safeguarding his position as a Muslim leader. Thus supporting a motion in the Central Assembly on 7 March 1930 to reduce the budget demand under the head 'Executive Council' to rupee one, he made a strong plea for the early introduction of self-government in India with due safeguards for Muslims and other minorities.[218] He similarly supported the motion to reduce the demand under the head 'Army Department' to rupee one on 8 March 1930.[219] On 10 March 1930 he again made a forceful speech in the Central Assembly in support of an adjournment motion moved to protest against an order issued under the Bombay District Police Act prohibiting Sardar Vallabhbhai Patel from addressing any public meeting for one month, whose defiance led to his arrest and conviction.[220] On the other hand, while initially willing to associate himself with Sapru and Jayakar in seeing Gandhi and the two Nehrus with a view to persuading them to call off the civil disobedience movement and agree to join the ensuing Round Table Conference of British and Indian leaders in London, Jinnah told the Viceroy in July that while he would do whatever the latter wanted, left to himself he was disinclined to join such a move, as he thought that nothing was likely to come out of it.[221]

Although Jinnah gave this reason for backing out of the proposed mediatory mission it is possible that his decision was also influenced by the then prevailing mood of the generality of the Muslim leaders who were quite upset by the recommendations of the Simon Commission published in June. They were, of course, satisfied with some of those recommendations, like, for instance, the abolition of dyarchy and the introduction of full responsible government in the provinces, subject to certain overriding powers of the Governors, in a federal set-up to be given shape in the future and the continuation of separate electorates for the constitution of the enlarged provincial councils. These gains, however, were nullified, in their view, by the proposal to introduce proportional representation in elections to the federal legislature and the absence of provision for statutory Muslim majority in the provincial councils of the Punjab and Bengal as well as one-third representation in the central legislature. The commission's failure to recommend the immediate separation of Sind from Bombay without any preconditions and the introduction of constitutional reforms, at par with other provinces of British India, in North-West Frontier and Baluchistan fell in the same category.[222] The Executive Board of the All India Muslim Conference immediately met in the first week of July, described the Simon Commission's Report as on the whole 'unacceptable' and 'retrograde and reactionary in spirit' and adopted a twelve-point resolution setting out in detail the Muslim objections.[223] Muslim leaders who had fully cooperated with the Simon Commission and asked their followers to keep away from the civil disobedience movement launched by the Congress thought that they had been given poor reward for their services. In that mood they even began to feel that the British were trying to please the Hindu Mahasabha and that their position in the provincial council, particularly in the Punjab and Bengal, would now be worse than what it was under the Montagu-Chelmsford Reforms. For under the latter there was an official bloc in every provincial council, whose backing was always available to the dominant Muslim group therein. Their feeling was most forcefully expressed by none other than the Muslim member of the Viceroy's Executive Council, Fazl-i-Husain, in a note addressed to the Viceroy on 18 August 1930:

> . . . in Muslim circles it is asked: is this the reward of ten years' cooperation with the Administration? and is this the reward of the Muslim cooperation both with the Simon Commission and with the British Government? In Muslim circles and in Muslim papers it is freely stated that the Simon Report has done injustice to Muslims in the hope of placating the Hindu Mahasabha Party and thus getting support from Muslims as well as from Mahasabha. It is futile to go into the question of motives. The fact remains that the Simon proposals render the position of Muslims in India much weaker than it has been under the Montford Reforms.[224]

While transmitting this note to the Secretary of State for India the Viceroy described it as 'a fairly good statement of . . . dominant Muslim opinion' and affirmed that he had 'considerable sympathy' with several of its points.[225] This sympathy was reflected in the Government of India's Despatch, dated 20 September 1930, on the proposals of the Simon Commission and in the subsequent notings and communications to the Secretary of State for India on the constitutional issues that came up for discussion at the Round Table Conference in London. The change in the person holding the office of the Viceroy from Lord Irwin to Lord Willingdon (18 April 1931) did not bring about any change in this situation. The only difference was that the latter was much more emphatic and persistent than the former in pressing the authorities in London to see to it that, whatever the cost, their decisions, on the whole, did not cause any serious disappointment to the Muslims. They pursued this line on the ground that the bulk of the Muslims had stood by the Government and could be counted upon to do so in future also. And Fazl-i-Husain functioned as the chief advisor on Muslim affairs and the chief interpreter of Muslim sentiments to both the Viceroys.[226]

As the day of the commencement of the Round Table Conference drew near the chief concern of Fazl-i-Husain was to ensure that the Government selected the right type of Muslims as delegates for that conference. Persons like the Aga Khan, Jinnah and Shafi were, of course, bound to be there because of their outstanding position in Muslim politics. Fazl-i-Husain had full faith in the Aga Khan, the veteran of separatist Muslim politics right from 1906, but the same could not be said about Jinnah and Shafi. Jinnah, with his old penchant for building bridges with the Congress as well as his keenness for Hindu-Muslim settlement and the early establishment of responsible government at the centre as well as in the provinces could not be relied upon to work for the advancement of Muslim interests to the exclusion of everything else and might even compromise them in the pursuit of his pet objectives. Shafi seemed more committed to Muslim interests than Jinnah, but like the latter, he too, being an all-India politician and for long interested in constitutional advance at the centre, might, under certain circumstances, cooperate with Jinnah in bringing it about. Fazl-i-Husain, on the other hand, was not much interested in constitutional advance at the centre and indeed preferred it to wait till provincial autonomy had taken firm roots and adequate safeguards had been devised to keep the Muslim majority provinces free from interference by a Hindu-dominated centre. Even if Shafi fully followed this line and opposed Jinnah that opposition might be construed as the product of his old rivalry with the latter and might not carry due weight with the other delegates. Fazl-i-Husain therefore, sponsored the name of Syed Muhammed Zafrulla Khan, a brilliant lawyer belonging to the Ahmediya sect in the Punjab, and Shafaat Ahmad Khan, an academic and a rising leader of Muslims in U.P., for inclusion among Muslim delegates. Explaining the grounds for his preference Fazl-i-Husain observed in course of a letter to Hailey, then Governor of U.P. and a close adviser to Irwin: 'Again, frankly, I do not like the idea of Jinnah doing all the talking and of course there being no one strong-minded enough to make a protest in case Jinnah starts expressing his views when those views are not acceptable to the Indian Muslims, I want some one who would frankly say that it is not the Indian Muslim view.'[227]

The main purpose of the letter, written at the suggestion of the Viceroy,[228] was to persuade Hailey to drop his insistence on including Hafiz Hidayat Husain and accept Shafaat Ahmad Khan in his place for representing U.P. Muslims (the other representative selected by

Hailey was the Nawab of Chhatari). Hailey thought that Shafaat Ahmad Khan 'with all his qualities of industry and keenness in debate' did not command among the U.P. Muslims the 'all round support in point of character' as was enjoyed by Hidayat Husain, but agreed to replace the latter by the former on the ground that he would be 'useful to Shafi and also form a somewhat effective counteraction to Jinnah'.[229]

Not content with success in securing the inclusion of persons of his choice, particularly Zafarulla Khan and Shafaat Ahmad Khan, Fazl-i-Husain went on sending them letters of advice, admonition and instruction, the gist of which was that they must remain firm on the Muslim demands as embodied in the resolutions of the All India Muslim Conference and in Jinnah's Fourteen Points and not show too much keenness for a Hindu-Muslim settlement. Thus, in one of his letters to Shafaat Ahmad Khan he observed:

> Now, who will benefit more by responsibility being introduced at the Centre at this stage? Hindus or Muslims? Undoubtedly, the Hindus. Therefore, who should be anxious to settle communal differences in order to secure the promised gain? Naturally the Hindus. Then why should Muslims, who are politically, educationally and economically weaker in the country, pretend that by ousting the British power from India and by introducing responsibility they stand to gain so much that, for it, they are prepared to sacrifice communal interests. The position has only to be visualised in a fair, judicial and common-sense way to notice the absurdity of it. The only explanation people here give of the attitude of some of the Muslim members of the Indian Delegation is—corruption. The Turkish nation was ruined over and over again by their Pashas. Is the Indian Muslim community going to be ruined by the Muslim Delegates at the Round Table Conference?[230]

The tone as well as content of this letter was provoked by the willingness of some of the leading members of the Muslim Delegation like the Aga Khan and Jinnah to give up their insistence on separate electorates if their other demands were met. This stand, identical with that of Jinnah at the All Parties National Convention in Calcutta in December 1928, ran counter to the view of Fazl-i-Husain that the issue of separate electorates was not negotiable and should be treated as a settled fact.[231] The liberal leaders were agreeable to the Aga Khan's and Jinnah's terms, but the two Hindu Mahasabha leaders, B.S. Moonje and M.R. Jayakar, adopted an extremely rigid and negative attitude just as they had done in 1928. So the discussions dragged on and no settlement could be arrived at. In the meanwhile, Fazl-i-Husain cracked the whip from Delhi; his proteges at the conference asserted themselves and prevented further negotiations on the issue of separate electorates. The Aga Khan plainly told the liberal leaders that the matter was no longer in his hands. 'A great opportunity', ruefully records Chimanlal Setalvad, a liberal delegate to the Round Table Conference, who had been involved in the negotiations with the Aga Khan and Jinnah, 'was thus lost'. According to him, if Sapru, V. Srinivas Sastri and he himself could have had their way, they would have at once conceded the demands of the Aga Khan and secured his and other Muslim representatives' agreement in favour of joint electorates.[232] It is, however, extremely doubtful if, in view of Fazl-i-Husain's rigid attitude on the issue of separate electorates and his firm hold over several Muslim delegates to the Round Table Conference, such an agreement would have really materialized even if the Mahasabha leaders had not adopted a negative attitude. Whatever that might be, the fact remains that the first Round Table Conference ended in January 1931 without any settlement of the communal problem.

IX

With the release of the Congress leaders in February 1931 and the signing of the Gandhi-Irwin Pact in the first week of March, providing for the suspension of the civil disobedience movement under certain conditions and the participation by the Congress in the Round Table Conference, there began a fresh effort to hammer out a communal settlement. Unlike in the recent past when he had been essentially a passive if also concerned onlooker, Gandhi now took the lead in this regard. He began by advising the Hindus to agree to whatever terms the Muslims wanted without any bargaining or haggling. Thus addressing a largely-attended public meeting in Delhi on 7 March 1931, just two days after signing the agreement with the Viceroy, Gandhi advised the Hindus, as constituting the majority community, to tell the Muslims: 'Have as big a share of the spoils as you want; we will be content to serve you.'[233] Gandhi reiterated this proposal in his address to the Jamiat-ul-Ulama Conference in Karachi on 1 April 1931. By that time Hindu-Muslim riots had taken place at Banaras, Mirzapur and Kanpur where Muslims had suffered heavily. Gandhi expressed his deep regret and sorrow at these outbreaks and especially mentioned his feeling of shame as a Hindu because of the atrocities committed by his co-religionists at Kanpur. 'I should feel ashamed', he observed, 'whenever either of the two communities commits atrocities, but those committed by the Hindus naturally put me to greater shame.' Stressing the urgency of a communal settlement, without which it might be futile for the

Congress to participate in the ensuing Round Table Conference, he added: 'As a Congressman and as a Hindu, I say that I wish to give the Muslims what they want. I do not wish to act like a Bania. I wish to leave everything to the honour of the Muslims.'[234]

This was easier said than done. In any case, such talk had hardly any practical significance. The Hindus, by and large, were in no mood to listen to such advice. Then there was the problem of the Sikhs, who too had become conscious of their position as an important minority in the Punjab and demanded weightage for themselves broadly in line with those given to the Muslims in provinces where they were in a minority. Above all, there were strong differences among Muslims themselves over at least one point—whether separate or joint electorates would best suit their interests. So Gandhi slightly modified his position through a clarification issued to the press on 6 April 1931. He still clung to his earlier stand regarding the beauty of surrender, but now made it clear that such surrender would be to an 'unanimously expressed wish of the Musssalmans and the Sikhs'. Before he could try to secure Hindu acceptance of a certain formula, he must first have such a formula. This, he further added, he did not have from the Muslims, as revealed by the failure of the talks of some prominent nationalist Muslims with the leaders of the All India Muslim Conference in Delhi on 4 April 1931. He had been warned, he said, by the nationalist Muslims not to accept any scheme that was not based on joint electorates and adult suffrage and had also been told that Muslim masses did not want separate electorates. Some of these nationalist Muslims were his oldest co-workers and he could not disregard their opinion. In any case, he could not identify himself with a solution that was frankly based on communalism and yet did not have the unanimous support of the community concerned. 'A solution that is admittedly defective and anti-national', he stressed, 'must, to be acceptable, have the merit at least of almost unanimous support from those affected by it.'[235] In spite of such clarifications Gandhi's utterances were causing unease to some of his close followers. Jawaharlal Nehru's letter to Gandhi written in the last week of April or first week of May 1931 is not available, but from the tenor of Gandhi's reply to the former it is clear that he had been subjected to some criticism for his utterances on the Hindu-Muslim question. While appreciating Nehru's frank observations on that question Gandhi observed: 'I have always taken good care to say that I was speaking for myself. So long as we have not evolved a concrete policy how could I help expressing my own personal views?'

Gandhi also added that the occasions had not been many when he had let himself go.[236] Soon he further clarified his position and remarked, in course of an interview to the press on 17 May 1931, that when he spoke of the Hindu-Muslim question he meant 'the entire communal question'. A settlement of this question, therefore, would also have to include the Sikhs.[237]

This might have been a logical position for Gandhi to take, but, as shown earlier, it was next to impossible to reconcile the rival claims of Muslims and Sikhs in the Punjab. The situation was not very different so far as the conflicting stands of the nationalist and separatist Muslims were concerned. The signing of the Gandhi-Irwin Pact was indeed followed, in quick succession, by not only a vigorous reiteration of both these stands, but also the failure of all efforts to reconcile them. Thus the All India Muslim Conference, the chief organization at that time of separatist Muslims, at its special session in Delhi in 5 April 1931, reiterated all the demands made by that body at the time of its foundation a little over two years earlier. These included continuation of separate electorates for Muslims at the centre as well as in the provinces, weightage in their favour in provinces where they were in a minority, provision for Muslim majority in the legislatures of the Punjab and Bengal, one-third Muslim representation in the central legislature and establishment of a federal system of government with residuary powers vesting in the provinces, who were to receive power directly from the British Parliament and to decide whether and on what terms to accede to the federation.[238] Feroz Khan Noon, who moved the resolution, said that Muslims would have to consider whether they had enough confidence in the majority community so as to accept all the powers being transferred to the federal legislature. Giving the example of defence, be maintained that if that became a transferred subject, Muslims would be reduced to the status of grass-cutters.[239] Such views were not aired merely for public consumption, but also communicated, in all earnestness, to the Viceroy when some of the leaders of the Muslim Conference called on him on 1 April 1931; Feroz Khan Noon went to the extent of demanding that if the control of the Army was going to be transferred to Indian hands, the transfer should be made not to the centre, but to the provinces.[240]

On the other hand, meeting at Lucknow on 18 and 19 April, the All India Nationalist Muslim Conference sang an entirely different tune. Sir Ali Imam, who presided, observed that although he had been a member of the Muslim Deputation which had called on the then

Viceroy, Lord Minto, in 1906, to demand separate electorates, he had subsequently come to the conclusion that such electorates represented a negation of nationalism and were positively harmful to Muslims themselves.[241] The resolution adopted by the Conference on the issue of Muslim representation in the legislatures opted for universal adult franchise, joint electorates and reservation of seats for minorities in the central as well as provincial legislatures on the basis of population, with the right to contest additional seats.[242] Ansari, who piloted that resolution, asserted that separate electorates were 'bound to prove the most effective method of perpetrating and accentuating communal bitterness and sectional exclusiveness'. Apart from national considerations, such electorates, according to him, would prove suicidal to the continuance of Muslims in India as a political and cultural force of any significance. Elucidating this point from the political angle he observed: 'If there is anybody anywhere anxious to see the Mussalmans reduced to absolute ineffectiveness in Indian politics, he must laugh in his sleeves at their own curious insistence on a measure so obviously calculated to bring about that result.'[243]

In view of such strong divergence of outlook between the separatist and nationalist Muslims it is not surprising that negotiations between their leaders, with the Nawab of Bhopal playing somewhat of a mediatory role, in order to hammer out an agreed solution to the communal problem, carried through various stages between March and June 1931, failed to produce any positive result.[244] Indeed the two groups now became further apart.[245] On the other hand, the Hindu Mahasabha adopted a position on the communal problem which it described as 'strictly national', strongly opposing not merely separate electorates but also reservation and weightage of any kind in any sphere of government in favour of any community. Similarly, it opposed any redistribution of provincial boundaries except through a detailed examination of all the relevant factors—linguistic, administrative, financial, etc.—by a committee of experts.[246] This meant really opposition to the immediate separation of Sind from Bombay, as demanded by almost all Muslim groups.

It is against this background of growing polarization on the communal issues that the Congress Working Committee, at its meeting in Bombay in July 1931, decided to set forth its stand on them. While doing so it affirmed that the Congress since its inception had set up 'pure nationalism' as its ideal and recalled the Lahore Resolution (1929) which had declared that in an independent India communal questions could only be settled on strictly national lines and assured Muslims, Sikhs and other minorities that the Congress would not accept any solution of the communal problem unless it was acceptable to all of them. Though thus precluded from 'any communal solution of the communal problem', at that critical juncture in the history of the nation it decided to suggest a solution which, 'though communal in appearance' was, in its opinion, 'as nearly national as possible and generally acceptable to the communities concerned'. The Working Committee's scheme contained the following points:

1. (a) The article in the Indian constitution relating to Fundamental Rights would include a guarantee to the communities concerned of the protection of their cultures, languages, scripts, education, profession and practice of religion, and religious endowments.
   (b) Personal laws would be protected by specific provisions to be embodied in the constitution.
   (c) Protection of political and other rights of minority communities in the various provinces would be the concern of and lie within the jurisdiction of the federal government.
2. The franchise would be extended to all adult men and women. Even if this principle was not adopted, the franchise would be uniform and so tailored as to reflect in the electoral roll the proportion in the population of every community.
3. (a) Joint electorates would form the basis of representation in the future constitution.
   (b) For the Hindus in Sind, Muslims in Assam and Sikhs in the Punjab and North-West Frontier Province, and for Hindus and Muslims in any province where they constituted less than 25 per cent of the population, seats would be reserved in the federal and provincial legislatures on the basis of population with the right to contest additional seats.
4. Appointments to public services would be made by non-party Public Service Commissions which would have due regard for efficiency as well as the principle of equal opportunity to all communities for a fair share in the public services of the country.
5. Interests of minority communities would be recognized by convention in the formation of federal and provincial cabinets.
6. The North-West Frontier Province and Baluchistan would have the same form of government and administration as other provinces.

7. Sind would be constituted into a separate province provided that the people of Sind were prepared to bear the financial burden of the separated province.
8. The future constitution of the country would be federal. The residuary powers would vest in the federating units, unless, on further examination, this was found to be against the best interests of the country.

As the Working Committee went on to clarify, it had prepared this scheme by way of a compromise between rival points of view: 'a compromise between the proposals based on undiluted communalism and undiluted nationalism'. While it hoped that its scheme would gain general acceptance by the Indian people, if this did not actually happen it expressed its readiness to unreservedly accept any other scheme which commanded the acceptance of all the parties concerned.[247]

It was this mandate which Gandhi carried with him to the second session of the Round Table Conference in London. He did not, however, have to wait till his arrival there to find out that it was not a mandate which was likely to enable him to bring about a settlement of the communal problem. The spokesmen of Hindu as well as Muslim interests made it clear soon after the publication of the Working Committee's scheme that it was totally unacceptable to them. Thus the Executive Board of the All India Muslim Conference, at its meeting at Allahabad on 9 July 1931, declared the scheme unacceptable to Muslims on almost every count.[248] The annual session of the All India Hindu Mahasabha, meeting about a month later at Akola acknowledged that the Congress Working Committee's scheme marked an advance towards a settlement of the communal problem on national lines, but found it on the whole unsatisfactory and unacceptable and reiterated its earlier position on almost all the issues in dispute.[249] At the Round Table Conference its representatives remained firmly attached to that position and refused to countenance any compromise. The leading Muslim representatives, on the other hand, showed their readiness to give up separate electorates and accept joint electorates if the Hindu side accepted the other Muslim demands. These included provision for statutory Muslin majorities in Bengal and Punjab, one-third Muslim representation in the central legislature, continued weightage for Muslims in the provinces where they were in a minority and residuary powers being vested in the provinces. Gandhi was willing to concede these demands provided the representatives of Hindu and Sikh interests agreed to them. He tried his best, even though only as a mediator, to bring about such an agreement, but failed. Some prominent Muslim leaders, including Shafi as well as Jinnah, were willing to move ahead towards a settlement if Gandhi agreed to go along and accepted all their demands. However, perhaps keeping in view the mandate of the Congress Working Committee which had permitted departure from its scheme of a communal settlement only if the alternative suggested was acceptable to all the parties concerned, he found himself unable to do so.[250] Whatever that might have been, it marked the end of all efforts to bring about a settlement of the communal problem through discussion among the Indian leaders attending the Round Table Conference. On 1 October 1931, Gandhi had secured a week's adjournment of the meeting of the Minorities Committee of the Conference for such efforts. When the Committee reassembled on 8 October, he announced their failure, 'with deep sorrow and deeper humiliation' and offered his apology to all the members for 'the waste of a precious week'.[251]

The representatives of Indian parties failing to reach an agreement over the communal question the matter was left to be settled through an award by the British Prime Minister, Ramsay MacDonald. By their decision, under the influence of the leaders of the Muslim Conference, not to invite Ansari, the acknowledged leader of the Congress or nationalist Muslims, to the Second Round Table Conference in spite of repeated requests by Gandhi and Irwin's assurance that this would be conceded,[252] the British had already indicated where their sympathies lay. The leaders of the Muslim Conference had, therefore, nothing to fear. Even so they remained on tenterhooks and did not feel sure about the nature of the Prime Minister's Award. In any case, they left nothing to chance and, adroitly using the loyalty card, did whatever they could to ensure that the Prime Minister's Award conceded their main demands. In this the key role was played by the Aga Khan. In a memorandum submitted to the new Secretary of State for India, Sir Samuel Hoare, in March 1932, he underlined the consistent Muslim policy of alliance with the British to safeguard their interests and asserted that the continued existence of Muslim identity in India depended on two factors: the permanence of real British authority in India and the minimum safeguards for the Muslims, as demanded, by the All India Muslim Conference in 1929. Both were equally necessary: 'One without the other will not prevent us from being submerged and absorbed by the Hindu majority.' The Aga Khan went on to assert that it was the inherent interest of Muslims not merely to work hand in hand with Britain, but also to ensure that the result of that cooperation was not their being handed over by the latter to Hindu domination. In this connection he narrated what had happened at the Second Round Table Conference. Gandhi was willing to concede the minimum demands of the Muslims provided they accepted the Congress ideal for India as a whole as well as washed their hands of the future of other minorities, but the Muslims 'deliberately, without any hesitation, refused any such union'. He, however, warned that Muslims were full of apprehensions about their future and a change was coming in their mood. They were beginning to say that if they did not get from Britain the safeguards which they required, it might be better for them to work along the lines of Ansari and the Congress Muslims instead of sticking on to the alliance with the British. While the Aga Khan himself would not join the other Muslims in following that line, there would be nothing left for him but to give up all political activity and turn to private life and his varied interests and occupations.[253]

The greatest advocate of the Muslim cause was, of course, the new Viceroy, Lord Willingdon, who was determined to crush the civil disobedience movement, restarted by the Congress in January 1932, and realized the value of keeping Muslims firmly out of it and on the side of the Government. In communication after communication he conveyed to the Secretary of State for India, Samuel Hoare, that the general Muslim mood was quite unsettled and that the only way to keep them aligned with the British was to satisfy their main demands, particularly with regard to the quantum of representation in Bengal and Punjab.[254] The continuation of separate electorates as also weightage for Muslims in the provinces where they were in a minority was, of course, taken for granted. When differences developed between the Viceroy and the Secretary of State on the quantum of Muslim representation in Punjab and Bengal, the former wrote to the latter:

> Do please visualise the political situation out here. The Congress are against us, the Moderates are not cooperating, and remember that these two bodies are nearly all Hindus. . . . The Muslims, who, on the whole, have generally supported Government, are, with the Princes, at present on our side. But if you give them less than de Montmorency [Governor] proposes for Punjab and I propose for Bengal, I am quite certain that they will non-cooperate too. . . . What we propose is, I think, fair and equitable. Anything else would spell disaster and I can only add that if owing to your decision I lost their [i.e. Muslim's] support as well, I should probably have to ask you to send out someone else to take up the role of Akbar which I have hitherto so inefficiently filled.[255]

There was really no difference with regard to Punjab, about which both London and New Delhi were agreed to give Muslims 51 per cent of seats in the legislature. The difference related to Bengal as the Secretary of State was inclined to accept what the new Governor, Anderson, recommended: 44.4 per cent of seats for Muslims and 42.8 per cent for Hindus. The Government of India on the other hand wanted 48.4 per cent for Muslims and only 39.2 per cent for Hindus. Willingdon's efforts were directed towards getting these figures accepted in London. In a telegram sent to the Secretary of State on the same day as the letter cited above the Viceroy again emphasized the danger involved in alienating the Muslims at that juncture. Here he argued that the substance of his proposals regarding Muslim representation in Bengal and Punjab had become known to important Muslim leaders. If the size of that representation was reduced at that stage the British would be faced with 'a very serious situation'. Muslims would be swept into opposition and thus friends would be turned into foes. Lest the Secretary of State should think that slight changes in the number of seats here and there could not produce such large results, the Viceroy added:

> But we are dealing with people emotional, suspicious, apprehensive of their future and apt to be hasty in opinion and violent in action. If the Muslims are now carried away in opposing we shall be faced with a situation in this country which almost certainly will demand measures more drastic than any we have yet taken. We should have the whole forces of the country against us. . . . We cannot afford to be wholly without friends.[256]

These pleadings were not without result. The Prime Minister's Award, issued on 16 August 1932, and becoming famous as the Communal Award, broadly accepted the Viceroy's suggestions.[257] Those Muslims who had followed the lead of Fazl-i-Husain and the All India Muslim Conference had reasons to feel happy. For the Award represented a great victory for the strategy planned by Fazl-i-Husain and vigorously pursued by the Muslim Conference: treating the continuation of separate electorates as also weightage for Muslim in provinces where they constituted a minority as settled facts, insisting on the constitutional recognition of Muslim dominance in Punjab and Bengal where Muslims constituted a majority, and relying primarily on British support to secure that objective. The strategy was based on a shrewd calculation of British predicament arising out of the growing momentum of the Indian nationalist movement and their determination to thwart it and prolong their rule over India as long as possible, underlining the obvious need for allies among the Indian population for that purpose. There can be no doubt that faith in the soundness of this calculation, by no means new, was immensely strengthened by the experience of negotiations for safeguarding the Muslim position in India during 1927-32. At the same time, the tenacity with which the Muslim Conference leaders, including the Aga Khan and Fazl-i-Husain, opposed the transfer of responsibility at the Centre to Indian hands until the provinces had acquired real power and the question of Muslim share in political power in the country as a whole had been settled, shows the widening horizons as well as the new concerns of Muslim nationalism. The leaders of that nationalism, among other things, left no one in doubt about their strong determination to ensure that Muslims in the provinces where they were in a majority became masters of their destiny, without any fear of interference by a Hindu-dominated Centre—something unavoidable in an undivided India having responsible government. The idea of Pakistan was to emerge and to gather momentum mainly out of this determination.

X

It was thought by some that one possible way to deal with a Hindu-dominated Centre was to form a big state (within India) consisting of all the Muslim dominated areas of the north and north-west. It was this idea which found expression in the presidential address of the poet-philosopher Mohammad Iqbal to the twenty-first session of the Muslim League held at Allahabad in December 1930:

> I would like to see the Punjab, the North-West Frontier Province, Sind and Baluchistan amalgamated into a single state. Self-government within the British Empire, or without the British Empire, the formation of a consolidated North-West Indian Muslim state appears to me to be the final destiny of Muslims at least of North-West India.[258]

This was, of course, not a blueprint for Partition. For Iqbal went on to affirm that the idea should not alarm the Hindus or the British and added:

> India is the greatest Muslim country in the world. The life of Islam as a cultural force in this living country very largely depends on its centralisation in the specified territory. Thus possessing full opportunity of development within the body-politic of India, the North-West Indian Muslims will prove the best defenders of India against a foreign invasion, be that invasion one of ideas or of bayonets.[259]

Although not advocating Partition, Iqbal's address cannot be brushed aside as of no consequence in the evolution of the thought-process which finally culminated in the widespread Muslim demand for Partition. On the contrary, by emphasizing the centrality of the bond of Islam in shaping a Muslim's political faith and the need for consolidating all the Muslim majority areas of the north-west into one large state Iqbal made a significant contribution towards the emergence of that demand. For even though not mentioning or demanding Partition he strongly underlined some of the basic points which were later used as the main ideological props for it.

In suggesting the consolidation of the Muslim majority areas of north-west India into one state Iqbal was not saying something startlingly new, but merely reflecting one of the strands of the then prevailing opinion among the Muslim intelligentsia in the Punjab. This is borne out by the despatch of 'A Correspondent in India' published in *The Times* (London) dated 14 March 1928. According to it, not only in the Punjab but also in the valley of the Indus and its tributaries there was to be found 'a practical vision of a constructive future, based on history'. That was the vision of 'effective Muslim rule'. He also mentioned that when the time came for the implementation of that vision the predominantly Hindu areas of the Punjab might be separated and added to Delhi. This would result in the creation of 'a solid Muslim bloc from the Peshawar valley to the mouth of the Indus'.[260]

Some others went beyond such consolidation and began thinking of India's Partition and the setting up of an independent Muslim State, thereby heralding the emergence of the Pakistan idea without, of course, mentioning that word. This too was not an entirely novel idea. Stray individuals had off and on suggested this earlier as the most suitable solution of the Indian problem. Thus, for instance, the Kheiri brothers, Abdul Jabbar and Abdul Sattar, had in a paper submitted to the Stockholm Conference of the Second International held in the autumn of 1917, suggested the Partition of India into a Muslim India and a Hindu India.[261] In March-April 1920, a local Urdu paper of Badaun (U.P.) called *Zulqarnain* published an open letter to Gandhi by one Muhammad Abdul Qadir Bilgrami advocating the division of India between Hindus and Muslims. The letter, subsequently published as a pamphlet running into 62 pages, contained a list of Muslim dominated districts 'fundamentally not too different from the present boundaries of Bangladesh and Pakistan'.[262] In 1921, a lawyer of Agra,

Nadir Ali, published a pamphlet in which he discussed the Partition of India as one of the means for settling the Hindu-Muslim problem.[263] In 1923, Sardar Gul Khan, President of the Islamic Anjuman, Dera Ismail Khan, in course of his deposition before the North-West Frontier Enquiry Committee, suggested the division of India between Hindus and Muslims. Asserting that Hindu-Muslim unity would never become a fact he added: 'we would very much rather see the separation of the Hindus and the Muhammedans, 23 crores of Hindus to the South and 8 crores of Muslims to the North'.[264] In 1924, Maulana Mohamed Ali declared at Aligarh: 'If the Hindu-Muslim problem is not settled, India will be divided into Hindu India and Muslim India.'[265] As mentioned in the previous chapter, doubts about prospects for Indian unity were not confined to Muslims. At least one prominent Congress as well as Hindu leader, Lajpat Rai, in 1924, envisaged India's Partition if Muslims continued to insist on asserting their dominance in those areas where they formed a majority of the population.

During the period covered by this chapter the idea of Partition apparently acquired a wide circle of adherents, particularly in the Punjab. In December 1927, Malcolm Hailey, then Governor of the Punjab, recorded that he noticed 'some curious movements going on in the Mohammedan world of Northern India'. Muslims in the Punjab were realizing that they never had the same interests as Muslims living in provinces where they were in a minority. This had set them thinking about the desirability of having a federation of their own embracing the Punjab, parts of U.P., the North-West Frontier Province, Sind and Baluchistan. They openly said that it was only a preparation for a larger federation which would embrace Afghanistan and perhaps Persia. Hailey was, of course, not sure how far these ideas would grow or shape themselves into a definite policy.[266] Within two years he reverted to this theme, as Governor of U.P., while reporting his conversation with Ross Masood, then Vice-Chancellor of the Aligarh Muslim University. According to that report, Masood told Hailey that the differences of Muslims from the Hindus were 'really very deep-seated', they being much more cultural than religious. Muslims felt that they would be swamped by the Hindus in a self-governing India. Their minds were turning more and more to the idea of a federation with Afghanistan, with Persia in the background, and with allies in the frontier independent territories. Hailey's own comment, after recording Masood's impression, is also significant, especially in the context of the long-prevailing myth that the idea of Partition first emerged in the

Muslim minority provinces, particularly U.P., and that Muslims of the Punjab supported it only towards the fag end of the Pakistan movement:

> Most of us, of course, have had schemes of this kind under view for some time. Circumstances have prevented their coming into the field of open discussion, and in any case I am not sure that they will gain much support in the U.P. or Bengal. But the Punjab Muslims have long been talking among themselves of a Union of Northern Punjab (which would give them a solid position against the Sikhs and Hindu Jats), Sind, Baluchistan and Afghanistan. A generation ago a union with Afghanistan would have been regarded with horror, for the Pathan is a very unpopular person in northern India; but the memory of his raids, etc., is dying out, and at present, at all events, it seems preferable to many of them to run the risk of engaging him as an ally rather than to accept the certainty of domination by a Hinduised Central Government.[267]

Hailey's impression is corroborated by some of the Muslim writings and speeches during 1928-9, which have recently come to light. Thus 1928 witnessed the publication in London of a book called *The Indian Moslems* by 'an Indian Mohammedan', whose identity was kept secret for a long time, but who has recently been identified as Nawab Sayyid Sardar Ali Khan of Hyderabad. Although not advocating Partition, he did speculate on a possible 'sub-division' of India, without which Muslims were not likely to receive their due: '. . . no doubt if India ever comes again to be subdivided, as was her usual lot before the Mogul arrived, they [Muslims] will be entitled to obtain their share in a general partition. But it would not be in an India that preserved its unity'.[268] Sardar Ali Khan was also a firm believer in the two-nation theory and emphasized that the future constitution must be based on it:

> Within the frontiers of India live two nations, the Moslem and the Hindu, which entertain for each other the same feelings as do, for instance, French and Germans, and who differ from one another more profoundly than any two nations in Europe. . . . This is the fundamental fact on which Indian society is based, and any constitution which is not founded on it will come to the ground.[269]

In December of the same year Maulana Murtaza Ahmed Khan Maikash a Punjabi journalist, wrote a series of four articles in the *Inquilab,* an Urdu daily of Lahore, asserting that the solution of the Indian communal problem lay in the establishment of 'a Muslim national homeland' consisting of the Punjab, Sind, Baluchistan and the North-West Frontier Province. In reply to criticism in a section of contemporary

Hindu press in Lahore, he emphasized that the demand for the creation of such a State was based on 'the internationally recognized principle of the right of self-determination' and that it was 'the only goal for which Muslims could make sacrifices'.[270]

About a year later, the Partition idea received powerful support from Nawab Sir Zulfiqar Ali Khan, a prominent political leader of the Punjab, associated with all the three important Muslim organizations—the Muslim League, Muslim Conference and Khilafat Conference—and also a member of the Central Legislature since 1921. In his address as chairman of the reception committee of the All India Khilafat Conference held at Lahore on 31 December 1929, he strongly affirmed the two nation theory and suggested a Partition of India on that basis, for the first time including Bengal also in the proposed Muslim homeland. In India, he argued, thanks to the Asian temperament, religion was an essential ingredient of nationality. India could, therefore, become a nation only if all its people accepted one common religion. However this was not possible as people do not choose their religion out of political considerations. The only practical way, therefore, to ensure peace in India was to divide the country between Hindus and Muslims. As he put it:

> India's freedom and progress depend on the fact that Muslims should be given such an area in northern India which should consist of two or three provinces, or be made one province. In this (Province), Muslims should not be less than 80 per cent (of the population). In the same way, in Eastern India, Bengal should be divided in such a manner that Muslims should form 80 per cent (of the population). Muslims themselves should, instead of rights, demand a (separate) country and a homeland.[271]

A Punjabi journalist, F.K. Khan Durrani, belonging to the Ahmediya sect and editor of *Muslim India* (Lahore), went beyond the vision of carving out a Muslim State out of India and looked forward to establishing Muslim rule over the whole of India as the only solution to the communal problem. In a book entitled *The Future of Islam in India,* published in February 1929, he observed:

> The idea of unity as a solution of India's problem is an unutterable folly, against which the history of the world stands as a witness. States have never been born of pacts, and the people of India are not so extraordinary[ly] wonderful that they should be able to achieve what the world has never been able to achieve. The idea of unity is based upon ignorance of the national characteristics of the two peoples. It is based upon ignorance of the very rudiments of political philosophy. The true solution of India's problem

is elimination of one of the two elements. Either the Muslims should commit suicide and remove themselves from the stage (or grow tufts of hair on their heads and become Hindus, which means the same thing) or assert themselves like Muslims and make a bid for the empire of India. There is no other alternative.[272]

While Durrani's dream of a Muslim empire over the whole of India may be brushed aside as representing the fantasies of a lunatic fringe among the Muslims, the recurrent talk of the establishment of an independent State of Muslims consisting of those areas of India where they constituted a majority, particularly in the north-west, clearly shows the emergence of a certain trend of thought which ultimately culminated in the Muslim League's formal adoption of the demand for Partition in 1940. In this connection it is significant that a seasoned, conservative politician like the Aga Khan, while criticizing the Nehru Report in October 1928 for envisaging the setting up of an unitary form of government in a self-governing India, in total disregard of its manifold diversities, suggested in its place 'an association of free states', with the latter having all the powers of governance, including control over the armed forces (on the Bavarian model in pre-1918 Germany). He further warned that if his suggestion was not accepted and a central government with plenary powers was set up in India, different peoples affected by it, including the Muslims in north-west India and Sind, would be justified in asserting their freedom under the principle of self-determination. In course of a letter, published in two parts in *The Times* (London), he observed:

It is not conceivable that when the strong arm of Britain had disappeared, great and compact races like the Maharattas, the Bengalis or the Mohammedans in the north-west and Sind would accept the control of a Central Executive and Legislature. Should such an authority at Delhi, dependent on a legislative majority of the other nationalities of the sub-continent dictate to some of these races, or even to lesser communities like the Sikhs, the aggrieved party would be justified, at least where it is territorially preponderant, in insisting on its freedom, according to the principle of self-determination which has been invoked against the continuance of British rule. The demand for self-determination can express itself in many forms against even a Swaraj majority among strata of peoples as varied in their outlook and standards as are the peoples of India.[273]

These lines may be read in conjunction with what the Aga Khan observed in course of his presidential address to the All Parties Muslim Conference in Delhi on 31 December 1928: 'The Muslims of India are not a community, but, in a special sense, a nation composed of many communities and of a population outnumbering in the aggregate the total even of the pre-war German Empire.'[274]

It is equally significant that a number of British observers of the Indian political scene were contemporaneously surmising that the ultimate destiny of India was likely to be Partition between a Hindu India and a Muslim India. Thus Sir Reginald Craddock, who had served in India as a member of the Indian Civil Service for a long time, observed in his book on the Indian problem published in 1929:

> Race and language are the great dividing features in India, as they are in Europe. The history of Europe has precluded the emergence of a single European nation; the same cause has the same effect in India. The tendencies of the time are entirely fissiperous and emphatically not coalescent. Coalescence, possible under empires and powerful monarchies, is impossible when men of various races and languages become democratic in their outlook. . . . To expect . . . union in a self-governing India is to fly in the face of history, experience and human nature. . . .
>
> The principle which underlines the difficulty of the democratic union of divergent races is surely plain . . . if Norway and Sweden could not keep together, if Ulster and the Irish Free state could not be got to combine, how can it be expected that the infinitely greater diversities and divergent racial elements to be found in India can be welded into one self-governing and democratic whole.[275]

About two years later, in June 1931, Sir Theodore Morison, a former Principal of the Mohammedan Anglo-Oriental College at Aligarh, expressed a similar view. Observing that far from being members of a single nation, Hindus and Muslims living on Indian soil actually constituted two nationalities in conflict, he remarked: 'Can a modern state which derives its authority from the consent of the governed be founded on the basis of two or more nationalities? A survey of the world today does not justify a positive answer to this question.'[276] On the 19th of the same month the *Manchester Guardian* published a report by one of its correspondents who observed: 'Many Muslims do not believe in the permanence of a Federal India, and they foresee a Muslim state in the north stretching from Karachi to North Bengal.'[277] A Cabinet Paper, dated 1 September 1931, similarly noted that it was a question whether the Muslim-dominated provinces should be under any degree of control of a centre which would be predominantly Hindu. It went on to observe that the 'primary object' of the Muslims was the creation of 'a Muslim India' and the secondary object the protection of Muslim interests elsewhere through the operation of the hostage theory.[278] Partly elaborating the same idea the *Economist* wrote in its issue of 7 November 1931:

Evidently the Muslims are manoeuvring already for an effective control of the entire Indus Basin from Kashmir to the NWFP through the Punjab to Sind inclusive. They may also reasonably look forward to making themselves masters of Eastern Bengal, where they have an overwhelming majority. In addition, they have fair chance of dominating a corridor between Eastern Bengal and the Punjab—a corridor which contains all the historic centres of the Muslim Raj in India, though numerically the Muslim element here is on a minority. With these great territories in their hands, the Muslims would hold a large Hindu population in pawn, as pledges for the safety of the scattered Muslim minority in other parts of India. In the worst event, they could retreat into their north-western and north-eastern citadels, pending reinforcements from the solid core of the Islamic world, which lies just on the other side of the Sulayman Mountains. That is how the Indian Muslims see the future, supposing that the British Empire in India were to go the way of the Manchu Empire in China. They do not seem to be afraid of the future.[279]

In April 1932, no less a person than Lord Irwin, who had till only a year back held the office of the Viceroy of India, remarked in course of a confidential letter: 'I must confess, though I should not dare say so publicly, that to me the prospects of an all-India federation seem to recede in favour of some division of India that would hold better hope of containing means of settling the communal difficulty.'[280] About the same time Theodore Morison, writing an essay on the Indian political situation, reiterated his view that the Muslims in India constituted a distinct nation by themselves:

It is not only in the customs and usages which mark their external life that the two peoples differ; the sources of their moral and intellectual inspiration are different. . . . But it is useless to enumerate the grounds of difference between Hindus and Muslims; the only thing that matters is that they do in fact feel and think of themselves as separate peoples. In all disquisitions on nationality this is the only test which is found to cover all cases. If a certain body of persons think of themselves as one nation and are willing to endure tribulations and material losses in order to remain together, then they are one people; if they cannot pass this acid test, they are not. Judged by this standard the Muslims of India are a nation. Communal differences, as they are called, are really national jealousies. That is why Sir Muhammed Iqbal declared 'the problem of India is international not national'.[281]

Yet another Englishman, John Coatman, who had recently retired as Director of Public Information, Government of India, remarked in the concluding chapter of his book surveying the political developments in India during 1926-32 that there was little hope of maintaining the political unity of India:

It may be that the die is already cast and that no united India, as we understand it today, will ever emerge. It may be that Muslim India in the north and north-west is destined to become a separate Muslim state or part of a Muslim empire. There is no reason yet to believe that this is so, but unless the processes which we have been watching at work are checked and reversed there is good reason for believing that this might be the ultimate outcome.[282]

As the next chapter will show, the processes hinted at here and sketched in the preceding pages, instead of being checked and reversed, acquired further momentum during the next five years.

NOTES

1. Jawaharlal Nehru, *An Autobiography* (New Delhi, 1984; first published 1936), p. 159.
2. Cited in *Indian Statutory Commission*, I (London, 1930), p. 27.
3. J. Coatman, *India in 1927-28* (Calcutta, 1928), p. 9.
4. Ibid., pp. 9-12. See also Mian Sir Muhammad Shafi to Sir Malcolm Hailey, 29 June, 1927, IOR, Mss. Eur. E220/11A, *Hailey Collection* and a note from the Chief Secretary to the Government of the Punjab, No. 10099-S, B., 29 September 1927, IOR, L/P&J/3/131, Private Office Papers.
5. Hailey to Muddiman, 1 July 1927, *Hailey Collection*.
6. *Indian Quarterly Register*, 1927, I, pp. 93-4.
7. Motilal Nehru to Jawaharlal Nehru, 7 July 1927, *Selected Works of Motilal Nehru,* Ravinder Kumar and Hari Dev Sharma, eds. (hereinafter referred to as *SWMN*), V (New Delhi, 1993), pp. 260-1.
8. Hailey to Muddiman, 23 June 1927, *Hailey Collection*, 10B.
9. Irwin to Birkenhead, 19 June 1928, IOR, Mss. Eur. C152/9, *Halifax Collection*. It may not be inappropriate to point out here that both Hindus and Muslims contributed to such writings. Thus *Rangila Rasul* and *Risala Vartman* had their counterparts in *Sita Ka Chhinal* (Depravity of Sita) and *Unniswi Sadi Ka Maharishi* (the Saint of the Nineteenth Century). See V.V. Nagarkar, *Genesis of Pakistan* (Bombay, 1975), p. 164.
10. J. Coatman, *India in 1928-29* (Calcutta, 1930), pp. 2-6.
11. Government of India, *India in 1929-30* (Calcutta, 1931), p. 9.
12. Government of India, *India in 1930-31* (Calcutta, 1932), pp. 19-20.
13. IOR, Mss. Eur. E220/21A, *Hailey Collection*.
14. *A History of the Hindu-Muslim Problem in India..., being the Report of the Committee appointed by the Indian National Congress (Karachi session, 1931) to enquire into the Cawnpore Riots of March, 1931* (Allahabad, 1931), p. 210.

15. Ibid., p. 180.
16. *Report of the Commission of Enquiry*, n. 13. See also Gyanendra Pandey, *The Ascendency of the Congress in Uttar Pradesh, 1926-34: A study in Imperfect Mobilisation* (Delhi, 1978), pp. 129-42.
17. *A History . . .*, n. 14, p. 378.
18. Hailey to Geoffrey Dawson, 26 April 1931, E220/20, Hailey Collection.
19. *A History . . .*, n. 14, p. 275.
20. AICC Papers, File G-39 (III), Nehru Memorial Museum and Library.
21. M.A. Jinnah, *History of the Origin of 'Fourteen Points'* (Bombay, n.d.), p. 3.
22. *Indian Quarterly Register*, 1927, I, p. 33.
23. Jinnah, n. 21, pp. 3-5.
24. Tara Chand, *History of the Freedom Movement in India*, IV (New Delhi, 1972), p. 107.
25. *Indian Quarterly Register*, n. 22, p. 34.
26. Ibid., pp. 34-5.
27. Ibid., pp. 36-7.
28. Ibid., pp. 422-3.
29. Irwin to Birkenhead, 11 May 1927, C152/3, *Halifax Collection*.
30. Ibid.
31. Ibid.
32. *Indian Quarterly Register*, n. 22., pp. 37-8.
33. Ibid., pp. 430-1.
34. Ibid., pp. 432-3.
35. Ibid., pp. 39-40.
36. Ibid., pp. 14-21.
37. Irwin to Birkenhead, 23 March 1927, *Halifax Collection*.
38. Irwin to Birkenhead, Telegram P. 26 March 1927, C152/8, ibid.
39. Irwin to Birkenhead, 11 May 1927, ibid.
40. Irwin to Birkenhead, 22 June 1927, ibid.
41. Motilal Nehru to Jawaharlal Nehru, 31 March 1927, *SWMN*, V, n. 7, p. 238.
42. Motilal Nehru to Sarojini Naidu, 22 June 1927, ibid., p. 256.
43. Gandhi to S. Srinivas Iyengar, 19 May 1927, *Collected Works of Mahatma Gandhi* (hereinafter referred to as *CWMG*), XXXIII (New Delhi, 1969), p. 343.
44. Gandhi to M.A. Ansari, 21 May 1927, ibid., p. 347.
45. *CWMG*, XXXIV (New Delhi, 1969), p. 3.
46. Ibid., p. 175.
47. *Indian Quarterly Register*, 1927, II, p. 39.
48. Irwin to Halifax, 15 September 1927, *Halifax Collection*.
49. *Indian Quarterly Register*, n. 47, pp. 40-50.
50. Ibid., pp. 50-8.
51. Ibid., pp. 25-31.
52. *Report of the Forty-Second Indian National Congress held at Madras, 1927* (Madras, 1928), pp. 60-93.
53. Ibid., pp. 28, 107.
54. See Syed Sharifuddin Pirzada, ed., *Foundation of Pakistan: All India Muslim League Documents: 1906-1947* (hereinafter referred to as *League Documents*), II, pp. 114, 119-21.

55. Ibid., p. 127.
56. Ibid., p. 120.
57. See *Report of the Forty-Second Indian National Congress,* n. 52, pp. 67-70.
58. *League Documents*, n. 54, p. 122.
59. Ibid., p. 123.
60. Ibid.
61. See Jinnah to Irwin, 31 October 1927 and Irwin to Jinnah, 1 November 1927, Syed Sharifuddin Pirzada, ed., *Quaid-e-Azam Jinnah's Correspondence* (Karachi, 1977), pp. 142-3.
62. G. Cunningham (Private Secretary to Viceroy) to D.T. Monteath (Private Secretary of State for India), 16 December 1927, *Halifax Collection.*
63. Irwin to Birkenhead, 22 December 1927, ibid.
64. Hailey to Brown, 14 December 1927, *Hailey Collection.*
65. Hailey to Irwin, 23 November 1927, ibid.
65a. For more details on this point, see Waheed Ahmad, *Road to Indian Freedom* (Lahore, 1979), pp. 160-2.
66. Firoz Khan Noon to Hailey, 13 November 1927, ibid.
67. Irwin to Birkenhead, 24 November 1927, *Halifax Collection.*
68. *League Documents,* n. 54, pp. 107-8.
69. Ibid., pp. 128-35.
70. Ibid., pp. 109-10.
71. Viceroy to Secretary of State, Telegram, 8 January 1928, C152/9, *Halifax Collection.*
72. Irwin to Birkenhead, 23 February 1928, C152/4, ibid.
73. See Motilal Nehru to Mahatma Gandhi, 21 February 1928, *SWMN*, V, n. 7, pp. 275-6.
74. Motilal Nehru to Gandhi, 24 February 1928, ibid., pp. 277-8.
75. Motilal Nehru to Tej Bahadur Sapru, 28 February 1928, ibid., p. 280.
76. Jawaharlal Nehru to Syed Mahmud, 17 March 1928, *Selected Works of Jawaharlal Nehru*, S. Gopal ed. (hereinafter referred to as *SWJN*), II (New Delhi, 1972), p. 37.
77. Viceroy to Secretary of State, Telegram, 14 March 1928, n. 29, C152/9, *Halifax Collection.*
78. Ibid.
79. Motilal Nehru to M.A. Ansari, 1 May 1928, *SWMN*, V, n. 7, pp. 302-3.
80. Motilal Nehru to Purshotamdas Thakurdas, 4 May 1928, ibid., p. 310.
81. See Mohammad Yaqub to M.A. Ansari, 9 May 1928 and Mohammad Ismail Khan to M.A. Ansari, 10 May 1928, Mushirul Hasan, ed., *Muslims and the Congress: Select Correspondence of Dr. M.A. Ansari 1912-1935* (New Delhi, 1979), pp. 53-4.
82. All Parties Conference, 1928, *Report of the Committee appointed by the Conference to determine the Principles of the Constitution for India* (Allahabad, n.d.), p. 17.
83. Ibid., p. 124.
84. Motilal Nehru to Gandhi, 27 June 1928, *SWMN*, V, n. 7, pp. 324-5. See also *All Parties Conference*, 1928, n. 82, p. 23.
85. See Motilal Nehru to Gandhi, 11 July 1928 and 19 July 1928, *SWMN*, V, pp. 328, 331.
86. *All Parties Conference*, 1928, n. 82, p. 43.

87. Motilal Nehru to Jawaharlal Nehru, 21 July 928, *SWMN*, V, n. 7, p. 338.
88. The full text of the Nehru Report with appendices, is reproduced in *SWMN*, VI (New Delhi, 1995), pp. 1-119.
89. *All Parties Conference*, 1928, n. 82, p. 124.
90. *SWMN,* VI, n. 88, p. 129.
91. Ibid., p. 126. These changes were incorporated in the Supplementary Report issued by the same Committee (reappointed by the Lucknow Conference) a few weeks later, See ibid., pp. 131-80.
92. Ibid., pp. 127-8.
93. Ibid., pp. 123-4, 190-4.
94. Ibid., p. 227.
95. Irwin to Birkenhead, 23 August 1928, C152/4, *Halifax Collection*.
96. Viceroy to Secretary of State, Telegram, 4 September 1928. C152/9, *Halifax Collection*.
97. M.C. Chagla's interview to the Press, 1 September 1928, *SWMN*, VI, n. 88, pp. 229-30. See also ibid., pp. 224-5 for the views of some other League leaders.
98. Ibid., pp. 230, 232-3.
99. Ibid., pp. 236-7. For Ansari's reply to Shaukat Ali's accusation and the latter's rejoinder see ibid., pp. 237-41, 243-5.
100. Ibid., pp. 246-8.
101. Irwin to Birkenhead, 23 August 1928, n. 95
102. Irwin to Birkenhead, 13 September 1928, ibid.
103. Motilal Nehru to Annie Besant, 30 September 1928, *SWMN*, V, n. 7, pp. 364-5.
104. Motilal Nehru to Purshotamdas Thakurdas, 29 September 1928, ibid., p. 363.
105. Irwin to Birkenhead, 8 March 1928, C152/4, *Halifax Collection*.
106. Irwin to Birkenhead, 6 September 1928, ibid.
107. Irwin to Birkenhead, 3 October 1928, ibid.
108. M.C. Chagla, *Roses in December: An Autobiography* (Bombay, 1973), p. 96.
109. David Page, *Prelude to Partition* (Delhi, 1982), p. 186.
110. Matlubul Hasan Saiyid, *Mohammad Ali Jinnah* (Lahore, 1962; first published 1945), p. 190.
111. Choudhry Khaliquzzaman, *Pathway to Pakistan* (Lahore, 1961), pp. 98-9. See also Chagla, n. 108, p. 96
112. *League Documents*, II, n. 54, p. 145.
113. Ibid., p. 143.
114. Ibid., p. 146.
115. Ibid., p. 147.
116. Khaliquzzaman, n. 111, p. 99.
117. *The Proceedings of the All Parties National Convention* (Allahabad, n.d.), pp. 73-4, 76-7. Gandhi as well as Sapru supported Jinnah's amendment asking for one-third representation for Muslims in the Central Legislature, but it could not be carried because of the opposition of the Hindu Mahasabha and Sikh members of the committee, Page, n. 109, p. 190.
118. *All Parties Conference*, 1928; Supplementary Report of the Committee (Allahabad, n.d.), p. 36.
119. *The Proceedings* . . . , n. 117, pp. 78-80.

120. Ibid., p. 84.
121. Ibid., pp. 84-5.
122. Ibid., pp. 85-6.
123. Ibid., p. 86.
124. Ibid.
125. Ibid., p. 86-92.
126. Ibid., pp. 92-5.
127. Ibid., p. 95.
128. Heotor Bolitho, *Jinnah, Creator of Pakistan* (London, 1956), p. 95.
129. Syed Hasan Riaz, *Pakistan Naguzeer Tha* (Karachi, 1967), 241-3, cited in Saad R. Khairi, *Jinnah Reinterpreted: The Journey from Indian National-ism to Muslim Statehood* (Karachi, 1995), p. 249.
130. This is how Jinnah had been described by Gopal Krishan Gokhale, one of the towering leaders of the Congress during the pre-Gandhi era, in the early twentieth century. 'He has the true stuff in him', said Gokhale, 'and that freedom from all sectarian prejudice which will make him the best ambassador of Hindu-Muslim unity.' Sarojini Naidu, 'A Pen Portrait', in *Mohammed Ali Jinnah; An Ambassador of Unity: His Speeches and Writings,* 1912-17 (Madras, 1918), p. 1.
131. Khaliquzzaman, n. 111, p. 98. He added in another connection: 'had once joint electorates been brought into the constitution it would have been impossible for the Muslims to secure Pakistan', ibid., p. 100.
132. Motilal Nehru to Mahatma Gandhi, 2 October 1928, *SWMN*, V, n. 7, pp. 368-9.
133. M.A. Ansari to Sarojini Naidu, 26 June 1927, Hasan, n. 81, p. 20.
134. Motilal Nehru to Annie Besant, 30 September 1928, *SWMN,* V, n. 7, p. 365.
135. Mushirul Hasan, *Nationalisms and Communal Politics in India, 1916-1928* (New Delhi, 1979), pp. 285-93. See also Page, n. 109, pp. 182-4.
136. See M.A. Ansari to Mahatma Gandhi, 13 February 1930 and Motilal Nehru to M.A. Ansari, 17 February 1930, Hasan, n. 81, pp. 96 and 104.
137. Motilal Nehru to Gandhi, 14 August 1929, *Motilal Nehru Papers,* Nehru Memorial Museum and Library. See also Uma Kaura, *Muslims and Indian Nationalism: The Emergence of the Demand for India's Partition, 1928-40* (New Delhi, 1977), pp. 46-7.
138. *SWMN, VI*, n. 82, p. 130.
139. M.A. Ansari to Gandhi, 13 February 1930, Hasan, n. 81, p. 96.
140. Shaukat Ali to M.A. Ansari, 6 September 1928, *SWMN*, VI, n. 82, p. 243.
141. Motilal Nehru to Gandhi, 27 June 1928, *SWMN,* V, n. 7, p. 325.
142. Ibid.
143. *SWMN,* VI, n. 82, pp. 123-4.
144. Ibid., p. 227.
145. Ibid., p. 243.
146. Hasan, n. 81, pp. 307-8.
147. Gandhi to Motilal Nehru, 3 March 1928, *CWMG*, XXXVI (New Delhi, 1970), p. 76.
148. Gandhi's Article in *Young India,* 16 August 1928, ibid., XXXVI (New Delhi, 1970), pp. 180-1.

149. 'I know', wrote Motilal to Gandhi, shortly after returning from Calcutta, offering his apology, for troubling Gandhi by insisting on his presence there, 'you are not at all satisfied with what we have been able to achieve in Calcutta but there can be no doubt as to how I would have fared without your support. You have saved a complete fiasco', Motilal Nehru to Mahatma Gandhi, 12 January 1929, *Motilal Nehru Papers*, Nehru Memorial Museum and Library.
150. *All Parties Conference,* n. 82, p. 29.
151. Ibid., p. 49.
152. See, for instance, Hasan, n. 137, pp. 301-3; Kaura, n. 139, p. 146; and Page, n. 109, pp. 172-4.
153. K.K. Aziz, ed., *The All India Muslim Conference, 1920-1935: A Documentary Record* (Karachi, 1972), pp. 1-39.
154. Ibid., pp. 53-6.
155. Page, n. 109, pp. 197-203.
156. M.A. Jinnah to Secretary, All India Muslim Conference, 25 September 1928, Aziz, n. 153, pp. 21-2.
157. *League Documents*, II, n. 54, pp. 148-9.
158. The Aga Khan, *The Memoirs of Aga Khan* (London, 1954), p. 210.
159. Sharif al Mujahid, *Quaid-e-Azam Jinnah: Studies in Interpretation* (Karachi, 1981), p. 391.
160. See Saiyid, n. 110, p. 195 and Syed Shamsul Hasan, *Plain Mr. Jinnah* (Karachi, 1976), p. 49.
161. *The Indian Quarterly Register*, 1929, I, pp. 262-373.
162. See Mujahid, n. 159, pp. 479-81. Both Saiyid (n. 110, p. 199) and Jamil-ud-din Ahmed, *Documents of the Muslim Freedom Movement* (Lahore, 1970, p. 100) mention the 15th point as 'an alternative', with slightly different wordings. Their versions tally with that given in *Indian Quarterly Register,* n. 163, p. 365, published not long after the Delhi Session of the League. This shows that that was how the points had originally appeared in the draft resolution introduced by Jinnah at the Delhi Session. However, shortly thereafter he himself slightly modified that paragraph's wording and placed it as point no. 15, see enclosure to M.A. Jinnah to Tej Bahadur Sapru, 14 December 1929, *Sapru Papers,* Series II, microfilm, Nehru Memorial Museum and Library. This conforms to the version given by Mujahid. See also *The Collected Works of Quaid-e-Azam Mohammad Ali Jinnah* (hereinafter referred to as *CWJ*), Syed Sharifuddin Pirzada, ed., III (Karachi 1986), pp. 352-4, 362-4.
163. Mujahid, n. 159, p. 480.
164. *The Indian Quarterly Register,* n. 161, p. 367.
165. See ibid., p. 363.
166. It is significant that the emerging unity in Muslim ranks as a result of their common opposition to the Nehru Report immensely pleased the then Secretary of State for India who wrote to the Viceroy: 'I am glad to know that the two wings of the Muslim Party have closed up and that they apparently will be no longer distracted by unnecessary division'. He also conveyed to the Viceroy the feeling in some British circles that there was need to pay greater attention to cultivating the Muslims: 'A little more nursing of the Muslim

Party, it is suggested, would give a much more stable element of support to Government in the Assembly', Peel to Irwin, 7 March 1929, C152/5, *Halifax Collection*.

167. Irwin to Peel, 21 March 1929, ibid.
168. *Indian Quarterly Register*, 1929, II, p. 350.
169. Jinnah's terms for settlement were one-third Muslim representation in the central legislature and separate electorates if the other twelve out of the Fourteen Points were not clearly accepted. Gandhi left it to Motilal Nehru to decide how Jinnah's demands could be met or whether they should be met, M.K. Gandhi to Motilal Nehru, 12 August 1929, *CWMG Supplementary Volume II* (New Delhi, 1991) pp. 55-6. Gandhi, of course, had not expected anything to come out of meeting Jinnah and remarked before going to see him: 'Nothing is possible with Jinnah', M.K. Gandhi to Vithalbhai J. Patel, 6 August 1929, ibid., p. 51. See also 'Interview with Mr. Jinnah', *CWMG,* XLI (New Delhi, 1970) p. 289; and M.K. gandhi to M.R. Jayakar, 24 August 1929, ibid., p. 319.
170. Motilal Nehru to Gandhi, 14 August 1929, *Motilal Nehru Papers,* Nehru Memorial Museum and Library.
171. *Indian Quarterly Register*, n. 160, pp. 359-60. While this was the public posture the Mahasabha leaders let it be known through private channels that they continued to accept the Nehru Report on all essential points and might even accept 'minor adjustments' if required to secure the adherence of bulk of the Muslims, but would do so only at the stage of finality when a settlement was being arrived at jointly by the representatives of Hindus, Muslims and the Government. See M.R. Jayakar to Mahatma Gandhi, 23 August 1929, *CWMG,* XLI, n. 172, pp. 574-5.
172. Mazharul Haq to M.A. Ansari, 3 September 1929, Hasan, n. 81, p. 85.
173. Ibid., See also Omar Sobani to M.A. Ansari, 4 July 1929, ibid., pp. 71-2.
174. M.A. Ansari to Mazharul Haq, 7 September 1929, ibid., pp. 86-7.
175. For the text of Jinnah's letter to Macdonald see Saiyid, n. 110, pp. 201-9. The text of the latter's reply, dated 14 August 1929, foreshadowing important political developments in the coming months, may be seen in Stanley Wolpert, *Jinnah of Pakistan* (Delhi, 1985), p. 109. Both the letters have been reproduced in *CWJ*, III, n. 162, pp. 365-71.
176. See Vallabhbhai Patel to Gandhi, 11 November 1929, *CWMG,* XLII (New Delhi), pp. 517-18. This was followed by a Gandhi-Jinnah meeting, with the Patel Brothers also present, in Bombay towards the end of November 1929, prompting Jinnah further to pursue his efforts for a conference of selected leaders with the Viceroy. See M.A. Jinnah to Tej Bahadur Sapru, 3 December 1929 and Tej Bahadur Sapru to M.A. Jinnah, 5 December 1929, *CWJ*, III, n. 162, pp. 407-9.
177. Viceroy to Secretary of State, Telegram, 20 December 1929, C152, 10, *Halifax Collection*.
178. See Minutes of Conversations between the Viceroy and Indian leaders (Gandhi, Nehru, Sapru, Jinnah and Patel) in 23 December 1929, prepared in 1930 by Sir George Cunningham, Private Secretary to Lord Irwin, *Motilal Nehru Papers*, 1930, Nehru Memorial Museum and Library. A copy is available in the National Archives of Pakistan (Vide Wolpert, n. 178, p. 380); this has been also reproduced in *CWJ*, III, n. 162, pp. 407-14.

179. In course of a press interview on 2 January 1930 Jinnah strongly criticized Gandhi and Motilal Nehru for their stand at the conference with the Viceroy and described the resolutions of the Lahore Congress as 'most misleading, impractical, unsound and unwise', and 'calculated to do enormous harm to the interests of India', *CWJ*, II, n. 162, pp. 420-1.
180. See Mujibur Rahman to M.A. Ansari, 21 July, 1929, Hasan, n. 81, pp. 73-4.
181. M.A. Ansari to Tassaduq Ahmad Khan Sherwani, 6 January 1930, ibid., pp. 90-1.
182. M.A. Ansari to Mahatma Gandhi, 13 February 1930, ibid., pp. 95-101.
183. Gandhi to M.A. Ansari, 16 February 1930, *CWMG*, XLII, n. 179, pp. 501-11. Also in Hasan, n. 81, pp. 101-2.
184. Motilal Nehru to M.A. Ansari, 17 February 1930, *Motilal Nehru Papers*, Nehru Memorial Museum and Library. Also in Hasan, n. 81, pp. 102-4.
185. Choudhary Khaliquzzaman to M.A. Ansari, 1 March 1930, Hasan, n. 81, p. 110.
186. Ibid.
187. T.A.K. Sherwani to M.A. Ansari, 3 March 1930, ibid., p. 113.
188. Syed Mahmud to M.A. Ansari, 1930 (no date mentioned, but must be one in the third week of February), ibid., pp. 105-7.
189. *The Encyclopedia of the Indian National Congress* (hereinafter referred to as *Congress Encyclopaedia)*, IX, A.M. Zaidi & S.G. Zaidi, eds. (New Delhi, 1980), p. 672.
190. Motilal Nehru to Maulana Mufti Mohammed Kifayatulla, 29 April 1930, *Motilal Nehru Papers*, Nehru Memorial Museum and Library.
191. *Congress Encyclopaedia,* X (New Delhi, 1980), n. 189, pp. 45-6.
192. *CWMG*, XLIII (New Delhi), 1971, pp. 306-8.
193. Judith M. Brown, *Gandhi and Civil Disobedience: The Mahatma in Indian Politics, 1928-34* (Cambridge, 1977), p. 139.
194. Geoffrey de Montmorency to Malcolm Hailey, 4 May 1930, E220/18A, *Hailey Collection*.
195. Hailey to Nawab Sir Muhammad Said Khan, 1 May 1930, ibid.
196. Hailey to Harry Haig, 6 May 1930, ibid.
197. Haig to Hailey, 6 May 1930, ibid.
198. Note of an Interview with Maulana Mohammad Ali on 12 May 1930, Enclosure to Irwin to Hailey, 12 May 1930, ibid.
199. See Ahmad Said (Chhatari) to Hailey, 4 May, 1930, ibid. The Nawab of Bhopal (Hamidullah Khan) too, at the prompting of the Viceroy, made 'a last minute effort' to see that a decision at Amroha was at least postponed, but failed. See Nawab of Bhopal to Irwin, 3 May 1930 and 10 May 1940, ibid.
200. *Indian Annual Register,* 1930, I, p. 43.
201. Mushirul Hasan, *A Nationalist Conscience; M.A. Ansari, the Congress and the Raj* (New Delhi, 1987), pp. 216-17.
202. Ibid., p. 188.
203. See Pandey, n. 16, pp. 111-12.
204. Irwin to Wedgwood Benn, 24 April 1930, C152/6, *Halifax Collection*.
205. Irwin to Benn, May 1930, ibid.
206. Irwin to Benn, 8 May 1930, ibid.

207. Irwin to Benn, 14 May 1930, and Enclosure to it entitled: 'Note by Mr. R.S. Bajpai', ibid.
208. Irwin to Benn, 12 June 1930, ibid. See Also *India in 1930-31* (Calcutta: Government of India, 1932), pp. 72, 76-7. The Government, of course, did its best to encourage those Muslims who were conducting a campaign against civil disobedience. Measures taken included printing a large number of copies of statements made by the Viceroy and the Secretary of State promising consideration of the claims of minorities, financing of itinerant preachers and paying for articles in the press, see Hailey to Irwin, 9 June 1930, 18B, *Hailey Collection*.
209. Some have contested this. See, for instance, Hasan, n. 201, p. 188.
210. *Indian Annual Register*, 1930, I, p. 27.
211. See M.A. Jinnah to Tej Bahadur Sapru, 14 December 1929, *Sapru Papers*, n. 164.
212. Tej Bahadur Sapru to M.A. Jinnah, 19 December 1929, ibid.
213. C.H. Setalvad to Tej Bahadur Sapru, 28 January 1930 and 6 February 1930, ibid. See also R.J. Moore, *The Crisis of Indian Unity, 1917-1940* (Oxford, 1974), pp. 105-6.
214. Kaura, n. 139, pp. 57-9.
215. Irwin to Wedgewood Benn, 6 March 1930, C152/6, *Halifax Collection*.
216. Irwin to Wedgewood Benn, 6 February 1930, ibid.
217. *CWJ*, III, n. 162, p. 424.
218. Ibid., pp. 437-41.
219. Ibid., pp. 442-55.
220. Ibid., pp. 456-9.
221. See Irwin to Wedgewood Benn, 10 July 1930, C152/6, *Halifax Collection*.
222. See *Report of the India Statutory Commission,* II (Calcutta, 1930), pp. 31-315.
223. Aziz, n. 153, 61.63.
224. 'Note by Sir Fazl-i-Husain', Enclosure to Irwin to Wedgwood Benn, 28 August 1930, C152/6, *Halifax Collection*.
225. Ibid.
226. See Page, n. 109, pp. 208-58.
227. Fazl-i-Husain to Hailey, 20 May 1930, Waheed Ahmad, ed., *Letters of Mian Fazl-i-Husain* (Lahore, 1976), p. 77.
228. See Irwin to Hailey, 20 May 1930, E220/18A, *Hailey Collection*.
229. Hailey to Fazl-i-Husain, 24 May 1930, Ahmad, n. 227, p. 80.
230. See Fazl-i-Husain to Mian Mohammad Shafi, 1 December 1930; to Zafrullah Khan, 1 December 1930; and to Shafaat Ahmad Khan, 1 December 1930, 20 December 1930 and 22 December 1930, ibid., pp. 109-17.
231. Ibid.
232. Chimanlal H. Setalvad, *Recollections and Reflections* (Bombay, 1946), pp. 357-9.
233. *CWMG*, XLIV (New Delhi, 1971), pp. 270-1.
234. Ibid., pp. 380-1.
235. Ibid., p. 394.
236. Gandhi to Jawaharlal Nehru, 8 May 1930, ibid., pp. 118-19. See also Mahatma Gandhi to Syed Mahmud, 4 May 1930, ibid., p. 80.

237. Ibid., p. 165.
238. *Indian Annual Register*, 1931, I, pp. 287-8.
239. Ibid., p. 288.
240. See Irwin to Wedgewood Benn, 2 April 1931, C152/6, *Halifax Collection.*
241. *Indian Annual Register*, 1931, I, p. 296.
242. Ibid., p. 299.
243. Ibid., 300-1.
244. For the respective versions of the two groups as to the course of these negotiations and the causes of their failure see the statements issued by T.A.K. Sherwani on 22 June 1931 on behalf of the Nationalist Muslim Party and that of Shafee Daudi about the same time on behalf of the All India Muslim Conference, ibid., pp. 303-7.
245. See in this connection the reports of the proceedings respectively of the All Bengal Muslim Conference held in Calcutta in May 1931 under the presidentship of Shaukat Ali and the All Bengal Nationalist Muslim Conference held at Faridpur in June 1931 under the presidentship of Ansari, ibid., pp. 309-16.
246. See the resolution on constitutional reforms adopted by the Hindu Mahasabha Working Committee in May 1931, ibid., pp. 318-9.
247 *Indian Annual Register*, 1931, II, pp. 66-7.
248. Ibid., pp. 222-3.
249. Ibid., p. 254.
250. See the Aga Khan, n 158, p. 229; Khaliquzzaman, n. 111, p. 113; and Jahanara Begum, Shah Nawaz, *Father and Daughter* (Lahore, 1971), pp. 127-31.
251. *CWMG*, XLVIII (New Delhi, 1971), pp. 102, 115. It may be added here that Gandhi had often affirmed his determination not to go to London to attend the Round Table Conference unless the communal question was settled, but had been overruled by the Working Committee, *CWMG*, XLVII (New Delhi, 1971), p. 243. At Marseilles, on the way to London, he observed in course of and interview to *The New York Times* on 11 September 1931, that, although the Hindu-Muslim question had by then become 'almost insoluble', he was still not without hope that a solution might be found, ibid., p. 416.
252. See *CWMG*, XLVI (New Delhi 1971), p. 413, *CWMG*, XLVII, n. 251, p. 434; Hasan, n. 81, p. 129; and Azim Husain, *Fazl-i-Husain: A Political Biography* (Bombay, 1946), p. 251.
253. Enclosure to Aga Khan to Samuel Hoare, 2 March 1932, IOR, L/PO/6/74, Private Office Papers.
254. See, for instance, Willingdon to Hoare, 6 March 1932, 14 March 1932 and 21 March 1932, IOR, Mss. Eur. E240/5, *Templewood Collection.*
255. Willingdon to Hoare, 10 July 1932, ibid.
256. Viceroy to Secretary of State, 10 July 1932, E24/11, ibid.
257. For the text of the Communal Award see *The Indian Annual Register*, 1932, II, pp. 233-7.
258. *League Documents*, II, n. 54, p. 159.
259. Ibid. For a detailed review as well as refutation of the view of several Pakistani scholars that the Allahabad Address contained the first exposition

from a public platform of the demand for India's Partition see K.K. Aziz, *A History of the Idea of Pakistan* (Lahore, 1987), I, pp. 224-327.

260. Ibid., p. 154. The 'Correspondent in India' was one J.M. Ewart, see ibid., p. 181, n. 49.
261. See Syed Sharifuddin Pirzada, *Evolution of Pakistan* (Lahore, 1963) , pp. 86-9. Also Majid Hayat Siddiqi, 'Bluff, Doubt and Fear: The Kheri Brothers and the Colonial State, 1904-45', *The Indian Economic and Social History Review,* XXIV, n. 3, July-September 1987, pp. 261-2.
262. Ishtiaq Husain Qureshi, *The Muslim Community of the Indo-Pakistan Subcontinent* (Karachi, 1977: 2nd edn), p. 338. Bilgrami's thesis rested primarily on the recurring Hindu-Muslim clashes over cow-killing, Aziz, n. 259, pp. 99-104.
263. Khaliquzzaman, n. 111, p. 238.
264. Pirzada, n. 261, pp. 95-6. See also Aziz, n. 259, pp. 116-17.
265. Khaliquzzaman, n. 111, p. 238.
266. Hailey to Sir Arthur Hirtzel, 15 December 1927, E220/11B, *Hailey Collection.*
267. Hailey to Irwin, 3 December 1929, E. 220/16B, ibid.
268. Aziz, n. 259, p. 152.
269. Pirzada, n. 261, pp. 118-19.
270. Aziz, n. 259, pp. 167-8.
271. M. Rafiq Afzal, 'Origin of the Idea of a Separate Muslim State: Nawab Sir Zulfiqar Ali Khan's Lahore Address, 1929', *Journal of the Research Society of Pakistan*, January-April, 1966, pp. 177-82.
272. Pirzada, n. 261, pp. 119-20. For speculation on the possible impact of Durrani's thinking on Iqbal and Rahmat Ali, see Aziz, n. 259, pp. 160-7. The full text of Durrani's book has been reproduced in K.K. Aziz, ed., *Prelude to Pakistan, 1930-1940: Documents and Readings Illustrating the Growth of the Idea of Pakistan* (Lahore, 1992), I, pp. 78-106.
273. The Aga Khan, 'A Constitution for India: The Bavarian Model', Letter to *The Times* (London), 13 October 1928. I am indebted to Professor S.R. Mehrotra for drawing my attention to this letter as well as for providing me with a photo-copy thereof. Reproduced in Appendix III.
274. *The Times of India*, 1 January 1929; cited in Ahmad, n. 65a, p. 172.
275. Reginald Craddock, *The Dilemma in India* (London, 1929), pp. 7-8.
276. Theodore Morison, 'The Hindu-Muslim Problem in India', *Contemporary Review,* June 1931: cited in Aziz, n. 259, II, pp. 331-2.
277. Cited in R.J. Moore, 'The Making of India's Paper Federation, 1927-35', C.H. Philips and M.D. Wainright, eds., *The Partition of India: Policies and Perspectives, 1935-1947* (London, 1970), p. 65.
278. Ibid., pp. 65-6.
279. Cited in Aziz, n. 274, pp. 335-6.
280. Irwin to Hailey, 16 April 1932, E220/24 A, *Hailey Collection*, n. 4.
281. Theodre Morison, 'Muhammadan Movements', J. Cumming, ed., *Political India, 1832-1932* (London, 1932), pp. 104-5.
282. J. Coatman, *Years of Destiny: India, 1926-1932* (London, 1932), p. 376.

CHAPTER VI

Further Widening of the Gulf and Spread of the Pakistan Idea, 1932-1937

THE ANNOUNCEMENT of the Communal Award by the British Prime Minister, Ramsay MacDonald, in August 1932, was expected by many to improve the situation on the communal front and help reduce the then prevailing tensions and animosities. Actually, the result was just the opposite. Similar expectations were aroused by the coming into force of the Government of India Act in August 1935, providing for the introduction of Provincial Autonomy as soon as elections were completed under it and the setting up of a Federation, bringing together the provinces of British India and the Indian States, at a future date, subject to the fulfilment of certain conditions. These expectations were, however, belied and the trends visible before the new Act came into force were further strengthened. The period between the announcement of the Communal Award in 1932 and the inauguration of Provincial Autonomy in 1937, witnessed not merely the wider dissemination of the Pakistan idea, buttressed by all the arguments which became an integral part of the League's campaign in later years, but also its adoption, albeit not yet public, by the great poet-philosopher of Muslim nationalism in India, Mohammad Iqbal, and the future founder of Pakistan, M.A. Jinnah. And this happened not after or as a consequence of the failure of the so-called Congress-League coalition talks in U.P. in 1937, as is generally assumed, but before those talks had even entered the final stage.

I

While issuing the Communal Award MacDonald had stipulated that changes could be made in it if an alternative could be produced through agreement among all the Indian parties concerned. Provision of separate electorates for the members of the scheduled castes which had been conceded in the Award as a result of the pleadings of B.R. Ambedkar at the Round Table Conference was replaced by joint electorates with reservation of seats as a result of Gandhi's fast in prison in September 1932 and the settlement arrived at in its wake between the leaders of caste Hindus and scheduled castes. Although efforts were made for a similar agreement among the leaders of Hindus and Muslims in order to do away with separate electorates for the latter, these could not succeed.

The crux of the matter was that, while Hindus and Sikhs were generally disappointed, Muslims, regardless of the posture adopted in public, were, on the whole, satisfied with the Communal Award. According to a confidential report prepared by the Government of India, although some liberal leaders expressed qualified approval for the Award, almost all the major organs of nationalist opinion in English ranging from the moderate *Hindu* and *Leader* to radicals like the *Free Press Journal, Bombay Chronicle, Hindustan Times* and *Advance* vehemently condemned it in general and the retention of separate electorates in particular and pointed out that it was 'expressly designed to disintegrate the nationalist movement and perpetuate communal strife'. Sikh denunciations were 'at least as vehement as the Hindu' and based on equally strong feelings. As for Muslim reaction to the Award, the Government's report mentioned that it could not altogether be judged from the press, for Muslims were naturally reluctant to declare themselves openly as satisfied. It had, however, little doubt that the Punjab Muslims were pleased, and the Bengal Muslims, 'though protesting and to some extent disappointed', were likely gradually to realize the solid advantage they had gained.[1] The forecast about Muslim opinion in Bengal proved to be literally true. Muslims in Bengal, at first ambivalent and divided in their reaction to the Award, ranged themselves fully behind it in due course, as they realized the significance of the fact that although not securing a majority of the seats in the Legislative Council, they had been given more seats therein than any other community. The vehement criticism levelled against the Award by the leading upper class Hindu (*Bhadralok*) politicians further underlined the value of the gains made by the Muslims.[2] The upper caste Hindus in Bengal were undoubtedly the most aggrieved section of the Indian population so far as the Communal Award was concerned. This was because that Award finally sounded the death-knell of their political predominance there. Under it, out of the total of 250 seats in Bengal

Legislative Council Hindus were given 80 seats and Muslims 119. After the Poona Pact their position became much worse, for 30 of the Hindu seats (as against 10 under the Communal Award) were now reserved for the scheduled castes. Thus the caste Hindus in Bengal were left with only 20 per cent of the seats (50 out of 250).[3] Their leaders, belonging to all shades of political opinion, started a powerful propaganda campaign against the Communal Award. Some of the leading Hindu intellectuals and poets, including the poet Rabindranath Tagore, the novelist Sarat Chandra Chattopadhyay, the philosopher Brajendra Nath Seal and the chemist P.C. Ray joined that campaign. It was argued that Hindus, though in a minority, were superior to Muslims in education, wealth and culture and, therefore, deserved a better deal. They also claimed that as a minority they deserved weightage in representation at par with Muslims where they were in a minority.[4] The leaders of Hindu opinion in the rest of the country, who were otherwise also unhappy with the Award and wanted it revised or withdrawn, could not but pay heed to the cry of their brethren in Bengal. Thus the quantum of Hindu representation in the Bengal legislature became one of the serious issues to be tackled in the negotiations which soon followed to hammer out a settlement to take the place of the Award.

These negotiations were facilitated by the realization, howsoever late, on the part of the Hindu leaders that after all heavens were not going to fall if the Muslims had a majority in the Punjab and Bengal. For in both these provinces that majority would be so small that it would not be possible for Muslims to form a government without the cooperation of Hindus. On the other hand, understanding with Muslims could lead the latter to give up their insistence on retaining separate electorates. This was naturally welcome to the Congress leaders, including both Hindus and Muslims, who had long since been ready for a settlement on that basis. The crucial factor in enabling the negotiations to take off was the support of the mercurial Maulana Shaukat Ali. He had only a short while ago toured U.P. asserting that separate electorates were essential to Muslims but now joined hands with Malaviya in the search for a formula which might do away with them.[5] The initial suggestion had, of course, come from Maulana Abul Kalam Azad, leader of the Congress or nationalist Muslims, with the active support of Syed Mahmud, belonging to the same camp. They met Malaviya and Shaukat Ali and impressed upon them the urgent need to join hands in finding a suitable substitute for the Communal

Award which might be acceptable to all the parties concerned. It was thus that Malaviya and Shaukat Ali came together and took the lead in convening an Unity Conference which met at Allahabad on 3 November 1932.[6]

The Unity Conference, however, seemed doomed to fail in securing its objective. Even while preliminary steps were underway for convening it, a discordant note was sounded by several prominent Muslim leaders, including Mohammad Iqbal, president of the Muslim Conference and Mohammad Yaqub, secretary of the Muslim League, who issued a joint statement on 7 October, stressing that it would be 'highly inopportune' to reopen the question of separate versus joint electorates as the Muslim community was not prepared to give up the former at that juncture. While they were not averse to considering any proposals which comprehensively dealt with all the vital issues concerning the community and not just the system of election, they pointed out that such proposals must come from the majority community. In a separate statement issued on the same date Mohammad Yaqub regretted that 'certain of the so-called nationalist Muslims' had sought to come into limelight through 'attempts to exaggerate or aggravate divisions in the Muslim community' and were reopening political sores to disturb the calm which had followed the publication of the Communal Award.[7]

The nationalist Muslims, however, remained undeterred and persevered with their efforts. They convened an 'All Parties' Muslim Conference at Lucknow on 16 October, which unanimously adopted a resolution welcoming negotiations with Hindus and others for the solution of the communal problem on a durable basis and appointed a committee for that purpose.[8] This was, of course, a necessary, preparatory step for the convening of the Unity Conference which met on 3 November at Allahabad and adjourned after appointing a committee to draft proposals for a communal settlement to take the place of the Communal Award. This committee met continuously from 3 to 17 November and came forward with comprehensive proposals covering almost all vital issues. In lieu of Hindus agreeing to statutory Muslim majority in the Punjab and Bengal, continuation of weightage for the Muslims in provinces where they were in a minority, Muslim representation of 32 per cent in the Central Legislature and separation of Sind from Bombay, Muslims were to whole-heartedly join others in demanding the setting up of a fully responsible government at the centre and agree to accept joint electorates on the basis of Mohamed Ali's formula (presented before his death in 1930 at the first session of the Round Table Conference). That formula stipulated election of minorities in two stages. Candidates would first seek the votes of the members of their own community. Out of those securing 30 per cent or more, that person would be declared elected who secured the highest number of votes polled on the basis of the general electoral roll. This system was to last for ten years, but could be given up earlier in favour of joint electorates pure and simple by any community in any province. The committee went much beyond the question of representation and tried to reassure the Muslims on various issues with which they were then concerned, including protection of religion, culture and personal laws and representation in cabinets and services.[9]

These proposals, however, failed to provide a basis for a settlement of the communal problem acceptable to all sections of the Indian people. The Muslims organized in communal organizations were certainly not impressed by them. Some of their members had attended the Unity Conference—a fact publicized by the organizers—but the leaders had kept aloof. This had been deliberately done in order to gain for their community all possible advantages that might accrue from it, particularly in their parleys with the Government, and at the same time retain the freedom to reject what did not appeal to them. As Hailey reported:

> . . . the Muslims who were at the conference were not really those who count; they had decided to allow a few Muslims to attend and gave them instructions from time to time to dig in their toes and obtain all the concessions possible from the Hindus. They hoped by this course to keep a free hand themselves, but at the same time to get from the Hindus such concessions as would enable Muslims to overcome the reluctance of the British Government to put in the constitution the kind of safeguards for the community that were comprised in the Jinnah Articles. They hoped to be able to point out to the British Government that if Hindus were prepared to make these concessions, there was no reason whatever why Government should stand in the way.[10]

Soon after the publication of the Unity Committee's proposals a joint conference of the Council of the All India Muslim league, the Working Committee of the All India Muslim Conference and the Working Committee of the Jamiat-ul-Ulama Hind (Kanpur) was held in Delhi on 20 November 1932 to consider them. Three leaders who had attended the Allahabad Unity Conference were also present. They explained that no final decisions had been taken at Allahabad, that even the Committee's report had not been signed by its members and that the Muslims attending the conference had given notice of important amendments.[11] The conference, through its resolution no. 5, made it 'quite clear' that no communal settlement would be acceptable to the Muslim community unless it conceded all the demands embodied in the All Parties Muslim Conference in January 1929 and amplified by it in April 1931. The resolution went on to record that the Allahabad Proposals fell short of Muslim demands and were, therefore, unacceptable.[12] On the same day, the secretaries of the three organizations represented in the Delhi Conference issued a joint statement describing the Allahabad Proposals as 'injurious to Muslim interests, impractical and unacceptable'.[13]

Although the nationalist Muslims did not lose heart and persevered in their efforts to clinch a settlement with the cooperation of the Congress and the Hindu Mahasabha leaders and whoever else were willing to join hands from sectional Muslim organizations and the Unity Conference resumed its deliberations, the joint stand of the three Muslim organizations virtually sealed its fate. Needless to add, the leaders of the Unity Conference also found it extremely difficult to carry along with them the Sikhs in the Punjab and the Hindus in Bengal.[14] Whatever hope there might have still been of the success of the efforts of the Unity Conference was extinguished by the declaration of the Secretary of State for India, Sir Samuel Hoare, at the closing session of the third session of the Round Table Conference in London on 24 December 1932 to the effect that the British Government was of the view that 'the Muslim community should have a representation of 33.3 per cent in the Federal Centre'.[15] This naturally pleased the Muslim leadership, especially in view of the fact that the Unity Conference had offered them only 32 per cent in the central legislature. The lesson was again reinforced that Muslims could always expect more from the British Government than they could ever get from the Congress or the Hindus. Besides, now there was hardly any issue on which the sectional Muslim leaders could hope to secure concessions from their Hindu counterparts in exchange for giving up separate electorates, which they continued to cherish above everything else, or lending a helping hand in improving the quantum of Hindu representation in Bengal.

In the meanwhile, communal tension and distrust between Hindus and Muslims went on increasing as a result of the Communal Award and the failure of all efforts to hammer out a formula, acceptable to all concerned, to take its place. This is how the situation appeared to Hailey in the second week of November 1932 while the committee set up by the Unity Conference was still continuing its labours:

The Communal Award and the complete failure in the attempt to find a readjustment seems to have driven both parties somewhat further apart. I do actually find that very many well-meaning Muslims and Hindus who have hitherto not been communal in their outlook are now hardening and each rather tends to look on the other party as irreconcilable.[16]

Within a year, the situation further deteriorated. Maulana Shaukat Ali, a powerful force behind the Unity Conference, had duly renewed his anti-Congress activities. In December 1933, he created an impression on the mind of the Governor of U.P. (on whom he had called) that his sentiments were all anti-Congress and that he would oppose any settlement based on joint electorates. At the same time his attitude betrayed considerable personal pique at the neglect by the Government of one who, to quote his own words, had 'smashed Gandhi'.[17]

Gandhi, who for some time had been concentrating solely on work relating to the problems of the scheduled castes, was, of course, far from being 'smashed'. However, he had begun feeling helpless again so far as the communal problem was concerned and turning to prayer as the only available remedy, just as he had done about a decade earlier in the wake of the developments following the Kohat riots and his disenchantment with the Ali brothers and the Unity Conferences. When it was reported to him that Ansari had 'a lurking fear' that he was not doing anything or as much as he should for bringing about communal unity, he wrote to Ansari in March 1934:

My views are just as strong as they were on the necessity of that unity. But I have come to the conclusion that this is the time for real lovers of unity to sit still and simply pray showing in their individual action what a living unity of hearts can mean. Do you not meet in your practice[18] boils which grow worse with teasing? I find communal discord such a boil. The more you tease it the worse it becomes. It needs a rest cure.[19]

In formulating its attitude towards the Communal Award the Congress in effect followed this formula. When the Award was announced (August 1932) the Congress was busy with the civil disobedience movement, and most of its leaders were in prison. However, those who were not in prison were quick to denounce it as one calculated to accentuate communal divisions in the country and serve British imperial interests. Malaviya, Rajendra Prasad, C. Rajagopalachari and

Ansari—all spoke in that vein.[20] Barring Malaviya and his Hindu-minded supporters, however, other Congress leaders considered it prudent to take into account the fact that in the country as a whole opinion on the Award was sharply polarized with the Hindus and Sikhs opposing and the Muslims, on the whole, supporting it. On the other hand, perhaps as a result of the controversy regarding it, there were 'distinct signs of the rise in communal feeling'.[21] In such a situation the Congress, in spite of its dislike for the Communal Award, could not afford to oppose it. As Gandhi observed in his address at the meeting of the Congress Parliamentary Board at Bombay on 16 June 1934, so long as a voluntary agreement on an alternative to the Award was not arrived at among all the parties concerned, it would be a 'betrayal of the Muslims' to take up a position of uncompromising opposition to it.[22] At the same time the Congress had also to be careful not to antagonize Hindus and Sikhs, most of whom were opposed to the Award. So the Working Committee, accepting Gandhi's advice, adopted a resolution on 17 June 1934, declaring that in view of division of opinion in the country regarding the Award, the Congress could 'neither accept nor reject' it as long as such division of opinion lasted. At the same time the Working Committee reiterated the old position of the Congress on the communal question since the Lahore Congress (1929), namely, that it could not propound any solution of the communal problem which was not 'purely national', but would accept any solution, even though falling short of national, which was agreed to by all the parties concerned. It also went on to declare that judged by the national standard the Communal Award was 'wholly unsatisfactory besides being open to serious objection on other grounds'. However, the way to make it ineffective was to explore the possibilities of arriving at an agreed solution and not to appeal to any external authority on that essentially domestic issue.[23]

Even with these additions the Working Committee's position was not found acceptable by two of its senior members, Malaviya and M.S. Aney, representing the Hindu point of view. Both of them resigned from the Working Committee and formed the Congress Nationalist Party based on unequivocal opposition to the Communal Award with a view to contesting the ensuing elections to the Central Assembly with that platform. Gandhi, however, remained firm on the policy of neither accepting nor rejecting the Award, describing it as 'the wisest' and 'the only correct attitude possible' for the Congress to adopt. One of the main reasons behind this firmness was his conviction that such a stand was best suited to leave the communal boil unteased for some time.[25]

The nationalist Muslims were pleased with Gandhi's firmness, for they saw in it 'a bold Congress stand' against the Hindus Mahasabha.[26] Even so there was no immediate abatement of the general Muslim distrust of the Congress. Keeping this in view many nationalist Muslims decided to contest the ensuing elections to the Central Assembly not on the Congress ticket but on that of a new organization, the Muslim Unity Board, set up by them specifically to deal with that situation. As Khaliquzzaman, a leading figure behind this move, explained his position to a fellow nationalist Muslim,

> Our Hindu friends do not seem to realise that it would not be possible for us to persuade Muslim candidates to stand on the Congress ticket because they know that it would be a dead weight for them in the election. The effect of the gesture made at Bombay [by the Congress Working Committee's resolution of 17 June 1934] will not be so sudden as to bring about a change in their mentality to have an effect in the present elections. No doubt in due course it will pacify the Muslims but it would take time.[27]

On the other hand, the bulk of Hindu Congressmen, regardless of the Working Committee's resolution of 17 June 1934, did not do anything to hide their utter dislike for the Communal Award and went on condemning it as before.[28] Perhaps keeping this in view the manifesto of the Congress Parliamentary Board for the elections to the Central Assembly, drafted by Gandhi himself and issued on 29 July 1934, while reiterating the policy of neither accepting nor rejecting the Award, thought it prudent to criticize it in much stronger terms than had been done in the resolution of the Working Committee and described it as 'intrinsically bad' and 'anti-national'.[29] This would certainly not have sounded reassuring to Muslims, who valued their gains under that Award, or helped in restoring their confidence in the Congress.

II

In the meanwhile, the temporary return of Jinnah to India in early 1934 after a stay for three years in the United Kingdom and his resumption of the leadership of the Muslim League had created a new hope in the hearts of many of those who were pinning for Hindu-Muslim understanding. For while seeking to revive the Muslim League and unite all politically conscious Muslims under its banner he, following his usual double-track strategy, also gave a fresh call for such understanding. He considered this particularly necessary at that time in order to forge an united front to facilitate a rapid advance towards self-government at the Centre as well as in the provinces and oppose the White Paper prepared by the British Government containing its proposals for the next instalment of constitutional reforms in India. Those proposals envisaged the introduction of full self-government in the provinces, subject to certain special powers vested in the Governors and the Governor-General, but left the Government of India broadly as it was before, with provision for dyarchy in the event of the coming into being of a federation consisting of both the provinces of British India and the bulk of the Indian states governed by the princes. Under Jinnah's guidance the Council of the League adopted a resolution on 2 April 1934 which, while accepting the Communal Award left the door open for its substitution by a new formula acceptable to all the parties concerned and expressed its 'readiness for cooperation with other communities and parties to secure such a future constitution for India as would be acceptable to the country'.[30] Summing up his impressions of the meeting of the League's Council Jinnah, in a press interview, emphasized the urgency of forging an united front against the White Paper:

> India looks forward to a real, solid united front. Can we even at this eleventh hour bury the hatchet, and forget the past in the presence of imminent danger, and close our ranks to get sufficient strength to resist what is being hatched both at Downing Street and in New Delhi? It is up to the leaders to put their heads together, and nothing will give me greater happiness than to bring about complete cooperation and friendship between Hindus and Muslims; and in this desire, my impression is that I have the solid support of Mussalmans.[31]

Such utterances naturally gave fillip to the hope in Congress circles that a substitute for the Communal Award might be worked out and an united front created to mount opposition to the White Paper and the Report of the Joint Select Committee which followed. However, Jinnah had often made such observations in the past, but in the face of opposition from dominant Muslim opinion which he was always keen to keep on his side, finally refused to make any significant departures from the stated Muslim positions so as to make a compromise settlement possible. The loyalist section of the Muslim leadership, therefore, had not yet given up hope that Jinnah could be persuaded to whittle down his opposition to the White Paper and the report of the Joint Parliamentary Committee and continue to stick firmly to the Communal Award. Fazl-i-Husain, the leader of that section, who had done so much to marginalize Jinnah in Muslim politics in the recent past, sent him an extremely warm and flattering letter after hearing from him and learning that he had recovered from illness in London where he had gone back after a short stay in India and was thinking of finally sailing for India to resume the leadership of the Muslim League:

> India and, in particular, Muslim India cannot afford to lose you. Men of clear vision, independent judgement and strength of character are very few, and when one sees efforts made in non-Muslim quarters not to help genuinely Muslim India with a view to secure their cooperation but simply to persuade the Muslim community to entrust its future to them, the need for a strong man of independent judgement, integrity and strength of character becomes apparent and overwhelmingly great.[32]

Congress or nationalist Muslims, on the other hand, were keeping their fingers crossed, not sure how far they could count on Jinnah's cooperation in turning the tide of Muslim opinion which was overwhelmingly in support of the Communal Award and hostile to the Congress. Ansari, then the top leader of nationalist Muslims as well as chairman of the Congress Parliamentary Board, thus found himself in a quandary. Analysing the situation in the Central Assembly for which elections had been completed in October 1934 and which had seen the uncontested return of Jinnah from his old Bombay Urban Mohammedan constituency, he calculated that as the Congress, after rallying all the nationalist-minded non-Congress members of various shades of opinion, would still fall short of seven members in order to marshal a majority against the report of the Joint Parliamentary Committee, Jinnah and his followers would constitute 'the decisive factor in the Assembly'. He was, however, not sure what role Jinnah would finally play. 'And you know Jinnah', Ansari wrote to a fellow nationalist Muslim leader, 'He is always led by his followers rather than lead them.'[33] There was, however, no escape from the fact that without Jinnah's cooperation the Congress could not gather majority support in the Central Assembly for its stand on the J.P.C. Report. Jinnah's position in Muslim politics at that time as well as his utterances also fuelled the hope that he might choose to play the nationalist game. For he knew that he could not count on the support of men like the Aga Khan and Fazl-i-Husain, who were firmly for supporting the Government, and that he had to build up a separate platform in order to rally the majority of Muslims under his own leadership. Besides, however much he might be interested in leading the Muslims, unlike many other leaders of the League, he was an ardent patriot at heart and felt an instinctive abhorrence for the loyalist line followed by them. Ansari, therefore, put aside his misgivings and in due course sent Jinnah a warm letter of greetings and expressed his keenness for a meeting:

> Now that you have been returned to the Assembly again at a very critical juncture in the history of constitutional changes, your usual patriotic outlook and political foresight would prove a great asset to the opposition. . . . It is more than obvious that a very great deal would depend on the attitude the Muslim members may adopt at this time, and it is equally clear that yours will be the greatest share in shaping their outlook and views.[34]

Jinnah was equally warm in his reply and fully reciprocated Ansari's desire for a meeting.[35] That this was not a mere formality and Jinnah at that time was really keen for an understanding with the Congress is borne out by Allama Iqbal's letter to Ansari and S.A. Brelvi's impressions after his meeting with Jinnah about the same time. 'I received a letter', wrote Iqbal, 'from Mr. Jinnah this morning. I think the time has come for Hindus and Muslims to work together.'[36] Brelvi reported after his conversation with Jinnah that the latter was 'prepared to go to any length to agree to an acceptable compromise on the question of the Communal Award'. As for the terms of such a compromise, although Jinnah did not commit himself to any formula Brelvi surmised that the former might agree to joint electorates provided the number of seats allocated to Muslims in various legislatures remained the same as provided for in the Communal Award.[37] Jinnah's keenness for a settlement with the Congress without, of course, giving away any of the gains made by the Muslims under the Communal Award,[38] comes out most forcefully in the following remarks made by him in conversation with a Congress leader, most probably Ansari, in the third week of January 1935:

> I have nothing in common with the Aga Khan. He is a British agent. I am devoted to my old policy and programme. . . . If the Congress can support the Muslims on the question of the Communal Award, I would be able to get all the Muslim members except 7 or 8. . . .
>
> As things stand, the practical way would be for just a few leaders of political thought to combine for the purpose of preparing a formula which both the communities might accept. The Congress I admit would have to change its attitude in some respects, but looking to the great interests at stake

Congress leaders should not flinch. I think the future is with the Congress Party and not with me or the Aga Khan.[39]

Thus was the ground prepared for talks between Jinnah and Rajendra Prasad, presidents respectively of the Muslim League and the Congress, which began at Ansari's house at Daryaganj in Delhi on 23 January 1935—underlining the key role played by Ansari in bringing them about[40] —and then continued with some interruptions at 13 Ashoka Road, until the end of February. [41] Jinnah, starting the talk on the first day, at Prasad's suggestion, observed that in his opinion that was an opportune moment for reopening the communal question, pointing out that this would have tremendous repercussions. There were, of course, difficulties in the way, but since the J.P.C. Report was in any case scheduled to be discussed in the Central Assembly in the first week of February the Communal Award was bound to figure there. If the Congress and the League could come to an agreement before that discussion, they would be able to present an united front. Prasad, stressing the difficulties presented by the communal problem, recalled the Congress stand formulated at the Lahore Congress (1929) stipulating that it would accept only a solution which was purely nationalistic in attitude and content; however, if that was not possible the Congress could accept any solution which was found acceptable by all the communities concerned. He also referred to the framework of a communal settlement adopted by the Congress Working Committee in 1931, which had been placed by Gandhi before the Round Table Conference, as well as the recent stand of the Working Committee neither rejecting nor accepting the Communal Award. Jinnah then remarked that if the Congress would accept only what was acceptable to others, there was nothing left for him and Prasad to negotiate. What Jinnah wanted was that 'the Congress and the Muslim League should come to an agreement leaving alone the Hindu Mahasabha on the one side and the Muslim Conference on the other'. The Congress and the League should adopt a common stand and if necessary, 'fight the communalists on both sides'. If, on the other hand, the Congress wanted to play only the role of a mediator, Jinnah's reply would be: 'Thank you for your good offices—but today is not the time—we shall utilize them when necessary.' Recalling what happened at the Round Table Conference in 1931 when Gandhi confined himself to playing a mediatory role between the leaders of different communities Jinnah again stressed that there was still time for the Congress and the League to come to an agreement and was sure 'the country would accept the joint lead'. In saying all this Jinnah was evidently trying to persuade Prasad to accept the Communal Award on behalf of the Congress and went on to assert, referring to the Working Committee's stand on it, that it had actually done so but did not have the boldness to declare it. He further reminded Prasad that at Lucknow (1916) the Congress had indeed accepted separate electorates, which constituted the main reason for its opposition to the Communal Award and asked Prasad not to make a fetish of joint electorates. When Prasad stuck to his position—emphasizing that experience since 1916 had shown that separate electorates had done great harm and 'the longer they remained the deeper would the poison go'—and asked Jinnah to let him know if he had some other proposals for a settlement, Jinnah retorted that it was for the Congress to make proposals if it wanted modifications in the Communal Award which was advantageous to Muslims, adding: 'Whoever heard a party which had obtained a decree coming forward with proposals to alter it? If the other party comes forward with suggestions, the decree-holder considering that it would be best to have a settlement, might consider them.'[42]

It is not known how Jinnah felt after the talks on the first day, but Prasad has recorded that the manner in which they proceeded did not raise much hope in him, though he did not despair and devoted himself whole-heartedly to the task set before them.[43] After the conversations on the first day he wrote to the former that 'the only way for progress' was to jointly formulate some proposals which both of them could present to their respective organizations as jointly emanating from them. After a few days Jinnah replied that he was prepared, 'in his individual capacity', to meet Prasad for the purpose mentioned by the latter. So the talks were resumed on 28 January.[44] After several meetings, on 14 February, the two were able to draft a formula, according to which separate electorates were to be replaced by joint electorates subject to the following conditions:

1. Franchise was to be so framed and adjusted as to reflect the proportion of population of the various communities in the electoral rolls for the provinces and the centre and for this purpose differential franchise was to be adopted wherever necessary.[45]
2. There would be no overlapping of electorates or constituencies.
3. In the Punjab the Sikhs would choose the constituencies for the seats allotted to them under the Communal Award. Thereafter Hindus would do the same. The remaining constituencies

would be awarded to the Muslims as per the Award, excluding the seats allotted to Europeans, Anglo-Indians, Indian Christians and Special Constituencies.

4. In Bengal if any seats were obtained from Europeans, for which joint efforts were to be made by Hindus and Muslims, the same would be divided between Hindus and Muslims in proportion to their population in the province. Subject to this, seats allotted to the Muslims under the Award were to remain reserved for them, excluding the seats given to Europeans, Anglo-Indians, Indian Christians and Special Constituencies.
5. As regards the other provinces the number of seats reserved for the Muslims were to remain the same as provided under the Award.
6. Similarly, seats allotted to Muslims by the Award in the Central Legislature were to remain reserved for them.[46]

Prasad would have liked a reduction of seats for the Muslims at the Centre where they would be able to secure more than one-third of the total, as they were expected to win in five or six special constituencies. He would also have liked reservation of seats to be limited to ten years. However, when Jinnah pointed out that neither of the two points would be acceptable to Muslims, Prasad did not press them as he had secured Jinnah's agreement to the replacement of separate by joint electorates—a point of cardinal importance for the Congress. Prasad explained his thinking in course of a letter to Patel on the same day that he and Jinnah were able to draft the above mentioned formula:

> Joint electorates are in themselves important in opening a way for joint action which had great possibilities for the future. Hindus have always attached great value to them and if they can be had they should be prepared to pay some price. The Musalmans have got separate electorates as also the seats. It will be difficult enough to induce them to give up even the first. I therefore feel that this formula furnishes a fair basis for agreement.[47]

Apart from the drawing up of the draft formula, Prasad and his important Congress colleagues, who were kept informed of the progress of the talks with Jinnah, had another ground to be optimistic about future relations with the Muslim League: Jinnah' adoption of a radical posture in the Central Assembly and voting in line with the Congress members on several issues. Thus when Prasad and Jinnah met for talks on 30 January, the latter, according to the record kept by Prasad, referred 'with pardonable pride' to the proceedings of he Central

Assembly that day when members of his party and the Congress had joined hands to throw out the Indo-British Trade Agreement (popularly known as the Ottawa Agreement).[48] Jinnah also explored with Prasad ways of presenting an united front when the J.P.C. Report came to be discussed in the Assembly. Although, because of differences on the Communal Award, the discussions on that day remained inconclusive, a partial united front did in fact emerge in the Central Assembly on 4 February. When the Government moved for consideration of the J.P.C. Report, Bhulabhai Desai, the leader of the Congress Party, moved for its total rejection and also pleaded that in view of the delicacy of the situation in India no opinion be expressed on the Communal Award. Having been defeated by a combination of government and almost all non-Congress members, including Jinnah and his supporters, the Congress remained neutral on Jinnah's first amendment calling for the acceptance on the Communal Award until an agreed substitute for it merged, but supported his remaining two amendments respectively describing the scheme regarding the provinces as 'most unsatisfactory and disappointing' and that regarding an all-India federation as 'fundamentally bad and totally unacceptable to the people of British India'. All of the three amendments proposed by Jinnah were, of course, carried, the first with the help of the Government members and the second and third with that of the Congress.[49] Although the debate on the J.P.C. Report primarily represented a victory for Jinnah's tactics and the Congress had only partial success—a Government report describing it as two-third defeat and one-third victory—the Congress circles were jubilant at the trend of the discussions.[50] They must have particularly been pleased by Jinnah's unequivocal support for the establishment of full responsible government at the centre and his opposition to the scheme of all-India federation primarily on the ground that it did not provide for such a government. His study of the scheme, he pointed out, had led him to conclude that it meant 'nothing but absolute sacrifice' of all that British India had stood for during the preceding 50 years in the development of democratic institutions. When a member pointed out that by opposing the scheme of all-India federation he was playing into the hands of Winston Churchill, Jinnah retorted:

> We are not agreeing with Mr. Churchill. Mr. Churchill's point is that he does not want any advance at the Centre. That is not my point. My point is that I do not want this scheme at the Centre, and I call upon you to review the whole position in consultation with Indian opinion and to

establish responsible government in my country. (Loud and prolonged applause)[51]

In course of the same speech, however, while pleading for acceptance of the Communal Award Jinnah underlined the separate identity of the Indian Muslims in a way in which he had never done before:

> Minorities mean a combination of things. It may be that a minority has a different religion from the other citizens of a country. Their language may be different, their race may be different, their culture may be different, and the combination of all these various elements—religion, culture, race, language, music, and so forth makes the minority a separate entity in the State, and that separate entity as an entity wants safeguards. Surely, therefore, we must face this question as a political problem, we must solve it and not evade it.[52]

Perhaps, in view of Jinnah's ardent plea for the early establishment of responsible government at the Centre as well as his continuing dialogue with Prasad for evolving a substitute for the Communal Award no one cared to analyse the significance of those words being uttered by Jinnah at that time. The hopes regarding Congress-League cooperation aroused by Jinnah's speech in the Central Assembly on 4 February as also the hammering of a joint formula by him and Prasad for replacing the Communal Award ten days later were, however, not fulfilled. The formula had been devised only as 'a basis for further discussion' and Prasad and Jinnah decided to ascertain opinion on it amongst Hindus, Sikhs and Muslims. As Prasad, joined in some cases by Govind Ballabh Pant, Bhulabhai Desai, J.B. Kripalani and G.D. Birla, talked to Hindu and Sikh leaders, he found strong opposition to differential franchise for Muslims as well as to statutory majority for them in the Punjab and Bengal. Malaviya insisted on the number of Muslim seats in the central legislature being reduced to 33.3 per cent as demanded earlier by Muslims. Representatives of Hindus in Bengal insisted that if any seats became available from Europeans they should go only to Hindus till they secured representation in the legislature commensurate with their population in the province.

Jinnah, on the other hand, told Prasad on 20 February that Muslims were asking him about the attitude of Hindu Mahasabha leaders, in particular Malaviya, and said that he would be able to secure the support of Muslims only if Prasad obtained their signatures accepting the formula. Two days later he pointed out that 'with propaganda being carried on his position was becoming very difficult and even negotiations were made very difficult'. Again, on 27 February, he 'complained at length that a tearing propaganda was being carried on and he was finding great difficulty in dissuading Mussalmans from attacking it [the formula]'. When Prasad asked if an agreement between the Congress and the League was a practical proposition, Jinnah replied that such an agreement would be useless. For the Government would not accept such an agreement and change the Communal Award.[53] That was the end of the Prasad-Jinnah talks.

In retrospect, it is ironical and at the same time revealing of Jinnah's continuing dilemma that, as noticed earlier, it was he who had, at the start of the talks with Prasad, suggested that the Congress and League should come to an agreement and go to the country with it, marginalizing the extremists on both sides. Later, he had agreed to a specific provision in this regard by Prasad in writing. Both thus agreed that they were holding talks for an agreement between the Congress and the League. However, when Jinnah saw opinion in Muslim circles turning against him he insisted on Prasad securing the support of Malaviya and other Hindu leaders before he could put the Prasad-Jinnah formula before Muslims, who were, of course, certain to be upset because it was based on the substitution of separate by joint electorates. Jinnah, on the other hand, was fully aware of the strong opposition of Malaviya and other Hindu Mahasabha leaders to the formula. His insistence on their support for the formula was, therefore, devised as providing him a somewhat plausible escape-route from his dilemma. For though he was as keen as ever on a Congress-League settlement, he was not prepared to risk his position of leadership among the Muslims for securing such a settlement. The excuse was to some extent plausible because, as pointed out earlier, Prasad and Jinnah had agreed upon a formula on 14 February only 'as a basis for further discussion' and they had also decided to 'ascertain opinion amongst Hindus, Sikhs and Muslims on it'. It would have been a different matter if they had prepared their formula with a view to being placed immediately before the Congress Working Committee and the League Council. It is, of course, true that even after ascertaining opinion among the different communities it was open to the two leaders, regardless of the attitude of the Mahasabha leaders, to go back to their initial understanding and submit their joint formula, revised if necessary, to their respective organizations. Prasad suggested this at the last stage, but Jinnah refused to go along, for reasons which are not difficult to imagine. After the success of the Congress in most of the general constituencies, except in Bengal, in the election to the Central Assembly in 1934, Prasad, unlike Motilal Nehru in 1928 or

Gandhi in 1931, could, without any fear, disregard extremist Hindu opinion, especially when armed with the Muslim League's approval for the burial of separate electorates. In contrast, Jinnah, seeking to revive a moribund organization and to unite all Muslims under its leadership, in the face of continuing challenge from hardliners like the Aga Khan and Fazl-i-Husain, could not afford to antagonize the generality of Muslim opinion by sticking to a formula based on the substitution of separate by joint electorates, especially when a section of apparently powerful Hindu opinion was not prepared to accept those portions of the formula which safeguarded the Muslim position. The chief cause of the failure of the Prasad-Jinnah talks, therefore, lay in their decision to depart from their initial understanding to work out a settlement between the Congress and the League and to search for consensus among the leaders of the different communities on the basis of the formula hammered out by them. Such a consensus had failed to materialize in spite of repeated efforts since 1927, and there was no basis for hope that it could do so in 1935. Jinnah, aware of the trend of Muslim opinion, which would not accept the substitution of separate by joint electorates, especially when no one was prepared to offer Muslims more seats in the legislatures than those allocated to them under the Communal Award, let Prasad do his bit first, before presenting the formula to Muslims for their consideration. If he had begun the exercise of ascertaining Muslim opinion on the joint formula and gone over to discuss it with Fazl-i-Husain and other leaders of the Muslim Conference, he too would have fared no better than Prasad had done in his discussions with Malaviya and other leaders of Hindu opinion. The brief obituary of the talks, issued on 1 March 1935, under the signatures of both Prasad and Jinnah accurately summed up the cause of their failure: 'We had made an earnest effort to find a solution of the communal problem which would satisfy all the parties concerned. We regret that in spite of our best efforts we have not been able to find such a formula.'[54]

Whatever the cause of the failure of the Prasad-Jinnah talks there can be no doubt that as a result of that failure the communal problem became even more intractable than before. Several months before their commencement Tej Bahadur Sapru, noted for his unbiased outlook, had observed that during the recent past several attempts had been made to compose differences among Indian leaders, but all had failed after coming within an inch of settlement and each attempt that had failed had made the position worse.[55] It could not be different this time.

III

Barely five months after the failure of the Prasad-Jinnah talks came the announcement that the Government of India Bill, based on the report of the Joint Parliamentary Committee, had received royal assent on 4 August 1935. The new Act provided for full provincial autonomy, subject to certain special powers of the Governor General. Dyarchy was abolished and the entire field of provincial administration, again subject to certain special powers of the Governor, was to be placed in the hands of ministers responsible to the lower house of the provincial legislature. The number of voters was also enlarged. At the Centre the Act provided for the establishment of a Federation, with partial responsible government, comprising both the provinces of British India and the Indian states. This was, however, made conditional on the accession to federation, by their own free will, of a sufficient number of states—enough to occupy 52 of the 104 seats allotted to the states in the upper house of the central legislature and to make up half of the total population of all the people living in the states. This was expected to take time and indeed, for one reason or another, never materialized. The provincial part of the Act, however, was enforced without much delay. Elections to provincial legislatures were held in the winter months of 1936-7 and responsible governments installed in all the provinces. The allocation of seats in he legislatures was strictly in accordance with the provisions of the Communal Award, as modified by the Poona Pact.

The major Muslim organizations had accepted the Communal Award, and the Congress too had practically acquiesced in it, with its formula of neither accepting nor rejecting it, and won a majority of general seats in the Central Assembly on that basis in 1934, thereby marginalizing the Hindu Mahasabha and its supporters. It could, therefore, be assumed with some plausibility by well-meaning persons, not fully conversant with all the complexities of the situation, that the stage was now set for a considerable easing of the communal tension, opening the way to harmonious Hindu-Muslim relations, or, at any rate, Congress-League relations. We find this assumption underlying almost all works dealing with India's Partition. That this did not happen and the communal problem actually got further aggravated with the inauguration of provincial autonomy has been generally ascribed in these works to the failure of the Congress to form coalition ministries in the provinces with the League's cooperation after the elections of 1936-7, particularly in U.P., in breach of an understanding arrived at earlier when prospects for a resounding Congress victory at the polls had not appeared bright. This is supposed to have so upset the leadership of the Muslim League as to turn its mind towards Partition. Even those who do not acknowledge the existence of any prior understanding for the setting up of coalition ministries tend to underestimate the difficulties in the way of such an endeavour and to emphasize that there was hardly any difference between the objectives and programmes of the Congress and the League at that time. They also consider the failure of the Congress in this regard as a turning point in the history of Congress-League relations and the shaping of the latter's policy.[56]

A close examination of the political situation in India between 1935 and 1937 shows that none of these assumptions has been based on facts. The general political situation in the country on the eve of provincial elections in 1936-7 was not at all relaxed, but continued to be pervaded by communal tension as before. Far from there being an understanding to have a coalition, the relations between the Congress and the Muslim League, not good to start with, had worsened as the election campaign gathered momentum and gone on deteriorating further after the end of that campaign. The failure of the so-called coalition talks in U.P. in July 1937 was the result of the conflict between the two organizations rather than its cause. Indeed, in view of all this what would be surprising is not that the talks failed, but that they were held at all. Actually what took place in U.P. were not talks for a coalition but for a merger of the provincial League in the Congress. Further, as a result partly of the evolution of Muslim politics and ideology between 1877 and 1937, and partly of the spectacle of a victorious Congress, which was indistinguishable for the League's leadership from a victorious Hinduism, in contrast to its own poor showing, that leadership had already, before the failure of the so-called coalition talks in U.P. in late July 1937, decided in favour of laying greater stress on Muslim nationalism or communalism as a means of building up its strength. At the same time, it had also begun to feel attracted towards the idea of the establishment of a sovereign Muslim State, mooted a few years earlier and rapidly spreading among the Muslim intelligentsia and youth, particularly in the Punjab, though because of purely tactical reasons, it did not consider it prudent to air it in public at that stage.

Thus although the Act of 1935 had fulfilled almost all the demands of the Muslim League, the continued opposition of most Hindu leaders, particularly in Bengal, to the Communal Award and the somewhat ambivalent attitude towards it adopted by the Congress—neither accepting nor rejecting it—continued to cause a good deal of tension among the Muslim elite. The failure of the Prasad-Jinnah talks in 1935 to provide a generally acceptable formula to take the place of the Communal Award further aggravated the situation and helped maintain an atmosphere of distrust and suspicion in Hindu-Muslim relations in politics. 'The communal question', reported G.D. Birla to Lord Linlithgow in December 1935, while the latter was preparing to assume his responsibilities in India as Viceroy and Governor-General, 'is getting worse from day to day without any sign of improvement.' He expressed the view that the situation would not calm down till the Hindus in Muslim-majority provinces and Muslims in Hindu-majority provinces realized that 'majority rule must prevail'.[57] Another perceptive observer of the Indian scene, Tej Bahadur Sapru, remarked in May 1936 that he could see 'no sign of a communal settlement in the present temper of the two communities'.[58]

While the controversy over the allocation of seats to different communities in the various legislatures had not been resolved to general satisfaction, a new controversy regarding the future national language of India had arisen. This was in some ways a continuation of the old conflict between the supporters of Hindi and Urdu. Gandhi had evolved a new formula to resolve this controversy by seeking to popularize the use of the term Hindustani instead of either Hindi or Urdu. He held the view that there was no basic difference between simple Hindi and simple Urdu and the language generally spoken by the common people in northern India could be called Hindustani and serve as the national language of India. In order to resolve the difference in script, he suggested that both Devnagari, in which Hindi was written, and Arabic, which was used for writing Urdu, could be accepted with freedom to the writer to decide which script he would use. At the same time, however, he also expressed the hope that a day might come when Devnagari would become acceptable to all sections of the Indian population. With this end in view, he supported a proposal made by the Akhil Bharatiya Hindi Sahitya Sammelan (All India Hindi Literary Association) for the popularization of the Devnagari script as the common script of all Indian languages, particularly those descended from Sanskrit.[59] Gandhi's suggestion regarding Hindustani did not find general acceptance and was opposed by the supporters of both Hindi and Urdu. There was so much tension on this issue that when in April 1936 at the inaugural conference of the Akhil Bharatiya Sahitya Parishasd (All India Literary Association) at Nagpur Gandhi in course of his speech mentioned Hindi or Hindustani, without making any reference to Urdu, as the future *lingua franca* of India;[60] he was subjected to a severe attack in the Urdu press. His bona fides, along with those of Nehru who also had been present at Nagpur, were attacked and the former was accused of a 'deep conspiracy to crush Urdu'.[61] Even the ardent Muslim supporters of Gandhi and Nehru remained silent and failed to say anything in their defence. Nehru expressed his deep anguish at this situation. 'Is it our fate', he wrote to a Muslim friend in the Congress, 'that always the reactionary Muslims should take the lead in everything and the nationalists should follow in their wake like dumb-driven cattle.'[62] Writing to another such friend he remarked: 'I can only conclude that most people, in connection with this matter or similar matters, are in a pathological condition and unable to act and think clearly.'[63] The fact was that most of these Muslim leaders, whom Nehru was expecting to speak up in defence of Gandhi, were themselves deeply concerned at what appeared to them as the latter's preference for Hindi.[64]

Gandhi understood the significance of this episode. 'The whole atmosphere', he wrote, 'is surcharged with suspicion. No person's declarations or acts are above suspicion.'[65] Writing a week later, he again remarked: 'The difficulty with us is that just now our hearts are not one and the best of us are affected by the virus of mutual suspicion.' In a bid to clarify his position he unequivocally declared:

> Hindi, Hindustani and Urdu are different names for the same speech just as the dialects of Cornwall, Lancashire and Middlesex are different names of the same speech. What is being aimed at today is not to evolve a new language but to adopt the language known under the three names as the inter-provincial language.

He also clarified his position on the question of script, clearly accepting both the Devnagari and Arabic scripts without, of course, dissociating himself from the movement for popularizing Devanagari as the common script of all Indian languages, particularly those derived from Sanskrit. As he put it:

> At the present moment insistence on Devnagari by Mussalmans is not to be thought of. Insistence on the adoption of Arabic script by the vast mass of Hindus is still less thinkable. What therefore I have suggested as the definition of Hindi or Hindustani is 'that language which is generally spoken by Hindus and Mussalmans of the North, whether written in Devnagari or Urdu'. I abide by that definition, in spite of protests to the contrary. But there is

undoubtedly a Devnagari movement with which I have allied myself wholeheartedly and that is to have it as the common script for all the languages spoken in the different provinces, specially those who have a large Sanskrit vocabulary.[66]

The suspicions, however, continued unabated. As late as May 1937, no less a person than Mian Iftikharuddin, then a prominent leader of the Congress in the Punjab, expressed doubts about Gandhi's fairmindedness on the Hindi-Urdu question as well as the efficacy of his views on it in allaying Muslim suspicions. In a confidential letter to K.M. Ashraf, who was incharge of the Muslim mass contact programme at the office of the All India Congress Committee, Iftikharuddin observed:

> I must confess that I regard Gandhi's view regarding Urdu-Hindi controversy typically evasive and confusing. I myself, in spite of my limited knowledge and lukewarm sympathies with Urdu, remain unconvinced of Gandhi's fairmindedness in this matter and I have my doubts if one could utilise Gandhi's views in convincing or converting the Muslim intelligentsia.[67]

Apart from issues like the Communal Award and the Hindi-Urdu controversy, which were poisoning the political atmosphere on the eve of 1937 elections, the basic divergence in the political outlook of the Congress and the Muslim League now became much sharper than ever before. From the very beginning the Congress had appealed to all Indians, without any difference of caste or creed, claimed to speak on behalf of all Indians and made particular effort to draw Muslims to its ranks. On the other hand, the Muslim League, again right from its birth, had tried to unite all Muslims under itself and made the safeguarding of the supposed special interests of Muslims as its main objective. Indeed it owed its very existence to the assumption that those interests could not be safeguarded without a separate political organization of Muslims. This naturally represented a challenge to the Congress claim to speak on behalf of all Indians. In spite of this basic divergence, however, the dividing line between the two organizations had not been too sharply drawn in their early years and some Muslim leaders continued to belong to both of them just as some Hindu leaders retained membership in both the Congress and the Hindu Mahasabha. As a result of the intensification of the Pan-Islamic movement in India, which had inculcated an anti-British outlook among Muslims, the two organizations had even cooperated together. The aftermath of the Khilafat movement, however, had gradually led not merely to a sharpening of Hindu-Muslim differences but also to a deterioration in Congress-League relations. The more negotiations and discussions took place for solving the communal problem, the more intricate it became. Gradually a view developed in the Congress that the best way of solving the communal problem was not to attach too much importance to it, but to concentrate on the struggle for freedom and appeal to all Indians, regardless of caste or creed, to join it. A natural corollary of this view was to avoid giving much importance to communal organizations. Although developing fitfully since 1930, this became a settled Congress policy after the failure of the Prasad-Jinnah talks in 1935. Jawaharlal Nehru, who assumed the presidency of the Congress in April 1936, emerged as its most articulate champion. Imbued with a secular approach to politics and full of enthusiasm for socialism and for viewing India's problems in the world perspective, he believed that the real problem of India was the economic problem, symbolized by the backwardness and poverty of the masses, and the solution of it lay in national freedom and socialism. The communal problem appeared to him as no genuine problem at all, but a phoney problem created by political and social reactionaries among both Hindus and Muslims, who had no interest either in India's freedom or in the welfare of the masses, but only wanted to increase their share in the loaves and fishes of office. According to him, the interest of the Congress could not be served by encouraging such groups. While he had expressed such views on several occasions in the past,[68] he gave a particularly forceful and cogent expression to them in course of his presidential address to the Congress session at Lucknow held in April 1936:

> . . . in my opinion, a real solution of the communal problem will only come when economic issues, affecting all religious groups and cutting across communal boundaries, arise. Apart from the upper middle classes, who live in hopes of office and patronage, the masses and the lower middle classes have to face identical political and economic problems. It is odd and significant that all the communal demands of any group, of which so much is heard, have nothing whatever to do with these problems of the masses and the lower middle classes.
>
> It is also significant that the principal communal leaders, Hindu or Muslim or others, are political reactionaries, quite apart from the communal question. . . . With them there can be no cooperation, for that would mean co-operation with reaction. But I am sure that with the larger masses and the middle classes, who may have temporarily been led away by the specious claims of their communal leaders, there must be the fullest cooperation, and out of that cooperation will come a fairer solution of this problem.[69]

Just at the time when the Congress, tired of endless negotiations, was adopting this approach to the communal problem in India, the Muslim League, under the leadership of Jinnah, decided to revive itself, make a reality of its claim to represent Muslims in all parts of the country and, for the first time, contest the forthcoming elections to the provincial legislatures under the new Act. Jinnah detested the political and social reactionaries, who constituted the bulk of the League's leadership and supported India's demand for freedom, but he had no liking for the path of struggle charted by the Congress under Gandhi's leadership and also believed that Muslims must have a strong organization of their own to safeguard their interests. While the former made him almost indistinguishable from Congress leaders as far as the objective of securing freedom from British rule was concerned,[70] the latter created a great barrier between him and the Congress, which was now more determined than ever before to strengthen its position as a national organization representing all sections of the Indian people, including the Muslims. Although the Congress did not have a large number of Muslims in its ranks, it always had some Muslims in it, in almost all parts of the country and at all levels of its vast organization. On the other hand, the Muslim League had become a moribund organization by 1934-5. The All India Muslim Conference, which had been active in recent years, was also then more or less in the same state. Other Muslim organizations were generally weak and their influence was confined to particular areas. In such a situation it was natural for the Congress to nourish the hope that, particularly with a president like Nehru, who had a pronounced secular image and was noted for his strong appeal to the youth, including the Muslim youth, it might be able to attract the Muslims in large numbers again just as it had done during the days of the Khilafat movement. But if Jinnah succeeded in reviving the League and turning it into a really representative organization of the Muslims, the political forces in the country would become polarized on communal lines and this could not but seriously weaken the cause of Indian nationalism. Indeed, in view of the recent accentuation of communal differences and the passionate espousal of a clearly separatist ideology of Muslim nationalism in its extreme form by such persons as Nawab Zulfiqar Ali Khan (1928), Mohammad Iqbal (1930) and Rahmat Ali (1933), the emergence of a strong, well-knit, all-India Muslim political organization, which could not materialize without appealing to and strengthening Muslim separatism, could have really dangerous possibilities from the point of view of Indian nationalism.

All this could not have been hidden from an extremely intelligent person like Jinnah. His stated position in 1936 was that India's freedom could not be attained without Hindu-Muslim unity, and that such unity could not be attained without a strong Muslim political organization. For, so long as the Muslims remained politically divided and unorganized, the Congress would not pay any serious attention to them. The Muslims, therefore, should first deserve to be taken seriously by organizing themselves before desiring a political settlement with the Hindus: 'If Muslims could speak with one voice, a settlement between Hindus and Muslims would come quicker.'[71] The desired terms of this settlement were, however, not spelled out. Some contemporary observers were baffled by this reasoning: 'Jinnah's nationalism' remarked one of them, 'is of a curious type. . . . It must be a wonderful brand of nationalism which believes in communal organisations with a view to negotiations on the basis of different communities and yet hopes for the consummation of a common nationhood irrespective of religious divergences.'[72]

All this while, as will be noticed in Section VII below, thanks to its forceful exposition by Rahmat Ali in Britain (1933) the Pakistan idea, based on the separate nationhood of Muslims and envisaging the Partition of India and setting up of a separate sovereign State comprising its Muslim majority areas, had been gathering momentum. Although not yet openly supported by any political leader or party of standing, the Pakistan National Movement, a new, small organization founded by Rahmat Ali in 1933, was actively engaged in spreading it. Besides, a number of individuals, particularly in the Punjab, were so enthused by it as to contribute articles and letters to the press ardently supporting it. On the other hand, Hindu nationalism, although lacking any large following, was acquiring a more strident tone rather than ever before. Thus presiding over the 18th annual session of the All India Hindu Mahasabha held at Lahore in October (21-3) 1936, Sankaracharya Kurkrote declared in his address that freedom would come to India only when people belonging to 'the alien faiths' were made to live here peacefully and on friendly terms with the Hindus and also realized that 'Hindustan is primarily for the Hindus'. He further affirmed that 'in Hindustan the national race, religion and language ought to be that of Hindus'.[72a] Such writings and speeches, although not representing the views of the majority in either community, could not in any way contribute to the relaxation of tension on the communal front. On the contrary, they were bound to considerably add to such tension by fostering mutual suspicion and distrust between the elites of both the communities, who had a tendency to treat such views as really reflecting majority opinion in each community.

IV

Whatever that might be, there is no doubt that in 1936-7 a clash between the Congress and the Muslim League, spearheaded respectively by Nehru and Jinnah, lay in the logic of history. It soon came into the open as the election campaign gathered momentum. Seeking to utilize the campaign for carrying the message of Indian nationalism to all parts of the country and raising its tempo, Nehru, the chief campaigner on behalf of the Congress as well as its president, emphasized wherever he spoke that what was taking place in India was not a routine contest between a number of political parties as happens during elections in free countries, but a contest between 'two forces—the Congress as representing the will to freedom of the nation, and the British Government in India and its supporters who oppose this urge and try to suppress it. Intermediate groups, whatever virtue they may possess, fade out or line up with one of the principal forces.'[73] This was a perfectly legitimate line for Nehru as the representative of the main political organization engaged in the struggle for freedom to take, but it caused offence to Jinnah, who in course of an election speech on 3 January 1937 remarked: 'There is a third party, namely Mussalmans. We are not going to be dictated to by anybody.' Although he said that the Muslims were ready 'as equal partners' to work for a settlement for the welfare of India, he regretted 'the Congress interfering in the affairs of Muslims by putting up Muslim candidates in opposition to the League candidates'.[74] This, said Nehru in course of a press statement issued on 10 January 1937, was 'communalism raised to the nth power'. For, carried to its logical conclusion Jinnah's stand meant that 'in no department of public activity must non-Muslims have anything to do with Muslim affairs'. The whole assumption behind this stand, emphasized Nehru, was that 'Muslims in India are indeed a nation apart and those who forget this fact commit a sin against the Holy Ghost and offend Mr. Jinnah'. Characterizing such ideas as medieval and out of date he reminded Jinnah that the latter's reference to Muslims as a third party was not at all complimentary to Muslims, for this meant that in the contest between British imperialism and Indian nationalism Muslims would function as 'a political group apart, apparently playing off one against the other, and seeking communal advantage even at the cost of the larger public good'.[75] There were several exchanges like this between the two leaders during 1936-7.[76]

The conclusion of the provincial elections in January-February 1937 did not see any improvement in Congress-League relations; on the contrary, they further drifted apart. The outstanding result of the elections was the emergence of the Congress as the dominant parliamentary party in India winning 716 out of a total of 1585 seats in the provincial legislatures. As only about half of the latter were general seats, open to be contested by all, this was quite an impressive showing. The Congress emerged as a clearly majority party in five provinces (Bihar, C.P., Madras, Orissa and U.P.), a virtually majority party in one more (Bombay, where it had won 86 seats in a house of 175) and as the largest single party in three others (Assam, Bengal and North-West Frontier Province). On the other hand, the League came out with a very poor showing, winning only 105 out of 482 total Muslim seats in all the provincial legislatures. So far as the Muslim majority provinces were concerned, it could not get a single seat in the North-West Frontier Province and Sind and got only one out of 86 Muslim seats in the Punjab; only in Bengal it acquired a respectable position to a certain extent, with 37 out of a total of 119 Muslim seats. In the Hindu-majority provinces, its scoreboard was only slightly better. In Bombay alone it secured a majority of the Muslim seats (20 out of 39). For the rest, it won 27 out of 64 Muslim seats in U.P., 11 out of 28 Muslim seats in Madras, 9 out of 34 Muslim seats in Assam and none at all in Bihar, Orissa and C.P. The Congress, however, had done much worse than the League so far as the Muslim seats were concerned. For it had contested only 58 and secured 26 Muslim seats all over India, acquiring a respectable position only in N.W.F.P. and having no representation on Muslim seats at all in a number of provinces.[77] The bulk of the Muslim seats had gone to local parties, like the Unionist Party in the Punjab, the Krishak Proja Party in Bengal and the National Agriculturist Party in U.P., and to Independents.[78] While their stand on the communal issues was not much different from that of the Muslim League, on political issues they were likely to adopt a more subservient attitude towards the British than the latter.

A realistic analysis of these election results might have placed the Congress in a sober mood. For the same results which set a seal on its dominant position in Indian politics also revealed that its support-base, except in the small north-western corner in India, was largely confined to Hindus. It may be argued that this called for a strategy based on seeking a cooperative relationship with as many Muslim groups as possible, including the League, based on a genuine sharing of power, with a view to winning them over to the cause of Indian nationalism. However, since such a policy had been tried in the past and failed, nobody was in a mood to turn to it again. This attitude was powerfully articulated by Nehru, who headed the Congress at that time and was determined to pursue its new policy based on an apparent rejection of the communal issue as a major factor in Indian politics, projection of the economic issue in its place and a direct appeal to the Muslim masses without paying much attention to the various Muslim parties and groups. His tours during the election campaign, in course of which he had travelled in all parts of India and drew enthusiastic crowds from all sections of the people, including Muslims, had convinced him that if only the Congress could reach the Muslim masses with its message of ending poverty and economic exploitation, the latter would flock to it in large numbers. As he put it in course of his presidential address to the All India Convention of Congress Legislators held in New Delhi on 19 March 1937:

> Only in regard to Muslim seats did we lack success. But our very failure on this occasion had demonstrated that success is easily in our grasp and the Muslim masses are increasingly turning to the Congress. We failed because we had long neglected working among the Muslim masses and we could not reach them in time. But where we reached, especially in the rural areas, we found almost the same response, the same anti-imperialist spirit, as in others. The communal problem, of which we hear so much, seemed to be utterly non-existent when we talked to the peasant, whether Hindu, Muslim or Sikh.[79]

Nehru strongly warned against reverting to the old policy of seeking understanding with separatist Muslim parties or groups. That, according to him, would further aggravate the communal problem and not solve it. The latter was possible only through a direct approach to the Muslim masses and an emphasis on solving their economic problems. To talk of Muslims as a group who might come to terms with Hindus as a group represented a medieval mentality which had no place in the modern world. The problems of poverty and unemployment and national freedom were common to all whether they were Hindus, Muslims, Sikhs or Christians. Once the Congress left the top fringe which was always talking about percentages of seats in the legislatures and state jobs, and reached the masses, those problems would come into limelight and put an end to what was commonly known as the communal problem.[80]

Nehru followed this up by a circular to the Provincial Congress Committees on 31 March 1937 asking them to make a special effort to enrol Muslim members of the Congress. He also suggested that each Provincial Congress Committee should appoint 'a special committee to consider and take in hand this work of increasing Congress contact with the Muslim masses, rural and urban' and to take particular care to issue notices in Urdu in all areas which had an Urdu-speaking population. He further informed the Provincial Congress Committees that the office of the All India Congress Committee was setting up a separate department to coordinate this effort and would gladly help with leaflets, pamphlets, etc.[81] This marked the formal launching of the Muslim mass contact programme of the Congress. Rajendra Prasad, Nehru's immediate predecessor as Congress President and one of the prominent members of the Congress Old Guard, extended his full support to it. In a statement issued to the press on 8 April 1937 he observed that 'Nehru's initiative had come not a day too soon' and exhorted all Congressmen to work most devotedly for its success, ensuring that there was no village without a Congress Committee and no such committee without Muslims.[82]

Nehru had mentioned in his circular on Muslim mass contact that he knew that a large number of Muslims were waiting to be approached by the Congress workers and would gladly join the Congress once they were approached. This might not have been literally true, but there is no doubt that the hectic tours of Nehru around the country with his emphasis on ending the poverty and exploitation of the masses as the primary objective before the Congress and the impressive Congress showing in the elections had created a favourable atmosphere for a general forward push by the Congress among all sections, including the Muslims. This is amply confirmed by British sources. 'I have been a little disturbed', wrote the Viceroy, Lord Linlithgow, to the Secretary of State, Lord Zetland, barely a week after the despatch of Nehru's circular to the Provincial Congress Committees regarding Muslim mass contact, 'to hear from more than one Muslim visitor that there is evident here and there a tendency on the part of the rank and file of Mohammadans to drift towards Congress.'[83] The confidential quarterly survey of the political situation in India, prepared by the Governor-General's Office in its first issue covering the period from 1 August to 31 October 1937, also reported that the efforts of the Congress to persuade the Muslims to join its ranks had 'met with some success, especially among young Muslims and minority sects in the

Muslim community'.[84] In U.P. in particular, the Congress seemed poised for success. According to the Governor, Sir Harry Haig, the League leaders were 'frankly alarmed at the Congress attempt on the Muslim masses and fear it may be successful'.[85] Such fears were not confined to U.P. Mohammad Iqbal reported to Jinnah from Lahore that the situation was 'becoming grave and the Muslim feeling in the Punjab . . . rapidly becoming pro-Congress'.[86] H.S. Suhrawardy followed suit from Calcutta: 'I do feel that the Congress mass-contact movement is spreading rapidly and will succeed in course of time unless we set up our own organizations.'[87] Reports from the Governors of C.P. and Bombay indicated initial Congress headway in those provinces also in enrolling Muslims as members.[88]

The initial promise was, however, not fulfilled. Indeed, it would not be wrong to say that the Congress mass contact campaign, on the whole, proved to be still born. A number of leaflets and pamphlets in Urdu were printed and distributed, but beyond it nothing much could be achieved. A party which could not get more than 58 Muslim candidates to put up in the whole of India out of no less than 482 Muslim seats could not immediately get enough Muslim workers to effectively carry on the work of Muslim mass contact. While most of the Provincial Congress Committees set up special committees for this work, the Gujarat Provincial Congress Committee declined to do so on this ground. 'The problem of Muslim mass contact', wrote Morarji Desai, then Secretary of the Gujarat Provincial Congress Committee, 'has to be very delicately handled in this province as there are no Muslim workers through whom the work can be done.' He further added: 'If non-Muslims take up the work of propaganda among the Muslims, it will meet with no response and it will perhaps give rise to a dangerous counter-propaganda by mischievous persons.'[89] Even in U.P., Nehru's home province and containing the headquarters of the All India Congress Committee, this problem was acutely felt. Urging K.M. Ashraf, in charge of the Muslim mass contact programme at the A.I.C.C. office, to find time to visit districts which badly needed Muslim Congressmen's presence on various occasions, a secretary of the U.P. Provincial Congress Committee considered it 'unfortunate that we have only two or three Muslim Congressmen, and even they do not find time for works which are more important'.[90] He must have meant Congress leaders when he was using the word 'Congressmen', but his letter does underline a serious difficulty faced by those in charge of implementing the Muslim mass contact programme of the Congress. In view of this situation it is not surprising that few

Provincial Congress Committees cared to report to the All India Congress Committee on either their progress or problems faced by them in implementing the programme and the latter could piece together a report about the setting up of special committees in most of the provinces only on the basis of 'stray correspondence and newspaper reports'.[91] The Muslim League, on the other hand, took the challenge posed by the announcement of the Congress programme quite seriously and its workers actively countered the Congress move. A Muslim worker sympathetic to the Congress reported from Meerut (U.P.), in August 1937, that contrary to the popular impression that the Muslim Leaguers were idle and arm-chair politicians they were working hard to gain favour among Muslims and were gaining strength day by day while the Congressmen responsible for Muslim mass contact work were inactive.[92] After Nehru ceased to be president of the Congress enthusiasm for the Muslim mass contact programme evaporated even from the headquarters of the Congress and its General Secretary, J.B. Kripalani, observed in course of a communication addressed to none other than Nehru himself that there had never been 'any separate department at the A.I.C.C. office for Muslim mass contact'.[93] K.M. Ashraf sadly reported to Nehru, then on a tour of Europe, in September 1938:

> Nearer at home in A.I.C.C. office Muslim contact work and the Political and Economic Department have been formally abolished and I have practically no work to do. I don's know, moreover, where I stand. There is no coordination between the A.I.C.C. and the provinces and at our best we have just to carry on the work for the W.C. [Working Committee]. The Congress President [Subhas Chandra Bose] has not even cared to visit us or given us any instruction whatever. I feel every day that I am a parasite on the A.I.C.C. funds. My life is being wasted. . . . Under these conditions I have decided to give up the office work in any case as soon as you are back in Allahabad.[94]

There is no evidence of any effort on Nehru's part to counter Kripalani or take recourse to any other step to revive the Muslim mass contact programme. The only inference one can draw from this is that by that time he had realized that the programme was beyond redemption. He was not wrong in coming to that conclusion.

In the meanwhile, the one result of the much publicised Muslim mass contact programme of the Congress had been to further embitter its relations with the Muslim League. The leaders of the latter considered it a serious challenge to the very existence of their organization and there followed a series of attacks and counter-attacks in the press. Thus Maulana Shaukat Ali in course of a statement to the press on the 21 April 1937, warned that the Muslim mass contact programme of the Congress would 'only widen the gulf and lead to a fearful catastrophe'.[95] This provoked Nehru to issue a lengthy statement to the press four days later explaining afresh the Congress position on Muslims. While doing so he again elaborated the rationale behind the programme of going to the masses and the futility of seeking understanding with communal leaders and groups. 'We have had enough experience of these in the past', he asserted 'and the experience does not call for repetition.'[96] This brought forth the comment from Jinnah on 29 April 1937, that Nehru was 'talking as if he were a sovereign authority'. Jinnah also emphasized that the Muslim League differed from the Congress on political issues in vital respects. Nehru again came out with a statement on 2 May 1937, clarifying the Congress policy and attacking the League's leadership. It was Jinnah, he emphasized, who was adopting a dictatorial attitude by objecting to the Congress carrying on ordinary political work among Muslims and issuing mandates to Muslims as a whole, regardless of their political attitudes or affiliations.[97] In course of a statement issued on 6 July 1937 Jinnah again warned that the Muslim mass contact programme of the Congress was 'fraught with very serious consequences'. There was plenty of scope for Nehru, he added, to improve his own people, the Hinds, just as the Muslim League had plenty of scope to improve the Muslims.[98] This again brought forth a strong rejoinder from Nehru, who claimed that the number of Muslim members of the Congress was enormously greater than the total membership of the Muslim League and affirmed that all the Indian people, regardless of the religion they professed, were his people.[99]

Side by side there developed a controversy—virtually impinging on each side's integrity—between Jinnah and the Congress leaders, notably Prasad and Nehru, on the real cause of the failure of the Prasad-Jinnah talks in 1935. It started with Jinnah observing in course of an address to a public meeting of Muslims in Bombay on 21 May 1937, that in 1935 he had spent four or five weeks holding conferences with Prasad and trying to get the Muslim viewpoint accepted at least by the Congress leaders if not also by those of the Hindu Mahasabha, but did not succeed.[100] When contradicted by J.B. Kripalani, then General Secretary of the Congress, Jinnah reiterated his stand even more forcefully through a statement to the press on 2 July:

At times it is very difficult to say who are Congress leaders and who are Mahasabha leaders, for the line of demarcation between the two with regard to a large number of them is very thin indeed.

Neither Babu Rajendra Prasad nor I had any authority to come to a binding agreement, as the talks were naturally subject to confirmation by the Congress and the Muslim League. Babu Rajendra Prasad tried to ascertain the consensus of opinion among Congress and Hindu Mahasabha leaders regarding the formula which he himself had approved but it was found that not only the Hindu Mahasabha leaders rejected it out of hands but even a certain section of influential Congress leaders were deadly opposed to the formula, which therefore, had to be dropped, as it was useless to proceed further.[101]

This brought forth a detailed rebuttal from Prasad on 11 July, asserting that he would have easily secured the assent of the Congress to the agreed formula, if Jinnah had so desired and further that the talks failed only because Jinnah insisted on the concurrence also of the leaders of the Hindu Mahasabha. Politely asking Jinnah to refresh his memory, Prasad observed:

In the conversation which I had with Mr. Jinnah in 1935 we were able to evolve a formula. I accepted it not only in my personal capacity, but as the President of the Congress and offered to have it ratified by the Congress. I was keeping in touch with prominent Congressmen while the conversations were going on and had received universal support of it from them. . . .

I had gone further and told Mr. Jinnah that the Congress and the League should accept the formula and the Congress would fight those Hindus who were opposed to it as it had fought them during the recent Assembly elections quite successfully in most of the Provinces. But this was not considered enough by Mr. Jinnah and as it was impossible to fulfil his demand that the Hindu Mahasabha should also join the matter had to be dropped. I dare say that Mr. Jinnah will himself recall all this conversation if he charges his memory a little. I kept full notes of the conversations from day to day and they are in the Congress office.[102]

The controversy went on and on, even while the talks on Ministry-making in U.P. were moving towards conclusion, with neither side showing any preparedness to budge from its position. At one stage it even became acrimonious. Nehru remarked in course of a statement to the press on 20 July that Jinnah's methods of controversy were getting 'curiouser and curiouser'.[103] Jinnah retorted by describing him eight days later as 'that busy body President' and remarking: 'What does he know what took place between me and Babu Rajendra Prasad? He seems to carry the responsibility of the whole world on his shoulders and must poke his nose in everything except minding his own business.'[104]

The issue which brought the relations between the Congress and the League to their lowest point till then related to the tactics employed by the League during the by-election in Bundelkhand (U.P.) in the beginning of July 1937, caused by the death of a member of the Muslim League. The Congress decided to challenge the League in that constituency and put up a well-known Congressman as its candidate. In view of the then prevailing political situation, that election was generally considered as a trial of strength between the two organizations.[105] The Muslim League leaders openly appealed to the religious sentiments of the voters and issued a statement declaring that Muslims should come together as they had 'been ordered . . . by God and his Prophet to support the Muslim League candidate to give a crushing reply to the non-Muslim organization' so that in future it would not dare to interfere in the affairs of Muslims.[106] To Nehru the use of such tactics appeared as tantamount to 'working for the Dark Age in India'.[107] This not merely widened further the gulf between the Congress and the League, but also created a hiatus between Nehru and Choudhary Khaliquzzaman, the leader of the League group in the U.P. Legislative Assembly, who had been in the Congress until recently, was generally considered to have pro-Congress sympathies even then, and had shown keen interest in joining the Congress Ministry, if and when formed. He had apparently had some political discussion with Nehru in April 1937 which had led the latter to believe that there was a lot of common ground between them. When Nehru found his name also among the signatories to the above-mentioned appeal, he was shocked. 'I could never have associated your name', he wrote to Khaliquzzaman on 27 June 1937, 'with a document of this kind. Under any circumstances this would have been difficult to believe, but after our talk in April last, I could hardly believe, my eyes.' It seems Khaliquzzaman had, during his meeting with Nehru, given him some assurance regarding the future. For Nehru proceeded to observe in his letter: 'Your assurance stuck to my mind and I valued it. Now that this assurance is gone, it is natural that I should experience some kind of a shock.'[108] Again, in reply to Khaliquzzaman's letter of 29 June 1937, Nehru wrote to him: 'It seems to me that there is a great difference between what you say in this letter and what you told me when we met.' Nehru also felt that Khaliquzzaman had clearly joined the communalist and reactionary camp and there was hardly any meeting ground between them. As he wrote further in his letter, he was rather glad that the Bundelkhand by-election had clarified the situation and revealed the real nature of the conflict then raging in India. That conflict, observed Nehru, was essentially political, between progress on one side and sheer communalism, religious bigotry and political reaction on the other. He was keen to do all that was possible to contribute to the solution of the communal problem, but he could not have any dealings with political reaction, because that would mean a surrender of all his principles and 'a divorce from the realities of the situation'.[109]

V

It was against this background of mounting tension and bitterness that the final round of negotiations for the formation of a so-called Congress-League Coalition Ministry took place in U.P. in the second half of July 1937. Before dealing with these negotiations, it is necessary to dispose of the oft-repeated assumption that there was some kind of understanding, arrived at during the election campaign, to the effect that the Congress and the Muslim League would jointly form a Ministry in U.P. This is absolutely baseless. On the face of it, it appears unreasonable to suppose that such an understanding existed at that stage when even this was not clear whether the Congress would agree to form a Ministry after the elections or not. But we need not depend only on this reasoning and may take other relevant factors into account. It is remarkable that Choudhary Khaliquzzaman, the most aggrieved person because of the failure of the negotiations in U.P., does not mention the existence of such an understanding in his memoirs. Though his phraseology is not unambiguous, it makes it clear that he does not claim the existence of such an understanding on an even informal basis. All that he is able to claim is that 'although there was no written pact between the Muslim League and the Congress for a coalition between the parties in the legislatures, yet the amicable manner in which the elections had been fought both by Congress and the League presaged a future settlement'.[110] He himself has also recorded that as early as 12 February 1937, when all the results of the elections were not known, Rajendra Prasad, who had been president of the Congress during 1935-6 and was one of the secretaries of its Parliamentary Board at that time, issued a statement to the press making it clear that the Congress would not cooperate within the legislatures with any other group or party.[111] The most authoritative contemporary account of the negotiations in U.P. is to be found in Nehru's detailed confidential letter to Prasad, dated 21 July 1937, tracing the Congress-League relations in U.P. since the time of elections; he too does not mention the existence of any such understanding.[112]

Nor is such an understanding referred to in any of the letters sent regularly by the Governor of U.P. to the Viceroy or by the latter to the Secretary of State for India during 1937-9. The first reference to such an understanding in a communication between British officials occurs in Linlithgow's letter to Zetland dated 29 March 1940 while reporting an interview with B. Shiva Rao, then a correspondent of the *Hindu*, two days earlier. According to it the latter had mentioned that as per his information, a 'Gentleman's Agreement' did exist between the Congress and the League in U.P. to the effect that they would form a Coalition Ministry, but the Congress had gone back on it after the elections as it had been able to secure an absolute majority by itself. He went on to assert that Nehru had himself mentioned this to him as the reason for what Shiva Rao described as a breach of faith.[113] For reasons mentioned in the preceding paragraph, Shiva Rao's testimony lacks credibility. Perhaps the Viceroy did consider it in this light. For a few months later he got the matter investigated. The testimony of his officials is telling. The matter was referred to J.C. Donaldson, who had been Secretary to the Governor of U.P. in 1937 and was then working in the Governor General's Secretariat (Reforms). He categorically affirmed in a note dated 13 August 1940 that 'he did not think that there was in the U.P. any definite agreement of the kind mentioned between the Congress and the Muslim League leaders'. After describing the various developments, in the light of the information possessed by him, he concluded:

> I have never heard it seriously alleged that the Muslim League had been tricked in the way suggested. It was, I think, sufficiently well known that while the League got valuable assistance from the Congress in the election, it had not been in a position to contribute to any large extent to the Congress success. The direct benefits of the election alliance went to the League. That body had at that time little to offer to the Congress in the U.P., and I do not think that a bargain over Ministerships of the kind suggested was either likely or did in fact take place.[114]

Thorne, the next senior official, agreed with this and added that while he had heard stories of the alleged pact and its violation and had seen occasional allusions to the matter in the press, his impression was that 'these stories had no currency (or very little) until a long time had passed and until the manufacture of Muslim League grievances had been organised'.[115]

VI

Having thus laid the ghost of a prior understanding regarding the formation of a coalition ministry in U.P. finally to rest, we can proceed to describe what actually happened. There is no doubt that there had been considerable cooperation between the Congress and the League during the elections. The main contest was between the Congress and the big landlords, both Hindu and Muslim, grouped under the National Agriculturist Party and enjoying encouragement and backing from the Government. The Congress apparently felt that it did not have much chance of defeating that party in Muslim constituencies through its own candidates and thought it wiser to support the candidates set up by the Muslim League in many of the Muslim constituencies, for it considered the National Agriculturist Party as the main opponent. There was no formal agreement or arrangement between the Congress and the Muslim League, and for some seats there was actually a contest between them, but by and large Congressmen, where they did not have their own candidate and the League's candidate was not considered an out-and-out reactionary, generally supported the League's candidates.[116]

As soon as the elections were over, rumours began to float that some Muslim Leaguers might join the Congress Party as well as the ministry, but nothing seemed certain. The talks between Govind Ballabh Pant and Khaliquzzaman, leaders respectively of the Congress and Muslim League Assembly Parties in U.P., were held on this basis—and not on that of a coalition between the two parties—right from the beginning. Even before all the election results were announced, but after it became clear that the Congress was being returned with a clear majority, Haig reported to Linlithgow in February 1937, that the Congress was likely to have some understanding with the left wing of the Muslim League from which two ministers were expected to be taken, taking with them about fifteen Muslim Leaguers into the Congress.[117] A few days later, however, he wrote that the situation was 'still obscure'. There were rumours that the Congress would make efforts to win over 'at least the whole of the Muslim League group and thus split the Muslims seriously'. The Congress seemed to be alive to the danger of having an active and united Muslim opposition to itself in the Assembly. On the other hand, it seemed doubtful that the Congress would 'pass over the handful of genuine Congress Muslims in favour of those who are clearly not in real sympathy with the Congress aims'.[118] Apparently the Congress leaders were hoping to solve this dilemma by asking those Leaguers whom they took in the Ministry to sign the Congress pledge. The position obtaining in March-April 1937 was thus described by the Governor:

> The Muslim League position is obscure and uncertain. When the Congress appeared contemplating taking office, they had adopted a very rigid attitude with regard to the Muslims and it was understood that they would not take in any Muslim who did not sign the Congress pledge. The Muslim League, under the leadership of Khaliq, were exceedingly ready to come to a settlement with them, but the Congress showed no signs of accepting this position. On the other hand, as soon as Mr. Pant had seen me on 24 March and office acceptance appeared to be impossible, overtures were immediately made by the Congress to the Muslim League and I am told they were offered two seats in the Cabinet. These negotiations have since continued and there is no doubt that the Muslim League are looking forward to an alliance with the Congress and taking office.[119]

This report is confirmed by the Congress and League sources, except in one important detail regarding the change in Congress stance. Actually, even after 24 March, the talks of Muslim Leaguers joining the Congress Ministry, if and when formed, proceeded only on the basis of their joining the Congress Party. Reporting on his talks with Khaliquzzaman at that time Pant informed Nehru:

> I saw him on the evening of the 29th March after the acceptance of office by the Congress had been finally ruled out. I did not like the idea of the Muslim League cooperating with any Ministry and got the desired assurance from Khaliq. I had a long talk with him and stressed the need and advisability of the Nationalist Mussalmans merging themselves in the Congress. Similarly I pressed him to join the Congress actively both inside and outside the legislature. He has well-nigh agreed to do so but wanted to examine the matter further before taking an irrevocable decision.[120]

That Khaliquzzaman was seriously considering joining the Congress with his supporters is also confirmed by the Governor who reported that the former had begun almost openly to identify himself with the Congress: he had a talk with Nehru to discuss the terms for joining the Congress and, as Chairman of the Lucknow Municipal Board, invited Pant to perform the hoisting of the Congress flag over its office building.[121] Reports of these goings on appearing in the press perturbed Jinnah, but his effort to secure clarification from Khaliquzzaman in April 1937 failed. When the latter did not reply to his communication even after three weeks, Jinnah issued a public warning to the Congress as well as to Khaliquzzaman. In a statement issued to the press on 25 April 1937, he observed that it was no use dealing with men who were in and out of the Congress and the League for securing personal advantages and that agreements arrived at with them would not improve matters in any way. He also expressed the hope that the Muslims of U.P. would not betray the Muslims of India and that Khaliquzzaman would not enter into any commitments which were likely to be repudiated not only by the Muslims of U.P., but by the Indian Muslims as a whole. Khaliquzzaman issued a rejoinder to this statement and alleged that Jinnah had been misled by half-truths conveyed to him by interested persons. The issue was finally settled only on 7 May 1937, when the U.P. Muslim League Parliamentary Board met in Lucknow with Jinnah himself in the chair and agreed upon a compromise formula according to which the Muslim League Party in the legislature was not to be merged with the Congress Party, but would be free to explore avenues of cooperation with it or with any other party on the basis of an agreed programme.[122] Khaliquzzaman accepted this decision with a brave face, but the fact could not be hidden that it meant a clear repudiation of the policy towards which he had been inclined for some time. 'Choudhury Kahliquzzaman's policy', reported the U.P. Governor, 'was completely defeated, but he professed to accept the policy laid down by the League under Mr. Jinnah's influence.'[123] The Governor had made a forecast at least two weeks earlier that some such thing was going to happen. He had then estimated that Khaliquzzaman was likely to be defeated at the meeting of the U.P. Muslim League Parliamentary Board and 'might be driven out of the League into the Congress', in which case not more than ten M.L.A.s were likely to follow him. 'On the other hand', added the Governor, 'Khaliq, who is nothing if not adroit, may not wish to burn his boats in this manner, and if he finds himself in danger of defeat may try to remain in the Muslim League by accepting some kind of compromise.'[124]

Whatever that may have been, Khaliquzzaman had now to be more circumspect in his negotiations with the Congress; it was in any case no longer possible for him to contemplate joining the Congress Party in the Assembly. He was still keen, however, to join the Ministry if he could do so together with his colleague, Nawab Ismail Khan, the new

Chairman of the League Parliamentary Board in U.P., and on the basis of terms which would not result in his isolation from other leaders of the League. The Congress, had its own problem in bringing Muslim League members into the Ministry at the cost of those Muslims, however small in number, who had stood by it, including some, like the leaders of the Jamiat-ul-Ulama, who had worked for the Muslim League in the Assembly elections, but had recently parted company from it on account of its pronounced anti-Congress postures. The dilemma before the Congress was very real, especially after the Bundelkhand by-election in which the League had carried on its campaign on the basis of the cry of 'Islam in danger' and even then a number of Muslims had supported the Congress, though, of course, they had not succeeded in securing victory. On the other hand, the Congress leaders, particularly Nehru and Azad, felt attracted by the prospect of the League ceasing to exist as a separate group in U.P. and being virtually absorbed by the Congress. Maulana Azad, supposedly recalling these events from memory, about twenty years later, is reported to have said that the final round of negotiations which took place in July 1937, broke down because of Nehru's opposition to having two Muslim League nominees in the Cabinet as demanded by Khaliquzzaman, instead of one.[125] Actually, Nehru, however reluctantly, was agreeable, as per his own contemporary account, to having two League nominees. What led to the breakdown of the negotiations was not the difference on the number of Ministers, but on the terms on which they were to be taken. There is no reason to doubt the veracity of Nehru's account recorded immediately after the event in course of a confidential letter. According to him, after much discussion of the pros and cons in which besides Nehru, Azad, Pant, J.B. Kripalani and Narendra Deva participated, it was decided that 'stringent conditions' should be offered to the Muslim League group in U.P. and if they were accepted, two of its members should be taken as ministers. These conditions included the League's acceptance of the Congress policy in the legislatures as settled by its Working Committee in March 1937; the winding up of the League group in the U.P. legislature, including the U.P. Parliamentary Board; all Muslim League members becoming full members of the Congress Party (though not being asked specifically to take the Congress pledge), and abiding by its discipline; no Muslim League candidates being set up in future elections; and League members also resigning from the ministry or the legislature in case of resignation by the Congress members. Although the League members were not asked to severe all connection with the parent Muslim League, the Congress leaders expected the U.P. League to break away from the parent body in due course. When Azad presented these conditions to Khaliquzzaman, the latter agreed to all of them except two: the winding up of the League's Parliamentary Board and not setting up separate candidates at the by-elections. He, of course, added that left to himself, he would agree to even them, but had no authority to do so and further that in effect what was being stipulated would happen any how. The Congress leaders, facing flak from Muslim Congressmen in U.P. for reopening up negotiations with the League leaders for their entry into the ministry, stuck to all their conditions and refused to whitle them down in any way. Khaliquzzaman, on the other hand, found himself unable to accept the Congress conditions. So the talks for cooperation broke down.[126]

While the attention of most of the historians of India's Partition who have touched upon ministry-making in 1937 has been concentrated solely on U.P., actually something similar happened in Bombay. The Muslim League had done the best there, securing 20 out of a total of 39 Muslim seats (better than U.P. where the League had secured 27 out of a total of 64). According to Kanji Dwarkadas, a friend and admirer of Jinnah, B.G. Kher, the leader of the Congress Assembly Party, sought Jinnah's cooperation in forming a ministry and asked him to nominate two persons from the League for appointment as ministers. Jinnah readily agreed and offered full cooperation to the Congress Ministry. However, the Congress High Command, particularly Vallabhbhai Patel, intervened and reprimanded Kher for having approached Jinnah. It began to be said that members of the League could be appointed as ministers only if they resigned from their organization and joined the Congress. Jinnah regarded this as humiliating and instantly rejected it.[127] This version has been contested by K.M. Munshi, who was one of the prominent members of the Congress Ministry in Bombay during 1937-9 and quite close to Kher. According to him, instead of Kher approaching Jinnah, it was Jinnah who had talked first to Munshi as well as Kher about such cooperation. Detailed discussions took place between Jinnah's emissary, Cowasji Jehangir, on the one hand and Patel and Azad on the other, with Kher and Munshi also present on several occasions during the discussions. The League wanted two ministers in the cabinet. Patel and Azad, however, rejected the offer of cooperation as it was made clear on Jinnah's behalf that his nominees would neither join the Congress legislature party nor accept its discipline. They would not also accept the principle of joint responsibility.[128] The Congress leaders felt that if the League members were taken into the Congress Ministry under such terms, 'Jinnah would have dictated the whole policy of the Government through his nominees, who, on every occasion, would threaten to resign'.[129]

VII

Now about the supposed result of the failure of the talks of Congress-League cooperation in ministry-formation in U.P. and Bombay on the mind of the League's leadership. The oft-repeated view that it was this which for the first time turned the latter towards the ideal of a separate, sovereign Muslim State is based on pure imagination and wishful thinking. There is incontrovertible evidence which shows that even before the beginning of the final round of talks for the formation of the so-called coalition ministries in these provinces, nay even before the publication of the Viceroy's statement of 22 June 1937, giving an assurance against the arbitrary use of special powers by the Governors and thereby opening the way for the formation of Congress ministries in the different provinces, Jinnah had felt decisively drawn towards the ideal of a separate, sovereign Muslim State, though for tactical reasons he had chosen not to reveal it to the public for the time being. It was at this time that in confidential letters addressed to him Iqbal, the great poet-philosopher of Muslim nationalism, finally declared that the only proper solution of the Indian problem lay in the Muslim majority areas of India emerging as an independent State or States. And we have Jinnah's own testimony that he himself had already arrived at the same conclusion.

Before dealing with Iqbal's letters to Jinnah and the latter's comments on them it would be appropriate to take note of the spread of the Pakistan idea between 1932 and 1937. As noted in the previous chapter, the Pakistan idea had emerged on the Indian horizon about ten years earlier, if not before, and had soon caught the imagination of enough adherents to lead some experienced British observers of the Indian political scene to conclude by 1931-2 that a self-governing India was not destined to be an united one. Rahmat Ali (1897-1951), a Punjabi Muslim student at Cambridge, contributed significantly to the further spread of the Pakistan idea during the following years. In 1933 he forcefully demanded the creation of a separate Muslim State out of the north-western areas of India and also gave it the name, Pakistan (first spelled Pakstan). Both the demand and the name were publicized through a four-page statement entitled *Now or Never,* drafted by Rahmat Ali and signed by him and three others, and forwarded on 28 January to important persons dealing with the Indian constitutional problem in Britain, including the members of the third session of the Round Table Conference on India then meeting in London. The signatories claimed that they were speaking 'on behalf of the 30 million Muslims of Pakstan', who then lived in the five northern units of India—Punjab, North-West Frontier Province, Kashmir, Sindh and Baluchistan—and representing 'their inexorable demand for the recognition of their separate national status, as distinct from the rest of India, by the grant of a separate federal constitution on social, religious, political and historical grounds'. They strongly attacked the Muslim delegates to the Round Table Conference (who included Iqbal) for having agreed to the setting up of an All-India Federation and characterized it as 'nothing less than signing the death-warrant of Islam and its future in India'. India, according to them, was neither the name of a single country nor the home of a single nation, but 'the designation of a State created for the first time in history, by the British'. In the five northern provinces of India, claimed for 'Pakstan', they emphasized, the Muslims constituted an over-whelming majority of the population and they had hardly anything in common with the Hindus:

> Our religion, culture, history, tradition, economic system, laws of inheritance, succession and marriage are basically and fundamentally different from those of the people living in the rest of India. The ideals which move our thirty million brethren-in-faith living in these provinces to make the highest sacrifices are fundamentally different from those which inspire the Hindus. These differences are not confined to the broad basic principles—far from it. They extend to the minute details of our lives. We do not inter-dine; we do not inter-marry. Our national customs and calendars, even our diet and dress are different.

They went on to clarify that what they were demanding was basically different from the suggestion made by Iqbal in 1930. While the latter had envisaged a consolidated Muslim state in the north-west to be a part of an All-India Federation, what was now being demanded was the setting up of a completely separate federation of their own for the Muslim majority areas of the north-west. 'There can be no peace and tranquility in the land', Rahmat Ali and his comrades finally warned, 'if the Muslims are duped into a Hindu dominated federation where we cannot be the masters of our destiny and captains of our own soul.'

This was not the last statement issued by this group. Rahmat Ali set up a small organization called the Pakistan National Movement in order to carry on a continuous propaganda campaign on behalf of the demand for Pakistan. In its name he continued to issue statements and brochures from time to time describing himself as the Founder-President, Pakistan National Movement. Thus while the Joint Select Committee of the British Parliament was considering proposals regarding Indian constitutional reforms, a statement issued on 1 November 1933, on behalf of the Pakistan National Movement drew attention to the demand contained in the first statement entitled *Now or Never* and declared that the Pakistan National Movement was irrevocably committed to it and determined to work by all constitutional means available to it for its realization. Pakistan and Hindustan, the statement observed, had given much to the world in the past and could give more in the future, but they could give anything of value only by remaining essentially themselves. 'Political fusion would destroy their national souls and would result in hybrid nationalism from which would issue nothing but degeneration, disruption, and disintegration.' Again, when the Parliament was giving consideration to the Government of India Bill, a statement dated 8 July 1935, issued under the signature of Rahmat Ali, declared that the Bill, embodying the scheme of an All-India Federation, had created 'an acute crisis in the national life of Pakistan', and had raised 'a supreme issue—an issue of life or death—for its national future'. Reiterating the basic ideology of the Pakistan movement it declared that the constitutional problem in India did not represent an inter-communal issue, but an international one and could be solved permanently only on that basis.[130]

At first the Pakistan idea did not have many takers—at any rate publicly— in the major Muslim political establishments in India. When in August 1933, the delegates of the Muslim Conference and the Muslim League, in course of their evidence before the Joint Select Committee on Indian Reforms in London, were asked whether they knew about a scheme of federation under the name of 'Pakistan', the replies were that it was 'only a students' scheme', was 'chimerical and impractical', and had not till then been considered by 'any representative gentleman or association'.[131] However, such replies need not be taken at their face value. B.R. Ambedkar, noted for his sharp intellect, who had attended the third session of the Round Table Conference as a delegate and later wrote a scholarly treatise strongly supporting the Pakistan idea, while mentioning that the Muslim members of the Conference did not countenance Rahmat Ali's scheme in any way, adds a footnote making an exception in the case of Mohammad Iqbal:

> If opposition to one common central government be taken as a principal feature of the scheme of Pakistan, then the only member of the R.T.C. who may be said to have supported it without mentioning it by name was Sir Muhammed Iqbal who expressed the view at the third session of the R.T.C. that there should be no central government for India, that the provinces should be autonomous and independent dominions in direct relationship to the Secretary of State in London.[132]

Proceeding to discuss the possible reasons for the generally negative attitude towards Rahmat Ali's scheme adopted by almost all the Muslim members of the Round Table Conference Ambedkar emphasizes tactical considerations and not lack of interest in the goal propounded therein:

> It is possible that the Muslims in the beginning thought that this destiny was just a dream incapable of realisation. It is possible that later on when they felt that it could be a reality they did not raise any issue about it because they were not sufficiently well organised to compel the British as well as the Hindus to agree to it. It is difficult to explain why the Muslims did not press for Pakistan at the R.T.C. Perhaps they knew that the scheme would offend the British and as they had to depend upon the British for a decision on the 14 points of dispute between them and the Hindus, the Musalmans, perfect statesmen as they are and knowing full well that politics, as Bismarck said, was always the game of the possible, preferred to wait and not to show their teeth till they had got a decision from the British in their favour on the 14 points of dispute.[133]

Ambedkar's footnote to this para is equally significant: 'It is said that it [Rahmat Ali's Scheme] was privately discussed with the British authorities who were not in favour of it. It is possible that the Muslims did not insist on it for fear of incurring their displeasure.'[134]

Whatever the calculations of the Muslim leaders attending the Round Table Conference or their peers at home, who adopted a similar stance, there can be little doubt that Rahmat Ali's impassioned advocacy of the Pakistan idea had considerable impact on the general Muslim opinion in India, particularly in the Punjab, the province which mattered most. For that idea soon began to be discussed in Muslim political circles there and several articles relating to it appeared in the press between 1933 and 1935. This was particularly true of *The Civil and Military Gazette,* the leading English daily of Lahore. Thus within less than two months of the issue of *Now or Never* the paper's 'Muslim Political Correspondent', obviously referring to it, reported in his regular column, 'Muslim World', that he had received 'a lengthy communication signed by some of the leading Muslims of the Northern provinces', and denouncing the setting up of an All-India Federation with responsibility at the centre as 'positively prejudicial to Muslim interests'. Without naming the leaflet, the correspondent proceeded to quote the following from *Now or Never*:

> If we the Muslims of Pakistan, with our distinct mark of nationality, are deluded into the proposed Indian Federation by friends or foes, we are reduced to a minority of one to four. It is this which sounds the death-knell of the Muslim nation in India for ever.[135]

The 'Muslim Political Correspondent' thus confined himself to just reporting in brief the idea proposed by *Now or Never* without supporting it. He did, however, lend his support next week to a scheme which he ascribed to Iqbal, and according to which India was to have not one but 'three separate federations, one of the Muslim provinces, another of the Hindu provinces and the third of the Indian States', which might 'eventually confederate'. As the correspondent put it, 'the only hope of an united India lies on these lines'.[136]

These brief references to Partition and confederation were followed by a series of articles and letters on the views propounded by Rahmat Ali and his friends. Some of them were critical, but most of them were quite laudatory and supportive. Thus a letter on 'The Pakstan Scheme' by one K.G. Ahmad published in May 1933, strongly refuted the contention of the generality of the Hindu press that the 'Pakstan Scheme' was inspired by the British diehards and remarked: 'The fact of the matter is that whatever is unpalatable to those who dream of establishing Hindu supremacy in the whole of India is always attributed by them to the influence of British conservatives.' Reacting to the fear expressed in the Hindu press that the 'Pakstan Scheme' represented another instance of Pan-Islamic outburst, the letter observed: 'In reality the myth of Pan-Islamism is the product of the disturbed imagination of non-Muslims. It is a bogey which has always terrorized those who gave birth to it.' Asserting that 'Pakstan' was going to be not a religious, but a cultural state, it nevertheless pointed out that in the case of Hindus and Muslims religion and politics could not be assigned to watertight compartments. The letter also refuted the criticism that 'Pakstan' would worsen the position of Muslims of the provinces where they were in a minority and pointed out that they would remain a minority whether 'Pakstan' was created or not. On the other hand, the creation of 'Pakstan' would 'save the soul of Islam in India'. It finally concluded:

> The Muslims want 'Pakstan' because they want to have full opportunity for their development along their own lines. History teaches us that slowly and gradually the ever-spreading tentacles of Hinduism have always succeeded in engulfing all foreign elements that came in its proximity. Not even a trace was left of them. Shall we not heed this warning held out to us by hoary centuries?[137]

Haji Rahim Bakhsh in his article entitled, 'The Two Distinct "Nations" of India' published in June 1933, without supporting the Pakistan idea in its entirety, lent a most powerful support to the two nation theory, the main prop for that idea. Arguing that a nation is formed not on the basis of a common subjection to a political authority, but on that of 'a sentiment of oneness fostered among a people by a variety of causes, the most important of which are a common race, a common language, common socio-religious prejudices, a common social life, a common culture, a common history and pride in common heroes', he remarked:

> Anyone who studies the effect of the sum-total of these factors which make a nation will readily recognise that in India Hindus and Sikhs on the one hand and Muslims on the other form two distinct nations in the truest sense of the term. The two live side by side but they do not interdine or intermarry, and practically lead two mutually exclusive social lives. In other words the corporate lives of the two nations run as two distinct and parallel currents. There is not a single event—not even a common festival—which stirs or disturbs the two currents alike. It is possible for the Sikhs, the Arya Samajists, the Sanatanists and other religious groups in the Hindu society to celebrate festivals which are common to all of them, but which either signify nothing to Muslims or only exasperate them. Again, it is possible for one to stir all sections of Hindus and Sikhs alike by referring to their common national heroes and to certain events from their common history, but one will have to invoke the aid of an entirely different set of heroes and historical events if one wants to make any appeal to Muslims. . . . In short, those powerful historical and social forces which unite individuals into nations have divided Indians into two distinct nations which may be broadly called the Muslim nation and the Hindu nation, to say nothing of certain small groups like the Parsis or Anglo-Indians who are outside the fold of both.[138]

Rahim Bakhsh did not advocate Partition, but only a recognition of the two nations with provision for both of them to develop along their natural lines within a federation with very limited powers. He, however, went on to emphasize that if this was not done, there was every likelihood of a revolt by one nation against domination by the other. 'The beginning of such a revolt', he added further, 'was indeed already visible in the current of thought among Muslims who were thinking of an isolated self-governing Muslim State or States in northern India.'[139] This really amounted to an indirect endorsement of the Pakistan idea. In a letter published in *The Civil and Military Gazette* in September 1933, Muhammad Anwar remarked with reference to that idea: 'It would allow the national culture of Hindus and Muhammadans to fructify instead of getting autumn blown, and the highest development of each of these two peoples, would be possible without one being subject to the other.' However, he also expressed certain doubts regarding the Pakistan idea and described it as a two-edged sword and as 'nothing short of a pious aspiration'.[140] Disagreeing with such a view Khalid Saifullah in course of his letter to the same paper published about two weeks later remarked:

> The idea of Pakistan is not to be attributed to the fancy or dreams of any visionary or poet. Its springs lie deep in the soul of the Mussalman people. It is simply and purely an expression of their will to live their own life. The right of self-determination has gained universal recognition and the people of North India only want to exercise this right to which like others they are perfectly entitled. In our own times the late Maulana Muhammad Ali and Dr. Sir Muhammad Iqbal—the two intellectual giants—well acquainted with the vital forces that animate groups and communities, made noble and laudable attempts to catch on the canvas, so to say, the latent wish of the people of Northern India. But it was reserved for Chaudhry Rahmat Ali of the Punjab and his devoted band of lieutenants, now at Cambridge, to clearly visualise the destiny in store for the people of Northern India and to formulate a concrete and practical scheme for its realisation.[141]

Writing in a similar vein Haider Ali Abbasi observed in course of his letter published in December 1933:

> The Pakistan movement represents the political and cultural aspirations and ideals of 40 millions inhabiting N.W. India. It is a positive, spontaneous and independent movement and its rise has nothing to do with such a poisonous and narrow-minded thing as Hindu communalism. The springs of the movement lie deep, in the soul of the Musalman people, and its roots spread far back to history. . . . What that man of destiny, Rahmat Ali, has really done is to have caught on the convas, so to say, what every Pakistani has cherished and nurtured in his heart from days immemorial.

Having such an approach to the Pakistan issue Abbasi brushed aside the argument advanced by a correspondent of *The Civil and Military Gazette* in one of its earlier issues that the administrative unification of India through, among other things, the installation of an uniform postal and telegraphic system in all parts of the country would stand in the way of separating the areas claimed for Pakistan from India. Pointing out that the life of a people was a billion times more important than the amount invested in setting up various types of administrative arrangements, he remarked: 'It is madness indeed to maintain that a nation of 40 millions should be annihilated on the altar of postal and telegraphic arrangements that have sprung up during the last hundred years.'[142]

In a letter to the same paper published in November 1934 Niaz Mahmood strongly refuted the criticisms of the Pakistan idea by some Hindu correspondents. Describing Rahmat Ali as 'the originator of this noble ideal', he expressed his amazement at the 'foolhardiness' of those correspondents in attacking the Pakistan scheme as the manifestation of Pan-Islamic sentiments and in expressing fear that Pakistan might become a tool in the hands of its Muslim neighbours and a source of danger to India. In his opinion, 'only a political idiot could ever think that the Muslims of Pakistan would subdue their own national pride and immediate interests in order to help some neighbouring Muslim state'. He further asserted that if the Muslims were clamouring for the secession of Pakistan from the rest of India, it was not because they wanted to become the subjects of Afghans or Persians, but because they justifiably dreaded 'the aggression of a selfish majority with whom they have absolutely nothing in common, not even their complexions'.[143] Gulshan Rai had expressed Hindu apprehensions on this point in *The Civil and Military Gazette* on more than one occasion. Answering him specifically Sayyid Shaukat Ali in his letter published in January 1935 pointed out that far from facing any danger from Pakistan, Hindus would in fact gain because the new state would be in a position to resist foreign aggression from the north-west and act as a buffer between the latter and what would be left of India.[144]

Although not to the same extent as in the Punjab the Pakistan idea expounded in *Now or Never* had its echo also in Bengal in spite of the fact that regardless of its Muslim majority it had not been included in the area claimed for Pakistan in that leaflet. Thus within two and a half months of its circulation in Britain *The Star of India* (Calcutta), generally considered an organ of Muslim opinion, published an article entitled 'Federation of Muslim States?', containing a detailed, sympathetic commentary on the Pakistan idea in its issue dated 14 April 1933. Without naming either the leaflet or its author the article declared: 'Considerable Muslim interest is being taken in a scheme which, however far-fetched it may seem at the present moment, may one day become a reality out of sheer force of circumstances.' After mentioning the large area and population sought to be included in the proposed federation of Muslim majority provinces in the north-west of India it went on to add:

> There is already a school of Muslim politicians in India who favour the idea of amalgamating these Provinces into a single State forming a unit of the proposed All-India Federation. To carry the proposal a step further, by forming a separate federation of these Provinces, appears rather more practical and fruitful of better results than forming them into a single unit of the All-India federation.
>
> There is no doubt that a separate Muslim Federal Dominion composed of the Punjab, the North-West Frontier Province, Kashmir, Sind and Baluchistan as different distinct units, would not only provide better opportunities for the progress and development of these states, but would also prove to be a buffer State against any incursion either of ideas or of arms from beyond the Himalaya and the Hindukush mountains.[145]

The word 'Pakstan' or 'Pakistan' had indeed become so current in political parlance by 1935 that the Aga Khan in a letter to Fazl-i-Husain in August that year—though not yet looking forward to Partition or the setting up of a fully sovereign Muslim State, but only to a confederal India, to be called United States of Southern Asia, with the provinces having their own armed forces—referred to the Muslim majority provinces in the north and west as 'the vast Pakestan block' and to Bengal as 'a second Pakestan'. It is also significant that the main emphasis in this letter was on strengthening Muslim position in these two regions.[146] That the Pakistan idea was steadily gaining ground during 1935-6 is also attested to by the industrialist, G.D. Birla, one of the most perceptive observers of the Indian political scene. Writing to Linlithgow, the Viceroy-designate of India, in January 1936, he remarked that 'the Pakistan dream' was being 'cherished by ambitious Mohammedan leaders in India with great vehemence'.[147] An article on Pakistan by F. Frenkow published in *Encyclopaedia of Islam* (1937) shows that Birla was not off the mark in underlining the growing popularity of the Pakistan idea among politically conscious Muslims.

Referring to the Pakistan Movement Frenkow remarked: 'For the first time since the fall of the Mughal Empire in India, the movement has reawakened the Muslims in the bi-national subcontinent of India to a sense of their national future; and its religious and patriotic character has deeply attracted the younger generation to its ideals.'[148]

VIII

Iqbal, the mirror of the Indian Muslim mind in the twentieth century, could not remain unaffected by this current of thought among his co-religionists, especially in view of the fact that it really represented the logical development of his own political thinking. On 21 May 1937 *The Star of India* published an article by F.K. Khan Durrani, who described it as in reality 'a call from Dr. Sir Mohammad Iqbal' for the formation of a new all-India politico-cultural organization of Indian Muslims to be known as the 'Muslim India Society', under his own (Iqbal's) personal guidance as president. Durrani recognized that the All-India Muslim League was already there and it was also showing signs of life at that time, but explained that the malady of Muslims lay deeper than could be cured by mere political leaders who, because of the very nature of their profession, had to function as 'opportunists', dealing with problems as they arose from day to day. Hence the need for a new organization animated by an unshakable faith in 'the political destiny of Islam' and 'that spirit of proud independence and militant aggressiveness which Islam engenders'. Durrani wrote further:

> The name of the society amply explains its nature and purpose. It is fashionable these days to make fine distinctions between 'full responsible government', 'dominion status', 'complete independence', and similar slogans. So far as the Muslims are concerned, these distinctions are meaningless and futile. The political idea[l] of Muslims was defined once for all times by the Holy Quran thirteen and a half centuries ago, and no man who believes in Islam and its Holy Founder can make a change in that ideal. The idea of subjection to non-Muslim rule is foreign to the whole ideology of Islam; the Holy Quran conceives of Muslims only as free and independent and never as a subject people, and it is not possible to serve and realise the purposes of Islam in a state of subjection. . . . Belief in Muhammad (God bless him) and belief in the Quran are incompatible with subjection to any rule or government which is not based on the Quran and has not the sanction behind it of the free opinions of the Muslims [149]

It is difficult to say whether Durrani was really airing his own views or those of Iqbal. In any case, it seems extremely doubtful that he had been asked by Iqbal to say all that he did in the latter's name. For Iqbal was not in any way deficient in expressing himself in English prose and there was no reason why someone else had to be chosen to give expression to certain views on his behalf. It seems probable that Durrani was conveying in his article something which Iqbal had mentioned or approved of in course of a private conversation, but which he was not till then ready to say publicly, without realizing that Durrani might use his name in the way he actually did.

Whatever that might have been, within a week of the publication of Durrani's article Iqbal wrote to Jinnah conveying certain views whose philosophical or ideological foundations were broadly similar to those propounded in Durrani's article. Indeed the kernal of the article, emphasizing the primacy of Islam in determining a Muslim's political faith and behaviour, really amounted to summing up Iqbal's own thinking since 1909-10, when he wrote *Shikwa* and *Jawab-i-Shikwa*. For some time past he had been devoting himself to the application of that thinking to the constitutional evolution of India. The Allahabad Address (1930), asking for the consolidation of the Muslim majority areas of north-west India into one political and administrative unit, even though within India, represented a significant stage in this respect. While concluding that address Iqbal had observed: 'I am not hopeless of an intercommunal understanding, but I cannot conceal from you the feeling that in the near future our community may be called upon to adopt an independent line of action to cope with the present crisis.'[150] The next stage, not generally noticed, is represented by his stand at the Third Round Table Conference (1933), mentioned earlier, that the new constitutional set-up being then devised should provid for transfer of power directly from the British Government to the Provinces without any provision for a central government. The articulation of his ideas on the constitutional issue in letters to Jinnah in 1937, after the elections to provincial Assemblies, constitutes the final stage. This again shows a progression from one step to another.

The first step is marked by Iqbal's letter to Jinnah dated 20 March 1937. Here he is concerned with the new Congress line expounded by Nehru at the All-India National Convention of the newly elected Congress legislators where the latter debunked the significance of the communal issue and gave primacy to the economic issue which, in his view, really affected the life of the people. Afraid that if this idea really gained ground, Muslim political identity would face a serious threat, Iqbal implored Jinnah in the name of Islam to immediately hold an All-

India Muslim Convention and to emphasize in his address there that the economic problem was not the only problem in the country and that for the Muslims the cultural problem was of 'much greater consequence' or at least 'not less important than the economic problem'. In the same letter Iqbal also emphasized that 'the whole future of Islam as a moral and political force in Asia rests very largely on a complete organization of Indian Muslims'.[151]

Jinnah, of course, did not accept Iqbal's suggestion regarding the holding of an All-India Muslim Convention. Although we do not have Jinnah's reply to Iqbal's letter, we can safely guess that the main reason must have been the former's awareness that an All-India Muslim Convention largely consisting of the newly elected Muslim legislators would have served only to expose the weakness of the Muslim League as only a small number of Muslim legislators had been elected on the League's ticket. Perhaps that prompted Iqbal to his next step which was to advise Jinnah on the means of transforming the League into a mass organization. It was while thinking about this that he realized the importance of the economic problem and this in turn led him to suggest the creation of 'a free state or states', with 'absolute Muslim majorities', without necessarily separating themselves from India. Pointing out that the League's future depended on the Muslim masses joining it and that this was not possible unless it offered a solution to the problem of poverty which severely afflicted them, he observed in course of his letter to Jinnah on 28 May:

> After a long and careful study of Islamic law I have come to the conclusion that if this system of law is properly understood and applied, at least the right to subsistence is secured to everybody. But the enforcement and development of the shariat of Islam is impossible in this country without a free Muslim state or states. This has been my honest conviction for many years and I still believe this to be the only way to solve the problem of bread for Muslims as well as to secure a peaceful India. If such a thing is impossible in India the only other alternative is a civil war which as a matter of fact has been going on for some time in the shape of Hindu-Muslim riots.[152]

Iqbal delineated the final destiny of his co-religionists in India in the north-west and east in his third important letter to Jinnah on 21 June. 'I know you are a busy man', he wrote by way of a preface, 'but I do hope you won't mind my writing to you so often, as you are the only Muslim in India today to whom the community has a right to look up for safe guidance through the storm which is coming to north-west India, and perhaps to the whole of India.' Reverting to the theme of the continuing civil war in India, this time he laid stress on the political aspect of the conflict between Hindus and Muslims. As he put it:

I tell you that we are actually living in a state of civil war which, but for the police and military, would become universal in no time. During the last few months there has been a series of Hindu-Muslim riots in India. In north-west India alone there have been at least three riots during the last three months and at least four cases of vilification of the Prophet by Hindus and Sikhs. In each of the four cases, the vilifier has been murdered. There have also been cases of the burning of the Koran in Sind. I have carefully studied the whole situation and believe that the real cause of these events is neither religious nor economic. It is purely political, i.e., the desire of the Sikhs and Hindus to intimidate Muslims even in the Muslim majority provinces.

According to Iqbal, such a situation had arisen because of the peculiar constitutional position in the Muslim-majority provinces where Muslims, in view of their slender majority, had to depend on non-Muslim support to run the government. The situation, he added, was further complicated by the fact that the Congress President (Nehru) had devalued the political existence of Muslims in unmistakable terms. Turning to the Hindu Mahasabha and describing it as 'the other Hindu political body' and as 'the real representative of the masses of the Hindus', Iqbal pointed out that it had declared more than once that a united Hindu-Muslim nation was impossible in India. In such a situation it was obvious to him that the only way to a peaceful India was 'a redistribution of the country on the lines of racial, religious and linguistic affinities'. It might be assumed from the context in which this suggestion was made that, though the language was slightly different, it was in substance the same old proposal of having provinces with absolute Muslim majorities, which Iqbal had made earlier and repeated to Jinnah less than a month ago. However, unlike in the past, Iqbal did not stop here, but went on to propose a separate federation of the Muslim majority provinces—with the Muslim element in the population further strengthened through reorganization—on the basis of the principle of self-determination of nations. This represented a clear advocacy of the Pakistan idea without, of course, any mention of the word 'Pakistan' or its most forceful promoter till then, Rahmat Ali. To quote Iqbal:

To my mind the new constitution with its idea of a single Indian federation is completely hopeless. A separate federation of Muslim provinces, reformed on the lines I have suggested above, is the only course by which we can secure a peaceful India and save Muslims from the domination of non-Muslims. Why should not the Muslims of North-West India and Bengal be considered as nations entitled to self-determination just as other nations in India and outside India are?[153]

Jinnah's replies to Iqbal's letters have not been found, but towards the end of his foreword to the publication containing them,[154] he underlines 'the very great historical importance', particularly of those letters which explain Iqbal's views on the future of Muslim India. Jinnah also makes it clear that he too had come to the same conclusions on the basis of his own study of the situation in India and further that this ultimately culminated in the adoption of the famous 'Pakistan Resolution' by the Muslim League in 1940. As Jinnah puts it:

His [Iqbal's] views were substantially in consonance with my own and had finally led me to the same conclusions as a result of careful examination and study of the constitutional problems facing India, and found expression in due course in the united will of Muslim India as adumberated in the Lahore Resolution of the All-Muslim League, popularly known as the 'Pakistan Resolution', passed on 23rd March 1940.[155]

Apart from this, there are some other pointers which indicate that Jinnah did not require to be converted by Iqbal to his views on the destiny of Indian Muslims. His consistent opposition to the scheme of an All-India Federation, coupled with support for the provincial part of the Act of 1935, was the result not merely of his opposition, which he shared with the Congress leaders, to the undemocratic provisions relating to the representation of the princely states in the Federation, but also of the concern which he shared with most other Muslim leaders of India with the prospect of Hindu domination of the federal government. This is borne out by the following report of a conversation with him in January 1936 as reported by a knowledgeable Indian:

Jinnah said that from 1930 he had been an unflinching opponent of the Federation Scheme between British India and the Indian States. He is convinced that the Federation plan will be disastrous to India and England. He is as determined as ever before to fight against Federation. In his opposition he feels he has the support of the country, *especially the Muslims*. But, he has no quarrel with the Reforms Scheme in the Provinces.[156]

The use of the phrase 'especially the Muslims' in connection with the opposition to the Federation indicates at least part of Jinnah's ground for opposing Federation. Although in his public speeches up to that time he had not clearly been mentioning the special reason for Muslim opposition to Federation, there was at least one experienced Indian leader, Sapru, who already in 1936, when several others saw in his opposition to Federation an approximation to the Congress stand, saw in it a reflection of the general Muslim concern with the prospect of Hindu domination of the federal government. As Sapru put it in May 1936:

> Jinnah's master passion seems to be to do everything he can to wreck the Federation. For the moment he is dominating Muslim politics. It is not difficult to understand why Jinnah should be so much opposed to the idea of Federation. In fact it is true to say of the Mohammadans generally that while they want Provincial Autonomy, as it places them in a position of advantage in certain Provinces, they do not want Federation as it will place them in no position of advantage at the Centre.[157]

The resounding Congress victory in the provincial elections of 1937, presaging a similar victory in the federal elections in future, if and when held, further strengthened Muslim opposition to the federal scheme. For the prospect of Hindus being divided into several parties had now disappeared and that had made the prospect of Hindu domination at the centre more detestable. It is not surprising in view of his preoccupation with safeguarding special Muslim interests in India that at the end of May or early June 1937 Jinnah told Lord Brabourne, then Governor of Bombay, that he was 'as keen as ever to work Provincial Autonomy and more firmly than ever against Federation'. This conversation also shows Jinnah determined to vigorously pursue a programme of intensified communalism even before the final talks for Congress-League coalition ministries had begun. To quote Brabourne:

> Jinnah went on to tell me some of his plans for consolidating the Muslim League throughout India and how he is doing his utmost to awaken the Muhammedans to the necessity of standing on their own feet more than they do now. His policy is to preach Communalism morning, noon and night and to endeavour to get the Muhammedans to found more schools, to open purely Muhammedan hospitals, Children's homes, etc., and to teach them generally 'to stand on their own feet and make themselves independent of the Hindus'.[158]

Here apparently Jinnah had referred to the Muslims as a community. This was his general practice those days when speaking to non-Muslims. But we have evidence now that when talking to his close colleagues and followers, at any rate after the elections of 1937, he had begun referring to Muslims as a nation. Thus when the Council of the All-India Muslim League was discussing the creed of that organization on 21 March 1937, Jinnah, from his presidential chair, explained that he believed in 'national self-government' and that 'the differences between the Hindus and the Muslims were due not to the lack of nationalism among the Muslims but because of the differences between their cultures'. Further he emphasized that 'the Muslims must unite as a nation, and then live or die as a united nation'.[159]

All this gives a lie to the theory that the failure to form a Congress-League Coalition Ministry in U.P. gave a new turn to Muslim politics in India. That new turn had already taken place as a result of the emergence of the Congress as the dominant parliamentary party in all the Hindu majority provinces, which contained the overwhelming majority of British India's population, foreshadowing the emergence of a similar Congress dominance at the Centre in the future and thereby strengthening the Muslim elite's attraction for a separate sovereign State of their own.

IX

What has been written above will, it is hoped, free us from the traditional, unhistorical view regarding the background, nature and significance of the failure of the Congress-League talks in U.P. Neither the general political situation nor the state of relations between the Congress and the Muslim League was conducive to the formation of a coalition between them. There had also been no prior understanding between them regarding it. Besides, the top leadership of the League had already, before serious negotiations for a so-called coalition had even commenced, veered round to the idea of a separate Muslim State, mooted several years earlier. We would not, however, be justified in going to the other extreme and assuming, as has been done by some, that the failure of these talks had 'no weighty consequences'.[160] Nehru who, contrary to the impression recently sought to be created by some historians,[161] had a major, though not the sole, hand in shaping the Congress policy in these talks[162] and had been opposed to a coalition with the Muslim League right from the beginning,[163] shows a better understanding of the consequences of their failure. Even while justifiably continuing to consider the decision of the Congress not to enter into a coalition with the Muslim League as 'natural and logical' in the then existing circumstances, he admits that 'the consequences of it on the communal question were unfortunate and it led to a feeling of grievance and isolation among many Muslims'.[164]

At the stage reached by Muslim politics by the summer of 1937 these consequences were weighty enough. They immensely helped the League in its drive to reinvigorate itself and increase its following among the masses as well as the elite. For what had happened in U.P. and Bombay could be shown as a model for what would happen when responsible government was established at the Centre: only those Muslims who were prepared to join the Congress could have a share in the Government. This was a most unwelcome prospect for the members of the Muslims elite, who were determined to maintain their separate political identity and at the same time secure a substantial share in power, not necessarily limited to the proportion of their co-regionalists to the total population of the country. The sceptre of Hindu domination, haunting their minds right from the beginning of the talk of responsible government in India and considerably magnified by the establishment of Congress dominance in the majority of Indian provinces, foreshadowing a similar dominance at the Centre, now began to appear much more menacing than ever before. This certainly helped the League in raising the cry of Islam in danger and spreading its message of Muslim nationalism in the Muslim majority as well as Muslim minority provinces; in establishing itself, for the first time in its history, as a really powerful political organization in all parts of the country; and in other ways preparing the ground for openly adopting, at an opportune moment, the demand for India's Partition and the setting up of a separate, sovereign Muslim State or States. It can, of course, be argued that the League leadership would not have been in a less advantageous position in carrying out its pre-determined task if it had succeeded in installing its nominees in the Congress-led Ministries in various Muslim minority provinces through the formation of Congress-League Coalition Ministries, with all the acquisition of prestige and power that would have gone with it. That, however, will be conjecture and not history.

NOTES

1. Government of India, Home Department, to Secretary of State for India, 22 August 1932, IOR, L/P&J/9/82, Private Office Papers. See also Hailey to Willingdon, 25 August 1932 and Hailey to Dawson (editor of *The Times*), 27 August 1932, IOR, Mss. Eu. E. 220/240, *Hailey Collection.*

2. See Joya Chatterji, *Bengal Divided: Hindu Communalism and Partition, 1932-1947* (Cambridge, 1995), pp. 30-3. Also Bidyut Chakrabarty, 'The Communal Award of 1932 and its Implications in Bengal', *Modern Asian Studies,* 23, 3(1989), pp. 503-4 and John Gallagher, 'Congress in Decline: Bengal 1930 to 1939', ibid., 7, 3(1973), pp. 615-25.
3. Chakrabarty, n. 2, pp. 499-502.
4. Chatterji, n. 2, pp. 23-9.
5. According to Hailey, at that time Governor of U.P., while some people attributed this change in Shaukat Ali to his desire to regain a position of leadership, others attributed it to the munificence of Birla, Hailey to Irwin, 3 November 1932, E220/25A, *Hailey Collection*.
6. *Indian Annual Register,* 1932, II, p. 281.
7. Ibid., pp. 283-4.
8. Ibid., pp. 288-9.
9. For the full text of the committee's proposals see IOR, L/P&J/9/82, Private Office Papers.
10. Hailey to Irwin, 4 December 1932, E. 220/25A, *Hailey Collection*.
11. Maulvi Sir Mohammad Yakub, Honorary Secretary, All India Muslim League to the Private Secretary to the Secretary of State for India, 21 November 1932, L/P&J/9/82, n. 9.
12. Ibid.
13. Ibid.
14. See *Indian Annual Register*, 1932, II, pp. 302-18.
15. Ibid., p. 474.
16. Hailey to Irwin, 9 November 1932, E. 220/25A, *Hailey Collection*.
17. Hailey to Harry Haig, 15 December 1933, E. 220/27A, ibid. The Government was, of course, not wanting in showing its appreciation for Shaukat Ali's services. The Home Member of the Government of India immediately responded after receiving the Governor's note and pointed out that actually the Maulana should be grateful to the Government for it had just treated him with 'considerable' liberality: it had granted his application for the restoration of his pension of Rs. 150 per month, suspended during the non-cooperation movement, and made it retrospective with effect from 1 October 1930, when he had gone to attend the first session of the Round Table Conference, Haig to Hailey, 20 December 1933, ibid.
18. Ansari was not merely a prominent political leader, but also an eminent medical practitioner.
19. Gandhi to M.A. Ansari, 18 March 1934, Mushirul Hasan, ed., *Muslims and the Congress: Select Correspondence of Dr. M.A. Ansari, 1912-1935* (New Delhi, 1979), p. 145.
20. *The Cummunal 'Award'? Examined and Criticised* (with a Foreword by C.Y. Chintamani) (Allahabad, 1934), pp. 49-51, 72-3.
21. Hailey to Willingdon, 10 April 1934, E. 220/27B, *Hailey Collection*.
22. *Collected Works of Mahatma Gandhi* (hereinafter referred to as *CWMG*), LVIII (New Delhi, 1974), p. 83.
23. Ibid., pp. 455-6.
24. Ibid., pp. 150, 173.
25. Gandhi to M.S. Aney, July (before 27), 1934, ibid., p. 253.

26. Khaliquzzaman to Asaf Ali, 18 July 1934. Choudhry Khaliquzzaman, *Pathway to Pakistan* (Karachi, 1961), p. 127.
27. Ibid.
28. Hailey to Brown, 19 July 1934, *Hailey Collection.*
29. *CWMG,* LVIII, n. 22, p. 255.
30. Syed Sharifuddin Pirzada, ed., *Foundation of Pakistan: All India Muslim League Documents, 1966-1947* (Karachi, 1970), II, pp. 231-2
31. Ibid., p. 233.
32. Fazl-i-Husain to Jinnah, 15 May 1934, IOR, Mss., Eur. E. 352, *Fazl-i-Husain Papers.*
33. M.A. Ansari to S.A. Brelvi, 3 December 1934, *S.A. Brelvi Papers*, National Archives of India.
34. Ansari to Jinnah, 30 December 1934, Hasan, n. 19, p. 231.
35. Jinnah to Ansari, 3 January 1935, ibid., p. 235.
36. Iqbal to Ansari, 1 January 1934, ibid., p. 233.
37. Brelvi to Ansari, 2 January 1935, p. 234.
38. Jinnah had told a group of Congress leaders in Bombay, in January 1934: 'All of you join me to formulate a hostile criticism . . . of the White Paper. But accept the Communal Award so that even Muslims might come around'. K.M. Munshi to Gandhi, 27 January 1934, K.M. Munshi, *Pilgrimage to Freedom* (Bombay, 1967), pp. 360-1.
39. 'Summary of conversation between Mr. Jinnah and myself', *Vallabhbhai Patel Papers*, Gallagher, n. 2, p. 628. Although Gallagher clearly mentions that the document is unsigned as well as undated and its authorship is not certain as several such documents emanating from other sources found their way to Patel's Papers, some have either directly or by implication, attributed the authorship to Patel. See, for example, Sharif al Mujahid, 'Jinnah and the Congress Party', D.A. Low, ed., *The Indian National Congress: Centenary Hindsights* (Delhi, 1988), p. 228; and Mushirul Hasan, *A Nationalist Conscience: M.A. Ansari, the Congress and the Raj* (New Delhi, 1987), p. 238. It is more likely, though by no means certain, that these remarks were made to Ansari, for they refer to the number of Muslim members, which could have meant only Muslim members of the Central Assembly and Ansari, as chairman of the Congress Parliamentary Board, was preoccupied with securing support from such members for the Congress position.
40. Rajendra Prasad, *Autobiography* (Bombay, 1957), p. 400.
41. 'Notes of Conversation between Mr. M.A. Jinnah and Rajendra Prasad', prepared by the latter from day today, *Rajendra Prasad Papers*, File XI/35, National Archives of India.
42. Ibid.
43. Prasad, n. 40.
44. Prasad, n. 41.
45. The principle of differential franchise was incorporated at the suggestion of Jinnah. He demanded that in constituencies where the number of Muslim votes was less than their proportion of the total population there should be provision for lowering the qualifications of franchise for them in order to rectify the situation, see Prasad, n. 40, p. 401.
46. *Prasad Papers*, n. 41.

47. Prasad to Vallabhbhai Patel, 14 February 1935, File VI/35, ibid.
48. *Prasad Papers*, n. 41.
49. For the texts of Jinnah's three amendments as well as his speech moving them see Waheed Ahmad, ed., *Quaid-i-Azam Mohammad Ali Jinnah: Speeches, Indian Legislative Assembly, 1935-1947* (Karachi, 1991), pp. 26-54.
50. Viceroy to Secretary of State, 9 February 1935, Home Poll. F.K.W. 83/35, National Archives of India.
51. Ahmad, n. 49, pp. 37, 39.
52. Ibid., p. 31.
53. *Prasad Papers*, n. 41.
54. Ibid., cited in Uma Kaura, *Muslims and Indian Nationalism: The Emergence of the Demand for India's Partition* (New Delhi, 1977), pp. 105-6.
55. Tej Bahadur Sapru to M.A. Ansari, 23 April 1934, *Sapru Papers*, Series II, Microfilm, Nehru Memorial Museum and Library (hereinafter referred to as NMML).
56. See, for example, R. Coupland, *Indian Politics 1936-1942* (London, 1943), pp. 110-12; Beni Prasad, *India's Hindu-Muslim Questions* (Allahabad, 1946), pp. 61-2; P.J. Griffiths, *The British Impact on India* (London, 1952), p. 342; Maulana Abul Kalam Azad, *India Wins Freedom* (Bombay, 1959), pp. 160-2; Penderal Moon, *Divide and Quit* (London, 1961), p. 146; R.C. Majumdar, *History of the Freedom Movement in India*, III (Calcutta, 1963), p. 563; Bimal Prasad, 'The Emergence of the Demand for India's Partition', *International Studies*, Vol. 9, No. 3, January 1968, pp. 251-2; Kaura, n. 54, pp. 112-13, 167-8; H.V. Hodson, *The Great Divide* (London, 1969), pp. 66-7; B. Shiva Rao, 'India, 1935-47', in C.H. Philips and Mary Doreen Wainwright, eds., *The Partition of India: Politics and Perspectives* (London, 1970), p. 419; B.B. Misra, *The Indian Political Parties* (Delhi, 1976), pp. 420-5; Waheed-uz-Zaman, *Towards Pakistan* (Lahore, 1978), pp. 85-91; Mushirul Hasan, ed., *India's Partition: Processes, Strategy and Mobilisation* (Delhi, 1993), pp. 9-12. For an exception to this general pattern see Anita Inder Singh, *The Origins of the Partition of India, 1936-1947* (Delhi, 1987), pp. 8-24.
57. G.D. Birla to Lord Linlithgow, 21 December 1935, IOR. Mss. Eu. F. 125/155 (c), *Linlithgow Collection*.
58. Sir Tej Bahadur Sapru to Lord Lothian, 4 May 1936, *Sapru Papers*, NMML.
59. *CWMG*, LXI (New Delhi, 1975), pp. 31-3, 87-8.
60. Ibid., LXII (New Delhi, 1975), p. 345.
61. Jawaharlal Nehru to Syed Mahmud, 24 September 1936, *Selected Works of Jawaharlal Nehru* (hereinafter referred to as *SWJN*), S. Gopal, ed., VII (New Delhi, 1975), p. 386. Also Nehru to Mahadeva Desai, 24 September 1936, ibid., p. 393.
62. Nehru to Syed Mahmud, 5 October 1936, ibid., pp. 397-8.
63. Nehru to S.A. Brelvi, 12 October 1936, ibid., pp. 399.
64. See the gist of Brelvi to Nehru, 5 October 1936 in ibid. Also the gist of Syed Mahmud to Rajendra Prasad, 24 April 1936 in Kaura, n. 54, p. 122. For a fuller view of the nature of the general Muslim attack on Gandhi at this time on the Hindi-Urdu issue, see K.K. Aziz, ed., *Prelude to Pakistan, 1930-1940: Documents and Readings Illustrating the Growth of the Idea of Pakistan* (Lahore, 1992), I, pp. 324-7, 341-4.

65. See the text of Gandhi's article entitled 'Hindi or Hindustani', published in *Harijan,* dated 9 May 1936 and reproduced in *CWMG,* LXII, n. 6, p. 383.
66. Ibid., p. 409.
67. Mian Iftikharuddin to K.M. Ashraf, 19 May 1937, *A.I.C.C. Papers*. File 47/ 1937, NMML.
68. See, for instance, Nehru's letter to Lord Lothian, 17 January 1936, *SWJN, VII*, n. 6, p. 69; his answer to a question on communalism while talking to the India Conciliation Group, London in February 1936, ibid., p. 97; and his article on 'A Constituent Assembly of India', also written in February 1936, ibid., p. 127.
69. Ibid., p. 190.
70. That is how Jinnah also appeared at that stage to the British. Referring to his support to the Congress in opposing the Ottawa Agreement on Imperial Tariff in 1936, the then Viceroy, Lord Willingdon, described him as 'really more Congress than the Congress'. In a sarcastic vein the Viceroy added that he thought Jinnah 'would go over to Congress entirely if he did not think that the Gandhi cap was not suitable for his style of dress'. See Willingdon to Zetland, 30 March 1936, IOR, Mss. Eu., D. 609/6, *Zetland Collection*.
71. Cited in Z.H. Zaidi, 'Aspects of the Development of Muslim League Policy, 1937-47, in Philips and Wainwright, n. 56, p. 250.
72. A.C. Mehta to Tej Bahadur Sapru, 28 April 1936, *Sapru Papers*, n. 58.
72a. *Indian Annual Register*, 1936, II, pp. 255-6.
73. Nehru's statement to the press, 18 September 1936, *SWJN,* VII, n. 61, p. 468.
74. Waheed Ahmad, ed., *Quid-i-Azam Mohammad Ali Jinnah: The Nation's Voice, Speeches and Statements, March 1935-March 1940* (Karachi, 1992), p. 108.
75. For text of Nehru's statement see *SWJN,* VIII (New Delhi, 1976), pp. 119-22.
76. These can be followed in ibid., pp. 124-32, 136-8, 149-52; Ahmad, n. 74, pp. 116-20; B.R. Nanda, 'Nehru, the Indian National Congress and the Partition of India, 1935-47'; and S.R. Mehrotra, 'The Congress and the Partition of India', in Philips and Wainwright, n. 56. pp. 158-9, 194. See Z.H. Zaidi, ibid., pp. 255-6, for a slightly different view of the Nehru-Jinnah exchanges.
77. For these figures see *Return showing the Results of Elections in India* (1937) cmd. 5589; there is a fairly detailed analysis in Gowher Rizvi, *Linlithgow and India* (London, 1978), pp. 25-7. Figures regarding the position of various parties in both houses of the provincial legislatures, which slightly vary from the figures given in the former, are also to be found in Appendix I, *Quarterly Survey of the Political and Constitutional Position in British India* (hereinafter referred to as *Quarterly Survey*), prepared by the office of the Secretary to the Governor-General (Public), New Delhi, No. 1, for the period ending 31 October 1937.
78. See *Quarterly Survey*, No. 1, F. 125/142, *Linlithgow Collection.*
79. *SWJN,* VIII, n. 75, p. 62.
80. Ibid. It may be added that at that time Gandhi also did not encourage any move for Congress-League dialogue. Thus when in May 1937, obviously

making an indirect bid to restart such a dialogue, Jinnah sent him a message through B.G. Kher, leader of the Congress Party in the Bombay Assembly, asking him to bestir himself in the cause of Hindu-Muslim unity, Gandhi wrote to Jinnah in reply: 'I wish I could do something, but I am utterly helpless. My faith in unity is as bright as ever; only I see no daylight out of the impenetrable darkness and, in such distress, I cry out to God for Light', Gandhi to Jinnah, 22 May 1937, *CWMG*, LXV (New Delhi, 1976), p. 231.

81. Nehru, n. 75, pp. 122-4.
82. S.A.I. Tirmizi, ed., *The Paradoxes of Partition (1937-47) I, 1937-39* (New Delhi 1998), pp. 149-50.
83. Linlithgow to Zetland, 9 April 1937, F. 125/4, n. 767.
84. *Quarterly Survey,* No. 1, *Linlithgow Collection.*
85. Haig to Linlithgow, 7 May 1937, F. 125/113, *Linlithgow Collection.*
86. Mohammad Iqbal to Jinnah, 22 April 1937, Mohammad Iqbal, *Letters of Iqbal to Jinnah* (Lahore, 1974), pp. 13-14.
87. S.H. Suhrawardy to M.A. Jinnah, 5 July 1937, *Quaid-i-Azam Papers* (hereinafter referred to as QAP), Reel 19, File 458, Quaid-i-Azam Academy, Karachi.
88. See Hyde Gowan to Linlithgow, 20 October 1937 and Lumley to Linlithgow 15 Nov. 1937, F. 125/112 and 113, *Linlithgow Collection.*
89. Morarji Desai to K.M. Ashraf, 12 June 1937, *A.I.C.C. Papers*, File 49/1937, NMML.
90. Damodar Swarup Seth to K.M. Ashraf, 1 May 1937, ibid., File 48/1937.
91. See an unsigned and undated report on the working of the Muslim Mass Contact Programme, obviously prepared in 1938, ibid., File G. 22/1938.
92. Ibid., File 47/1937.
93. J.B. Kripalani to Jawaharlal Nehru, 30 July 1938, ibid., File G. 71/1938.
94. K.M. Ashraf to Jawaharlal Nehru, 2 September 1938, *Jawaharlal Nehru Papers,* NMML.
95. Cited in *SWJN,* VIII, n. 75, p. 125.
96. Ibid., pp. 127-8.
97. Ibid., pp. 129-32, Ahmad, n. 74, pp. 137-40.
98. *SWJN,* VIII, n. 75, p. 150; Ahmad, n. 74, pp. 108, 134, 142-4.
99. *SWJN,* VIII, n. 75, pp. 150-1.
100. Ahmad, n. 74, pp. 151-2.
101. Tirmizi, n. 82, pp. 204-5.
102. Ibid., p. 207.
103. *SWJN,* VIII, n. 74, pp. 164-5.
104. Ahmad, n. 74, pp. 164-5.
105. Haig to Linlithgow, 23 June 1937, n. 57. See also Nehru to Rafi Ahmad Kidwai, 1 July 1937, *SWJN,* VIII, n. 75, p. 146.
106. Cited in *SWJN,* VIII, n. 75, p. 135.
107. Ibid., p. 137.
108. Ibid.
109. Ibid., pp. 142-3.
110. Khaliquzzaman, n. 26, p. 153.
111. Ibid.
112. See Jawaharlal Nehru to Rajendra Prasad, 21 July 1937, *SWJN*, VIII, n. 75,

pp. 165-71; also available in Valmiki Choudhary, ed., *Dr. Rajendra Prasad: Correspondence and Select Documents,* I (New Delhi, 1984), pp. 63-7; reproduced in Appendix V.

113. Linlithgow to Zetland, 29 March 1940, D. 609/19, *Zetland Collection.*
114. File No. 89/40-R, Secretariat of the Governor-General (Reforms), National Archives of India.
115. Ibid.
116. Nehru, n. 112.
117. Haig to Linlithgow, 13 February 1937, F. 125/112, *Linlithgow Collection.*
118. Haig to Linlithgow, 17 February 1937, ibid.
119. Haig to Linlithgow, 17 April 1937, F. 125/113, ibid. Haig reiterated this assessment two years later in a slightly different language without, of course, mentioning any definite agreement regarding the formation of a coalition: 'The Congress had since the general election been flirting with the Muslim League and suggesting some form of coalition. These conversations resulted in the Muslim League holding aloof from my minority Ministry. But when the Congress took office they decided to reject the idea of a coalition with the Muslim League and to pursue instead a policy of direct approach to the Muslim masses,' Enclosure to Haig to Linlithgow, 3 June 1939, IOR, Mss. Eu. 115/6, *Haig Collection.* As is well-known, the Muslim mass contact programme of the Congress was launched at the end of March 1937 while the Congress Ministry in U.P. was formed in July 1937. This shows that Haig was inadvertently mixing up things to prove a pre-conceived point. After relinquishing office as Governor of U.P. Haig said in 1940 that at the time of general elections in U.P. 'there was a widespread belief that after the elections there would be some sort of an alliance between the Congress and the Muslim League', see Sir Harry Haig, 'The United Provinces and the New Constitution', *Asiatic Review* (London, 1940), XXXVI. This also does not amount to saying that there was an agreement between the Congress and the League regarding the formation of a coalition ministry in U.P.
120. Govind Ballabh Pant to Jawaharlal Nehru, 3 April 1937, *Jawaharlal Nehru Papers,* File No. P-27 (i), NMML. This was written in reply to Nehru's to Pant, 30 March 1937, in which the former had mentioned an information communicated to him by one of his Muslim friends in U.P. that efforts were being made to bring about a coalition between the Congress and League parties in the U.P. Assembly and remarked: 'I am surprised to read this and I can hardly believe that there is anything behind it. . . . I am personally convinced that any kind of pact or coalition between us and the Muslim League will be highly injurious. It will mean that we almost lose our right to ask the Muslims to join us directly. . . . Abul Kalam Azad, as you know, is strongly opposed to it.' *SWJN,* VIII, n. 75, p. 78.
121. Haig to Linlithgow, 23 April 1937, F. 125/113, *Linlithgow Collection.*
122. Zaidi, n. 71, pp. 256-8. See also Tirmizi, n. 82, pp. 161-2; Kaura, n. 54, pp. 115-16, and Singh, n. 56., pp. 17-18.
123. Haig to Linlithgow, 24 May 1937, F. 125/113, *Linlithgow Collection.*
124. Haig to Linlithgow, 23 April 1937, ibid.
125. Azad, n. 56, p. 161.
126. Nehru to Prasad, 21 July 1932, *SWJN,* VIII, n. 112, pp. 165-71. It may be

added here that in March 1937 the All India Congress Committee while keeping the option open of forming ministries in Provinces where the Congress had gained a majority of seats, had reiterated that the immediate objectives of the Congress were to combat the new constitution and to lay stress on its demand for the setting up of a Constituent Assembly. See *Indian Annual Register*, 1937, I, pp. 177-8.

127. Kanji Dwarkadas, *India's Fight for Freedom, 1913-1947: An Eye-Witness Story* (Bombay, 1966), p. 467.
128. K.M. Munshi, *Pilgrimage to Freedom, 1902-1950* (Bombay, 1967), pp. 47-8.
129. K.M. Munshi, Oral History Transcript, No. 15, NMML.
130. IOR, L/P&J/8/689. All the three documents bearing the signatures of Rahmat Ali and his friends, cited here, have been reproduced in full in K.K. Aziz, ed., *Complete Works of Rahmat Ali,* I (Islamabad, 1978), pp. 1-20.
131. *Joint Committee on India Constitutional Reform: Minutes of Evidence*, II (London, 1934) p. 1496.
132. B.R. Ambedkar, *Pakistan or the Partition of India* (Bombay, 1946; 3rd edn.), p. 329. Iqbal's stand is not at all surprising in view of the resolution adopted by the Executive Board of the All India Muslim Conference, of which he was then president in August 1932: 'The Board most emphatically adds that the Moslems of India will not accept any constitution unless it creates completely autonomous Federal States of equal status and accepts the principle that the transfer of power shall be from Parliament to the Provinces and not from Parliament to the Central Government', *The Times of India*, 22 August 1932, cited in Waheed Ahmad, *Road to Indian Freedom* (Lahore, 1979), p. 201.
133. Ibid., pp. 329-30.
134. Ibid., p. 329.
135. *The Civil and Military Gazette* (Lahore), 20 March 1933.
136. Ibid., 27 March 1933.
137. Ibid., 28 May 1933.
138. Ibid., 15 June 1933.
139. Ibid.
140. Ibid., 7 September 1933.
141. Ibid., 19 September 1933.
142. Ibid., 22 December 1933.
143. Ibid., 1 November 1934.
144. Ibid., 7 January 1935.
145. Aziz, n. 64, p. 170.
146. Aga Khan to Fazl-i-Husain, 13 August 1935, IOR, Mss. Eu. E. 352, Box III, *Fazl-i-Husain Papers*.
147. G.D. Birla to Lord Linlithgow, 17 January 1936, IOR, Mss. Eu. F. 125/155 (C), *Linlithgow Collection*.
148. Aziz, n. 64, p. 351.
149. Ibid., pp. 370-3.
150. Pirzada, n. 30, p. 171.
151. Iqbal, n. 86, pp. 11-12.
152. Ibid., pp. 15-17. In an obvious bid to remove possible misunderstanding and distance himself from the article by Durrani, who had claimed to speak

on behalf of Iqbal and castigated the Muslim political leaders as opportunists, Iqbal wrote at the end of his letter: 'Muslim India hopes that at this serious juncture your genius will discover some way out of our present difficulties.' He also added a post-script mentioning that he had originally intended to write an open letter to Jinnah in the press, but felt on further consideration that 'the present moment was not suitable for such a step', ibid., p. 18.

153. Ibid., pp. 18-23. It may be worth mentioning here that Iqbal was so obsessed with the future of the Muslim-majority provinces that he suggested to Jinnah in his letter of 21 June that the Muslims therein would best serve their own interests as also those of Muslims in the minority provinces by ignoring the latter.
154. The first edition of Iqbal's letters to Jinnah carried no date, but was published in 1943; see Syed Shamsul Hasan, *Plain Mr. Jinnah* (Karachi, 1976), p. 171.
155. Iqbal, n. 86, pp. 4-5. In spite of the evidence presented here some scholars continue to hold that Iqbal was not in favour of India's Partition and the setting up of a separate, sovereign Muslim State; see Saad R. Khairi, *Jinnah Reinterpreted: the Journey from Indian Nationalism to Muslim Statehood* (Karachi, 1995), pp. 343-6 and Iqbal Singh, *The Ardent Pilgrim: An Introduction to the Life and Work of Mohammad Iqbal* (Delhi, 1977, 2nd edn.), pp. xii-xiii. Rafiq Zakaria held the same view earlier, but he is not sure now; see his *Iqbal: The Poet and the Politician* (New Delhi, 1993), pp. 144-9.
156. D. Madhava Rao to H.A. Gwynne, 27 January 1936, F. 125/153(c), *Linlithgow Collection.* Italics added.
157. Tej Bahadur Sapru to Lord Lothian, 4 May 1936, *Sapru Papers*, NMML.
158. Lord Brabourne to Lord Linlithgow, 5 June 1936, F. 125/113, *Linlithgow Collection.*
159. All India Muslim League, Proceedings of the meetings of the Council, 1936-7, vol. 222, Archives of the Freedom Movement, University of Karachi.
160. See, for instance, Sarvepalli Gopal, *Jawaharlal Nehru: A Biography,* I (Bombay, 1976), p. 229.
161. Ibid., pp. 222, 228. Also B.R. Nanda, *Jawaharlal Nehru: Rebel and Statesman* (Delhi, 1995), pp. 177-8.
162. Jawaharlal Nehru to Rajendra Prasad, 21 July 1937, *SWJN,* VIII, n. 126.
163. See Jawaharlal Nehru to Govind Ballabh Pant, 30 March 1937, n. 120.
164. Jawaharlal Nehru, *The Discovery of India* (Bombay, 1969), p. 369.

APPENDIX I

SYED AHMAD KHAN'S SPEECH AT MEERUT, 16 MARCH 1888

I think it expedient that I should first of all tell you the reason why I am about to address you on the subject of to-night's discourse. You know, gentlemen, that, from a long time, our friends the Bengalis have shown very warm feelings on political matters. Three years ago they founded a very big assembly, which holds its sittings in various places, and they have given it the name "National Congress". We and our nation gave no thought to the matter. And we should be very glad for our friends the Bengalis to be successful if we were of opinion that they had by their education and ability made such progress as rendered them fit for the claims they put forward. But although they are superior to us in education, yet we have never admitted that they have reached that level to which they lay claim to have attained. Nevertheless, I have never, in any article, or in any speech, or even in conversation in any place, put difficulties or desired to put difficulties in the way of any of their undertakings. It has never been my wish to oppose any people or any nation who wish to make progress, and who have raised themselves up to that rank to which they wish to attain and for which they are qualified. But my friends the Bengalis have made a most unfair and unwarrantable interference with my nation, and therefore it is my duty to show clearly what this unwarrantable interference has been, and to protect my nation from the evils that may arise from it. It is quite wrong to suppose that I have girded up my loins for the purpose of fighting my friends the Bengalis: my object is only to make my nation understand what I consider conducive to its prosperity. It is incumbent on me to show what evils would befall my nation from joining in the opinions of the Bengalis: I have no other purpose in view.

The unfair interference of these people is this—that they have tried to produce a false impression that the Mohammedans of these Provinces agree with their opinions. But we also are inhabitants of this country, and we cannot be ignorant of the real nature of the events that are taking place in our own North-West Provinces and Oudh, however their colour may be painted in newspapers, and whatever aspect they may be made to assume. It is possible that the people of England, who are ignorant of the real facts may be deceived on seeing their false representations, but we and the people of our country,

Source: Sayyid Ahmad Khan, *The Present State of Indian Politics: Speeches and Letters* (Allahabad, 1888).

who know all the circumstances, can never be thus imposed on. Our Mohammedan nation has hitherto sat silent. It was quite indifferent as to what the Babus of Bengal, the Hindus of these Provinces, and the English and Eurasian inhabitants of India might be doing. But they have now been wrongly tampering with our nation. In some districts they have brought pressure to bear on Mohammedans to make them join the Congress. I am sorry to say that they never said anything to those people who are powerful and are actually *Raises* and are counted the leaders of the nation; but they brought unfair pressure to bear on such people as could be subjected to their influence. In some districts they pressed men by the weight of authority, in others they forced them in this way—saying that the business they had at heart could not prosper unless they took part—or they led them to suppose that they could not get bread if they held aloof. They even did not hold back from offering the temptation of money. Where is the man that does not know this? Who does not know who were the three or four Mohammedans of the North-West Provinces who took part with them, and why they took part? The simple truth is they were nothing more than hired men (Cheers). Such people they took to Madras, and having got them there, said: "These are the sons of Nawabs, and these are *Raises* of such-and-such districts, and these are such-and-such great Mohammedans," whilst everybody knows how the men were bought. We know very well the people of our own nation, and that they have been induced to go either by pressure, or by folly, or by love of notoriety, or by poverty. If any *Rais* on his own inclination and opinion joins them, we do not care a lot. By one man's leaving us our crowd is not diminished. But this telling of lies that their men are landlords and Nawabas of such-and-such places and their attempt to give a false impression that the Mohammedans have joined them, this is a most unwarrantable interference with our nation. When matters took such a turn, then it was necessary that I should warn my nation of their misrepresentations in order that others should not fall into the trap; and that I should point out to my nation that the few who went to Madras, went by pressure, or from some temptation, or in order to help their profession, or to gain notoriety, or were bought (Cheers). No *Rais* from here took part in it.

This was the cause of my giving a speech at Lucknow, contrary to my wont, on the evils of the National Congress; and this is the cause also of to-day's speech. And I want to show this that except Badruddin Tyabji[1] who is a gentleman of very high position and for whom, I have great respect, no leading Mohammedan took part in it. He did take part, but I think he made a mistake. He has written me two letters, one of which was after the publication of my Lucknow speech. I think that he wants me to point out those things in the

[1]Badruddin Tyabji was born in 1844. In 1876, he founded Anjuman-e-Islam of Bombay, an institution intended for the betterment of the Muslims of India. In 1882 he was nominated a member of Bombay Legislative Council. He presided over the third deliberations of the Indian National Congress. [Madras, 1887].

Congress which are opposed to the interests of Mohammedans in order that he may exclude them from the discussion. But in reality the whole affair is bad for Mohammedans. However, let us grant that Badruddin Tyabji's opinion is different from ours; yet it cannot be said that his opinion is the opinion of the whole nation, or that his sympathy with the Congress implies the sympathy of the whole community. My friend there, Mirza Ismail Khan, who has just come from Madras, told me that no Mohammedan *Rais* of Madras took part in the Congress. It is said that Prince Humayun Jah joined it. Let us suppose that Humayun Jah, whom I do not know, took part in it, yet our position as a nation will not suffer simply because two men stand aside. No one can say that because these two *Raises* took part in it that therefore the whole nation has joined it. To say that the Mohammedans have joined it is quite wrong and is a false accusation against our nation. If my Bengali friends had not adopted this wrong course of action, I should have had nothing to do with the National Congress, nor with its members, nor with the wrong aspirations for which they have raised such an uproar. Let the delegates of the National Congress become the stars of heaven, or the sun itself—I am delighted. But it was necessary and incumbent on me to show the falsity of the impression which, by taking a few Mohammedans with them by pressure or by temptation, they wished to spread that the whole Mohammedan nation had joined them (Cheers).

Gentlemen, what I am about to say is not only useful for my own nation, but also for my Hindu brothers of these Provinces, who from some wrong notions have taken part in this Congress. At last they also will be sorry for it, although perhaps they will never have occasion to be sorry; for it is beyond the region of possibility that the proposals of the Congress should be carried out fully. These wrong notions which have grown up in our Hindu fellow country-men, and on account of which they think it expedient to join the Congress, depend upon two things. The first thing is this: that they think that as both they themselves and the Bengalis are Hindus, they have nothing to fear from the growth of their influence. The second thing is this: that some Hindus—I do not speak of all the Hindus but only of some—think that by joining the Congress and by increasing the power of the Hindus they will perhaps be able to suppress those Mohammedan religious rites which are opposed to their own, and, by all uniting, annihilate them. But I frankly advise my Hindu friends that if they wish to cherish their religious rites they can never be successful in this way. If they are to be successful, it can only be by friendship and agreement. The business cannot be done by force; and the greater the enmity and animosity the greater will be their loss. I will take Aligarh as an example. There Mohammedans and Hindus are in agreement. The Dasehra and Moharrum fell together for three years, and no one knows what took place. It is worth notice how, when an agitation was started against cow-killing, the sacrifice of cows increased enormously, and religious animosity grew on both sides, as all who live in India well know. They should understand that those things that can be done by friendship and affection cannot be done by any pressure or force. If these ideas which I have expressed about the Hindus of these provinces be correct and their condition be similar to that of the Mohammedans, then they ought to continue to cultivate friendship with us. Let those who live in Bengal eat up their own heads. What they want to do, let them do it. What they don't want to do, let them not do it. Neither their disposition nor their general condition resembles that of the people of this country. Then what connection have the people of this country with them? As regards Bengal, there is, as far as I am aware in Lower Bengal, a much larger proportion of Mohammedans than Bengalis. And if you take the population of the whole of Bengal, nearly half are Mohammedans and something over half are Bengalis. Those Mohammedans are quite unaware of what sort of thing the National Congress is. No Mohammedan *Rais* of Bengal took part in it, and the ordinary Bengalis who live in the districts are also as ignorant of it as the Mohammedans. In Bengal the Mohammedan population is so great that if the aspirations of those Bengalis who are making so loud an agitation be fulfilled, it will be extremely difficult for the Bengalis to remain in peace even in Bengal. These proposals of the Congress are extremely inexpedient for the country which is inhabited by two different nations, who drink from the same well, breathe the air of the same city, and depend on each other for its life. To create animosity between them is good neither for peace, nor for the country, nor for the town.

After this long preface I wish to explain what method my nation, nay, rather the whole people of this country, ought to pursue in political matters. I will treat in regular sequence of the political questions of India, in order that you may have full opportunity of giving your attention to them. The first of all is this—In whose hands shall the administration and the Empire of India rest? Now, suppose that all English and the whole English army were to leave India, taking with them all their cannon and their splendid weapons and everything, then who would be rulers of India? Is it possible that under these circumstances two nations—the Mohammedans and the Hindus—could sit on the same throne and remain equal in power? Most certainly not. It is necessary that one of them should conquer the other and thrust it down. To hope that both could remain equal is to desire the impossible and the inconceivable. At the same time you must remember that although the number of Mohammedans is less than that of the Hindus, and although they contain far fewer people who have received a high English education, yet they must not be thought insignificant or weak. Probably they would be by themselves enough to maintain their own position. But suppose they were not. Then our Mussalman brothers, the Pathans would come out as a swarm of locusts from their mountain valleys, and make rivers of blood to flow from their frontier on north to extreme end of Bengal. This thing—who after the departure of the English would be conquerors—would rest on the will of God. But until one nation had conquered the other and made it obedient, peace cannot reign in the land. This conclusion is based on proofs so absolute that no one can deny it. Now, suppose that the English are not in India and that one of the nations of India has conquered the other, whether the Hindus the Mohammedans, or the Mohammedans the Hindus. At once some other nation of Europe, such as the French, the Germans, the Portuguese, or the Russians, will attack India. Their ships of war, covered with iron and loaded with flashing cannon and weapons, will surround her on all sides. At that time who will protect India? Neither Hindu can save nor Mohammedans; neither the Rajputs nor my brave brothers the Pathans. And what will be the result? The result will be this—that foreigners will rule India, because the state of India is such that if foreign powers attack her, no one has the power to oppose them. From this reasoning it follows of necessity that an empire, not of any Indian race, but of foreigners, will be established in India. Now, will you please decide which of the nations of Europe you would like to rule over India? I ask if you would like Germany, whose subjects weep for heavy taxation and the stringency of their military service? Would you like the rule of France? Stop! I fancy you would, perhaps, like the rule of the Russians, who are very great friends of India and of Mohammedans, and under whom the Hindus will live in great comfort, and who will protect with the tenderest care the wealth and property which they have acquired under English rule? (Laughter). Everybody knows something or other about these powerful kingdoms of Europe. Everyone will admit that their governments are far worse, nay beyond comparison worse, than the British Government. It is, therefore, necessary that for the peace of India and for the progress of everything in India the English Government should remain for many years—in fact for ever!

When it is granted that the maintenance of the British Government, and of no other, is necessary for the progress of our country, then I ask whether there is any example in the world of one nation having conquered and ruled over another nation, and that conquered nation claiming it as a right that they should have representative government? The principle of representative government is that it is government by a nation, and that the nation in question rules over its own people and its own land. Can you tell me of any case in the world's history in which any foreign nation after conquering another and establishing its empire over it has given representative government to the conquered people? Such a thing has never taken place. It is necessary for those who have conquered us to maintain their Empire on a strong basis. When rulers and ruled are one nation, representative government is possible. For example, in Afghanistan, of which Amir Abdur Khan[2] is the ruler, where all the people are brother-Afghans, it might be possible. If they want they can have representative government. But to think that representative government can be established in a country over which a foreign race rules, is utterly vain, nor

[2]Amir Abdur Rahman, nephew of Sher Ali, Amir of Afghanistan. He was a refugee in Samarkand under Russian protection. He helped Roberts in his famous march from Kabul to Qandahar (in about 1880) which led to defeat of Ayub. He later on became the Amir of Afghanistan.

can a trace of such a state of things be discovered in the history of the world. Therefore to ask that we should be appointed by election to the Legislative Council is opposed to the true principles of government, and no government whatever, whether English or German or French or Russian or Mussalman, could accept this principle. The meaning of it is this : "Abandon the rule of the country and put it in our hands." Hence, it is in no way expedient that our nation should join in and echo these monstrous proposals.

The next question is about the Budget. They say: "Give us power to vote on the budget. Whatever expenses we may grant shall be granted, whatever expenses we do not grant shall not be granted." Now, consider to what sort of government this principle is applicable. It is suited to such a country as is, according to the fundamental principles of politics, adapted also for representative government. The rulers and the ruled must be of the same nation. In such a country the people have also the right of deciding matters of peace and war. But this principle is not adapted to a country in which one foreign race has conquered another. The English have conquered India and all of us along with it. And just as we made the country obedient and our slave, so the English have done with us. Is it then consonant with the principles of empire that they should ask us whether they should fight Burma or not? Is it consistent with any principle of empire? In the time of the Mohammedan empire, would it have been consistent with the principles of rule that, when the Emperor was about to make war on a Province of India, he should have asked his subject-peoples whether he should conquer that country or not? Whom should he have asked? Should he have asked those whom he had conquered and had made slaves, and whose brothers he also wanted to make his slaves? Our nation has itself wielded empire, and people of our nation are even now ruling. Is there any principle of empire by which rule over foreign races may be maintained in this manner?

The right to give an opinion on the Budget depends also on another principle, which is this: that in a country in which the people accept the responsibility for all the expenses of government, and are ready with their lives and property to discharge it,—in such a country they have a right to give their opinion on the Budget. They can say, "undertake this expense or leave that alone". And whatever the expense of the state affairs, it is then their duty to pay it. For example, in England in a time of necessity the whole wealth and property of every one, from the Duke to the cobbler, is at the disposal of the Government. It is the duty of the people to give all their money and all their property to the Government, because they are responsible for giving Government all that it may require. And they say: "Yes, Yes, take it! Yes, take it. Spend the money. Beat the enemy. Beat the enemy." These are conditions under which people have a right to decide matters about the Budget. The principle that underlies the Government of India is of a wholly different nature. In India, the Government has itself to bear the responsibility of maintaining its authority and it must, in the way that seems to it fittest, raise money for its army and for the expense of the empire. Government has a right to take a fixed proportion of the produce of the land as land-revenue, and is like a contractor who bargains on this income to maintain the empire. It has not the power to increase the amount settled as land-revenue. However great its necessity, it cannot say to the zamindars:[3] "increase your contributions". Nor do the zamindars think that, even in a time of necessity, Government has any right to increase its fixed tax on land. If at this time there were a war with Russia, would all the zamindars and taluqdars be willing to give double their assessment to Government? They would not give a pice more. Then what right have they to interfere and say: "So much should be spent and so much should not be spent?" The method of the British Government is that of all Kings and Asiatic Empires. When you will not, even in time of war, give a pice more of your land-revenue, what right have you to interfere in the Budget.

The real motive for scrutinising the Budget is economy. Economy is a thing of such a nature that everyone has a regard for it in his household arrangements. It is a crude notion that Government has no regard for economy and squanders its money, Government practises economy as far as possible. Our Government is so extremely miserly that it will not uselessly give any one a single pice. Until great necessity arises and great pressure be brought to bear on it, it will not spend a pice. It has completely forgotten the generosity of the former Emperors. The Kings of later times presented poets and authors with estates and lakhs of rupees. Our Government does not spend a pice in that way. What greater economy can there be than this? Instead of rewards it gives authors copyright. That also it does after taking two rupees for registering. It writes a letter as a sanad,[4] and says that, for forty years, no other man may print the book. Print it, sell it, and make your profit: this is a reward to you from Government.

People look at the income of the Government and say it is much greater than that of former empires, but they don't think of the expenses of Government and how much they have increased. In the old days, a sword of fifteen or twenty rupees, a gun a ten or fifteen rupees, a card-board ammunition bag, and a coil of fuse was enough equipment for a soldier. Now look and see how the expenses of the army have increased in modern times, and what progress has been made in arms, and how they are daily improving, and the old ones becoming useless. If a new kind of gun or cannon be invented in France or Germany, is it possible for Government not to abandon all its old kinds of guns or cannon and adopt the new? When the expenses have grown so much, the wonder is how on earth Government manages to carry on its business on the small tax which it raises (Cheers). Perhaps many people will not like what I am going to say, but I will tell them openly a thing which took place. When after the Mutiny, the Hon'ble Mr. Wilson was Finance Minister, he brought forward a law for imposing a tax, and said in his speech that this tax would

[3]Landholders.

[4]Certificate.

remain for five years only. An honourable English friend of mine showed me the speech and asked me if I liked it. I read it and said that I had never seen so foolish a Finance Minister as the Hon'ble Mr. Wilson. He was surprised. I said that it was wrong to restrict it to five years. The condition of India was such that it ought to be imposed for ever. Consider for a moment that Government has to protect its friends the Afghans, and their protection is necessary. It is necessary for Government to strengthen the frontier. If in England there had been any need for strengthening a frontier, then the people would themselves have doubled or trebled (sic) their taxes to meet the necessity. In Burma there are expenses to be borne, although we hope that in future it will be a source of income. If, under such circumstance, Government increases the salt-tax by eight annas per maund, is this thing such that we ought to make complaints? If this increase of tax be spread over everybody it will not amount to half or quarter of a pice. On this to raise an uproar, to oppose Government, to accuse it of oppression—what utter nonsense and injustice! And in spite of this they claim the right to decide matters about the Budget.

When it has been settled that the English Government is necessary, then it is useful for India that its rule should be established on the firmest possible basis. And it is desirable for Government that for its stability it should maintain an army of such a size as it may think expedient, with a proper equipment of officers; and that it should in every district appoint officials in whom it can place complete confidence, in order that if a conspiracy arises in any place they may apply the remedy. I ask you, is it the duty of Government or not to appoint European officers in its empire to stop conspiracies and rebellions? Be just, and examine your hearts, and tell me if it is not a natural law that people should confide more in men of their own nation. If any Englishman tells you anything which is true, you remain doubtful. But when a man of your own nation, or your family, tells you a thing privately in your house, you believe it at once. What reason can you then give why Government, in the administration of so big an empire, should not appoint, as custodians of secrets and as givers of every kind of information, men of her own nationality, but must leave all these matters to you, and say: "Do what you like?" These things which I have said are such necessary matters of State administration that, whatever nation may be holding the empire, they cannot be left out of sight. It is the business of a good and just Government, after having secured the above mentioned essentials, to give honour to the people of the land over which it rules, and to give them as high appointments as it can. But, in reality, there are certain appointments to which we can claim no right; we cannot claim the post of head executive authority in any zila.[5] There are hundreds of secrets which Government cannot disclose. If Government appoint us to such responsible and confidential posts, it is her favour. We will certainly discharge the duties faithfully and without divulging her secrets. But it is one thing to claim it as a

[5]District.

right and another for Government, believing us to be faithful and worthy of confidence, to give us the posts. Between these two things there is a difference between Heaven and Earth. How can we possibly claim as a right those things on which the very existence and strength of the Government depends? We most certainly have not the right to put those people in the Council whom we want, and to keep out those whom we don't want, to pass those laws that we want, and to veto those laws that we dislike. If we have the right to elect members for the Legislative Council, there is no reason why we should not have the right to elect members for the Imperial Council. In the Imperial Council thousands of matters of foreign policy and State secrets are discussed. Can you with justice say that we Indians have a right to claim those things? To make an agitation for such things can only bring misfortune on us and on the country. It is opposed to the true principles of government, and is harmful for the peace of the country. The aspirations of our friends the Bengalis have made such progress that they want to scale a height to which it is beyond their powers to attain. But if I am not in error, I believe that the Bengalis have never at any period held sway over a particle of land. They are altogether ignorant of the method by which a foreign race can maintain its rule over other races. Therefore, reflect on the doings of your ancestors, and be not unjust to the British Government to whom God had given the rule of India; and look honestly and see what is necessary for it to do to maintain its empire and its hold on the country. You can appreciate these matters; but they cannot who have never held a country in their hands nor won a victory. Oh, my brother Mussalmans! I again remind you that you have ruled nations, and have for centuries held different countries in your grasp. For seven hundred years in India you have had Imperial sway. You know what it is to rule. Be not unjust to that nation which is ruling over you, and think also on this: how upright is her rule. Of such benevolence as the English Government shows to the foreign nations under her, there is no example in the history of the world. See what freedom she has given in her laws and how careful she is to protect the rights of her subjects. She has not been backward in promoting the progress of the natives of India and in throwing open to them high appointments. At the commencement of her rule, except clerkships and ***kaziships*** there was nothing. The ***kazis***[6] of the pargana, who were called commissioners, decided small civil suits and received very small pay. Up to 1832 or 1833 this state of things lasted. If my memory is not wrong, it was in the time of Lord William Bentinck that natives of India began to get honourable posts. The positions of Munsif, Subordinate Judge and Deputy Collector on respectable pay were given to natives, and progress has been steadily going on ever since. In the Calcutta High Court a Kashmiri Pandit was first appointed equal to the English Judges. After him Bengalis have been appointed as High Court Judges. At this time there are, perhaps, three Bengalis in the Calcutta High Court, and in the same

[6] *Kazi* = Judge.

way some Hindus in Bombay and Madras. It was your bad fortune that there was for a long time no Mohammedan High Court Judge, but now there is one in the Allahabad High court (Cheers). Native High Court Judges can cancel the decision of English Judges and Collectors. They can ask them for explanations. The subordinate native officers also have full authority in their posts. A Deputy Collector, a Sub-Judge, or a Munsif decides cases according to his opinion, and is independent of the opinion of the Judge or Collector. None of these things have been acquired by fighting or opposition. As far as you have made yourselves worthy of the confidence of Government, to that extent you have received high positions. Make yourselves her friends and prove to her that your friendship with her is like that of English and the Scotch. After this what you have to claim, claim—on condition that you are qualified for it.

About this political controversy, in which my Hindu brothers of this Province, to whom I have given some advice, and who have, I think, joined from some wrong notions, have taken part, I wish to give some advice to my Mohammedan brothers. I do not think the Bengali politics useful for my brother Mussalmans. Our Hindu brothers of these provinces are leaving us and are joining the Bengalis. Then we ought to unite with that nation with whom we can unite. No Mohammedan can say that the English are not "people of the Book". No Mohammedan can deny this: that God has said that no people of other religions can be friends of Mohammedans except the Christians. He who had read the Koran and believes it, he can know that our nation cannot expect friendship and affection from any other people. (Thou shalt surely find the most violent of all men in enmity against the true believers to be the Jews and the idolators; and thou shalt surely find those among them to be the most inclinable to entertain friendship for the true believers, who say "we are Christians." Koran, Chap. V.) At this time our nation is in a bad state as regards education and wealth, but God has given us the light of religion, and the Koran is present for our guidance, which has ordained them and us to be friends. Now God has made them rulers over us. Therefore we should cultivate friendship with them, and should adopt that method by which their rule may remain permanent and firm in India, and may not pass into the hands of the Bengalis. This is our true friendship with our Christian rulers, and we should not join those people who wish to see us thrown into a ditch. If we join the political movement of the Bengalis our nation will reap loss, for we do not want to become subjects of the Hindus instead of the subjects of the "people of the Book". And as far as we can we should remain faithful to the English Government. By this my meaning is not that I am inclined towards their religion. Perhaps no one has written such severe books as I have against their religion of which I am an enemy. But whatever their religion, God has called men of that religion our friends. We ought not on account of their religion but because of the order of God to be friendly and faithful to them. If our Hindu brothers of these Provinces, and the Bengalis of Bengal, and the Brahmans of

Bombay, and the Hindu Madrasis of Madras wish to separate themselves from us, let them go, and trouble yourself about it not one whit. We can mix with the English in a social way. We can eat with them, they can eat with us. Whatever hope we have of progress is from them. The Bengalis can in no way assist our progress. And when the Koran itself directs us to be friends with them, then there is no reason why we should not be their friends. But it is necessary for us to act as God has said. Besides this, God has made them rulers over us. Our Prophet has said that if God places over you a black negro slave as ruler you must obey him. See, there is here in the meeting a European, Mr Beck. He is not black. He is very white (laughter). Then why should we not be obedient and faithful to those white-faced men whom God has put over us, and why should we disobey the order of God?

I do not say that in the British Government all things are good. Nobody can say that there is any Government in the world, or has ever been, in which there is nothing bad, be the Government Mohammedan, Hindu, or Christian. There is now the Sultan of Turkey, who is a Mohammedan Emperor, and of whom we are proud. Even his Mohammedan subjects make complaints of his government. This is the condition of the Khedive of Egypt. Look at the Governments of Europe, and examine the condition of the Government of London itself. Thousands of men complain against Government. There is no Government with which every body is satisfied.

If we also have some complaints against the English Government, it is no wonderful thing. People are not even grateful to God for His government. I do not tell you to ask nothing from Government. I will myself fight on your behalf for legitimate objects. But ask for such things as they can give you, or such things to which, having due regard to the administration of the country, you can claim a right. If you ask for such things as Government cannot give you, then it is not the fault of Government, the folly of the askers. But what you ask, do it not in this fashion: that you accuse Government in very action of oppression, abuse the highest official, use the hardest words you can find for Lord Lytton and Lord Dufferin, call all Englishmen tyrants, and blacken columns on columns of newspapers with these subjects. You can gain nothing this way. God had made them your rulers. This is the will of God. We should be content with the will of God. And, in obedience to the will of God you should remain friendly and faithful to them. Do not do this: bring false accusations against them and give birth to enmity. This is neither wisdom nor in accordance with our holy religion.

Therefore the method we ought to adopt is this, that we should hold ourselves aloof from this political uproar and reflect on our condition, that we are behindhand in education and are deficient in wealth. Then we should try to improve the education of our nation. Now our condition is this, that the Hindus, if they wish, can ruin us in an hour. The internal trade is entirely in their hands. The external trade is in possession of the English. Let the trade which is with the Hindus remain with them. But try to snatch from their hands the trade in the produce of the county which the English now enjoy and draw profit from. Tell them: "Take no further trouble. We will ourselves take the leather of our country to England and sell it there. Leave off picking up the bones of our country's animals. We will ourselves collect them and take them to America. Do not fill ships with the corn and cotton of our country. We will fill our own ships and will take it ourselves to Europe!" Never imagine that Government will put difficulties in your way in trade. But the acquisition of all these things depends on education. When you shall have fully acquired education, and true education shall have made its home in your hearts, then you will know what rights you can legitimately demand of the British Government. And the result of this will be that you will also obtain honourable positions in the government, and will acquire wealth in the higher ranks of trade. But to make friendship with the Bengalis in their mischievous political proposals, and join in them, can bring only harm. If my nation follows my advice they will draw benefit from trade and education. Otherwise, remember that Government will keep a very sharp eye on you because you are very quarrelsome, very brave, great soldiers and great fighters.

APPENDIX II

MUSLIM LEADERS' ADDRESS TO THE VICEROY, LORD MINTO, AND THE LATTER'S REPLY, SIMLA, 1 OCTOBER 1906

A. Muslim Leaders' Address

Availing ourselves of the permission accorded to us, we, the undersigned nobles, jagirdars, taluqdars, lawyers, zamindars, merchants and others representing a large body of the Mohammedan subjects of His Majesty the King-Emperor in different parts of India, beg most respectfully to approach your Excellency with the following address for your favourable consideration.

We fully realise and appreciate the incalculable benefits conferred by British rule on the teeming millions belonging to diverse races and professing diverse religions who form the population of the vast continent of India, and have every reason to be grateful for the peace, security, personal freedom and liberty of worship that we now enjoy. Further, from the wise and enlightened character of the Government, we have every reasonable ground for anticipating that these benefits will be progressive and that India will in the future occupy an increasingly important position in the comity of nations.

One of the most important characteristics of British policy in India is the increasing deference that has so far as possible been paid from the first to the views and wishes of the people of the country in matters affecting their interests, with due regard always to the diversity of race and religion, which forms such an important feature of all India's progress.

Beginning with the confidential and unobtrusive method of consulting influential members of important communities in different parts of the country, this principle was gradually extended by the recognition of the right of recognised political or commercial organisations to communicate to the authorities their criticisms and views on measures of public importance, and finally by the nomination and election of direct representatives of the people in Municipalities, District Boards, and above all in the Legislative Chambers of the country. This last element is, we understand, about to be dealt with by the Committee appointed by Your Excellency with the view of giving it further extension, and it is with reference mainly to our claim to a fair share in such

Source: John Morley Papers, Mss. Eur. D. 573/35, India Office Library and Records (London).

extended representation and some other matters of importance affecting the interests of our community, that we have ventured to approach your Excellency on the present occasion.

The Mahommedans of India number, according to the census taken in the year 1901, over sixty-two millions or between one-fifth and one-fourth of the total population of His Majesty's Indian dominions, and if a reduction be made for the uncivilised portions of the community enumerated under the heads of animist and other minor religions, as well as for those classes who are ordinarily classified as Hindu but properly speaking are not Hindu at all, the proportion of Mahommedans to the Hindu majority becomes much larger. We, therefore, desire to submit that under any system of representation, extended or limited, a community in itself more numerous than the entire population of any first class European power except Russia may justly lay claim to adequate recognition as an important factor in the State.

We venture, indeed, with Your Excellency's permission, to go a step further, and urge that the position accorded to the Mahommedan community in any kind of representation, direct or indirect, and in all other ways affecting their status and influence should be commensurate, not merely with their numerical strength, but also with their political importance and the value of the contribution which they make to the defence of the empire, and we also hope that your Excellency will in this connection be pleased to give due consideration to the position which they occupied in India a little more than hundred years ago and of which the traditions have naturally not faded from their minds.

The Mahommedans of India have always placed implicit reliance on the sense of justice and love of fair dealing that have characterised their rulers; and have in consequence abstained from pressing their claims by methods that might prove at all embarrassing, but earnestly as we desire that the Mahommedans of India should not in the future depart from that excellent and time-honoured tradition, recent events have stirred up feelings, especially among the younger generation of Mahommedans, which might, in certain circumstances and under certain contingencies, easily pass beyond the control of temperate counsel and sober guidance.

We, therefore, pray that the representations we herewith venture to submit, after a careful consideration of the views and wishes of a large number of our co-religionists in all parts of India, may be favoured with your Excellency's earnest consideration.

We hope your Excellency will pardon our stating at the outset that representative institutions of the European type are new to the Indian people; many of the most thoughtful members of our community in fact consider that the greatest care, forethought and caution will be necessary if they are to be successfully adapted to the social, religious and political conditions obtaining in India, and that in the absence of such care and caution their adoption is likely, among other evils, to place our national interests at the mercy of an unsympathetic majority. Since, however, our rulers have, in pursuance of their immemorial instincts and traditions, found it expedient to give these institutions an increasingly important place in the Government of the country, we Mahommedans cannot any longer in justice to our own national interests hold aloof from participating in the conditions to which their policy has given rise. While, therefore, we are bound to acknowledge with gratitude that such representation as the Mahommedans of India have hitherto enjoyed has been due to a sense of justice and fairness on the part of your Excellency and your illustrious predecessor in office and the heads of Local Governments by whom the Mahommedan members of Legislative Chambers have almost without exception been nominated, we cannot help observing that the representation thus accorded to us has necessarily been inadequate to our requirements, and has not always carried with it the approval of those whom the nominees were selected to represent. This state of things was probably under existing circumstances unavoidable, for while on the one hand the number of nominations reserved to the Viceroy and Local Governments has necessarily been strictly limited, the selection on the other hand of really representative men has, in the absence of any reliable method of ascertaining the direction of popular choice, been far from easy.

As for the results of election, it is most unlikely that the name of any Mahommedan candidate will ever be submitted for the approval of Government by the electoral bodies as now constituted unless he is in sympathy with the majority in all matters of importance. Nor can we in fairness find fault with the desire of our non-Muslim fellow-subjects to take full advantage of their strength and vote only for members of their own community, or for persons who, if not Hindus, are expected to vote with the Hindu majority on whose goodwill they would have to depend for their future re-election. It is true that we have many and important interests in common with our Hindu fellow-countrymen and it will always be a matter of the utmost satisfaction to us to see these interests safeguarded by the presence in our Legislative Chambers of able supporters of these interests, irrespective of their nationality. Still, it cannot be denied that we Mahommedans are a distinct community with additional interests of our own which are not shared by other communities, and these have hitherto suffered from the fact that they have not been adequately represented. Even in the provinces in which the Mahommedans constitute a distinct majority of the population, they have too often been treated as though they were inappreciably small political factors that might without unfairness be neglected. This has been the case, to some extent, in the Punjab, but in a more marked degree in Sind and in Eastern Bengal.

Before formulating our views with regard to the election of representatives, we beg to observe that the political importance of a community to a considerable extent gains strength or suffers detriment according to the position that the members of that community occupy in the service of the State. If, as is unfortunately the case with the Mahommedans, they are not adequately represented in this manner, they lose in the prestige and influence which are justly their due.

We, therefore, pray that Government will be graciously pleased to provide that both in the gazetted and the subordinate and ministerial services of all Indian provinces a due proportion of Mahommedans shall always find place. Orders of like import have at times been issued by Local Governments in some provinces, but have not, unfortunately, in all cases been strictly observed on the ground that qualified Mahommedans were not forthcoming. This allegation, however well-founded it may have been at one time, is, we submit, no longer tenable now, and wherever the will to employ them is not wanting the supply of qualified Mahommedans, we are happy to be able to assure Your Excellency, is equal to the demand.

Since, however, the number of qualified Mahommedans has increased, a tendency is unfortunately perceptible to reject them on the ground of relatively superior qualifications having to be given precedence. This introduces something like the competitive element in its worst form, and we may be permitted to draw Your Excellency's attention to the political significance of the monopoly of all official influence by one class. We may also point out in this connection that the efforts of Mahommedan educationists have from the very outset of the educational movement among them been strenuously directed towards the development of character, and this we venture to think is of greater importance than mere mental alertness in the making of good public servants.

We venture to submit that the generality of Mahommedans in all parts of India feel aggrieved that Mahommedan Judges are not more frequently appointed to the High Courts and Chief Courts of Judicature. Since the creation of these Courts only three Mahommedan Lawyers have held these honourable appointments, all of whom have fully justified their elevation to the Bench. At the present moment there is not a single Mahommedan Judge sitting on the Bench of any of these Courts, while three Hindu Judges in the Calcutta High Court, where the proportion of Mahommedans in the population is very large, and two in the Chief Court of the Punjab, where the Mahommedans form the majority of the population. It is not, therefore, an extravagant request on our part that a Mahommedan should be given a seat on the Bench of each of the High Courts and Chief Courts. Qualified Mahommedan lawyers eligible for these appointments can always be found, if not in one province then in another. We beg permission further to submit that the presence on the Bench of these courts of a Judge learned in the Mahommedan Law will be a source of considerable strength to the administration of justice.

As Municipal and District Boards have to deal with important local interests affecting to a great extent the health, comfort, educational needs and even the religious concerns of the inhabitants, we shall, we hope, be pardoned if we solicit for a moment Your Excellency's attention to the position of Mahommedans thereon before passing to higher concerns. These institutions form, as it were, the initial rungs in the ladder of self-government and it is here that the principle of representation is brought home intimately to the intelligence of the people, yet the position of Mahommedans on these Boards is not at present regulated by any guiding principle capable of general application, and practice varies in different localities. The Aligarh Municipality, for example, is divided into six wards and each ward returns one Hindu and one Mahommedan Commissioner, and the same principle we understand is adopted in a number of Municipalities in the Punjab and elsewhere, but in a good many places the Mahommedan tax-payers are not adequately represented. We would, therefore, respectfully suggest that the local authority should in every case be required to declare the number of Hindus and Mahommedans entitled to seats on Municipal and District Boards, such proportion to be determined in accordance with the numerical strength, social status, local influence and special requirements of either community. Once their relative proportion is authoritatively determined, we would suggest that either community should be allowed severally to return their own representatives as is the practice in many towns in the Punjab.

We would also suggest that the Senates and Syndicates of Indian Universities might be similarly dealt with, that is to say, there should, so far as possible, be an authoritative declaration of the proportion in which Mahommedans are entitled to be represented in either body.

We now proceed to the consideration of the question of our representation in the Legislative Chambers of the country. Beginning with the Provincial Councils, we would most respectfully suggest that as in the case of Municipalities and District Boards the proportion of Mahommedan representatives entitled to seats should be determined and declared with due regard to the important consideration which we have ventured to point out in paragraph 5 of this address, and that the important Mahommedan landowners, lawyers, merchants and representatives of other important interests, the Mahommedan members of District Boards and Municipalities and the Mahommedan graduates of universities of a certain standing, say five years, should be formed into Electoral Colleges and be authorised, in accordance with such rules of procedure as Your Excellency's Government may be pleased to prescribe in that behalf, to return the number of members that may be declared to be eligible.

With regard to the Imperial Legislative Council whereon the due representation of Mahommedan interests is a matter of vital importance, we crave leave to suggest (1) that in the cadre of the Council the proportion of Mahommedan representatives should not be determined on the basis of the numerical strength of the community, and that in any case the Mahommedan representatives should never be an ineffective minority; (2) that as far as possible, appointment by election should be given preference over nomination; (3) that for the purposes of choosing Mahommedan members, Mahommedan landowners, lawyers, merchants and representatives of other important interests of a status to be subsequently determined by your Excellency's Government, Mahommedan members of the provincial Councils and Mahommedan fellows of universities should be invested with electoral powers to be exercised in accordance with such procedure as may be prescribed by your Excellency's Government in that behalf.

An impression has lately been gaining ground that one or more Indian Members may be appointed on the Executive Council of the Viceroy. In the event of such appointment being made we beg that the claims of Mahommedans in that connection may not be overlooked. More than one Mahommedan, we venture to say, will be found in the country fit to serve with distinction in that august chamber.

We beg to approach your Excellency on a subject which must closely affect our national welfare. We are convinced that our aspirations as a community and our future progress are largely dependent on the foundation of a Mahommedan University which will be the centre of our religious and intellectual life. We, therefore, most respectfully pray that your Excellency will take steps to help us in the undertaking in which our community is so deeply interested.

In conclusion, we beg to assure your Excellency that in assisting the Mahommedan subjects of His majesty at this stage in the development of Indian affairs in the directions indicated in the present address, your Excellency will be strengthening the basis of their unswerving loyalty to the Throne and laying the foundation of their political advancement and national prosperity, and your Excellency's name will be remembered with gratitude by their posterity for generations to come, and we feel confident that your Excellency will be gracious enough to give due consideration to our prayers. We have the honour to subscribe ourselves, Your Excellency's most obedient and humble servants. . . .

B. Minto's Reply

Your Highness and gentlemen, allow me, before I attempt to reply to the many considerations your address embodies, to welcome you heartily to Simla. Your presence here today is very full of meaning. To the document with which you have presented me are attached the signatures of nobles, of Ministers of various States, of great landowners, of lawyers, of merchants, and of many other of His Majesty's Mahommedan subjects. I welcome the representative character of your deputation as expressing the views and aspirations of the enlightened Muslim community of India. I feel that all you have said emanates from a representative body basing its opinions on a mature consideration of the existing political condition of India, totally apart from the small personal or political sympathies and antipathies of scattered localities, and I am grateful to you for the opportunity you are affording me of expressing my appreciation of the just aims of the followers of Islam, and their determination to share in the political history of our Empire. As your Viceroy I am proud of the recognition you express of the benefits conferred by British rule on the diverse races of many creeds which go to form the population of this huge continent. You yourselves, the descendants of a conquering and ruling race, have told me today of your gratitude for the personal freedom, the liberty of worship, the general peace and the hopeful future which British administration has secured for India. It is interesting to look back on early British efforts to assist the Mahommedan population to qualify themselves for the public service. In 1782 Warren Hastings founded the Calcutta Madrassah, with the intention of enabling its students 'to compete on more equal terms with the Hindus for employment under Government'. In 1811 my ancestor Lord Minto advocated improvements in the Madrassah and the establishment of Mahommedan Colleges at other places throughout India. In later years the efforts of the Mahommedan Association led to the Government Resolution of 1885 dealing with the educational position of the Mahommedan community and their employment in the public service, whilst Mahommedan educational effort has culminated in the college of Aligarh, that great institution which the noble and broadminded devotion of Sir Syed Ahmed Khan—(applause)—has dedicated to his co-religionists. It was in July 1877, that Lord Lytton laid the foundation stone of Aligarh, when Sir Syed Ahmed Khan addressed these memorable words to the Viceroy: 'The personal honour which you have done me assures me of a great fact, and fills me with feelings of a much higher nature than mere personal gratitude. I am assured that you who upon this occasion represent the British rule have sympathy with our labours. To me this assurance is very valuable and a source of great happiness. At my time of life it is a comfort to me to feel that the undertaking which has been for many years and is now the sole object of my life, has roused on the one hand the energies of my own countrymen, and on the other has won the sympathy of our British fellow-subjects, and the support of our rulers, so that when the few years I may still be spared are over, and when I shall be no longer amongst you, the College will still prosper and succeed in educating my countrymen to have the same affection for their country, the same feelings of loyalty for the British rule, the same appreciation of its blessings, the same sincerity of friendship with our British fellow-subjects as have been the ruling feelings of my life.' (applause). Aligarh has won its laurels, its students have gone forth to fight the battle of life strong in the tenets of their own religion, strong in the precepts of loyalty and patriotism, and now when there is much that is critical for the future of India the inspiration of Sir Syed Ahmed

Khan and the teachings of Aligarh shine forth brilliantly in the pride of Mahommedan history, in the loyalty, commonsense, and sound reasoning so eloquently expressed in your address.

But, gentlemen, you go on to tell me that sincere as your belief is in the justice and fair dealings of your rulers, and unwilling as you are to embarrass them at the present moment you cannot but be aware that recent events have stirred up feelings amongst the younger generation of Mahommedans which might pass beyond the control of the temperate counsel and sober guidance. Now I have no intention of entering into any discussion upon the affairs of Eastern Bengal and Assam, yet, I hope that without offence to any one I may thank the Mahommedan community of the new Province for the moderation and self-restraint they have shown under conditions which were new to them and as to which there has been inevitably much misunderstanding, and that I may, at the same time, sympathise with all that is sincere in Bengali sentiments. But above all what I would ask you to believe is that the course the Viceroy and the Government of India have pursued in connection with the affairs of the new Province—the future of which is now I hope assured—(applause)—has been dictated solely by a regard for what has appeared best for its present and future populations as a whole, irrespective of race or creed, and that the Mahommedan community of Eastern Bengal and Assam can rely as firmly as ever on British justice and fair play for the appreciation of its loyalty and the safeguarding of its interests.

You have addressed me, gentlemen, at a time when the political atmosphere is full of change. We all feel it would be foolish to attempt to deny its existence. Hopes and ambitions new to India are making themselves felt, we cannot ignore them, we should be wrong to wish to do so. But to what is all this unrest due? Not to the discontent of misgoverned millions—I defy anyone honestly to assert that; not to any uprising of a disaffected people. It is due to that educational growth in which only a very small portion of the population has yet shared, of which British rule first sowed the seed, and the fruits of which British rule is now doing its best to foster and to direct. There may be many tares in the harvest we are now reaping, the Western gram which we have sown may not be entirely suitable to the requirements of the people of India, but the educational harvest will increase as years go on, and the healthiness of the nourishment it gives will depend on the careful administration and distribution of its product. You need not ask my pardon, gentlemen, for telling me that 'representative institutions of the European type are entirely new to the people of India' or that their introduction here requires the most earnest thought and care. I should be very far from welcoming all the political machinery of the Western world amongst the hereditary instincts and traditions of eastern races. Western breadth of thought, the teachings of Western civilization, the freedom of British individuality, can do much for the people of India. But I recognise with you that they must not carry with them an impracticable insistence on the acceptance of political methods. (Applause).

And now, gentlemen, I come to your own position in respect to the political future of the position of the Mahommedan Community for whom you speak. You will, I feel sure, recognise that it is impossible for me to follow you through any detailed consideration of the conditions and the share that the community has a right to claim in the administration of public affairs: I can at present only deal with generalities. The points which you have raised are before the committee which, as you know, I have lately appointed to consider the question of representation, and I will take care that your address is submitted to them. But at the same time I hope I may be able to reply to the general tenor of your remarks without in any way forestalling the Committee's report. The pith of your address, as I understand it, is a claim that in any system of representation—whether it affects a Municipality, a District Board, or a Legislative Council in which it is proposed to introduce or increase an electoral organisation—the Mahommedan Community should be represented as a community, you point out that in many cases electoral bodies as now constituted cannot be expected to return a Mahommedan candidate and that if by chance they did so it could only be at the sacrifice of such a candidate's views to those of a majority opposed to his own community whom be would in no way represent; and you justly claim that your position should be estimated not merely on your numerical strength but in respect to the political importance of your community, and the service it has rendered to the Empire. I am entirely in accord with you. (Applause). Please do not misunderstand me, I make no attempt to indicate by what means the representation of communities can be obtained, but I am as firmly convinced as I believe you to be, that any electoral representation in India would be doomed to mischievous failure which aimed at granting a personal enfranchisement regardless of the beliefs and traditions of the communities composing the population of this continent. (Applause). The great mass of the people of India have no knowledge of representative institutions. I agree with you gentlemen, that the initial rungs in the ladder of self-government are to be found in the Municipal and District Boards, and that it is in that direction that we must look for the gradual political education of the people. In the meantime, I can only say to you that the Mahommedan community may rest assured that their political rights and interests as a community will be safeguarded in any administrative organisation with which I am concerned, and that you and the people of India may rely upon the British Raj to respect, as it has been its pride to do, the religious beliefs and the national traditions of the myriads composing the population of His Majesty's Indian Empire. (Applause).

Your Highness and gentlemen, I sincerely thank you for the unique opportunity your deputation has given me of meeting so many distinguished and representative Mahommedans. I deeply appreciate the energy and interest in public affairs which have brought you here from great distances, and I only regret that your visit to Simla is necessarily so short.

APPENDIX III

LALA LAJPAT RAI'S SOLUTION FOR THE HINDU-MUSLIM PROBLEM, 1924

It is suggested on behalf of Muslim leaders that

(a) Communal representation with separate electorates in all the legislatures, local bodies, universities and other official or semi-official bodies should be provided. Mr. M.A. Jinnah is the latest recruit to this party, and I really cannot understand how he calls himself a nationalist still. The euphemism that, this is only tentative and that a time will come when the Muslims will be ready to give up communal representation should deceive no one. Once you accept communal representation with separate electorates, there is no chance of its being ever abolished, without a civil war. A civil war, will again, actually mean the supremacy of one of the communities over the other. This lends weight to the fear entertained by some Hindus that some at least of the Muslim leaders are counting on the help of foreign Muslim states to establish Muslim rule throughout Hindustan. Whether this fear is or is not well-founded, it is only natural that those who entertain it should oppose communal representation with all the strength they can command. Their opposition, however, cannot be effective as the Government seems determined to adopt their course. Therein they see the best guarantee of the permanence of the present conditions. Communal representation with separate electorates is the most effective reply to the demand for Swaraj, and the surest way of India never getting it. I have never been able to appreciate the mentality of those who constantly talk of turning out the British and at the same time insist on communal representation with separate electorates. I really don't understand what they mean. The second is the surest way of the first being never realized. The experience of the last three years is the most conclusive proof of it. The Muslim demand strengthens the position of anti-Swarajists both among the Hindus and the Muslims, and supplies an effective reply to the contention that India is ripe for Swaraj. Communal representation by itself is a sufficiently bad principle, destructive of, and antagonistic to, the idea of a common nationhood, but separate electorates make this vicious principle immeasurably worse. If our Muslim countrymen are really earnest in their belief in nationalism and in their demand for Swaraj, the least they can do is not to insist on separate electorates.

(b) Representation in provincial legislatures and local bodies should be on

Source: *The Tribune* (Lahore), 14 December 1924; reproduced in V.C. Joshi, ed., *Lala Lajpat Rai: Writings and Speeches* (Delhi, 1966), pp. 210-13.

the basis of population in provinces and places where the Mussalmans are in a majority. In other provinces and places they should have "effective" minority representation.

(c) Posts and offices under Government should also be distributed on the principle stated in clause (b).

(d) In the provinces where the Muslims are in a minority as well as in the All-India departments the Muslims ought to have 25 per cent to 33 per cent of the total posts.

We will take these clauses one by one, in their serial order.

The principle of clause (a) is both theoretically and practically a negation of the united nationhood. It provides for a complete division of India, as it is, into two sections: a Muslim India and a non-Muslim India. I say deliberately non-Muslim India because all that the Muslims are anxious for is a guarantee of their own rights. All the other communities they lump into one as non-Muslims. Let those who demand communal representation with separate electorates in all the representative institutions of the land honestly confess that they do not believe in nationalism or in a united India. The two things are absolutely irreconcilable.

(b) The demand for proportionate representation in the Legislatures is perfectly reasonable provided the principle is accepted through and through. The plea for "effective" minority representation is, however, untenable. Mr. Jinnah has placed a special interpretation of his own on this term. Let us examine it in the light of facts. In Bengal and the Punjab, the Mussalmans are in a majority, and if this principle is accepted, they will rule over these Provinces. The Hindus in these Provinces, according to the interpretation of Mr. Jinnah are an effective minority already; so they are not entitled to any special representation. But what about the Sikhs? Are they or are they not entitled to special representation? And from whose share are they to get it? From the share of the Hindus or that of the Muslims? Under no principle can they get it from the share of the Hindus. They must get it, if they must, from the Muslims' share on the same principle on which the Muslims themselves claim it in the U.P., or the other Provinces where they are in a minority. This will interfere with the absolute majority which Muslims demand over the Hindus and Sikhs combined. Some Mussalmans realize this and contend that they will be content with a bare majority of one or two. But it is obvious that they cannot have every thing in their own way. Assuming, however, that they are allowed their own way, do they imagine that they will be able to make their rule effective in the Punjab? The Punjab occupies a unique position among the Provinces of India. It is the home of a community who were the rulers of the Province when the British took possession of it. That community is virile, strong and united. Will this community readily consent to occupy the entirely subservient position which this arrangement involves? If nothing else helps them, they may oppose Swaraj, as they did not long ago. Under the circumstances I would suggest that a remedy should be sought by which the Muslims might get a decisive majority without trampling on the sensitiveness of the Hindus and the Sikhs. My suggestion is that the Punjab should be partitioned into two provinces, the Western Punjab with a large Muslim majority, to be a Muslim-governed Province; and the Eastern Punjab, with a large Hindu-Sikhs majority, to be a non-Muslim governed Province. I do not discuss Bengal. To me it is unimaginable that the rich and highly progressive and alive Hindus of Bengal will ever work out the Pact agreed to by Mr. Das. I will make the same suggestion in their case, but if Bengal is prepared to accept Mr. Das's Pact, I have nothing to say. It is its own look-out.

Maulana Hasrat Mohani has recently said that the Muslims will never agree to India's having Dominion Status under the British. What they aim at are separate Muslim States in India united with Hindu States under a National Federal Government. He is also in favour of smaller States containing compact Hindu and Muslim populations. If communal representation with separate electorates is to be the rule, then Maulana Hasrat's scheme as to smaller provinces seems to be the only workable proposition. Under my scheme the Muslims will have four Muslim States (1) The Pathan Province or the North-West Frontier, (2) Western Punjab, (3) Sindh, and (4) Eastern Bengal. If there are compact Muslim communities in any other part of India, sufficiently large to form a Province, they should be similarly constituted. *But it should be distinctly understood that this is not a united India. It means a clear partition of India into a Muslim India and a non-Muslim India.*

APPENDIX IV

THE AGA KHAN ON THE FUTURE CONSTITUTION FOR INDIA, 1928

In a previous article I dwelt on the unsatisfactory treatment in the Indian Constitution proposed in the Nehru Report of the three great problems of the independent Indian States, the protection of the Moslem and other minorities, and the provision of an adequate national Army in Swaraj India. But by far most serious, in fact the insuperable, defect of the Constitution recommended is that it predicates a unitary All-India Government, very much on the lines of the present central authority, yet without its safeguards and guarantees, moral and material, and its scope for the development oi provincial autonomy and racial developments. The draft Constitution overlooks the consideration that the *raison d'être* of the call for political freedom is that peoples should govern themselves and not have an outside authority imposed upon them—whether it be that of the British electorate or that of an executive, controlled by an Indian Parliament at Delhi or Simla, inevitably accentuating the dominance in India as a whole of a particular raci. l or cultural portion.

The Burmese people, by faith and race and history, are so distinct from India that they could not possibly accept the dictation of a Swaraj Parliament at Delhi. The immediate result of adoption of the Left Parties' scheme could be to unite the Burmans in insistent appeals to the English people for separation and independence—appeals that could not in fairness and equity be refused.

The difficulties which would arise in India proper would hardly be smaller. It is not conceivable that, when the strong arm of Britain had disappeared, great and compact races like the Mahrattas, the Bengalis, or the Mahomedans of the north-west and Sind would accept the control of a Central Executive and Legislature. Should such an authority at Delhi, dependent on a legislative majority of the other nationalities of the subcontinent, dictate to some or other of these races, or even to lesser communities like the Sikhs, the aggrieved party would be justified, at least where it is territorially preponderant, in insisting on its freedom, according to the principle of "self-determination" which has been invoked against the continuance of British rule. The demand for "self-determination" can express itself in many forms against even a Swaraj majority among strata of peoples as varied in their outlook and standards as are the peoples of India.

Source: *The Times* (London), 13 October 1928; courtesy Professor S.R. Mehrotra.

While not entirely unconscious of this fundamental objection to their scheme, the framers of the Commonwealth Constitution have evaded the issue, and have not proposed even half measures to meet it. Serious thinkers about the future of my country have realized that the present distribution of provinces—grown haphazard out of British Imperialism and administrative history or convenience—cannot be reconciled with a self-governing India. During his long association with India, the late Edwin Montagu (than whom no one was more responsible for making Indian autonomy a question of practical politics) often remarked to me that units like the Bombay Presidency and the Central Provinces would be impossible anomalies under self-government. But, mindful of the difficulties Lord Curzon encountered in partitioning Bengal, he wisely refused to take up the question of provincial redistribution before the inauguration of his Reforms. Determined to make a beginning with Indian responsibility, he framed the Reforms in the hope and expectation that at later stages the approach of self-government would render the present distribution not only absurd but impossible. Mr. Lionel Curtis, the real parent of dyarchy, also saw the difficulty and made the idealistic proposal of a division of British India into a considerable number of small provinces with a few million inhabitants each. Such a grouping would cut up many real nationalities and make India administratively another, if greater, France, for the provinces would be little more than the French departments. No one with practical knowledge of the various Indian nationalities, with their passion for individual expression, can believe that such a scheme would go through without strife or could succeed.

The solution I urge for the consideration of my countrymen, as well as the British people (who, inevitably, whether rightly or wrongly, must be associated with the next two or three 'successive stages' of advance to self-government to which they are pledged), is frankly to face the facts and boldly to accept the consequences.

India, when freed from any outside control, cannot have a unitary, non-federal Government. The country must accept in all its consequences its own inevitable diversities, not only religious and historical, but also national and linguistic. It must base its constitution on an association of free states, such as the German Empire was before the crash ten years ago. Each Indian province must enjoy to the full the freedom and independence of, say, Bavaria, in the years before the Great War. The Indian Free States would resemble the self-governing British Dominions in being ultimately held together by the bond of monarchy, represented by the present British Sovereign and his heirs. As a convinced monarchist I am indifferent whether the India of that day is regarded as a kingdom or an empire. The downfall of Russia, Austria, and Germany in our time, and of the two French Empires and the Roman Empire in former generations, may be said to give to the word "Emperor" less happy associations than the word "King". But, after all, this is today a matter of fashion. In Rome "Emperor" was a popular term and the Kingdom was unpopulár. In our own day, the happy consequences of Kingship in Great Britain, Holland, Belgium and the Scandinavian empire have endeared the word "King" to the people immediately concerned.

By frank acceptance of the idea of an association of free states almost all the difficulties in the way of a Swaraj India would sooner or later be overcome. Each free state would be based, not on considerations of size, but on those of religion, nationality, race, and language plus history. Thus Burma would be one state, while Bengal, with its Mahomedan East and Hindu West, would be two. The Mahratta country would be an entity in this regrouping. Where there exists a distinct race, such as the Gujeratis, the mere fact that it occupied a relatively small area would not prevent its acquisition of the status of a free state. On the other hand, the Mahomedan provinces of the North and the West would probably coalesce and make one important free state.

The burning question of the protection of minorities would in large measure be solved. The compact bodies of Mahomedans in the North-West and the East of India proper would have free states of their own. In provinces where they are a small minority they would have some guarantee of fair play in the fact of propinquity by language and residence to their Hindu neighbours, and also by being too small numerically to bid for political control. Other minorities would have similar practical safeguards. The free states would not be mere provinces with Legislatures and Executives liable to be overruled by a Central Government in which the Hindus would have a permanent majority. They would be secure from all kinds of interference, except in matters in which they would be freely associated with other states; and, if the Bavarian examples were taken, these would be few and far between. The Indian principalities could come into a free association of states, because in practice their semi-autonomy would be augmented and not decreased. The larger states, such as Hyderabad, Kashmir, and Mysore, could enter into the association as distinct units, while groups of smaller principalities like those of Kathiawar, Rajputana, and Central India could confederate and enter the union as free and independent members. If thought desirable the states of, say, Central India could constitute two groups of free states.

To revert to the position of Burma: she would stand to gain substantially by the new system without any corresponding loss. There would be no incentive for her to separate from Eastern dominions with which she would have close economic ties and from which she would derive commercial advantage. I have little doubt that, if the objective I have sketched is adopted, the Gujeratis, or the Mahrattas, or a union of the Northern Provinces and Sind, could in the relatively near future establish, within their own well-defined areas, free state administrations with good hope at success.

The popular authority would be based on rational facts and have that immense asset—the nearness of the governing body in sentiment and ideas to the people. The difficulty of providing adequate defence would be overcome by stages. Initially, all that would be required would be the removal of British troops and officials from the one or two well-defined areas where the new system was taking effect. Rightly conservative and cautious, the British would be willing to start the experiment of transfer of full responsibility over one or two areas, with a view to successive extensions of the system, as it succeeded, to other units.

The success or failure of this approach to self-government would depend on the position of each unit being akin to that of Bavaria in the former German Confederation, rather than that of an American state or a Swiss canton. Anyone with a knowledge of political history must be aware of the immense difference here implied and its consequences, and must realize that it will immediately go a long way to appeal not only to the ruling Princes, but to the various races and religions, as well as to Burma. By freeing the Moslem majorities in the North-West and East from ultimate Hindu control it will give them something worth having. Glaring injustice to any community is improbable, because nowhere in the free states of India will one nationality, race, be at the mercy of a semi-foreign majority dictating its orders from a distance.

APPENDIX V

MUHAMMAD IQBAL'S LETTERS TO M.A. JINNAH, MAY-JUNE 1937, AND THE LATTER'S COMMENT ON THEIR HISTORICAL SIGNIFICANCE, 1943

A. Iqbal's Letters

I

Confidential

Lahore
28th May, 1937

My dear Mr. Jinnah,

Thank you so much for your letter which reached me in due course. I am glad to hear that you will bear in mind what I wrote to you about the changes in the constitution and programme of the League. I have no doubt that you fully realise the gravity of the situation as far as Muslim India is concerned. The League will have to finally decide whether it will remain a body representing the upper classes of Indian Muslims or Muslim masses who have so far, with good reason, taken no interest in it. Personally I believe that a political organization which gives no promise of improving the lot of the average Muslim cannot attract our masses.

Under the new constitution the higher posts go to the sons of upper classes; the smaller ones go to the friends or relatives of the ministers. In other matters too our political institutions have never thought of improving the lot of Muslims generally. The problem of bread is becoming more and more acute. The Muslim has begun to feel that he has been going down and down during the last 200 years. Ordinarily he believes that his poverty is due to Hindu money-lending or capitalism. The perception that it is equally due to foreign rule has not yet fully come to him. But it is bound to come. The atheistic socialism of Jawaharlal is not likely to receive much response from the Muslims. The question therefore is: how is it possible to solve the problem of Muslim poverty? And the whole future of the League depends on the League's activity to solve this question. If the League can give no such promises I am sure the Muslim masses will remain indifferent to it as before. Happily there is a solution in the enforcement of the Law of Islam and its further development in the light of modern ideas. After a long and careful study of Islamic Law I have come to the conclusion that if this system of Law is properly understood and applied, at least the right to subsistence is secured to everybody. But the enforcement

Source: *Letters of Iqbal to Jinnah*, with a Foreword by M.A. Jinnah (Lahore, 1974; first published 1943).

and development of the Shariat of Islam is impossible in this country without a free Muslim state or states. This has been my honest conviction for many years and I still believe this to be the only way to solve the problem of bread for Muslims as well as to secure a peaceful India. If such a thing is impossible in India the only other alternative is a civil war which as a matter of fact has been going on for some time in the shape of Hindu-Muslim riots. I fear that in certain parts of the country, e.g., N.W. India, Palestine may be repeated. Also the insertion of Jawaharlal's socialism into the body-politic of Hinduism is likely to cause much bloodshed among the Hindus themselves. The issue between social democracy and Brahmanism is not dissimilar to the one between Brahamnism and Buddhism. Whether the fate of socialism will be the same as the fate of Buddhism in India I cannot say. But it is clear to my mind that if Hinduism accepts social democracy it must necessarily cease to be Hinduism. For Islam the acceptance if social democracy in some suitable form and consistent with the legal principles of Islam is not a revolution but a return to the original purity of Islam. The modern problems therefore are far more easy to solve for the Muslims than for the Hindus. But as I have said above in order to make it possible for Muslim India to solve these problems it is necessary to redistribute the country and to provide one or more Muslim states with absolute majorities. Don't you think that the time for such a demand has already arrived? Perhaps this is the best reply you can give to the atheistic socialism of Jawaharlal Nehru.

Anyhow I have given you my own thoughts in the hope that you will give them serious consideration either in your address or in the discussions of the coming session of the League. Muslim India hopes that at this serious juncture your genius will discover some way out of our present difficulties.

Yours sincerely
(Sd.) Mohammad Iqbal

P.S. On the subject-matter of this letter I intended to write to you a long and open letter in the press. But on further consideration I felt that the present moment was not suitable for such a step.

II

Private and Confidential *Lahore*
21st June, 1937

My dear Mr. Jinnah

Thank you so much for your letter which I received yesterday. I know you are a busy man; but I do hope you won't mind my writing to you so often, as you are the only Muslim in India today to whom the community has a right to look up for safe guidance through the storm which is coming to North-West India, and perhaps to the whole of India. I tell you that we are actually living in a state of civil war which, but for the police and military, would become universal in no time. During the last few months there has been a series of

Hindu-Muslim riots in India. In North-West India alone there have been at least three riots during the last three months and at least four cases of vilification of the Prophet by Hindus and Sikhs. In each of these four cases, the vilifier has been murdered. There have also been cases of burning of the Koran in Sind. I have carefully studied the whole situation and believe that the real cause of these events is neither religious nor economic. It is purely political, i.e. the desire of the Sikhs and Hindus to intimidate Muslims even in the Muslim majority provinces. And the new constitution is such that even in the Muslim majority provinces, the Muslims are made entirely dependent on non-Muslims. The result is that the Muslim Ministry can take no proper action and are even driven to do injustice to Muslims, partly to please those on whom they depend, and partly to show that they are absolutely impartial. Thus it is clear that we have our specific reasons to reject this constitution. It seems to me that the new constitution is devised only to placate the Hindus. In the Hindu majority provinces, the Hindus have of course absolute majorities, and can ignore Muslims altogether. In Muslim majority provinces, the Muslims are made entirely dependent on Hindus. I have no doubt in my mind that this constitution is calculated to do infinite harm to the Indian Muslims. Apart from this it is no solution of the economic problem which is so acute among Muslims.

The only thing that the communal award grants to Muslims is the recognition of their political existence in India. But such a recognition granted to a people whom this constitution does not and cannot help in solving their problem of poverty can be of no value to them. The Congress President has denied the political existence of Muslims in no unmistakable terms. The other Hindu political body, i.e. the Mahasabha, whom I regard as the real representative of the masses of the Hindus, has declared more than once that a united Hindu-Muslim nation is impossible in India. In these circumstances it is obvious that the only way to a peaceful India is a redistribution of the country on the lines of racial, religious and linguistic affinities. Many British statesmen also realise this, and the Hindu-Muslim riots which are rapidly coming in the wake of this constitution are sure further to open their eyes to the real situation in the country. I remember Lord Lothian told me before I left England that my scheme was the only possible solution of the troubles of India, but that it would take 25 years to come. Some Muslims in the Punjab are already suggesting the holding of a North-West Indian Muslim Conference, and the idea is rapidly spreading. I agree with you, however, that our community is not yet sufficiently organized and disciplined and perhaps the time for holding such a conference is not yet ripe. But I feel that it would be highly advisable for you to indicate in your address at least the line of action that the Muslims of North-West India would be finally driven to take.

To my mind the new constitution with its idea of a single Indian federation is completely hopeless. A separate federation of Muslim provinces, reformed on the lines I have suggested above, is the only course by which we can secure a peaceful India and save Muslims from the domination of non-Muslims. Why should not the Muslims of North-West India and Bengal be considered as nations entitled to self-determination just as other nations in India and outside India are?

Personally I think that the Muslims of north-West India and Bengal ought at present to ignore Muslim minority provinces. This is the best course to adopt in the interests of both Muslim majority and minority provinces. It will therefore be better to hold the coming session of the League in the Punjab, and not in a Muslim minority province. The month of August is bad in Lahore. I think you should seriously consider the advisability of holding the coming session at Lahore in the middle of October when the weather is quite good in Lahore. The interest in the All-India Muslim League is rapidly growing in the Punjab, and the holding of the coming session in Lahore is likely to give a fresh political awakening to the Punjab Muslims.

Yours sincerely,
(Sd.) Mohammad Iqbal
Bar-at-Law

B. Jinnah's Comment[1]

It is . . . much to be regretted that my own replies to Iqbal are not available. During the period under reference I worked alone unassisted by the benefit of a personal staff and so did not retain duplicate copies of the numerous letters that I had to dispose of. I made enquiries from the Trustees of Iqbal's estate at Lahore and was informed that my letters are not traceable. Hence I had no alternative but to publish the letters without my replies as I think these letters are of very great historical importance, particularly those which explain his views in clear and unambiguous terms on the political future of Muslim India. His views were substantially in consonance with my own and had finally led me to the same conclusions as a result of careful examination and study of the constitutional problems facing India, and found expression in due course in the united will of Muslim India as adumberated in the Lahore Resolution of the All-India Muslim League, popularly known as the "Pakistan Resolution", passed on 23rd March, 1940.

M.A. Jinnah

[1]Concluding paragraph of Jinnah's Foreword to *Letters of Iqbal to Jinnah.*

APPENDIX VI

JAWAHARLAL NEHRU'S LETTER TO RAJENDRA PRASAD ON MINISTRY-MAKING IN U.P., 21 JULY 1937

Allahabad
21-7-1937

My dear Rajendra Babu,

Thank you for your letter about Orissa affairs. I have been wanting to write to you for the last four days about a curious situation that has arisen here but as the urgency seemed to pass, I delayed writing. I shall now put you briefly in possession of the facts.

During the general elections in the U.P. there was not much conflict between the Congress and the Muslim League. It was the desire of both parties to avoid a conflict as much as possible and to accommodate each other. In the early stages of the election campaign a number of Muslims who were more or less Congressmen were doubtful if they would stand on behalf of the Congress or the League. If they had been pressed to do so they would have probably stood on the Congress ticket. But as there was no such pressure they drifted gradually to the League side under the vague impression that it was much the same thing. The League election board in the U.P. was a curious affair. There were some fairly good and old Congressmen in it, there were hopeless reactionaries, and there were middling people who drifted hither and thither.

As we looked upon the election campaign it was a tussle with the Agriculturist Party which was a wholly government party of big zamindars. The League also was opposing them and so inevitably our opposition to the League weakened. We did not want to split the forces opposed to pure reaction.

I did not know much about all this and had practically nothing to do with it. As the election campaign developed and our strength became apparent, some Muslims came to us wanting to stand on our ticket. But they were not obviously desirable from the Congress point of view and we allowed matters to drift, although we began to regret not having run more Congress Muslim candidates.

There was no kind of arrangement between the U.P. Congress and the League, but a kind of convention developed. In one or two instances we opposed League candidates and came near to success.

Source: *Selected Works of Jawaharlal Nehru*, S. Gopal, ed., vol. VIII (New Delhi, 1976).

During the election campaign the outstanding and most powerful worker on behalf of the League was Maulana Husain Ahmad who has always been very near to the Congress. During my tours where there was no Congress Muslim candidate, I usually supported the League candidate if he was not an obvious reactionary, as sometimes he was.

After the elections there was a tussle inside the League and the reactionary elements seemed to gain the upper hand. Relations between the U.P. Congress and the U.P. League became more strained. During the convention at Delhi this matter was discussed by us with the Jamiat leaders who had so far supported the League fully but who were now worried at the reactionary turn it was taking.

After the convention the U.P. League board became even more reactionary and its president, the Raja of Salempur, joined the interim ministry. This created a crisis in the League which resulted in the resignation of many members from its parliamentary board. Among those who resigned was Maulana Husain Ahmad. Most of those who resigned were not M.L.A.s but one M.L.A., Hafiz Ibrahim, also resigned and formally joined the Congress Party. There were at least four or five other M.L.A.s in the League group who were keen on joining the Congress Party but who for various reasons refrained at the time.

During the months that followed there was much controversy between the two groups of Muslims—those of the League and those who had resigned and their sympathisers, who were supporting the Congress. Bitterness grew, and the success of the Congress appeal to the Muslim masses irritated the Muslim Leaguers. So matters stood and the distance between the League and the Congress went on widening. This came to a head in the recent Bundelkhand election. This election, although we lost it, was an eye-opener to everybody. All manner of Muslims from maulvies and members of the Jamiat to young students trooped up, often uninvited, to help the Congress candidate. The reactionary methods of the League irritated them and they grew quite enthusiastic in their opposition to it. We lost the election for two reasons: (1) the cry of 'Islam in danger' and (2) bribery on an extensive scale. Many voters came to us and told us that they would vote for the Congress candidate if we paid them a little more than the other side was paying. There was a third reason also—the strength of caste feeling. Quite 25% of the voters were Malkhan Rajputs and the Muslim League candidate belonged to the same brotherhood. Their biradari decided to support him and threatened to punish any member who did not do so. People were made to take the oath on the *Qoran*. This solid block of votes went wholly against us almost without a single exception. But for it we had a comfortable majority. There was also shameless personation in regard to women voters, the same persons voting again and again.

In spite of all this the election was a most hopeful sign of a growing political consciousness among the Muslims. All our workers are sure that if the election was held again in the same area we would win. Last time we only put in about ten days' intensive effort. We got the real rural vote of the peasant but the residents of the *qasbas* were far more difficult. It was interesting to find that the Muslim peasant was not carried away by the cry of 'Islam in danger'. When asked why he was voting for the Congress he confessed frankly that he did so because he expected the Congress to reduce his rent.

Generally speaking therefore our position has been considerably strength-ened by the election. We have discovered to our pleasant surprise that there is a strong band of Muslim workers all over the province who are determined to fight reaction and to support the Congress. Quite a number of the leading lights of the Jamiat have helped us enthusiastically. They were disgusted by the tactics of the League's supporters in Bundelkhand. We have collected a large number of leaflets and posters issued by the League and they are instructive reading.

It is true that we have still to face a solid mass of reaction and the cry of religion carried off many people. It is also true that bribery is rampant during Muslim elections. The voters are very poor and are smaller in number. We cannot and will not compete in these corrupt practices. Still the outlook is hopeful.

I have, without intending to do so, discussed at some length the Bundelkhand election. Still it will help you to form a background.

Towards the end of June , a little before the Working Committee meeting the U.P. Muslim League leaders, Khaliquzzaman and Nawab Ismail Khan, made an approach towards the Congress. This had obviously some connection with the possibility of ministries. They pointed out that last March their parliamentary board had offered cooperation to the U.P. Congress Party on the basis of the 'Wardha programme' as laid down by the Working Committee, and were prepared to work under the discipline of the Congress Party. You will remember the Working Committee resolution on the Congress policy in the legislatures passed at the Wardha meeting prior to the convention. It was not clear whether the Muslim League board accepted the whole resolution or only the particular items of the legislative programme. If the former, then they accepted the Congress policy 100% including independence, fighting the Act, constituent assembly, etc., etc.

I knew nothing about all this, nor did Maulana till it was vaguely hinted at Wardha early this month by Pantji. But it was all very vague and I did not like the look of this angling for ministries.

When Maulana Abul Kalam went to Lucknow from Wardha he saw Khaliq who told him that he was practically prepared to give him a blank cheque ***provided*** two of their number were included in the ministry—himself and Nawab Ismail Khan, the president of the U.P. board. Maulana looked at all this with some suspicion but he felt attracted by the possibility of the whole Muslim League ceasing to exist as a separate group and being practically absorbed by the Congress.

He and Pant came to Allahabad and we discussed the matter at great length. I disliked (we all did) this bargaining for seats in the ministry. We disliked taking in two persons who, form the Congress point of view, were weak. We feared reaction among the Congressmen in general, and Congress Muslims in particular, who would have been irritated at their being excluded in preference for those who had been fighting the Congress. What of those who had severed their connection with the League and joined us? What of those Muslims of ours who had stood by the Congress during all these years? What of the Jamiat which was supporting us and opposing the League? You must remember that we have always had a strong and staunch group of Muslims with us in the U.P. They have not been many but they are growing in influence and younger Muslims are now strongly attracted to us. Were we going to ignore those who were with us and favour our opponents who joined us just to get the spoils of office? And then there was the risk of conflicts arising within the ministry or the party—conflict of a communal or political nature—resulting in resignations and the creation of an awkward situation.

All this and more we considered and we hesitated. And yet the alternative was worth having if it could be secured. This was the winding up of the Muslim League group in the U.P. and its absorption in the Congress. This would have a great effect not only in the U.P. but all over India and even outside. This would mean a free field for our work without communal troubles. This would knock over the British Government which relied so much on these troubles.

After much discussion in which two other members of the U.P. (Kripalani and Narendra Deva) joined, we came to the conclusion that we should offer stringent conditions to the U.P. Muslim League group and if they accepted them in toto then we would agree to two ministers from their group. Besides them one minister would be Rafi Ahmad [Kidwai].

We drew up these conditions. The March resolution of the Working Committee on Congress policy in the legislatures was to be accepted from A to Z after full consideration, so that there might be no misapprehension. The Muslim League group will be wound up, including the U.P. parliamentary board. All the Muslim League M.L.A.s to become full members of the Congress Party (but there was this that they were not specially asked to take the Congress pledge). All of them to abide by the discipline of the Party. In bye-elections, no separate candidates; all to support the Congress candidates, and generally to endeavour to increase the prestige of the Congress. If the Congress decided on resignation from the ministry or from the legislature, they would follow suit. And some others. You will agree that these were pretty stringent conditions and in effect amounted to something more than the Congress pledge. But we did not ask them to sever all connection with the parent Muslim League. The position would have been a peculiar one involving a dual loyalty to some extent. It could not last and we expected the U.P. Leaguers to break away from the parent League.

We decided to offer these conditions and also that if any condition was not agreed to, then not to come to terms with them.

Maulana and Pant went to Lucknow. They sent for Nawab Ismail Khan but he was ill in Meerut and could not come. There were talks with Khaliq who agreed to all the conditions except two: the winding up of the parliamentary board and not to set up separate candidates at bye-elections. These were vital conditions. Khaliq said that he personally would agree but he had no authority to do so. In effect, he pointed out, this might happen anyhow. Therefore Maulana said he could not give a final answer and came to Allahabad.

Meanwhile rumours had spread that we were talking with the Muslim League. Of course the details were not known. There was consternation among all our people, especially the Muslim Congressmen, the Jamiat people and young Muslims. Not only consternation but anger for the Bundelkhand election was fresh in everybody's mind. Maulana Husain Ahmad sent a special messenger and so on and so forth.

I was feeling very uncomfortable and was instinctively repelled by all this talk on an opportunistic basis. I felt trouble would follow and the settlement would be temporary only. Maulana was also distracted. Ultimately we sent word that we regretted we could not alter our previous conditions at all; if they were accepted in toto we would agree, not otherwise. We had no authority to go beyond this without consulting the Working Committee. So the matter dropped and Maulana Azad went off to Bombay. Khaliq said he was unable to agree.

Today Khaliq made another approach. He suggested that he would call an emergent meeting of his executive to consider the question of the bye-elections if we could postpone decision for some days. I spoke to him on the phone. I referred him to Pantji but did not encourage him at all.

That is how matters stand now. Maulana Azad is keen on Hafiz Ibrahim being taken into the cabinet. He is a good and competent man and used to belong to the Swaraj Party. He might be described as a moderate Congressman. Pantji knows him well. There is just one difficulty about him and that is this. It might be said that he left the League and joined us in order to get into the ministry. This would not be true as he left the League in March or early April when the question of ministry was not in the air. He left with a group including Maulana Husain Ahmad. He is intimately connected with the Jamiat. Still it is possible that the torrent may be hurled against him.

I am tired of writing this long letter. By the time you reach the end of it you will appreciate the humour of my saying at the beginning that I would give a brief account. But the matter was complicated and I wanted you to be in full possession of the facts in case of possible developments. Vallabhbhai has already had a chance of discussing this with Maulana Azad.

I am sending copy of this letter to Bapu.

Maulana Azad has not returned yet from Bombay, nor is there any news of him.

Yours sincerely,
Jawaharlal Nehru

Bibliography

MANUSCRIPT SOURCES

INDIA OFFICE LIBRARY AND RECORDS (IOR) LONDON

L/P&J/3/131, Private Office Papers.
L/P&J/6/74, Private Office Papers.
L/P&J/8/698, Private Office Papers.
L/PO/9/82, Private Office Papers.
MSS Eu. E. 220, *Hailey Collection.*
MSS Eu. C. 152, *Halifax Collection.*
MSS Eu. E. 352, *Fazl-i-Husain Collection.*
MSS Eu. F. 125, *Linlithgow Collection.*
MSS Eu. D. 573, *Morley Collection.*
MSS Eu. 238, *Reading Collection.*
MSS Eu. E. 240, *Templewood Collection.*
MSS Eu. D. 609, *Zetland Collection.*

NATIONAL ARCHIVES OF INDIA, NEW DELHI

Home Pol File no. 82/1925.
Home Pol File no. 83/85.
Home Pol File no. 89/40-R.
Home Pol File no. 144/1925.
Home Public no. 145/1920.
Rajendra Prasad Papers, Files VI-XI/1935.
S.A. Brelvi Papers.

NEHRU MEMORIAL MUSEUM AND LIBRARY, NEW DELHI

AICC Papers 1924 to 1939.
Jawaharlal Nehru Papers.
K.M. Munshi, Oral History Transcript no. 15.
Motilal Nehru Papers.
Tej Bahadur Sapru Papers (Microfilm).

GANDHI NATIONAL MUSEUM, NEW DELHI

Gandhi Papers.

QUAID-I-AZAM ACADEMY, KARACHI

Quaid-i-Azam Papers.

PRINTED SOURCES—OFFICIAL PUBLICATIONS

COUNCIL OF STATE DEBATES, 1927, I (CALCUTTA, 1927).

Government of India, *India in 1929* (Calcutta, 1931).

Government of Bombay, *Source Material for a History of the Freedom Movement in India*, II (Bombay, 1958).

Indian Statutory Commission I (London, 1930).

Indian Statutory Commission II (London, 1930).

Indian Statutory Commission IV (London 1930).

Joint Committee on Indian Constitutional Reform: Minutes of Evidence, II (London, 1934).

Report of the Administration of the Punjab (1922).

Return Showing the Results of Elections in India (1937).

PROCEEDINGS AND REPORTS OF SOME CONFERENCES AND POLITICAL PARTIES

All Parties Conference, 1928, *Report of the Committee appointed by the Conference to determine the Principles of the Constitution for India* (Allahabad, n.d.).

All Parties Conference, 1928: *Supplementary Report of the Committee* (Allahabad, n.d).

All Parties National Convention: Proceedings (Allahabad, n.d.).

History of the Hindu-Muslim Problem in India . . . being the Report of the Committee appointed by the Indian National Congress (Karachi Session 1931) *to enquire into the Cawnpore Riots of March 1931* (Allahabad, 1933).

Pirzada, Syed Sharifuddin, ed., *Foundation of Pakistan: All India Muslim League Documents,* 2 Vols. (Karachi, 1969-1970).

Report of the Forty-Second Indian National Congress held at Madras, 1927 (Madras, 1928).

Zaidi, A.M., *Congress Presidential Addresses*, 4 Vols. (New Delhi, 1985).

———and Shaheda Zaidi, eds., *The Encyclopaedia of Indian National Congress* 12 Vols. (New Delhi, 1976-80).

WRITINGS OF PROMINENT THINKERS, POETS AND LEADERS

Ahmad, Jamil-ud-din, *Historic Documents of the Muslim Freedom Movement* (Lahore, 1970).

Ahmad, Waheed, ed., *Letters of Mian Fazl-i-Husain* (Lahore, 1976).

———, ed., *Quaid-i-Azam Mohammad Ali Jinnah: Speeches, Indian Legislative Assembly, 1935-1947* (Karachi, 1991).

———, ed., *Quaid-i-Azam Mohammad Ali Jinnah, The Nation's Vioce: Speeches and Statements*, March 1935-March 1940 (Karachi, 1992).

Aziz, K.K., *Ameer Ali: His Life and Works* (Lahore, 1968).

——, ed., *The All India Muslim Conference, 1920-1935: A Documentary Record* (Karachi, 1972).

———, ed., *Complete Works of Rahmat Ali*, I (Islamabad, 1978).

———, ed., *Prelude to Pakistan, 1930-1940: Documents and Readings Illustrating the Growth of the Idea of Pakistan*, 2 Vols. (Lahore, 1992).

Choudhary, Valmiki, ed., *Dr. Rajendra Prasad: Correspondence and Select Documents* I (New Delhi, 1984).

Collected Works of Mahatma Gandhi, Vols. XX-LXII (New Delhi, 1966-1975); Supplementary Vol. II (New Delhi, 1991).

Gandhi, M.K., *Autobiography* (Ahmedabad, 1969; first published 1927).

Gopal, S., ed., *Selected Works of Jawaharlal Nehru*, Vols. II-VIII (New Delhi, 1972-1976).

Haque, Enamul, ed., *Nawab Bahadur Abdul Lalif: His Writings and Related Documents* (Dacca, 1968).

Hardinge, Lord, *My Indian Years, 1910-1916* (London, 1948).

Hasan, Mushirul, ed., *Muslims and the Congress: Select Correspondence of Dr. M.A. Ansari, 1912-1935* (New Delhi, 1979).

———, ed., *Muhammed Ali in Indian Politics: Select Writings*, 3 Vols. (New Delhi, 1983).

Iqbal, Mohammad, *Letters of Iqbal to Jinnah* (Lahore, 1974; first published 1943).

Jayakar, M.R., *The Story of My Life*, II: *1922-1925* (Bombay, 1959).

Jinnah, M.A., *History of the Origin of 'Fourteen Points'* (Bombay, n.d.).

Khan, The Aga, *The Memoirs of Aga Khan: World Enough and Time* (London, 1954).

———, 'A Constitution for India: The Bavarian Model', Letter to *The Times* (London), 13 October 1928.

Kumar, Ravinder and Hari Dev Sharma, eds., *Selected Works of Motilal Nehru*, V-VI (New Delhi, 1993-1995).

Mary, Countess of Minto, *India, Minto and Morley, 1905-1910* (London, 1934).

Naidu, Sarojini, 'A Pen Portrait', in *Mohammad Ali Jinnah: An Ambassador of Unity: His Speeches and Writings, 1912-1917*, I (Madras, 1918).

Nehru, Jawaharlal, *The Discovery of India* (Bombay, 1969; first published 1946).

Patwardhan, R.P. and D.V. Ambedkar, ed., *Speeches and Writings of Gopal Krishna Gokhale*, I (Poona, 1962).

Pirzada, Syed Sharifuddin, ed., *Quaid-e-Azam Jinnah's Correspondence* (Karachi, 1977).

———, ed., *The Collected Works of Quaid-e-Azam Mohammad Ali Jinnah*, 3 Vols. (Karachi, 1986).

Prasad, Rajendra, *Autobiography* (New Delhi, 1984; first published 1957).
Joshi, Vijaya Chandra, ed., *Lala Lajpat Rai, Writings and Speeches*, II (Delhi, 1966).
Setalvad, Chimanlal H., *Recollections and Reflections* (Bombay, 1946).
Wasti, Syed Razi, ed., *Memoirs and other Writings of Syed Ameer Ali* (Lahore, 1968).

OTHER CONTEMPORARY PUBLICATIONS

The Indian Annual Register, 1922-1937 (from 1924 to 1929 named the Indian Quarterly Register), Calcutta.

SECONDARY SOURCES: BOOKS AND ARTICLES

Abbasi, Muhammed Yusuf, *Muslim Politics and Leadership in South Asia, 1876-92* (Islamabad, 1981).
Afzal, M. Rafiq, 'Origin of the idea of Separate Muslim State: Nawab Sir Zulfiqar Ali Khan's Lahore Address, 1929', *Journal of the Research Society of Pakistan,* January-April 1966.
Ahmad, Jamil-ud-din, *Muslim Political Movements: Early Phase* (Karachi, 1963).
Ahmad, Sufia, *Muslim Community in Bengal 1884-1912* (Dacca, 1974).
Ahmad, Waheed, *Road to Indian Freedom: The Formation of the Government of India Act 1935* (Lahore, 1979).
Ali, Mohamed, *Green Book, No. 1* (Lucknow, 1907).
Ambedkar, B.R., *Pakistan or the Partition of India* (Bombay, 1946; 3rd edn.).
Azad, Maulana Abul Kalam, *India Wins Freedom: The Complete Version* (Hyderabad, 1988; first published Bombay 1959).
Aziz, K.K., *The Making of Pakistan: A Study in Nationalism* (London, 1967).
———, *A History of the Idea of Pakistan*, I & II (Lahore, 1987).
Bamford, P.C., *History of the Non-Cooperation and Khilafat Movements* (Delhi, 1974).
Chatterji, Joya, *Bengal Divided: Hindu Communalism and Partition, 1932-1947* (New Delhi, 1995).
Chattopadhyaya, Gautam, *Bengal Legislative Politics and Freedom Struggle, 1862-1947* (New Delhi, 1984).
Chintamani, C.Y., *Communal 'Award'? Examined and Criticized* (Allahabad, 1934).
Choudhry, B.M., *Muslim Politics* (Calcutta, 1946).
Choudhry, Khaliquzzaman, *Pathway to Pakistan* (Karachi, 1961).
Coatman, J., *India in 1927-28* (Calcutta, 1928).
———, *India in 1928-29* (Calcutta, 1930).
———, *Years of Destiny: India, 1926-1932* (London, 1932).
Coupland, R., *Indian Politics, 1936-1942* (London, 1943).

Craddock, Reginald, *The Dilemma in India* (London, 1929).
Dale, Stephen Frederic, *Islamic Society on the South Asian Frontier: The Mappilas of Malabar, 1498-1922* (Oxford, 1980).
Das, M.N., *India under Morley and Minto* (London, 1964).
———, *Indian National Congress versus the British,* I (Delhi, 1978).
Das, Suranjan, *Communal Riots in Bengal, 1905-1947* (New Delhi, 1991).
Desai, Mahadev H., *Day to Day with Gandhi: Secretary's Diary*, Vol. IV (Varanasi, 1969).
Dwarkadas, Kanji, *India's Fight for Freedom, 1913-1947: An Eye-Witness Story* (Bombay, 1966).
Engineer, Ashgar Ali, *Islamic Perspective,* Vol. II, No. II, July 1986.
Gallagher, John, ed., *Locality Province and Nation: Essays on Indian Politics 1870-1940* (Cambridge, 1973).
———, 'Congress in Decline: Bengal 1930 to 1939', *Modern Asian Studies,* 7, 3 (1973).
Ghosh, Pansy Chaya, *The Development of the Indian National Congress* (Calcutta, 1985; 2nd edn.).
Gilbert, Martin, *Servant of India* (London, 1966).
Gopal, S., *British Policy in India 1858-1905* (Cambridge, 1965).
———, *Jawaharlal Nehru: A Biography,* I (Bombay, 1976).
Gorden, Leonard A., *Bengal: The Nationalist Movement, 1876-1940* (Delhi, 1974).
Gordon, Richard, 'Hindu Mahasabha and the Indian National Congress, 1915 to 1926', *Modern Asian Studies* IX, 2 (1975).
Griffiths, P.J., *The British Impact on India* (London, 1952).
Hardgrave, Rober L.J., 'The Mapilla Rebellion, 1921: Peasant Revolt in Malabar', *Modern Asian Studies,* XI, 1 (1977).
Hasan, Mushirul, *Nationalism and Communal Politics in India, 1916-1928* (New Delhi, 1979).
———, ed., *Communal and Pan-Islamic Trends in Colonial India* (New Delhi, 1985; 2nd edn.).
———, ed., *India's Partition: Processes, Strategy and Mobilisation* (Delhi, 1993).
Hasan, Shamsul, *Plain Mr. Jinnah* (Karachi, 1976).
Hodson, H.V., *The Great Divide* (London, 1969).
Husain, Azim, *Fazl-i-Husain: A Political Biography* (Bombay, 1946).
Hyde, H. Montgomery, *Lord Reading* (London, 1967).
Ikram, S.M., *Modern Muslim India and the Birth of Pakistan* (Lahore, 1965).
Islam, Mustafa Nurul, *Bengali Muslim Public Opinion as Reflected in the Bengali Press, 1901-1930* (Dacca, 1973).
Islam, Zafrul, 'Two Historic Letters', *Journal of the Punjab University Historical Society* (Lahore, 1960).
——, 'A Note on the Central National Muhammedan Association', *The Proceedings of Pakistan History Conference* (Ninth Session) (Karachi, 1962).

Jain, M.S., *The Aligarh Movement* (Agra, 1965).

Kabir, Mafizullah, 'Nawab Salimullah and Muslim Politics, 1871-1915', *Bangladesh Historical Studies*, II, 1977.

Khairi, Saad R., *Jinnah Reinterpreted: The Journey from Indian Nationalism to Muslim Statehood* (Karachi, 1995).

Khaliquzzaman, Choudhry, *Pathway to Pakistan* (Lahore, 1961).

Karim, A., *Letters on Hindu-Muslim Pact* (Calcutta, 1924).

Kaura, Uma, *Muslims and Indian Nationalism: The Emergence of the Demand for India's Partition, 1928-1940* (New Delhi, 1977).

Kripalani, J.B., *Gandhi: His Life and Thought* (New Delhi, 1970).

Kumar, R., ed., *Essays on Gandhian Politics: The Rowlatt Satyagraha of 1919* (London, 1971).

Low, D.A., *The Indian National Congress: Centenary Hindsights* (Delhi, 1988).

Lytton, Earl of, *Pundits and Elephants* (London, 1942).

Majumdar, Bimanbehari and Bhakat Prasad Majumdar, *Congress and Congressmen in the Pre-Gandhian Era* (Calcutta, 1967).

Majumdar, R.C., *History of the Freedom Movement in India*, III (Calcutta, 1963).

Malik, Hafeez, *Sir Sayyid Ahmed Khan and Muslim Modernisation in India and Pakistan* (New York, 1980).

McPherson, Kenneth, *The Muslim Microcosm, Calcutta, 1918-1935* (Wiesbaden, 1974).

Mehrotra, S.R., *The Emergence of the Indian National Congress* (New Delhi, 1971).

———, *History of the Indian National Congress, 1885-1918* (New Delhi, 1995).

Mehta, Asoka and Achyut Patwardhan, *The Communal Triangle in India* (Allahabad, 1942).

Menon, M. Gangadhar, *Malabar Rebellion, 1921-1922* (Allahabad, 1989).

Minault, G., *The Khilafat Movement* (Delhi, 1982).

——— and David Lelyveld, 'The Campaign for Muslim University, 1896-1920', *Modern Asian Studies*, 8, 2 (1974).

Misra, B.B., *The Indian Political Parties* (Delhi, 1976).

Moon, Penderal, *Divide and Quit* (London, 1961).

Moore, R.J., *The Crisis of Indian Unity, 1917-1940* (Oxford, 1974).

———, 'The Making of India's Paper Federation, 1927-35', in C.H. Philips and M.D. Wainright, eds., *The Partition of India: Politics and Perspectives, 1935-1947* (London, 1970).

Morison, Theodore, 'The Hindu-Muslim Problem in India', *Contemporary Review*, June 1931.

———, 'Muhammadan Movements', in J. Cumming, ed., *Political India, 1832-1932* (London, 1932).

Mujahid, Sharif al, *Quaid-i-Azam Jinnah* (Karachi, 1981).

———, 'Jinnah and the Congress Party', in D.A. Low, ed., *The Indian National Congress: Centenary Hindsights* (Delhi, 1988).

Mukhopadhyaya, Manik, ed., *The Golden Book of Saratchandra: A Centenary Commemorative Volume* (Calcutta, 1977).

Munshi, K.M., *Pilgrimage to Freedom, 1902-1950* (Bombay, 1967).

Nagarkar, V.V., *Genesis of Pakistan* (Bombay, 1975).

Nanda, B.R., *The Nehrus: Motilal and Jawaharlal* (London, 1962).

———, *Gokhale: The Indian Moderates and the British Raj* (New Delhi, 1977).

———, *Gandhi: Pan-Islamism, Imperialism and Nationalism in India* (Bombay, 1986).

———, *Jawaharlal Nehru: Rebel and Statesman* (Delhi, 1995).

Niemeijer, A.C., *The Khilafat Movement in India, 1919-1924* (The Hague, 1972).

Owen, Hugh F., 'Negotiating the Lucknow Pact', *Journal of Asian Studies*, XXXI, May 1972.

Page, David, *Prelude to Partition* (Delhi, 1982).

Pande, B.N., *Nehru* (New York, 1976).

Pandey, Gyanendra, *The Ascendency of the Congress in Uttar Pradesh, 1926-34: A Study in Imperfect Mobilisation* (Delhi, 1978).

Panikkar, K.N., *Against Lord and State: Religion and Peasant Uprising in Malabar, 1836-1921* (Delhi, 1989).

———, ed., *Peasant Protests and Revolt in Malabar* (New Delhi, 1990).

Parvate, T.V., *Bal Gangadhar Tilak* (Ahmedabad, 1958).

Philips, C.H. and B.N. Pandey, eds., *The Evolution of India and Pakistan 1858 to 1947: Select Documents* (London, 1962).

——— and Marg Doreen Wainwright, eds., *The Partition of India: Politics and Perspectives* (London, 1970).

Pirzada, Syed Sharifuddin, *Evolution of Pakistan* (Lahore, 1963).

Prakash, Indra, *Where we Differ? The Congress and the Hindu Mahasabha* (New Delhi, 1942).

Prasad, Beni, *India's Hindu-Muslim Questions* (Allahabad, 1946).

Prasad, Bimal, 'The Emergence of the Demand for India's Partition', *International Studies*, Vol. 9, No. 3, January 1968.

———, 'Congress versus the Muslim League, 1935-1937', Richard Sisson and Stanley Wolpert, eds., *Congress and Indian Nationalism: The Pre-Independence Phase* (Berkeley, 1988), pp. 305-29.

———, 'Jawaharlal Nehru and Partition', in Amrik Singh, ed., *The Partition in Retrospect* (New Delhi, 2000), pp. 27-47.

Prasad, Rajendra, *India Divided* (Bombay, 1946).

Prasad, Yuvaraj Deva, *The Indian Muslims and World War I* (New Delhi, 1985).

Qureshi, Ishtiaq Husain, *The Muslim Community of the Indo-Pakistan Subcontinent* (Karachi, 1977; 2nd edn.).

Rahman, Matiur, *From Consultation to Confrontation: A Study of the Muslim League in British Indian Politics, 1906-1912* (London, 1970).

Ram Gopal, *Indian Muslims* (Bombay, 1959).

Rani, Sheila, 'Indian Public Opinion and the Crisis in the British Empire', unpublished Ph.D. Thesis, University of Delhi, 1985.

Rao, B. Shiva, 'India, 1935-45', in C.H. Philips and Marg Doreen Wainwright, eds., *The Partition of India: Politics and Perspectives* (London, 1970).

Ray, Prithwi Chandra, *Life and Times of C.R. Das* (London, 1927).

Ray, Rajat Kanta, *Social Conflict and Political Unrest in Bengal, 1875-1927* (Delhi, 1984).

Riaz, Syed Hasan, *Pakistan Naguzeer Tha* (Karachi, 1967).

Rizvi, Gowher, *Linlithgow and India* (London, 1978).

Robinson, Francis, *Separatism Among Indian Muslims* (Delhi, 1975).

Saiyid, Matlubul Hasan, *Mohammad Ali Jinnah* (Lahore, 1962; first published 1945).

Sarkar, Sumit, *The Swadeshi Movement in Bengal, 1903-1908* (New Delhi, 1973).

Sen, Shila, *Muslim Politics in Bengal, 1937-1947* (New Delhi, 1976).

Shahnawaz, Jahan Ara, *Father and Daughter* (Lahore, 1971).

Siddiqi, Majid Hayat, 'Bluff, Doubt and Fear: The Kheri Brothers and the Colonial State, 1904-45', *The Indian Economic and Social History Review*, XXIV, July-September 1987.

Singh, Anita Inder, *The Origins of the Partition of India, 1936-1947* (Delhi, 1987).

Singh, G.N., *Landmarks in Indian Constitutional and National Development*, I (Delhi, 1973).

Singh, Hiralal, *The British Policy in India* (Meerut, 1982).

Singh, Iqbal, *The Ardent Pilgrim: An Introduction to the Life and Work of Mohammed Iqbal* (Delhi, 1977; 2nd edn.).

Tara Chand, *History of the Freedom Movement in India*, IV (New Delhi, 1972).

Tirmizi, S.A.I., ed., *The Paradoxes of Partition (1937-47)* I (New Delhi, 1998).

Tripathi, Amales, *The Extremist Challenge* (Bombay, 1967).

Wasti, Syed Razi, *Lord Minto and the Indian National Movement* (Oxford, 1964).

———, *The Political Triangle in India, 1858-1924* (Lahore, 1976).

Williams, L.F. Rushbrook, *India in 1921-1922* (Calcutta, 1922).

——, *India in 1923-1924* (Calcutta, 1924).

Wolpert, Stanley A., *Morley and India* (Berkeley, 1967).

——, *Jinnah of Pakistan* (Delhi, 1985).

Wood, Conard, *The Moplah Rebellion and its Genesis* (New Delhi, 1987).

Zaidi, A.M., ed., *Evolution of Muslim Political Thought in India*, I (New Delhi, 1975).

Zakaria, Rafiq, *Rise of Muslims in Indian Politics* (Bombay, 1970).

——, *Iqbal: The Poet and the Politician* (New Delhi, 1993).

Zaman, Waheed-uz-, *Towards Pakistan* (Lahore, 1978, 3rd edn.).

Index